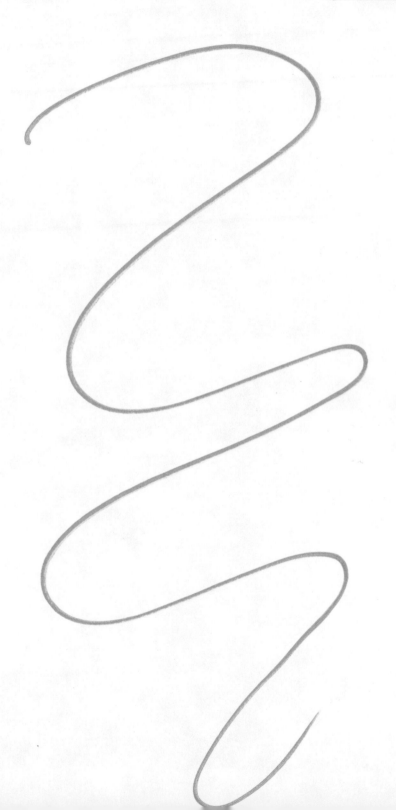

Successful Direct Marketing Methods

Fourth Edition

Bob Stone

Chairman Emeritus, Stone & Adler, Inc.

NTC Business Books

a division of *NTC Publishing Group* • Lincolnwood, Illinois USA

To Dorothy, my "one and only" for over forty years, who did extra duty in raising five wonderful kids while her husband was almost constantly "in flight." This book is but another manifestation of a wonderful partnership.

This edition published by NTC Business Books, a division of NTC Publishing Group, 4255 West Touhy Avenue, Lincolnwood (Chicago), Illinois 60646-1975 U.S.A. 1988 by Bob Stone. All rights reserved. No part of this book may be reproduced, stored in a retrieval system, or transmitted in any form, or by any means electronic, mechanical, photocopying or otherwise, without the prior permission of NTC Publishing Group. Manufactured in the United States of America. Library of Congress Catalog Card Number: 86-61333

8 9 0 MP 9 8 7 6 5 4 3 2 1

Contents

S E C T I O N   I
The World of Direct Marketing

CHAPTER ONE
The Scope of Direct Marketing

CHAPTER TWO
Data Base Marketing

SECTION II
Choosing Media for Your Message

CHAPTER EIGHT

Mailing Lists   164

CHAPTER NINE

Magazines   192

CHAPTER TEN

Newspapers   224

CHAPTER ELEVEN

Electronic Media   241

CHAPTER TWELVE

Co-ops   266

CHAPTER EIGHTEEN

Mathematics of Direct Marketing 441

CHAPTER NINETEEN

Idea Development and Testing 469

Foreword

A new edition of the "Bible" of direct marketing has a significance all of its own. It signals that direct marketing has taken another quantum leap that must be defined.

This, the fourth edition of Bob Stone's landmark book, reflects the growing sophistication of direct marketing, with new chapters on business-to-business direct marketing, data base marketing, and fund raising for worthy causes. These additions do indeed reflect areas of explosive growth in the industry.

Since it was first published in 1974, when it was absolutely unique, *Successful Direct Marketing Methods* has remained state-of-the-art both for educators and practitioners. The over 100,000 copies in print have guided the knowledgeable and educated the student, and thereby contributed significantly to the successful practice of direct marketing.

In terms of education, the importance of Bob Stone's book cannot be overstated. In the year of its publication, there were fewer than a dozen courses in the subject matter available nationwide. With the advent of this book (and the others that followed it) and its teacher's manual, direct marketing has gained gradual acceptance as an academic discipline. Today, there are more than 130 courses, one undergraduate degree, two graduate degrees, and one certification program available in the most prestigious American universities. The direct marketing industry now, for the first time in its history, has a pool of academically trained personnel upon which to draw. The implications for excellence in the field are obvious.

Bob Stone, direct marketer sine qua non and educator par excellence, has made formidable contributions. He has donated thousands of dollars in royalties from this book to the Direct Marketing Educational Foundation, which is devoted to the education of future industry executives.

He is also a teacher in the true sense of that word. He has taught at Direct Marketing Educational Foundation's Collegiate and Professors' Institutes for over twenty years. In addition, Bob Stone teaches direct marketing courses at both University of Missouri/Kansas City and Northwestern University, Evanston, Illinois.

Direct marketing owes him an unpayable debt, and I am delighted to be able to sing his—and the book's—praises at the beginning of this new edition.

Jonah Gitlitz, President
Direct Marketing Association

About the Author

Bob Stone

Position
Chairman Emeritus of Stone & Adler, Inc.

Articles
Author of more than 200 articles on direct marketing, which have appeared in *Advertising Age* magazine since 1967.

Awards
Six-time winner of the Direct Marketing Association's Best of Industry Award. The firm he cofounded, Stone & Adler, has received Direct Marketing Association's highest honors, including the Silver and Gold Echo Awards as well as the International Direct Marketing & Mail Order Symposium's Bronze Carrier Pigeon Award. Member of Direct Marketing Hall of Fame. Recipient of the Edward N. Mayer, Jr. Award for contributions to direct marketing education, the Charles S. Downes Award for direct marketing contributions, and the John Caples Award for copy excellence.

Affiliations
Former director of the Direct Marketing Association
Former president of the Chicago Association of Direct Marketing
Former membership chairman of the Direct Marketing Association
Former president of the Associated Third Class Mail Users
Board member of the Direct Marketing Educational Foundation
Adjunct Professor at University of Missouri
Adjunct Professor at Northwestern University

Preface

When I started work on this, the fourth edition of *Successful Direct Marketing Methods,* I announced the task before me at a family gathering which included our daughter and four sons. Jeff, the oldest son and the sage of the group, asked, "Dad, haven't you got that thing right yet?"

"I had it right in 1975, 1979, and 1984," I replied, "but a few years after each update new applications and new technologies emerged. So I have to update." That's good. In a way the four editions are a recorded chronicle of unprecedented growth of a single marketing discipline.

The first edition in 1975 contained fourteen chapters; this edition contains twenty-one chapters. Lifestyle selection was in its infancy in 1975; lifestyle identification and selection is commonplace today. And so it was with data base marketing, business-to-business direct marketing, cable TV, direct marketing education, and all the rest. Tremendous progress in little more than a decade.

Targeted Relationship Marketing (TRM) was a concept yet to be conceived. Home shopping shows were but a glimmer of an idea. Software that can analyze, answer the "what-ifs," and pinpoint direction were little more than a dream. Back in 1975, only one major direct marketing agency had merged into a major general agency. Today each of the top twenty major general agencies has a direct marketing unit! Clearly, direct marketing continues to be a rapidly growing and moving target with change and improvements the norm.

But of all the changes, none have been more marked than the change in people entering the direct marketing stream: college bred majors in marketing, and now, just beginning to reach meaningful numbers, majors in direct marketing. What these entry-level people are bringing to the party is a foreknowledge of business planning and strategic planning, regression analysis, lifestyle segmentation, data base marketing, research, and creative development and execution. The skills they have acquired foretell the future. A bright future indeed.

At the twenty-second Spring Conference of the Direct Marketing Association, Stan Rapp of Rapp & Collins, New York City, identified five signposts, present today, that will be major factors in shaping the bright future.

1. Push-button Shopping (shopping by phone)

2. Video Brochures (VCRs as the medium)

3. One-to-One Publishing (configurations of merchandise in catalogs and magazines targeted to individual needs of the marketplace)

4. World Direct Trade (global marketing, using direct marketing methods)

5. Maximarketing (traditional channel marketers harnessing the power of multi-channel distribution)

To cash in on the future, practitioners and entry-level people alike must be abreast of all that is available. And that is why the fourth edition of *Successful Direct Marketing Methods* has been written.

Best of success to you!

Bob Stone

Acknowledgments

As w.th all editions of *Successful Direct Marketing Methods,* the materials in this, the fourth edition, in no way reflect the sole thinking of the author. Instead, this book is a reflection of all that is happening in direct marketing, with generous contributions from a host of people and organizations.

Thanks to Direct Marketing Association for the statistics it has provided. To Pete Hoke, publisher of *Direct Marketing,* for his contributions. To Rose Harper, president of the Kleid Co., Inc., for her input on mailing lists. To Stan Rapp and Tom Collins of Rapp & Collins for their contributions on magazines and the techniques of creating print advertising.

And my thanks go likewise to Jo-Von Tucker, president of Jo-Von Tucker & Associates, for her input on catalogs. To Bob Kestnbaum, president of Kestnbaum & Company for his input on the mathematics of direct marketing. And to Bob Hutchings of IBM for his contributions on lead generation programs.

Numerous present and former staff members of Stone & Adler contributed to this book. Special thanks go to Jerry Wood for his contributions on strategic planning. To Don Kanter for his input on creating mail packages. And to Vince Copp for his contributions on direct marketing research.

Thanks also go to Frank Daniels for his input on idea development. And finally—a special thank you to Aaron Adler, cofounder of Stone & Adler, for lending his wisdom to the chapter on selecting and selling merchandise.

The World of Direct Marketing

CHAPTER ONE

The Scope of Direct Marketing

The widening scope of direct marketing has been both evolutionary and revolutionary. The traditional applications have been refined. New applications have emerged.

The explosive growth of direct marketing in the 50s, 60s, and 70s must be credited, for the most part, to entrepreneurs—pioneers who saw direct marketing as another channel of distribution for traditional marketers in particular. But widening the scope of direct marketing must be credited to the new breed of direct marketing talent who have broadened the scope to include *Targeted Relationship Marketing* (TRM).

Joel Tucciarone, director of strategic marketing of Wunderman, Ricotta & Kline, New York, states that "TRM means cultivating consumers into loyal customers through proprietary persuasion systems."

The three building blocks of Targeted Relationship Marketing, as Mr. Tucciarone sees it, are:

1. Prospect/user identification/enhanced data base

2. Relationship management

3. Customized persuasion

Continuing, Joel Tucciarone states that "a central TRM premise is that true knowledge about individual customers, users and prospects for a given product category is capturable in a proprietary data base. Most brand marketers," he points out,

> have not realized the asset value of knowing who their actual or competitive users are. And while many direct marketers recognize the asset value of their list, many have not yet moved to a richer profiling of customers and prospects with an *enhanced data base*.

Shortly we will present mini case histories of TRM as well as refined traditional applications of direct marketing. But first let us define this unique marketing discipline.

Direct Marketing Defined

A hint of the scope of direct marketing is found in the official definition provided by the Direct Marketing Association.

> *Direct Marketing* is an interactive system of marketing which uses one or more advertising media to effect a measurable response and/or transaction at any location.

When we dissect this simple straightforward definition we come upon key words that separate direct marketing from other marketing disciplines.

- "Interactive": Interaction, one-on-one communication between marketer and prospect/customer, is an important key.
- "One or more advertising media": Direct marketing is not restricted to any one media. As a matter of fact, direct marketers have discovered there is a synergism between media. A combination of media often is far more productive than any single medium.
- "Measurable response": Measurability is a hallmark of direct marketing. Everything we do is measurable. We know what we spend; we know what we get back.
- "Transaction at any location": The world is our oyster. Transactions can take place by phone, at a kiosk, by mail, by personal visit.

The total scope of media from which direct marketers can choose appears on the direct marketing flow chart (Exhibit 1-1), published by *Direct Marketing* magazine. Interspersed with the media scope are the disciplines involved in a successful direct marketing operation.

Unique Direct Marketing Applications

Now let us look at some mini case histories indicative of the broadening scope of direct marketing as well as the refinement of long-standing applications. As with all case histories in this book, the reader is urged to reflect on each with a key question: *How can I adapt that idea to my line of business?*

Customer Loyalty Programs

The epitome of Targeted Relationship Marketing is best exemplified by customer loyalty programs—a rather recent development in direct marketing applications.

Based upon the premise that all customers are not created equal—approximately 80 percent of all repeat business for goods and services

Exhibit 1-1. Direct Marketing Flow Chart

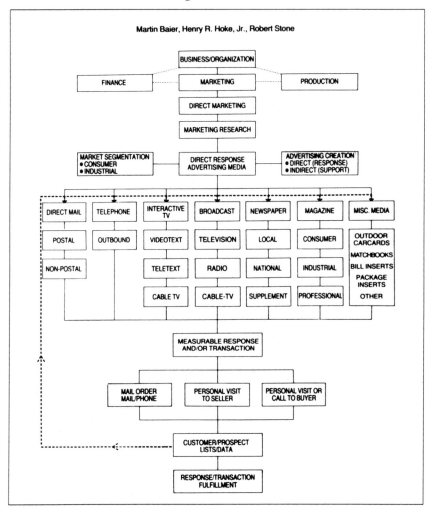

comes from 20 percent of a customer base—proponents of customer loyalty programs target specific marketing efforts to the rich 20 percent of their data base.

Among the first to recognize the opportunities existent with TRM were the airlines. They too find that approximately 80 percent of their revenue comes from 20 percent of their customer base, their frequent flyers.

In a speech before the Chicago Association of Direct Marketing in January 1987, Ray Cohen, formerly in charge of the United Airlines "Mileage Plus" Program, outlined how United maintains a special relationship with their special customers and thereby retains the loyalty of those customers.

"Mileage Plus" was launched in April 1981. The marketing premise was simple: the more a customer purchases your product, the greater the rewards, and the greater the incentive to keep purchasing your product. "Fortunately," said Ray Cohen, "as an airline we could provide one of the most desirable rewards in the world . . . *free travel.*"

Suffice it to say that United's "Mileage Plus" program could not have been launched had they not had the ability to identify frequent flyers through an enhanced data base—the first building block in Joel Tucciarone's TRM procedures. Likewise they had to create procedures and develop personnel to bring off relationship management—the second building block.

The heart of building and maintaining customer loyalty—the third building block—is *customized persuasion.* "Mileage Plus" members have received special treatment from the outset. Each member is given a membership card with a unique number. Each member receives frequent statements (Exhibit 1-2) showing flight activity, miles flown, bonus miles, and total miles that can be applied to upgrades and free travel.

Customized persuasion doesn't stop there. "Mileage Plus" members are given a special toll-free phone number. They get frequent newsletters which offer unique trips and special bonuses. What's more, if a "Mileage Plus" member reaches the upper levels of miles traveled, that member is upgraded to "Premier" status; upgrading brings with it more bonuses!

Actual results figures are confidential, of course. But it is a known fact that membership is in the millions. And customer loyalty is at an all-time high.

Let's look at some categories of business that have indeed adapted the customer loyalty marketing concept, keeping in mind our admonition to ask the question, how can this idea be adapted to my line of business?

AT&T, a communications giant who never knew true competition until deregulation, now embraces the customer loyalty program concept. Their program—"Opportunity Calling"—targets "heavy users" of long distance services and rewards them with bonus points tied to the amount of long distance services they use each month. These points can be used to discount the cost of merchandise and services offered through "Opportunity Calling" catalogs.

Hotels, not unlike airlines, are dependent upon the frequent business traveler for the lion's share of their business. Their reward programs are modeled after those of the airlines.

Because heavy users carry two or more cards, credit card companies face fierce competition. Loyalty programs have been structured to reward cardholders for the preferred usage of one card.

Reward programs have likewise been structured in business categories as disparate as car rental and consumer catalog sales. Customer loyalty is an imperative for all: it's most often the difference between profit and loss.

Kiosks as a Direct Marketing Tool

The mini case history that follows describes a massive direct marketing breakthrough at retail for a plethora of products and services not regularly

Exhibit 1-2. "Mileage Plus" Statement

UNITED AIRLINES

MileagePLUS®

Scandinavian Airlines	Air France	Holland America Line	Cathay Pacific	Alitalia	Lufthansa	Swissair	British Airways

MILEAGE PLUS
ACCOUNT NO.   00085 471 457

STATEMENT
CLOSING DATE   03/31/87

Robert Stone
1630 Sheridan Rd No 8g
Wilmette, Il. 60091

See reverse side for additional information and to claim award.   Retain bottom portion for your records

Robert Stone   ACCOUNT NO.   00085 471 457   STATEMENT CLOSING DATE   03/31/87

If you have returned your Premier Reservations questionnaire, your profile should be
available for your use soon. You'll see a special notice on your statement when your
personal information has been entered into United's reservation system. Notification
will begin with next month's statement.

PREVIOUS BALANCE	UNITED FLIGHT MILES	PARTNER TRAVEL MILES	FLIGHT BONUSES	SPECIAL BONUSES	AWARD MILES	NEW BALANCE	YEAR-TO-DATE UNITED MILES
10935	11366	500	5684	0	0	28485	13598

ACTIVITY DATE	REF. NO.	TRAVEL ITINERARY	FLIGHT MILES	BONUS MILES (SEE BONUS KEY BELOW)	TOTAL MILES
*** FLIGHT ACTIVITY ***					
03/02/87	160	UA 0547 K ORD-PHX	1440	PRM 720	2160
03/09/87	161	UA 0256 K PHX-ORD	1440	PRM 720	2160
03/17/87	162	UA 0001 K ORD-HNL	4243	PRM 2122	6365
03/23/87	163	UA 0002 K HNL-ORD	4243	PRM 2122	6365
03/25/87	164	UX 2849 Y ORD-LSE	500		500
*** AWARD ACTIVITY ***					
03/29/87		PREMIER UPGRADE			

carried in inventory by retailers. Its potential boggles the mind.

The marketer is the Sylvania light bulb division of GTE Products Corp. Sylvania has about 20–25 percent of the light bulb market, but General Electric controls about 60 percent of the U.S. market. So gaining shelf space is a severe problem for Sylvania and all of GE's competitors.

Researching the problem, Sylvania's direct marketing agency, Rapp & Collins of New York City, came up with a unique marketing concept. The development of a kiosk that could offer the complete line of 6,000 varieties of light bulbs and lighting systems without any inventory requirements by retailers. Research indicated that home-products centers, a growing retail category, would prove to be ideal outlets.

The kiosks (Exhibit 1-3) eat up only about two square feet of selling space, require no staffing by store personnel, and give the retailer a commission of roughly 25 percent on every sale GTE makes.

Equipped with an extensive catalog and a direct toll-free telephone line to GTE's telemarketing group in West Seneca, New York, consumers can place orders or inquire about products they see in the catalog. Payment is made via Visa or MasterCard. Goods are shipped to the home overnight!

Once again asking our magic question—how can I adapt that idea to my line of business?—think of the possibilities.

Shoe stores, stocking only the most popular styles and sizes, could install a kiosk which would show *all* styles on a screen. The consumer could then give the style number and size to the sales clerk, who would arrange for overnight shipment from the warehouse. (As a matter of fact, Florsheim Shoes is already doing this.)

Retailers could install "Video Kiosks"—next day pickup, just like film processing—of any video tape the consumer may want.

Just to mention a few more possibilities: sporting goods stores, apparel stores, costume jewelry stores could all increase their lines and sales by applying direct marketing methods.

Home Shopping Shows

The big direct marketing story of the mid 1980s has been home shopping shows—a dynamic TV vehicle for moving hundreds of millions of dollars of merchandise.

The estimated 1988 sales for home shopping shows is $4 billion, up from $90 million in 1985.

The word "spectacular" seems to be a mild superlative when attempting to describe the rapid growth of home shopping shows. The driving force in this direct marketing phenomenon has been Home Shopping Network (HSN), Inc., of Clearwater, Florida (Exhibit 1-4).

Part of the phenomenal growth of HSN is explained by its rapid expansion into areas serviced by cable TV and its penetration of local broadcast markets. Penetration as of January 1, 1987, was approximately forty-one million homes, representing 52 percent of homes with TV in America.

Exhibit 1-3. The Sylvania Kiosk

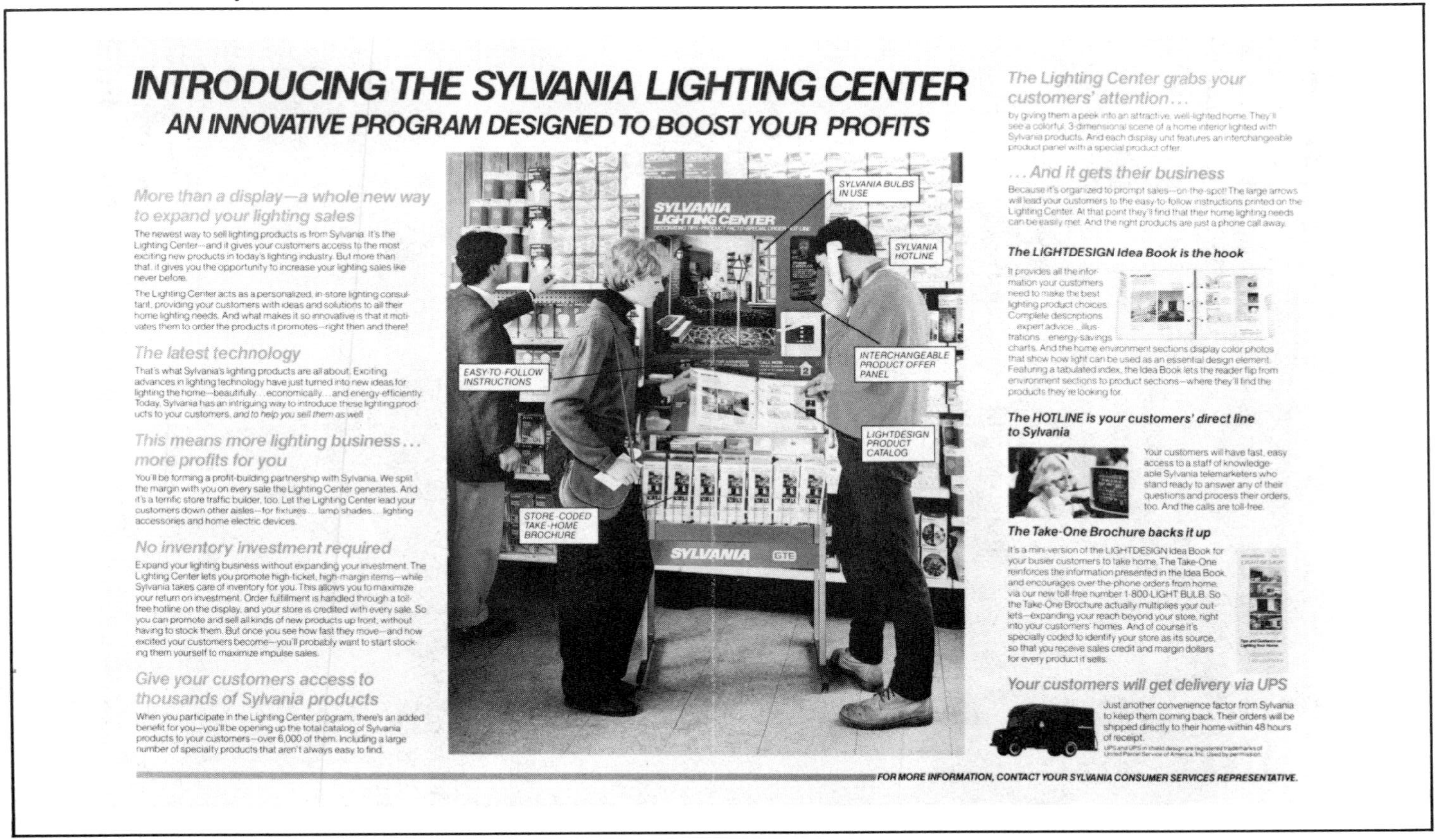
INTRODUCING THE SYLVANIA LIGHTING CENTER
AN INNOVATIVE PROGRAM DESIGNED TO BOOST YOUR PROFITS
More than a display—a whole new way to expand your lighting sales
The newest way to sell lighting products is from Sylvania. It's the Lighting Center—and it gives your customers access to the most exciting new products in today's lighting industry. But more than that, it gives you the opportunity to increase your lighting sales like never before.
The Lighting Center acts as a personalized, in-store lighting consultant, providing your customers with ideas and solutions to all their home lighting needs. And what makes it so innovative is that it motivates them to order the products it promotes—right then and there!
The latest technology
That's what Sylvania's lighting products are all about. Exciting advances in lighting technology have just turned into new ideas for lighting the home—beautifully . . . economically . . . and energy-efficiently. Today, Sylvania has an intriguing way to introduce these lighting products to your customers, and to help you sell them as well.
This means more lighting business . . . more profits for you
You'll be forming a profit-building partnership with Sylvania. We split the margin with you on every sale the Lighting Center generates. And it's a terrific store traffic builder, too. Let the Lighting Center lead your customers down other aisles—for fixtures . . . lamp shades . . . lighting accessories and home electric devices.
No inventory investment required
Expand your lighting business without expanding your investment. The Lighting Center lets you promote high-ticket, high-margin items—while Sylvania takes care of inventory for you. This allows you to maximize your return on investment. Order fulfillment is handled through a toll-free hotline on the display, and your store is credited with every sale. So you can promote and sell all kinds of new products up front, without having to stock them. But once you see how fast they move—and how excited your customers become—you'll probably want to start stocking them yourself to maximize impulse sales.
Give your customers access to thousands of Sylvania products
When you participate in the Lighting Center program, there's an added benefit for you—you'll be opening up the total catalog of Sylvania products to your customers—over 6,000 of them. Including a large number of specialty products that aren't always easy to find.
SYLVANIA LIGHTING CENTER
SYLVANIA BULBS IN USE
SYLVANIA HOTLINE
INTERCHANGEABLE PRODUCT OFFER PANEL
EASY-TO-FOLLOW INSTRUCTIONS
LIGHTDESIGN PRODUCT CATALOG
STORE-CODED TAKE-HOME BROCHURE
SYLVANIA
GTE
The Lighting Center grabs your customers' attention . . .
by giving them a peek into an attractive, well-lighted home. They'll see a colorful, 3-dimensional scene of a home interior lighted with Sylvania products. And each display unit features an interchangeable product panel with a special product offer.
. . . And it gets their business
Because it's organized to prompt sales—on-the-spot! The large arrows will lead your customers to the easy-to-follow instructions printed on the Lighting Center. At that point they'll find that their home lighting needs can be easily met. And the right products are just a phone call away.
The LIGHTDESIGN Idea Book is the hook
It provides all the information your customers need to make the best lighting product choices. Complete descriptions . . . expert advice . . . illustrations . . . energy-savings charts. And the home environment sections display color photos that show how light can be used as an essential design element. Featuring a tabulated index, the Idea Book lets the reader flip from environment sections to product sections—where they'll find the products they're looking for.
The HOTLINE is your customers' direct line to Sylvania
Your customers will have fast, easy access to a staff of knowledgeable Sylvania telemarketers who stand ready to answer any of their questions and process their orders, too. And the calls are toll-free.
The Take-One Brochure backs it up
It's a mini-version of the LIGHTDESIGN Idea Book for your busier customers to take home. The Take-One reinforces the information presented in the Idea Book, and encourages over-the-phone orders from home, via our new toll-free number 1-800-LIGHT BULB. So the Take-One Brochure actually multiplies your outlets—expanding your reach beyond your store, right into your customers' homes. And of course it's specially coded to identify your store as its source, so that you receive sales credit and margin dollars for every product it sells.
Your customers will get delivery via UPS
Just another convenience factor from Sylvania to keep them coming back. Their orders will be shipped directly to their home within 48 hours of receipt.
UPS and UPS in shield design are registered trademarks of United Parcel Service of America, Inc. Used by permission.
FOR MORE INFORMATION, CONTACT YOUR SYLVANIA CONSUMER SERVICES REPRESENTATIVE.

Exhibit 1-4. Home Shopping Network Studio

The HSN1 studio which is located in Clearwater, Florida. As many as 420 operators man computer terminals taking telephone orders that come in from around the country for merchandise offered on HSN1 and HSN2.

But penetration is a matter of scale. We must look into the merchandising concept and the program format to discover the most important ingredients of the success story. HSN advertises themselves as "America's original, live, discount shop at home TV service."

Their ingredients for success are best described by quoting from their annual report.

> Our approach to retail buying is a whole new experience for consumers; and they love it. Broadcast live 24 hours a day on two networks, Home Shopping Club (HSC) wows viewers with an amazing array of retail items often priced substantially below the retail prices they are accustomed to. In addition to the convenience of shopping in their own homes, customers are treated to a mixture of shopping and entertainment—in other words, it's just plain fun.
>
> Home Shopping Club knows no limit to inventive and entertaining merchandising. Each item appears for a few minutes, encouraging viewers to make a buying decision. Truly interactive television programming, HSC's television hosts frequently encourage viewers to call and participate in the show. Contests and prizes such as HSC's "Spendable Kash" generate excitement and keep programming lively. With the aid of the computer, HSC celebrates members' birthdays and anniversaries by sending out "Spendable Kash" on each occasion.

Viewers are served a variable menu of merchandise on the two HSN Networks. Club member purchases are carefully tracked. The entire relationship with an HSC member is stored within our computer database and allows our Customer Service Department to insure customer satisfaction. This allows the Networks to continue to provide on an ongoing basis the kind of merchandise and programming necessary to keep viewers tuned in and buying.

Home Shopping Network, Inc., offers a never-ending stream of merchandise, featuring deeply discounted products, including close-outs, overruns, overstocks, branded merchandise and specially manufactured products. The secret of our product success is innovation, coupled with our buying power.

Buyers scour the world for goods that are being liquidated by manufacturers, distributors, and retailers. HSN buyers also develop close relationships with manufacturers of the types of products which are popular with viewers. This new concept of electronic merchandising is, in fact, changing the way America buys and suppliers are eager to be part of this emerging industry. The potential for moving large volumes of merchandise gives manufacturers a whole new outlet for their products and allows Home Shopping Network, Inc., to buy at greatly advantaged prices.

A wide assortment of items are available to Club members. Jewelry, electronics, designer fashions, appliances, tools, housewares, and gifts are only a few of the more than 25,000 different products offered annually. Every item offered is available for immediate shipment. HSN has uniquely demonstrated a consistent ability to turn its inventory very rapidly.

The home shopping concept is too new to be certain, but there are those in direct marketing who view home shopping shows as a much-needed source for a massive injection of new mail order buyers who will continue to be responsive to a wide variety of merchandise offers.

Then there are those who view home shopping shows as a "fad" with HSN, in particular, living off of close-outs and off-brand merchandise. Time will tell, but indications are there will continue to be a massive audience out there for heavily discounted merchandise offered via TV.

At the other end of the spectrum are home shopping shows offering upscale merchandise, QVC Network of West Chester, Pennsylvania, for example. (See Chapter 11, "Electronic Media.") My conclusion is that home shopping shows are here to stay.

Membership Programs

Let's discuss the more traditional applications of direct marketing.

Development of membership programs for trade associations and other nonprofit organizations has long been a charge for direct marketing professionals. It is rare to find direct marketing professionals on a trade association staff, but the more astute associations hire professionals to mount their membership programs. The American Film Institute of Washington, D.C., is an excellent example.

Wishing to improve upon the response they were getting from their standard direct mail membership solicitation, the Institute turned to Donna Baier Stein, an outstanding free-lance copywriter in McLean, Virginia. Donna Baier Stein's credentials include successful membership programs for such renowned organizations as the Smithsonian, the World Wildlife Fund, and the National School Boards Association.

The American Film Institute is the only independent, nonprofit organization dedicated to advancing the art of film and television in the United States. One hundred percent of each member's dues is designated for a subscription to *American Film* magazine, the country's only consumer magazine specializing in the art of the moving image.

The Market   The market for American Film Institute is defined as professionals in film, TV, and video; upscale frequent film-goers; other art and culture enthusiasts; and predominantly young and affluent segments of the population.

The Mailing Package   The new package Donna Baier Stein developed consisted of a four-page letter signed by Francis Ford Coppola, an official membership nomination certificate, a personalized membership acceptance form, business reply envelope, and personalized outer envelope with Coppola's name above the AFI corner card address (see Exhibit 1-5).

Results   This mailing package was a big winner. It outpulled the standard mailing package (the control) by 34 percent.

The professionalism that made the difference may not be apparent to a neophyte. Using a well-known figure—Francis Ford Coppola—got the immediate attention of the target audience. The magnificent writing style held the interest of the reader. The membership benefits described in the letter created a strong desire to join a select group. And the time limit placed upon the offer spurred action.

Moral: For best results, use a professional.

Lead Generation Programs

An ever-expanding need in business is for expertise in developing qualified leads for dealers and salespeople (see Chapter 17, "Managing a Lead Generation Program").

Actually the need to generate qualified leads has always existed. But the ability to zero in on the best prospects, rate inquiries by potential, and

Exhibit 1-5. The American Film Institute "Package"

The American Film Institute

The John F. Kennedy Center for the Performing Arts, Washington, D.C. 20566

You are one of a select group

recently nominated for National Membership

in The American Film Institute.

Dear Mr. Cohen:

A darkened room, a parting curtain. Even now--after years
in the profession, after directing The Godfather and Apocalypse
Now--the opening moments of a movie never fail to cast their
spell on me.

That's why I'm delighted to invite you to join a group of
people who want to be closer to, and better enjoy, an art form
that touches all our lives.

Your new membership in The American Film Institute will put
you in this picture...an insider to the exciting arts and dynamic
industries of film, TV, and video.

On behalf of AFI's Board of Trustees, I
need to hear in the next ten days
if you will accept their special nomination.

But first, let me tell you about some of the many member
benefits they've already reserved for you:

* Invitations to film screenings, motion picture
  premieres, lectures, seminars, festivals, and many
  other AFI-sponsored events hosted by acclaimed
  performers and professionals.

* Generous discounts on the AFI Desk Diary and
  other unique gift merchandise, car rentals...
  plus two FREE passes to Landmark Theatres.

* Reduced-price admission to the AFI Theater in Washington's
  Kennedy Center, the Los Angeles County Museum of Art,
  and London's British Film Institute Theatre.

And if you're the ardent movie/TV buff or industry
professional I think you are, there's even more good news.

Because when you join AFI you'll also receive a full year's
(10 issues) subscription to American Film magazine--a thought-
provoking, graphically exciting, and acclaimed magazine on the

Exhibit 1-5. The American Film Institute "Package"

-2-

film, television, and video arts.

The American Film Institute was first established in 1967 by the National Endowment for the Arts, with Gregory Peck our founding chairman.

Today, the institute is nearing the end of its second decade of service to the film and television arts. Our magazine American Film, has just celebrated its own tenth anniversary.

I'd like you to be part of the year ahead which promises to be one of our most exciting ever.

In this Decade of Preservation (1983-1993), vital work is now being done at AFI's National Center for Film and Video Preservation--coordinating a national effort to preserve classic films that, as time goes by, are in danger of crumbling to dust or bursting into flames.

The need to save these rare prints is urgent...so your favorite movies and TV shows aren't lost forever. So we can "Play It Again, Sam" for many years to come.

With your support, we can save the magic moments of Gene Kelly's Singing in the Rain, and Fred Astaire dancing in Swing Time. Bogey coming face to face with Bergman, Judy Garland on the road to Oz, even Lucy and Ethel stuffing chocolates into their uniforms as the conveyor belt speeds by.

The American Film Institute's archival collection in the Library of Congress now contains nearly 20,000 titles of classic films and kinescopes like these.

But the commendable work of film preservation is only one part of our mission.

Film is alive and well--in movies, TV, cable, and video. (In fact, if you own a VCR, you'll want to read American Film regularly--for its "must-see" recommendations for cassette viewers.)

So in many ways, in cities around the world, AFI and American Film magazine stay at the forefront of today's filmmaking revolution.

With style and substance, American Film
educates...enlightens...and entertains
people in, and interested in, this art form.

In its colorful, stimulating pages, you'll watch film magic step off the screen as literally as the dashing Egyptologist in

(continued)

Exhibit 1-5. The American Film Institute "Package"

-3-

Woody Allen's The Purple Rose of Cairo.

You'll meet a cast of many--through interviews and profiles of Woody, Steven Spielberg, George Lucas, Gillian Armstrong, John Sayles, Martin Scorsese, Rebecca de Mornay, Lillian Gish.

Listen as Gregory Hines taps his way from Broadway to Hollywood, and Repo Man Emilio Estevez pushes at the limits of his craft. Be among the first to spot bright new stars in celluloid skies. And learn what young, independent filmmakers are up to--how much creative control the new technologies bring them, and why they're not "underground" any more.

Time and again, American Film takes you behind the scenes-- into a world of final cuts, deals, and budgets. Onto the stage sets of Grand Illusion. And into the anticipatory quiet of screening rooms, and the executive talk of board rooms at major TV networks.

It lets you stand during shooting with the late, great Sam Peckinpah. Watch John Waters, Baltimore's Prince of Trash, teach film appreciation to inmates of a maximum security prison. And survey the smorgasbord of TV...the world of paperback tie-ins...the past and future of MTV.

Yet neither American Film--nor the activities of AFI--stop with the winding credits of a darkened screen.

They go out to meet the world: to measure the societal impact of this most powerful communications media.

They analyze the way films shape our styles, give substance to our dreams. And they encourage important cultural exchange through historic China Film Week, and our popular national touring film programs which have included unusual new films from East Germany, Japan, and the Arab world.

In short, your institute membership and magazine subscription will make all your film-going and TV watching more fun, rewarding, and meaningful.

There's an intangible benefit of membership as well: the satisfaction of knowing you're helping to preserve and encourage one of the most vital, living parts of our culture.

As a National Member of The American Film Institute, you lend a hand to developing tomorrow's talent--through grants, internships, and AFI's Center for Advanced Film Studies.

You enable us to stock and maintain the extraordinary

Exhibit 1-5. The American Film Institute "Package"

-4-

research holdings of the Louis B. Mayer Library at the AFI campus in Los Angeles, devoted to the motion picture, television, and video arts.

You support-- and are most welcome to attend--classes, film workshops, and seminars taught by giants of the profession.

If you accept our invitation to join the institute, you will be part of all this...and your patronage of inestimable value to the entire film community.

Because our Board of Trustees has nominated you, you can now join The American Film Institute for 25% less than customary membership dues--only $15 for the year.

Your subscription to American Film is included in these dues--at a cost far less than the single cover copy price!

$15: A small amount to pay when it can enrich your life, enhance the art form, and preserve a treasured part of our cultural heritage.

I hope you'll join other AFI members who share these special commitments... and enjoy the wealth of privileges AFI membership brings.

Say yes to our nomination, won't you? Simply complete and return the enclosed acceptance form to become the newest National Member of The American Film Institute. I look forward to welcoming you.

Sincerely,

Francis Ford Coppola

increase the number who become customers is the result of refinements in target marketing.

Encyclopaedia Britannica USA is a prime example of sophisticated lead generation programs. Encyclopaedia Britannica, the reference standard of the world for more than two centuries, is sold in the home by a large national sales force.

To meet targeted sales forecasts and to prevent creative wear-out, hundreds of direct marketing lead-generating tests are conducted annually. We are indebted to Dave Hefter, corporate president of MARCOA DR GROUP of New York, Chicago, Boston, and Newport Beach for this mini case history.

TV Guide, with its enormous circulation and geographic targeting capabilities, is used as a testing ground for front-end and back-end premium offers, copy, involvement devices (stamps, tokens); everything from testing the color of the reply card to brand new creative themes.

This is done with four-color, four-page preprinted inserts which can be printed eighteen-up on the press, premixed, and distributed to all regions. Each test is, of course, uniquely keyed, tracked, and measured on the basis of pull percent, cost per lead, conversion ratio (number of sales calls needed to close a sale), cost per sale, and total unit sales.

What appears to be winning creative the first time out is retested several times, each time with increased circulation, to confirm results before it is tested in other media: Sunday supplements, consumer magazines, direct mail, television, and the like. That's how Dennis the Menace came to be tested against another cartoon character, who first made his appearance in *TV Guide* in October 1982.

"Freckles" was created by MARCOA DR GROUP as the creative approach that offered a new low-cost premium free to lead respondents: a twelve-page, two-color booklet entitled, *Make Your Child a Winner!*

After a number of tests, it was clear that the premium wasn't working, but the creative approach was very strong. In fact, in August 1983, when Freckles was tested with another control premium—a three-volume Britannica desk reference set—he changed the course of lead history. He became the control in January 1985, and through the years has had more than twenty different creative themes tested against him.

In view of these results, the objective for July 1986 was a real challenge: beat the Freckles control creative approach by at least 10 percent "across the board" (lead pull, unit sales, conversion ratio, cost per sale). The offer was to remain the same as the control: a free Britannica booklet mailed to the prospect, plus the three-volume desk reference set offered free for an in-home presentation by a Britannica sales representative.

The first test was launched in the July 19, 1986 issue of *TV Guide* (Exhibit 1-6). It was a resounding success: Dennis not only outpulled his stiff competition by over 16 percent, but outsold and outconverted Freckles by nearly *70 percent!* Dennis was, in fact, the number one winner across the board.

Exhibit 1-6. Britannica *TV Guide* Lead Generation Approach

	Lead Pull	Total Sales	Conversion Ratio	Reduced Cost
Freckles Control	—	—	—	—
vs.				
Dennis	+16.5%	+69.5%	+68.5%	+69.5%

In two subsequent tests, Dennis again beat Freckles by wide margins.

Issue	Lead Pull	Total Sales	Conversion Ratio	Reduced Cost
11/29/86	+20.1%	+25.0%	+29.6%	+25.0%
01/31/87	+13.3%	+10.9%	+16.1%	+10.9%

The Dennis creative has been extended to a consumer on-page ad and bind-in business reply card to appear in *Disney Channel Magazine* and a direct mail package has been created around him.

Pretty good for a kid who can't even read yet.

Six Big Keys to Direct Marketing Success

The expanded scope of direct marketing begs the question, "What does make direct marketing successful?" An oversimplified answer might be: *offering the right products or services via the right media, with the most enticing propositions, presented with the most effective formats, proved successful as a result of the right tests.*

Sounds pretty simple. But, of course, it isn't! Let's explore the six big keys to direct marketing success and some basic questions relating to them.

1. *Right products or services.* Success in any endeavor start with the product. No matter what the selling medium, no business can long survive unless the product is *right*. Time was when direct sale of products via mail, space, or broadcast advertising was looked upon as a means of "dumping" merchandise that did not sell well through retail channels. Time was when off-brand merchandise, which couldn't get shelf space in retail stores, was offered direct to the consumer. That's all changed today. Successful direct marketers offer quality merchandise of good value.

2. *Right media.* Some authorities give half or more of the credit for the success of a mailing to the lists that are used. You can't prove the figure. But you can bet on this: one of the most important keys to success is lists! Likewise, selection of the publications used for print ads and the stations used for broadcast are vital keys to success. (Chapters 8 through 13 cover each major medium in depth.)

3. *Right offer.* There is no key to success more important than the offer. You can have the right product, the right mailing lists, the right print and broadcast media. But you still won't make it big if you don't have the right offer. You've got to overcome human inertia, whatever the medium. (Chapter 4 covers offers designed to overcome human inertia.)

4. *Right formats.* The number of formats for presenting offers is almost endless. This is particularly true of direct mail, where there are few restrictions on format. The marketer can use anything from a simple post card to a 9″ × 12″ mailing package which could include a giant four-color brochure, letter, giant order card, tokens, stamps, pop-ups, and so on.

   Restrictions on print and broadcast advertising are, of course, more stringent, because of controls by the publishers and the stations. But the important point is that there is a *right* format for a given mailing package, a given ad, and a given commercial. Depending on format selected, the results can be anywhere from disastrous to sensational.

5. *Right tests.* With literally thousands of chances to do the wrong thing, the way to achieve direct marketing success is to test to determine the *right* thing. Indeed, direct marketing is the most *measurable* type of marketing there is.

   Mailing packages can be tested scientifically to determine such vital factors as best offer, best format, best lists, best copy, best postage, and so on.

   The print medium, with the advent of regional editions, has also made an endless variety of tests possible. Direct marketers now test by regions. They test for size and color. They test for position. They test bind-in cards, bingo cards. They test special against general interest magazines. Newspapers can be tested to learn all you have to know.

   It is also possible to test the efficiency of broadcast on a control basis. Testing is likewise possible when the telephone is used as a selling medium. (Chapter 19 clearly spells out the techniques that enable you to test for the right answers.)

6. *Right analyses.* The final element essential to a successful direct marketing program is right analyses. Direct marketers live by figures, but misinterpretation of figures often leads to erroneous conclusions. Fortunes have been lost by counting *trial orders* instead of counting *paid-ups.* Fortunes have been lost by *averaging* response, by not re-

ally knowing break-even points, by never determining the value of a customer, by never preparing cash-flow charts.

Chapter 18 is devoted to applying the mathematics of direct marketing properly.

Checklist for Applying the Six Big Keys to Direct Marketing Success

1. The product or service you offer

   ☐ Is it a real value for the price asked?
   ☐ How does it stack up against competition?
   ☐ Do you have exclusive features?
   ☐ Does your packaging create a good first impression?
   ☐ Is the market broad enough to support a going organization?
   ☐ Is your product cost low enough to warrant a mail order markup?
   ☐ Does your product or service lend itself to repeat business?

2. The media you use

   Customer lists
   ☐ Is your customer list cleaned on a regular basis?
   ☐ Do you keep a second copy of your list in a secure place to avoid loss?
   ☐ Have you developed a profile of your customer list, giving you all the important demographic and psychographic characteristics?
   ☐ Have you coded your customer list by recency of purchase?
   ☐ Have you worked your customer list by the classic mail order formula: recency-frequency-monetary?
   ☐ Have you thought of what other products or services may appeal to your customer list?
   ☐ Do you mail your customer list often enough to capitalize on the investment?

   Prospect lists
   ☐ Do you freely provide facts and figures to one or more competent mailing list brokers, enabling them to unearth productive lists for you?
   ☐ Have you worked with competent list compilers in selecting names of prospects who match the profile of those on your customer list?
   ☐ Do you test meaningful, measurable, projectable quantities?
   ☐ Have you measured the true results of prospect lists, computing for each list the number of inquiries, the quantity of returned goods, net cash receipts per thousand mailed, and repeat business?

☐ Have you determined how often you can successfully mail to the same prospect lists?

Print

☐ Have you matched your offers with your markets and used print publications with good direct response track records?

☐ Have you measured the true results of print media, computing for each newspaper or magazine the number of inquiries, the amount of returned goods, net cash receipts per insertion, and repeat business?

☐ Have you determined how often you can successfully use the same print media?

Broadcast

☐ Have you selected broadcast media that best fit your objective: (a) to get inquiries or orders, (b) to support other advertising media?

☐ Have you measured the true results of broadcast media, computing for each station the number of inquiries, the amount of returned goods, net cash receipts per broadcast schedule, and repeat business?

☐ Have you determined the proper times and frequency for broadcast schedules?

3. The offers you make

☐ Are you making the most enticing offers you can within the realm of good business?

☐ Does your offer lend itself to the use of any or all of these incentives for response: free gift, contest, free trial offer, installment terms, price savings, money back guarantee?

☐ Does your offer lend itself to the development of an "automatic" repeat business cycle?

☐ Does your offer lend itself to a "get-a-friend" program?

☐ Have you determined the ideal introductory period or quantity for your offer?

☐ Have you determined the ideal introductory price for your offer?

☐ Have you determined the possibility of multiple sales for your offer?

4. The formats you use

Direct mail

☐ Are your mailing packages in character with your product or services and the markets you are reaching?

☐ Have you developed the ideal format for your mailing packages,

with particular emphasis on mailing envelope, letter, circular, response form, and reply envelope?
- ☐ Do you work with one or more creative envelope manufacturers?
- ☐ Are your sales letters in character with your offers?
- ☐ Are your circulars graphic, descriptive, and in tune with the complete mailing package?
- ☐ Does your response form contain the complete offer? Is it attractive enough to grab attention and impel action?

Print
- ☐ Are your ads in character with your product and services and the markets you are reaching?
- ☐ Have you explored newspaper inserts, magazine inserts, bind-in cards, tip-on cards, Dutch door newspaper inserts, plastic records?

Broadcast
- ☐ Are your commercials in character with your products and services and the markets you are reaching?
- ☐ Have you determined the efficiency of stand-up announcer commercials vs. staged commercials?
- ☐ Have you explored the efficiency of noted personality endorsements?

5. The tests you make

- ☐ Do you consistently test the big things: products, media, offers, and formats?
- ☐ Have you tested to determine the best timing for your offers, the best frequency?
- ☐ Have you determined the most responsive geographical areas?
- ☐ Do you consistently test new direct mail packages against control packages, new ads against control ads, new commercials against control commercials?
- ☐ Do you use adequate test quantities?
- ☐ Do you follow your test figures through to conclusion, using net revenue per thousand as the key criterion?
- ☐ Do you interpret your test figures in the light of the effect on the image and future profits of your company?

6. The right analyses

- ☐ Do you track results by source, computing front-end and back-end response, returned goods factors, and bad debt factor for each source?
- ☐ Do you analyze results by ZIP codes, by demographics, and by psychographics?
- ☐ Do you compute the level of repeat business by original source?

Ten Major Responsibilities

The world of direct marketing is a big world, an exciting world, an awesome world for those who have never operated within it. And the scope keeps expanding.

As more and more major corporations and agencies enter direct marketing (and they are doing so at a rapidly accelerating rate), it is becoming clear that those who are succeeding are doing so by setting up direct marketing separate and apart from other marketing and advertising functions.

It is safe to predict that in the next decade all major corporations and agencies will have staffs of direct marketing experts. Following is a detailed list of the ten major responsibilities of the direct marketing executive—a total of eighty-eight individual functions.

Exhibit 1-7. Direct Marketing Evaluations and Functions Checklist

1. Product selection and development
   Market potential
   Competition
   Reliability of sources
   Value comparison
   Packaging
   Shipping costs
   Unit of sale
   Profit margin
   Ease of use
   Instructions
   Refurbishing costs
   Repeat potential
   Evaluation of syndication

2. Strategic planning
   Establishing objectives
   Developing planning models
   Doing business planning
   Developing strategies
   Implementation of strategies

3. Markets and media selection
   Mailing lists
   Magazines
   Newspapers and supplements
   Radio and television
   Co-ops
   Telemarketing
   Car cards, match books, etc.

4. Creative development and scheduling
   Strategy and concept
   Offers
   Copy
   Layouts
   Formats
   FTC regulations
   Scheduling of ads and mailing packages

5. Research
   Exploratory research
   Pretesting
   Evaluative research
   Qualitative research
   Quantitative research
   Focus groups
   Survey research

6. Testing procedures
   Compiled vs. direct response lists
   Regional testing
   Testing by ZIP codes
   Testing by socioeconomic factors
   Seasonal testing
   Price testing
   Offer testing
   Establishing control ads and control mailing packages

(continued)

Exhibit 1-7. Direct Marketing Evaluations and Functions Checklist

Determining media
  duplication
Using probability scales
Preevaluation of ads and
  mailing packages
Measuring readership

7. Fulfillment
  Shipping facilities
  Replacement procedures
  Returned goods procedures
  Distribution centers
  Shipping method (carriers)

8. Budgeting and accounting
  Cash flow charts
  Bad debt reserves
  Financing costs
  Attrition scales
  Forms and systems
  Commercial credit card
    affiliations
  Credit and collection procedures

Recency, frequency, and
  monetary criteria

9. Customer service
  Sales correspondence
  Complaints and adjustments
  Activation and reactivation

10. Personal and supplier relations
  Advertising department
  Fulfillment sources
  Accounting department
  Customer service
  Advertising agency
  List brokers
  Space reps
  Suppliers of merchandise and
    services
  Printers, engravers, and
    typesetters
  Artists and art studios
  Envelope houses

Self-Quiz

1. Define TRM.

   T _____

   R _____

   M _____

2. The three building blocks of TRM are:

   a. Prospect/user identification/enhanced data base

   b. _____

   c. _____

3. Define direct marketing.

   _____

   _____

   _____

4. Approximately _____ percent of all revenue comes from _____ percent of a customer base.

5. What is the most important question to ask when you read about a unique idea like United Airline's loyalty program?

   _____

   _____

   _____

6. Why should direct marketing kiosks appeal to retailers?

   _____

   _____

   _____

7. Home shopping shows via TV have been the mail order breakthrough of the 80s. Name three categories of merchandise that sell well on these shows.

   a. _____

   b. _____

   c. _____

8. When conducting a lead generation program, four areas must be measured.

   a. Lead pull   c. Conversion _____

   b. Unit _____   d. Cost per _____

9. What are the six big keys to direct marketing success?

   a. Right products or services   d. _____

   b. _____   e. _____

   c. _____   f. _____

10. What are the ten major responsibilities of direct marketing executives?

    a. Product selection and development

    b. Strategic planning

    c. Markets and media selection

    d. _____

e. _____

f. _____

g. _____

h. _____

i. _____

j. _____

Pilot Project

You are the catalog manager of a women's apparel catalog. You have a 200,000 customer base. You learn that 80 percent of your business is coming from 20 percent of this base. So you decide that in order to protect your franchise with the precious 20 percent a *loyalty program* is in order.

Your assignment is to (a) establish a name for your loyalty program, and (b) list the special benefits you will give members for remaining loyal to your company.

CHAPTER TWO

Data Base Marketing

There are those who say that data bases are the "secret weapon" of direct marketing. To a major degree this is true for direct marketers know who raises their hands expressing interest in the marketers' products and services. Direct marketers know who their buyers are, what they buy, how often they buy, whether they buy by phone or by mail, how much they spend, by what methods they pay.

Such is not the case with most traditional marketers. Millions of people trade at supermarkets each day, but they are not known by name or by what they purchase. Department stores get a step closer to their clientele by identifying those customers who use the stores' credit cards.

Business-to-business marketers who sell through jobbers and distributors know the names of their jobbers and distributors, but they don't know the names of the firms to whom they sell. Nor do they know exactly what products those firms buy from the line, how often they buy, how much they spend. The manufacturer's destiny, to a major degree, is left in the hands of their jobbers and distributors. In the final analysis only the pure direct marketer can exercise complete control over inquiry and customer data bases.

Gathering Source Data

Data base management starts with measuring the efficiency of advertising and promotions, knowing which radio and TV commercials, which print ads, and which mailing lists are most cost efficient from a customer acquisition standpoint.

Let's say you are mounting a lead generation program. You decide to use six different mailing lists (Table 2-1). By tracking sources for each, you might come up with a table that would look something like this:

Table 2-1. Lead Generation Program (Direct Mail)

List	Quantity Mailed	Total List	Percentage of Response	Percentage Sold	Average Order
A	5,000	24,000	5.0	10	$300.00
B	5,000	30,000	2.5	20	340.00
C	5,000	50,000	10.0	2	120.00
D	5,000	40,000	3.5	6	350.00
E	5,000	40,000	5.0	5	300.00
F	5,000	15,000	6.0	10	280.00
Averages	5,000	199,000	5.33	8.9	$281.66

If we throw everything into the pot, we find that our lead generation mailing averages a response of 5.33 percent, that we sell an average of 8.9 percent, and that our average order comes to $281.66. But those are *averages.* By tracking each source, we quickly discover we have at least one "loser."

List C, front-end, looks great: 10 percent in inquiries—the best response. But look at the back end: only 2 percent sold and an average order of only $120.00. With no back-end tracking, the marketer would most certainly have mailed the balance of 50,000 names on List C. Not only would this pull down the average percentage sold and the average order, but it would have devastated the telephone salespeople handling the low quality leads from this list source.

Now let us say that we decide upon a continuation mailing to all the lists with the exception of List C and that we get the same type of response. Table 2-2 shows the picture.

Table 2-2. Continuation Mailing for Lead Generation Program

List	Mailing Quantity	Response	Percentage Sold	No. of Sales	Average Order	Total Sales
A	19,000	5.0	10.0	95	$300	$ 28,500
B	25,000	2.5	20.0	125	340	42,500
D	35,000	3.5	6.0	73	350	25,500
E	35,000	5.0	5.0	87	300	26,100
F	10,000	6.0	10.0	60	280	16,800
	(T)124,000	(A)4.4	(A)10.0	(T)440	(A)$314	(T)$139,450

T = Total; A = Average.

Our percent and number of leads is down. But our closure rate and average order—the two factors that count—are up. And let us not overlook the money saved in the telemarketing program by not processing poor quality leads, plus the money saved by not mailing 45,000 pieces to List C. Only by tracking responses by sources and putting this information in your data base is it possible to know which mailing lists and which publications lead to the best end result.

Tables 2-1 and 2-2 deal specifically with getting new customers—first orders. Once a prospect becomes a customer, it's important that the original source of inquiry be carried right into the *customer data base.*

Lists A and B, for example, look extremely good with closure rates of 10 percent and 20 percent, respectively. But the true test is, how well do these customers perform after the first order? By punching the original source into the customer data base, the answer to this all-important question can be called up any time. And what the computer tells you is often a shocker.

Developing a Customer Data Base

The data base requirement varies greatly by category of business, to be sure. But regardless of category of business, there is a guideline to follow that should lead to a meaningful data base. Ask this question: "What data will I need in order to carry on a meaningful dialogue with my customers either by phone, or mail, or both?" Depending upon the nature of a business, here is basic data which should go into the data base:

- Name of individual
- Mailing and shipping address
- Telephone number
- Time Zone
- Standard industrial classification (SIC) number (if a business firm)
- Source of inquiry card/or order
- Date of inquiry/or order
- Cost of inquiry/or order
- History of purchases
    By dates
    By what items purchased
    By dollar amounts of purchases
    By cumulative sales dollars

Manipulating Data Bases

By putting basic data into your customer base the opportunity to maximize profit by manipulating the data increases a hundred fold. You will know precisely what your investment in each new customer is, by medium. You will know the dates and amounts of purchases for each customer and exactly what they bought. You will have a running profit and loss statement for each customer. And ultimately you will be able to measure the average lifetime value of each customer. (See Chapter 18, "Mathematics of Direct Marketing.")

The concept of manipulating customer data came about almost out of sheer desperation during the Great Depression. Catalog giants like Sears and Wards were feeling the impact of bread lines, as were all businesses. Working against the maxim that "All customers are not created equal," they developed a formula that changed the way mail-order customers were promoted. And this formula, with refinements, is being used to this day.

The R-F-M Formula

This magic formula was tagged as R-F-M (recency, frequency, monetary). Best customers, and therefore those most likely to buy again, were identified as those who had bought most recently, those who bought most frequently within a specified period, and those who had spent specified amounts.

Through testing, the mail-order giants learned that these three criteria—recency, frequency, monetary—were the basis for maximizing profits. Indeed, they soon found it possible to develop pro-forma statements that enabled them to predict with deadly accuracy what their profits would be based upon which customers they selected to receive their current catalog and which customers they excluded from their current circulation.

In its simplest form, the R-F-M formula calls for a point system to be established with purchases broken down by quarter of the year. A typical formula might be as follows:

Recency points:
- 24 points—current quarter
- 12 points—last six months
- 6 points—last nine months
- 3 points—last twelve months

Frequency points: Number of purchases × 4 points.

Monetary points: 10 percent of dollar purchase with a ceiling of 9 points. (The ceiling avoids distortion by an unusually large purchase.)

Number of points allotted varies among those using R-F-M formulas, but the principle is the same. Once the system is established and point values are assigned, the opportunities for maximizing profits are almost phenomenal. I've seen sophisticated systems that have scores of categories with profit figures ranging from $50 per thousand catalogs mailed to $1,500 and more. Under the system, each account is isolated from all other accounts. Buying habits dictate how frequently an account is solicited.

Once the R-F-M system is computer programmed, producing a monthly update is a simple matter. Table 2-3 shows what a hypothetical partial printout might look like for a representative group of accounts. The table shows the activity of five accounts for December 1987. Account number 16,441 bought twice in September and once in December. Recency points were computed in relation to the time interval since each purchase.

Table 2-3. Analysis of Accounts by Recency, Frequency, Monetary—December 1987

Account Number	Month	Recency Points	No. of Purchases	Frequency Points	Dollar Purchases	Monetary Points	Total Points	Cumulative Total Points
16,441	9	12	2	8	32.17	3.21	23	39
16,441	12	24	1	4	46.10	4.61	32	71
16,521	1	3	3	12	87.09	8.71	23	23
16,608	7	12	1	4	21.00	2.10	18	28
16,708	4	6	1	4	33.60	3.36	13	18
16,708	8	12	2	8	71.00	7.10	27	45
16,708	11	24	1	4	206.00	9.00	37	82
16,921								68

Frequency points were computed by multiplying the number of purchases by four. Monetary points were computed by multiplying the dollar amount of purchases by 10 percent. Note that under "Cumulative Total Points" this marketer had carried over sixteen accumulated points from the previous calendar year, indicating that his customer first bought in calendar year 1986.

In reviewing the list of accounts, note that account number 16,708 spent $206 in November but was given only nine monetary points. This reflects the arbitrary decision of the marketer to give no more than nine monetary points regardless of amount of purchase. Finally, note that account number 16,921 shows no activity for calendar year 1987 but has a total of 68 points for 1986.

The opportunities for manipulating a data base under the R-F-M system are immense. And, of course, the system need not be restricted to catalog firms. It is clearly applicable to telemarketing.

The R-F-M System Expanded

Robert Kestnbaum, a noted authority on data base management, has altered and added to the R-F-M formula. He has found for his clients—those engaged in direct marketing and telemarketing as well—that profits are maximized even further by employing his altered formula, which goes under the acronym FRAT.

F stands for frequency or purchase within a specified period. (Kestnbaum gives the greatest weight to frequency.) He follows this factor with R, recency of purchase. Then A, amount of purchase, followed by T, type of merchandise, or service, purchased. The T is an important addition to the R-F-M formula, for what a person buys currently serves as a statement about what else that person is likely to buy in the future. For example, subsequent purchases of a woman who just bought support hose are likely to be quite different for the woman who just bought jogging shoes.

Being given a data base that provides almost unlimited manipulation fires the flames of imagination. Think of the commands that can be made of the computer on behalf of a telemarketing center.

- "Give me a list of all our customers who have bought two or more times in the last six months."
- "Give me a list of all our customers who first bought within the last three months."
- "I want all the names of those who bought Product X in the last 12 months so we can phone them about preference treatment in testing our new model."
- "Let me have a list of everyone who bought a personal computer from us in the last year. I want to mount a mail campaign to sell our new software program."

If you've got the data base, the computer will give you whatever you ask for. Fast.

A specific example of maximizing profits by drawing upon *type of purchase* from the FRAT formula comes from Bureau of Business Practice in Waterford, Connecticut. I received a mailing from this publisher offering a card file of anecdotes for public speakers. Because I fulfill speaking engagements regularly, I ordered the card file. In the process of ordering I made a statement about myself: I said, in effect, "I am interested in public speaking material." The publisher obviously noted this by punching what I bought into his data base.

Evidence of this astute application is Exhibit 2-1: Note how Bureau of Business Practice plays off of my expressed interest in public speaking materials. This is target marketing at its finest.

Before data base marketing, the Bureau of Business Practice or any other publisher would have simply offered me a wide variety of books and pamphlets based on the simple fact that I bought *something*. To dramatize the difference: suppose they had offered me a card file on foreman training (a subject in which I have no interest) following my purchase of the public speaking card file? In no way would I be a prospect, even though I would be included in the Bureau of Business Practice customer data base.

Cross-Selling

Our exploration of data base manipulation continues.

One of the most exciting potentials is in the area of cross-selling. When you know what every customer buys, it's a simple matter to cross-sell related products.

Consider banks, for example. The computer can easily segment out all accounts by class and dollar amounts.

- Savings Accounts
- Personal Checking Accounts
- Commercial Checking Accounts
- Money Market Checking Accounts
- Home Mortgages
- Commercial Real Estate Loans
- Inventory Loans
- Accounts Receivable Loans
- Car Loans
- Home Improvement Loans

Pinpointing accounts by class and amount leads to cross-selling opportunities. Commercial checking accounts, for example, are prime prospects for inventory loans. Savings accounts are prime prospects for car loans. Those who have paid down, or paid off home mortgages are prime prospects for equity loans. Opportunities for cross-selling abound.

Major insurance firms have mastered cross-selling. And they have the data bases to make it happen. They know about their policy-holders: ages, home ownership, marital status, children and their ages. And they know which policies each policyholder has with the company.

These insurance companies can get a printout any time they want of all policyholders turning sixty-five, say within six months. Their cross-selling opportunity in this instance would be supplemental medicare insurance.

These insurance companies can get a printout any time they want of families with preschool children. The cross-sell opportunity in this instance would be an educational insurance program.

The data base manipulation opportunities are practically endless. Cross-sell hospital insurance to accident insurance policyholders. Cross-sell cancer insurance to hospital insurance policyholders. Cross-sell homeowner's insurance to mortgage insurance policyholders. And on and on.

Enhanced Data Bases

Our concern thus far has been with capturing data about those who inquire and those who buy. But other types of data bases have emerged which can help to enhance the value of existing lists—both rental lists and compiled lists—by matching demographics and lifestyles to the customer profiles of given marketers.

National Demographics & Lifestyles (NDL) of Denver, Colorado is in the forefront of compiling and providing massive compiled lists of consumers with precise selections of demographics and lifestyles. Jock Bickert, president of NDL, illustrates the importance of enhanced demo-

Exhibit 2-1. Bureau of Business Practice Mailing

24 ROPE FERRY ROAD • WATERFORD, CT 06386 • PHONE 203-442-4365 • TELEX 966420

BUREAU OF BUSINESS PRACTICE • DIVISION OF SIMON & SCHUSTER, INC. • A GULF+WESTERN COMPANY

Telephone your order toll free!
Just dial 800-243-0876
Connecticut residents call 442-4365

DECEMBER 27, 1986

BOB STONE INC.
MR. ROBERT STONE, PRES.
1630 SHERIDAN RD. 8G   + SS
WILMETTE IL.   .60091

DEAR MR. STONE,

WE HAVE A VERY SPECIAL OFFER FOR YOU BECAUSE OF YOUR
INTEREST AND RECENT PURCHASE OF THE SPEAKERS CARD FILE.

A FEW YEARS AGO WE DEVELOPED AN EXCITING 1-YEAR
CASSETTE PROGRAM CALLED THE EXECUTIVES SHORTCUT COURSE
TO SPEECH IMPROVEMENT. I HAVE ENCLOSED A PROMOTIONAL
BROCHURE THAT WE USED TO DESCRIBE THE COURSE. FROM
IT, I THINK YOU CAN SEE WHY THE IDEA WAS RECEIVED
WITH SUCH TREMENDOUS SUCCESS.

NOW WE ARE PACKAGING THE ENTIRE 12-PART COURSE ON 6
EXTENDED PLAY CASSETTES, ALONG WITH OUR *EXECUTIVES
HANDBOOK OF HUMOR FOR SPEAKERS,* IN A CONVENIENT AND
HANDSOME BINDER, AND OFFERING IT TO YOU AT THE REDUCED
RATE OF ONLY 69.00--A BIG SAVINGS OF OVER 35 PERCENT OFF
THE MONTHLY PROGRAM PRICE. AND IF YOU PREFER, WE WILL BILL
YOU IN TWO MONTHLY INSTALLMENTS OF 34.50. JUST INITIAL
THE APPROPRIATE BLANK BELOW.

        INITIALS...... SEND ME THE COMPLETE EXECUTIVES SHORT
                       CUT COURSE TO SPEECH IMPROVEMENT, THE
                       HANDBOOK AND BINDER IN ONE SHIPMENT,
                       AND BILL ME ONLY 69.00, PLUS A SMALL
                       CHARGE FOR POSTAGE AND HANDLING.
                            (ETI7-083)

        INITIALS...... BILL ME IN TWO MONTHLY INSTALLMENTS
                       OF 34.50 EACH, PLUS A SMALL CHARGE
                       FOR POSTAGE AND HANDLING.
                            (ETI7-091)

THIS IS THE FIRST IN A SERIES OF VERY SPECIAL OFFERS.
FROM TIME TO TIME YOU WILL RECEIVE OTHER ONE-TIME
SPECIALS.

SINCERELY,

David M. Atwood

DAVID M. ATWOOD

ETI-(X199-DB08)

David Day—Bloomington, Minnesota		Nick Night—Bloomington, Minnesota	
Demographics		*Demographics*	
Sex	Male	Sex	Male
Household income	$40,000	Income	$40,000
Age	34	Age	34
Marital status	Married	Marital status	Married
Occupation	Sales/marketing	Occupation	Professional/technical
Spouse occupation	Clerical	Spouse occupation	Homemaker
Home ownership	Single family home	Home ownership	Single family home
Length of residence	Eight years	Length of residence	Four years
Children at home	Two, ages four and one	Children at home	One, age five
Lifestyle Activities		*Lifestyle Activities*	
Golfing		Fishing	
Foreign travel		Working on automobiles	
Physical fitness exercise		Camping	
Investing in stocks and bonds		Watching sports on TV	
Home workshop		Personal computing	

graphics and lifestyle data by comparing two men from the same city—same age, same income, same marital status—but with major differences in other demographics and in their lifestyles as well.

Looking at the profiles of David Day and Nick Night, their "differences" are easily apparent: Day is in sales/marketing; Night is a professional/technical person. Day's wife works at a clerical job; Night's wife is a homemaker. But the really significant differences are in lifestyle activities.

Day is a golfer; Night likes to fish. Day is interested in foreign travel; Night likes to work on automobiles. Day is a physical fitness devotee; Night likes to camp. Day is a serious investor in stocks and bonds; Night, on the other hand, devotes a lot of time to watching sports on TV. Day devotes free time to his home workshop; while Night works on his personal computer.

It is through the selection of lifestyle criteria that direct marketers can match prospects to customer profiles. Let's look at the profiles of David Day and Nick Night and translate them to prospecting opportunities.

David Day:
- Golfing—golf equipment, golf magazines, golf books, golf trips, golf club memberships
- Foreign travel—tours, travel books, travel magazines

- Physical fitness—jogging apparel, physical fitness magazines, physical fitness equipment
- Stocks and bonds—investment services, brokerage houses, investment books and publications
- Home workshop—workshop equipment, do-it-yourself books and magazines

Nick Night:
- Fishing—fishing equipment, fishing trips, books and magazines on fishing
- Working on automobiles—auto repair manuals, auto equipment catalogs, auto books and publications
- Camping—camp site directories, camping equipment, camping apparel, camping books and publications
- Sports on TV—subscription to cable sports network, sports books and publications
- Personal computer—computer programs, PC equipment, PC books and publications

National Demographics & Lifestyles maintains a "lifestyle inventory" of 57 activities and interests based upon data compiled from responses to consumer questionnaires. Over 14 million questionnaires are returned each year. Their master list is appropriately called "The Lifestyle Selector"®. The massive data base size also permits NDL to accurately profile small areas of geography—even down to the postal carrier route level.

Successful use of "The Lifestyle Selector"® is very much dependent upon marketers being able to provide a precise definition of demographic and lifestyle characteristics of their target markets. But the sad fact is that most marketers are unable to come up with precise definitions.

So in 1981 NDL introduced NDL F/O/C/U/S, by which mailers can determine the precise demographic and lifestyle characteristics of their target markets. The process is relatively simple. NDL compares the mailer's customer file (or subsegments of the file such as "high ticket" buyers, new subscribers, etc.) to "The Lifestyle Selector"® data base, identifies the matches between both of the comparison files, and then profiles the matches.

Those match profiles are extrapolated to a description of the mailer's entire file. With a match rate that consistently falls between 15 and 25 percent, the analysis is highly reliable. Another way of thinking of the process is that it represents a customer survey which generates an average response rate of 20 percent.

The large match sample sizes which ensue (e.g., 200,000 for a million name customer file) not only insure reliability, but also allow NDL to apply sophisticated multivariate analytic techniques that are precluded with small samples. Those multivariate analyses lead to the identification of important secondary and tertiary markets which may be very different from the obvious, primary market.

Once the NDL F/O/C/U/S analysis is complete, NDL applies the profile criteria to the remaining noncustomer portion of "The Lifestyle Selector"® data base and supplies the mailer with the names of likely prospective customers, customer "twins," so to speak.

In their fascinating, futuristic book titled, *MaxiMarketing* (McGraw-Hill, 1987), Stan Rapp and Tom Collins of Rapp & Collins detail some of the other mass data bases now available:

Select and Save distributes questionnaires to 50 million households via Valassis free-standing inserts and targeted direct mail. Consumers are promised price-off coupons and/or samples for filling out and returning a questionnaire. The questionnaire inquires about category usage, brand preference, volume of consumption, length of purchase cycle, number of users per household, multiple-brand users, and special usage information such as the size of the family pet. All this information is entered in the company's data base. Then, in co-op mailings, advertisers can enclose custom-tailored offers that reflect how the advertiser wants to treat each name. For instance, people known to be users of a competitor's product might receive a coupon with a larger cents-off value.

Donnelley's Carol Wright direct mail co-op, which reaches approximately 45 million households in 351 metro markets, now offers advertisers a targeting service called "Share Force." Questionnaires on product and brand usage are distributed through the Carol Wright co-op twice a year. The response rate is about 14 percent, providing data on six million households. Respondents are rewarded with a small box of samples and coupons. In this way advertisers can give samples or coupons to self-identified nonusers of their products.

Even local supermarkets, drugstores, and other retailers can use this new technique of nonwaste marketing. Until now, most supermarkets have joined with brand advertisers in wastefully distributing coupons or circulars to both customers and noncustomers throughout an entire market area.

CSI Telemarketing does telephone surveys of homes in a given area around a supermarket that wants to build its customer base. Respondents are asked what supermarket and drug store they patronize and what brands they use. Then only noncustomers can be selected to receive a mailing of coupons designed to woo them to pay the store a visit.

Retailers pay CSI about one dollar for each name of a competitive store's customer, manufacturers pay about ten or twelve cents for the name of the user of another brand. CSI recently went public and hoped to expand its survey base to 20 million names in 1987.

JFY is responsible for perhaps the most ambitious undertaking in profiling households by name and address. This company began in 1979 with a pilot data base of 20,000 households which had answered a questionnaire about product and brand usage. By 1983 JFY was mailing out a fairly elaborate questionnaire to 40 million households a year and getting back 8 million replies (response is stimulated by a vague promise of coupons and samples).

Which toothpaste do you use? Which coffee? How many smokers are in the family and which brands do they smoke? Do you color your hair? Do you diet? Do you own a dog? Do you often order products by mail? How many credit cards do you carry? Which ones? Do you have a universal life insurance policy? With which company? Do you plan to buy a new American-made car in the next six months? A house? A personal computer? A trip to Europe? How old are family members? What is the family income bracket? All this and more is entered in the JFY data base for use by mailers.

Advertisers can obtain the names and addresses of respondents in their category on an exclusive or nonexclusive basis. Unlike one-time list rentals, clients receive a computer tape of the names and addresses which they can keep and use as often as they wish.

Even a data base of 8 million households with information on which services and products each uses is not large enough to interest some advertisers with full national distribution. Thus in mid-1985 JFY's president, Harry Dale, announced that by using both mail and phone surveys the company is now able to make available data on 14 million households and expected to increase that number to 20 million in the future.

Among the early users attracted by JFY services were R.J. Reynolds, Seagram, and General Foods.

Data Base Overlays

Mass data bases and their enhancements are leading the way to refined target marketing. Target marketing makes it possible to increase response dramatically. Likewise, by using targeted segments of mailing lists the direct marketer can expand the number of lists which will produce a satisfactory response. (For a thorough discussion of mailing lists, see Chapter 8.)

Still another technique for data base enhancement is the use of *data base overlays.*

Overlays are computer programs that are run against existing lists—compiled or direct response lists—to ferret out those names known or suspected to have characteristics which match certain characteristics of a direct marketer's customer base. Here is an example of the application:

The Catholic Guild for the Blind in Chicago obviously has their strongest appeal among Catholics. They know from experience that their best response comes from Catholic donor lists. Yet, to build their donor base they are dependent, for the most part, on using lists of donors from other philanthropic organizations which do not appeal to any particular religious affiliation.

The Guild achieved a major breakthrough when they were able to apply a Catholic overlay to some major donor lists. The program for the Catholic overlay identified areas by ZIP codes which have a high concentration of Catholics (certain ZIPs in Boston and Chicago, for instance). By mailing exclusively to these identified ZIPs the Guild, on average, doubled their response.

Another example of using overlays to better target prospects comes from business-to-business direct marketing. Business-to-business direct marketers who profile their customer base learn who their best customers are and therefore know who their best prospects are. A typical profile might read "Our best customers are in the wholesale and service fields, employing from 10 to 250 people in towns or cities under 750,000 population."

With this profile at hand, selections can be made from a compiled list of business firms that will match the profile precisely. Or a business-to-business direct response list can be run against a compiled list, identifying a high percentage of business firms which match the profile.

Considering the value of data bases and the opportunity to maximize profits with proper application, it's small wonder that the data base is so often referred to as direct marketing's "secret weapon."

Self-Quiz

1. Why is it important to track mailing and space advertising for lead generation programs from cost per inquiry to cost per sale?

_____

_____

_____

2. In addition to the name, address, phone number of a customer, name four additional pieces of data that should be captured for a data base.

a. _____

b. _____

c. _____

d. _____

3. Define the R-F-M formula.

R _____

F _____

M _____

4. Define the FRAT formula.

F _____

R _____

A _____

T _____

5. What is the theory of "cross-selling"?

_____

_____

_____

6. What is the difference between "demographics" and "lifestyle activities"?

_____

_____

_____

7. Describe how packaged goods companies can use enhanced data bases to reach target prospects for a particular product category.

_____

_____

_____

8. If a direct marketer doesn't know the precise demographic and lifestyle characteristics of his or her customer base, how might a profile be developed?

_____

_____

_____

9. Define a "data base overlay."

_____

_____

_____

10. Name three characteristics that business-to-business direct marketers should know about their customer base.

    a. SICs (standard industrial classifications)

    b. _____

    c. _____

Pilot Project

You are the direct marketing manager for a women's apparel catalog operation. The apparel you sell is high fashion. Your company has never profiled their customer base. They don't know the average age, family income, marital status, geographic distribution, or lifestyle activities of their clientele.

You have told your management that before you can present a program to increase the customer base it will be essential that you develop a customer profile.

Your assignment is to write a letter to management telling them the exact steps that you will take to develop a precise demographic and lifestyle profile.

CHAPTER THREE

Strategic Business Planning

With the new professionalism that has come to direct marketing the discipline is being treated more and more as a "business." And with this new viewpoint the need for strategic business planning has emerged. Major traditional marketers who have established direct marketing units as separate profit centers have insisted upon strategic business planning for these centers just as they do for their traditional operations. But strategic business planning is quite foreign to those who have built businesses based solely upon direct marketing methods. Yet the rewards that can come from strategic business planning can be as great proportionately for the entrepreneur as for the giant corporation.

When facing the reality that large- and medium-size companies have been the stimulus for recent growth, it behooves today's direct marketer to take heed to the signals and make sure that their approaches are as contemporary as their potential targets. Since accountability is one of the key elements in direct marketing programs, it is necessary for us to ensure that we remain on track with our own marketing plans, up to date with the emerging technologies, and, finally, with optimizing our own organization's resources.

Strategic Business Planning Defined

First of all, let's define our terms. *Strategic business planning* is a formal method to consider alternatives related to the growth, development or other options of an enterprise, organization, or business. It has application for large and small companies in direct marketing, ranging from fund raising to lead generation to product sales. When properly developed, a strategic business plan should provide:

- A comprehensive review of the current business
- A description of the problems and opportunities that must be dealt with in the short term
- Clear direction
- A practical action plan

A strategic business plan is *not* a marketing plan. It is much broader in scope, but it does address marketing issues related to a business or company. A well-designed plan will permit much greater control over one's business, enabling the individual to deal with critical situations in a pro-active rather than a reactive manner.

Direct marketers have countered the strategic planning issue with a number of comments such as:

- "It's expensive and time-consuming."
- "My plan is based on past experience and current expectations."
- "We don't have the availability of talent in our organization to make planning work."

These comments seem quite valid, especially for smaller firms. Many are hard pressed to look out further than three months at a time. However, when the following questions are asked, companies of all sizes are likely to agree on the impact:

- Has your company felt the impact of new or revised federal regulations over the past few years?
- Is the current economic environment having an impact on profitability?
- Are sales increasing at the rate you forecasted?
- Are you comfortable with your organization's ability to adapt to change?

These questions, and many more like them, apply to virtually every business endeavor. Managing these responses and affiliated actions are the key to success in direct marketing today.

How to Develop a Plan

After disposing of the questions on what strategic business planning entails and how it applies to direct marketers, the next step is how to develop a plan and what should be included. Let's agree on one more fact. There are countless methods used for developing strategic business plans. They range from the efforts of a single, specially trained planning executive to extensive committee approaches. The range of the information developed is equally broad. A plan in some industries may dictate a company's action for a ten-year period, whereas in other cases, it may suggest very specific actions for a twelve-month period. Depending upon the purpose and expectations, any approach may benefit an organization.

There does not seem to be any evidence that better results are achieved through any one methodology. However, for direct marketers, I feel that a more simplified and practical approach will yield the most actionable information. Further, while it would be nice to be able to project, with infinite wisdom, what will happen to our industry and organization or company over the next five years, it is next to impossible. Just review recent growth, technological change, and new applications of direct marketing and you will understand the difficulty of accurate long-term planning. Also, the array of information to be included in a strategic business plan should be subject to the criteria of what is absolutely necessary, rather than what you would like to include. The simpler the plan and the process for developing it, the higher the likelihood of success.

To provide a clearer understanding of a business plan, look at the planning model in Exhibit 3-1. It has proven successful with a number of direct marketing operations. Initial examination of the model suggests a planning time span of three years. However, the meat of the plan is in the annual action plan that covers a twelve-month time frame. As stated, a twelve-month planning horizon seems to provide more than enough opportunity to manage change.

Let's examine each of the components of the model in more detail.

Exhibit 3-1. A Model for Strategic Business Planning

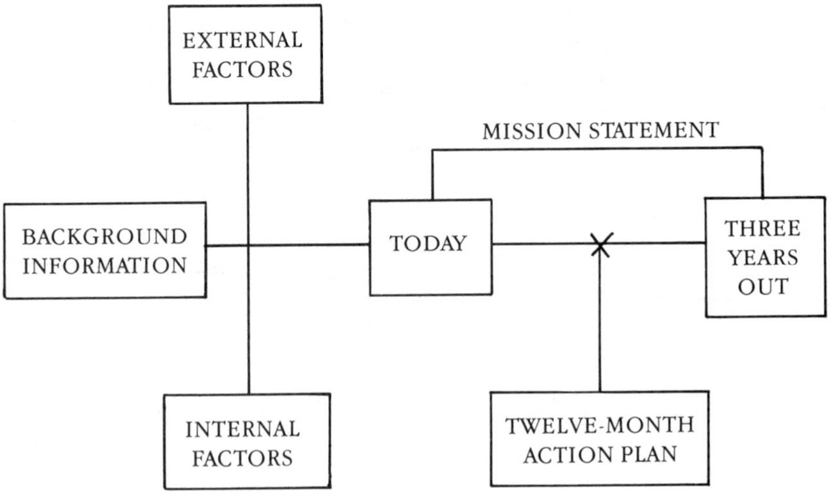

Background Information

In order to develop a strategic business plan, it is necessary to carefully and thoroughly investigate a company's performance. In effect, you are trying to take a "snapshot" of activities covering the current situation and extending back two or three years. As this is performed, you can separate data into two categories: (a) Financial and Marketing/Sales and (b) Organizational Data.

In the first case, you are looking for the following types of information:

- Growth
- Market share
- Expenditures in specific categories
- Seasonality of sales
- Profit levels
- Product/service line
- Financial resources
- Allocation of resources
- How you rate against your competition

In the second case, you must review how the organization and staff conduct the business. You must determine how the organization works rather than how it looks on the formal organization chart. You must get a "fix" on the company's personality.

For example, is the good work being accomplished on a daily basis spread evenly across the staff or is it really accomplished by a core of dedicated people. Or, do the key employees understand what the business is trying to accomplish, rather than just reporting the "party line." This case is every bit as important as knowing the financial operations of the business. However, it is the one most often overlooked in business planning.

After collecting the raw data on business, marketing and organizational issues, we are ready to proceed to the next step in the model.

External Factors

Simply stated, *external factors,* sometimes referred to as exogenous factors, are all of those activities and actions that have an impact on your business, but are out of your immediate control. You might quickly say, "If we cannot exert any control over these factors, why include them at all?" The answer to that is twofold: positioning and contingency.

Examples of external factors are:

- Current economy
- Federal regulation
- Competition
- Availability of resources
- Postal rates
- Technology

If we examine one external factor, you will get a clearer understanding of why it is important to determine what they are and how they impact your business:

The Current Economy   We certainly cannot control this complex and far-reaching situation. However, consider for a moment the action we can take to optimize our position. To name just a few, we can:

- Better manage cash flow
- Reduce inventory
- Tighten receivables

As you can see, we have been able to reduce some of the impact of this external factor on our business.

When developing a list of external factors, two considerations are important:

1. Limit the list to only the most important factors—ten or less for many companies. There is nothing more frustrating or less rewarding than considering all of the perils outside of your control and never getting to the major issues that affect your firm directly.

2. As you discuss and decide on each major external factor, be specific in defining what impact it has on your business. If this is impossible, discard the factor.

After looking outside your company or business and sifting through the relevant information, it is time to move to the next phase of plan development.

Internal Factors

Internal factors are those you do have control of and influence over. Such factors are probably best described as the strengths and weaknesses of your company. The identification of strengths and weaknesses are often referred to as the "building blocks" of a sound strategic business plan. Experience has indicated it is easier and more productive to start with the positive aspects—therefore the strengths.

Basically stated, they include those activities that you consistently complete extremely well—the things that give you an edge on your competition. They can include, but are not limited to:

- Technology
- Product
- Marketing
- Process
- Service
- Systems
- People
- Organization
- Attitude
- Flexibility
- Management
- Communication
- Leadership

For example, in direct marketing, a company might refer to its preeminence in product development, production innovations, back-end service and performance, and so forth. All of these are significant attributes and must be defined. This will allow for leveraging real strengths against stated goals. One note of caution. Make sure your description of a strength is accurate. Oftentimes the definition of these considerations is completed in a cavalier manner, and what is described by some as being a strength turns out to be of less value than previously reported.

The next move in the development of internal factors is defining weaknesses. Actually, this is the toughest part in developing a strategic business plan. However, this part of the inspection will yield the greatest return. It is difficult to elaborate on the shortfalls of a business. In this case, we are often getting at subpar performance levels. How many executives really want to define what's wrong with the operation, the staff, or even their direction of them? Weaknesses can be described as what a company does poorly and can include the following:

- Technology
- Product
- Marketing
- Process
- Service
- Systems

- People
- Organization
- Attitude
- Flexibility
- Management
- Communication
- Leadership

A comprehensive review of internal factors will provide an accurate picture of the company as it is today. More often than not, when completed objectively, it is quite revealing. In content alone, it can include a number of documents and summary sheets. Gathering the data is only one step. The next is to condense it into an accurate, readable document. And that brings us to the next component of the planning model.

Mission Statement

The *mission statement* is a condensation of what the company is today and what we want (expect) it to be tomorrow. Let's separate the mission statement into those parts and describe each individually.

Mission Statement—Today. The purpose of this statement is to accurately define in business shorthand the position of the company as it now exists. It is derived from the microscopic review discussed earlier. It usually is restructured in length to one or two typewritten pages. If it is honest, it will probably sound somewhat pessimistic. But that's okay. Actually, more often than not, where the company is today is not where it wants to be tomorrow.

Let's take a look at a mission statement. After considerable discussion, one direct marketing company, which for the sake of this discussion we'll call Leisure Time Activities, developed this statement of where they are today:

LEISURE TIME ACTIVITIES Today—1988

Today we are an established mail order company operating in the U.S. and Canada with a preeminent niche in the leisure activities market. In 1987, we had sales of $17 million and an embarrassing shortfall of $1.5 million in profits. Our recent growth has been sluggish and has not met our expectations. We have limited information on the market, but we do know we have a dominant share of the hobby segment. We have not extended this strength into the larger market of sporting goods.

The competition is intensifying especially for sporting goods. Major companies have an edge and they are expanding the market. This is all taking place in a market where there is little current product innovation. We feel technological change is coming, but don't know when. As a company, we have moved from a leadership position to a company that follows.

Although we have good products and a good customer base, we have become complacent. We have not leveraged our small size and financial strength to the best advantage. Our marketing approach is lackluster. We have experienced a breakdown in leadership, management, and communications. This has confused our direction and has had a negative impact on company spirit and teamwork; and as a result, we have had a breakdown in company performance in several areas.

Although we perceive our company and organization to be in a growth mode, we have not taken effective actions to make it happen. We have discussed an appetite for change and have developed a consensus on the major issues that must be resolved.

In summary, we are at a turning point. We must leverage our good name and products which have enabled us to become a major force in this industry, develop innovative marketing plans, and move in one direction, collectively.

Mission Statement—Tomorrow   The purpose of this statement is to define reasonable goals to be achieved within a specific period. The length of time to cover for this type of statement varies. A three-year period for goal setting is often an agreeable compromise.

But let's take a look at Leisure Time Activities again—where do they see themselves in three years?

LEISURE TIME ACTIVITIES—Three Years Out

By the end of 1991 we will be recognized as an aggressive, multiline direct marketing company. We will have demonstrated state-of-the-art marketing programs, a collective winning attitude, and financial results in line with written plans. We will have a sales volume of $20 million with a minimum of 25% R.O.I. And we will generate a profit on sales of 10%.

Our growth will be carefully planned. We will have expanded our capabilities and increased our share of the sporting goods market. Our product lines will include, but not be limited to, equipment and supplies, clothing, related gift items, and tend to have more proprietary products.

Our management has become a cohesive team which is directing a qualified, experienced, and motivated staff. This collective effort has provided a competitive edge and the flexibility to use our strengths in the best possible way.

Our financial performance has enabled the company to easily secure capital for further investment opportunities.

In summary, we have turned Leisure Time Activities around. This has been recognized by our stockholders, our employees, and the industry. We have replaced our former complacency with a demonstrated winning attitude.

If you manage to plan correctly, you will revisit these goals on an annual basis to make sure you remain on track and that changing conditions are updated. Remember, a plan is not a document that is put on the shelf and dusted off each December. In developing this section of the mission statement, you may wish to include:

- Sales/Income
- Markets
- Technology

- Organization/Size
- New Products
- Position in Market

The checklist in Exhibit 3-2 is provided to assist in structuring your mission statement.

You are now at a critical point in the planning model—you have developed:

What You Are Today ← → What You Want to Be in Three Years

The next step is to deal with the "gaps" in the mission statement, the differences between your strengths/weaknesses now and your expected position in three years.

Action Plans

The fundamental output from any good strategic business plan is the identification of those actions or activities that must be accomplished in order to reach your intended position. These actions or activities spring forth from your examination of internal and external factors and are summarized in the today section of the mission statement.

Exhibit 3-2. Mission Statement

General Information	Today	Three Years Out
Volume		
Profit		
Growth		
Market position		
External Factors		
Competition		
Industry factors		
Geography		
Internal Factors		
Strengths		
Weaknesses		
Product		
Summary		

The question is, how do you prepare an action plan that guarantees progress against your stated goals? There may be several ways to develop this kind of plan. However, there are a few fundamentals to success:

- Top management endorsement
- Clearly stated tasks
- Complete understanding by those who must implement the plan
- Realistic and attainable actions

If the above criteria can be met, the likelihood of success is greatly increased. Now, let's move on to the development of an action plan. An action plan defines the "must-do" tasks for completion, usually over a twelve-month period. These are the problems or opportunities that must be handled in order to achieve planning goals. They must be specific and precisely worded to ensure that those responsible for achievement have a clear understanding of the tasks to be accomplished. Participants must know *what* is to be accomplished, *how* it will be accomplished, by *whom,* and *within what time frame.* Anything short of these conditions will negatively impact performance against the plan.

There are some guidelines for developing objectives and strategies that detail the action plan. Let's start out the right way and clearly define what we mean when using the following terms:

- *Objective.* A statement that accurately describes *"what"* is to be accomplished over the next twelve months. In almost all cases, it is a must-do task.
- *Strategies.* A listing of methods, events, and so forth, that describe *"how"* an objective will be achieved. Completed strategies always list who is responsible, for what, and when.

To simplify the discussion, let's divide it into two parts:

- How to develop good objectives
- How to develop effective strategies

How to Develop Good Objectives

The very first step in moving toward the development of action plan objectives is to review any notes developed during the strength and weakness identification. Determine the problems, not the symptoms. After this is completed, review the problems and define them as clearly as possible. It is necessary at this stage to move from the general to the specific. It is easier to reduce a general concept by listing all situations or actions relating to the problem prior to specifically pinpointing it. Perhaps the following example will make this clearer.

Example 1.   Let's take a look at the Leisure Time Activities company again. In the general area, one of the problems is the need to increase profits.

"A definite need to increase profit"

If we dig deeper, we can expand this area to include:

1. We need a 10 percent profit on all sales made in 1988-89.

2. We must improve our marketing approach.

3. We must regain our leadership position.

4. We lack specific controls—financial, purchasing, inventory, marketing programs.

5. We need to develop systems to accurately project our financial future.

6. We need a minimum of 25 percent R.O.I.

While all of the above comments are valid, they do not relate directly to the same specific problem: (1) gets at the heart of the problem—how much and when. It further describes the scope of what is to be done. The others, steps (2)-(6), may either be strategies (how to do it) or may be related to another problem.

It is necessary to use this process for all problem areas so that accurate descriptions of the problems are developed.

The next step is to take the refined list for each problem and write an objective. As this is completed, consider whether the problem or task is realistic and achievable. If you should feel that nothing can practically be done in a given situation, why continue working on it? While this situation doesn't happen very often, it should be acknowledged. Let's assume that the problem can be dealt with. You must now put it in a clear statement that describes what is to be accomplished. We have found that there are three integral parts in defining problems. They are:

1. A clear, concise statement of the *task*

2. The *purpose* for completing the task

3. Reasonable *time* measurement(s)

Further, we have found that when these factors are included, the probability of successful completion is greatly increased.

The outline method seems to be the easiest approach in applying the factors. Here's an example:

Task	Purpose	Time
• What do we want to do?	• Why are we doing it?	• When do we want it completed or what interim time checks should we use?

Going back to an earlier situation, we can develop an objective that meets the criteria. (For sake of discussion, we have stated the real problem as the need to increase profits through planning.)

Task	Purpose	Time
• Achieve a sales volume of $20MM with a minimum 25 percent R.O.I.	• To increase profits	• Within next twelve months
	• Regain leadership position	• By December 1989
• Develop short and long term plans		• Monitor progress quarterly

Using this information, we can develop an objective statement that clearly reflects our intention:

By December 1989, we must develop short and long term plans
<u>TIME</u>   <u>TASK</u>

to achieve a sales volume of $20MM with a minimum 25% R.O.I.
<u>PURPOSE</u>

and regain a leadership position in our market. Progress on this

will be formally monitored on a quarterly basis.
<u>ADDITIONAL MEASUREMENTS</u>

At this point you may ask the question—is all this really necessary? The best answer is simply this: if you do not take the time to clearly select and write the plan objectives, not much will happen. One other example might help.

Example 2. Leisure Time Activities found that after a comprehensive assessment, there were a number of internal problems related to morale and communications. As they focused on the problem, it seemed that improved communications would really clear up the situation. They then developed this objective:

"We must improve company internal communications."

From this point, they further identified five strategies that would be necessary to achieve the objective. After additional discussion, they felt that even if all of the strategies were implemented, they would only, at best, achieve a partial solution to the problem. In reanalyzing the objective, they found some critical flaws as listed below:

1. Only part of the task was identified.

2. The purpose of the action was not specified.

3. There were no time measurements or checkpoints.

They went back to discuss the objectives. The following revision makes the point quite well:

> Within six months, we will improve the interchange of information and ideas throughout the company about plans and activities affecting operations and policies, in order to encourage feedback and involvement of all employees.

You will notice when we move into strategy development that a clear objective reduces the difficulty of strategy selection.

How to Develop Effective Strategies

Now that you know what must be done, we will discuss approaches and methods to describe *how* it should be done. Strategies are events, methods, and so forth, that crisply define the kinds of actions that should be taken to solve a problem; that is, complete an objective. If an objective has been clearly written, the strategies are easily developed.

One way to look at strategies is to think of an action plan. What kind of actions should you take to rectify this problem or improve a given situation? At this point, you are not trying to get down to details. Rather, you are looking for a logical sequence of activity that will outline actions for the next twelve months or so. By the way, some strategies may extend beyond a twelve-month period. To get a better fix, let's continue with the objective just discussed in Example 2:

> Within six months, we will improve the interchange of information and ideas throughout the company about plans and activities affecting operations and policies, in order to encourage feedback and involvement of all employees.

While this objective may be typical of any number of companies, the methods used to achieve it may vary considerably. A group must consider all of the problems, resources, and other considerations. Let's list some facts that seem apparent:

1. We know when we want to accomplish it.

2. We know the type of communication we want to disseminate (plans and activities).

3. We know what areas it will affect (operations and policies).

4. We know we need to encourage feedback and involvement.

What seems to emerge is that Leisure Time Activities needs to improve interchange of information on a companywide basis. They now know what they want to do and need to develop how they are going to do it. In discussing the matter further, they came up with the following action recommendations:

- Set up a departmental activities program
- Set up an Operations Improvement Committee to answer questions and get employee feedback
- Provide a forum for departmental information interchange
- Meet informally with employees
- Deliver a "State of the Company" message
- Provide feedback on progress of plans and activities

These were refined and expanded as shown in Exhibit 3-3.

As you can see, the group went from the general to the specific. When approaching it in this manner, you can see where the plan stands at all times. This company turned a normal problem into a reasonable and practical opportunity.

Exhibit 3-3. Executing Strategies

Strategies	Responsibility	Due Date
1. Company orientation to department activities: set up program and schedule.	Personnel and division managers	Monthly
2. Operations Improvement Committee to be set up to answer questions and obtain feedback from employees.	A representative from each department	5/15
3. Management Committee will be the forum for interchange of departmental information and in turn inform their department and get feedback.	Management Committee	3/23
4. "State of the Company" message: where we are, how we are doing, etc.	President	4/1 and annual
5. Informal meeting of all employees.	Executive Committee	6/1 and 12/1 and semiannual
6. Memo from Executive Committee to employees on how we are doing.	Executive Committee	Monthly
7. Staff luncheons with informal meetings— opportunity for employees to ask questions.	Management Committee	When necessary
8. New employee orientation.	Personnel and department peer level	5/1
9. Social/athletic activities: a. set up program b. schedule an "activity day."	Personnel Personnel Management Committee	5/1 4/15

How to Manage the Plan

Once a strategic business plan is written, there is a tendency to forget about it and to return to the normal everyday grind. This happens in spite of the fact that the objectives that were developed during the process were *must-do* tasks. To assure that must-do tasks are acted upon and to make certain the plan functions as a road map, proceed as follows:

1. Set up a small planning coordination function (1-2 people). This function is responsible for managing the plan from the meeting to back on the job. The function should:
    A. Coordinate with each person responsible for an objective and make sure their assigned objective is in final form with realistic due dates, strategy assignments, and so forth. (During the planning meeting, appoint one or two people to be responsible for each objective developed.)
    B. Consolidate all objectives and review background data (developed in the meeting).
    C. Submit it for management approval.
    D. Develop a short typewritten overview of the planning meeting which describes the highlights of the plan (no confidential information) for all employees. After the management's approval, this should be discussed with all employees as appropriate.
    E. Stay on top of the plan. The coordination group should establish a practical method to evaluate progress against strategies. This should be put into a two-page report and presented to management on a quarterly basis.

2. There are a number of other practical approaches which can be utilized. These range from getting lower level organizational participation on strategies to individual departmental plans.

In summary, strategic business planning is a management tool that enables an organization to focus on problems and opportunities, on current position and future direction, and, finally, on what to do about it. Participating in the development of a strategic business plan is only one phase. Making it work is another.

Self-Quiz

1. Define strategic business planning.

_____

_____

_____

_____

2. What are the two types of data required for background information pertinent to developing a strategic business plan?

   a. _____

   b. _____

3. List six external factors that can have an impact on a direct marketing operation, but cannot be directly controlled.

   a. _____   d. _____

   b. _____   e. _____

   c. _____   f. _____

4. List six internal factors over which a direct marketing operation can exercise control.

   a. _____   d. _____

   b. _____   e. _____

   c. _____   f. _____

5. Define a mission statement.

   _____

   _____

   _____

   _____

6. What are the four fundamentals to making an action plan work?

   a. _____

   b. _____

   c. _____

   d. _____

7. Define an objective as it relates to a business plan.

   _____

   _____

   _____

   _____

8. Define a strategy as it relates to a business plan.

_____

_____

_____

_____

9. In moving toward the development of action plan objectives one should determine the _____, not the _____.

10. What are the three integral parts involved in defining a problem?

a. _____

b. _____

c. _____

Pilot Project

Your company has had a mail order catalog for three years that offers ladies' apparel, home furnishings, and gift items. You are no match for competitors like Horchow and Neiman-Marcus. Your resources, both personnel and financial, are limited. It is obvious that you are fighting a losing battle as you are now positioned.

Your objective is to change direction and establish a clearly defined niche in the marketplace, changing your merchandise mix to items not generally available from your competition.

It is your assignment to develop strategies and an action plan that will reposition your catalog in the marketplace over the next twelve months. (Among the strategies you might consider are: positioning your catalog as *the source* for apparel, home furnishings and gifts for the career woman, or positioning your catalog as *the source* for apparel and gift items for those engaged in outdoor activities.)

CHAPTER FOUR

Importance of the Offer

The propositions you make to customers—more often referred to as *offers*—can mean the difference between success or failure. Depending on the offer, differences in response of 25, 50, 100 percent, and more are commonplace.

Not only is the offer you make the key to success or failure, but the manner in which an offer is presented can have an equally dramatic effect. For example, here are three ways to state the same offer.

1. Half price!

2. Buy one—get one *free!*

3. 50% off!

Each statement conveys the same offer, but statement number 2 pulled 40 percent better than statement number 1 or number 3. Consumers perceived statement number 2 to be the most attractive offer.

Offers with Multiple Appeals

Exhibit 4-1 illustrates what appears to be a very innocent order card. But the multiple appeals used are certain to have a strong effect on front-end response. And the "conditions" for accepting are certain to have an immediate and long-term effect on how well the publisher does both front end and back end.

Let's examine the appeals and conditions. "Please send me, free, the Premier issue of GEO." That's strong: You can't beat the appeal of something free. But note the slight condition ". . . and reserve a money-saving Charter Subscription in my name."

The first appeal is followed by another appeal and a condition: "At the end of thirty days, if I have not instructed you to cancel my reservation, you may enter my subscription at the Charter Rate of $36 for one year (12 more monthly issues)—a savings of $12 off the annual cover price of $4 per issue."

So the *basic* offer breaks out like this: First issue free (appeal); right to cancel at the end of thirty days (appeal); enter twelve-month subscription at $36 unless instructed otherwise (condition); save $12 off the annual cover price (appeal).

But the offer doesn't end there. "As a Charter Subscriber, I am entitled to renew annually at savings of 25% off the newsstand price" (appeal). "Please bill me automatically each year" (condition). "If at any time, for any reason, I elect to cancel my subscription, I will receive a full refund on all unmailed issues. The Premier issue is mine to keep in any case" (appeal).

Finally, "In addition, when I pay for my Charter Subscription, as a special gift I will receive a limited-edition copy of the GEO Premier Issue Cover Poster" (both a condition and an appeal). In total, a brilliantly conceived and well thought through offer.

Exhibit 4-1. Offer with Multiple Appeals and Conditions

FREE PREMIER ISSUE/CHARTER SUBSCRIPTION RESERVATION

Please send me, free, the Premier Issue of GEO, and reserve a money-saving Charter Subscription in my name. At the end of thirty days, if I have not instructed you to cancel my reservation, you may enter my subscription at the Charter Rate of $36 for one year (12 more monthly issues)—a savings of $12 off the annual cover price of $4 per issue.

As a Charter Subscriber, I am entitled to renew annually at savings of 25% off the newsstand price. Please bill me automatically each year. If at any time, for any reason, I elect to cancel my subscription, I will receive a full refund on all un-mailed issues. The Premier Issue is mine to keep in any case.

In addition, when I pay for my Charter Subscription, as a special gift I will receive a limited-edition copy of the GEO Premier Issue Cover Poster.

Please make any necessary corrections in your name or address. Return this reservation form in the postage-paid reply envelope enclosed.

H-PF-R   P.O. BOX 2552, BOULDER, COLORADO 80322

The Effects This offer, one of many tested by *Geo* in the introduction of its international magazine, can have a tremendous effect on immediate and long-term results.

Geo and its agency know that offering the premier issue free will almost certainly bring a greater response than "tighter" offers that don't allow for cancellation after the first issue. But it also knows that, historically, its "loose" offer can result in cancellations as high as 65 percent. So, to be determined is whether the superb quality of its magazine will overcome the historically poor conversion rate of this type of offer.

Guaranteeing in perpetuity a renewal rate of 25 percent off the newsstand price is a "safe" offer in that it is a more or less standard discount for the publishing industry. I don't see any long-term problems with that offer.

But—"Please bill me automatically each year"—could be a problem, or a bonanza. This condition allows *Geo* to bill automatically without employing a renewal series, often six to eight efforts. Yet to be determined, however, is whether (a) the cancellation rate will be the same, better, or worse than when a renewal series is used and (b) whether the pay-ups will be the same, better, or worse than when a renewal series is used.

The sign-off offer—"In addition, when I pay for my Charter Subscription, as a special gift I will receive a limited-edition copy of the Premier Issue Cover Poster"—is smartly conceived. It is clear recognition on the part of *Geo* and its agency that not only do "loose" offers like this one historically result in a low conversion rate, but that pay-ups for those who don't cancel tend to be lower than for "tighter" offers. To be learned is whether the lure of the free cover poster upon payment will hype the conversion rate and the payment rate.

So this "innocent" offer is loaded with immediate and long-term implications. And so it is with all direct response offers. That's why no direct response person worth his salt would consider starting creative until offers are clearly thought through.

Factors to Consider

Basically, there are ten factors to consider when creating an offer.

1. *Price.* This is a toughie. Does the price you settle upon allow for a sufficient markup? If you have competition, is the price competitive? Is the price you settle upon perceived by the consumer to be the right price for the value received?

   If you want to sell your item for $7.95 each, how about two for $15.90 (same price, but you get twice the average sale)? How about selling the first for $11.95 and the second for $3.95 (same total dollars if you sell two units—and if you don't sell two units you get a higher price for a single unit)?

Pricing. There's nothing more important. Testing to determine the best price is vital to maximizing long-term payoff.

2. *Shipping and handling.* Where applicable (and it's usually not applicable when selling a publication or service), shipping and handling charges can be an important factor in pricing. It's important to know how much you can add to a base price without adversely affecting sales.

   Many merchandisers follow a rule of thumb that shipping and handling charges should not exceed 10 percent of the basic selling price. But again, testing is advisable.

3. *Unit of sale.* Will your product or service be offered "each"? "Two for?" "Set of X?" Obviously, the more units you can move per sale, the better off you are likely to be. BUT—if your prime objective is to build a large customer list fast, would you be better off to offer single units if you got twice the response over a "two for" offer?

   In the case of *Geo,* suppose it had offered six months for $18? Would it be better off long term?

4. *Optional features.* Optional features include such things as special colors, odd sizes, special binding for books, personalization.

   Optional features often increase the average order. For example, when the publisher of a dictionary offered thumb indexing at $2 extra, 25 percent of total purchasers opted for this added feature.

5. *Future obligation.* Subscribers to *Geo,* returning the illustrated order card, have agreed to automatic billing, if they don't elect to cancel.

   More common are book and record offers that commit the purchaser to future obligation. ("Take ten records for $1 and agree to buy six more in the coming twelve months.") A continuity program offer might state: "Get volume one free—others will be sent at regular intervals."

   Future obligation offers, when successful, enable the marketer to "pay" a substantial price for the first order, knowing there will be a long-term payout.

6. *Credit options.* Many marketers feel a major factor in the direct marketing explosion during the past decade has been the proliferation of credit cards. It's rare today to receive a catalog that does not contain one or more of these credit options: "Charge to American Express, Diners Club, Carte Blanche, VISA, MasterCard, Discover." It pays: The average order is usually 15 percent or more larger than a cash order.

Offer Credit

Some major direct marketers offer credit for thirty days (*Geo* did this), others offer installment credit with interest added (oil companies are a good example). Whether it be commercial credit cards or house credit, history says credit options increase revenue.

7. *Incentives.* Incentives include free gifts, discounts, and sweepstakes. (*Geo* offered two incentives, the premier issue free with a conditional subscription and a free poster upon payment.)

   Toll-free ordering privilege is likewise an incentive—ease of ordering. Not unlike credit options, toll-free ordering privileges tend to increase the average order 15 percent and more.

   But incentives must be tested front-end and back-end. Are people "buying" the free gift or sweeps? Will they be as good repeat customers as those who bought in the first instance without incentive?

8. *Time limits.* Time limits add urgency to an offer. (*Geo,* for example, could have applied a time limit to its charter offer—with good logic.)

   One word of caution: If you establish a time limit, stick to it!

9. *Quantity limits.* One of the major proponents of quantity limits is the collectibles field. ("Only 5,000 will be minted. Then the molds will be destroyed.") There is something in the human psyche that says, "If it's in short supply, I want it!" Even "Limit—two to a customer" often outperforms no limit.

   But, if you set a limit, stick to it.

10. *Guarantees.* Of the ten factors to be considered in structuring an offer, there is one which should never be passed up—*the guarantee. Geo* has two guarantees: Cancel the subscription if not pleased with the free Premier issue and "if at any time, for any reason, I elect to cancel my subscription, I will receive a full refund on all unmailed issues."

Hundreds of millions of people have ordered by phone or mail over the decades with the assurance their satisfaction is guaranteed. Don't make an offer without a guarantee!

Nothing should happen in the creative process until you have structured an offer, or offers, which will make the creative process work. But let's remember this—what you offer is what you live with!

Checklist of Basic Offers

The following checklist briefly describes thirty-one basic offers that may be used singly or in various combinations, depending on the marketer's objectives. Variations on some of these basic offers are illustrated in Exhibits 4-2 through 4-6.

1. *Free information.* This is often the most effective offer, particularly when getting leads for salespeople is the prime objective or nonprospects must be screened out at low cost before expensive literature is sent to prime prospects.

2. *Samples.* A sample of a product or service is often a very effective sales tool. If a sample can be enclosed in a mailing package, results often more than warrant the extra cost. Consideration should be given to charging a nominal price for a sample. The recipient's investment in a sample promotes trying it, and this usually results in a substantial increase in sales.

3. *Free trial.* Bellwether of mail order. Melts away human inertia. Consider fitting the length of the trial period to the nature of the product or service, rather than the standard fifteen days.

4. *Conditional sale.* Prearranges the possibility of long-term acceptance based on a sample. Example: "Please send me, free, the Premier issue of *Geo,* and reserve a money-saving Charter Subscription in my name. At the end of the thirty days, if I have not instructed you to cancel my reservation, you may enter my subscription at the Charter Rate of $36 for one year (twelve more monthly issues)—a savings of $12 off the annual cover price of $4 per issue."

5. *Till forbid.* Prearranges for continuing shipments on a specified basis. The customer has the option to forbid future shipments at any specified time. Works well for business services offers and continuity book programs.

6. *Yes-no.* An involvement offer. The prospect is asked to respond, usually through a token or stamp, including whether he accepts or rejects the offer. Historically, more favorable responses are received with this offer than when no rejection option is provided.

Exhibit 4-2. Involvement Device

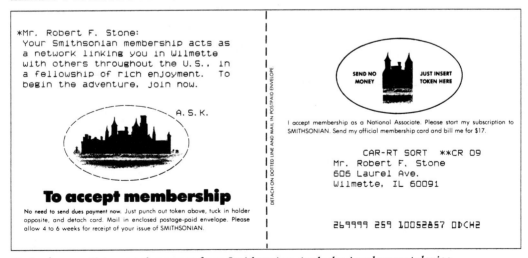

Order form, with personal message from Smithsonian, includes involvement device.

7. *Time limit.* Setting a time limit on a given offer *forces* action, either positive or negative. Usually it is more effective to name a specific date rather than a time period. It is important to test for the most effective time limit because a short period may not allow sufficient time for deliberation. Too long a period, on the other hand, may promote inertia.

8. *Get-a-friend.* Based on the axiom that the best source for new customers is one's present list of satisfied customers. Many get-a-friend offers get new customers in a large volume at low acquisition cost. The best response for a get-a-friend offer usually results from limiting the number of friends' names requested and offering a reward for providing names or securing new customers.

Exhibit 4-3. Postcard Mailing with Multiple Devices

Simple postcard mailing from Newsweek includes sales message, yes-no offer, discount offer, and subscription card.

SAVE 75% WITH NEWSWEEK'S GOLDEN ANNIVERSARY SUBSCRIPTION OFFER!

Dear Mr. Stone,
No big sales pitch. Subscribe to Newsweek now and take advantage of our special 50th Anniversary Offer -- the lowest rate available -- a full 75% off the cover price and 50% off the basic subscription rate. Act now!

Mr. Robert Stone
606 Laurel Ave
Wilmette, Il. 60091

☐ **I do**
☐ **I do not**   34471215   Offer ends 7/15/82

accept this special invitation to receive **26 weeks** of Newsweek for **$9.75** (only 37.5¢ a copy)—75% off the $1.50 cover price, 50% off the 75¢ basic subscription rate. I prefer this alternate term ☐ **52 weeks** for **$19.50** (I still pay only 37.5¢ a copy).

Please check one: ☐ Bill me ☐ Payment enclosed   ☐ Charge ☐ American Express   ☐ Diners
                            (put form in envelope)   (put form in envelope) ☐ VISA ☐ Master Card   1159714485

Card # _____ Expires _____

Interbank   # (Master Card) _____ Signature _____
                                    Good only in the 50 states of the U.S.A.

Newsweek
P.O. BOX 411 • LIVINGSTON, N.J. 07039
Tell us, Mr. Stone,
whether you will
accept this special
HALF-PRICE OFFER!

FIRST CLASS PRESORTED

Mr. Robert Stone
606 Laurel Ave
Wilmette, Il. 60091

Exhibit 4-4. Three-Tier Offer

FREE SOCIAL SECURITY FACT KIT

Here is what you get in your FREE Fact Kit:

50-page Handbook tells you all about your rights, benefits, and privileges under Social Security. It even explains how to collect the money you're entitled to.

Benefits Computer makes it easy to calculate the approximate monthly benefits you'll collect.

Official Social Security Request Form Send it in, and the government reports directly to you on the Social Security earnings credited to your account for each of your working years. It's important to check this report for accuracy, since there's a 3-year time limit for correcting any errors.

1982 GUIDE TO SOCIAL SECURITY

SOCIAL SECURITY FACT KIT

As a free gift to you, Old American invites you to accept a 3-piece Social Security Fact Kit. To receive this no-obligation gift, place Label A here.

**BOX A
AFFIX LABEL A HERE**

TRIP-AID ACCIDENT POLICY CERTIFICATE

APPLICATION

☐ YES Send me your policy. I have enclosed 10¢ with my application.

Date of Birth _____
Month   Date   Year

Beneficiary _____
First Name   Middle Initial   Last Name

Relationship of Beneficiary _____

To the best of my knowledge and belief, I am sound mentally and physically. I understand that the policy (Series ID3077) becomes effective when issued.

Signature X _____
First Name   Middle Initial   Last Name

Licensed Resident Agent, if applicable
ID2000   Old American Ins. Co. • 4900 Oak • PO Box 573 • K.C., MO 64141

**BOX B
AFFIX LABEL B HERE**

Indicate any change to name and/or address by crossing out and inserting correct information.

OLD AMERICAN
TRIP-AID ACCIDENT POLICY

For persons 40 to 85 years of age
30 DAYS COVERAGE FOR 10¢
(Regular premium is $5.40 monthly)

TRIP-AID ACCIDENT POLICY CERTIFICATE

APPLICATION

☐ YES. Send me your policy. I have enclosed 10¢ with my application.

Date of Birth _____
Month   Date   Year

Beneficiary _____
First Name   Middle Initial   Last Name

Relationship of Beneficiary _____

To the best of my knowledge and belief, I am sound mentally and physically. I understand that the policy (Series ID3077) becomes effective when issued.

Signature X _____
First Name   Middle Initial   Last Name

Licensed Resident Agent, if applicable
ID2000   Old American Ins. Co. • 4900 Oak • PO Box 573 • K.C., MO 64141

**THIS APPLICATION FOR USE
BY SPOUSE OR OTHER
FAMILY MEMBER, AGE 40 TO 85,
WHO ALSO WISHES TO APPLY**

Name _____
Please Print

Address _____

City _____

State _____ **Zip** _____

DP:AP1082:25T

Three-tier offer from Old American Insurance Company offers: (1) a free Social Security Fact Kit; (2) an opportunity for the mail recipient to accept a 10¢ introductory offer for a Trip-Aid Accident Policy; and (3) the same opportunity for a spouse or other family member.

9. *Contests.* These create attention and excitement. Stringent FTC rules apply. Highly effective in conjunction with magazine subscription offers and popular merchandise offers.

10. *Discounts.* A discount is a never-ending lure to consumers as well as businesspeople. Discounts are particularly effective where the value of a product or service is well established. Three types of discounts are widely offered: (a) for cash, (b) for an introductory order, and (c) for volume purchase.

Discounts for volume purchases are often tied to levels of purchase. For example, "5 percent discount on orders up to $25.00; 10 percent discount on orders from $25.00 to $50.00; 15 percent discount on orders of $50.00 and over."

Exhibit 4-5. Get-A-Friend Offer

Get-a-friend offer from the Literary Guild: Member encourages a friend to fill in new application. Member fills in the balance of card, indicating bonus desired as a reward for acquiring a new member.

The Literary Guild

231-3

New Applicant: Choose 4 books for $1 with membership!

Please accept my application for membership in The Literary Guild. Send me the 4 books indicated and bill me just $1, plus shipping and handling. I agree to the membership plan described in the enclosed circular and understand that I need buy only 4 more books at the regular low club prices whenever I want them. After buying 4 more books I may resign or remain a member for as long as I wish without further obligation to purchase books.

SATISFACTION GUARANTEED: If not completely satisfied with your Introductory package, return all four books within ten days. Your membership will be canceled and you'll owe nothing.

Write in code numbers of your 4 books here

Mr.
Mrs.
Miss
Ms.

(please print)

Address _____ Apt. _____

City _____ State _____ Zip _____

Present Member: Take 2 books FREE for each friend who becomes a member!

Write in code numbers of your 2 books here:

SPECIAL BONUS: Take one of these gifts free for each friend you introduce to The Literary Guild. Check one box for each friend:

☐ 88278 "Foot Notes" Memo Board
☐ 81075 The Literary Guild Book Jacket
☐ 85597 The Literary Guild Mini-Bag

81075

88278

85597

PRESENT MEMBER: In addition to your 2 FREE books, take one of these gifts free for each member recruited.

IMPORTANT: To avoid delay, please enter your current book club account number.

Name _____
(please print)

Address _____ Apt. _____

City _____ State _____ Zip _____

53   Order cannot be processed unless this card is filled in by both Present Member and New Applicant   FG033

Exhibit 4-6. Use of Token with Free Offer

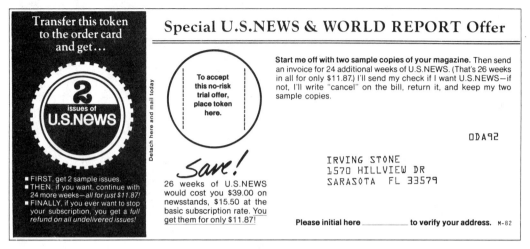

U.S. News and World Report *offers the first two issues free, with the right to cancel the conditional subscription for twenty-four additional issues. Token dramatizes the free offer.*

Another play on basic discount offers is what is commonly referred to as *multiple time-dated discount offers.* The objective here is to get the customer into the habit of using your product or service. (Exhibit 4-7 is a good example of the technique.)

11. *Negative option.* This offer prearranges for shipment if the customer doesn't abort the shipment by mailing the rejection form prior to deadline date. In popular use by book and record clubs. FTC guidelines must be followed carefully.

12. *Positive option.* Every shipment is based on a *direct action* by the club member, rather than a *nonaction* as exemplified by the negative option feature of most book and record clubs. Front-end response to a positive option is likely to be lower, but long-pull sales are likely to be greater.

13. *Lifetime membership.* Under this plan, the member pays one fee, $5, for instance, at the time of becoming a member. In return the member is guaranteed substantial reduction from established retail prices. There is no requirement that the respondent make a specified number of purchases. But the safeguard to the marketer is that the member is more likely to make purchases because of his front-end investment.

14. *Load-ups.* This proposition is a favorite of publishers of continuity series. Example: The publisher offers a set of twelve books, one to be released each month. After the purchaser has received and paid for

Exhibit 4-7. Multiple Time-dated Discount Offer

MANUFACTURER COUPON | EXPIRES 6/20/87

72270

Winston.
America's Best.
$2⁰⁰ OFF
a carton of Winston.
—Any style, any length—

463076806

$2

$2

72270

LIMIT: ONE COUPON PER CARTON

REDEEM BY JUNE 20, 1987   USE FIRST

MANUFACTURER COUPON | EXPIRES 6/27/87

72271

Winston.
America's Best.
$2⁰⁰ OFF
a carton of Winston.
—Any style, any length—

463076806

$2

$2

72271

LIMIT: ONE COUPON PER CARTON

REDEEM BY JUNE 27, 1987   USE SECOND

MANUFACTURER COUPON | EXPIRES 7/4/87

72272

Winston.
America's Best.
$2⁰⁰ OFF
a carton of Winston.
—Any style, any length—

463076806

$2

$2

72272

LIMIT: ONE COUPON PER CARTON

REDEEM BY JULY 4, 1987   USE THIRD

the first three books, the publisher invites him to receive the remaining nine, all in one shipment, with the understanding that payments can continue to be made monthly. This load-up offer invariably results in more *complete sets* of books being sold.

15. *Free gift.* Most direct response advertisers have increased response through free gift offers. For best results, you should test several gifts to determine the most appealing. There's no set criterion for the cost of a gift as related to selling cost. The most important criteria are: (a) appropriateness of the gift, (b) its effect on repeat business, and (c) net profit per thousand circulation or distribution including cost of the gift.

16. *Secret gift.* Lester Wunderman, chairman of Wunderman, Ricotta & Kline, invented the secret gift offer, commonly known as the "Gold Box offer." Conceived to measure the impact of TV upon the pull of a newspaper or magazine insert, the viewer was told that there was a secret gold box on the insert order form and that by filling in the box the prospect would receive an extra free gift over and above the regular free gift offer.

17. *Cash-up free gift.* Used primarily by publishers, cash-up offers stimulate cash with order. Incentives for advance cash payment usually involve one or two extra issues of a publication, or a special report not available to charge subscribers.

18. *Add-on offers.* One of the most innovative offers ever developed for increasing the unit of sale was first developed, I believe, by the "Horchow Collection." The offer was directed to catalog buyers about to place a phone order, toll-free. The direction was, "When you place your phone order ask about our Special-of-the-Month." The special was always a discount on a catalog item. One catalog marketer I know of adapted this idea and consistently sold the "special" to 10 percent to 15 percent of phone order inquirers.

19. *Deluxe alternative.* Related to the famous Sears tradition of *good, better, best* are offers for deluxe alternatives. A classic example would be a dictionary offered in a regular edition or in a thumb-indexed edition for $2 more. By giving the prospect the choice, the advertiser often increases total response and total dollars.

20. *Charters.* A charter offer by its very nature denotes something special. The offer plays on the human trait that many people want to be among the first to see, try, and use something new. The most successful charter offers include special rewards or concessions for early support.

21. *Guaranteed buy-back.* "Satisfaction guaranteed" is the heart of mail order selling. But the guaranteed buy-back offer goes much further.

This guarantee pledges to buy back the product (if the customer so requests) at the original price for a period of time after original purchase.

22. *Multiproduct.* Multiproduct offers may take the form of a series of postcards or a collection of individual sheets, each with a separate order form. Each product presentation is structured to stand on its own feet.

23. *Piggybacks.* These are "add-on" offers that ride along with major offers at no additional postage cost. The unit of sale is usually much smaller than the major offer. Testing is advocated to determine whether piggybacks add to or steal from sales of the major offer.

24. *Bounce-backs.* Bounce-back offers succeed on the premise, "the best time to sell a person is right after you have sold him." Bounce-back order forms are usually included in shipments or with invoices or statements. Bounce-backs may offer (a) more of the same, (b) related items, or (c) items totally different from those originally purchased.

25. *Good-better-best.* The essence of the offer is to give the prospect a choice between something and something. Example: For their State of the Union series, the Franklin Mint gave the prospect three choices: 24k gold on sterling at $72.50 monthly, solid sterling silver at $43.75 monthly, and solid bronze at $17.50 monthly.

26. *Optional terms.* The technique here is to give the prospect the option of choosing terms at varying rates. The bigger the commitment, the better the buy.

27. *Flexible terms.* A derivative of optional terms is flexible terms. The potential subscriber to a magazine is offered a bargain weekly rate of, say, 25 cents a week for a minimum period of 16 weeks. But, if he wishes, the subscriber may choose to enter his subscription for any number of weeks beyond the minimum at the same bargain rate.

28. *Exclusive rights.* This is an offer made by publishers of syndicated newsletters. Under the term of such an offer, the first to order—an insurance broker, for example—has exclusive rights for his trading area so long as he remains a subscriber.

29. *Upgrade offers.* Upgrade offers are particularly effective when applied to a customer base. Insurance companies are very adept at applying this technique, "Double the daily benefits on your cancer policy for a small additional premium" is typical of upgrade offers by insurance companies. A response rate of 25 to 30 percent isn't unusual.

   Credit card companies have done a remarkable job of upgrading members based upon their activities with existing card membership.

American Express is a classic example, starting with their Green Card and moving up to their Gold and Platinum Cards.

30. *Kiosks.* In Chapter 1 you were introduced to kiosks as a distribution channel. The offer to take orders or request information through a kiosk increases selling opportunities dramatically.

31. *Promotional video cassettes.* Direct marketers have been among the first to see the promotional opportunities through the medium of advertising video cassettes. It is estimated that by the end of this decade 66 percent of television households will be equipped with a VCR. This gives the direct marketer the opportunity to use the demonstration power of television without TV's time restraints.

An offer to send a video cassette, either free or for a small charge, gives the marketer a unique opportunity for a professional, "live," in-depth, presentation of a product, or service. Cruise lines, exercise equipment manufacturers, art gallaries, and luxury apartment complexes are among business categories benefiting from video cassette offers.

Merchandising the Offer

Each of the thirty-one offers we have just reviewed have wide application. As a matter of fact, many of the offers can be used successfully in combination. However, as powerful as many of these offers are, one must keep ever in mind that to maximize success the *offers must be merchandised properly to target markets.*

Anatomy of an Upgrade Offer

We are indebted to Jim Schmidt, senior vice president and creative director of McCann Direct, New York City, for a fascinating case history of an *upgrade offer* which illustrates concisely the degree of thinking and quality of execution which must be applied to make an offer truly successful.

Client   American Express

Product   The Platinum Card

Background and Specific Opportunity   In 1982, American Express decided to develop a "super premium" charge card which would serve to

- reinforce the American Express franchise among the most important Card Member segment—heavy billers
- retain leadership in the top-end charge card category
- act as an additional revenue-generating product for American Express Travel-related Services, Inc.

Target Prospects Based on research and judgment, the criteria for solicitation were established as

- existing American Express Personal and Gold Card members
- achievement of a minimum of two years tenure as an American Express Card member
- expenditures totaling a minimum of $10,000 on their American Express Card(s) annually
- maintenance of an impeccable payment history with American Express

Product Strategy To offer a new "exclusive" charge card to a select group of American Express Card members who entertain and travel extensively.

The customized array of benefits and services afforded these *Platinum Card* prospects meets the criteria of their lifestyles, as well as appeals to their need for recognition and prestige.

Research A study was conducted among American Express Card members in 1983 to gauge interest in the *Platinum Card* concept. Fifteen percent of all qualified responders indicated an interest in holding this "super premium" card. In addition, psychographic profiling was executed to define more clearly the primary target segments to aid in product positioning and communications development.

Subsequently, the initial test mailing for the *Platinum Card* product was initiated in May, 1984. The cost of the product was set at $250 per Platinum Card.

Communications Strategy The target market was a relatively small one clearly defined by American Express membership criteria. Information on these potential customers was available in American Express's own data base.

Therefore, the exclusive utilization of direct mail—with the support of a public relations effort to hype awareness for this initial launch—was determined to be the most efficient method for extending the offer. This direct mail effort was sent to a random selection of American Express Gold Card members who met the qualification criteria.

Executional Points

- Utilize a "preapproved" and "best customer" message
- Incorporate a "by-invitation-only" approach to reinforce the highly personalized nature of the product
- Issue only one offer per year per qualifier to reinforce the unique positioning and limited availability of the Platinum Card
- Extend the offer from the president of the Consumer Card Division to establish a sense of recognition from American Express
- Use of personalization (closed-face outer envelope, letter, acceptance form, reference to the Card member's date of original membership) to differentiate the offer as unique and reinforce the product positioning as an exclusive payment instrument for a small group of American Express Card members

Format

- Outer Envelope (personalized by a computer driven word processing system)
- Letter (personalized by a computer driven word processing system)
- Brochure—a simple, straightforward presentation of *Platinum Card* benefits (in keeping with the "invitational" concept, graphics were not used.)
- Acceptance Form (personalized by a computer-driven word processing system, thus requiring only the Card member's signature for enrollment)
- Business Reply Envelope
- Personal "invitation" from the president of the Consumer Card Division enclosed in an envelope

Note that particular attention was paid to the tone and look of each element of the package to reflect the positioning of the Card itself and increase appeal to this select market. All elements, except the brochure, were silver foil embossed on textured stock.

Test   Three different tests were executed for the letter copy only. All other elements remained the same.

Results   The initial test mailing generated an outstanding response which was five times the response projected. The "sharing important news" letter (Exhibit 4-8) slightly outperformed the other two test cells.

In addition, annual Card member spending substantially increased postpurchase of the Platinum Card, thus meeting the initial business objective.

Exhibit 4-8. The "Sharing the Important News" Letter

The Platinum Card^{SM}

James F. Calvano
President
Payment Systems Division

Mr. H. L. Clark
123 Main Street
Anywhere, USA   12345

Dear Mr. Clark:

I would like to share with you some important news about a Card from American Express that is planned for introduction in August of this year.

This new Card is and will continue to be beyond the aspirations and reach of all but a few of our Card members. Appropriately called The Platinum Card, it is reserved solely for those whose long association with American Express and annual volume of travel and entertainment charges indicate that they require and deserve to command the best.

Receipt of this Invitation certifies that you are among them.

As you would expect, the new Platinum Card^{sm} will continue to secure Card member services to which you are already accustomed. Worldwide charge privileges. Assured Reservations. No pre-set spending limit. Duplicate receipts. Emergency card replacement. Emergency check cashing at hotels, motels, airline counters. Travel Accident Insurance. And Express Cash.

What distinguishes The Platinum Card and sets its possessor on a new plateau of recognition, service and convenience are the newly customized services it will provide.

First and foremost, it will command immediate recognition and respect at the finest hotels, restaurants and selected private clubs worldwide.

Secondly, The Platinum Card Personalized Travel Service will also assure customized attention to your travel needs and arrangements

AMERICAN EXPRESS TRAVEL RELATED SERVICES COMPANY, INC.   POST OFFICE BOX ONE, BOWLING GREEN STATION, NEW YORK, NEW YORK 10274

(continued)

Exhibit 4-8. The "Sharing the Important News" Letter

24 hours a day. We'll keep a record of your travel preferences --
what hotels, airlines, and ground transportation (limousines and
car rentals) you like to use -- so many of the bothersome travel
details are easily taken care of in advance. And we'll be happy to
make en route changes to the original itinerary we booked for you
should you have a change in plans.

What's more, in keeping with The Platinum Card level of
service, you will have increased Travel Accident Insurance
protection -- to a full $500,000 -- every time you charge your
common carrier travel tickets to The Platinum Card. And should
the need arise, you will now be able to cash your personal check for
up to $10,000 at participating American Express (R) Travel Service
Offices worldwide.

You will also be able to obtain up to $10,000 in Travelers
Cheques from our network of automated dispensers and up to $1,000
in cash from automated teller machines at participating U.S.
financial institutions.

Arrangements for billing are similarly customized:

o You may choose the billing time most convenient for you --
   the beginning, middle or end of the month.

o And at year end, you may receive a customized summary of
   all charges itemized by category of expense: retail, hotel,
   restaurants, and the like.

Should you have questions or problems concerning Card
membership and its services, you will have a Customer Service
Representative available any hour of the day or night via an
exclusive toll-free 800 telephone number reserved for Platinum
Card members only. You will also have access to a special number
you can call collect when outside the U.S. You are assured prompt,
one-stop personal attention to all your inquiries.

Please read the enclosed brochure which more fully explains
the privileges and benefits of the new Platinum Card.

You've earned The Platinum Card and we recognize that. To
obtain one in your name, simply complete and return the enclosed
request by July 31, 1984. Assuming your American Express account

Exhibit 4-8. The "Sharing the Important News" Letter

has remained in good standing, The Platinum Card will be mailed to you in August, 1984 and the annual fee of $250 will then be billed to your account. Along with The Platinum Card, we'll give you instructions for canceling your present account if you wish to do so.

I look forward to hearing from you soon, and including you in the privileged company of Platinum Card members.

Cordially,

James F. Calvano

PS. One further thought -- lest it be a matter of concern. Let me assure you that your original Membership Date will remain intact and will be shown on the new Platinum Card.

Additional Offer Considerations

The American Express case history is a classic example of all the elements involved in conceiving, targeting, and executing an offer. But there are still other considerations, particularly as they relate to *free gift offers* and *get-a-friend offers.*

Free Gift Offers

Giving free gifts for inquiring, for trying, and for buying has got to be as old an incentive as trading stamps. It is not unusual at all for the right gift to increase response by 25 percent and more. On the other hand, a free gift offer can actually reduce response or have no favorable effect on the basic offer. This is particularly true where the unit of sale or amount of sale consideration overshadows the appeal of the free gift.

What's more, there is a tremendous variance in the appeal of free gifts. For example, the Airline Passengers Association tested two free gifts along with a membership offer: an airline guide and a carry-on suit bag. The suit bag did 50 percent better than the guide.

A fund-raising organization selling to schools tested three different gifts: a set of children's books, a camera, and a thirty-cup coffee maker. The coffee maker won by a wide margin; the children's books came in a poor third.

Testing for the most appealing gifts is essential because of the great differences in pull. In selecting gifts for testing purposes, follow this good rule of thumb: Gifts that are suited to personal use tend to have considerably more appeal than those that aren't.

There is yet another consideration about free gifts: Is it more effective to offer a selection of free gifts of comparable value than to offer only one gift? The answer is that offering a selection of gifts of comparable value usually reduces response. This is perhaps explained by the inability of many people to make a choice.

Adopting the one-gift method (after testing for the one with the most appeal) should not be confused with offering gifts of varying value for orders of varying amounts. This is quite a different situation. A multiple-gift proposition might be a free travel clock for orders up to $25, a free transistor radio for orders from $25 to $50, and a free Polaroid camera for orders over $50.

Offering gifts of varying value for orders of varying amounts is logical to the consumer. The advertiser can afford a more expensive gift in conjunction with a larger order. His prime objective is accomplished by increasing his average order over and above what it would be if there were no extra incentive.

The multiple-gift plan works for many, but it can also boomerang. This usually happens when the top gift calls for a purchase over and above what most people can use or afford. The effect can also be negative if the gift offered for the price most people can afford is of little value or consequence.

The multiple-gift plan tied to order value has good potential advantages, but careful tests must be conducted. An adaptation of the multiple-gift plan is a gift, often called a "keeper," for trying (free trial), plus a gift for keeping (paying for the purchase). Under this plan the prospect is told he can keep the gift offered for trying even if he returns the product being offered for sale. However, if the product being offered is retained, the prospect also keeps a second gift of greater value than the first.

Still another possibility with gift offers is giving more than one gift for either trying or buying. If the budget for the incentive is $1, for example, the advertiser can offer one gift costing $1, two gifts costing $1, combined, or even three gifts totaling $1. From a sales strategy standpoint, some advertisers spell out what one or two of the gifts are and offer an additional "mystery gift" for prompt response. Fingerhut Corporation of Minneapolis is a strong proponent of multiple gifts and "mystery" gifts.

Free gifts are a tricky business, to be sure. Gift selection and gift tie-ins to offers require careful testing for best results. The $64 question always is, "How much can I afford to spend for a gift?" Aaron Adler, co-founder of Stone & Adler, maintains that most marketers make an erroneous arbitrary decision in advance, such as "I can afford to spend 5 percent of selling price." He maintains that a far more logical approach is to select the most appealing gift possible, without being restricted by an arbitrary cost figure, rather than to be guided by the net profit figures resulting from tests. For example, Table 4-1 shows a comparison of net profits for two promotions, one with a gift costing $1.00 and the other with a gift costing $2.00 on a $29.95 offer, given a 50 percent better pull with the $2.00 premium.

It is interesting to note that, in this example, when the $1.00 gift was offered, the mailing just about broke even. But when the cost of the gift was doubled, the profit jumped from $4.52 to $52.16 per thousand mailed.

Another advantage of offering more attractive gifts (which naturally cost more) is to offer gifts of substantial value tied to cumulative purchases. This plan can prove particularly effective when the products of services being offered produce consistent repeat orders. A typical offer under a cumulative purchase plan might be: "When your total purchases of our custom-made cigars reach $150, you receive a power saw absolutely free."

Get-a-Friend Offers

Perhaps one of the most overlooked and yet most profitable of all offers is the get-a-friend offer. If you have a list of satisfied customers, it is quite natural for them to want to let their friends in on a good thing.

The basic technique for get-a-friend offers is to offer an incentive in appreciation for a favor. Nominal gifts are often given to a customer for the simple act of providing friends' names, with more substantial gifts awarded to the customer for friends who become customers.

Based on experience, here is what you can expect in using the get-a-friend approach: You will get a larger number of friends' names if the customer is guaranteed that his name will not be used in soliciting his friends. Response from friends, however, will be consistently better if you are allowed to refer to the party who supplied their names.

Table 4-1. Comparison of Profits from Promotions with Free Gifts of Different Costs

Item	$1 Gift	$2 Gift
Net pull of promotion	1%	1.5%
Sales per thousand pieces	$299.50	$449.25
Less		
Mailing cost	$120.00	120.00
Merchandise cost (45%)	134.98	202.16
Administrative cost (10%)	30.00	44.93
Premium cost	10.00	30.00
Total costs	294.98	397.09
Profit per thousand pieces	$ 4.52	$ 52.16

To get the best of two worlds, therefore, you should allow the customer to indicate whether his name may be used in soliciting his friends. For example: "You may use my name when writing my friends," or "Do not use my name when writing my friends."

Response from friends decreases in proportion to the number of names provided by a customer. One can expect the response from three names provided by one person to be greater than the total response from six names provided by another person. The reason is that it is natural to list the names in order of likelihood of interest.

Two safeguards may be applied to getting the maximum response from friends' names: (1) limit the number of names to be provided, for example, to three or four, and (2) promote names provided in order of listing, such as all names provided first as one group, all names provided second as another group, and so forth. Those who have mastered the technique of getting friends' names from satisfied customers have found that, with very few exceptions, such lists are more responsive than most lists they can rent or buy.

Short- and Long-Term Effects on Offers

A major consideration in structuring offers is the effect a given offer will have on your objective.

- Is it your objective to get a *maximum* number of new customers for a given product or service as quickly as possible?

- Is it your objective to determine the *repeat business factor* as quickly as possible?
- Is it your objective to break even or make a profit in the shortest possible period?

So, the key question to ask when designing an offer is, "How will this offer help to accomplish my objective?"

Offers Relate to Objectives

Say you are introducing a new hobby magazine. You have the choice of making a short-term offer (three months, for instance) or a long-term offer (say twelve months). Since you want to determine acceptances as quickly as possible (your objective), you would rightly decide on a short-term offer. Under the short-term offer, after three months you will be getting a picture of renewal percentages. If you have made an initial offer of twelve-month subscriptions, you would have to wait a year to determine the publication renewal rate. In the interim, you would be missing vital information important to your magazine's success.

If the three-month trial subscriptions are renewed at a satisfactory rate, you could then safely proceed to develop offers designed to get initial long-term subscriptions. It is axiomatic in the publishing field that the longer the initial term of subscription, the higher the renewal rate is likely to be. Professional circulation men know from experience that if they are getting, say, a 35 percent conversion on a three-month trial, they can expect a conversion of 50 percent or more on twelve-month initial subscriptions. This knowledge, therefore, can be extrapolated from the short-term objective to the long-term objective.

Sol Blumenfeld, a prominent direct marketing consultant, when addressing a Direct Mail/Marketing Association convention, made some pertinent remarks about the dangers of looking only at front-end response. Blumenfeld stated, "Many people still cling to the CPA (cost per application) or CPI (cost per inquiry) response syndromes. In their eagerness to sell now, they frequently foul up their chances to sell later."

He then asks, "Can the practice of those who concern themselves only with front-end response at least partially explain book club conversions of only 50 to 60 percent? Magazine renewal rates of only 30 percent? Correspondence school attrition factors of as much as 40 percent?"

Blumenfeld gives us a case in point. A control for the Britannica Home Study Library Service (a division of Encyclopaedia Britannica) was run against several test ads developed by the agency. Control ads offered free the first volume of *Compton's Encyclopedia.* Major emphasis was placed on sending for the free volume; small emphasis was place on the idea of ultimately purchasing the balance of the 24-volume set. Front-end response was excellent; the rate of conversion to full 24-volume sets was poor. Profitability was unacceptable.

Against the control ad, the agency tested several new ads that offered Volume I free but also revealed the cost of the complete set—right in the headline. Here's what happened: The cost per coupon for the new ads was 20 percent higher than the control ad, but conversions to full sets improved a full 350 percent!

Ways to Hype Response

Once you have decided on your most appealing offer, either arbitrarily or by testing, you should ask a very specific question: How can I hype my offer to make it even more appealing? There are several ways.

Terms of Payment

Where a direct sale is involved, the terms of payment you require can hype or depress response. A given product or service can have tremendous appeal, but if payment terms are too stringent—beyond the means of a potential buyer—the offer will surely be a failure. Five general categories of payment terms may be offered: (1) cash with order, (2) C.O.D., (3) open account, (4) installment terms, and (5) revolving credit.

If a five-way split test were made among these categories, it is almost certain that response would be in inverse ratio to the listing of the five categories. Revolving credit would be the most attractive and cash with order the least-attractive terms. With each loosening of terms, the appeal of the offer is hyped. In a four-way split test on a merchandise offer, here's how four terms actually ranked (the least-appealing terms have a 100 percent ranking): cash with order, 100 percent; cash with order—free gift for trying, 144 percent; bill me offer (open account), 177 percent; and, bill me offer (open account) and free gift, 233 percent.

As the figures disclose, the most attractive terms (bill-me offer and free gift) were almost two-and-one-half times more appealing than the least attractive terms (cash with order).

While C.O.D. terms are generally more attractive than cash-with-order requirements, the hazard of C.O.D. terms is refusal on delivery. It is not unusual to sustain an 8 percent refusal rate when C.O.D. terms are offered. (Many C.O.D. orders are placed emotionally, and emotion cools off when the delivery man or letter carrier calls and requests payment.)

When merchandise or services are offered on open account, payment is customarily requested in fifteen or thirty days. Such terms are naturally more appealing than cash with order or C.O.D. Open account terms are customary when selling to business firms. When used in selling to the consumer, however, such terms, while appealing, can result in a high percentage of bad debts, unless carefully selected credit-checked lists are used.

The best appeals lie in installment terms and revolving credit terms. Both mechanisms require substantial financing facilities and a sophisticated credit collection system. Installment selling in the consumer field is virtually essential for the successful sale of "big ticket" merchandise—items selling for $69.95 and up.

One can have the best of two worlds—most appealing terms and no credit risk—by making credit arrangements through a sales finance firm or commercial credit card operations, such as American Express, Diners Club, Discover, or one of the bank cards—VISA or MasterCard.

Bank cards and travel-and-entertainment cards have proved a boon to mail order operations, especially catalog operations. It is not unusual to hype the average order from a catalog by 20 percent when bank card privileges or travel-and-entertainment card privileges are offered. Not only do these privileges tend to increase the amount of the average order, they also tend to increase the total response.

When arrangements are made through commercial credit card operations, any member may charge purchases to his card. The credit of all members in good standing is ensured by the respective credit card operations. The advertiser is paid by the agency for the total sales charged less a discount charge, usually about 1 to 3 percent for bank cards and 3 to 7 percent for travel-and-entertainment cards.

Sweepstakes

Perhaps the most dramatic hype available to direct marketers is sweepstakes. (See Exhibit 4-9.) A sweeps overlaid on an offer adds excitement and interest. Two major direct marketers who have used sweepstakes through the 1960s and 1970s and on into the 1980s are *Reader's Digest* and Publishers Clearing House. The techniques they use are the ultimate in sophistication.

Both *Reader's Digest* and Publishers Clearing House use TV support as an integral part of their sweepstakes promotions. Success depends upon (1) heavy market penetration of the printed materials, (2) time-controlled delivery of the printed offer to coincide with TV support, and (3) sufficient TV impact to excite interest in the printed promotion. Careful testing is required to determine the most cost-efficient amount of TV laid over the print offer. "Keep TV commercials simple," cautions Publishers Clearing House. Current PCH commercials prove they practice what they preach: They feature the sweepstakes, using past winners to carry the message, leaving the magazine savings story to the mailing package.

Astute direct marketers like RD and PCH know incentives for prompt response tend to increase total response. Each has built incentives for prompt response into its sweepstakes contests. *Reader's Digest,* for example, has offered the following bonus award incentive: "$1,000 a day for every day your entry beats the deadline of January 31." This means that, if the grand prize is $50,000 and your entry is postmarked before January 21, you, as the grand prize winner, will win an extra $10,000. Another technique is reader involvement. "Seven Chances to Be a Winner," PCH announces in promoting a $400,000 sweepstakes. The entrant was given seven prize numbers.

Umbrella Sweepstakes

A big sweepstakes requires a bushel of money for prizes and administration. Direct marketers, bottom-line people that they are, have found ways to overlay a major sweeps on more than one proposition. *Reader's Digest,* for example, can overlay the same sweeps on a magazine subscription offer, a book club offer, and a record offer—each falling under the umbrellas of one prize budget.

D. L. Blair, the largest sweepstakes judging agency in the country, points out that there are many questions to be answered for anyone contemplating a sweepstakes. Here are questions D. L. Blair has answered for us.

Q.   Currently, what are the most popular prize structures?

A.   Cash, automobiles, travel, and home entertainment appliances—in that order—continue to be the most appealing and popular prize structures. According to our most recent research, apparel (fur coats, designer dresses) has virtually no appeal. As for other merchandise, we generally prefer to eschew the use of merchandise prizes except when we have conclusive research indicating greater consumer preference for the prize item than for its equivalent cash value.

Q.   When a sweeps is tested against a nonsweeps, what range of increase might be expected for a magazine subscription offer or catalog offer?

A.   Using a sweepstakes overlay, we have never seen less than a 15 percent increase in orders for either a catalog or a magazine subscription. The greatest increase we have ever seen is 350 percent. Generally, the increment falls between 30 and 100 percent.

Q.   Can a low-budget sweeps be successful?

A.   Though it is generally true that the success levels of any sweepstakes are importantly impacted by prize budget, we have seen low-budget programs work extremely well when directed at special interest groups. Thus, while a $3,500 value grand prize would provide little or no motivation to most broad audience segments, a $3,500 home flight simulator would be highly appealing to an audience comprised solely of private pilots; a $3,500 hunting carbine would be highly appealing to NRA members; a $3,500 one-of-a-kind Wedgwood bud vase would be extremely appealing to Wedgwood collectors.

Q.   From a legal standpoint, must all prized be awarded in a sweepstakes offer?

A. Speaking solely from the narrow area of what is strictly legal, it is only necessary to award prizes to those who have submitted entry numbers that the judges have preselected as winning numbers. There are, however, very compelling business and ethical reasons that strongly suggest that any direct marketer would be ill-advised to consider awarding fewer than the full number of prizes which he has advertised.

Q. Is the average order from a catalog, for example, likely to be smaller with a sweeps entry?

A. It depends on whether the order is from a former buyer or a new customer. The average order from former buyers tends to be larger. I've seen a sweepstakes increase the value of each catalog order by more than 40 percent. New customer orders, on the other hand, tend to be lower than average, probably because these are fringe buyers coming in as a result of the sweepstakes overlay.

Q. Having acquired a new customer with a sweepstakes contest, would you say that repeat business is likely to depend on additional sweepstakes contests?

A. Yes, to some degree it is true that continuing sweepstakes promotions might be necessary to maintain a normal level of repeat business. (See Exhibit 4-10.) I would say this is true to the same extent that a customer first acquired with incentives such as price-off coupons, free gifts, discount offers, and the like would be conditioned to such offers in the future.

Q. What is the profile of sweepstakes entrants these days?

A. It's becoming broader with more geographic, economic, and educational homogeneity. This "flattening" process extends to the sex of respondents: men account for almost 47 percent of sweepstakes entrants.

Q. Is the appeal of sweepstakes to direct marketing customers increasing, declining, or holding flat?

A. Almost without exception, our direct mail marketing clients are reporting greater new customer and current buyer penetration from their sweepstakes programs. Since we are seeing comparable response increases in programs run by our package goods clients, it would appear that there is significantly more consumer interest in sweepstakes than has ever been the case before.

Telephone Toll-free telephone response (800 numbers) offers the opportunity to hype the response from just about any offer, particularly offers involving free information or the sale of merchandise. (See Chapter 13, "Telemarketing.")

Exhibit 4-9. Sweepstakes Offer

Playboy Great Escape Sweepstakes offers a $72,235 grand prize and an array of lesser prizes on the front cover of a four-page folder and personalized entry coupon for the same group of prizes.

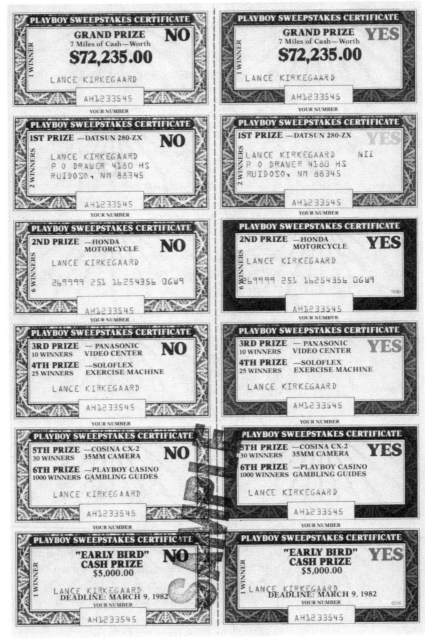

Exhibit 4-10. Devices to Hype Response

Read this only if youve decided to say "no".

Dear Friend,

Before you decide not to subscribe to PLAYBOY, please take one more minute to reconsider. Why? Because there are at least <u>three</u> good reasons to say "YES" instead.

(1.) PLAYBOY'S EDITORIAL. PLAYBOY is recognized as the world's best forum for male entertainment.

(2) PLAYBOY'S GREAT HALF-PRICE OFFER. You can have 12 issues of PLAYBOY delivered to your door for just $15.50. That's half the $31.00 newsstand rate -- you save $15.50.

(3.) PLAYBOY'S NO-RISK GUARANTEE. If at any time you aren't delighted with PLAYBOY, you can cancel your subscription. We'll send you a full refund for all remaining issues -- no questions asked.

If you think about all the benefits, you really have nothing to lose by saying "YES". And you have PLAYBOY to gain. So insert your 6 YES Sweepstakes Certificates into the Official Entry Envelope and return them to us today.

Thank you. And good luck in The $165,000.00 Great Escape Sweepstakes.

Doug Robinson

Doug Robinson

DR/bl

"EARLY BIRD" BONUS $5,000.00

To qualify for the "Early Bird" Bonus Prize Drawing, detach your 6 YES or 6 NO Certificates — whichever you choose — and return them in the preaddressed reply envelope before March 9th.

TO ENTER, ACT BEFORE MARCH 9, 1982

If you're the lucky winner, you will receive a check for $5,000.00 . . . and you'll still be eligible to win any one of the other prizes to be awarded in

THE PLAYBOY $165,000.00 GREAT ESCAPE SWEEPSTAKES

Included in the Playboy Great Escape Sweepstakes mailing package are two devices: a "Publisher's Letter" and an "Early Bird" bonus offer.

Publisher's Letter

Another innovative device that has been developed for hyping responses during the past decade is an extra mailing enclosure known as the "publisher's letter." It gets its name from its first usage—a short letter from a magazine publisher enclosed in the basic mailing package.

The publisher's letter usually carries a headline: "If you have decided not to respond, read this letter." The letter copy typically reinforces the offer made in the basic mailing package, assures the reader it is valid, and guarantees the terms. This extra enclosure often increases response by 10 percent and more. While the publisher's letter was originated for subscription letters, this device was soon adopted by other direct marketers selling goods and services. Results have been equally productive.

The Guarantee

No matter what the terms or basic offer may be, a strong guarantee is essential when selling products or services direct. For more than ninety-five years, Sears, Roebuck and Company has guaranteed satisfaction, for every article offered (Exhibit 4-11). Over the years, no one else has ever succeeded in mail order operations without duplicating the Sears guarantee or offering a similar assurance.

The importance of the guarantee is perhaps best understood by recognizing a negative fact of life. It is this. Over ninety-five years after Sears first established its ironclad guarantee, it is still a fact of human nature that one is hesitant to send for merchandise unless one knows that the product may be returned for full credit if it does not meet expectations. Guaranteed satisfaction should be a part of any offer soliciting a direct sale.

Many marketers have developed unique guarantees that go beyond the trial period. Madison House, for instance, advertised a new fishing lure in a March issue of *Family Weekly.* The company knew, of course, that in northern areas, lakes were frozen over and that there would be no opportunity to test and use this lure before spring. Madison House overcame the problem beautifully by urging the fishing buff to send for the lure *now,* with the proviso that the lure could be returned any time within six months for a full cash refund. This guarantee had two advantages: It assured the fishing buff that, even though he was ordering the lure out of season, he could return it after he tried it in season; and it enabled Madison House to advertise and get business out of season.

One of the most successful manuals ever produced at National Research Bureau was the 428-page *Retail Advertising Sales Promotion Manual.* It was offered on a ten-day free trial basis with the guarantee: "If this manual isn't all we say it is, you may return it any time within twelve months for full refund." National Research Bureau sold over 20,000 manuals at $19.95. It is significant that, after several years, no one has ever asked for a refund!

Many marketers reinforce their own guarantees with a "third-party" guarantee. "Approved by Underwriters Laboratory" can make the difference where electrical appliances are concerned. The *Good Housekeeping* Seal of Approval has long been accepted as a guarantee of validity of claim.

Publishers Clearing House has made this statement, "In addition to the publisher's own warranties, Publishers Clearing House makes you this unconditioned guarantee: You may have a full cash refund at any time, or for any reason, on the unused part of any subscription ordered through the clearing house. This guarantee has no time limit. It is your assurance that you can order from Publishers Clearing House with complete confidence."

In direct sales, the right proposition and the right terms of payment are only two-thirds of the impetus. A clear, strong guarantee completes the equation.

Danger of Overkill

The power of an offer cannot be overestimated. But there's such a thing as too much of a good thing—offers that sound too good to be true or that produce a great front-end response but make for poor pay-ups or poor repeat customers. Here are two thought-provoking examples:

A comprehensive test was structured for a fund-raising organization to determine whether response would best be maximized by (a) offering a

Exhibit 4-11. Sears Guarantee

SEARS GUARANTEE

Your satisfaction is guaranteed or your money back.

We guarantee that every article in this catalog is accurately described and illustrated.

If, for any reason whatever, you are not satisfied with any article purchased from us, we want you to return it to us at our expense.

We will exchange it for exactly what you want, or will return your money, including any transportation charges you have paid.

SEARS, ROEBUCK AND CO.

free gift as an incentive for an order; (b) offering a combination of free gift plus a cash bonus for completing a sale; or (c) offering a cash bonus only. The combination of free-gift-plus-cash-bonus pulled the lowest response by far; the free-gift proposition far outpulled the cash-bonus proposition.

The second example: A $200 piece of electronic equipment was offered for fifteen-day free trial. This was the basic proposition. But half the people on the list also were invited to enter a sweepstakes contest. The portion of the list who were not invited to enter a sweepstakes responded 25 percent better than the portion who were invited to enter.

In both these examples, the more generous offer proved to be "too much." One must be most careful not to make the offer so overwhelming that it overshadows the product or services being offered. Another important consideration in structuring offers is the axiom, "As you make your bed, so shall you lie in it." Here's what we mean. If you obtain thousands of new customers by offering free gifts as incentives, don't expect a maximum degree of repeat business unless you continue to offer free gifts. Similarly, if you build a big list of installment credit buyers, don't expect these buyers to respond well to cash-basis offers, and vice versa.

Given offers attract given types of customers. Make sure these are the types you really want. Here is an illustration of our axiom. A firm selling to businesses built a large customer list based on a series of soft-sell offers. The firm then went into another product line, offering products to their customers and to cold prospect lists. Three offers were tested: (1) a free gift for ordering, (2) a discount for ordering, and (3) no incentive. The results of the three offers against cold lists and against the customer list are provided in Table 4-2.

Table 4-2. Results of Testing Three Types of Offers with Both
Cold and Customer Lists

	Results (in Percent)	
	Cold Lists	Customer List
Free gift	2.2	3.2
Discount	5.2	3.1
No incentive	2.5	3.9

Note the dramatic differences in response between cold lists and the customer list. The discount offer was more than twice as attractive to cold lists. But, to the customer list, not nurtured in this manner, the discount offer was the least attractive. Note also that the offer with no extra incentive was the most attractive to the customer list.

Effect on Bad Debts

It is rarely mentioned that a misleading offer can have a devastating effect on bad debts. A misleading offer causes the consumer, without consciously thinking about it, to feel that he has been rooked and often leads him to conclude, "They can whistle for their money." The justice, if it may be called that, is that those who would mislead usually end up paying dearly for their misdeeds.

The fact that it is poor business to make misleading offers is underscored by the following true story. For many years two large publishers exchanged mailing lists—each making noncompeting offers to the list of the other. The two publishers exchanged bad-debt lists. Time after time, the publisher known for its misleading offers would send the other publisher a list of customers with whom it had bad-debt experience. When the names were compared, it was found that, in over 80 percent of the cases where both publishers had the same customers, the publisher who practiced forthrightness had no bad-debt experience with the identical customers. Honesty does pay.

Make It Easy to Order

The structure of an offer should not be taken lightly. The impact an offer can have on immediate and long-term results can be tremendous. Sad, but true, some of the most brilliant offers fail, not because the offers aren't appealing, but because they are poorly presented, verbally or graphically, or both. The greatest sins of execution are to be found in coupon space ads.

Tony Antin, who directed creative services for *Reader's Digest,* laid down this mandate for coupon order forms: "A coupon (order form) should be—*must be*—an artistic cliché. Rectangular. Surrounded by dash lines. Not even dotted lines. Because one connects dots. One cuts along dashes. Moreover, the coupon should be where it belongs, at the lower outside. The coupon should stand out from the rest of the ad."

So, construction of offers boils down to this: Your primary job is to overcome human inertia. Your offers should relate to objectives. Consider the short- and long-term effects. And, by all means, make it easy to order!

Self-Quiz

1. An ad, TV or radio commercial, or direct mail piece can't be regarded as direct marketing unless there is an offer. ☐ True   ☐ False

2. Basically, there are ten factors to consider when creating an offer. They are:

   a. _____   f. _____

   b. _____   g. _____

   c. _____   h. _____

   d. _____   i. _____

   e. _____   j. _____

3. Of the ten factors, which one should *always* be applied to a direct sale offer?

   _____

4. What is a "till forbid" offer?

   _____

   _____

   _____

5. What is the difference between a "negative option" and a "positive option"?

   _____

   _____

   _____

6. What is the basic rule to follow in testing a variety of free gifts to determine which is most appealing?

_____

_____

_____

7. Here are five terms of payment: (1) cash with order, (2) C.O.D., (3) open account, (4) installment terms, and (5) revolving credit. Which is likely to have the most appeal?

_____

8. What is an "Umbrella Sweepstakes"?

_____

_____

_____

9. Currently, what are the most popular prize structures for sweepstakes?

_____

_____

_____

10. Define a "Publisher's Letter."

_____

_____

_____

11. Why is the guarantee in direct sale offers so essential?

_____

_____

_____

12. What is a "third-party" guarantee?

_____

_____

_____

13. Under what conditions can an offer be "too attractive"?

_____

_____

_____

14. Check the requirement for an effective coupon (order form):
Coupons should be ☐ rectangular   ☐ oval. Coupons should be surrounded by ☐ dotted lines   ☐ dash lines.

Pilot Project

You have been given an important assignment: to launch a new publication for the over-fifty market called *Prime Time*.

This is to be a monthly publication carrying a cover price of $2.50, with a mail subscription rate of $24 a year. The publisher is anxious to: (a) reach a subscription base of 100,000 subscribers before the first issue appears and (b) determine the renewal rate as quickly as possible. There will be no newsstand distribution.

Keeping the publisher's objectives in mind, develop three different offers that might be tested.

CHAPTER FIVE

Selecting and Selling Merchandise

The urge to enter the mail order business is an urge that just won't go away for thousands of entrepreneurs. Yet most who enter the arena fail—miserably. The reasons for failure are multitudinous. A false belief one can get rich quick. Lack of intuitive feelings about mail order products. No sense of necessary ratios of cost to selling price. Failure to test properly. A dearth of knowledge about appropriate media. Poor merchandise sources. Insufficient capital. And on and on and on.

How then does one find hot mail order items? Where do you go? What do you look for? What should you avoid? How do you start?

There is no greater authority to answer these questions than Len Carlson of Los Angeles who has pioneered and marketed about 10,000 mail order items over the past thirty years. His sage advice could pay the cost of this book hundred of times over.

The first tip from Len Carlson is that you look for items whose benefits you can demonstrate with photos and graphics and copy that dramatize the end use.

And where do you find such items? Rarely in general merchandise stores. More often in boutiques—off-beat stores that offer the unusual. Boutiques in this country and particularly boutiques abroad.

Then there are the trade shows, the Housewares Show in Chicago, the hardware and stationery shows, the premium shows. And the foreign trade shows, too. He calls his escapades "treasure hunts."

He doesn't just look. He asks questions: "What items are you selling to mail order companies now?" "Can you add this feature?" "What are the requirements for getting an exclusive on this item?" "What kind of a backup inventory can you guarantee?"

Most manufacturer's representatives are startled when he asks, "What do you have in your big briefcase that doesn't sell well?" Often he finds items that bombed out on retail shelves that he can bring to life in catalogs and promote with demonstrable benefits.

Along the same line, he recommends resurrection of oldies but good-
ies, taking them out of mothballs for new generations of buyers. An anal-
ogy he gives is a technique Walt Disney employed to bring back his
successful kid movies every seven years.

The tips for finding mail order items continue. "You have to become a
great reader, subscribing to jillions of consumer and trade magazines,"
says Mr. Carlson. "Not only U.S. magazines, but foreign magazines, as
well." Many of the magazines are available in libraries. Then there is what
he calls "the rule of two." Here's how that works. You religiously accumu-
late mail order catalogs. When you see a new item, you record it as a test. If
you see the same item in a subsequent catalog, you assume the test worked
and your interest should be piqued. If you don't see the item a second
time, you can assume the item bombed.

One of the top mail order secrets Mr. Carlson learned years ago is the
appeal of personalization. Few stores personalize. So a mail order operation can take a standard stock item, personalize it and change the appeal
from "ho-hum" to "exciting." Such mundane items as dog and cat dishes,
floor mats, and paper napkins are good examples.

But there is one rule for selecting hot mail order items he uses that is
my favorite. It goes like this: Show all new items to your wife. If she says
"no"—go with them!

Gloria Carlson, based upon years of experience, agrees with Len.

The checklist that follows summarizes the sources for discovering viable mail order items.

Where to Discover Mail Order Items

1. Study competitive catalogs and solo offers.

2. Read consumer magazines.

3. Subscribe to pertinent trade journals.

4. Cover U.S. trade shows.

5. Browse retail stores constantly.

6. Write to manufacturers listed in directories.

7. Talk to manufacturers' representatives.

8. Periodically visit book stores and the library.

9. Attend foreign trade fairs; shop foreign stores.

10. Read foreign magazines and catalogs.

11. Contact foreign commercial attachés.

12. Revive your old successes.

13. Set up and refer to your "idea file" frequently.

14. Add on features to existing items.

15. Personalize if pertinent to product.

- Use your instincts!
- Keep your eyes open!
- Hustle! Work!
- Innovate!
- Think MERCHANDISE—all the time!
- *The search never ends!*

One of the most invaluable checklists developed by Mr. Carlson is his list of thirty-four factors to consider when selecting mail-order items. This checklist follows.

Thirty-Four Factors to Consider when Selecting Mail Order Items

1. Is there a perceived need for the product?

2. Is it practical?

3. Is it unique?

4. Is the price right for my customer or prospect?

5. Is it good value?

6. Is the markup sufficient to assure profit?

7. Is the market large enough? Does it have broad appeal?

8. Or . . . are there specific smaller segments of my list that have a strong desire for the product?

9. Is it new? Or . . . will my customers perceive it to be new?

10. Will it photograph/illustrate interestingly?

11. Are there sufficient unusual selling features to make the copy exciting?

12. Is it economical to ship? Too fragile? Odd-shaped? Too heavy? Too big?

13. Can it be personalized?

14. Are there any legal problems to overcome?

15. Is it safe to use?

16. Is the supplier reputable?

17. Will backup merchandise be available for fast shipment on reorders?

18. Might returns be too huge?

19. Will refurbishing of returned merchandise be practical?

20. Is it, or can it be, packaged attractively?

21. Are usage instructions clear?

22. How does it compare to competitive products?

23. Will it have exclusivity?

24. Will it lend itself to repeat business?

25. Is it consumable (for repeat orders)?

26. Is it faddy? Too short-lived?

27. Is it too seasonal for mail order selling?

28. Can an add-on to the product make it more distinctive and saleable?

29. Will the number of stock-keeping units (sizes and colors) create inventory problems?

30. Does it lend itself to multiple pricing?

31. Is it too readily available in stores?

32. Is it like an old, hot item, that guarantees its success?

33. Or . . . is it doomed because similar items failed before?

34. Does my mother/wife/brother/husband like it? (If so, it probably should be discarded!)

Let's take checkpoint number 6, for example: Is the markup sufficient to assure profit? On this Mr. Carlson says, "The books say you need four or five times cost in order to sell profitably. I don't think that's necessarily true. Certainly you need to more than double the cost of an item to come out."

On checkpoint number 24: Will it lend itself to repeat business? Here is what he says: "You should search for items that lend themselves to repeat business. Otherwise you've got to keep coming up with new items for repeat business. Consumable items are the ideal."

Knowing how to evaluate products is a key to mail order success. But not the only key. Finding a niche for yourself in the marketplace is at the top of the list.

"Your first question," says Mr. Carlson, "should be: 'What's missing from the market?'" When he launched Sunset House, he perceived a void in the marketplace that could be filled by bringing hundreds of gadgets together in one catalog. A multi-million-dollar business grew from the recognition of this void.

Years later another entrepreneur perceived there was no one place in the market where one could buy hard to find tools. Thus the highly successful Brookstone Catalog operation was born.

Finding a void and the right items to fill that void are key. But even these steps are short of achieving success. The entrepreneur, in particular, must be a total businessman. The final checklist from Len Carlson is the coup de grâce. It's the "moment of truth" for would-be mail order millionaires. Careful study of this comprehensive checklist could lead many to conclude "mail order is not for me." And that could be good!

Merchandise Selection and Product Development

1. Set marketing objective.

2. Select products.

3. Perform market research.

4. Evaluate potentials.

Media Selection

1. Make budget decisions.

2. Decide on direct mail circulation.

3. Select appropriate house list segments.

4. Arrange rental/compilation of outside lists (list brokers).

5. Decide timing of campaign.

6. Buy space/time (ad agencies, reps, media).

7. Arrange for inserts/co-ops/package inserts/other media.

8. Consider telephone selling.

Creative Decisions

1. Develop the offers and formats.
2. Get copy prepared.
3. Arrange for photography/illustrations.
4. Typography, design, and layout considerations.
5. Production and scheduling.
6. Set printing and mailing program.
7. Buy envelopes.
8. Work with creative consultants.

Testing Projects

1. Offers
2. Prices
3. Lists
4. Geographic areas
5. Formats

Buying Procedures

1. Negotiate with vendors and purchase products.
2. Follow up vendors for delivery.
3. Re-buy.
4. Maintain inventory control.
5. Control inspection of incoming merchandise.
6. Dispose of overstock inventory.

Management Functions

1. Estimate costs, potentials, and profitability.
2. Analyze response and sales.
3. Check legal aspects re merchandising.

4. Double-check record-keeping and data-capture activity.

5. Decide if credit/credit cards to be offered.

6. Decide if telephone orders should be accepted.

7. Study if foreign sales are possible.

8. Sell house products, wholesale, to others.

9. Maintain liaison with fulfillment, accounting, and customer service departments.

An Entrepreneurial Success Story

With caution hopefully well established, it's time to give living proof that entrepreneurs can succeed in spite of the hazards involved. Let me tell you about a beautiful, intelligent, and charming young lady by the name of Annie Hurlbut. She is a classic example of getting into mail order by serendipity. A neophyte in every sense, but she has performed like she wrote Len Carlson's checklists!

Annie Hurlbut is an anthropologist who, when she was at Yale, spent her sophomore summer working at an archeological dig in Peru. There she encountered the alpaca, a cameloid animal related to the vicuna and the llama. Although the alpaca has an unpleasant disposition (it spits at people, she says), it is the mainstay of the economy of the Andes, serving as food and, along with the llama, as beast of burden. (The alpaca can carry up to a fifty-lb. load. "Put fifty-one lbs. on it and it balks," Ms. Hurlbut says.) But the alpaca is raised mainly for its extraordinary wool, which is lightweight, warm, and grows naturally in a variety of colors, from white to beige, brown, and gray.

Ms. Hurlbut returned to Peru again as a graduate student in anthropology, but this time for her thesis research on women who sell in primitive markets. Among their wares were handloomed alpaca garments, which were warm and practical but not exactly stylish.

So, Annie Hurlbut turned designer. She worked with the Peruvians to design sweaters with more flair so they would be more acceptable to North American women. With her first stock, she returned to the Hurlbut farm in Tonganoxie, Kansas, and started a mail order catalog business called, "The Peruvian Connection," with her mother as a partner. They produced a catalog and did some ads. And with this, Annie Hurlbut was in the mail order business.

Some of Annie's early ads were primitive. And the first "catalog" was really no more than an amateurish flyer. But the first ads and catalogs sold enough merchandise to pay the bills with some left over to reinvest. Clearly, alpaca styled by Peruvians overcame any lack of sophistication in mail order techniques. Annie Hurlbut's sense of style, plus alpaca's uniqueness, worked. Annie learned quickly that the secret to building a mail order business was in developing a customer file as quickly as possible. Then to offer those customers other items.

Peruvian Connection's first offering outside of apparel was pure alpaca blankets. (See Exhibit 5-1.)

There are a couple of other noteworthy tried-and-true mail order techniques that Annie Hurlbut used in conjunction with this mailing. Enclosing a swatch of the blanket was a brilliant stroke. (I couldn't resist running my fingers over the swatch—it is really soft!) Also, Annie encouraged ordering by phone and charging to a credit card.

Would you like to guess what the pull was from the customer list? Five percent? No. Ten percent? No. Twenty-five percent? No. It pulled 43 percent—a pull the "professionals" would give up their birthright to get.

Expanding Existing Mail Order Operations

It has been said with considerable validity—"No mail order item, or mail order line is forever." It is certainly a truism that every mail order item— not unlike items sold through traditional channels—is subject to product life cycles. (See Exhibit 5-2.) Hence there is the ever-present need to come up with new products and services. How does one do that?

When someone asks Aaron Adler, cofounder of Stone & Adler, how to determine what new product or service to offer, he asks, "What business are you in?" Nine times out of ten, the person will say, "Oh, I'm in the catalog business," or, "I sell collectibles," or, "I sell books," or something similar. That type of answer is true, of course, so far as it goes. But it probably doesn't go far enough if you really want to explore all the possibilities of your operation. The executive of a company who thinks of himself as being in the "catalog business" or in the "record business" limits his options severely. His thinking is confined so narrowly that it becomes difficult to come up with new offers for customers. On the other hand, if he gives serious thought to the total character of his business, new avenues of possibility are opened, perhaps leading to the development and promotion of a wider range of products and services.

To illustrate: Is a mail order insurance company merely in the business of selling insurance? Not at all. It is really in the business of helping to provide financial security to its policyholders and prospects. From that perspective, management of an insurance company can think of offering not only other kinds of insurance policies but also financial planning services, loans, and the sale of mutual funds, assuming, of course, there is no conflict with insurance or investment laws and regulations.

More and more successful mail order companies have adopted this kind of thinking. A classic example is the Franklin Mint, whose management recognized that the company was not simply in the business of sell-

Exhibit 5-1. The Peruvian Connection

December 26th, 1979

Dear Special Customer:

In early December, on a trip to Peru for Christmas orders,
I stumbled across some extraordinary 100% alpaca blankets, a
swatch of which I'm enclosing in this envelope. I was aston-
ished by the quality of the fibre used and impressed with the
workmanship, even to the blanket-stitched edges. When I heard
the prices (under half of what we pay for the $250 Mon Repos
blankets we import), I called the States to consult with my
partner, and bought up every one. A few hours later The Peruvian Connection was launched into the market of luxury blankets.
As far as I know, we are the first and only U.S. importers
of 100% alpaca blankets, although they have been exported to
Europe for some time.

Our plan is to sell these blankets at direct-importer
WHOLESALE prices in order to compete with the $75 to $95 prices
of the 50%alpaca/50% sheep's wool blankets currently available
in stores and through catalogues such as Gumps, Brookstone,
Shopping International and others. These half. alpaca blankets
are beautiful, warm and sturdy. We know, we've been importing
them for years. But for weightless warmth and silky softness,
no natural fibre-- not mohair, not angora, not even cashmere--
competes with pure alpaca. The secret lies in the high lanolin
content of this wool from the Andes.

The reason you rarely see 100% alpaca blankets in this country
is simple: Alpacas, which live almost exclusively in the Andes,
produce a limited amount of wool (they are sheared only once
every two years during the rainy season). The global demand for
scarce alpaca fibre, however, is insatiable. In the four years

distributed in the united states by
canaan farm tonganoxie kansas 66086 (913) 845-2750

*Two-page letter gets attention at the outset, and quickly establishes value
through the technique of favorable comparison.*

Exhibit 5-1. The Peruvian Connection

of our import business, the Peruvian market price of alpaca has
more than quadrupled.

Since Inca times, when by law only nobility could wear clothing
of fine alpaca, alpaca has been valued over the hair of its coarser
cousin, the llama. Now even lesser quality llama sells for astounding prices. In the December, '79 issue of Smithsonian, the domestic price of llama was quoted at $32 a pound, compared to the 75¢
a pound price quoted for sheep's wool. The article didn't mention
alpaca, probably because even in Andean marketplaces, the latter
sells for considerably more than the highest grade of llama. Predictions are that the price of this once royal fibre will continue
to climb. Alpaca is, in effect, Peru's golden fleece.

The small number of blankets I brought back in December were
bought just ahead of a substantial mid-December price rise. As
a test market, between now and January 31st, we are offering 64
of these blankets at prices well below our own Wholesale prices.
Because our supply at this price is limited, we are offering this
special discount to only a fraction of our mailing list, most of
whom are old customers. You are one of 100 people in on this
sneak preview.

If you love alpaca, don't wait for the price rise to buy one
of these blankets. As are all of our exotic exclusives from Peru,
our new 100% alpaca blankets are fully guaranteed.

We at the Peruvian Connection send you our warmest, softest
wishes for a Happy New Year.

SPECIAL PRICE
THROUGH JAN 31st

WHOLESALE PRICES FOR 100% ALPACA BLANKETS:

    Blanket (86"x65") .... $148.00 $125.
        (pictured, in natural alpaca stripes)

    Throw Blanket (75"x57") $103.50 $92.50
        (pictured, in natural alpaca stripes)

    Lap robe (or child's blanket) (43"x35")...... $42.00 $37.50
        (not pictured, in solid color soft brown)

(continued)

Exhibit 5-1. The Peruvian Connection

Four-color circular was included with two-page letter.

Exhibit 5-2. Concept of the Product Life Cycle

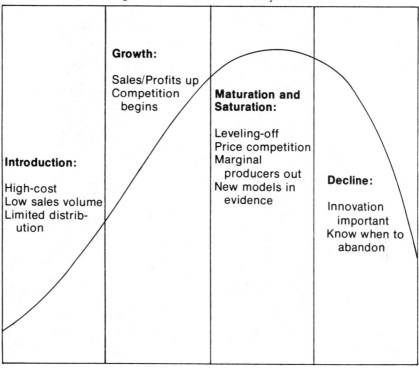

ing limited-edition medallions. Franklin Mint was actually in the business of producing fine art objects on a limited-edition basis for those who enjoy the pleasure and status provided by owning handsome objects not available to the majority of the general public. In addition, the possibility existed that the value of these objects would increase as time went on. As a result, the company has successfully offered limited-edition art prints, books, glassware, porcelain, and a myriad of other items. (See Exhibit 5-3.)

Another example is Baldwin Cooke Company. This firm for many years had offered an executive planner (desk diary) that businesspeople found made an excellent Christmas gift for their clients and friends. Then came the realization that the company was not simply in the business of selling desk diaries, but rather was in the business of selling executive gifts. This led to the development of a broad line of successful new products. The company's gift catalog today runs thirty-two pages with a circulation of one million plus.

An outstanding example of this broad-based thinking is the Meredith Publishing Company, publishers of *Better Homes and Gardens,* among other publications. Recognizing that the company was not simply in the magazine publishing business but rather in the business of disseminating

Exhibit 5-3. Expanding Your Product Line

Ad from Franklin Porcelain typifies new product expansion program.

The renowned illustrator of "Little Women" creates her first porcelain sculptures . . .

Amy by Tasha Tudor

Inaugurating Tasha Tudor's first collection of porcelain sculptures. Individually crafted, hand-painted and issued in limited edition. Art of enchanting beauty, at the very attractive price of $75.

In today's world of fine book illustrators, there is one name that stands out among the rest—*Tasha Tudor*. An artist who, for almost fifty years, has been capturing the hearts of millions with art that is happy, innocent and filled with old-fashioned charm. With delicate use of colors and a wealth of detail, her illustrations create a magical world of make-believe with characters as loveable as they are unforgettable.

Now, to celebrate the 150th anniversary of author Louisa May Alcott's birth, Tasha Tudor has created her very first works in porcelain. A collection of limited edition "Little Women" sculptures that are sure to be of exceptional interest to collectors.

"Amy", portraying Louisa May Alcott's charming, blue-eyed beauty, inaugurates the collection. Crafted in fine, hand-painted porcelain, it is a thoroughly delightful work of art. And it will be issued at the very modest price of just $75—which may itself be paid in convenient monthly installments.

The figure that Tasha Tudor has designed is so vivid, so alive, it's as if "Amy" had invited you into the pages of "Little Women" to come pay a special visit. There she sits with dreamy eyes fixed on the sketchpad in her lap. From her cascading golden curls, to the ruffled pinafore she wears as an artist's smock—she's the very vision of loveliness. A captivating and compelling sculpture as charming and full of grace as Louisa May Alcott's young artist.

To ensure that every small detail of Tasha Tudor's art—every nuance of expression—is faithfully captured, each sculpture will be individually crafted by master porcelain artisans in Japan. Each sculpture will be hand-cast . . . hand-assembled . . . and hand-painted with uncompromising care.

In the tradition of classic works in fine porcelain, "Amy" will be issued in a single limited edition, reserved exclusively for those who order from the collection by November 29, 1982—the 150th anniversary of Louisa May Alcott's birth. When all valid orders from these individuals have been filled, the edition will be closed.

"Amy" will bring her own personality and charm to your home and any room in which you choose to display her. And in time to come, this engaging work of art is likely to become a treasured family heirloom, lovingly passed on from mother to daughter.

To acquire your own hand-painted fine porcelain sculpture of "Amy" by Tasha Tudor, it is important to act promptly. Please be sure to mail the accompanying advance reservation application by May 31, 1982.

Figure shown actual size

- - - - - ADVANCE RESERVATION APPLICATION - - - - -

Amy by Tasha Tudor

Valid only if postmarked by May 31, 1982 · Limit: One sculpture per person.

Franklin Porcelain
Franklin Center, Pennsylvania 19091

Please accept my reservation for "Amy" by Tasha Tudor, to be handcrafted for me in fine, hand-painted porcelain.

I understand that I need send no money now. I will be billed in four equal monthly installments of $18.75* plus 75¢ for shipping and handling, with the first payment due in advance of shipment.

*Plus my state sales tax

Signature _____
ALL APPLICATIONS ARE SUBJECT TO ACCEPTANCE

Mr.
Mrs.
Miss _____
PLEASE PRINT CLEARLY

Address _____

City _____

State, Zip _____

3165

useful, helpful information to large segments of middle America, management moved into such product areas as geographic atlases, world globes, gardening books, cookbooks, and a whole range of similar materials.

So, if you are exploring new products or services you can offer your customers or those you can use to reach new prospects, think about what kind of business you are really in. When you make that determination, you'll find that many new areas will open for you.

For the moment, let's pursue the idea that you are in direct marketing, that you have a list of customers built by offering products or services that they have found eminently satisfactory, and that you would like to expand your sales to those customers with new offerings. Let's also assume that you have answered the question of what business you are really in and have concluded that there are broader areas of endeavor available than you had previously realized. What then?

What Are Your Capabilities?

First, review your capabilities and those of your organization and, again, try to think in the broadest possible terms.

The G.R.I. Corporation, which originally launched the World of Beauty Club, decided to utilize the ability it had developed in working with cosmetic manufacturers to set up a similar arrangement of sampling with a group of food manufacturers. In this case the market consisted of large numbers of people who wanted to sample new foods and save money on a regular basis.

Other companies that have looked at their own expertise and facilities to determine what new products and services they could develop range all the way from the Donnelley Company, which utilized its co-op mailings to include the sale of its own products, to Time-Life, which used its editorial and photographic expertise to produce probably the most successful series of continuity books in the publishing industry. (See Table 5-1.)

So along with determining the business you're in, probably the second most important factor to investigate is your company's capabilities. As you can see, determining what business you are in and examining your capabilities go hand in hand in helping you pinpoint new merchandise or services. But there are significant differences between these areas and they must be considered individually. By doing so, you will be able to broaden your horizons even more.

What Is Your Image with Your Prospect?

A third area to consider in this entire process is one that, paradoxically, instead of expanding your horizons is more likely to limit them or at least put some boundaries on them. Unlike the first two considerations—determining the business you are really in and examining your capabilities—this third area requires you to carefully analyze the "image" customers have of your company. (See Exhibit 5-4.)

Every customer has an image of the company he or she deals with. This image may differ from customer to customer (and probably does in degree if not in kind), based on the relationship each customer has had with that company. If one customer has had nothing but satisfactory dealings with a company, that customer's image would differ from that of one who may have had an unsatisfactory experience, regardless of the cause. But the company's basic image will vary only slightly from customer to customer and will be essentially the same for all customers.

Table 5-1. Leading Mail Order Businesses

Name of Business	Sales Segments
1. Sears, Roebuck	Catalog retail
2. J.C. Penney	Catalog retail
3. United Services Automobile Association	Insurance
4. Geico	Insurance
5. Colonial Penn	Insurance
6. Time-Life—Books	Books
7. Spiegel	Catalog retail
8. Reader's Digest Magazines	Magazines
9. Reader's Digest—Multiproducts	Multiproducts
10. Franklin Mint	Collectibles
11. National Liberty	Insurance
12. Fingerhut	Multiproducts
13. Reader's Digest Books	Books
14. New Process	Apparel
15. Time—Magazines	Magazines
16. Signature	Multiproducts
17. Columbia Record Club	Records
18. Lane Bryant	Apparel
19. Doubleday	Books
20. American Express	Multiproducts
21. Grolier	Books
22. L.L. Bean	Sporting goods
23. TV Guide	Magazines
24. Physician's Mutual	Insurance
25. Olan Mills	Photography
26. Old American Insurance	Insurance
27. RCA Music Service	Records and tapes
28. Union Fidelity	Insurance
29. National Geographic Society	Magazines
30. Ambassador	Multiproducts
31. United Equitable	Insurance
32. Unity Buying Service	Multiproducts
33. Commerce Clearing House	Business services
34. Bradford Exchange	Collectibles
35. Avon Fashions	Apparel
36. Eastern Numismatics	Collectibles
37. Meredith	Magazines
38. Department of Commerce	Educational
39. Dreyfus Corp.	Financial services
40. Federal Express	Business services
41. Garden Way	Gardening
42. Warshawsky	Automotive
43. Comp-U-Card	Multiproducts
44. Shopsmith	Hardware/tools
45. Looart	Stationery

Table 5-1. Leading Mail Order Businesses

Name of Business	Sales Segments
46. AT&T Long Lines	Business services
47. Spencer Gifts	Gifts
48. Swiss Colony	Food
49. Union Fidelity	Insurance
50. Xerox Family Service	Books
51. Jackson & Perkins	Gardening
52. Eddie Bauer	Sporting goods
53. Harry & David	Food
54. Burpee	Gardening
55. Haband	Apparel
56. Figi's	Food
57. Rodale—Magazines	Magazines
58. Miles Kimball	Gifts
59. Sharper Image	Consumer electronics/science
60. Talbot's	Apparel
61. SAVE	Multiproducts
62. Hirchene Photo Products	Photography
63. Eastern Mountain Sports	Sporting goods
64. Brookstone	Hardware/tools
65. C&H Materials Handling	Industrials
66. Drawing Board	Business supplies
67. Healthkit	Consumer electronics/science
68. Hudson Pharmaceuticals	Health
69. Sturdee	Health

Source: Adapted from Direct Marketing *(July 1987) magazine. This chart lists sixty-nine firms engaged in mail order. Sales segments indicate the diversity of goods and services sold via mail order.*

For example, General Motors has a particular image with most Americans. That image exists even for those who have never owned a GM car. The buyer of a GM car who was not happy with his or her purchase may have a somewhat different image of that company based on how his or her complaints were treated. But, in general, the American public believes that General Motors is a responsible, reputable company selling various forms of transportation among which are cars they enjoy using and driving.

Another example in an entirely different field is International Business Machines. Here is a company with which, I dare say, the majority of Americans have never had direct contact. But the image of IBM with most people is probably that of a major American, multinational corporation with unsurpassed technical and scientific skill in the development of the most advanced computers. As in the case of Henry Ford of an earlier day,

IBM is probably regarded by most Americans as the developer and the most advanced proponent of a particular technology. In the case of IBM, this technology is concerned with sophisticated computers and with office equipment such as typewriters.

This perceived image is a vitally important factor when you are considering what new products or services to offer your customers or your prospects, if your company is sufficiently well known. It has been proved over and over in direct marketing as well as in other distribution channels that a company has great difficulty selling merchandise or services that do not fit the public's preconceived image of that company. This can be illustrated in the case of one company that built its customer list on the sale of power tools and then failed dismally in an offer of books of general interest to the same audience.

Let's take the case of the Minnesota-based Fingerhut Company. This firm has built a fine reputation by offering good values in medium- to low-priced merchandise ranging from power tools to tableware. While the company was able successfully to sell medium- to low-priced men's and women's wear to the same audience, it is highly doubtful that they could just as successfully sell fine bound books or Yves St. Laurent clothing. This is true not only because the demographics of the Fingerhut list probably are not suited to the higher-priced category, but also because the Fingerhut image does not conform to that high-priced merchandise.

Unless your customers or prospects are willing to believe that you are a qualified source for the products you are offering, they are unlikely to buy. But if those prospects *expect* certain products from you, because they fit your company image, your chances of success are vastly enhanced.

Thus, it is extremely important that you fully recognize the image you present to your customers and that you select offerings that are appropriate to that image. This recognition, as mentioned earlier, narrows your choices. But it narrows them to your ultimate advantage if it keeps you from going so far afield that what you offer will stand little chance of success.

At this point we might discuss the kinds of factors that tend to create a company's image. The combination of such factors consists of approximately equal parts of the following:

- The products or services offered in the past.
- The style and quality of the new product itself.
- The price level.
- The presentation of the product, whether it is an ad, a commercial, or a mailing piece. The "sound" of the copy and the appearance of the graphics send a definite message to the prospect.
- The "look" of the merchandise package received by the customer.
- The "sound" and appearance of any other communication with your customer, for example, the invoice, the way complaints are handled, and the way telephone communications are conducted.
- The "tone" of any publicity your company receives.

An excellent example of the difference a company's image can make can be given in a comparison of two companies featuring outdoor products: L.L. Bean of Maine and Norm Thompson of Seattle, Washington. Just as they are at opposite ends of the country, both companies successfully present different, yet equally acceptable, images. L.L. Bean's image is that of an old-line, conservative company with the Yankee habit of underplaying its product, a company featuring timeless styles that appeal primarily to a mature audience. Norm Thompson, on the other hand, shows an image of a company that appeals to men and women with a more youthful lifestyle. The company prides itself on its ability to come up with interesting, often exotic new products from abroad.

Examine the Characteristics of Your Customer List

Another most important "mine" to explore for products or services is your own customer list. Study your list from a number of different perspectives, such as:

- How your list was developed
- How your customers have been "educated"
- What they are buying, if you give them choices
- The demographics and psychographics of your customers
- The "product experience" of your list

Let's start with the first point, how your list was developed. In other words, what type of merchandise have your customers been buying? At what prices? How have they paid: cash, charge, time payment? These may appear to be obvious questions, but it is surprising how often they are overlooked when new product planning is under consideration.

Your customers are constantly "telling" you what they like and are interested in every time they make a purchase. Catalog companies are following this rule every time they analyze each product in their catalog for profitability. By doing this, they automatically determine which products are most popular and, as a corollary, which new products they should add to their line and at what prices.

If you are successfully selling a vacuum cleaner through direct marketing, it is likely your customers would be logical prospects for such products as sets of dishes, tableware, glassware, and similar items. If you are selling clothing through the mail, as does the Haband Company and New Process, your customers might well be tempted by offerings of economical housewares, luggage, towel sets, and so forth.

Moreover, the price levels of your merchandise are standards by which to judge any new offering. There is one proviso: You should be constantly testing higher price levels to determine the upper pricing limits of your customer list. Just a 10 to 15 percent increase in the price level your customers will accept may open many more profitable products or services for you to offer.

Exhibit 5-4. The Importance of Image

This classic McGraw-Hill ad, directed to prospects for business publication advertising, applies with equal force to those who would enter the mail order field.

I don't know who you are.

I don't know your company.

I don't know your company's product.

I don't know what your company stands for.

I don't know your company's customers.

I don't know your company's record.

I don't know your company's reputation.

Now—what was it you wanted to sell me?"

MORAL: Sales start **before** your salesman calls—with business publication advertising.

McGRAW-HILL MAGAZINES
BUSINESS•PROFESSIONAL•TECHNICAL

This, of course, raises the question of methods of payment used by your customers. If they pay in cash or by credit card, they will probably prefer to continue to purchase on that basis. This will probably add to the difficulty of introducing a new item that requires a higher purchase price. On the other hand, if your customers are used to paying on the installment plan, they more likely will be willing to purchase higher-priced merchandise, especially if you can increase the number of installments. Customers who prefer to pay for their merchandise on a monthly basis are, generally speaking, more likely to be concerned with the amount of the individual payment rather than the total price of the product.

The second point is, "How have your customers been educated?" The way in which you first got your customers has an important influence on what they expect of you in future offers. An example of the power of this "educating" process is the Fingerhut Company, whose customers have been conditioned to expect a host of free gifts with every purchase. It is unlikely that Fingerhut would be successful with a new offering that did not include such free gifts.

The Grolier Corporation has built a large list of book customers by offering free the first volume of a set of books, whether or not the prospect decides to continue with the series. Again, an offering to these customers of a new series without the free volume would probably fail. At the same time, Time-Life Books has been extremely successful in a program of selling books with an offer that only permits the prospect to examine a new volume for a limited time, without getting it free.

Especially if you are just starting in business, give serious thought to your front-end offer. Be sure you are clear on how you want your customers "educated." The way you start out is probably the way you will have to continue. If you'd rather not adopt the pattern of free gifts, free volumes, and sweepstakes, you probably ought not to start with such an offer.

What Are the Lifestyles of Your Customers?

Now we get to your customers themselves. What kind of a lifestyle do they have? If you haven't already, you should do a comprehensive analysis to develop a "profile" of your "typical customer."

More and more we are finding that the demographic profiles of customers combined with their psychographic (lifestyle) profiles give many clues to successful new product development and sales.

With such a profile, you will find all kinds of "road signs" to new products or services. How your customers live, the kinds of vacations they take, the type of entertainment they enjoy, whether they prefer books to movies, as well as their income level, education, size of family, whether they live in a house or apartment, and other demographic characteristics—all are hints as to the new products or services they might be interested in.

Obviously, people who live in an apartment are less likely to be prospects for a set of power tools than people who live in a house. Similarly, people who prefer movies to books are not very good prospects for a best seller.

What New Products Are People Buying?

When you want to determine whether an offering will work in direct marketing, review the products that people are currently buying at retail. Examples are LED watches and paperback books.

Formerly, direct marketers tended to shy away from products available at retail. But that is no longer true. A wide variety of products ranging from Polaroid cameras to General Electric toasters have been and are being sold through the direct response method in increasing volume. Only a few years ago the Quality Paperback Book Club was started, successfully, on a direct response basis, to take advantage of the tremendous popularity of paperbacks. When you consider that paperbacks are sold in virtually every drugstore, cigar shop, candy store, railroad station, and airport—as well as every bookstore—QPB's success can be seen as a tribute to the convenience and acceptance of direct marketing.

Look at the New Lifestyles

American lifestyles seem to be changing more rapidly all the time. A few years ago the women's liberation movement initiated a continuing change in the lifestyles of many women that influences the lifestyles of a great many men as well. Over half of all women in America now work outside the home. Obviously, employed women have different needs from those who don't work. More convenient food preparation products, for instance. The number of unmarried women who head households also keeps growing. Their needs, too, are different. Their need for financial advice, for example, is certainly different from that of married women. For many years senior citizens have constituted a growing segment of U.S. society. Older people have many needs that differ from those of younger age groups. An example of how one group is addressing those needs is the American Association of Retired Persons. The association offers people over fifty-five years of age a wide variety of services ranging from travel opportunities to insurance. Membership is in the multimillions. All of these groups have particular needs that frequently can be met by the perceptive direct marketer.

Price/Value Relationships

Once you have selected your product or service, you are faced with the problem of pricing it. How much can you get for it? Whatever price you select, it must appear to the prospect as the "right" price for that item. He or she must perceive your price as being a value. And that perception depends on the item and the person to whom you are appealing.

A person earning $250 per week has one set of price/value relationships. Another earning $750 per week has a different set. To the first person, a $7 tie may have just the right price/value relationship. To the second, the tie may seem "cheap."

A piece of merchandise in itself has a perceived price/value relationship with the consumer. One expects a set of cookware to cost less than a set of bone china dishes. A price of $49 for a set of cookware might sound just right. But $49 for a bone china dinnerware set sounds suspiciously inexpensive.

As an example of how people establish a price/value relationship for a product, here's a test conducted by a direct marketer selling a set of four kitchen knives. Five offers were tested with the results indicated.

- Offer 1—four knives at $19.95 plus $1.00 shipping and handling. Pull: 1.3 percent.
- Offer 2—four knives at $19.95, plus hanging board at $1.50 (optional), plus $1.00 shipping and handling. Pull: 1.3 percent; 80 percent took the hanging board.
- Offer 3—four knives, plus hanging board, plus shipping and handling at $24.95. Pull: 0.9 percent.
- Offer 4—three knives at $19.95, plus $1.00 shipping and handling. Pull: 0.8 percent.
- Offer 5—five knives at $29.95, plus hanging board at $1.50, plus $1.00 shipping and handling. Pull: 0.7 percent.

As you can see, the prospects saw offer 2 as the best in terms of price and value, far better than offer 3, which was only $2.50 more.

We have been through this time after time, and we have found that the assumption that there is a right price for every item invariably holds true. Certain cookware sets can only be sold at $39.95. Certain clock radios can only be sold at $49.95. Certain sets of stainless tableware can only be sold at $24.95.

Conversely, we have also found that the customer will, in some cases, accept a higher price than you would have chosen as the proper price/value relationship. For example, a paint gun was tested at both $49.95 and $59.95. And sales at the $59.95 price were better. So, while you may think you have a good idea what the right price for an item should be, you should test that price, but also test at a higher and lower price. You may be pleasantly surprised.

Price/value relationships change, too. Inflation has an effect on them. So does competition. And the relative popularity of the item is important. The same paint gun that sold successfully at $59.95 now sells for $89.95 in about the same quantities as it did at the lower price. Remember when

Sharp came out with the first electronic calculator? It was only a four-function model, but American Express sold thousands at $300. Today you'd be lucky to get $15 for it.

Other Areas to Consider

Finally, let's consider several other marketing factors apart from the product or service itself. These are such factors as the offer, the advertising medium to be used, and how to use research in reaching your decisions.

So far as the offer is concerned, regard it as an opportunity to say to the prospect, "Here is a special reason for acting now rather than waiting to order at a future date." The best offers flow from the product or service being offered. A good example is the original Franklin Mint five-year buy-back guarantee, an offer that corresponded perfectly with the firm's assumption that their products might increase in value. Book club and record club offers of X number of books or records for as little as ten cents are other examples. Free gift offers, limited time or quantity offers, free trial periods, and a wide variety of others can be useful. Try to develop an offer that relates to the general character of your merchandise best. It can pay big dividends.

Products May Determine Media

When it comes to deciding which advertising medium to use, a number of basic factors must be considered. Generally speaking, if the product doesn't carry at least a $15.00 profit at a $29.95 retail price, you probably won't be successful in a solo mailing, unless the pull is really sensational.

A further consideration in your decision as to whether to use the direct mail system is the amount of copy and illustration you need. The more of both you require, the more likely your product belongs in the mail. If your item is suited to a visual demonstration, television becomes a likely medium, especially if the item's price is under $29.95.

Newspaper inserts should not be overlooked as a viable medium today. Inserts have brought a new dimension that offers as much copy space as needed with a wide variety of interesting formats, plus a return envelope, quality reproduction, and, often, market segmentation. Newspaper inserts have opened opportunities for a wide range of offers—from insurance to limited-edition commemoratives and free credit cards.

The Use of Research

Over the past few years an activity that has been receiving more attention in determining product selection is market research. For many years, direct marketers believed that the only way to determine the appeal of a product or service was to put it in the mail or run an ad and see if it sold. Today, sophisticated direct marketers are more and more turning to research as a means of helping to determine whether an item stands a chance of success. (See Chapter 20.)

Consider the various research techniques available to help in selecting your product or service so as to increase your prospects for success. Research such as focus group testing can give you valuable insights into the appeal (or lack thereof) of your offering. It can also help you determine which one or two or more items have the strongest appeal. Often this procedure can even help you add to the appeal of your product or service by suggesting benefits to be added.

Reliable Sources

Everything we've said so far presupposes that you have a dependable source for supplying your product or that you will have a supplier once you determine what you are going to sell. Seasoned direct marketers always make certain they are ready to deliver when they put a promotion in the mail, or advertise in a magazine, or offer the item via broadcast. A cardinal point to remember is: the product must be on hand before you start your promotion. Once you have mailed or placed your ad, you have committed yourself fully. You can't recall the mailing or magazine. And in the direct response business, if you can't deliver in a reasonable length of time, you will lose a large percentage of your orders. You will create much expensive, time-consuming correspondence. You will engender a lot of ill-will and undoubtedly lose the bulk of your investment.

Mining Your Customer Base

While direct marketers must be on a relentless, continuous search for new products and services, there is the ever-present danger that the excitement of new product development will take attention from the product or products that built the business in the first place. No established direct marketer can afford to overlook this danger because their customer bases are the lifeblood of their businesses.

Self-
Quiz

1. The first tip in selecting mail order items is that you should select items whose benefits you can _____ with photos and graphics.

2. List ten sources for discovering mail order items:

a. _____   f. _____

b. _____   g. _____

c. _____   h. _____

d. _____   i. _____

e. _____   j. _____

3. List ten factors to consider when selecting mail order items:

a. _____   f. _____

b. _____   g. _____

c. _____   h. _____

d. _____   i. _____

e. _____   j. _____

4. What are the four phases of the product life cycle?

a. _____   c. _____

b. _____   d. _____

5. In attempting to expand your business with new products or services, what is the first question you should ask yourself?

_____

_____

6. How does the image of your company influence your selection of products?

_____

_____

7. In determining what other products you might offer your customers, you should look at your house list from five different angles. They are:

a. _____

b. _____

c. _____

d. _____

e. _____

8. Define price/value relationships.

_____

_____

_____

_____

9. The more copy and illustration you need to adequately present your product, the more likely it is that:
☐ space is your best medium.
☐ direct mail is your best medium.

10. A major source of gaining new customers is _____
_____.

Pilot Project

You are Annie Hurlbut. You have developed a customer base of 50,000 women who have purchased handloomed alpaca garments made in Peru.
   The question you face is, "What else might I offer to my customer list?" Make a list of ten products you think would be most attractive to this customer base.

CHAPTER SIX

Business-to-Business Direct Marketing

Those "in the know" regard business-to-business direct marketing as the fastest growing segment of the industry. Many refer to it as a "sleeping giant."

When one seeks out the underlying reason for dramatic growth, the answer is almost unanimous—*the accelerating cost of sales calls.* The last available figures from McGraw-Hill Research indicated that the cost of an industrial sales call had passed the $200 mark.

And, keeping in mind the generally accepted number of sales calls necessary to consumate a sale as five, we're looking at an average cost of $1,000 to consumate a sale. That's where direct marketing comes into the picture: done right, *it reduces cost per sale dramatically.*

Business-to-Business Expenditures

Proving the accuracy of figures for advertising, promotion, and training is difficult, but knowing the ranking of various categories is of extreme value. *Business Marketing,* in their July 1986 issue, published a meaningful article with the "tongue-in-cheek" title "Here Is What Business-to-Business Marketers Spend Their Money On. We Think." Table 6-1 divulges the relative ranking of expenses. Direct marketing tops the list. But Table 6-2 is the real shocker. Over 90 percent of direct marketing expenditures, according to the study, are credited to telemarketing! (More on this later.)

The Ogilvy & Mather Study

In October of 1986 Ogilvy & Mather Direct published findings, based upon an extensive study of business-to-business direct marketing. Their findings were truly revealing.

Table 6-1. Business-to-Business Advertising Promotion and PR Expenditures

Advertising	$8,589,371,000
Direct Marketing	30,850,000,000
Trade Shows	21,000,000,000
Sales Promotion	7,616,900,000
Incentives	15,065,871,000
Sales Force Management	5,920,000,000
Public Relations	2,405,300,000
Research	2,190,200,000
Total	$93,637,642,000

Source: Business Marketing, *July 1986.*

Table 6-2. Direct Marketing Expenditure by Business-to-Business Marketers

Direct Mail	$ 3,100,000,000
Telemarketing	27,750,000,000
Total	$30,850,000,000

Source: Business Marketing, *July 1986.*

One of their goals was to study the buying behavior and attitudes of executives at different levels of management. Therefore they conducted the study among top management, middle management, and technical executives, such as engineers and data processing executives.

Another objective of the study was to determine whether buying behavior and attitudes of executives varied by company size.

Annual expenditures by business executives was divided into three spending levels: (1) spent less than $1,000, (2) spent $1,000 to $9,999, and (3) spent $10,000 or more. Ogilvy found that those whose annual expenditures were less than $1,000 accounted for only 1 percent of the total dollar volume; the 23 percent who spent between $1,000 and $10,000 accounted for only 5 percent of dollar volume. But the heavy spenders—those who spent over $10,000 via direct response in a twelve-month period—accounted for 94 percent of total dollar volume.

The study showed that annual sales of a company is a reliable indicator of executive spending via direct response: an executive of a company that has over $100 million in sales will spend nearly six times as much as an executive from a company with less than $5 million in sales.

Ogilvy research also helped to determine which product categories offered the best direct marketing opportunities. Respondents to the survey were read a list of thirty-two product and service categories. They were asked to indicate the categories in which they bought something via direct response or responded to an offer for information, a demonstration, or a visit from a sales representative.

As one might expect, business magazines and books, seminars, and office supplies are at the top of the respondents' list. The percentage of executives purchasing via direct response for the top eight categories of products and services was as follows:

- Business magazines   65%
- Business books   54%
- Seminars, conferences, and conventions   54%
- Office supplies and stationery   47%
- Manufacturing materials and parts   44%
- Computer software   43%
- Airline travel   42%
- Hotel accommodations   42%

The propensity to inquire, buy, ask for a demonstration, or have a representative call for the remaining twenty-four product and service categories is shown in Table 6-3.

As one might expect, there was a definite correlation between product and service categories and level of management likely to initiate a direct response transaction. For example, if you are selling airline travel, office equipment, office furniture, or credit cards, you are likely to find that those in middle management represent your best target market. But if you are selling manufacturing machinery and equipment, technical management is likely to be your target market.

Finally, the Ogilvy survey confirmed the major difference between consumer direct marketing and business-to-business direct marketing—*the decision-making process*. The survey confirmed that, depending upon the product or service being considered, as many as three or more individuals within a company might be involved in some aspect of the decision. Thus each sphere of influence must be taken into account in developing the direct marketing strategy. This is rarely the case in consumer direct marketing.

Table 6-3. Ogilvy & Mather Survey Results

Category	Percentage
Manufacturing machinery and equipment	40
Membership in professional associations	40
Business newsletters	38
Personal computers	38
Office equipment such as typewriters and copiers	37
Office furniture such as desks and chairs	34
Packaging materials	32
Long distance telephone service	29
Telephone systems and equipment	27
Delivery services	27
Credit cards	26
Car rentals/leasing	26
Courses via video or audio cassette	24
Gifts for clients or employees	23
Facilities for company meetings	22
Office furnishings such as lamps, pictures, and clocks	21
Mainframe computers	20
Audio-visual equipment	18
Information systems	18
Vans and trucks	17
Corporate insurance	15
Corporate banking services	13
Leather goods and luggage	6
Real estate or plant relocation	6

Business-to-Business Direct Marketing Objectives

There are five major objectives for business-to-business direct marketing:

1. To sell direct without any other distribution channels

2. To supplement sales through other distribution channels

3. To get qualified leads for salespeople, dealers, and distributors

4. To serve "after-markets"

5. To inform or educate

We will deal with each objective separately.

Direct Sales to Business Markets

Selling direct, without any other distribution channels, is commonplace today in business-to-business marketing. From the marketer's standpoint, he or she is freed from the high cost of face-to-face selling and the difficult task of developing a dealer and/or distributor organization. What's more, the marketer can "contact" prospects and customers as often as desirable from an economics standpoint.

Mailing list usage is a major factor in success. Compiled lists can be selected by sales volume, number of employees, standard industrial classifications (SICs), and ZIP codes. When a business-to-business marketer has a true profile of the customer base, mailings can be targeted to the most likely prospects—even by management names and titles.

The business-to-business direct marketer is not restricted to compiled lists. Many have found direct response lists—inquiry and buyer names of other business marketers—to be highly productive. What makes direct response lists so productive is the fact that these lists contain the names of business people who have proven their propensity to inquire or buy by mail or telephone. (For a more complete understanding, see Chapter 8, "Mailing Lists.")

Supplementary Sales

Few business-to-business marketers have sales forces or dealer/distributor organizations of sufficient size to contact all likely prospects. Indeed, even if they could, the sales potential of thousands of prospects dictates that a sales organization can't afford to call upon "marginal" prospects. That's where direct marketing comes into the picture.

Direct marketing methods can also be brought to bear for "orphan territories" (territories temporarily without sales representation). Rather than let competition walk away with existing customers, the business-to-business marketer uses direct marketing methods—telemarketing in particular—to hold customers until another representative is in place.

To Get Qualified Leads

The big breakthrough in business-to-business direct marketing has been the development of systems and methods for getting *qualified* leads for salespeople. Proper applications drives down the cost per sale dramatically.

Chapter 17, "Managing A Lead Generation Program," will take you through a model step-by-step program for efficient lead generation and follow through.

To Serve "After-Markets"

The term *after-market* requires definition. An after-market is a market for supplies or materials that exists after firms have purchased what is generally referred to as "capital equipment." Because capital goods sales are usually substantial, salespeople can afford to make several calls to complete a sale. But rarely do they feel they can afford to make service calls to sell supplies after the initial sale. The following example illustrates how direct marketing methods can solve the problem.

The A. B. Dick Company, a pioneer in the office duplicating equipment field, found they had in excess of 200,000 users of their equipment, too small to warrant pursuing for supply sales—ink and paper primarily—by their sales force. Market research disclosed the after-market for supplies was being serviced mainly by office supply dealers who were selling supplies from competitive manufacturers.

Direct marketing helped to solve this marketing problem for A. B. Dick. A combination telephone and direct mail program was launched to small businesses, churches, and fraternal organizations who had A. B. Dick equipment. Some A. B. Dick regions got supplies orders from as much as 14 percent of those they phoned. And an unexpected bonus was the sale of thousands of dollars of new equipment to replace outmoded equipment.

To Inform or Educate

The fifth major objective for business-to-business direct marketers is to *inform* or *educate*. The way must be paved adroitly, particularly in the case of capital goods sales—sales of $50,000, $100,000 and into the hundred of thousands of dollars. And direct marketing methods have proved to be uniquely suited to the task.

We are indebted to two sophisticated business-to-business direct marketers for providing unique case histories which prove the value of direct marketing methods for informing and educating. The two marketers are Harris Corporation and Apple Computer, Inc.

Harris Corporation Educational Lead Generation Program

The Harris Corporation is known the world over as manufacturers of state-of-the-art printing equipment. But like so many major corporations, through product development and acquisitions, they have grown far beyond their original franchise.

Early in 1986, Harris came to Stone & Adler with a charge: develop a lead generation program to produce qualified leads for marketing a state-of-the-art office automation system. This new office automation system performed both word processing and data processing functions from a single workstation and could function as a compatible component of the current user's data processing network.

Both the client and the agency felt that before any program could be developed, considerable research had to be conducted. Scores of questions had to be answered. Two of the key questions were: What are the spheres of influence involved in a considered purchase of this magnitude? What effect would the low recognition level of Harris in this market have upon key prospects?

The Harris Corporation research findings are detailed in Chapter 20, "Research for Direct Marketers," starting on page 511. Reading those findings prior to reviewing the promotion plan which follows will help you to appreciate how research dictates marketing strategy.

Mission   Develop a direct mail lead generation program directed at *Fortune* 1000 companies which will introduce the Harris Concept III Information Processing System and generate qualified leads for Harris sales representative follow-up.

Marketing Environment   There are two major issues which were especially important in the development of this program.

1. The selection of an information systems vendor in *Fortune* 1000 companies is based on a complex decision-making process. Although the main decision-maker is usually the director of Information Systems (or M.I.S. director, or various other titles) there are numerous other "influencers" in the decision-making process, notably, the CEO and lower level information systems managers.

2. There is very low recognition of Harris Corporation as a vendor of information systems in this marketplace—in particular, as a vendor of office automation products.

Advertising Strategy   Given the complexity of the market and its low awareness of Harris as a possible vendor, the following strategy was developed for the program:

*   *Create impact* with unusual and dramatic materials—audio and video tapes.
*   *Utilize synergy* to generate added interest with the use of "support" advertising plus multiple mailings to several levels at each company.
*   *Offer incentives* to the main decision-makers for agreeing to a product demonstration.

***Wall Street Journal* Teaser Ad**   The purpose of the ad was to stimulate interest in the direct mail packages and to insure that the materials were opened and read when delivered. The ad served the added purpose of generating additional leads from companies who were not on the initial mailing list. (See Exhibit 6-1.)

Three-Pronged Direct Mail   In order to reach both the main decision-maker and the major "influencers" in the vendor selection decision process, three different direct mail packages were developed. For each company, different packages were sent to the CEO, the director of Information Systems and up to three Information Systems managers.

A number of persons with different titles received packages at the Information Systems manager level. Some representative titles were:

- Information Services/Center manager
- Micro/Personal Computer evaluator
- Data Communications manager
- Applications manager
- Systems/Programming manager

Package No. 1: Information Systems Managers (Exhibit 6-2). This package contained the following materials:

- *A two-page letter* from C. Lance Herrin, vice president of Harris Integrated Systems Marketing Group, introducing the Concept III System.
- *A twelve-page brochure* describing Concept III, the components of the system and the main technical innovations, such as Perspective.
- *An eight-minute audio cassette* entitled "Faster and Faster: A Brief History of Information Processing," which explains the key benefits of the Concept III System in an entertaining format.
- *A gift flyer* which describes the choice of two incentives being offered for seeing a demonstration of Concept III in action.
- *A business reply card/800 toll-free number* for requesting a visit from a Harris representative.

Package No. 2: Directors of Information Systems (Exhibit 6-3). This package contained the following materials:

- *A two-page letter* from Wesley E. Cantrell, senior vice president of Harris Business Information Systems. The letter introduced the Concept III System and informed the recipient that he/she would be receiving a follow-up call from a Harris representative within a few days to set up an appointment.

Exhibit 6-1. *Wall Street Journal* Full Page Ad

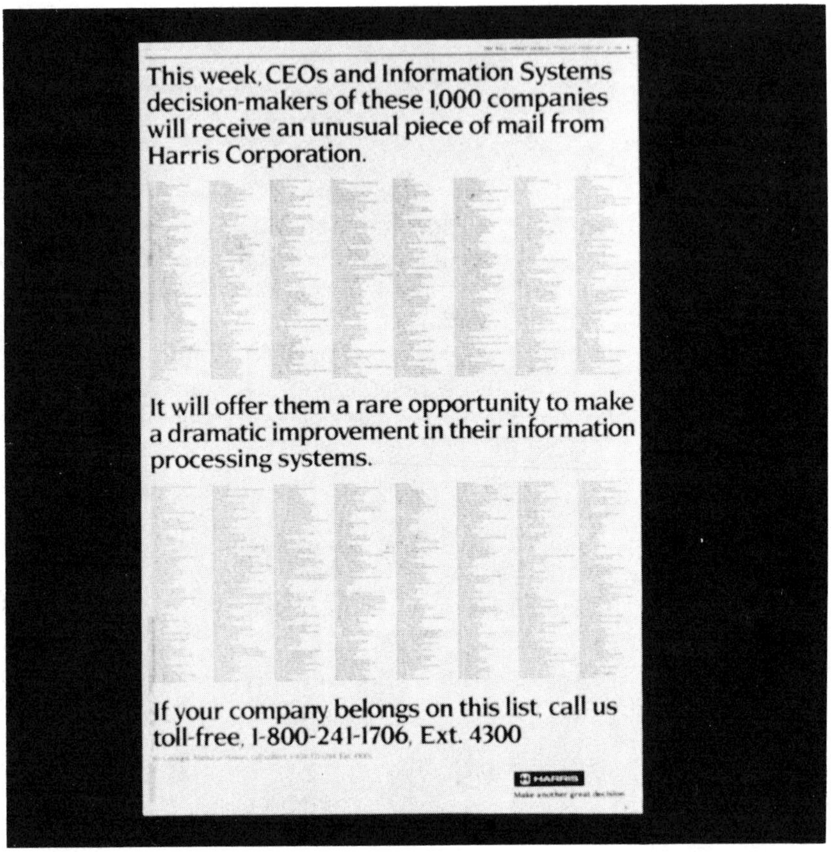

- *A twelve-page brochure* (same as for the Information Systems Manager package).
- *A twelve-minute video cassette tape* ("Make Another Great Decision") which described the Concept III System and demonstrated how it can improve productivity and performance.
- *A gift flyer* which described the choice of two different incentives being offered for seeing a demonstration of Concept III in action.

Package No. 3: Chief Executive Officers (Exhibit 6-4). This package contained the following materials:

- *A two-page letter* from Dr. Jospeh A. Boyd, chairman of Harris Corporation, introducing the Concept III System.
- *A four-page brochure* which gave an overview of Concept III and described the main technical innovations, such as Perspective.

- *A three-minute micro tape* in a Harris-Lanier *Pocket Caddy* which elaborated on the benefits of the Concept III System.

Sales Representative Follow-up   The Harris National Accounts sales representatives telephoned each of the Directors of Information Systems within a few days of the packages delivery to set up an appointment to talk about Concept III.

Results   Sales results are confidential, of course, but a good measure of the success of the program is the fact that demonstration requests were so heavy that it was necessary to schedule appointments weeks in advance.

Exhibit 6-2. Information Systems Managers' Mailing

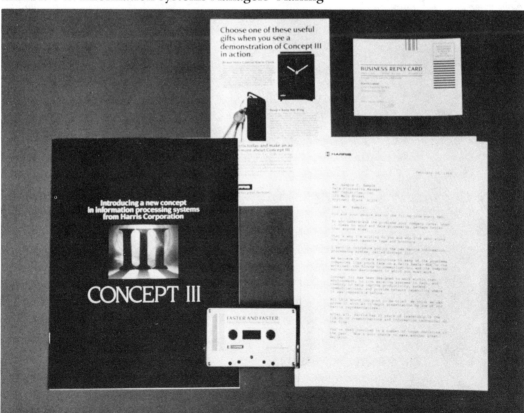

Exhibit 6-3. Directors' of Information Systems Mailing

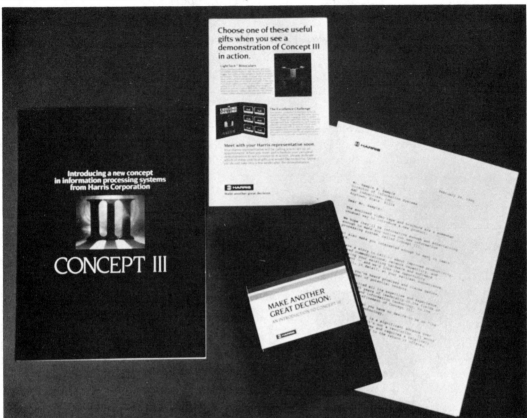

Apple Computer's New Product Introduction

And now we come to a case history that is similar to Harris Corporation—except in one major respect.

The similarity was that like the Harris Corporation, Apple Computer was introducing a new computer application—Apple Desktop Publishing—with a market potential that was hard to gauge. The estimates of the market's potential in 1985 ranged wildly from a projected high of $10 billion by 1990 to a low of $2 billion. And not unlike Harris Corporation, Apple Computer could only guess at their target audience.

The dissimilarity was that Apple was introducing a new product that combined a Macintosh personal computer, an Apple Laserwriter printer, and appropriate software—all products that had contributed to their reputation. Acceptability of a new, related product seemed more likely.

To launch Apple Desktop Publishing, Apple worked with Krupp/Taylor USA, a leading West Coast direct marketing agency. The agency's

Exhibit 6-4. Chief Executive Officers' Mailing

charge was to help develop a program that would ultimately drive prospects into dealers for live demonstrations. We are indebted to Craig Campbell, a vice president in the Krupp organization, for providing the background on this unique case history.

Direct Response Objective Through various forms of research, we learned that certain audiences were very likely to make a purchase if they understood the benefits of Apple Desktop Publishing and then had these values reinforced through hands-on experience. Therefore, Krupp/Taylor USA saw its primary objective as the development of a dialogue designed to educate various target audiences about the benefits of Apple Desktop Publishing, and then encourage this audience to visit an Apple authorized retail dealer for a demonstration.

Direct Response Strategy   To complement Apple's "Trojan Horse" strategy of developing a vertical beachhead with communications professionals so that we could later move laterally into more traditional business functions, it was necessary to create a model for such a progression.

Our strategy recognized that, with a low threshold of knowledge about desktop publishing, our first task was to educate. We proposed accomplishing this by a "curriculum" marketing approach targeted to what we all believed would prove to be the "innovator" portion of the market.

The MAP© Curve   This thinking led to the development of a concept we came to call the MAP© Curve. The operative principal of MAP is a combination of two well-known marketing theories. The first is the Product Adoption Curve. Simply stated, the premise is that in the early stages of a new product's market acceptance, its support comes from *Innovators.* As one moves up the curve, support then comes from *Early Adopters,* then the *Early Majority,* and so on, until eventually, as the product reaches a saturation point, its support is a function of *Laggards.*

The second element of the MAP Curve model recognizes the tried-and-true direct response principle that one develops markets with vertical audiences and then expands the market by moving increasingly to horizontal audiences.

When combining these ideas a rather dramatic but simple notion becomes evident. Namely, that the progression of market adoption for a new product defines the corresponding audience selection.

Direct Response Tactics   As a result of various national research and dealer-supplied input, we came to know that a qualified prospect had a much stronger propensity for purchase after a demonstration of the system.

In addition, we knew that it was incumbent upon us to offer as much predemonstration education as possible. This led to a three-pronged program design.

- We decided initially to focus on service industry communicators as our innovators. Our audience would be comprised of graphic design firms, advertising agencies, magazine, book, and newsletter publishers, and several other markets that need to effectively communicate on paper.
- We would solicit these targets with heavily informative material at least three times in an effort to open a dialogue of education, action, and transaction.
- Finally, the offer used to drive prospects to dealers for the purpose of demonstrating Apple Desktop Publishing should assist in the education process. We envisioned a classic example of "information as offer," and of qualifying prospects by creating offers that *did not* have a high perceived value in a financial sense.

The Mailing Package   The mailing package was designed to lead to an Apple Desktop Publishing demonstration. Big and impressive, the package contained a memo from the executive vice president telling the reader that an Apple Desktop Publishing system helped produce the entire contents of the package, a four-page letter extolling the uniqueness and cost-saving advantages of the system; a twelve-page, four-color brochure illustrating the system's applications; and a four-color certificate for presentation to the dealer, entitling the prospect to a free demonstration and a free one-year subscription to *Personal Publishing* magazine. Exhibit 6-5 illustrates the introductory memo; Exhibit 6-6, the dealer certificate.

Results   Response information is proprietary, but can be reported as follows: if the unit sales break-even index is 100, the total sales-to-date index is 750. Suffice it to say, at this writing Apple Computer had 90 percent of the desktop publishing market:

Business-to-Business Direct Response Media

When we reviewed estimated expenditures for business-to-business marketers earlier in this chapter, we noted that direct marketing accounted for approximately one-third of total expenditures. But we should also note that *Business Marketing* identified only two media as constituting direct marketing: direct mail and telemarketing. A more accurate break-out of media would include the following:

- Trade paper advertising soliciting an inquiry or sale
- Direct mail
- Trade shows
- Telemarketing

A few comments about each medium are in order.

Trade Paper Advertising

Most trade paper advertising appears in *vertical* publications, that is publications which cater to specific industries: metals, plastics, electronics, banking, computers, office systems—to give a few examples.

There are generally two types of trade paper advertising, institutional and direct response. Institutional advertising serves a genuine purpose in that it establishes an important presence in specific markets. Direct response advertising, although it often carries an institutional message, puts the emphasis on getting an inquiry or consumating a sale.

Business-to-business direct marketers using trade paper advertising to get inquiries or make direct sales are often disappointed at the relatively

Exhibit 6-5. Memo Announcing an Apple Innovation

From the desk of Del Yocam

Dear Friend,

Product innovation is a full-time job at Apple. I know because I'm responsible for it.

That's why I take a great deal of pride in telling you that an Apple desktop publishing system was used to help produce the entire contents of this package; brochure, letter, certificate, this note, everything.

And we did it faster, at less expense, and with more creative flexibility than ever before. And you can too. All with one affordable, reliable, state-of-the-art system that will forever change the way you think about the printed word —or the printed picture, or nearly anything else that's printed.

To learn more about the system that is revolutionizing printed communications, read the enclosed letter and brochure, then call your participating authorized Apple dealer. You'll find your nearest one by calling 800-446-3000. Ask for extension 508. You won't be disappointed.

Thanks for your time.

Sincerely,

Del Yocam

Del Yocam
Executive Vice President
Group Executive, Product Operations

Exhibit 6-6. Certificate Redeemable at Apple Dealer

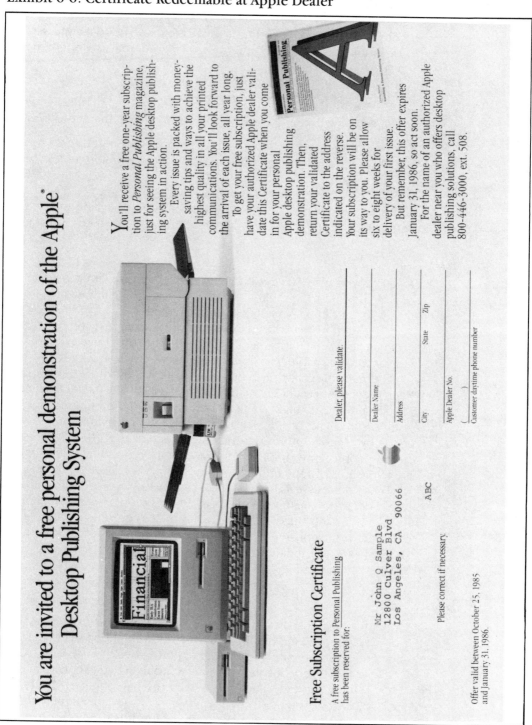

You are invited to a free personal demonstration of the Apple® Desktop Publishing System

You'll receive a free one-year subscription to *Personal Publishing* magazine, just for seeing the Apple desktop publishing system in action.

Every issue is packed with money-saving tips and ways to achieve the highest quality in all your printed communications. You'll look forward to the arrival of each issue, all year long.

To get your free subscription, just have your authorized Apple dealer validate this Certificate when you come in for your personal Apple desktop publishing demonstration. Then, return your validated Certificate to the address indicated on the reverse. Your subscription will be on its way to you. Please allow six to eight weeks for delivery of your first issue.

But remember, this offer expires January 31, 1986, so act soon.

For the name of an authorized Apple dealer near you who offers desktop publishing solutions, call 800-446-3000, ext. 508.

Free Subscription Certificate

A free subscription to Personal Publishing has been reserved for:

Mr John Q Sample
12800 Culver Blvd
Los Angeles, CA 90066

ABC

Please correct if necessary.

Offer valid between October 25, 1985 and January 31, 1986.

Dealer, please validate.

Dealer Name

Address

City   State   Zip

Apple Dealer No.

(   )
Customer daytime phone number

small response rate they achieve. There is a way to substantially increase response rates: use *preprint mailings*.

The mechanics of preprint mailings are really quite simple. Say that you are running a full-page inquiry ad in a trade journal two months hence. You take the following steps:

1. You ask the trade journal for an advance proof of your ad.

2. You arrange to rent the entire subscription list of the trade journal.

3. You send a direct mail piece with a preprint of your forthcoming ad to all subscribers, giving them an opportunity to inquire or buy before the ad appears.

The technique is so simple, and yet the results are usually outstanding. Being let in on something in advance seems to be the motivating factor.

Direct Mail

If getting responses in large numbers is an imperative, direct mail, including catalogs, is an essential medium. An outstanding advantage of direct mail is that it can be personalized and targeted.

Where getting leads is the objective, direct mail can be programmed to produce just the lead flow a sales or dealer organization can handle efficiently. A manageable lead flow assures that leads won't get "cold."

The really big growth area in business-to-business direct marketing has been in the use of catalogs. Such renowned business marketers as IBM and 3M have embraced catalogs as a cost-efficient way to sell supplies and light equipment. Many business marketers sell their products and services solely by catalog. Quill Corporation of Lincolnshire, Illinois, the office supply people, for example, mails over 20 million catalogs a year. Its sales are in the area of $100 million.

There is one caveat about business catalogs: most of them are dull. This need not be. As a matter of fact, it should not be. For the same techniques that motivate a business executive to buy from a consumer catalog applies to buying from a business catalog. The techniques that motivate catalog shopping are covered thoroughly in Chapter 15, "Techniques of Creating and Marketing Catalogs."

Trade Shows

One could be accused of "stretching it" when trade shows are identified as a direct response medium. More accurately, it might be stated that trade shows offer unique direct marketing opportunities.

First of all, every business person attending a trade show is an upper strata member of a target audience. Their firms have spent easily $1,000 or more for them to attend. Business persons who attend are there to learn what is new; to negotiate vendor relationships. It is serious business.

The exhibitors, on the other hand, have spent thousands to show their wares. Without exception, these exhibitors capture the names of those who frequent their booths. And thus direct marketing opportunities emerge. The bottom line is that scores of business-to-business marketers report that names captured at trade shows are the most productive of all the lists they use.

Telemarketing

Telemarketing is made to order for business-to-business marketers. Proof of its usefulness is the fact that telemarketing accounts for a major portion of business-to-business direct marketing budgets.

There are three major reasons why telemarketing is so effective for business marketers: (1) telemarketing cuts cost per sale; (2) even though telemarketing is the most expensive advertising medium, its cost per sale is relatively low when compared with the size of the average order; and (3) the business person is receptive to telemarketing because he or she is accustomed to transacting business by telephone. (The applications and techniques of telemarketing are covered thoroughly in Chapter 13. For business-to-business direct marketers, that chapter warrants special study.)

Self-Quiz

1. The size of a company has no effect on the buying behavior of executives. ☐ True   ☐ False

2. Name five product/service categories which offer the best direct marketing opportunities.

    a. Business magazines

    b. Seminars

    c. _____

    d. _____

    e. _____

3. There are five major objectives for business-to-business direct marketing.

    a. To sell direct without any other distribution channels

    b. To supplement sales through other distribution channels

    c. _____

    d. _____

    e. _____

4. Define SIC.

   _____

   _____

   _____

5. Why are business-to-business direct response lists often highly productive?

   _____

   _____

   _____

6. Define an "orphan territory."

   _____

   _____

   _____

7. Define an "after-market."

   _____

   _____

   _____

8. What is a "preprint mailing"?

   _____

   _____

   _____

9. There are generally two types of trade paper advertising:

   a. Institutional

   b. _____

10. If getting large numbers of responses is an imperative, which one of the following mediums is likely to produce the largest numbers:
    ☐ Trade paper advertising ☐ Direct mail ☐ Trade shows ☐ Telemarketing

Pilot Project

You have obtained exclusive rights to marketing over 100 business-to-business direct marketing case histories. You have indexed all case histories along with a brief description of *objective accomplished* for each case history. You have determined that the selling price for each case history will be $25.

Your task is to develop a complete marketing plan. Among questions to be answered in your marketing plan are:

- Who is your target market?
- What mailing lists will you use?
- What trade papers will you use?
- Will you exhibit at trade shows? Which trade shows?
- Will you use telemarketing? To whom and how?
- Will you offer a discount for two or more case histories? What will your discount structure be?

CHAPTER SEVEN

Fund-raising for Worthy Causes

Few people associate fund-raising with direct marketing. But the fact is fund-raising is a major part of the total scope of direct marketing. Estimates are that well over $40 billion is raised each year for philanthropic organizations alone. This staggering figure does not include multimillions raised for worthy business-related causes.

Corporate America is sympathetic to worthy causes, both philanthropic and business related. As a matter of fact, scores of major corporations insist that their top executives become actively engaged in local and national causes.

The contributions that executives with direct marketing know-how can make to fund-raising efforts can be phenomenal. Facing the sad fact that most fund-raising efforts are inept in the hands of well-intentioned amateurs increases the importance of applying direct marketing know-how.

Fund-raising Basics

The classic way to raise funds for a worthy cause is to take a three-step approach.

1. Form a committee of influentials with the charge to make face-to-face contacts with potential large contributors, establishing a targeted contribution amount for each potential donor.

2. Mount a direct mail campaign to an identified prospect list (data base) of potential contributors.

3. Organize a telephone campaign either in support of the direct mail campaign and/or to those who have not responded to the direct mail campaign.

This is the classic three-step approach, but a few other basic facts are in order, as well.

1. Direct mail is now the primary fund-raising method used by nonprofit organizations, accounting for about one-third of all dollars contributed.

2. The highest percent of response in a fund-raising effort comes from previous contributors.

3. The cost of direct mail in ratio to dollars raised can range from a very low percentage—3 percent to 5 percent, for example—for mailings to a select list of previous donors to 100 percent and more for mailings to people who have never contributed before.

4. Favorable response to telephone solicitations usually can be enhanced when calls are made by people of stature in a community, or in an industry.

5. It generally is agreed that people respond best to emotional appeals, backed by *rationale* for giving.

6. People tend to respond more readily to appeals for specific projects rather than for general needs. Example: "Will you help us to raise $92,000 so we can give Braille books to the blind?"

7. When pledges are made by telephone, it can be expected that 75 percent to 80 percent of the pledges will be collected, if properly followed up.

8. When a telephone campaign is done properly to selected lists, the pledge rate can be as much as ten to twelve times that of direct mail.

9. The average contribution tends to increase when specific contribution amounts are suggested. Example: "You contributed $20 last year. May we suggest you contribute $25 this year to help our expanded needs."

10. Total amount pledged tends to be greater when a multipayment plan is offered.

11. Setting a specific date for meeting a fund-raising goal tends to increase response and total contributions.

The Mathematics of Fund-raising

The uninitiated in fund-raising often criticize philanthrophic organizations for spending a major portion of their money received from contributions on mailing efforts to get new donors. In most instances this criticism is due to sincere ignorance about the mathematics of fund-raising. Investing in new donors, when done right, produces a substantial return on investment.

In a remarkable book, titled *Billions By Mail* (Published by Tabor Oaks, P.O. Box 637, Lincoln, Massachusetts 01773), Francis S. Andrews, chairman, American Fund Raising Services, Inc., Waltham, Massachusetts, provides all the evidence one would need to prove the validity of investing in new donors. Here, from his book, is what "Andy" Andrews has to say about investing in new donors.

Investment Method of Fund-raising

Just as an investor is interested in the net income he will receive over the useful life of his asset, an institution measures its return on donor investment by the amount of net income it receives over the life of a donor.

Investment portfolio managers can invest an institution's funds in a broad-based list of stocks and bonds, with a substantial element of risk, and secure annual yields ranging from 5% to 20%.

Fund-raising managers can invest an institution's funds in a broad based list of contributors, with *no* risk, and secure annual yields ranging from 50% to 200%.

An investment in new donors is self-financing. Within 90 to 120 days, often earlier, the total "investment" needed to establish a donor list will be returned to the bank.

Investing in a large donor base is one of the fastest and surest ways of pyramiding capital.

The donor investment process calls for a systematic screening of "mass" mailing lists in search of those families who are willing to support an organization with a continuing series of annual and special gifts.

Donor acquisition carries a high initial commitment of cash or credit. Only a small fraction of all families solicited can be attracted as donors in one year. These percentages range from 1% to 5%, depending on the popularity of the institution or cause. However, over a period of 5 to 10 years, total penetration can grow to 10% or 20% of the total family universe.

The degree of possible penetration is dependent on the socioeconomic mix of the population and the duration and intensity of the fund-raising effort.

The economic justification for direct mail donor investment rests on the premise that a new donor is an investment in future income. Otherwise, such an investment would be classified as an unwarranted churning of institutional dollars.

A lifetime of philanthropy adds up to an impressive return on original investment. If this were not the case, there would be little justification for soliciting new donors or members at costs which sometimes exceed the value of the first friendship gift.

Annual giving and membership programs are analogous to a business investment. They are made not for today but for the future. And, since donor income is reliable and predictable, this puts donor investment way ahead of the vagaries of Wall Street.

Lifetime Cumulative Gift

Donors acquired by mail, cultivated by mail, and renewed by mail, will contribute in a consistent pattern over a long period of years.

A donor base represents a significant source of income for a nonprofit organization.

The long-term value of a donor was first verified by a ten-year computerized research study conducted by American Fund Raising Services for the Massachusetts General Hospital.

The MGH, one of the major research-teaching hospitals, agreed to cooperate in a decade-long project to document the giving habits of donors.

A computerized fund-raising system, the first for hospitals, was designed and programmed. The system made it possible to retrieve information such as year of first gift, annual gift, cumulative gift, and mail code. Lost or deceased donors were assigned bypass codes and retained in the system to keep all original donor groups intact for the period of the study.

Changes of address were carefully handled and an intensive investigation of each "loss" was made to assure that all records were maintained perfectly during the life of the study.

Contributors of $500 or more were removed from the general file and set up on a major donor list for special development and tracking.

The results of this *10-Year History of Annual Giving, Massachusetts General Hospital, 1963-1973,* are shown on page [144].

Separate records were kept for each year's donor group. The example shown in this book is for donors acquired in the 1963-64 fundraising year. That first year, 3,396 new donors contributed a total of $85,806, with an average gift of $25.27.

At the end of ten years, the "class of 63-64" had contributed $831,761. This total was for annual giving only. The hospital estimated, based on its own tracking of major gifts and bequests, that more than $1 million also came in from special gifts.

No investment portfolio would have returned an equal annual income or appreciation of original capital.

Over the ten-year period, a base of more than 175,000 donors was built from annual mailings to Massachusetts families. At the peak of the program, more than $1,000,000 in net income was received annually.

The table reveals some interesting facts about donor renewal rates in the 1960s. First, there is a sizeable drop-off in the renewal rate—from 100% to 56.1%. Second, once the initial drop has taken place, normal attrition takes over. Third, the average gift tends to increase over the years, cancelling out the decline in rate.

If 44% of the original donor base did not repeat in the first renewal year, does this mean that these donors were lost forever?

The Study of Lifetime Contributing Patterns, Massachusetts General Hospital—1962-1972, shown on page [145] answers this question.

This study reveals a remarkable degree of donor loyalty. Eleven years after acquisition, only 6% of the original donor group had given just one gift. 43% had given nine or more gifts and 52% had given eight or more gifts.

Massachusetts General Hospital
10-YEAR HISTORY OF ANNUAL GIVING
1963-1973

Research Project

Officers and directors of the Massachusetts General Hospital, embarking on a major direct mail program which involved a considerable investment in the building of a donor base, wished to confirm the fact that such an investment was a prudent use of funds. American Fund Raising Services was engaged to conduct a long-term project to document the long-term value of new donor acquisitions. The table below traces the contributing records of donors whose first gift was received in 1963 and for nine years thereafter.

Research Results

Year	Number of Donors	Renewal Percentage	Yearly Contributions	Cumulative Gift Totals
1963-64	3,396	100	$ 85,806	—
1964-65	1,905	56.1	$ 78,252	$ 164,058
1965-66	1,927	56.7	$ 107,095	$ 271,153
1966-67	1,847	54.4	$ 92,388	$ 363,541
1967-68	1,790	52.7	$ 96,656	$ 460,197
1968-69	1,708	50.2	$ 94,697	$ 554,894
1969-70	1,482	43.6	$ 96,380	$ 651,274
1970-71	1,214	35.7	$ 65,411	$ 716,685
1971-72	1,177	34.7	$ 69,272	$ 785,957
1972-73	1,040	30.6	$ 45,804	$ 831,761

Conclusion

More than 175,000 donors were included in the 10-year research project which established the wisdom of investing in a base of donors whose annual gifts equalled the return on a multimillion dollar endowment. The tabulation shows the performance of only one donor group—those acquired in 1963-64. A similar tabulation, with similar results, was maintained for all new donors. Here, the small group of only 3,396 new donors, contributing $85,806 in their first renewal year, eventually contributed $831,761 to annual giving campaigns over 10 years.

Massachusetts General Hospital
STUDY OF LIFETIME
CONTRIBUTING PATTERNS
1962-1972

Research Project

Proof of donor loyalty had not been documented in 1962 when the Massachusetts General Hospital commissioned American Fund Raising Services to conduct a computerized study of long-term donor contributing patterns. This study was a by-product of the 10-Year History of Annual Giving. The necessity for a donor loyalty study was the unsettling contention among some that half of all new donors are lost in the first renewal year, presumably forever. This study, conducted under strict research standards, would confirm or deny this alleged high loss among new donors.

Research Results

First Gift	One Gift	Two Gifts	Three Gifts	Four Gifts	Five Gifts	Six Gifts	Seven Gifts	Eight Gifts	Nine Gifts	Ten Gifts	Eleven Gifts
1972	100%										
1971	54%	46%									
1970	39%	26%	35%								
1969	33%	20%	18%	29%							
1968	29%	19%	16%	15%	21%						
1967	28%	18%	14%	12%	16%	12%					
1966	25%	16%	13%	13%	10%	11%	12%				
1965	23%	16%	12%	11%	10%	9%	9%	9%			
1964	20%	13%	11%	11%	10%	8%	8%	8%	11%		
1963	16%	10%	9%	9%	8%	9%	9%	9%	9%	12%	
1962	6%	5%	6%	7%	7%	8%	9%	9%	11%	14%	18%

Conclusion

This research project established the fact that the first-year "drop-off" of approximately 50% does not represent a permanent loss of support. On the contrary, the study proved the exceptional loyalty of newly acquired donors. 10 years after acquisition, only 6% of the original donor group had given one gift only. Unlike membership groups where a non-renewing member cuts his ties with a group, contributors to annual appeals give on an irregular basis.

Educational Foundation Campaign

More often than not, business executives get involved in a fund-raising program when their trade association identifies a worthy industry effort for which funds are required over and above funds normally generated from members.

Such was the case a few years ago with the Direct Mail/Marketing Educational Foundation. Annual income from members covered the cost of bringing college students—all expenses paid—to the Lewis Kleid Institute twice each year. But the foundation had a much larger goal: to establish direct marketing degree programs at three major universities.

For this goal, the foundation had no funds. And it was calculated that it would be necessary to raise a capital fund of $1.2 million to underwrite the program. A tremendous task.

How did the foundation organize to reach their ambitious goal? They followed the classic three-step approach.

1. They formed a committee of influentials to make person-to-person approaches with major organizations having a vested interest in direct marketing, organizations capable of pledging $15,000 to $30,000 and more over three years.

2. They developed a mailing package to go to the 2,400 members of the Direct Marketing Association, all of whom also had a vested interest in the future of direct marketing.

3. They made arrangements with CCI, a leading telemarketing agency to phone all members who did not pledge as a result of person-to-person contact, or as a result of the direct-mail effort.

The letter—a five pager, plus pledge card—follows (Exhibit 7-1). Much of the story behind the fund-raising effort is told in the letter, as you will see.

Exhibit 7-1. Educational Foundation Mailing

STONE & ADLER INC.

150 NORTH WACKER DRIVE
CHICAGO, ILLINOIS 60606
(312) 346-6100

June 1st, 1982

Mr. Jerry Greenberg
The Finals
149 Mercer Street
New York, New York 10012

Dear Mr. Greenberg,

Remember when you were a kid. A "dreamer" was put down
as someone who would never amount to anything—destined
to be a "non-achiever" for life.

What a myth!

Let me tell you about some "dreamers" who became super
achievers in direct marketing. They succeeded beyond
their wildest dreams.

There's the thrilling story of L. L. Bean in Maine. For
years they ran a successful mail order business...catering
to outdoorsmen.

But Leon Gorman dreamed of new horizons...a new world out
there of men and women who never fished or hunted—dressed
the way outdoors people dress. A pipe dream? Hardly, Leon
Gorman turned dream to reality. Sales—plateaued at the
$50 million level—boomed past the $100 million level in a
few short years.

What about the legendary "kitchen table" people? Len
Carlson, out in California, is a part of the legend.

(continued)

Exhibit 7-1. Educational Foundation Mailing

Len and his wife Gloria shared a dream. They dreamed they could put together a catalog of hard-to-find gadgets that would appeal to the masses. Thus Sunset House was born.

Fifteen years and a customer base of 6.5 million names later, the press announced Sunset House had been acquired by a major corporation for a price reported to be in the millions.

The most remarkable dream story on the agency side is that of Lester Wunderman. Les was an account person with the Max Sackheim agency. He dreamed of having his own agency.

But an agency that would apply sophisticated direct response techniques to all media—including a "new" medium called television. Today his firm—Wunderman, Ricotta & Kline—has billings in excess of $100 million, with offices in New York and 12 foreign countries.

As you read of these dreams-come-true I hope you are recalling your own. The dreams you have had which have helped you to get to where you are today.

> But of all the dreams-come-true which I have witnessed over the years there is one which supersedes all others. A dream-come-true which has touched all our lives, a dream which will live on beyond our lifetimes.

The year was 1965. Lewis Kleid, a leading list broker in his day, was a close friend of Edward N. Mayer, Jr., known around the world as "Mr. Direct Mail."

Lew made a proposition to Ed. He said, "Ed—if you will devote time to teaching the rudiments of direct marketing to college kids, I'll provide the seed money to make it happen."

Thus, with the simplicity that was a trademark of Ed Mayer, the Lewis Kleid Institute was launched. Today, almost 17 years later, The Direct Mail/Marketing Educational Foundation, a non-profit organization which sponsors Kleid Institutes, continues in the Ed Mayer image.

Exhibit 7-1. Educational Foundation Mailing

Over the past 17 years over 1,000 bright college students have taken the 5-day intensive course, sponsored by the Foundation ...all expenses paid. It is estimated that over 50% of these students have entered into a direct marketing career.

As one of the privileged few who has had the honor of lecturing each new group of candidates over many years—I only wish you could witness, as I have, the excitement that comes to each as they are introduced to the wonders of direct marketing disciplines.

"I learned more in five days than in my four years as a marketing major," is a somewhat typical statement from one of these exuberant students.

But let me give you just a few quotes from hundreds in file.

"I learned so very much—the week just set my spark for direct marketing into a big roaring fire!"

> Marilee Gibson
> Yorchak
> New Mexico State
> University

"The Institute has greatly increased my awareness and understanding of direct marketing, and furthered my career interest."

> Tim Harrison
> University of North
> Carolina

"If one of your objectives was to stimulate young, ambitious people to enter your field, you succeeded with me."

> Paula Miante
> College of William and
> Mary

(continued)

Exhibit 7-1. Educational Foundation Mailing

I guess from all of this one would have to conclude our dream
has truly come true. Well—not exactly.

None of us ever dreamed that direct marketing would have the
explosive growth we have all experienced. (As an aside—
when I wrote my first book I trumpeted that total sales of
goods and services via the direct marketing method had reached
the staggering figure of $300 million. The estimated figure
for 1981 is $120 *billion!*)

So now we realize that if our true dream is to be realized—
growing our own at the college level to people our future
growth—we are going to have to raise our sights beyond the
far horizon.

Where we are bringing the gifted student to the Institute—
only one each from about 35 colleges twice each year—we've
got to get Direct Marketing taught on the college campus in
full semester courses. Not to three score and ten for five
days. Instead—to hundreds for full semesters.

Is this "The Impossible Dream"? No!

I'm going to tell you about what some regard to be an
emerging "miracle," which is in the process of happening as
I pen this letter.

At a Board of Directors meeting a few months ago in the
offices of The Direct Mail/Marketing Educational Foundation,
Richard L. Montesi, President, made a startling proposal.
A proposal which he stated would make our ultimate dream
come true.

The ultimate dream, as he expresed it, is to establish a
Chair for a Direct Marketing Center in three major universities: one in the Middle West; one in the East; and one in the West.

The full-scale curriculums will be structured to earn a
degree in Direct Marketing for each graduate, carrying with
them a stature similar to that enjoyed by a graduate from
the Wharton School of Business or Harvard Business School.

Exhibit 7-1. Educational Foundation Mailing

"An exciting idea," we said. "But how are we going to fund these centers?" "From a capital fund of $1.2 million," Dick said. "$1.2 million. Good God!" was the reaction.

Well then the miracle started happening. Andy Andrews, one of the directors, said—"Why don't we go around the table right now and see how much commitment we can get over the next three years from the small group of directors at this table?"

Would you believe we raised $120,000.00—10% of our goal—within five minutes!

When we left that day a few of us agreed to write some letters and make some phone calls. And what happened as a result surpasses anything in my experience.

Remember those "dreamers" I talked about earlier? Well let me tell you what happened with some of them.

Remember Leon Gorman of L. L. Bean? He's committed $15,000 over three years. And Len Carlson—another $15,000. And Les Wunderman—$15,000. They're putting their money where their dreams are.

The list goes on. "Dusty" Loo of Looart Press—a major commitment. John Flieder of Allstate Insurance—"Count us in." Kiplinger Washington Editors. The Kleid Company. Jim Kobs of Kobs & Brady—"Absolutely!" Publishers Clearing House. Grolier. Colonial Penn. Rodale Press. Spiegel. American Express.

John Yeck of Yeck Brothers Group—"You can count on us." Eddie Bauer. Rapp & Collins. Ogilvy & Mather. Alan Drey. The DR Group. Hanover House. And on and on.

> To this moment, these people and some others we have contacted bring total commitments to $725,000. So we have reached 60% of our goal!

(continued)

Exhibit 7-1. Educational Foundation Mailing

This is exciting in itself, but equally exciting is the
fact that we have two formal proposals from two major
universities detailing how a Chair would be established
for Direct Marketing. And the cost.

One proposal is from UMKC—University of Missouri, where
Martin Baier of Old American has taught Direct Marketing
classes for a number of years. The other proposal is from
New York University. Both universities are ready when we are.

So we are this close to bringing off a 20th Century miracle!

Now we come to you to ask you to share in this dream of
dreams. There is a pledge card inside of the enclosed envelope. The amount suggested is just that. A suggestion. You
are the best judge of what your company should pledge against
the future.

I have asked for and have gotten approval to have your
response come back to me personally. I'd like to hear from
you even if there is some unforeseen circumstance under which
you cannot make a pledge.

We must decide very soon upon the first university to
establish a Direct Marketing Center. Therefore I will
appreciate it if you will reply within the next 10 days.
Thank you so very much.

                                        Sincerely,

                                        Bob Stone

P.S. It is my fondest dream that you and I will be
     there to witness the commencement exercises of
     the first graduating class with a degree in
     Direct Marketing.

Exhibit 7-1. Educational Foundation Mailing

"A Margin of Excellence"

THE DIRECT MAIL/MARKETING EDUCATIONAL FOUNDATION
CAPITAL FUND RAISING PROGRAM

Our organization wishes to participate in the DMMEF Capital Fund Raising Program. Our 3-YEAR PLEDGE is indicated to the right.

Company _____

Officer Name _____

Address _____

Signature _____

YOUR TAX DEDUCTIBLE GIFT WILL MAKE A DIFFERENCE

Contribution Category	Payment Schedule
☐ Leadership Gift $10,000 annually $_____	payable by July 15, 1982
☐ Major Gift $5,000 annually $_____	payable by 1983
☐ Special Gift $2,500 annually $_____	payable by 1984
☐ Supporting Gift $1,000 annually	

Pledges are for three years only and are nonbinding commitments. Reminders will be mailed thirty days prior to the payment dates indicated above.

A couple of comments about the letter and pledge card before we talk about the telephone campaign: First, most neophytes would be aghast at a five-page letter; but the fact is that no letter is too long if written to the interest of the reader.

Second, the letter encouraged pledges by telling what the reader's peer group had already pledged, confirming the acceptance of the worthy goal. And finally, the letter had a sense of urgency—"We must decide very soon upon the first university to establish a Direct Marketing Center."

The pledge card employed two fund-raising principles: (1) pledges will be larger if you spread them over time (three years in this case), and (2) suggesting a specific amount (amounts suggested were in ratio to the dues a member paid) improves the chances of a pledge in that amount.

The mailing package was a huge success. Only a handful of those who responded favorably pledged less than the requested amount. But the foundation was still short of their goal. And this is where telemarketing techniques put the campaign over the top.

The Telemarketing Program

The strategy for the telephone effort was developed by the late Murray Roman, founder of Campaign Communications Institute, a pioneer in telemarketing. He first reviewed the membership prospect list, eliminating those who had already pledged, and then selected from those remaining the ones he considered most likely for telephone solicitation.

This list agreed upon, he then prepared a script for a taped message from Bob DeLay, president of the Direct Marketing Association, and Bob Stone, chairman of Stone & Adler, Inc. The taping completed, his agency started making calls within a few days.

The procedure was for the CCI telephone communicator to ask the prospect permission to play a taped message from Bob DeLay and Bob Stone. The taped message follows:

> BOB DELAY: This is Bob DeLay. I am asking that you take a few minutes to hear Bob Stone and me talk about an industry opportunity that depends so much on your good will and support. We are talking to you on tape via telephone to be sure you personally get our message and because we like to reach our members as quickly as possible while there is still time for decision making. But here is Bob Stone to tell you more about that opportunity.

> BOB STONE: Thanks, Bob. I really appreciate your kindness in allowing me time to bring you up to date on the progress that has been made in the Educational Foundation fund-raising drive. One word that I think describes the progress best is *terrific!*

> It's amazing to me that in the most trying of times direct marketers of all sizes across the nation have responded so favorably. This has convinced me that our objective of growing our own talent is absolutely right. I have seen many pledges come through for $15,000; many for $7,500 and scores for $3,000. On the other hand, one company contributed $30,000 and another $52,000.

> These major contributions are great but some of the smaller pledges have thrilled me the most. One was from a 24-year old by the name of Michael Gersen who said, "At age 24, recently experiencing the lack of specialization in our university system, I feel your dreams and the steps you have taken are of the utmost importance. I am not in a position to commit an annual gift; however, I would very much like to show my support with the enclosed contribution." And enclosed was his personal check in the amount of $50.00. Isn't that great?

> So here's where we are at this point in time. We are approaching the $900,000 mark with a little over $300,000 to go. To fall short of our goal now, to fail to educate the talent we will need in the future would be tragic.

> As I said in my letter to you, the amount of the pledge suggested was just that—a suggestion. I am going to ask the telephone communicator to repeat the suggested pledge for you in a moment.

> Let me say, whatever amount you consider adequate from your standpoint will be a profitable investment in the future. And what a great day it will be for you and me and everyone else in direct marketing when we see bright young talent graduating with B.A.s and M.B.A.s in direct marketing. Then our futures will indeed be secure. Thank you for listening.

Upon completing the playing of the taped messages, the CCI telephone communicator came back on the line and asked for a three-year pledge in the exact amount suggested in the mailing piece. Results were astounding: 18 percent of those called made a pledge. The campaign went over the top.

So here is a classic example of putting the three-step approach into practice. The person-to-person phase raised $725,000; the direct mail/telephone phase raised $505,000. Grand total: $1,230,000—all from 2,400 prospects!

"Freedom to Mail" Campaign

Actually the Direct Marketing Educational Foundation fund-raising campaign was preceded by a few years by an *emergency campaign* sponsored by the Direct Marketing Association, then known as the Direct Mail/Marketing Association. (The need to raise emergency funds, particularly to fight threatening legislation, is common among trade associations.)

In the mid-1970s, the association and its members were faced with the growing threat of restrictive and potentially crippling privacy legislation, both at the national and state levels. Various individual educational programs and projects were planned to combat this threat to the freedom of the mails: total financial needs were estimated at about $500,000 annually for at least three years. Since this sum was substantially in excess of the association's ability to budget, it was decided by the board of directors to initiate a mail/solicitation program seeking capital gifts from members.

The "Freedom to Mail Program" was launched in 1979 and largely completed in that year, with $1,700,000 raised from approximately 300 member firms. Under the direction of Bob DeLay, then president of DMMA, and Andy Andrews, board member and fund-raising counselor, a mail/solicitor program was organized along classic capital fund-raising guidelines. A "military" structure was formed with various levels of solicitation from leadership gifts down to the "captain" level soliciting gifts in the $1,000 range.

As in standard capital-fund-raising practice, an early step was the writing and designing of a campaign kit and a "case statement." Such a kit was produced under the logo and slogan, "Preserving Our Freedom to Mail." The information kit contained a booklet, *Action Program,* a question and answer sheet, a pledge card, and a reply envelope.

Association officers and a small group of top level executives from member companies conducted a personal solicitation of leadership gifts in the $10,000 to $20,000 range, annually, for three years. A precall letter was prepared for prominent members to send to key prospects prior to personal solicitation (Exhibit 7-2).

The remaining membership was classified into prospect levels of $5,000 to $10,000, $2,500 to $5,000, and $1,000 to $2,500 annually. These prospects, in groups of ten to twenty, were assigned to twenty-five captains and solicitors.

Rather than sending one "blockbuster" letter responsible for arousing interest and stimulating gifts, capital-fund-raising practice prefers to use an advance educational program followed by personal solicitation. In this instance each of the key prospects was invited to a regional luncheon where the "Freedom to Mail Program" was discussed after a slide presentation on the projects chosen to meet the threat of crippling legislation. No direct solicitation took place at these luncheons.

The information kit was distributed at the luncheons, and mailed with a covering letter to those who were unable to attend. After ten days, an assigned solicitor either saw the prospect in person or talked with her/him by phone. Seventy-five percent of the campaign total was raised in this

Exhibit 7-2. "Freedom to Mail" Solicitation

Dear :

Columbia House is an active member of the Direct Mail Marketing Association which has recently launched a program to raise $1.5 million to finance a comprehensive three-year "Freedom to Mail" action program. This program is designed to head off both federal and state legislation which would adversely affect direct mail marketing organizations.

This greatly expanded program includes not only a positive action effort to head off future legislatures, but it also includes direct intervention at both state and federal levels. The enclosed folder describes the program in more detail.

Columbia House has become convinced that the time has come to make a major commitment in the direction of privacy, and we have made a three-year pledge at the leadership contribution level.

In addition, I have agreed to be active in the solicitation program. This letter is to give you a few days to think about your own commitment. I will call and discuss the matter in the next week or so. Naturally, I hope you join with Columbia House and other companies which have a stake in direct marketing in making this program a success.

Sincerely,

two-step solicitation process. In addition, direct mail solicitation letters were sent to individuals classified as likely to give less than $1,000. This continuing effort netted 25 percent of the campaign total.

During the campaign, dozens of different letters were used, each tailored to the personality and preference of the solicitor. Suggested letter copy to solicit and thank the contributor was provided by the committee. During the campaign and for the three-year payment period, a monthly newsletter kept donors abreast of the successful use of the funds collected.

The successful "Freedom to Mail Program" illustrated a coordinated direct marketing effort in which calls, telephone solicitation, personal visits, and direct mail were used interchangeably to achieve the campaign's goal.

Applying Business Thinking to Worthy Causes

Most philanthropic organizations have two things in common: a severe shortage of funds and a distinguished board of directors to whom they look for guidance. Fund-raising expertise among directors rarely exists, however.

A case in point is the Guild for the Blind in Chicago. They are always pressed for funds to provide the many services they want to perform. Although they have a fine board of directors, I am the only board member with some direct mail fund-raising experience.

Applying the "problem-solution" technique, which is typical of a businessperson's approach, I asked this question of myself: How can we get an extremely high response with practically no investment on the part of the Guild? The solution seemed to be—*ask each director to send a fund-raising letter to fifty friends and acquaintances.*

To test the idea I decided to be the "guinea pig." I compiled a list of fifty likely prospects and wrote a two-page letter to be processed on my personal letterhead (Exhibit 7-3). Enclosed with the letter was a folder describing activities of the Guild and a donor form recommending contributions of varying amounts, tied to specific projects. In addition, a stamped return envelope was enclosed; the return address was my home.

There were several strategies employed in this mailing:

1. Instead of using the Guild for the Blind letterhead I opted to use my letterhead because I felt it would be more personal.

2. Since I was trading on friendship, I strategized that the best approach was to admit it, without shame, in the very first paragraph.

3. Using one of the tenets of successful fund-raising procedures, I selected one program—the Mobility Program—as the focus of my appeal.

4. Finally, instead of asking my friends to send their contributions directly to the Guild, I decided that a stamped return envelope with my home address would have more impact.

Those were the strategies. Now the results: Response rate was 64 percent, with the average contribution in excess of $75.00. Hallelujah!

Flushed with my "success story," I presented the plan, the findings, and the results to the board. Several agreed to compile a list of fifty friends and to use the mailing package I had created.

Several weeks later the results from mailings made by other directors were in. My bubble burst with a loud thud! Where I had enjoyed a response rate of 64 percent, mailings by other directors pulled 3 to 5 percent. I couldn't believe it. One thing I did know: my friends were no more wealthy or more sensitive to worthy causes than the friends of other directors.

The reasons for poor response became abundantly clear with further investigation.

1. Most directors opted to use the Guild's letterhead rather than their own, thus taking the heart out of the personal one-on-one approach.

2. Only a couple had the "courage" to use the first paragraph of the letter, a direct appeal for help. Most used an indirect "weasel approach" instead.

3. Likewise, only a couple enclosed a stamped response envelope addressed to their home address. Most opted for the Guild response envelope instead.

There is a real moral to this "good news-bad news" story. It is this: *If we violate the precepts of sound fund-raising techniques, results are likely to be dismal.*

The Guild's need to raise funds didn't go away. The ability to acquire new donors continued to be severely hampered by a pitifully small amount of money available to invest in an expanded donor base. But there is a happy ending to this story.

Again applying the problem-solution approach I came up with a new brainstorm. Suppose we were to ask directors to make loans to the Guild, offering to repay them out of proceeds from contributions? To make it a business proposition, we would pay interest on the unpaid balance until the loans were fully repaid? After that, all future revenue would be retained by the Guild.

Knowing I couldn't sell the concept to the directors without proof of practicality, I decided to make the first loan. Based on what "Andy" Andrews said in his book, *Billions by Mail,* I would have my money back in 90 to 120 days.

Exhibit 7-3. Guild for the Blind Mailing

BOB STONE, INC.

1630 SHERIDAN ROAD #8G • WILMETTE, ILLINOIS 60091

Mr. and Mrs. Pat Cunningham
205 9th
Wilmette, Illinois 60091

Dear Mick and Pat:

Frankly this is an appeal for help. And I'll admit without shame that
I am, in effect, trading on our friendship in making this appeal to you.

To get right to the point, I'm proud to be a board member of The Guild
For The Blind, the most unique organization I have ever served. I say
unique because this wonderful organization is showing the blind people
the way to dignity, self respect and a life of fulfillment.

The goal of the Guild is best explained in the words of Stephen Benson,
Assistant Director.

> "I am blind and it is likely that I will remain blind for the
> rest of my life. It seems to me that blind people have at
> least two life options:
>
> "One - to sit and wait for a cure, or for someone to take care
> of them, push and pull them around like a doll, with nothing
> to do with directing their own lives, thus perpetuating all the
> stereotypes of blind people.
>
> "Two - blind people can be active, contributing human beings,
> loving life, participating in it to the fullest extent. As
> far as I'm concerned option number two is the only one that
> makes sense. Not only does it offer the opportunity to be a
> wholly vital people, it also offers the opportunity to partici-
> pate in changing the public's mind about blindness.
>
> "I believe this is an obligation each of us must fulfill so
> blind people who follow will have richer, fuller lives."

This program of fulfillment is called the Mobility Program. To teach it
to blind people Steve Benson has prepared a text which will be available
in braille for the totally blind, in large print for those with sight
impairment and a cassette for those who cannot read braille or large print.

In addition, the Guild will provide instructors to teach blind people how
to travel with the ease that you and I take for granted. Instructors will
show students how to travel with the long white cane...a recent development
which allows them to walk with confidence.

(continued)

Exhibit 7-3. Guild for the Blind Mailing

So as each student completes the Program walking up or down steps, boarding buses, and trains, even walking on ice or snow will be as natural as for the sighted person. And, most important of all, many of these good people will be able to travel to work, enjoying gainful employment.

But there is just one thing. No Federal funds are available to make the Mobility Program reality. As a matter of fact - no funds whatever. The future of the Program is solely dependent upon the generosity of fortunate people like you and I.

That's why I have had no hesitancy in sending you this urgent appeal. Whatever you can do at this time will be greatly appreciated by the Guild For The Blind, those they serve and yours truly.

Sincerely,

Robert Stone

P.S. Please use the enclosed form and return to me in the stamped, self-addressed envelope. Thank you so much.

As Andy had predicted, the new donor mailing, with subsequent follow-ups, made it possible for the Guild to repay me in full within 120 days. And, happily, the Guild will profit from these new donors for years to come.

Armed with these results, I had no difficulty arranging for loans from other directors. As a matter of fact, loans from directors led to the largest Christmas mailing in the forty-year history of the Guild for the Blind.

Like so many of the ideas presented in this book, the idea of getting seed money from directors to finance new donor mailings has to be viewed as an *adaptable idea*. For philanthropic organizations this particular idea can solve a persistent major problem.

The need to raise funds for worthy causes will never go away. The concept of applying business acumen with direct marketing know-how can make a major difference in the effort.

Self-Quiz

1. Describe the classic three-step approach to raising funds for a worthy cause.

   a. _____

   _____

   _____

   _____

   b. _____

   _____

   _____

   _____

   c. _____

   _____

   _____

   _____

2. The highest percent of response in a fund-raising effort comes from _____contributors.

3. It is generally agreed that people respond best to ☐ rational ☐ emotional appeals.

4. Total amount pledged for a cause tends to be greater when a ☐ single payment   ☐ multipayment is offered.

5. The average gift to a philanthropic organization tends to ☐ decrease ☐ increase over the years.

6. If you had a list of donors all of whom originally contributed $10.00, how much of an increase would you ask for in your next solicitation? ☐ $5.00   ☐ $10.00   ☐ $15.00   ☐ $20.00   ☐ $25.00.

7. In structuring a fund-raising letter which appeal is generally more effective?   ☐ Selling one particular cause.   ☐ Selling the many causes of a philanthropic organization.

8. Why is it "good business" to "invest" in new donors?

   _____

   _____

   _____

9. The highest percent of response comes from ☐ new contributors ☐ previous contributors.

10. When pledges are made by telephone it can be expected that about _____ percent of pledges will be collected, if properly followed up.

Pilot Project

You are on the fund-raising committee of your local church. The roof is in serious disrepair. It is estimated that the work will cost $100,000. But the church does not have the funds to do the necessary work. The contractor is willing to accept payment over a three-year period. Therefore you can ask for pledges over a thirty-six-month period.

Your assignment is to write a letter to go to fifty of your friends and acquaintances soliciting pledges.

Choosing Media for Your Message

CHAPTER EIGHT

Mailing Lists

Chapter 2 "Data Base Marketing"—emphasized the importance of developing and working data bases from all media sources. This chapter is devoted solely to mailing lists—major sources of input for data bases.

What is a list? The *Random House Dictionary* defines a list as "a series of names or other items written or printed together in meaningful groupings so as to constitute a record." The operative words are "meaningful groupings." The list, then, is simply a way to organize otherwise random material into market segments.

In general terms, there are three things that are both central and indispensable to direct marketing through lists:

1. Identifying the best customers on internal (house) lists

2. Finding more of them through outside lists

3. Selling to them at a maximum profit with minimum waste

Types of Lists

There are two broad categories of lists: internal (house) lists and external (outside) lists. *Internal lists* (a company's own files) include customers, former customers, subscribers, former subscribers, donors, former donors, inquiries, prospects, and warranty cards. *External lists* include compiled and direct response lists from sources outside the company.

Your best customer is the one you already have. Internal lists, popularly known as house files, should be considered an *information data base*. It is essential, in the data collection process, to include as much relevant information as possible about your customers. Remember that this data base (house file) is a company asset as valuable to direct marketers as any asset the company has.

In every instance, the first expense—and usually the most costly—is the acquisition cost. Over the life of the customer, subscriber, member, contributor, and so forth, the acquisition cost isn't really the payoff—the revenue will come from persistency—its lifetime value. Therefore, the data base must be structured to serve as a marketing information system. This will enable you to make marketing decisions based on facts.

With certain exceptions, if a product or service can't be sold to your in-house names, it can't be sold anywhere. But even a house file is not effective unless you have the ability to segment it productively and use it selectively.

House File Segmentation

Let's start with the definition of *segment:* one of the constituent parts into which an entity or quantity is divided as if by natural boundaries.

With lists, then, segmentation works on the theory that parts of a list have more sales potential for a particular product or service than other parts of a list. The art in getting more sales from existing customers is to be able to match offers to the customers' buying preferences. It goes without saying that segmentation is practical in relation to the size of a list. If the list constitutes a few hundred names, segmentation is hardly worthwhile. But if a list runs as few as 5,000 names, segmentation can prove very worthwhile. And if the list runs into the hundreds of thousands, segmentation becomes essential to maximizing profits. In the classic questions of journalism, each mailer must continually ask:

- *Who* are my customers?
- *What* do they buy from me?
- *Why* do they respond to my mailings?
- *How* do I retain them and increase their purchases?
- *Where* do I find others like them?
- *When* do I sell them more effectively?

The answers to these questions can only be found in careful attention to the specifics of planning. In list utilization, planning is defined in three basic areas: selection, analysis, and budgeting (forecasting). These subjects will all be covered later in this chapter.

The first of this vital trio—selection—begins with the internal lists.

Customer value or definition of a good customer depends on the dynamics of the company. The function of the marketing effort must be geared to converting first-time buyers into loyal, repeat customers. This can be described as target marketing. One approach to target marketing is to use the customer's past history to project future purchases.

If the data base is programmed to store certain bits of information about each customer, the data base is not just a list of customers—it's a gallery of portraits. The art is to get more sales from existing customers by being able to match your offers to their buying preferences.

In addition to the behavioral characteristics of RFM, or FRAT (defined in Chapter 2), other psychodynamic factors that should be included are:

- *Mode of payment:* cash, open account, installments, credit card.
- *Geographics:* not only where your customer lives, but also correlating recency, frequency, monetary to geographic areas.
- *Type of product purchased:* labeled by product categories—household, leisure, recreation, fashions, gourmet, travel, sports, do-it-yourself, and so forth.
- *Length of time on the file:* an indication of interest in your publication, book club, catalog, and so forth.
- *Source:* direct mail, radio, TV, space, telephone, cable TV, inserts, co-ops, and so forth. It is important to note that the use of multimedia contributes another lifestyle statistic to the data base.
  Date of last transaction: includes payment, change of address, correspondence, renewal, and unsolicited contributions.

These are just some of the variables. Others should be determined based on what the company sells. A magazine publisher, for example, will not use the same factors as a catalog company or a fund-raising organization.

Several mathematical regression techniques allow the marketer to relate each element of customer data on the file to other transactional data and, thus, to predict customer behavior. It is important to realize that there is no universal equation that applies to all types of regression analysis. Every equation must be custom-designed based on the dynamics of the particular company and must be used, evaluated, and updated on a continuing basis.

Properly structured, this type of research will lead to customer demand analysis and segmentation on the theory that parts of a list have more sales potential (hence more profit) for a particular product than others. You must do all you can to optimize the segmentation of your customer file for internal use and for list rental to others because both aspects will contribute substantially to your profit picture.

External Lists

This information from your house file can be extended to your use of outside lists. There are two basic kinds of outside or external lists: compiled lists (usually by some common interest) and list of inquiries and/or customers from other companies. With literally thousands of lists to choose form, the dominant characteristics of the internal file will prevail and establish direction for selection of external lists. (See Table 8-1.)

List of other companies' customers have one advantage over compiled lists if those companies sell by direct response: they have one discriminant characteristic—they are direct mail buyers. While compiled lists do not necessarily represent direct response buyers, they do have discriminant characteristics. There are extensive compilations in the business, professional, educational, technical, agricultural markets—and the consumer market. If you want to reach college students, the biggest universe is represented by compiled lists. If you want to reach presidents of firms by number of employees, compiled lists will give you the most complete coverage. If your market is to "new mothers," compiled lists offer the biggest universe. And likewise for accountants, engineers, farmers, and scores of categories.

In the business category (used by business-to-business advertisers, mail order companies selling to the business community, and business and financial services), these compilations offer the opportunity to reach any segment of U.S. industry. Selections are available by SIC (Standard Industrial Classification) code, size of company, number of employees, occupational level, individual name, title, and almost any configuration of selection factors required for the particular promotion.

In the professional market, there exists a multitude of choices. For example: doctors (by specialty, age, in private practice, intern, affiliated with hospital practice, hospital administrator, etc.); lawyers (by size of firm, specialty, one-man firm, senior partners, ABA members, etc.); educators (by discipline, elementary, secondary, college teachers, administrators, pupil enrollment, etc.).

Most business/professional compilations are derived from printed sources: directories, rosters, registrations at trade shows, Dun & Bradstreet. There is a *Directory of Directories* that lists over 5,200 directories of various types. (Note that because lists deteriorate rapidly, it is important to find out when the list was compiled.)

In the consumer market, companies such as Polk, Metromail, and Donnelley, among others, offer the capability of reaching almost every household in the U.S. with an overlay of Census tract statistics. Census tracts are comprised of relatively small areas with the purpose of making each tract as homogeneous as possible. One important use of compiled lists is to match external files against the house list to get a better feel for the demographics of the external file for segmentation purposes. For example, one group that can be segmented is super spot subscribers—those who live in high-income areas. With properly structured tests and in-depth analysis, you can establish a market for your product by demographics such as income, education, number of children in the family, and so on. This type of compilation usually can't be tested with small quantities and/or without carefully structured response analysis. This will be discussed at greater length later in this chapter.

Table 8-1. External List: *Better Homes & Gardens**

Selections available by:

1. Subscribers (Length of Residence)

2. Income
   Under $10,000
   $11,000 - $19,000
   $20,000 - $49,000
   Over $50,000

3. Age   18-35;   36-49;   50-64;   65+

4. Household Size

5. Address Changes (Monthly)

6. Super-Spot Subscribers (High-Income ZIPs)

7. Multiple Purchasers (Actives who purchased one-plus book within last two years)

8. Ethnic/Religious
   Catholic
   Jewish
   Italian
   Spanish

List drawn from 7,500,000 subscribers.

Why do companies rent their lists? Profit. And the recognition that there is no such thing as a "captive audience." The fact that a person buys by mail is an indication of a "mail order buying characteristic." That person is likely to appear on many lists, which is why duplication elimination is an established technique used by most volume mailers (see "Duplication Elimination": merge/purge).

Let's look at potential profit. Assuming a list of 500,000 names, turned over twenty times per year:

> 10,000,000 names at a net to the list owner of $36 per M ($45 per M, less 20% broker's commission) = $360,000. At a running cost of about $2/M, we are talking about $340,000 that goes right down to the bottom line. Depending on the quality and size of the list, this could really be a very conservative estimate.

How does outside list rental affect internal sales? There have been very carefully structured tests conducted over the years to answer this question. Results show over and over again that there is no effect or, at the most, a minimal effect upon internal sales. The number of kinds of lists available for rental boggles the mind. To get a feel for list availability, refer to Table 8-2: Review of Consumer Lists by Category.

Demographics

People of like interests tend to cluster ("birds of a feather flock together"). While the impact of societal changes does affect this theory, demographics is still a valid method by which to add another dimension to the customer profile.

Table 8-2. Review of Consumer Lists by Category

	1986	
Category	No. of Lists	Universe (000)
Hobbies and Special Interests	1,046	223,245
Female-Oriented How-To (Cooking, Sewing, etc.)	145	35,819
Sports/Outdoors	430	77,759
Photography	58	13,438
Male-Oriented Hobbies & How-To	120	32,556
Other Subsegments	293	63,673
Entertainment	398	97,026
Music	66	20,913
Gourmet Food	111	27,917
Travel	70	16,122
Other Subsegments	151	32,074
Reading	462	75,286
General & Cultural	96	35,972
News & Politics	60	12,143
Regionals	152	10,336
Other Subsegments	154	16,835
Self-Improvement	552	182,580
Opportunity Seekers	157	41,730
Health & Fitness	166	48,790
Other Subsegments	229	92,060
Home Interest	822	436,630
Catalogs & Merchandise	252	125,058
Parents/Children	251	191,773
Female Personal Merchandise (Cosmetics, Jewelry, etc.)	204	58,570
Shelter Magazines	48	52,491
Male Merchandise	67	8,738
Total All Categories	3,280	1,014,767

ZIP codes, which many mailers once feared, have proven to be a boon instead of a burden. They brought list maintenance into the computer age. This step made it possible to identify duplicate names in a mailing and also led to analysis of response by ZIP codes.

It then led to a further refinement in geographical analysis by *Census tract overlays.* Unlike geopolitical districts (cities, counties, states, and even ZIP codes) Census tracts are relatively small and homogeneous. Most residents in the Census tract will exhibit more demographic similarities than differences—age, marital status, income, occupation, education, home ownership, home value, number of children in the household, and so forth. As mentioned previously, this type of analysis can lead to further house file segmentation. In some instances, inferential lifestyle values are added based on the resulting demographics.

Psychographics (Lifestyle)

Veblen's theory of "conspicuous consumption" at one point in time was a sharp behavioral definition. But now we see that consumers, although demographically related, have been showing marked tendencies to spend their discretionary income quite differently. To identify our target market, it is essential to capture lifestyle details. This concept is not new—it has been recognized for a long time that societal changes have *influenced demographics.*

If we look at Table 8-3: The Target Is Moving, we see that these socio-economic changes are quite evident. The significance of these trends can't be ignored. In a highly advanced and rapidly expanding technological environment, we must recognize that socioeconomic changes will come even more rapidly. In marketing, societal change is a subject you can never know enough about.

List Brokers and List Selection

A broker, as the name implies, serves two sides: the client (mailer) and the list owner. If you have a product or service that is to be sold to a vertical market—for example, doctors, lawyers, or accountants or any other pinpointed, highly specialized market—finding the right lists is simple. In almost every field, there is a compiler, trade publication, or list owner who has the precise list.

It gets decidedly more complex when you are selling a product that has a broader appeal. Here is where the broker can offer invaluable assistance in suggesting those lists that appear to represent the market you are trying to reach. You get the benefit of experts who make mailing lists their full-time specialization.

A professional relationship doesn't work if the list consultant is asked to operate in a vacuum or in abstract terms. You must view the broker as part of the total marketing process. You must specify your needs and objectives well enough in advance to permit the broker to research the list marketplace. (This research is also a valuable tool for the creative people. Working without a clear, complete knowledge of the list market makes it difficult to properly focus the promotional copy.)

To emphasize—here are some factors necessary to establish a competent working relationship with a list broker:

1. Bring the list broker into the picture at an early stage to help define the market.

2. Give the broker *time* to do a professional job. Specific, targeted list recommendations take time. Information such as balance counts, selectivity, segmentation, and geographical counts, is essential to proper list selection.

3. List rental orders (accompanied by the mailing piece and a requested specific mail date) must be cleared for approval with the list owner. Allow time for this process. (Refer to List Tests, Market Tests, this chapter, for further list selection strategies.)

List Managers

During the past few years there has been a trend toward list management whereby a given list broker takes over the complete management of a list for rental purposes. Under this arrangement, the list manager performs all or almost all of the following functions:

1. Handles contacts with list brokers.

2. Clears sample mailing piece and mail date with list owner.

3. Processes list rental orders.

4. Follows up on completion of list rental orders to assure delivery of order within the specified return date.

5. Bills the broker on behalf of the list owner.

6. Collects payment and remits to list owner less broker's commission and list management fee.

7. Assumes responsibility for all promotions of the list and sales activity without charge (over and above the established fee) to the list owner.

8. If the list owner so desires, the manager assumes responsibility for the maintenance of the list either in-house or with an outside computer service bureau.

9. Provides the list owner with a detailed activity report—including billing and collecting information—on a predetermined time frame.

The list rental business is, for some list owners, a part-time activity. Being relieved of the voluminous details involved and the time required to promote the list usually more than warrants the extra compensation the manager receives for the specialized services rendered.

Table 8-3. The Target Is Moving

Working Women
1. Half the labor force
2. More than half of all married women work. Over 50% of married couples have dual income.
3. By 1990—only one out of four married women will be a full-time homemaker.

Families (Preliminary Report from Census 1970 vs. 1980)
1. Number of children in a household decreasing
2. Number of children increasing (more women of child-bearing age)
3. Size of household declined sharply since 1970. Nearly 23% of all U.S. households consist of one person.
4. Total number of households increased from 63.4 million to 80.4 million
5. Surprising number of single people living in units which once accommodated families
6. Households maintained by women increased by 51% vs. 11% growth in families. Families maintained by a man increased by 33.6%. Over 8,000,000 men and women are raising children alone.

Age Distribution of the Population
1. Majority of U.S. population (as a result of "baby boom" between 1946 & 1954) is past 30 years old and represents about 53.4 million.
2. 45-54 market represents 25% of spending in U.S. The over-45 group represents the largest pool of *purchasing power* ever to impact on U.S. economy.

Geographical Shifts (The "Where" of the Market)
1. Distant *exurbs* are growing residential areas
2. Rural areas now have executive homes where pastures once were
3. Some states struggling with industrial decline—other trying to cope with industrial growth

Recreation
1. More leisure time makes relaxation one of America's most serious businesses. Represents about 8-9% of gross national product.
2. *Recreational learning* a major trend
3. *Electronic recreation room* with mini-computers linked to the TV set

List Information

List brokers and list managers present list information on what is known as a data card. The *data card* shows the price of the list. The rate is quoted on a per-thousand-name (per M) basis. The price range averages $40 to $50 per thousand for direct response lists, exclusive of selection charges. Compiled lists usually rent at a far lower rate per thousand. Exhibit 8-1 typifies specific data available to the prospective list renter.

List Rental Procedures

Lists can be ordered directly from a list owner, but most list rental orders are placed through list brokers. The broker handles all the details with the list owner: clearances, order placement, follow up for order completion, billing, collecting, and payment to the list owner, less the usual 20 percent commission that accrues to the list broker.

The rental of lists involves certain conditions:

1. The names are rented for *one time use* only. No copy of the list is to be retained for any purpose whatsoever.

2. Usage must be cleared with the list owner in advance. The mailing piece which is approved is the only one that can be used.

3. The mail date approved by the list owner must be adhered to.

4. List rentals are charged on a per-thousand-name basis.

5. Net name arrangements vary, but most list owners will specify the percentage (of the names supplied) for which the full list rental charge per M must be paid plus a specific running cost for the names not used.

6. Most list owners charge extra for selections such as: sex, recency, ZIP, state, unit of sale, or any segmentation available on the particular list. Prices vary.

List Tests

Test: The means by which the presence, quality or genuineness of anything is determined, a means of trial. As any crossword puzzle fan knows, a test is an experiment, an attempt to determine by small-scale trial, whether something will or won't work consistently or universally.

How big should a sample be? The proper sample size is determined by two factors: sampling tolerance (or deviation) and the degree of risk that the user is willing to accept. As long as we have perfect random samples, we can keep the sampling tolerance small by taking large samples. This part of the equation is scientific.

The risk factor is much harder to deal with because this involves subjective judgments. Some people can't tolerate much risk.

Some practitioners advocate that the sample size should be based on the number of responses needed. The caution here is that some mailers, particularly on a new product, have what might be termed "unreasonable expectations." The higher the price of the product, the lower the response is likely to be. Under these circumstances, a small test quantity will not yield the numbers needed to project with a degree of confidence. If, for example, you expect three orders per thousand, you should test 20,000 to give you a sense of response validity.

Some others advocate the ideal sample as a constant percentage of the entire list. This is impractical and expensive when the list is a large one. Believe it or not, your sampling tolerance is hardly affected at all by the size of the list.

List testing, unfortunately, is not conducted under laboratory conditions. For starters, we can't get a true random sampling in most instances. The best we can do is systematic sampling—an nth name sample. And even this is not always executed properly.

For example, here are the results from a total mailing of 35,000 pieces, all mailed to the identical list, all mailed the same day, but broken out under five different keys.

Key Code	Quantity	Percentage of Response
91035	7,500	1.48
91036	7,500	1.29
91037	7,500	1.39
91038	7,500	1.48
91039	7,500	1.25

Theoretically, the percent of response should have been identical for all five keys, but actually there was a variation of 18 percent from high to low response. So one way to get a feeling for the validity of a test is to use a checking system whereby you give a separate key to each one-fifth of a test quantity. If the response is quite equal, you can feel comfortable. If there are substantial variations within the subsets, you must proceed cautiously.

Another universal practice is to reconfirm the test with a larger sample. Actually, this type of sequential sampling is the most reliable schematic because you can schedule quantities on each successive usage in an orderly fashion, supported by monitored results. Thus you are able to control and minimize the risk.

Exhibit 8-1. Data Card

House & Garden (Condé Nast)

454,016 Subscribers	@ $85/M	Feb. 1987	K01 Y02
13,308 Canadian Subscribers	@ $85/M		D01
10,162 Address Changes (Quarterly)	@ $95/M		
71,259 Expires (Last 4 Months)	@ $55/M	Minimum:	

(Hotline Selection not available at this time.)

(Add $15 per reel for nonreturnable magtape.)

Minimum:

10,000 (Actives)
5,000 (Expires)

Data   Published monthly by Condé Nast Publications, *House & Garden* is the magazine of creative living, international, interior decoration, art, architecture and gardens, travel, dealers, and collectors.

Magtape or Cheshire from:

Neodata Services
Att: Larry Cline
833 W.S. Boulder
   Road
Louisville, CO 80027

Unit $24.00/year

Profile   Median Age: 43.4.
Median Household Income: $65,200.
Median Net Worth of Household: $494,500.
93% own their own home.
Median value of home is $156,100.
21% own a weekend/vacation home or condominium.
45% are professional or managerial.
93% are married.
70% attended/graduated from college.

Two complete samples required in advance for all new tests and continuations.

No phone clearances.

Sex   Mostly women. Can select @ $5/M: 256,678 women Subscribers; 71,823 men Subscribers; balance unidentified.

Allow 3 weeks to process orders.

Media   100% Direct Response. No source select.

Signed agreement form from Mailer required for initial test order.

Filed   ZIP sequence / 4-up Cheshire / 9T/1600 Magtape. DMA Mail Preference Service Names suppressed.

Selections   Nth name @ N/C.
State / SCF / ZIP @ $3.50/M. Can use ZIP tape.
Pressure sensitive levels @ $8/M.

Net Name Arrangement (100,000 minimum): 85% + $6/M with computer verification.

Keying $2.00/M (up to 4 digits).

Note: List owner requires payment 30 days after mail date.

Note: List owner will not rent to sweepstakes offers.

Note: For Canadian Subscribers, see Kleid data card no. 20806 (Condé Nast Master Canadian Active file).

Note: Orders cancelled five days prior to or after original mail date will require full payment.

Another very important factor to be considered in the "how big" question is the back-end (persistency) factor. If you must track these customers (frequency of purchase, collections, conversions, renewals, average take), you need to test in larger quantities. For example, if each test list is 5,000 names and response is 2 percent, tracking future activity of an average of only 100 respondents from each list can prove unreliable from the standpoint of mathematical analysis. In tracking studies of book, record, and tape clubs, the number of *starts* to be analyzed is critical to the evaluation process.

In general terms, then, based on experience, a 5,000 quantity is usually adequate and more than 10,000 doesn't seem to be worthwhile.

I'm afraid that the testing question of "how many" will always be with us. It can't be answered in an absolute way because there are no consistent elements that are universally applicable to every product or service being sold by mail. When you think about it, continuation mailings rarely yield the same response as the test because there are variables from test to continuation that cannot be controlled—time lapse, seasonality, change in list sources, economics, weather conditions, consumer behavior, and a host of other factors.

Market Tests

If you are introducing a new product, it is essential to use the direct mail test to determine the potential universe for the product. Initial preconceptions about ultimate sales penetration and about target markets are usually restrictive and rarely accurate.

In addition, the initial test mailing is sometimes too small to be projectable to a large continuation mailing. For example, an initial test of 50,000, which usually will include offer and package tests, is not projectable to a continuation mailing of 500,000 or more. Yet in many instances, this is the stated objective. So, it is recommended that no less than a 100,000 quantity be used and preferably 150,000, particularly if tests, other than the market test, are being conducted.

To be able to identify the market, a "spectrum test" is recommended. Working with twenty to thirty lists, you construct a ladder of three tests—a sort of X, Y, Z arrangement. Your middle group, the Y of the spectrum, is drawn from lists that appear to be right on target. Your X panel is drawn from those which, because of certain affinity factors, could be considered good prospects. The Z group, while it reflects a very different profile, inferentially could have reasons for being interested. This type of spectrum testing yields clues about how deeply you can mail because it is a two-dimensional sample. You are sampling the universe of lists as well as the people on the particular lists chosen.

Then there is always the question of what to do on a test mailing of, say, 150,000. Are we better off testing thirty lists with 5,000 or fifteen lists with 10,000? This depends on the growth pattern established in the original forecast plan.

Let's run through, as an example, a magazine called the *Glory of Art*.

The first step was an "Overview of List Markets." The intention of this overview is to provide a feel for the potential universe—and to decide on the specific lists to be selected from each category. (See Table 8-4.) On the *Glory of Art* it was decided to go with thirty lists, because the market testing was most crucial in determining whether or not this was a viable publication in the marketplace. (See Table 8-5.)

You will note that, while the schedule is concentrated in the more targeted categories, other categories, such as women's fashions, were explored with an eye toward market evaluation and expansion.

In analyzing by category in the initial stages, it is better to look at the number of lists tested in each category and the success ratio—rather than averaging response on each category. Averages can be misleading. One list in a particular category that responded dramatically higher or lower than the other lists can influence the overall average.

This type of analysis should be considered directional—and not an absolute. In some instances the ratios are reliable, in some instances they're not. For example, where only one list was tested in a category and it proved responsive, that category must be approached more cautiously than the category where five lists were tested and they were all responsive. (See Table 8-6.)

Table 8-4. Overview of List Markets (*Glory of Art*)

Category	No. of Lists	Potential Universe
Art/Antiques/Collectibles	31	2,995,900
Up-Scale Gifts & Decorating Items	24	2,088,600
Luxury Foods & Gifts	16	3,316,200
Photography	5	968,900
Women's High Fashions	8	843,500
Cultural Books & Magazines	31	5,232,200
Regional Publications	20	2,732,100
Cultural Arts	7	485,400
Miscellaneous (credit card)	5	1,732,000
Total	147	20,394,800*

©*Copyright by Rose Harper, The Kleid Company, Inc.*
Can be reduced by approximately 25% due to the duplication factor.

Table 8-5. *Glory of Art* **List Test Schedule 150,000**

Category	Universe	Test Quantity	No. of Lists
Art/Antiques/Collectibles	1,215,600	45,000	9
Up-Scale Gifts & Decorating Items	383,000	20,000	4
Luxury Foods & Gifts	1,871,900	25,000	5
Photography	150,000	5,000	1
Women's High Fashions	185,000	5,000	1
Cultural Books & Magazine	876,900	25,000	5
Regional Publications	267,000	10,000	2
Cultural Arts	245,000	10,000	2
Miscellaneous (credit card)	125,000	5,000	1
Total	5,319,400	150,000	30

©Copyright by Rose Harper, The Kleid Company, Inc.

The most important element to consider, however, is that the dynamics of each testing situation are dissimilar—particularly the objectives, the time frame, and the financials. These variables must be studied and given consideration in structuring the initial test.

Duplication Elimination

The advent of the ZIP code in 1967 forced list owners into the computer age. This led to the breakthrough in the ability to remove duplicate names (dupes) within a mailing. The popular term is "merge/purge"—and what it means is the matching of two or more mailing lists by electronic means to remove duplication and to insure that each addressee receives only one mailing piece. This is accomplished by the use of a match code that is a series of characters extracted on a consistent basis from the name and address which fully identifies that person to the computer.

Aside from avoiding the irritation to the recipient of receiving several of the same mailings at almost the same time and sending a solicitation to a present customer, there are considerable dollar savings involved. (See Table 8-7.)

Another factor that needs to be considered because of merge/purge is the resulting true or actual list cost per thousand. This is essential information in projecting a mailing plan—and an *actual* list cost per order. (See Table 8-8.)

Table 8-6. *Glory of Art* **Analysis Success Factor by Category**

	No. of Tests	No. of Continuations	Percentage of Success
Y (of the Spectrum)			
Art, Antiques, Collectibles	9	7	77.8
Cultural Books & Magazines	5	5	100.
Cultural Arts	2	1	50.
Subtotal	16	13	81.3
X			
Upscale Gifts & Decorating Items	4	1	25.
Photography	1	1	100.
Regional Publications	2	2	100.
Subtotal	7	4	57.1
Z			
Luxury Foods & Gifts	5	2	40.
Women's High Fashions	1	1	100.
Miscellaneous (credit card)	1	—	—
Subtotal	7	3	42.9
Total	30	20	66.6

©Copyright by Rose Harper, The Kleid Company, Inc.

Table 8-7. Dollar Savings on Dupe Removal*

Percent Duplication	Mailing Quantity			
	1,000,000	*2,500,000*	*5,000,000*	*10,000,000*
5	$10,000	$ 25,000	$ 50,000	$100,000
10	20,000	50,000	100,000	200,000
15	30,000	75,000	150,000	300,000
20	40,000	100,000	200,000	400,000
25	50,000	125,000	250,000	500,000
30	60,000	150,000	300,000	600,000
35	70,000	175,000	350,000	700,000

©Copyright by Rose Harper, The Kleid Company, Inc.
Savings achieved by eliminating duplicate names from a mailing (based on a mailing cost of $200 per thousand pieces).

In most instances the house file (or segments of the house file) is the primary list against which the rental lists are matched. Then, all lists are matched against each other. In the process, intralist duplication is also discovered. Since the mailing tape, after the match, is in ZIP code sequence, it provides the opportunity to:

1. Analyze response by ZIP code by matching the tape of response against the mailing tape.

2. Omit all ZIP codes which, from previous experience, have not been responsive or have proved to have a high bad-pay factor.

At what quantity it makes sense to merge/purge against the house file is a knotty question. Some managements maintain a strict policy against any duplication of their house file regardless of the quantity of the rental names. In such instances merge/purge is an imperative.

Judgment dictates that the larger your house file becomes, the higher the percentage of duplication you can expect from rented lists. Thus if a direct marketer has a house list of 1,000,000 names, for example, merge/purge is almost always advisable, no matter what the quantity of rented names. On the other hand, if the house list is, say, only 50,000 names, it hardly makes sense to merge/purge 5 lists of 5,000 each against the house file because the duplication factor would be very small.

However, the duplication factor should not be the sole consideration in deciding for or against merge/purge. A firm with a house file of 50,000 names might elect to build its house file fast and, therefore, test 20 lists of 5,000 names simultaneously. The chances of heavy duplication between these 100,000 names could be in the 25 percent range. Therefore, merge/purge would make sense even though duplication against the house file would probably be small.

Tape-to-tape matching offers other marketing opportunities. For example, an insurance company has been reaching "golden age" prospects via Census tract addressing by using tracts with the highest density of older people. There was waste, however, in reaching everyone in a Census tract. By tape-to-tape matching against a list of families with young children in the same areas, it was possible to refine the selections by suppressing the young families. Tape-to-tape matching also allows for file overlay analysis to take advantage of various types of information available on consumer files. For example, refer back to the selections available on the *Better Homes & Gardens* file. Much of this detailing was accomplished in this manner.

Another example is the overlay on the *McCall's* magazine subscriber file that was done by Donnelley marketing. This enabled selection by age, income, dwelling unit size, length of residence, ethnic, and religious preference. Lifestyle Selector (Denver, Co.), through the information they collect on consumer information cards, will overlay their master file on your house file. The names that match are then analyzed to produce a lifestyle

MAILING LISTS 181

Table 8-8. Actual List Cost per Thousand after Merge/Purge Assuming Gross Quantity of 50,000 Names and a 25% Duplication Factor

Gross Quantity	List Cost per M	Running Charges per M	Selection Charges per M	Billing 85% on Basic List Rental	Running Costs	Selection Charges	Total Billing	Actual List CPM (assuming 75% qty. mailed)
50,000	$40.00	$5.00	—	$1,700.00	$37.50	—	$1,737.50	46.33
50,000	40.00	5.00	$6.50	1,700.00	37.50	$325.00	2,062.50	55.00
50,000	45.00	5.00	—	1,912.50	37.50	—	1,950.00	52.00
50,000	45.00	5.00	4.50	1,912.50	37.50	225.00	2,175.00	58.00
50,000	50.00	5.00	—	2,125.00	37.50	—	2,162.50	57.67
50,000	50.00	5.00	7.50	2,125.00	37.50	375.00	2,537.50	67.67
50,000	55.00	5.00	—	2,337.50	37.50	—	2,375.00	63.33
50,000	55.00	5.00	6.50	2,337.50	37.50	325.00	2,700.00	72.00

©Copyright by Rose Harper, The Kleid Company, Inc.

profile of your house file—demographically by age, income, occupation, marital status, home ownership, etc.—plus a lifestyle profile including forty-eight interest and hobby categories, such as foreign travel, gardening, cooking, photography, physical fitness, among others.

PRIZM, a division of Claritas Company, Roslyn, Virginia, represents a new generation of market targeting systems made possible through the massive data resources of the U.S. Census and some important developments in the field of demographic research. The PRIZM (Potential Rating Index by Zip Markets) service was formed by combining two independent data bases: The Claritas Cluster System (a "geodemographic" market segmentation system that has classified all of the thousands of neighborhoods and communities in the United States into forty different homogeneous types or "clusters") and The Simmons Market Research Bureau Annual Surveys (a series of syndicated surveys of product usage and media readership/viewership). Using the address of every respondent in the SMRB surveys, the respondents were assigned to their respective clusters. These subsets of respondents then provided measurements of cluster behavior towards all major products, services, and media. The thrust of this system is "a new way to use ZIP codes for market targeting."

Some of the terminology used in the merge/purge process is:

- Contribution to Multibuyers—names appearing more than once that are transferred to the multibuyer file
- Quantity Ordered—by the mailer
- Gross Input—actual quantity processed into the system
- Unordered Names—(could involve requested omits such as state, SCF, ZIP)
- Edit Errors—usually mistakes in the address (City, State, ZIP)

- Net Records into Merge/Purge—after omitting unordered names and edit errors
- Internal Duplication—also described as intrafile duplicates that represent names and addresses appearing more than once within one file
- Pander File Matches—usually from the DMA Mail Preference Service tape (These are people who have written to DMA indicating that they prefer *not* to get any mail.)
- Suppression Matches—usually an internal file of customers, plus those people who requested that their name not be used for list rental purposes, bad-pay file, and so forth
- Unique Records—names that remain on the mailing tape only one time

Scheduling and Analysis of Direct Mail Programs

The attraction of direct mail is its *measurability.* Direct mail is not inexpensive. On a cost per thousand exposure, aside from telephone, it is probably the most expensive medium. But unlike most media, the response per thousand is not extrapolated. It is an arithmetical fact.

Let's go back to the *Glory of Art,* where thirty lists were tested in the initial mailing.

In order to plan the continuation mailing, there is the need to analyze the test results. Here are the factors considered—and a review of the overall test mailing:

Actual Mail Quantity	150,040
Number of Orders	3,256
Percent Response	2.170
Package Cost per M	$180
List Cost per M	$45.56
Total Cost per M	$225.56
Total Cost	$33,843
Gross Cost per Subscriber	$10.39
Percent Credit	90.40
Percent Bad Pay	28.10
Net Subscribers	2,428
Net Percent Response	1.61
Net Cost per Subscriber	$13.93
Total Revenue (on Net)	$43,702
Net Revenue (Total Revenue minus Total Cost)	$9,859
Net Revenue per Subscriber	$4.06

Important: *These same factors were considered on a* list-by-list basis.

Another important step is to consider the assumptions that need to be applied when projecting the roll-out response. This qualifier is necessary for a variety of reasons: the test quantity of 5,000 on each list; the test mailing was made at a different time (see seasonality); the increase in merge/purge factor due to the larger mailing quantity.

In this instance the following assumptions were used:

1. 12% loss through merge/purge

2. 10% lift for seasonality

3. 7% decrease for test to continuation

4. Credit and Bad-Pay at Actual for each list

These assumptions were applied on a *list-by-list* basis with the starting point being previous response. (See Table 8-9—*Glory of Art* Continuation Mailing—which shows a sampling of the list-by-list analysis).

Now let's look at the summary of the continuation mailing (see Table 8-10), using the same factors that were used to analyze the test mailing.

You will note that 100,000 in new list tests was included. In order to sustain a continuing and ongoing direct mail program, it is essential to develop an inventory of profitable lists. Therefore, in most instances, 10 percent of the total mailing should be devoted to list testing.

Remember that mailing plans are budgets or pro-forma profit plans. And, in direct mail, it all starts with list history. The ability to review the history of a list on an each-time-used basis is critical to structuring a sound mailing plan because in direct mail, the list is the medium.

One of the most helpful evaluation tools is the use of "break-even" analysis. This measures the response needed for total revenue to meet total promotional cost. At this point, obviously there is no profit. Each company, then, must add other constants (overhead, cost of money, cost of product, bad-pay, returns, refurbishing, customer lifetime value, etc.) to determine how much it can afford to pay for an order.

There are many variations in the analytical process. The charts refer to magazines—but with some variations, could apply to books, catalogs, etc. It all boils down to the absolute necessity of measuring results within the parameters of the financial dynamics of the particular situation. If direct mail is measurable, then the message must be loud and clear. And it doesn't stop with front-end response.

One precaution: There is a danger in working with averages. The "average" is a handy mathematical device, but remember, there are several kinds of averages, all different and each revealing a wholly different aspect of the same set of figures. Let's look at how a group's typical income would be, computing just four of the more simple averaging methods. (See Table 8-11.)

Table 8-9. *Glory of Art* Continuation Mailing (Art/Antique/Collectibles)*

Lists	Mail Qty.	Percent of Resp.	Mail Qty.	No. Orders	Percent of Resp.	Pkg. C.P.M.	List C.P.M.	Total C.P.M.	C.P.O.	Percent of Credit	Percent Bad Pay	Net Orders	Percent Net Resp.	Net C.P.O.	Total Cost	Total Revenue	Net Revenue	Net Revenue per Subs.
1	5,004	2.90	44,300	1,315	2.97	$180	$45.45	$225.45	$7.59	91.0	27.6	985	2.22	$10.15	9,987	17,730	7,743	7.86
2	4,950	3.10	35,250	1,117	3.17	180	63.85	243.85	7.69	88.0	28.1	841	2.38	10.24	8,595	15,138	6,543	7.78
3	5,007	3.00	44,000	1,350	3.07	180	45.47	227.47	7.34	89.0	23.0	1,074	2.44	9.32	10,008	19,332	9,324	8.68
4	5,100	2.90	43,200	1,278	2.96	180	63.66	243.66	8.23	91.0	29.3	937	2.17	11.22	10,562	16,866	6,304	6.72
5	4,999	2.80	43,100	1,232	2.86	180	50.72	230.72	8.06	82.0	21.0	1,020	2.37	9.74	9,944	18,360	8,416	8.25
6	5,060	3.00	47,600	1,461	3.07	180	63.02	243.02	7.91	85.0	26.0	1,138	2.39	10.17	11,567	20,484	8,917	7.83
7	4,975	3.10	30,800	976	3.17	180	51.13	231.13	6.72	92.0	28.0	725	2.35	9.84	7,118	13,050	5,932	8.18

© Copyright by Rose Harper, The Kleid Company, Inc.
*Sample of List-by-List Evaluation.

There is no intention here to dispute the use of averages. That would be impractical. What is being suggested is that the nuances behind averages be observed. You need, to use a statistical term, to be aware of the "outliers," the freaks, that can influence the average unduly and lead to incorrect interpretation of results.

Seasonality

Seasonality has been a priority subject in direct mail for a long time. Have seasonality patterns been changing? During the past five years it appears so, from the seasonality study conducted by The Kleid Company, Inc. (See Table 8-12.)

While the dynamics of budgeting and other considerations can, and do, influence mailing periods, there are strong reasons why seasonality studies should be conducted by companies using direct mail on a consistent basis. The same type of names (such as changes of address), the same quantity, offer, and mailing package should be mailed at the same time each month to measure seasonality.

Statistical and Analytical Techniques

Statistics is a branch of mathematics dealing with the collection, analysis, and interpretation of masses of numerical data. In some instances, it is easy, for example, descriptive statistics. These represent numbers that yield an efficient summary of some type of information, for example, batting averages, unemployment rates, Dow-Jones averages.

In direct mail, it is essential to segment and define our market. And to do this, it becomes necessary to look at the techniques available for use in analysis and as market research tools.

Multivariate methods are not new, but the proliferation of these techniques in marketing research has been spurred by the ability of the computer to perform enormous numbers of calculations in a short time. Factor analysis, a member of the family of multivariate methods, is based on the following proposition. If there is a systematic interdependence among a set of variables, it must be due to something fundamental that created the interdependence. These underlying factors will tend to cluster the variables into categories. The categories are not mutually exclusive. Factor analysis will perform the identification of underlying factors and the grouping of manifest (observed) variables under each factor.

Table 8-10. *Glory of Art* Continuation Mailing

	Continuations	List Tests	Total
Mail Quantity	866,702	100,000	966,702
Number of Orders	23,759	2,000	25,759
Percent Response	2.74	2.00	2,66
Package CPM	$180.00	$180.00	$180.00
List CPM	$51.73	$45.00	$51.03
Total CPM	$231.73	$225.00	$231.03
C.P.O.	$8.45	$11.25	$8.67
Percent Credit	89.4	89.3	89.4
Percent Bad Pay	26.6	27.3	26.6
Net Orders	18,105	1,513	19,618
Net Percent Response	2.09	1.51	2.03
Net C.P.O.	$11.09	$14.90	$11.38
Total Cost	$200,842	$22,500	$223,342
Total Revenue	$325,890	$27,234	$353,124
Net Revenue	$125,048	$4,734	$129,782
Net Revenue per Subscriber	$6.91	$3.12	$6.61

For example, Old American Insurance Company of Kansas City, Missouri, has a unique data bank that stores up to 103 bits of manifest data about each ZIP code. The data bank lists potential marketing units (ZIP code areas) in terms of their environmental characteristics which, when combined into factors, provide the inferential dimension of lifestyle and are thus used to predict consumer behavior. Using factor analysis, Old American can mathematically correlate the 103 environmental variables of the ZIP code areas of interest with each other and thus condense them into a dozen or more uncorrelated factors that are much more meaningful and manageable in subsequent analysis.

Regression analysis and correlation analysis enable us to deal with variables that are stated in terms of numerical values rather than in qualitative categories. These methods provide the bases for measuring the strength of the relationships among the variables. The term *regression analysis* refers to the methods by which estimates are made of the values of a variable from a knowledge of the values or one or more other variables and to the measurement of the errors involved in this estimation process. The term *correlation analysis* refers to methods for measuring the strength of the association (correlations) among these variables. Equations are used in both instances to express the relationship among the variables.

There are many variations of these mathematical, analytical systems. The direct marketer must be aware of the importance of statistical analysis for decision making. And, to make it worthwhile, the direct marketer needs to establish the marketing concepts or criteria so that the statisticians can decide on the technique to be used in order to get actionable information—information from the data base that will help you manage your other resources better.

Table 8-11. Averaging Methods for Group Income

Family Income*	Income-Averaging Methods
1. $60,000	*Arithmetic Mean* $30,000†
2. $50,000	The most common kind of average. Computed by taking the sum of all the families divided by the number of families. In this example, three families earn more than the mean and six earn less.
3. $40,000	
4. $30,000	
5. $25,000	*Mid-Range* $37,500†
6. $20,000	The richest earns four times more than the poorest. Add the bottom and top and divide by 2. Three families earn more than the midrange and seven earn less.
7. $20,000	
8. $20,000	*Median* $22,500†
9. $20,000	If you want to represent the group by what a family in the exact middle gets, you must locate the median—the income that will be higher than the incomes of the lower half and lower than the upper half. If there were eleven families, the median income would be the sixth highest. With only ten—no family is in the middle, so you find the dividing line by adding the fifth and sixth and dividing by 2. In this example, the median is less than both the midrange and the mean.
10. $15,000	
	Mode $20,000†
	Also called the *Norm*. Mode in statistical work equals that value, magnitude or score which occurs the greatest number of times in a given series of observations. In this example, the modal income is $20,000. If there had been no set of two or more, there would have been no mode.

©Copyright by Rose Harper, The Kleid Company, Inc.
*Total = $300,000.
†"Typical" income for group.

Table 8-12. Seasonality Study: Five-Year Summary by Category Showing Top Two Months

Categories	1981-82	1982-83	1983-84	1984-85	1985-86
Business & Finance (Top)*	Dec	Dec	Dec	Dec	Dec
(2)†	Jan	Jan	Jan	June	Jan/June
Cultural Reading	Dec	Dec	Dec	Dec	Dec
	June	June	June	June	June
General Reading	July	Dec	Dec	Dec	Dec
	Dec	June	July	June	June
Self-Improvement	Dec	Dec	Dec	Dec	Dec
	Sept	Jan/Sept	Jan	July	Jan
Home Interest	Feb	Dec	Dec	July	July
	Jan	Jan	July	Oct	Dec
Parents & Children	July	July	July	July	July
	Jan	Dec	Jan	Jan	Jan
Hobbies	July	Dec	Dec	Dec	Dec
	Dec	July	July	July	June
Entertainment	July	Dec	Dec	Dec	Dec
	Aug	Jan	Jan	Jan/July	Sept
Education	June	Jan	Dec	June	Apr
	Dec	Nov/Dec	Jan	Dec	Dec
Fund-Raising	Nov	Sept	Dec/Feb	Sept	Feb
	Feb	Feb	Oct	Oct	Sept

©Copyright by Rose Harper, The Kleid Company, Inc.
*First Line = Top; † Second line = Second place

Mathematical Modeling

Modeling techniques have been used in direct mail for some time now, but today's advanced technology allows for marketing information systems with predictive capabilities. In the magazine field, for example, the Promotion Evaluation Model (designed by Policy Development Corp., LaJolla, Ca.) is a tool for source evaluation. The initial gross cost of acquiring a new subscriber is not the key to the real value of the subscription. Back-end performance (pay-ups, conversion, renewal rates) provide the definitive measurement of response. Source evaluation is a method for examining the renewability and profitability of a new subscriber/product through a variety of sources within a particular time frame.

Then there are marketing decision models. In general, a "model" allows exploration of various alternatives by profit ratios, return on investment, and any other pertinent statistics. You can play the "what if" game by making a number of changes to see their effect on the overall plan. It's a simulation technique. And it all starts with a data base of past experience, data, and history. The data collection and processing activity is extremely important and will be directional in the selection of the model to be developed.

The heart of every direct marketing operation is a data base. The degree of success you achieve in the use of mailing lists will be measured by your ability to extract the most profitable segments from your data base and those of others.

Self-Quiz

1. What three things are both central and indispensable to direct marketing through lists?

   a. _____

   b. _____

   c. _____

2. The two broad categories of lists are _____

   and _____.

3. Your best customer is _____.

4. The art of getting more sales from existing customers is to be able to

   match _____

   to customer buying _____.

5. Define the RFM formula:

   R stands for _____.

   F stands for _____.

   M stands for _____.

6. Define Super-Spot Subscribers:

   _____

   _____

7. More than _____ of all married women work.

8. List brokers serve two sides: the _____
   and the _____.

9. In testing a new list a _____
   quantity is usually adequate.

10. However, if a mailer is testing offers and mailing packages simultane-
    ously, a quantity of at least _____
    names is recommended.

11. Define a "spectrum test."

    _____

    _____

    _____

12. Define "merge/purge."

    _____

    _____

    _____

13. How does one best establish the seasonality factor of a mailing pro-
    gram?

    _____

    _____

    _____

Pilot Project

You are the circulation director of a consumer magazine. You have agreed to conduct a mailing list seminar for the marketing class of a leading uni-versity.

In preparation for this seminar define all aspects of the following outline.

A.   Definition of a list

B.   The three things central and indispensable to direct marketing through lists

C. Definition of internal and external lists

D. The theory of segmentation

E. Definition of RFM formula

F. Value of Census tracts

G. Value of ZIP codes

H. Functions of a list broker

I. Functions of list managers

J. Components of list data cards

K. Purpose of list tests

L. Test quantities

M. Theory of a "spectrum test"

N. Duplication elimination

O. Break-even analysis

P. Seasonality

Q. Factor analysis

R. Regression and correlation analysis

S. Modeling techniques

CHAPTER NINE

Magazines

Where Do You Go First?

The advertising pages of magazines are to the direct response advertiser what the retail outlet is to the manufacturer selling through the more traditional channels. A magazine that performs consistently well for a variety of direct response advertisers is like a store in a low-rent, high-traffic location. It's far more profitable than a store selling the same merchandise on the wrong side of town.

Such a magazine just seems to have an atmosphere that is more conducive to the mail response customer. The mail order shopping reader traffic is high in relation to the publication's cost per thousand. Magazines in this category (and this is by no means a complete list) are *National Enquirer, Parade,* and the mighty *TV Guide.* Women's publications also doing well for mail order advertisers are *Family Circle, Better Homes and Gardens, Good Housekeeping, Cosmopolitan, Woman's Day, Seventeen,* and *Redbook.* Men's publications include *Home Mechanix, Moose, Playboy,* and *Penthouse.* (For a comprehensive list of magazines that provide a structured mail order atmosphere, see Table 9-1.)

But just as retail locations come into and go out of favor with each passing decade, so do the trends that determine which publications work well in the mail order marketplace at a particular time. For example, coming into favor right now are *New Yorker, Country Living, Family Circle,* and *Smithsonian.* In the 1960s there was must greater interest in such publications as *McCall's, Ladies' Home Journal, House & Garden, House Beautiful,* and the *National Observer.* And I can remember in the 1950s looking to *Living for Young Homemakers, Harper's/Atlantic,* and *Saturday Review*—and the *Saturday Evening Post* could be counted on for good results.

There are some publications that one might assume at first glance to be just great for the mail order advertiser. But close examination of performance figures for many different advertisers in these publications causes a red flag to be raised for the direct marketing advertiser. Here are a few places to go right now at your own risk: *Reader's Digest, National Geographic, New York,* and *Town & Country.* Some of these publications, though, have done well for high-ticket items like collectibles.

Regional Editions: When Is the Part Bigger than the Whole?

For the buyer of space in magazines today, most publications with circulations of over 1.5 million offer the opportunity to buy a regional portion of the national circulation. But it was not always so.

Although it has been said that the *New Yorker* was the first to publish sectional or regional editions in 1929, it wasn't until the late 1950s that major magazines began selling regional space to all advertisers, not just to those who had distribution limited to a particular section of the circulation area.

The availability of regional editions for everyone opened important opportunities to the mail order advertiser. Here are a few of the things you can do with regional buys:

1. You don't have to invest in the full national cost of a publication to get some indication of its effectiveness for your proposition. In some cases, such as *Time* or *TV Guide*, by running in a single edition you can determine relative response with an investment at least 20 percent less than what it costs to make a national buy.

2. Some regions traditionally pull better than others for the mail order advertiser. For many mail order products or services, nothing does better than the West Coast or worse than the New England region. You can select the best response area for your particular proposition.

   Remember, in most publications you will be paying a premium for the privilege of buying partial circulation. If you are testing a publication, putting your advertising message in the better-pulling region can offset much of this premium charge.

3. Availability of regional editions makes possible multiple copy testing in a single issue of a publication. Some magazines offer A/B split-run copy testing in each of the regional editions published. For example, in *TV Guide,* you can test one piece of copy against your control in one edition, another against your control in a second edition, another against your control in a third, and so on. As a result, you can learn as much about different pieces of copy in a single issue of one publication as you could discover in several national A/B copy splits in the same publication over a time span of two years or more.

4. When testing regionally, don't make the mistake of testing too small a circulation quantity. It is essential that you test a large enough circulation segment to provide readable results that can be projected accurately for still larger circulations.

   Warning: Buying regional space is not all fun and games. You will have to pay for the privilege in a number of ways. As mentioned, regional space costs more. How much more? You can get an idea of what to expect from these representative examples: *Woman's Day* from 53 to 124 percent: *Time* from 5 to 279 percent; *Popular Science* from 28 to 59 percent; *TV Guide* from 5 to 163 percent; and *Reader's Digest* from 52 to 188 percent.

The minimum and maximum figures relate to the number and circulation size of regions you may be buying for any one insertion.

Another factor to keep in mind is the relatively poor position regional ads receive. The regional sections usually appear far back in the magazine or in a "well" or signature of several consecutive pages of advertising with no editorial matter to catch the reader. As you will see later in our discussion of position placement, the poor location of an ad in a magazine can depress results as much as 50 percent below what the same advertisement would pull if it were in the first few pages of the same publication. If you are using regional space for testing, be certain to factor this into your evaluation.

An example of how various factors must be weighed in utilizing regional circulation for text purposes follows:

Regional Test Schedule for XYZ Yarn & Craft Company

REDBOOK

Space:	Full-page four-color insert
Position:	Back of main editorial (regional forms)
Issue:	June 1987
Space Cost:	$13,355 (printing cost not included)
Editions Used:	Central (670,000)
	North Central (395,000)
Total test circulation:	1,065,000 (27.0 percent of total circulation)
Regional premium:	None

FAMILY CIRCLE

Space:	Full-page four-color insert
Position:	Back of main editorial (regional forms)
Issue:	June 1987
Space Cost:	$3,662.55 (printing cost not included)
Editions Used:	Los Angeles (532,000)
	San Francisco (305,000)
Total test circulation:	837,000 (13.3 percent of total circulation)
Regional premium	$450 ($225/region)

Since full-page four-color inserts have been extremely profitable for some of the larger mail order advertisers, this size unit was tested for the

XYZ Yarn & Craft Co. to see if such inserts could bring in a lower lead cost than obtained from a black-and-white page and card.

Because women's publications are the most successful media for this advertiser, the company went to two that offered the mechanical capabilities for regional testing of such an insert. Although May and June are not prime mail order months, it was necessary to test then in order to allow turnaround time for the next season's scheduling. Therefore, the following factors would have to be taken into consideration in projecting test results to learn whether this unit would be successful in prime mail order months with full circulation: (1) regional premium, (2) month of insertion, (3) position in book, and (4) relative value of specific media.

Pilot Publications: The Beacons of Direct Response Media Scheduling

When planning your direct marketing media schedule, think about the media universe the way you think about the view of the sky in the evening. If you have no familiarity with the stars, the sky appears to be a jumble of blinking lights with no apparent relationship. But as you begin to study the heavens, you are soon able to pick out clusters of stars that have a relationship to one another in constellations.

You will recognize the stars that make up the Big Dipper in Ursa Major, the Hunter, the Swan, the Bull, and other familiar constellations. If you were to go on to become a professional astronomer, you would eventually recognize eighty-nine distinctly different groups. Once you know the various constellations, a star within a particular grouping inevitably leads your eye to the other related stars.

The magazine universe is no different. There are nearly 400 consumer magazines published with circulations of 100,000 or more. The first step in approaching this vast list is to sort out the universe of magazines into categories. Although this process is somewhat arbitrary, and different experts may not agree entirely as to which magazines fall into which category, we are going to set down a chart of the major publications that you can use like a chart of the skies to map out particular magazine groupings. Once you begin to think of magazines as forming logical groupings within the total magazine universe, you can begin to determine the groupings offering the most likely marketplace for your product or proposition. Table 9-2 is a basic magazine category chart and lists some of the publications currently available for the direct response advertiser.

Table 9-1. U.S. Consumer Magazines with Mail Order and/or Shopping Advertising Pages

Class Publication

A

10A A+
33 Absolute Sound, The
23 Accent on Living
8 Across the Board
30A Adirondack Life
8A Adventure Magazine
46 Adventure Road
21A Advocate, The
4 Aero
10A Ahoy
23 Aimplus
22 Air & Space, Smithsonian
31 Air Force Times
4 Air Line Pilot
4 Air Progress
1 Air Travel Journal
30A Alaska
1 Alaska Airlines Magazine
9B Alcalde
46 Aloha
2 American Artist
5 American Baby
18 American Brewer
8 American Business
13 American Cage-Bird Magazine
2 American Collector's Journal
13 American Field
17A American Film
19 American Handgunner
23 American Health
22 American Heritage
23A American History Illustrated
21 American Horticulturist
19 American Hunter, The

20 American Legion Auxiliary's National News, The
20 American Legion Magazine, The
31A American Motorcyclist
39 American Photographer
19 American Rifleman
21 American Rose Magazine
26 American Scholar, The
19 American Shotgunner, The
41 American Spectator, The
12 American Square Dance Magazine
1 American Way
22 American West
24 Americana
1 Amtrak Express
35 Animal Kingdom
28 Antaeus
10A Antic
2 Antique Market Report
2 Antique Monthly
2 Antique Trader Weekly, The
2 Antiques Directory
4 AOPA Pilot
25 Appaloosa Journal
25 Appaloosa World
25 Arabian Horse World
25 Arabians
22 Archaeology
19 Archery World
24 Architectural Digest
30A Arizona Living
31 Army Times
31 Army Times Military Group

2 Art & Antiques
2 Art & Auction
2 Art & Crafts Catalyst
2 Art in America
2 Artist's Magazine, The
2 Artnews
2 Art Now Gallery Guide
2 Art/World
2 Artforum
30A Atlantic City Magazine
22 Atlantic, The
22 Attenzione
33 Audio
35 Audubon
24 Austin Homes & Gardens
3 Auto Racing Digest
3 Autobuff
3 Automobile Magazine
3 AutoWeek
4 Aviation Digest

B

20 B'nai B'rith International Jewish Monthly, The
30A Back Home in Kentucky
8B Backpacker
25 Backstretch, The
51 Barbie
8 Barron's-National Business and Financial Weekly
45 Baseball Digest
45 Basketball Digest
19 Bassmaster Classic Report
19 Bassmaster Magazine
6 Bay & Delta Yachtsman

Source: Consumer Magazine and Agri-Media Rates and Data (May 27, 1987).

Table 9-1. U.S. Consumer Magazines with Mail Order and/or Shopping Advertising Pages

23 Bestways
13 Better Beagling
24 Better Homes and
   Gardens
24 Better Homes and
   Gardens All-Time
   Favorite Recipes
24 Better Homes and
   Gardens Building
   Ideas
11 Better Homes and
   Gardens
   Christmas Ideas
11 Better Homes and
   Gardens Country
   Crafts
24 Better Homes and
   Gardens
   Decorating
24 Better Homes and
   Gardens Do-It-
   Yourself Home
   Improvement and
   Repair
21 Better Homes and
   Gardens Garden
   Ideas and Outdoor
   Living
43A Better Homes and
   Gardens
   Grandparents
24 Better Homes and
   Gardens Holiday
   Cooking
11 Better Homes and
   Gardens Holiday
   Crafts
24 Better Homes and
   Gardens Home
   Plan Ideas
24 Better Homes and
   Gardens Kitchen
   & Bath Ideas
24 Better Homes and
   Gardens Low
   Calorie

49 Better Homes and
   Gardens
   Microwave Recipes
14 Better Homes and
   Gardens
   Needlecraft Ideas
24 Better Homes and
   Gardens
   Remodeling Ideas
24 Better Homes and
   Gardens
   Traditional Home
24 Better Homes and
   Gardens Window
   and Wall Ideas
 8 Better Investing
22 Better Living
44 Beverly Hills (213)
45 Bicycle Guide
45 Bicycle Rider
45 Bicycle USA
19 Big Three, The
45 Billiards Digest
13 Bird Talk
35 Bird Watcher's Digest
 8 Black Enterprise
11 Blade Magazine, The
25 Blood-Horse, The
1A Blum's Farmers &
   Planters Almanac
   and Turner's
   Carolina Almanac
45 BMX Action
45 BMX Plus
 6 Boating
 6 Boatracing
30A Boca Raton
45 Body Boarding
18 Bon Appetit
30A Boston Magazine
49 Boston Woman
30A Bostonia Magazine
19 Bowhunter
45 Bowling
45 Bowling Digest

51 Boys' Life
 1 Braniff's Destination
 7 Bride's
23A British Heritage
 8 Business Month
 8 Business Week
10A Byte

C

30B Cable Choice
30A California
45 California Bicyclist
25 California Horse
   Review
43A California Senior
   Citizen
8B Camping and RV
   Magazine
8B Canoe
30A Cape Cod Life
24 Capper's
 3 Car and Driver
 3 Car and Driver
   Buyers Guide
 3 Car Collector/Car
   Classics
 3 Car Craft
46 Caribbean Travel &
   Life Magazine
 3 Cars & Parts
   Magazine
13 Cat Fancy
42 Catholic Twin Circle
13 Cats Magazine
45 Century Sports
   Network
16 Change
24 Changing Homes
22 Changing Times
42 Charisma
 6 Chesapeake Bay
   Magazine
19 Chevy Outdoors
38 Chicago Tribune
   Magazine Sunday
49 Child

(continued)

Table 9-1. U.S. Consumer Magazines with Mail Order and/or Shopping Advertising Pages

18	Chocolatier
42	Christian Century, The
42	Christian Herald
42	Christianity Today
25	Chronicle of the Horse, The
42	Church Herald, The
30A	Cincinnati
3	Circle Track
33	Circus Magazine
44	City & Country Club Life
8	City & State
23A	Civil War Times Illustrated
15	Classified, Inc.
30A	Cleveland Magazine
11	Coin World
11	Coins
2	Collector Editions
2	Collectors Mart
2	Collectors News
2	Collectors' Showcase
9B	College Woman
24	Colonial Homes
45	Colorado SportStyles
41	Commonweal
10A	Compute!
10A	Compute!'s Apple Applications Special
10A	Compute!'s Gazette
10A	Computer Digest
10A	Computer Graphic
10A	Computer Living/New York
10A	Computer Shopper
46	Conde Nast's Traveler
30A	Connecticut Magazine
22	Connoisseur, The
22	Consumers Digest
33	Contemporary Christian Music
1	Continental Airlines Magazine

49	Cooking Light
18	Cook's Magazine, The
49	Cosmopolitan
24	Country Home
24	Country Journal
24	Country Living
18	Country Living/Country Cooking
30B	CPI Guide Network, The
11	Craft Art Needlework Digest
11	Crafts 'N Things
11	Crafts Magazine
8	Crain's Chicago Business
8	Crain's New York Business
49	Creative Ideas for Living
41	Crisis, The
45	Cross Country Skier
6	Cruising World
31A	Cycle
31A	Cycle Guide
31A	Cycle News
31A	Cycle World
31A	Cycle World 1987 Annual & Buyer's Guide
45	Cycling U.S.A.
45	Cyclist

D

30A	D Magazine
24	Dallas-Fort Worth Home & Garden
17A	Dancemagazine
17A	DancScene
39	Darkroom & Creative Camera Techniques
39	Darkroom Photography

11	Dell Puzzle Magazine Group
30A	Denver Magazine
30A	Detroit Monthly
30B	Dial
9B	Directions
31A	Dirt Bike
31A	Dirt Rider Magazine
31A	Dirt Wheels
45	Disc Sports
43	Discover
46	Discovery
20	Discovery YMCA
49	Disney Channel Magazine, The
46	Diversion
13	Dog Fancy
13	Dog World
11	Dolls
9B	Dorm Magazine
33	Down Beat
30A	Down East
11	Dragon
17A	Dramatics
33	Drum Corps World
19	Ducks Unlimited
3	Dune Buggies & Hot VWs

E

20	Eagle Magazine
24	Earth Shelter Living
22	East West
6	Eastern Boating
25	Eastern Horse World
31A	Easyriders
50	Electricity
20	Elks Magazine, The
50	Elle
46	Endless Vacation
6	Ensign, The
8	Entrepreneur
42	Episcopalian, The
25	Equus
34	Espionage Magazine
30	Esquire

Table 9-1. U.S. Consumer Magazines with Mail Order and/or Shopping Advertising Pages

49 Essence	19 Florida Sportsman	22 Globe
42 Eternity	21 Flower & Garden	45 Golf Digest
46 European Travel & Life	4 Flying	45 Golf Illustrated
	11 Flying Models	45 Gold Magazine
16 Exceptional Parent, The	30A Folsom World & Northlake News, The	49 Good Food Magazine
		49 Good Housekeeping
49 Executive Female, The	18 Food & Wine	8A Good Sam's Hi-Way Herald
5 Expecting	45 Football Digest	
51 Eye, The	8 Forbes	18 Gourmet
	41 Foreign Affairs	19 Gray's Sporting Journal
F	41 Foreign Service Journal	
3 Fabulous Mustangs and Exotic Fords		6 Great Lakes Sailor
	8 Fortune	30A Great Lakes Travel & Living
	3 4WD Action	
49 Fairfield County Woman	3 4 Wheel & Off-Road	30A Greenville Magazine
	3 Four Wheeler	1A Grier's Almanac
49 Family Circle	16 4-H Leader—The National Magazine For 4-H	22 Grit
49 Family Circle Great Ideas		42 Group
		5 Guide for Expectant Parents
24 Family Handyman, The	45 Freestylin'	
	8 Frequent Flyer	21A Guide Magazine/Gay Life
8A Family Motor Coaching	46 Friendly Exchange	
	19 Full Cry	5 Guide To Your Child's Development
21 Farmstead Magazine	19 Fur-Fish-Game	
34 Fate	8 Futures	
20 Federal Times	22 Futurist, The	33 Guitar World
2 Fiberarts		19 Gun Dog
19 Field & Stream	**G**	19 Gun Week
43A 50 plus	30 Gallery	30 Gung-Ho
11 FineScale Modeler	20A Gambling Times	19 Guns & Ammo
30B Fine Tuning	19 Game & Fish Magazine	19 Guns & Ammo Annual 1988
11 Fine Woodworking		
19 Fins and Feathers	11 Games	19 Guns Magazine
46 First Class	20A Gaming International Magazine	
5 First Year of Life, The		**H**
19 Fish Sniffer, The		20 Hadassah Magazine
19 Fisherman, The	4 General Aviation News	47 Ham Radio Magazine
19 Fishing & Hunting News		47 Hands-On Electronics
	23 Generations	
19 Fishing Facts	30 Genesis	50 Harper's Bazaar
19 Fishing World	30 Gentlemen's Quarterly	22 Harper's Magazine
19A Flex		24 Harrowsmith
45 Florida Golfweek	7 Getting Married: A Planning Guide	9B Harvard Magazine
45 Florida Racquet Journal		46 Hawaii
	50 Glamour	23 Health
		3 Hemmings Motor News

(continued)

Table 9-1. U.S. Consumer Magazines with Mail Order and/or Shopping Advertising Pages

21 Herb Quarterly, The	24 It's Your Move	8B Lost Treasure
33 High Fidelity	9B Ivy League	20A Lottery Player's
8 High Technology	Magazines	Magazine
23A Highlander, The		42 Lutheran Standard,
8 Hispanic Business	**J**	The
24 Historic Preservation	1A J. Gruber's Almanack	42 Lutheran, The
45 Hockey Digest	30A Jacksonville	
24 Home	Magazine	**M**
29 Home Mechanix	30A Japanese-American	30 M
11 Home Shop	Yellow Pages	42A Macfadden Women's
Machinist, The	33 Jazziz	Group
24 Homeowner, The	33 Jazztimes	10A Macworld
24 Homes International	20 Junior League	50 Mademoiselle
30A Honolulu Magazine	Review	2 Magazine Antiques,
25 Hoof Beats	51 Junior Scholastic	The
2 Horizon		34 Magazine of Fantasy
11 Horoscope	**K**	and Science
25 Horse Digest, The	8B KOA Directory Road	Fiction, The
25 Horse Illustrated	Atlas and	11 Magical Blend
25 Horseman	Camping Guide	30A Manhattan
25 Horse World	30A KS. Magazine	30A Manhattan Living
25 Horseman's Service		6 Marine and
Directory and	**L**	Recreation News
Desk Reference,	30A L.A. Weekly	19 Marlin
The	30A L.A. West	10 Marvel Comics
25 Horsemen's Journal	1 LACSA'S World	Group
25 Horseplay	1A Ladies Birthday	43A Mature Outlook
25 Horsetrader, The	Almanac, The	49 McCall's
	49 Ladies' Home	49 McCall's Beauty,
I	Journal	Diet & Health
44 Illustrated, The	49 Lady's Circle	Guide
46 In-Fisherman	6 Lakeland Boating	49 McCall's Cooking
Angling	5 Lamaze Parents'	School
Adventures,	Magazine	14 McCall's
The	11 Lapidary Journal	Needlework &
8 Inc.	16 Learning 87	Crafts
8 Income	23 Let's Live	23 Medical Self-Care
Opportunities	24 Life & Home	30 Men's Health
30A Indianapolis	10A Link-Up	45 Met Golfer, The
Monthly	11 Linn's Stamp News	24 Metropolis
45 Inside Sports	11 Live Steam	30A Metropolitan Detroit
16 Instructor	42 Living Church, The	24 Metropolitan Home
45 International	11 Llewellyn New	30A Miami Mensual
Gymnast	Times, The	30A Miami/South Florida
46 International Travel	6 Log, The	Magazine
News	30A Los Angeles	19 Michigan
46 Islands	Magazine	Out-Of-Doors

Table 9-1. U.S. Consumer Magazines with Mail Order and/or Shopping Advertising Pages

30A Mid-Atlantic Country	11 National Doll World	41 New Republic, The
4 Midwest Flyer Magazine	3 National Dragster	49 New Woman
	22 National Examiner	24 N. Y. Habitat
24 Midwest Living	46 National Geographic Traveler	36A New York Magazine
19 Midwest Outdoors		28 New York Review of Books, The
27 Milwaukee Labor Press AFL-CIO	25 National Horseman, The	
11 Miniature Collector	11 National Knife Magazine, The	38 The New York Times Magazine
11 Model Railroader		30A New York Woman
7 Modern Bride	30 National Lampoon	22 New Yorker, The
33 Modern Drummer	45 National Masters News	44 Newport Beach (714)
47 Modern Electronics		38 Newsday Magazine, The
43A Modern Maturity	8 National OTC Stock Journal, The	
33 Modern Percussionist	8B National Parks	42 Nor'easter
	45 National Racquetball	19 North American Hunter
39 Modern Photography	41 National Review	
22 Moneysworth	3 National Speed Sport News	30A North Shore
22 Mother Earth News		30A Northeast Magazine
22 Mother Earth News American Country	22 Natural History	8B Northeast Outdoors
	31 Navy News	31A Northeast Riding
	31 Navy Times	35 Not Man Apart
22 Mother Jones	14 Needle & Thread	43A NRTA/AARP News Bulletins
5 Mothers Today	14 Needlecraft For Today	
5 Mothers Today Sourcebook		22 Nuestro
	11 Needlepoint News	11 Numismatic News
31A Motocross Action	30A Nevada Magazine	11 Nutshell News
6 Motor Boating & Sailing	22 New Age	51 NYC
	30A New Dominion	**O**
3 Motor Trend	30A New England Monthly	3 Off-Road
31A Motorcyclist		6 Offshore: New England's Boating Magazine
8A Motorhome	43A New England Senior Citizen	
46 Motorland		
9B Moving Up	24 New Homeowner Guide, The	30A Ohio Magazine
49 Ms.		3 Old Cars Weekly
51 Muppet Magazine	6 New Jersey Boater	1A Old Farmer's Almanac, The
19A Muscle & Fitness	19 New Jersey Hunting and Fishing Guide	
3 Muscle Car Review		34 Old West
3 Muscle Cars		24 Old-House Journal, The
33 Music City News	30A New Jersey Monthly	
N	30A New Mexico Magazine	43 Omni
30A Nashville		3 On Track
41 Nation, The	30A New Orleans Magazine	24 1,001 Home Ideas
42 National Catholic Register		3 Open Wheel
	22 New Realities	30A Orange Coast
		30A Oregon Coast

(continued)

Table 9-1. U.S. Consumer Magazines with Mail Order and/or Shopping Advertising Pages

30A Orlando Magazine	30A Pittsburgh	47 Radio-Electronics
30 Oui	4 Plane&Pilot	11 Raitfan & Railroad
42 Our Sunday Visitor	30 Playboy	11 Railroad Model
19 Outdoor America	30 Players	Craftsman
19 Outdoor Life	25 Polo	10A Rainbow, The
39 Outdoor	3 Pontiac	46 Rand McNally Road
Photographer	3 Popular Cars	Atlas
19 Outdoor Press, The	11 Popular Ceramics	17A Rave
19 Outdoor Sports &	3 Popular Hot Rodding	22 Reader's Digest
Recreation	29 Popular Mechanics	49 Redbook Magazine
45 Outside	39 Popular Photography	31 Retired Officer, The
33 Ovation	29 Popular Science	31A Rider
24 Owner Builder, The	24 Popular	3 Road & Track
	Woodworking	31A Road Rider
P	6 Power and	22 Robb Report, The
25 Pacific Coast Journal	Motoryacht	33 Rock Magazine
30A Pacific Northwest	6 Powerboat	33 Rocket, The
25 Paint Horse Journal	24 Practical	30A Rockford Magazine
44 Palm Beach Social	Homeowner	46 Rocky Mountain
Pictorial	25 Practical Horseman	Motorist
45 Parachutist	42 Presbyterian Survey	19 Rod & Reel
22 Parade	23 Prevention	34 Rod Serling's The
20 Paraplegia News	4 Private Pilot	Twilight Zone
49 Parenting	51 Progressive Forensics	Magazine
49 Parents	45 Prorodeo Sports	49 Rodale's Children
11 Passenger Train	News	21 Rodale's Organic
Journal	22 Psychic Guide	Gardening
10A PC World	22 Psychology Today	33 Rolling Stone
10A PCM, The Personal	13 Pure-Bred Dogs	9A Rotarian, The
Computer	American Kennel	3 Rotary Rocket
Magazine for	Gazette	45 Rugby
Tandy Computer	51 Purple Cow	10A Run
Users		45 Runner's World
30A Peninsula	**Q**	45 Running Times
19 Pennsylvania	47 QST	25 Rural Heritage
Sportsman, The	25 Quarter Horse	
25 Performance	Journal, The	**S**
Horseman	25 Quarter Horse News	30A Sacramento
8 Personal Investor	25 Quarter Racing	Magazine
39 Petersen's	Record, The	25 Saddle & Bridle
Photographic	18 Quick & Healthy	25 Saddle Horse Report
Magazine	Cooking	19 Safari
30A Philadelphia		6 Sail
Magazine	**R**	6 Sailboat &
30A Phoenix Metro	45 Racquet	Equipment
11 Pipe Smoker	45 Racquetball in	Directory
	Review	

Table 9-1. U.S. Consumer Magazines with Mail Order and/or Shopping Advertising Pages

6	Sailing	45	Ski	45	Sports Collectors
6	Sailing World	45	Ski America		Digest
30A	St. Louis Magazine	45	Ski X-C	45	Sports History
23	Saint Raphael's	45	Skiers Directory	41	Spotlight, The
	Better Health	1	Skies America	9B	Stanford Magazine,
6	Salt Water Sportsman	45	Skiing		The
30A	San Francisco Focus	45	Skin Diver Magazine	46	State, The
30A	San Jose Metro	16	Skip	3	Street Rodder
47	Satellite Orbit	45	Skydiving	30A	Summit
47	Satellite TV Week	49	Slimmer	24	Sunset
22	Saturday Evening	6	Small Boat Journal	3	Super Chevy
	Post, The	43C	Snow Week	47	Super Television
22	Saturday Review	43C	Snowmobile	45	Surfing
8	Savvy	49	Soap Opera Digest	43B	Swank
45	Scholastic Coach	4	Soaring	45	Swimming
51	Scholastic Magazines	45	Soccer Digest		World-Junior
	High School	30	Soldier of Fortune		Swimmer
	Network	6	Soundings		
20	Scouting	24	South Florida Home		**T**
45	Scuba Times		& Garden	49	Taxi
6	Sea Magazine	24	Southern Accents	43	Technology Review
30A	Seacoast Life	6	Southern Boating	49	'Teen
49	Self	17	Southern California	49	Teenage
43A	Senior American		Guide	30A	Tempo
	News	24	Southern Living	45	Tennis
43A	Senior Golfer,	30A	Southern Magazine	9B	Texas College
	The	19	Southern Outdoors		Student
49	Seventeen	2	Southwest Art	21	Texas Gardener
14	Sew News	3	Special Interest	24	Texas Homes
10A	Sextant		Autos	30A	Texas Monthly
49	Shape	43	Spectrum Magazine,	25	Thoroughbred
33	Sheet Music		IEEE		Record, The
	Magazine	1	Spirit of Aloha	25	Thoroughbred Times
19	Shooting Times	45	Sport	14	Threads
24	Shop-At-Home	4	Sport Aviation	31A	3&4 Wheel Action
	Directory, The	19	Sport Fishing	22	Tiffany
19	Shotgun Sports	19	Sporting Classics	49	Today's Chicago
39	Shutterbug	36A	Sporting News, The		Woman
2	Shuttle Spindle &	45	Sports 'N Spokes	49	Today's Christian
	Dyepot	19	Sports Afield		Woman
35	Sierra	19	Sports	11	Tole World
14	Simplicity Magazine		Afield/Special	30A	Toledo Metropolitan
51	16 Magazine		Publications	23	Total Health
19	Skeet Shooting	3	SportsCar	46	Tours & Resorts
	Review	3	Sports Car Illustrated	22	Town & Country

(continued)

Table 9-1. U.S. Consumer Magazines with Mail Order and/or Shopping Advertising Pages

45 Track & Field News	**V**	49 Washington Woman
1A Trail Blazers' Almanac and Pioneer Guide Book	20 V.F.W. Magazine	30A Washingtonian Magazine, The
	30A Valley Magazine	45 Water Skier, The
	22 Vanity Fair	6 Waterfront
8A Trailblazer	23 Vegetarian Times	36A Weekly, The
6 Trailer Boats	45 Velo-News	18 Weight Watchers Magazine
8A Trailer Life	8 Venture	
11 Trains	3 Vette	17 Welcome to Miami and the Beach
19 Trap & Field	43A VFW Auxiliary	
19 Trapper, The	24 Victorian Homes	28 West Coast Review of Books
46 Travel & Leisure	47 Video	
46 Travel/Holiday	47 Video Review	6 Western Boatman, The
25A Travelhost	47 Videomaker	
1 Travelling on Business	18 Vintage	4 Western Flyer
	30A Virginian, The	25 Western Horseman
8B Treasure	42 Virtue	19 Western Outdoor News
11 Tropical Fish Hobbyist	50 Vogue	
	14 Vogue Patterns	46 Westways
3 Truckin'	45 Volleyball Monthly	1 What's Up?
34 True West	3 VW & Porsche, Etc.	3 Wheel, The
3 Turbo	3 VW Trends	23 Whole Life
19 Turkey		35 Wildbird Magazine
30A Twin Cities	**W**	35 Wilderness
	49 W	19 Wildfowl
U	25 Walking Horse Report	22 Wilson Quarterly, The
9B UCLA Monthly, The	19A Walking Magazine, The	
4 Ultralight Flying!		45 WindRider
45 Ultrasport	41 Washington Monthly, The	19 Wing & Shot
45 Underwater USA		45 Winning Bicycle Racing Illustrated
24 Unique Homes	38 Washington Post Magazine, The	
22 USA Today		11 Winning!
30A Utah Holiday Magazine	36A Washington Post National Weekly Edition, The	49 Woman's Day
22 Utne Reader		

Table 9-1. U.S. Consumer Magazines with Mail Order and/or Shopping Advertising Pages

49 Woman's Day Special
     Interest
     Magazines
11 Woman's Day Best
     Ideas For
     Christmas
19A Woman's Day Diet &
     Fitness
49 Woman's Day Family
     Holiday
     Favorites
14 Woman's Day Granny
     Squares &
     Crafts
49 Woman's Day Great
     Holiday Baking
24 Woman's Day Home
     Decorating
     Ideas
24 Woman's Day Home
     Improvements
24 Woman's Day
     Kitchens & Baths
19A Woman's Day 101
     Ways to Lose
     Weight and Stay
     Healthy

49 Woman's Day Simply
     Delicious
     Meals in Minutes
14 Woman's Day 101
     Sweater & Craft
     Ideas
23 Women's Health
49 Women's Record,
     The
49 Women's Sports and
     Fitness
29 Wood
8A Woodall's 1988 RV
     Buyer's Guide
8B Woodall's 1988
     Tenting Directory
6 WoodenBoat
24 Woodheat
     Woodstove
     Directory
20 Woodmen of the
     World Magazine
11 Woodworker's
     Journal, The
49 Workbasket
24 Workbench
49 Working Mother

49 Working Mother
     Digest
49 Working Parents
49 Working Woman
4 World Airshow News
22 World Press Review
45 World Tennis
46 World Traveling
47 Worldradio
28 Writer's Digest

Y

6 Yachting
6 Yachting's Boat
     Buyers Guide
22 Yankee
49 YM
23 Yoga Journal

Within each category there are usually one or more publications that perform particularly well for the direct response advertiser at a lower cost than other publications in the group. We call those magazines the pilot publications for the group. If you use the pilot publications and they produce an acceptable cost per response, you can then proceed to explore the possiblity of adding other magazines in that category to your media schedule.

Table 9-2. Basic Consumer Magazine Categories

Demographic	Category	Sample Publications
Dual Audience	General Editorial/ Entertainment	Grit, National Enquirer, National Geographic, New York Times Magazine Section, Parade, People, Reader's Digest, TV Guide
	News	Time, Newsweek, Sports Illustrated, U.S. News & World Report
	Special Interest	Architectural Digest, Business Week, Elks, Foreign Affairs, High Fidelity, Modern Photography, Natural History, Ski, Travel & Leisure, Wall St. Journal, Yankee
Women	General/Service/ Shelter (Home Service)	Better Homes & Gardens, Cosmopolitan, Ebony, Family Circle, Good Housekeeping, House Beautiful, House & Garden, Ladies' Home Journal, McCall's, Redbook, Sunset, Woman's Day
	Fashion	Glamour, Harper's Bazaar, Mademoiselle, Vogue
	Special Interest	Brides, MacFadden Women's Group, McCall's Needlework & Crafts, Parents, Working Woman
Men	General/ Entertainment/ Fashion	Esquire, Gentlemen's Quarterly, Penthouse, Playboy
	Special Interest	Field & Stream, Home Mechanix, Outdoor Life, Popular Mechanics, Popular Science, Road & Track, Sports Afield
Youth	Male	Boy's Life
	Female	Teen, YM
	Dual Audience	Scholastic Magazines

In selecting the pilot publications in a category, keep in mind that you are not dealing with a static situation. As indicated earlier, a publication's mail order advertising viability changes from year to year, and what is a bellwether publication this season may not be the one to use next year. What is important is that you check out your own experience and the experience of others in determining the best places to advertise first in each category, and the next best, and the next best, and so on.

Think of your media buying program as an ever-widening circle, as illustrated in Exhibit 9-1. At the center is a nucleus of pilot publications. Each successively larger ring would include reruns in all profitable pilot publications plus new test books. In the same way, you can expand from campaign to campaign to cover wider levels of the various media categories until you have reached the widest possible universe.

Bind-In Cards

The reason for the success of the insert card is self-evident. Pick up a magazine, thumb through its pages, and see for yourself how effectively the bound-in-cards flag down the reader. Each time someone picks up the

Exhibit 9-1. Circle Approach to Media Selection

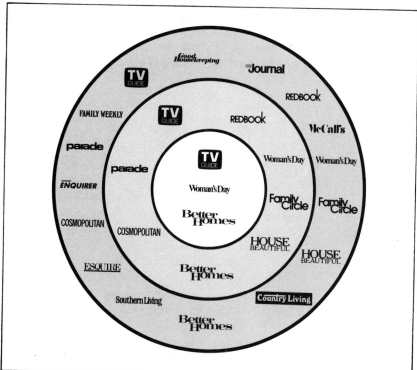

publication, there is the insert card pointing to your message. Another reason is the ease with which the reader can respond. The business reply card eliminates the trouble of addressing an envelope, providing a stamp, and so on.

Before the development of the insert card, the third and fourth covers of a magazine were the prime mail order positions and were sold at a premium. The bind-in insert card has created a world in which three, four, five, or more direct response advertisers can all have the position impact once reserved for the cover advertisers alone.

When you go to purchase space for a page and an accompanying insert card, you must face the fact that the best things in life are not free. Insert card advertising costs more. You must pay a space charge for the page and the card and sometimes a separate binding charge, and you must then add in the cost of printing the cards. How much you pay, of course, depends on the individual publication, the size of the card, and a number of other factors. There is no rule of thumb to follow in estimating the additional cost for an insert card. Space charges alone for a standard business reply card can be as little as 40 percent of the black-and-white page plus additional binding charges.

When the cost of the insert unit adds up to as much as four times the cost of an ordinary black-and-white page, you will have to receive four times the response to justify the added expense.

For most direct response advertisers, the response is likely to be six to eight times as great when pulling for an order and as much as six to eight times as great in pulling for inquiries. As a result, you can expect to cut your cost per response by 50 percent or more with an insert card as opposed to an ordinary on-page coupon ad.

Bingo Cards

While insert cards have a dramatic effect upon response, so do bingo cards. Bingo cards, often referred to as "information cards," are a unique device developed by magazine publishers, both consumer and business, to make it easy for the reader to request more information. "Bingo card" is really a generic term for any form—a reply card or printed form on a magazine page—on which the publisher prints designated numbers for specified literature. The reader simply circles the number designated for the literature desired. (See Exhibit 9-2.)

Typically an advertiser placing a specified unit of space in a magazine is entitled to a bingo card in the back of the publication. Ads reference these bingo cards with statements such as, "For futher information circle Item No. 146." The cards are sent directly to the publisher who, in turn, sends compiled lists of inquiries to participating advertisers. The respective advertisers then send fulfillment literature to all who have inquired.

A neat system, to be sure, but a caveat is in order. "We get tons of requests for literature from bingo cards, but they're not worth a damn," is a frequent advertiser complaint.

On the other hand, "Bingo cards can be very productive," states Adolph Auerbacher, who has been publisher of twenty-two special interest publications, for *Better Homes & Gardens*. Auerbacher points to two prime reasons for poor sales conversions: (1) failure of advertisers to respond to inquiries quickly, and (2) failure of advertisers to qualify prospects properly. Pointing to a survey by *Better Homes & Gardens* among 203 companies to whom they responded, Auerbacher reports the following response times. During the first week 13 percent sent literature. At the end of the first month they had heard from 62 percent. Thirty-eight percent of the companies had not responded a month after the first response was received. And 10 percent were never heard from. (For maximum effectiveness all advertisers should have responded within two weeks.)

Exhibit 9-2. Bingo Card for *Better Homes & Gardens*

Information

WORTH WRITING FOR

Better Homes and Gardens®
REMODELING IDEAS,
Summer 1987 Dept. SURI7
P.O. BOX 2611
CLINTON, IA 52732

Issue 66

TO ENSURE PROMPT HANDLING OF YOUR ORDER FOLLOW THESE INSTRUCTIONS:

- Circle your choice
- Enclose cash, check, money order for cost of booklets plus $1.00 service charge (no stamps/foreign)

- Send coupon and remittance to address above
- ALLOW 4-6 WEEKS FOR DELIVERY
- Coupon expires July 19, 1988

FREE LITERATURE

Circle numbers below corresponding to items in this issue.
Please include $1.00 for handling charge

5.	214.	323.	400.	406.	1321.	1810.
9.	300.	324.	401.	602.	1602.	4056.
55.	301.	330.	402.	613.	1664.	
59.	303.	344.	403.	919.	1666.	
71.	322.	376.	405.	1205.	1668.	

PRICED LITERATURE

Numbers below refer to items on which there is a charge.
Please include proper remittance.

25 .... 35¢	73 .... 50¢	332 .... 50¢	762 .... $2.00	1256 .. $10.00	1305 .... $2.95	1679 .... $2.00
27 .... 25¢	74 .... $3.00	407 .... $1.25	802 .. $14.50	1271 .... $3.95	1306 .... $2.95	1808 .... $1.00
35 .... $3.00	75 .... $1.00	410 .... 25¢	821 .... $3.00	1272 .... $4.95	1307 .... $2.95	1816 .... 50¢
57 .... $2.00	94 .... $1.99	415 .... 15¢	827 .... $5.95	1273 .... $5.95	1335 .... $1.00	1824 .... $2.00
60 .... $1.00	95 .... $1.99	420 .... 75¢	828 .... $1.00	1274 .... $4.95	1359 .... $1.00	4011 .... $1.00
61 .... $1.00	150 .... 35¢	426 .... 50¢	844 ...... 25¢	1275 .... $3.95	1361 .. $12.00	4012 .... $1.00
62 .... $1.00	205 .... 25¢	430 .... 25¢	855 .... $1.99	1290 .... $9.75	1362 .. $12.00	4013 .... $1.00
63 .... 50¢	217 .... $1.00	437 .... $2.00	902 .. $14.50	1291 .... $8.75	1363 .. $12.00	4014 .... 25¢
67 .... 50¢	310 .... 25¢	438 .... $1.00	911 .... 25¢	1293 .... $8.75	1364 .. $12.00	
68 .... $1.00	316 .... 35¢	612 .... $1.00	1001 ...... 40¢	1294 .... $3.75	1365 .. $12.00	
69 .... 25¢	321 .... $1.00	614 .... $1.00	1005 ...... 40¢	1296 .. $28.00	1604 .... $2.00	
70 .... $1.00	327 .... $1.00	616 .... $1.00	1217 .... $5.00	1303 .... $2.95	1672 .... $2.00	
72 .... $1.00	329 .... 50¢	744 .... $1.00	1244 .... $5.00	1304 .... $2.95	1673 .... 25¢	

Name (please print) _____

Address _____

City _____

State_____ Zip Code _____

I AM ENCLOSING:

$_____for priced items

$___1.00___for handling

$_____total remittance

To the question of qualifying prospects properly for a better likelihood of sales conversion, Auerbacher gives some interesting theories and facts. To the age old question, "Should the advertiser charge for literature or send it free?" he makes this key point:

> If an air conditioner advertiser, for example, has a literature cost of $1, he has a natural tendency to want to get his dollar back. But he may lose sight of the fact that his real objective is to sell a $500 air conditioner.
>
> Even taking into account that those who pay $1 for the literature might be more qualified, the ratio of free requests to dollar payments may be so overwhelming that more air conditioners in total might be sold to consumers who requested free literature.

But often it is best to charge for literature as a qualifier. The "$64 question" is "how much?" Here Adolph Auerbacher provides some hard facts. Citing Table 9-3, he refers to three titles among their stable of special interest books with the details of response by amount charged for literature. Free literature requests had the greatest response in every case, as one would expect. But note the differences in response between varying amounts requested. For *Remodeling Ideas,* for example, a 10¢ request pulled 22 percent as many requests as free. But 25¢ pulled more requests than 10¢. And in the case of *Building Ideas,* a 50¢ request pulled as well as a 25¢ request. With the exception of *Decorating Ideas,* both a $1 and a $2 request got a very poor response, suggesting upper limits of resistance perhaps.

So, as Mr. Auerbacher points out, success in the use of bingo cards depends, to a major degree, upon rapid fulfillment of literature requests and qualifying prospects in the most cost-efficient way. Two additional factors must be taken into account: (1) the closer the literature offered ties to the special interest of the book, the better the response is likely to be; and (2) advertiser awareness is an important response factor (an Armstrong will most always outpull a Joe Blow).

Magazine Advertising Response Pattern: What Do These Early Results Mean?

There is a remarkable similarity from one insertion to another in the rate of response over time for most magazines. Monthly publications generally have a similar pattern for the rate of response from week to week. However, the pattern of response for publications in different categories can vary. For example, a mass circulation weekly magazine *(TV Guide* or *Parade)* will pull a higher percentage of the total response in the first few weeks than a shelter book (such as *House & Garden* or *Better Homes &*

Gardens). A shelter book has a slower response curve but keeps pulling for a long period of time because it is kept much longer and is not so short-lived as a mass circulation magazine.

Table 9-3. Tabulation of Literature Requests

Price	Median Response	Percentage of Free	*High	†Low	‡Ratio H/L
Better Homes & Gardens Remodeling Ideas, Spring '80					
Free	672		1171	192	6:1
10¢	148	22	373	113	3:1
25¢	213	32	408	51	8:1
50¢	130	19	540	51	10:1
$1	82	12	240	3	80:1
$2	19	3	129	2	65:1
Better Homes & Gardens Building Ideas, Spring '80					
Free	781		1501	252	6:1
10¢	108	14	199	60	3:1
25¢	298	38	430	109	4:1
50¢	297	38	722	97	7:1
$1	95	12	431	3	143:1
$2	31	4	164	3	55:1
Better Homes & Gardens Decorating Ideas, Spring '80					
Free	491		1420	21	67:1
10¢	62	13	72	49	1.5:1
25¢	193	39	400	68	6:1
50¢	138	28	646	35	18:1
$1	102	21	282	17	16:1
$2	79	16	123	19	6:1

"Information Worth Writing For" section arranged to show median, highest response, lowest response, and ratio between highest and lowest response.
**High means the highest number of requests for the literature of a given advertiser in a particular issue; †Low means the lowest number of requests; ‡Ratio H/L means the ratio of response of the best puller contrasted to the worst puller.*

Also, subscription circulation will pull faster than newsstand circulation. Subscribers usually receive their copies within a few days while newsstand sales are spread out over an entire month. Consequently the response pattern is spread out as well.

If you are running an ad calling for direct response from a monthly magazine, here is a general guide to the likely response flow:

After the first week	3-7%	After two months	.75-85%
After the second week	20-25%	After three months	.85-92%
After the third week	40-45%	After four months	.92-95%
After one month	50-55%		

From a weekly publication, such as *Time* or *TV Guide,* the curve is entirely different; 50 percent of your response usually comes in the first two weeks.

These expectations, of course, represent the average of many hundreds of response curves for different propositions. You may see variations up or down from the classic curve for any single insertion.

As a general rule for monthlies, you can expect to project the final results within 10 percent accuracy after the third week of counting responses. If you are new to the business, give yourself the experience of entering daily result counts by hand for dozens of ads. Before long you will develop an instinct for projecting how an ad for your particular proposition is doing within the first ten days of measured response.

Timing and Frequency: When Should You Run? How Often Should You Go Back?

Once you determine where you want to run, timing and frequency are the two crucial factors in putting together an effective print schedule.

Of course, there are some propositions that have a time of the year when they do best, for example, novelty items are likely to be purchased in October and November or even as early as late September for Christmas gifts. But for the nonseasonal items, you can look forward to two major print advertising seasons for direct response.

The first and by far the most productive for most propositions is the winter season, which begins with the January issue and runs through the February and March issues. The second season begins with the August issue and runs through the November issue.

The best winter months for most people are January and February. The best fall months are October and November. For schools and book continuity propositions, September frequently does as well or better.

If you have a nonseasonal item and you want to do your initial test at the best possible time, use a February issue with a January sale date or a January issue with a late December or early January sale date of whatever publication makes the most sense for your proposition.

How much of a factor is the particular month in which an ad appears? It could make a difference of 40 percent or even more. Here is an example of what the direct response advertiser may expect to experience during the year if the cost per response (CPR) in February were $2; January $2.05;

February, $2; March, $2.20; April, $2.50; May, $2.60; June, $2.80; July, $2.60; August, $2.40; September, $2.60; October, $2.20; November, $2.20; December, $2.40.

These hypothetical relative costs are based on the assumption that the insertion is run one time in any one of the twelve issues of a monthly publication. But, of course, if you are successful, you will want to run your copy more than once. So now we are faced with the other crucial question: What will various rates of frequency do to your response? Should you run once a year? Twice? Three times? Or every other month?

The frequency factor is more difficult to formulate than the timing factor. Optimum frequency cannot be generalized for print media advertising. Some propositions can be run month after month in a publication and show very little difference in cost per response. At one time, Doubleday & Company had worked out optimum frequency curves for some of its book club ads that required a twenty-four-month hiatus between insertions.

How, then, do you go about determining ideal frequency of insertions? Try this procedure. The first time your copy appears in a publication, run it at the most likely time of the year for your special appeal. If you have a non-seasonal proposition, use January or February issues.

If the cost per response is in an acceptable range or up to 20 percent better than expected, wait six months and follow with a second insertion. If that insertion produces results within an acceptable range, you probably are a twice-a-year advertiser.

If the first insertion pulls well over 20 percent better than the planned order margin, turn around and repeat within a three or four-month period.

If the response to the test insertion in January or February was marginal, it usually makes sense to wait a full year before returning for another try in that publication.

The best gauge of how quickly you can run the next insertion aimed at the same magazine audience is the strength of the response from the last insertion. What you are reading in the results is a measurement of the saturation factor as it relates to that portion of the circulation that is interested in your selling message.

Of course, like all the other factors that affect response, frequency does not operate in a vacuum. The offer of a particularly advantageous position in a particular month or a breakthrough to better results with improved copy can lead you to set aside whatever carefully worked out frequency you had adopted earlier.

Determining Proper Ad Size: How Much Is Too Much?

A crucial factor in obtaining an acceptable cost per response is the size of the advertising unit you select. Ordinarily, the bigger the ad the better job the creative people can do in presenting the selling message. But there is one catch. Advertising space costs money. And the more you spend, the greater the response you need to get your money back.

What you want to find is the most efficient size for your particular proposition and for the copy approach you have chosen. Just as with frequency, there is no simple rule of thumb here.

Generally speaking, advertising for leads or prospects or to gain inquiries requires less advertising space than copy that is pulling for orders. Many companies seeking inquiries or running a lead item to get names for catalog followup make use of advertising units of less than one column. Only a handful of companies looking for prospects can make effective use of full-page space. Going one step further and using a page and insert card to pull for leads runs the risk of being too effective. This unit can bring in inquiries at very low cost, but there is always the danger that the quality will be very poor. Find out at your own peril.

For example, if you use a black-and-white page with a tear-off coupon that generates leads at $5 each and that convert at a 10 percent rate, then your advertising cost per sale is $50. Take the same insertion and place it as a page and insert card, and the cost per response may be as low as $3. If the conversion rate held up at 10 percent, the advertising cost per sale would be only $30. But it is more likely that the advertiser would experience a sharp conversion rate drop to perhaps 5 percent, with a resultant $60 cost per sale plus the cost of processing the additional leads.

When a direct sale or a future commitment to buy is sought, the dynamics usually are different from those when inquiries are sought. As a general rule, the higher the unit of sale or dollar volume commitment, the larger the unit of space that can be afforded, right up to the double page spread with insert card. However, there are a number of additional factors to be considered as well:

1. The nature of the product presentation may inherently require a particular space unit. For example, in record club and book club advertising, experience has shown that a maximum number of books and records should be displayed for best results. As a consequence, many of these clubs run a two-page spread as their standard ad unit. And in a small-size publication such as *TV Guide,* they may take six or even eight pages to display the proper number of books and records.

2. Some propositions, such as Time-Life Books in the continuity bookselling field, require four-color advertising in order to present the beautiful color illustrations that are an important feature of the product being sold.

3. Usually full-page ads appear at the front of a publication and small-space ads at the back. So going to a full-page unit is often related to the benefits you can expect from a premium, front-of-book position.

4. If you are successful with a single-page ad with coupon, test using an insert card before you try to add a second page. If the page and insert card work for you, give the spread and card a try.

5. Most mail order advertising falls into one of three size categories: (a) the spectacular unit—anything from the page and standard card insert to the four-page preprinted insert; (b) the single full-page unit; and (c) the small-space unit less than one column in size.

The awkward sizes in pulling for an order appear to be the one-column and two-column units. These inserts seldom work better than their big-brother pages or little-sister 56-line, 42-line, and 21-line units, although a "square third" (2 columns by 70 lines) can be a very efficient space unit.

Always remember, space costs money. The objective is to take the minimum amount of space you need to express your proposition effectively and to return a profit.

Start by having the creative director at your advertising agency express the proposition in the amount of space needed to convey a powerful selling message. Once you have established the cost per response for this basic unit, you can experiment with other size units.

If you have two publications on your schedule that perform about equally well for the basic unit, try testing the same ad approach expressed in a smaller or larger space size in one of those two publications while running the basic control unit in the same month in the other publication.

Four-Color, Two-Color, Black-and-White: How Colorful Should Your Advertising Be?

All magazines charge extra for adding color to your advertising. And remember there will be additional production expense if you go this route.

Usually the cost of adding a second color to a black-and-white page does not return the added costs charged by the publication for the space and the expense of producing the ad. If the copy is right, the words will do their job without getting an appreciable lift from having headlines set in red or blue or green. An exception might be the use of a second color tint as background to provide special impact to your page.

It is with the use of four-color advertising that the direct response advertiser has an opportunity to profit on an investment in color.

A number of publications (for example, *Esquire, Time, Woman's Day, Ladies' Home Journal*) allow you to run a split of four-color versus black-and-white, in an alternating copy A/B perfect split-run. Test results indicate an increase of anywhere from 30 percent to almost 60 percent where there is appropriate and dramatic utilization of the four-color process.

Given a striking piece of artwork related to the proposition or an inherently colorful product feature to present, you can expect an increase in response when you use four-color advertising. Since you will need more than a 20 percent increase in most publications to make the use of color profitable, it is wise to pretest the value of this factor before scheduling it across the board. Some products such as insurance simply do not require color.

Now just what can you expect the cost of four-color advertising to be? Table 9-4 shows four-color charges from a representative group of consumer publications.

Table 9-4. Four-Color Rate Examples

Publication	Black-and-White Page Rate	Four-Color Page Rate	Percentage Increase for Four-Color
Woman's Day	$53,465	$ 62,450	16.8%
Family Circle	49,240*	55,990*	13.7
Ladies' Home Journal	52,300	60,600	15.9
Seventeen	21,100	26,300	24.6
Redbook	43,875	58,020	32.2
McCall's	51,400	63,300	23.1
Good Housekeeping	53,572*	67,220*	25.4
Glamour	29,540	41,630	40.9
Newsweek	54,095	86,500	59.9
Time	77,010	120,130	56.0
Sports Illustrated	57,350	89,470	56.0
Popular Mechanics	18,125*	30,510*	68.3
Home Mechanix	13,470*	20,215*	50.1
Reader's Digest	91,350	109,830	20.2
Esquire	12,733	19,040*	49.5

*Mail order rates.

If you plan to use four-color advertising, the increase in publication space cost is only one of the cost factors to be weighed. The cost of the original four-color engravings for a 7″ × 10″ page runs from $3,000 to $5,000 depending on the copy and artwork being used. This compares with a black-and-white engraving cost that could be from $200 to $300. In addition, any dye transfers or other four-color preparatory work will probably increase mechanical preparation costs by 50 percent or more over a comparable black-and-white insertion.

The Position Factor Can Mean as Much as What You Say

Position in life may not be everything, but in direct response it often means the difference between paying out or sudden death. By "position" we mean where you advertisement appears in the publication. There are two rules governing the position factor. First, the closer to the front of the book an ad is placed, the better the response will be. Second, the more visible the position, the better the response will be.

The first rule defies rational analysis. Yet it is as certain as the sun's rising in the morning. Many magazine publishers have offered elaborate research studies demonstrating to the general advertiser than an ad in the editorial matter far back in a publication gets better readership than an ad placed within the first few pages of the publication. This may well be true for the general or institutional advertiser, but it is not true for the direct response advertiser.

Whatever the explanation may be, the fact remains that decades of measured direct response advertising tell the same story over and over again. A position in the first seven pages of the magazine produces a dramatically better response (all other factors being the same) than if the same insertion appears farther back in the same issue.

How much better? There are as many answers to this question as there are old pros in the business. However, here is about what you might expect the relative response to be from various page positions as measured against the first right-hand page arbitrarily rated at a pull of 100.

First right-hand page 100	Back of book (following main)
Second right-hand page 95	body of editorial matter) 50
Third right-hand page 90	Back cover 100
Fourth right-hand page 85	Inside third cover 90
Back of front of the book	Page facing third cover 85
(preceding editorial matter) .. 70	

The second rule is more easily explained. An ad must be seen before it can be read or acted on. Right-hand pages pull better than left-hand pages, frequently by as much as 15 percent. Insert cards open the magazine to the advertiser's message and thereby create their own "cover" position. Of course, the insert card introduces the additional factor of providing a postage-free response vehicle as well. But the response from insert cards, too, is subject to the influence of how far back in the magazine the insertion appears. Here is what you can expect in most publications (assigning a 100 rating to the first card):

First insert card position 100
Second insert card position 95
Third insert card position 85
Fourth insert card position 75*
Fifth insert card position 70*

If position follows main editorial matter.

The pull of position is as inexorable as the pull of gravity. Well, almost, that is. There are a few exceptions. In the fashion and the mechanics magazines, card positioning seems to make little or no difference. Another exception may involve the placement of an ad opposite a related column or feature article in a publication (for example, a *Home Handyman's Encyclopedia* ad opposite the Home Handyman column). Another exception may involve placement of your ad in a high-readership shopping section at the back of a magazine.

How to Buy Space

Because mail order advertising is always subject to bottom-line analysis, the price you pay for space can mean the difference between profit and loss. Mrs. Florence Peloquin, head of Florence Peloquin Associates, New York City, provides some basic questions the advertiser should ask the publisher or his or her agency before placing space.

1. Is there a special mail order rate? Mail order rates are usually 10 to 30 percent lower than general rates.

2. Is there a special mail order section, a shopping section where mail order ads are grouped? (Usually in the back of the book.)

3. Does the book have remnant space available at substantial discounts? Many publishers offer discounts of up to 50 percent off the regular rate.

4. Is there an insertion frequency discount, or dollar volume discount? Is frequency construed as the number of insertions in a time period or consecutive issues? Many publishers credit more than one insertion in an issue toward frequency.

5. Do corporate discounts apply to mail order? Sometimes the corporate discount is better than the mail order discount.

6. Do you have seasonal discounts? Some publishers have low-volume advertising months during which they offer substantial discounts.

7. Do you offer spread discounts when running two pages or more in one issue? The discount can run up to 60 percent on the second page.

8. Do you have a publisher's rate? Is this in addition to or in lieu of the mail order rate? It can be additive.

9. Will you accept a per-inquiry (P.I.) deal? Under P.I. deals the advertiser pays the publisher an amount for each inquiry or order, or a minimum flat amount for the space, plus so much per inquiry or order.

10. Do you accept "umbrella contracts"? Some media buying services and agencies own banks or reserves of space with given publications and can offer discounts even for one-time ads.

11. Do you barter for space? Barter usually involves a combination of cash and merchandise.

When bought properly, tested properly, and used properly, magazine advertising represents a vast universe of sales and profit potential for the direct response advertiser.

Self-Quiz

1. Name five magazines that provide a conducive atmosphere for direct response advertisers.

   a. _____

   b. _____

   c. _____

   d. _____

   e. _____

2. Name the four major advantages of using regional editions of magazines.

   a. _____

   b. _____

   c. _____

   d. _____

3. What are the two negative factors involved in buying regional space?

   a. _____

   b. _____

4. Name five basic consumer magazine categories.

   a. _____

   b. _____

   c. _____

   d. _____

   e. _____

5. Give the definition of a pilot publication.

_____

_____

_____

6. What is the theory of an expanded media-buying program based on an ever-widening circle?

_____

_____

_____

_____

7. What is the principal advantage of an insert card in a magazine?

_____

_____

_____

8. When direct response advertisers use insert cards, the response is likely to be: _____ to _____ times as great when pulling for an order and as much as _____ to _____ times as great in pulling for inquiries.

9. What are the two prime reasons for poor sales conversions to "bingo cards"?

a. _____

b. _____

10. As a general rule, when a direct response advertiser uses a monthly magazine, he or she can usually expect to have about 50 percent of his or her total response after _____ weeks.

11. For weekly publications 50 percent of total response can be expected after _____ weeks.

12. From a timing standpoint, which is the most productive season for most direct response propositions?

_____

_____

13. Which is the second most productive season?

_____

14. When is the best possible time to test a nonseasonal item?

_____

_____

15. How much is the cost per response (CPR) likely to vary between the best pulling month and the poorest pulling month? _____

_____ percent

16. Provide guidelines for frequency factors in magazine advertising.

a. If the cost per response is in an acceptable range or up to 20 percent better than expected, wait _____ months and follow up with a second insertion in the second half of the year.

b. If the first insertion pulls well over 20 percent better than allowed order margin, turn around and repeat within a _____ or _____ month period.

c. If response to the test insertion in January or February was marginal, it usually makes sense to wait _____ before returning for another try in that publication.

17. Generally speaking, which requires more space for effective direct response advertising?

_____ Pulling inquiries

_____ Pulling orders

18. What is the prime advantage of a full-page ad vs. a small ad in a magazine?

    _____

    _____

19. If a single-page ad with coupon is successful, what is the next logical test?

    _____

    _____

    _____

    _____

20. What are the three size categories for most mail order advertising?

    a. _____

    b. _____

    c. _____

21. When four-color versus black-and-white is tested, results indicate an increase of anywhere from _____ percent to almost _____ percent where there is appropriate and dramatic utilization of the four-color process.

22. What are the two rules governing the "position" factor for the direct response advertiser?

    a. _____

    b. _____

23. Right-hand pages pull better than left-hand pages by as much as _____ percent.

24. If a 100 rating is assigned to a first insert card position in a publication having five insert card positions, what would the fifth insert card rating be?

    _____

25. Mail order rates are usually _____ percent to _____ percent lower than general rates.

Pilot Project

You are the advertising manager for a publisher of children's books. It is your assignment to test market a new continuity series of 10 books written for age levels 6 to 10. Each book in the series will sell for $4.95. Outline a plan for test marketing in magazines.

1. What pilot publications would you schedule for testing?

2. Will you use any regional editions?

3. Do a circle approach to media selection indicating what additional publications you will expand to if the pilot publications prove successful.

4. Prepare a timing schedule, indicating when your pilot ads will break and when your expanded media-buying program will take place.

5. What ad size will you use and will the ad be black-and-white, two color, or four color?

CHAPTER TEN

Newspapers

For sheer circulation in print, there is nothing to compare with the daily and Sunday newspapers. There were 1,632 daily newspapers in the United States with an average daily circulation of 63 million as of May 1, 1987. Thus the circulation available through newspapers offers an exciting opportunity for direct response advertisers. It is significant that many direct response advertisers spend all or a major portion of their budgets in newspapers.

Newspapers are unique in that they can serve as a vehicle for carrying direct response advertising formats foreign to their regular news pages. Remarkable results have been achieved by using these special formats.

Newspaper Preprints

Use of preprints by direct response advertisers is a phenomenon of this decade. The Newspaper Advertising Bureau of New York estimates that 51.5 billion preprints circulated in 1986. Preprints became a viable method for direct marketers in 1965. In the first five months of that year there was only one preprint mail order advertiser (Time-Life Books) in million-circulation newspapers.

Columbia Record Club followed Time-Life Books in 1965. Wunderman, Ricotta & Kline, the club's agency, first tested preprints in newspapers in six markets (*Akron Beacon, Dallas Times Herald, Des Moines Register, Minneapolis Tribune, Peoria Journal Star*, and *Seattle Times*). Hundreds of millions of preprints have since been run in newspapers by Columbia Record Club. There are two obvious advantages to preprints such as those used by Columbia. First, they provide abundant space for the detailed listing of items available. Second, a perforated postpaid return card may be imprinted, which, because of the weight of the stock used, closely resembles an ordinary post card and can be easily mailed by the respondent.

The dramatic impact of preprints in a newspaper must be measured against the greatly increased cost. Comparing a four-page preprint with a fourth cover in a syndicated Sunday supplement, one finds the preprint costs almost four times as much. The tremendous volume of preprints found in the Sunday newspaper is good evidence that the increased cost often is more than warranted.

The Newspaper Advertising Bureau furnishes the following estimated space costs for inserts in the top 100 markets based on a tabloid size of 10¾″ × 12¾″: Two pages plus flap, $40.60 per M; four pages, $40.60 per M; eight pages, $46.43 per M; twelve pages, $52.32 per M; sixteen pages, $57.01 per M; twenty-four pages, $65.40 per M.

It should be noted that these estimated costs in the 100 top markets are for *space only.* Printing costs of the inserts must be added. A breakdown of costs for space, depending on the sizes of preprint, for representative newspapers is given in Table 10-1. Careful note should be taken of the fact that the CPM tends to be lower for large metro papers. Thus, if a direct marketer has a proposition that appeals only to small towns, the chances for successful use of preprints are greatly diminished.

Acceptable Size

Size depends on the newspaper's policy and equipment, but, generally speaking, minimum size is 5½″ × 8⅛″. Maximum size is 10¾″ × 14½″. These minimum and maximum sizes are folded sizes—unfolded size could be larger. For example, a standard format size of 21½″ × 14½″ printed on heavy stock could fold in half to 10¾″ × 14½″.

Sunday versus Weekday Inserts

Figures for 1986 show that weekday preprints constitute about 41.7 percent of total preprint circulation in the U.S.

Syndicated Newspaper Supplements

Imagine placing three space insertion orders and buying newspaper circulation of 65 millions plus! This is indeed possible if you place insertion orders in the three major syndicated newspaper supplements. Branham Newspapers, Inc., major newspaper representative, presents the figures in Table 10-2.

Table 10-1. National Estimated Tabloid (10¾" × 13") Insert Costs
for Sunday Newspapers Published within PMSA

PMSA (Top)	Number of Newspapers	Total Circulation (000)	2 Pages	4 Pages	8 Pages	12 Pages	16 Pages	24 Pages
10	46	15,496.60	$38.97	$39.58	$45.95	$51.78	$56.25	$63.11
25	107	23,895.60	39.01	39.67	45.97	51.98	56.51	64.66
50	167	33,476.30	38.51	40.02	46.11	52.09	56.69	64.93
75	221	39,219.70	39.06	40.56	46.31	52.23	56.86	65.30
100	259	42,570.50	39.07	40.57	46.41	52.30	56.98	65.36
150	327	47,535.40	39.10	40.73	46.75	52.49	57.30	65.84
200	387	50,650.80	39.15	40.89	47.03	52.68	57.44	65.91
250	431	52,395.70	39.23	41.13	47.29	52.97	57.63	66.06
315	493	54,384.00	39.45	41.42	47.55	53.20	57.81	66.17

Source: Newspaper Advertising Bureau, Inc., 1987.

Distribution of the three syndicated supplements breaks down about this way. Sunday Mag/Net is distributed by about 43 member newspapers. Those carrying Sunday Mag/Net supplements offer a choice of thirty-nine top metro areas for advertising.

USA Weekend is generally carried by the newspapers with smaller circulations, many of which publish within the top metro areas but basically "C" and "D" counties. The majority of the newspapers distributing *USA Weekend* are outside the top 150 metro areas.

Parade is included in some of the Sunday Mag/Net newspapers, but generally it is more evenly distributed among the top 100 metro areas. Obvious advantages of syndicated supplements are their relatively low cost per thousand circulation and the possibility of reaching top metro areas as well as smaller cities, depending on the supplement used.

One thing going for the syndicated supplements is their mail order atmosphere. *Parade,* for instance, points out that 60 percent of its advertising carries some kind of coupon that enables the advertiser to get a measurement of results.

Among the syndicated supplements, *Parade* and *USA Weekend* offer a mail order booklet inserted on a regular basis. This booklet, commonly called a Dutch Door, usually runs twelve pages. Its page size is one half that of the supplement. Some issues are taken over entirely by one advertiser. Other issues contain a variety of small mail order ads.

It is obvious that a direct marketer who has no previously placed space in one of the syndicated supplements would not go full run without testing. *Parade,* for example, offers remnant space to mail order advertisers at 20 percent discount. Remnant space is advertising space left over when package goods advertisers buy only in those markets where they have distribution. Second to testing in remnant space is testing in regions.

With about 717 Sunday and weekend magazines, both syndicated and locally edited, a direct response advertiser has an incredible amount of distribution available at low cost. (See Exhibit 10-1.)

Comics as a Direct Marketing Medium

Perhaps the biggest sleeper as a medium for direct marketers is the comic section of weekend newspapers. Comics are not glamorous, nor are they prestigious. But their total circulation, readership, and demographics constitute an exciting universe for the direct response advertiser. Here are some of the fascinating facts and figures about comics as an advertising medium.

Each week, usually on Sunday, 50.3 million color comics are distributed through 450 different newspapers. These comics literally saturate the major and secondary markets, providing 61 percent or better coverage in 278 of the 300 strategic metropolitan markets of the country. There are two major comic groups—Puck and Metro.

The Puck Group is available through two networks: the National Network and the American Network. The National Network, made up of newspapers that almost all have circulations of over 100,000, is distributed through sixty-five papers in sixty-five cities. The American Network, made up of newspapers with circulations of under 100,000, is distributed in ninety-three papers in ninety-two cities. Also available through Puck are four geographically concentrated editions: the Pacific Group, made up of eleven West Coast newspapers; the California/Nevada/Washington group, with eleven papers; the Texas Group of eleven papers; and the Ottaway newspapers with seven papers.

Metro Sunday comics are available on the basis of newspaper networks. There are two networks: a basic network of eighty-five newspapers, and a selective network of nineteen newspapers. Total circulation is 26,684,000 for the two networks, comprising 104 newspapers. Standard Rate and Data Service also lists other smaller comic groups, regionally oriented. The size of these groups ranges from the Texas Sunday Comic Section, with a circulation of 727,099, to the Wyoming Color Comic Group, with a circulation of 39,815. Combined, Metro and Puck have a total circulation of 45,406,394. Metro's cost per thousand for a four-color page is $13.14; Puck's is $18.33.

The demographic characteristics of comics readers are quite a surprise to most advertisers, who seem to have ill-conceived ideas about this type of reader. The median age of the adult comics reader is 39 years, slightly younger than the U.S. median age of 40.2 years.

Table 10-2. Summary of Circulation and Rates for Sunday Newspaper Supplements

Publication	Circulation	Four Color		Black-and-White	
		Page	CPM	Page	CPM
Sunday Mag/Net	20,100,000	$217,490	$10.82	$177,291	$8.82
Parade	31,787,000	311,700	9.81	252,500	7.94
USA Weekend	13,744,916	127,300	9.26	110,300	8.02
Total	65,631,916	$656,490	$10.00	$540,091	$8.23

Source: Sunday Magazine Network, Parade, USA Weekend, 1987.

One of the major misconceptions about comics readership is that the higher one's education, the less likely one is to read the comic pages. Statistics from Simmons Total Audience Study, as illustrated in Table 10-3, dispute this.

Finally, there is the misconception that the higher one's income, the less likely one is to read comics. Again, the figures refute this.

Among direct response advertisers, the largest users of comic-page advertising in the past have been photo finishers. Huge photo finishing businesses have been started from scratch using comics as a prime advertising medium. The availability of the ad-and-envelope technique in conjunction with comic-page advertising serves a genuine need of photo finishers because they are able to provide an envelope in which the prospect can return completed film rolls. The standard charge for a free-standing envelope or for affixing a card or envelope to the ad averages about $15 per thousand, plus the cost of printing the response vehicle. With ad-and-envelope, the direct response advertiser provides the same impetus to response with a reply card or reply envelope.

Following the photo finishers with comic-page advertising have been insurance companies and land developers. Opportunities obviously are there for a host of other direct response advertisers seeking mass circulation at low cost. Comic-page advertising traditionally limits advertising to one advertiser per page. Thus full-page advertising is not essential to gain a dominant position. Comics, not unlike syndicated supplements, should be tested before one goes full run. You can test individual papers among the Metro Group, the Puck Group, and the independent groups.

ROP Advertising

We have been exploring formats carried by newspapers—preprints, syndicated supplements, and comics. Not to be overlooked, of course, is run-of-paper (ROP) advertising. Generally, direct response advertisers have failed to get the results with ROP advertising that they have obtained from newspaper preprints and syndicated newspaper supplements. One obvious reason is that four-color advertising is not generally available for ROP. Another is that ROP ads don't drop out for individual attention. But many successes can be cited for small-space ROP advertising, small-space ads that have run frequently year after year in hundreds of newspapers. When small-space ads are run over a long period of time with high frequency, the number of reader impressions multiplies rapidly in proportion to the cost.

Effect of Local News on Results

A major difference between newspaper advertising and all other print media is that the newspaper reader is more likely to be influenced by local news events. All newspaper advertising appears within the atmosphere of the local news for a given day. A major scandal in local politics or a catastrophe in a local area such as a tornado can have a devastating effect on the advertising appearing in a given issue. Magazines, on the other hand, do not

Exhibit 10-1. First Page of a Six-Page Newspaper Insert for Columbia House

Exhibit 10-2. Comic-Page Advertising

Calls attention to an envelope inserted loose in newspaper.

Table 10-3. Demographic Characteristics of Readers of
Comics Compared with U.S. Population

Characteristics	Comics Readers	U.S. Population
Age		
18-24	20.5%	18.4%
25-34	21.7	22.1
35-49	23.9	23.3
50-64	20.9	21.5
65 and above	13.0	14.7
	100.0%	100.0%
Education		
Graduated from college/attended college	39.1%	33.3%
Graduated from high school	40.3	39.5
Did not graduate from high school	20.6	27.2
	100.0%	100.0%
Income		
$50,000 and above	22.6%	18.5%
$40,000-49,999	15.3	13.6
$35,000-39,999	9.3	8.4
$30,000-34,999	10.1	9.6
$25,000-29,999	9.2	9.7
$20,000-24,999	9.3	9.9
$10,000-19,999	16.3	18.7
$ 9,999 and under	7.9	11.6
	100.0%	100.0%
Median Income	$31,837	$22,415

tie in closely with local events. Magazines are normally put aside to read during hours not taken up by involvement in local events. Because local events have a strong effect on response, positively or negatively, markets with similar demographics don't always respond in the same manner. All newspaper advertising tends to be *local,* even though a schedule may be national.

Developing a Newspaper Test Program

When a direct response advertiser first considers testing newspapers as a medium, he or she has a myriad of decisions to make. Should he or she go ROP, the newspaper preprint route, local Sunday supplements, syndicated supplements, TV program supplements, comics? What papers should he or she test? Putting ad size and position aside for the moment, we have two initial considerations: the importance of advertising in a mail order climate and the demographics of markets selected as they relate to the product or service you are offering.

If you had one simple product, say a stamp dispenser, for instance, and a tiny budget, you might place one small ad in one publication. You could run the ad in the mail order section of the *New York Times Sunday Magazine.* Generally if you don't make it there, you won't make it anywhere. Running such an ad would give a "feel." If it works, it would be logical to test similar mail order sections in major cities such as Chicago, Detroit, and Los Angeles. (See Exhibit 10-3.)

Simple items, which are suited to small-space advertising in mail order sections, greatly simplify the testing procedure. But, more often than not, multicity testing in larger space is required.

Prime direct response test markets in the United States include Atlanta, Buffalo, Cleveland, Dallas-Fort Worth, Denver, Des Moines, Indianapolis, Omaha, and Peoria. In the selection of test markets, you should analyze the newspaper to make certain it has advertising reach and coverage and offers demographics that are suitable to your product. If there are two newspapers in a market, it is worthwhile to evaluate both of them. Let us say that because of budget limitations advertising can be placed in only a limited number of markets. Such criteria as circulation, household penetration, women and men readers, and advertising lineage relating to the product to be advertised should be measured.

A number of sources will provide the data necessary for evaluation. You would begin with SRDS's *Newspaper Rates and Data* for general cost and circulation information. *SRDS Circulation Analysis* would provide information about metro household penetration. *Simmons Total Audience Study* could then be used to isolate men or women readers of a particular age group. Other criteria to be measured include retail lineage in various classifications and spendable income by metro area.

Demographics are a major consideration market by market whether you are going ROP, preprints, local supplements, syndicated supplements, or TV program supplements. Once an advertiser develops a test program that closely reflects the demographics for his or her product or service, expansion to like markets makes possible the rapid acceleration of a full-blown program. But selecting newspapers is tedious, because there are hundreds from which to choose as compared with a relative handful of magazines whose demographics can be more closely related to the proposition. As an example, a test newspaper schedule could be placed in the following markets: Atlanta, preprint; Cleveland, Metro comics; Dallas-Fort Worth, ROP; Denver, preprint; Des Moines, ROP; Indianapolis, preprint; Omaha, Metro comics; and Peoria, *Parade* remnant. If there is more than one newspaper in a test market, the paper with the most promising demographics should be selected.

Exhibit 10-3. Mail Order Shopping Guide from the *Chicago Tribune Sunday Magazine*

A test schedule like this would be ambitious in terms of total dollars, but it would have the advantage of simultaneously testing markets and formats. Once a reading has been obtained from the markets and formats, the advertiser can rapidly expand to other markets and will have the advantage of using the most productive formats.

Advertising Seasons

As in direct mail and magazine direct response advertising, there are two major newspaper direct response advertising seasons. The fall mail order season begins roughly with August and runs through November. (A notable exception is a July insertion which is often useful especially when using a pretested piece.) The winter season begins with January and runs through March.

Exceptions to the two major direct response seasons occur in the sale of seasonal merchandise. Christmas items are usually promoted from September through the first week of December. A nursery, on the other hand, will start promoting in late December and early January, then again in the early fall. Many nurseries follow the practice of promoting by geographical regions, starting earlier in the south and working up to later promotion in the north.

Timing of Newspaper Insertions

Beyond the seasonal factor of direct response advertising in newspapers, timing is important as it relates to days of the week. According to the *E&P Yearbook, Bureau of Advertising Circulation Analysis,* the number of copies of a newspaper sold per day is remarkably constant month after month—despite such events as summer vacations and Christmas holidays. And people buy the newspaper to read not only the editorial matter but also the ads. According to an *Audits & Surveys Study,* the percentage of people opening an average ad page any weekday, Monday through Friday, varies less than 3 percent, with Tuesday ranking the highest at 88 percent.

There is no question that the local newspaper is an integral part of practically everyone's daily life. While magazines may be set aside for reading at a convenient time, newspapers are read the day they are delivered or purchased or are not read at all. Monday through Thursday are favorite choices of many direct response advertisers for their ROP advertising. Many direct response advertisers judiciously avoid the weekday issue containing grocery advertising.

As we have seen, more and more newspapers are accepting preprints for weekday insertions. This can be a major advantage considering the larger number of preprints appearing in most big Sunday newspapers.

Newspaper Response Patterns

Newspapers have the shortest time lapse from closing date to appearance date of all print media. In most cases, ads can appear in the newspaper within seventy-two hours after placement. Depending on the format used, up to 90 percent or more of responses will be reached for a typical direct response newspaper ad within these time frames: ROP, after the second week; preprints, after the third week; syndicated newspaper supplements, after the third week; and comics, after the second week.

Naturally, response patterns vary according to the proposition. Thus, it is important for each advertiser to develop his own response pattern. But the nature of newspaper advertising permits a quick turn-around. *Dow Theory Forecasts,* for instance, has run ads in hundreds of newspapers. Dow is able to project results, giving you the option of deciding whether to repeat an ad, within a week after the first orders are received.

Determining Proper Ad Size

In direct response newspaper advertising, as in retail or national newspaper ads, few people dispute the claim that the larger advertisement generally will get more attention than a smaller one. But whether the full-page ad gets twice the attention of the half-page ad or four times the attention of the quarter-page ad is debatable. It is cost per response that counts. Just as in magazine advertising, less space is usually indicated for inquiry advertising and more space is dictated for a direct order ad.

According to a study conducted by the Bureau of Advertising in 1971 relating to mail-back newspaper coupons, the size of the space seems to be a factor in reader response only to the extent that it is a factor in initial reader attention. In this study, 85 percent of newspaper inserts ran ads of 1,000 lines or more. Only half used fewer than 1,000 lines, with a minimum of 500 lines per ad.

A low-budget advertiser often must choose between a single full-page ad and several small ads over an extended time. The proper guide to follow in determining the initial size of ads is to base the size on the space required to tell the *complete story.*

Trying to sell membership in a record and tape club in a small space would be ludicrous. Experience shows that one must offer a wide selection of records in the ad to get memberships. The same is true for a book club. On the other hand, if you are selling a single item at a low price—say, a cigarette lighter for $4.95—the complete story can be told in a small space. Where small-space advertising can tell the whole story, consistency and repetition often prove to be keys to success.

Aside from the obvious requirement of using a full page or more for a proposition, constant testing of ad sizes will establish the proper size to produce the most efficient cost per inquiry or per order.

The Position Factor

Newspapers and magazines have many similarities in respect to the importance of position in direct response advertising. Research has demonstrated high readership of newspaper ads, whatever the position. However, direct response advertisers still prefer right-hand pages. Generally, such advertisers find that ads are more effective if they appear in the front of the newspaper than in the back. And placement of coupon ads in the gutter of any newspaper page is almost always avoided.

All newspapers are printed in sections. Special consideration should be given to the reading habits of men and women as they relate to specific sections of a newspaper. Three major sections of any given newspaper are sports, women's pages, and general news. Table 10-4 shows results of a study by *Million Market Newspapers* of 32,000 ads. What this study obviously shows is that any appeals to sports-minded men will get high readership on the sports pages. If you have a product that appeals to women, you will get high readership in the women's section. A product that appeals to both men and women calls for running the ad in the general news section.

Table 10-4. Newspaper Advertisements Featuring Products of Interest to Men or Women by Section Placement

Section Placement	Median Performance	
	Men	Women
Sports	114	49
Women's	63	101
General news	100	101

Source: "Million Market Newspapers," Starch studies of 32,000 ads (1961-63).

Color versus Black and White

The possibilities of using color in newspaper advertising may be regarded as similar to those for magazine advertising with one major exception. If you plan to use one or more colors other than black in an ROP ad, you simply can't get the quality that you can in a color magazine ad. This does not mean that ROP color should not be tested. A majority of newspapers that offer color will allow A/B splits of color versus black and white.

Studies have been made via split-runs and the recognition method to test the attention-getting power of both two-color and full-color ROP. Such studies have shown increases of 58 percent for two color and 78 percent for full color above the level of results for black-and-white versions of the same ads. Comparable cost differences are 21 percent and 25 percent.

When Starch "noting score" norms are used to estimate the same attention-getting differential, a different conclusion is reached. The differences are about 10 percent and about 30 percent (when size and product category are held constant). Using norms means comparing a black-and-white ad for one product in another city at another time. These variables inevitably blur the significance of comparisons.

For the direct response advertiser, these studies are interesting. However, you should remember that genuine controlled testing is the only way to get true figures.

Self-Quiz

1. Name the two obvious advantages of preprints.

   a. _____

   b. _____

2. Which is the most popular format for a preprint?

   ☐ Card   ☐ Multipage

3. Name the three major syndicated newspaper supplements.

   a. _____

   b. _____

   c. _____

4. Define a Dutch Door.

   _____

   _____

   _____

   _____

5. What is remnant space?

   _____

   _____

   _____

   _____

6. The higher one's education, the less likely one will read the comic pages.   ☐ True   ☐ False

7. The higher one's income, the less likely one will read the comic pages.   ☐ True   ☐ False

8. What is the advantage of the ad-and-card and ad-and-envelope for comic-page advertisers?

_____

_____

_____

9. How many advertisers will comics groups allow per page?

_____

10. What major advantage to direct response advertisers is offered by preprints and supplements over ROP advertising?

_____

_____

_____

11. What is the major difference between newspaper advertising and all other print advertising as related to potential results?

_____

_____

_____

12. What are the two initial considerations in the development of a newspaper test program?

a. _____

b. _____

13. If you have a single item that is suitable for advertising in a small space and a limited budget for testing, which publication would you test first?

_____

14. What are the two main seasons for newspaper direct response advertising?

a. _____

b. _____

15. Give the preferred weekdays for ROP advertising:

_____

_____

16. Depending on the format used, up to 90 percent or more of responses will be reached for a typical direct response newspaper ad within these time frames:

    ROP ....   after_____week(s)

    Preprints...................   after_____week(s)

    Supplements ....   after_____week(s)

    Comics ....   after_____week(s)

17. The size of newspaper space seems to be a factor in reader response only to the extent it is a factor in:

    _____

    _____

18. When running ROP, direct response advertisers should specify:

    ☐ Left-hand page   ☐ Right-hand page

19. What is the major disadvantage of running color ROP?

    _____

    _____

    _____

    _____

Pilot Project

You are the advertising manager of a mail order operation selling collectibles. You have been successful in magazines offering a series of historic plates. You have never used newspapers, but now you have a $75,000 budget to test the medium.

Outline a newspaper test plan.

1. Select your test cities.

2. Will your tests run in the Sunday edition or the weekday edition, or both?

3. What formats will you test—preprints, supplements, comics, local TV books, ROP?

4. What size preprints or ads will you test?

5. At what time of the year will you run your tests?

Note: Remember that if you use preprints, your total space budget should cover printing costs.

CHAPTER ELEVEN

Electronic Media

Broadcast TV. Cable TV. AM-FM radio. Computer networks. Video cassettes and video discs. These are the major electronic media available to direct response advertisers. To get a quick insight as to how these mediums are being used, let's take a look at some applications.

Electronic Media Applications

Broadcast TV

Selling magazine subscriptions, tapes and records, merchandise, and financial services via direct response TV is commonplace today. But some of the applications are truly unique. White Castle is a case in point.

Hundreds of thousands of midwesterners were practically raised on White Castle hamburgers. Each year many of those same midwesterners move to other regions of the country. Even without a White Castle nearby the taste lingered on.

White Castle solved the availability problem with a unique TV campaign with the theme—"White Castle has the taste some people won't live without" (Exhibit 11-1). Outside of the White Castle trading area commercials ended with this tag line: "Hamburgers to Fly. Call 1-800-W CASTLE." Over 10,000 hamburgers were being sold a week with a minimum order of fifty hamburgers for $57!

Cable TV

Broadcast TV, both local and network, has long been a major medium for consumer direct response advertisers—producing inquiries, supporting other mediums, and selling goods and services to the consumer. But in the last five years, in particular, cable has come on strong.

Cable TV *looks* like broadcast TV, but it is different in many ways. First, the cable TV audience is highly defined. The cable operator knows who is tied into the system—he or she sends them a bill every month. This demographic information, and some psychographic information, is available to the advertiser.

Exhibit 11-1. White Castle Campaign

DAUGHTER: I miss you, momma. I miss the city, too.

MOMMA: What if we sent you a little bit of your home town.

DAUGHTER: Now, how are you gonna do that?

White Castle hamburgers from back home! You can't get them out here.

My folks sent them!

ROOMMATE: Hey! Johnson's got White Castles!

GANG: White Castles!

DAUGHTER: You know, on my first date we stopped at a White Castle.

SINGERS: WHITE CASTLE HAS THE TASTE SOME PEOPLE WON'T LIVE WITHOUT.

With many more channels available than are available for broadcast TV, cable, not unlike the audience selectivity traits of radio and special interest magazines, provides more special interest programming. Thus the direct response advertiser can tie offers to predefined audiences who have a proclivity toward special interests such as sports, news, and entertainment.

One of the most firmly established special interest channels is Home Box Office (HBO). Their appeal is to those who have a particular interest in movies, sports, and special events. To be successful, not only must HBO offer superior programming, but they must sell subscriptions for the programs as well. We are indebted to Jim Kobs, chairman of Kobs & Brady, Chicago, for the case history that follows.

HBO Campaign When you are the leading cable TV premium channel, and you're selling a visual product, it seems only natural that TV advertising would be an important part of your marketing program. And it is for Home Box Office.

But that wasn't always the case. Until a few years ago, HBO had relied primarily on consumer direct mail to generate leads for the local cable system operators, who serve as distributors for the HBO channel.

TV had been considered prior to that, but it simply wasn't cost efficient. In a typical local media market, most TV households were not wired or eligible to receive cable TV. So TV spots would be wasted on too many viewers who had no opportunity to sign up for the movies, sports, and special events that HBO offered. But as cable's distribution grew (it is now available to over 70 percent of U.S. TV households), and as cable operators saw the benefits of cooperating in areawide promotions, direct response TV became a viable medium for selling cable TV and HBO.

With the help of its direct marketing agency, Kobs & Brady Advertising, HBO began running TV spots in a few small media markets in the early 1980s. The purpose of the spots was to generate leads for the cable companies, who, in turn, followed up with their own pricing and installation details. So HBO felt that sixty-second spots were sufficient to put across its message and elicit a response. (Ninety-second spots were later tested, but they didn't pay out as well. Also, they were more likely to be "preempted" by advertisers paying the full standard rate than the sixty-second spots were.)

Leads from the spots were received via telephone, with a separate 800 number assigned to each station for tracking purposes. These leads were then sorted and sent, via overnight or electronic mail, to the appropriate cable companies for follow-up. Lead information was also sent to HBO and the agency for evaluation. When a cable company closed a sale, this too was reported.

After a few years of limited activity, enough data had been accumulated both to justify, and implement, an expanded direct response TV campaign. By evaluating such factors as number of spots aired, length of flight, type of station (independent or affiliated), cost per spot, and cable penetration, it was determined that a few facts were important for planning future TV efforts:

- *What doesn't work in week one won't work in subsequent weeks.* Traditional direct response television theory holds that advertisers should let a spot air for at least two or three weeks, allowing the frequency of the message to build before making any judgment. HBO, however, has found that if a spot doesn't work in week one, it will never work; little or no improvement can be seen in subsequent weeks of airing. Why? HBO is a product that already has high consumer awareness. And there are few details to explain. Thus frequency of message is far less important in generating a lead.

- *The 1st quarter is consistently the strongest.* The fact that January-March saw the highest response rates of any season should be no surprise to traditional users of direct response TV. But in the broadcast industry, where new programming has been historically introduced in the fall, it *was* a surprise to see another period do so much better.

- *Large urban media markets are more successful than small rural media markets.* Large urban media markets obviously have more potential cable subscribers than smaller ones. But HBO had always had difficulty in reaching them via direct mail because many mailing lists were supplied by cable operators, who found it hard to come by reliable lists of apartment dwellers and new residents. TV, on the other hand, is a mass medium that reaches both these segments very well.

In 1986, HBO's use of direct response spots contributed a significant number of new subscribers to cable TV and HBO, at a lead cost that was most efficient. In addition, this success led to a breakthrough in another important area: the use of support TV.

Like many other direct marketers, HBO had previously used only thirty-second TV spots to support its mail and *TV Guide* print campaigns, paying full standard rates for guaranteed time. Upon evaluation of the sixty-second direct response spots, however, Kobs & Brady recommended that HBO begin using sixty-second support TV spots as well—even though they would be preemptible—because they could be bought at much lower direct response media rates. Mary Pat Ryan, vice-president and management supervisor at Kobs & Brady, explained the reasons for this recommendation as follows:

First, HBO has a fairly mass audience, with little differentiation based on lifestyle or psychographics. In addition, mail is dropped to almost every household in the cabled area—again, not to demographically or psychographically targeted lists. As a result, targeted support TV buys are not necessary for supporting HBO's mail pieces.

Also, experience had shown that sixty-second preemptible spots were not, in fact, preempted often enough to be a real problem for HBO. On the contrary, with smart media planning and buying, a large market could be reached at a highly efficient cost.

In addition, everything HBO had done in the media market had proved that prominent display of their product—their movies, sports, and entertainment specials—was crucial. A sixty-second spot allowed time enough both to display the HBO product *and* support the mail/print campaign.

Finally, HBO was moving toward "integrated" campaigns, with every promotion—from mail to TV, from general awareness to direct response—utilizing the same creative themes and graphic looks. The

Exhibit 11-2. "Summer Entertainer" Spot

HOME BOX OFFICE

"SUMMER ENTERTAINER"

1. (MUSIC UNDER) ANNCR: (VO) This summer, some of the greatest names in Hollywood will gather here,

2. and here's your chance to see them.

3. The world's heavyweight championship will be a

4. the nation's top comedians and most exciting events will be seen here,

5. all at great savings if you act now.

6. This summer,

7. one of the major entertainment centers will be your home.

8. With HBO, your summer entertainer.

9. And you can bring HBO into your home by calling this toll-free number.

10. You'll get installation at special savings.

11. Savings that connect you to the blockbusters

12. and show stoppers,

13. crowd thrillers

14. and bone chillers on HBO.

15. Plus on cable TV, the risk takers

16. newsbreakers

17. and music makers 24 hours a day.

18. So call now and you'll get installation for only $9.95.

19. A big saving off the regular price. Call 1-800-346-3000.

20. This is a limited time offer, so call 1-800-346-3000. HBO. We're your summer entertainer.

"Summer Entertainer" theme is used in both response and support spots for HBO.

sixty-second spot, therefore, became useful in achieving their integration of an overall image and a specific call to action: "Look for this announcement in your mail or *TV Guide*." A good example of this is HBO's 1987 campaign called "Your Summer Entertainer." Both mail and print used similar graphics to dramatize the programming that HBO would bring into the viewer's home. TV support used the same theme, coupled with dramatic aerial graphics, to build expectation for the mailings. (See Exhibit 11-2.)

To sum up, HBO and Kobs & Brady found that by utilizing sixty-second support TV spots at lower-cost preemptible rates, they could get double the air time for about the same cost of thirty-second nonpreemptible spots. And, they could use this extra time not only to give extra support to their mail campaigns—but to better tell the whole HBO story.

Today, HBO sends out over 100 million direct mail pieces a year, utilizes four-page inserts in national *TV Guide* runs, and supports both efforts with sixty-second spots in over 120 markets, three times a year. According to Steve Janas, vice president of direct marketing at HBO, results show that in those media markets where mail and *TV Guide* advertising is supported by TV, subscriber acquisition is over 100 percent higher than in similar media markets using no TV at all!

Here is one final example of how cable is being promoted to the advantage of direct response advertisers. In Chapter 1, "The Scope of Direct Marketing," we presented a mini case history about the phenomenal growth of Home Shopping Network, which sells millions of dollars of liquidated merchandise to consumers. Now we present facts about a competing home shopping show—QVC Network, Inc.

Founded by Joe Segel, the founder of the Franklin Mint, a classic mail order success, QVC features high-quality consumer products at substantially reduced prices. The fact sheet shown in Exhibit 11-3 gives an insight into the program structure.

Equally significant is the manner in which *continuing interest* in the program is promoted. Exhibit 11-4 shows a two-page letter which goes to cable subscribers, making them members of the QVC Shoppers Club. Weekly prizes offered are the lure for daily viewing.

From the standpoint of the direct marketer, home shopping shows provide the media without the investment in TV advertising, and, depending upon agreements with show sponsors, an opportunity to build a large mail order customer base.

Radio

Radio has two things going for it over broadcast TV: (1) program formats to which advertisers can better target, and (2) much lower costs for like time periods.

Exhibit 11-3. QVC Fact Sheet

INFORMATION FOR PUBLIC USE

 FACT SHEET

THE COMPANY	QVC is a direct response marketing company which offers high quality consumer products, at substantially reduced prices, to cable television viewers via a continuous cable shopping program.
PRODUCTS	Products presented by QVC are as varied as consumer tastes but, in all cases, are of high quality. Home decor, jewelry, collectibles, sports and leisure items, and consumer electronics are among items offered …frequently well-known brand names, including selected merchandise from Sears, the nation's largest retailer.
TO ORDER	Orders may be placed by phone via QVC's toll free number 1-800-345-1515. No need to trudge out to the mall. Just pick up your phone to save time and money. QVC accepts Discover, Carte Blanche, VISA, MasterCard, American Express and Diners Club credit cards. For Sears products, we also accept Sears credit cards. And your personal check is always welcome at QVC.
ORDER SHIPMENT	Orders are processed and shipped promptly and carefully upon check or credit card approval. UPS will normally deliver to your front door within 5 to 10 days of shipment from QVC.
WARRANTIES	Satisfaction guaranteed or your money back! In addition to the manufacturers' warranty, if you're not 100% satisfied with your purchase for any reason, return it within 30 days for full credit or refund. And you can call our toll-free customer service number, 1-800-367-9444, if you have any questions.
LOCATION	QVC Network Goshen Corporate Park West Chester, PA 19380
GENERAL	QVC is a publicly held company which is traded on the NASDAQ National Market System under the symbol, QVCN.

QVC NETWORK, INC.• GOSHEN CORPORATE PARK • WEST CHESTER, PA 19380

Exhibit 11-4. QVC Shoppers Club Solicitation

SAMPLE CABLE TV
QVC NETWORK
CHANNEL 99

QVC SHOPPERS CLUB

★ DOUBLE DISCOUNT CARD ★

CHARTER MEMBERSHIP NO.   1234-5678

1-800-345-1515
QVC CHARTER MEMBERSHIP NO.
1234-5678

1-800-345-1515
QVC CHARTER MEMBERSHIP NO.
1234-5678

1-800-345-1515
QVC CHARTER MEMBERSHIP NO.
1234-5678

1-800-345-1515
QVC CHARTER MEMBERSHIP NO.
1234-5678

Mr. John Sample
1 Sample Street
Sample City NY 10001

LIMITED TO ONE MEMBERSHIP PER HOUSEHOLD

To make sure you don't miss your share of QVC's weekly $25,000 jackpot, place these stickers where you'll see them while watching TV.

Mr. John Sample
1 Sample Street
Sample City NY 10001

Dear Mr. Sample:

Because you're a Sample Cable TV subscriber, we're pleased to award you a FREE Charter Membership in the QVC Shoppers Club.

Your exclusive membership number is valuable. No one else has that number. It's your key to winning a share of our weekly $25,000 cash jackpot. And you'll have at least 10 chances to win EVERY DAY -- 70 or more opportunities to win every week.

Yes, every week we're handing out a total of $25,000 cash, just to encourage you to get acquainted with the new QVC Home Shopping Program on Channel 99.

QVC stands for Quality, Value and Convenience. Turn on Channel 99 - any time of the day or night -- and you'll see an exciting parade of quality products to help you look your best, to beautify your home, and to make life easier. At big savings. And you can order any item by phone, with a 30-day return privilege. It's the most convenient way of shopping you've ever seen.

But you don't have to buy anything to share in our weekly jackpot. Here's how easy it is for you to win.

At least 10 times every day, live on Channel 99, we'll draw a 4-digit number at random.

Every time that number matches the first 4 digits OR the last 4 digits of your membership number, YOU ARE A WINNER!

Your membership number is **1234-5678**. So you have two chances at each drawing -- at least 10 times a day. Whenever either 1234 or 5678 is drawn, you've won.

Exhibit 11-4. QVC Shoppers Club Solicitation

If you're the only winner to call in during the week, the whole $25,000 is yours. If 10 winners call in, each gets $2,500. The cash pool will be divided evenly by the number of winners who have called in and identified themselves before the next number is drawn.

And that's not all. Once a week we'll also spin a wheel of fortune to select a GRAND PRIZE -- such as a new car, vacation, cruise or home entertainment center. All the daily winners who have claimed their share of the jackpot during the past week will be entered in this drawing and can <u>also win this super bonus prize</u>.

We've made it very easy for you to win. You don't even have to pay for a postage stamp, walk out of your home -- or do anything to enter. Your number is already entered. And after each drawing, the lucky number will be shown frequently -- at about 5 minute intervals -- until the next number is drawn.

But you do have to phone in to claim your prize -- before the next number is drawn. So I suggest that you watch the QVC Program as often as possible.

In fact, it makes good sense to leave the QVC Channel on whenever your family is around the house -- even <u>right now</u>. You may find that you're entitled to a share of $25,000 this very minute.

What's more, as a <u>Charter</u> Member, you're entitled to even greater savings -- savings the general public will not know about. <u>You're in on a secret</u> revealed only to Charter Members who have DOUBLE DISCOUNT cards like yours. This secret will not be mentioned on the air --

Every time you see a <u>STAR in the upper right corner of the TV screen</u> on the QVC Program, Charter Members are entitled to <u>double the discount</u> on the item currently being shown. For example, if the regular price of a <u>STARRED</u> item is $29.95 and it is being offered for $19.95, <u>YOU</u> can take off another $10.00 and order it for only $9.95.

In brief, shopping through QVC means really big dollar savings. You also save shopping time and effort. It's like having a shopping mall right in your own living room -- with super fast delivery and a 30-day <u>unconditional return privilege.</u>

And remember, <u>you don't have to buy anything</u> to win your share of the $25,000 weekly drawings. Just watch as often as possible, since we're drawing a new number at least ten times a day.

Sincerely yours,

Bill Johnston
Senior Vice President
QVC Network, Inc.

BJ:aa

Targeting to the right program formats is the key. For example, if an advertiser is soliciting phone-in orders for a rock album or tape, there's no problem running a radio commercial on scores of stations that feature rock music; these listeners are the very audience the advertiser is seeking.

Or if a financial advertiser is soliciting inquiries from potential investors, there are program formats that help the advertiser reach a target audience: "Wall Street Report," for example, or FM stations with a high percentage of upper-income listeners.

This sixty-second radio commercial by Merrill Lynch was run in conjunction with program formats with a high percentage of listeners who match their customer profile.

(MUSIC UP AND UNDER)
ANNOUNCER: A word on money management from Merrill Lynch. Today, many banks are trying to copy our revolutionary Cash Management Account financial service. Here's why they can't. Bank money market accounts are simply that: bank accounts. A Merrill Lynch CMA gives you access to the entire *range* of our investment opportunities. Instead of just an account, you get an Account Executive, backed by the top-ranked research team on Wall Street. Idle cash is automatically invested in your choice of *three* CMA money market funds. You enjoy check writing, a special VISA card, automatic variable rate loans up to the full margin loan value of your securities—at *rates* banks aren't likely to match. So give your money sound management, and *more* to grow on. The all-in-one CMA financial service. (MUSIC) From Merrill Lynch. A breed apart.

LOCAL ANNOUNCER: For more complete information and a free prospectus, including sales charges and expenses, call 000-0000. Read it carefully before you invest or send money. That's 000-0000.

Computer Networks

Another electronic medium available to the direct marketer, but not widely used, is the computer network. There are over 14 million home computers in place in the U.S. today; most have been purchased by business people who rationalize the cost as an extension of their business activities. Many are connected via telephone lines to central data bases such as the Source and the Dow Jones News Retrieval Service.

These networks are used essentially for business-to-business purposes; this use does not exclude opportunities to program consumer product information. One of the largest and most successful "programs" available to the computer networker is CompuServe's comparative shopping service.

Various brands of merchandise offered for sale by various merchants can be called up from the data base. The user can make an item-by-item, feature-by-feature comparison, including price—all done with the calculating aid of the computer. The user can actually order the item he or she wants, via the return leg of the telephone line, for later delivery to home or office. In this sense, we are dealing with an electronic sales directory or catalog. It differs from a printed catalog in that, for the most part, computer networks are limited to text-only displays.

Video Cassettes and Video Discs

It is estimated that by 1990 more than half of all TV homes will have one or more VCRs. This could be bad news for movie theaters: close to $3 billion annually is spent on movie rentals. The onslaught of VCRs isn't good news for TV networks either: millions use their TV sets to watch taped movies, sporting events, and special events . . . *sans commercials.*

But for the direct marketer, VCRs offer an opportunity rather than a threat: direct marketers have the opportunity to become sponsors of video cassette programming.

By incorporating commercial messages in the programs, producers can defray the high cost of production and sell their tapes at a lower price. In addition, they may be able to open new distribution outlets. As an example, the hour long "Mr. Boston Official Video Bartender's Guide," sponsored by Glenmore Distilleries, is available through liquor stores as well as the more usual outlets. Along with the cassette goes an eight-page catalog of each Glenmore product.

With such a catalog, or with specific sales and response information incorporated into a taped presentation, a sponsored video cassette might prove so productive for an advertiser that it could afford to sell the tape cheaply, use it as a self-liquidating premium, or even give the tape to video cassette outlets for low-rate rental. Video cassette catalogs also show potential for high-ticket items that benefit from demonstration.

While video discs haven't attained the popularity of video cassette recorders, they have been gaining ground with consumers over the past few years.

For catalogs, and for many other types of electronic publishing, the technology of choice may soon be the compact random-access optical video disc. These digitally encoded discs pack an enormous amount of audio and/or video information in a small space. For example: Grolier's twenty-one-volume *Academic American Encyclopedia* was issued on a single 4.7-inch disc in the fall of 1985. It costs less than half as much as the printed version and it uses only one-fifth of the total capacity of the disc!

Video discs can store sound, still pictures, and moving images as well as computer data. There appear to be limitless commercial applications—from the ultimate Sears catalog to ad-supported cooking courses.

Direct Response TV

Buying and scheduling TV and radio time is best left to the experts—direct marketing agencies and some select buying services. But for a direct marketer to recognize the opportunities and pitfalls of advertising in these media, it is imperative that the basics be understood. Let's start with TV.

Ratings

It is important to keep in mind that the cost of a commercial time period is based on its "rating." This is a measure of its share of the total TV households viewing the show. The more highly rated the show, the higher the cost. One rating point equals one percent of the total households in the market. A show with a 20 rating is being watched by 20 percent of television households.

When the total ratings of all the time periods in a schedule are combined, the result is called gross rating points (or GRPs). Simply stated, if a television schedule has 100 GRPs per week, it is reaching the equivalent of 100 percent of TV households in the market in that week. Obviously, this is a statistical reach with varying degrees of duplication. It does not guarantee 100 percent of the individual homes will be reached.

Commercial Lengths

While thirty seconds is the most common time length for general or image advertising, direct marketers seldom find that adequate to tell their selling story in a persuasive way. Ninety to 120 seconds is usually required for a direct sale commercial, while sixty to ninety seconds are usually required for lead generation commercials. On the other hand, support commercials with sufficient GRPs prove effective with a combination of ten-second and thirty-second commercials. But key outlet marketing usually requires longer lengths.

Of course, with the popularity of thirty-second announcements and the premium broadcasters can get for them, it is not always possible to clear longer length commercials, particularly during periods of high demand.

Reach and Frequency

Television advertisers use two terms in measuring the effectiveness of their television schedules. *Reach* refers to the number of *different* homes exposed to the message within a given time segment. *Frequency* is a measure of how many times the average viewer will see the message over a given number of weeks. Frequency also can be measured against viewer quintiles (e.g., heaviest viewers, lightest viewers, etc.).

The combination of reach and frequency will tell you what percentage of the audience you are reaching and how often on average they will see your message. Television schedules often are purchased against reach and frequency goals and actual performance measured in postanalysis.

For most direct marketers, reach and frequency are not as important as actual response rates, which represent a true return on the media dollar. But a knowledge of what reach and frequency are is critical when television is used in a supporting role.

Buying Time

Buying time for very specific time periods is the most expensive way to purchase it. You pay a higher price to guarantee your message will run at a precise time within a predetermined program environment. Television time also can be bought less expensively. Stations will sell ROS (run-of-station) time, time available during periods the station has been unable to sell at regular rates. This is particularly true with independent (non-network) stations, which often have sizable inventories of unsold time. If the station, however, subsequently sells the time to a specific buyer, your commercial will be preempted.

Preemptible time can be an excellent buy for direct response advertisers because of the combination of lower cost and quite respectable response rates. When buying preemptible time, it also is possible to specify the day-parts (daytime, early fringe, late fringe, etc.) for slightly more than straight ROS rates. This can be important for the direct marketer with a specific target audience for his product. Such spots still may be preempted at any time, however.

Television time also may be purchased on the basis of payment per inquiry (or PI) and bonus-to-pay-out. PI allows the station to run as many commercials as it wishes, whenever it wishes. There is no charge for the time, but the station receives a predetermined sum for every inquiry or sale the advertisement generates for the advertiser. The advertiser is not committed to pay for a spot until it delivers an inquiry or sale and then only in relation to responses.

But there are disadvantages. It is almost impossible to plan methodically for fulfillment. Such programs cannot be coordinated reliably with other efforts or promotion timetables. And, since the station will run the commercials that it feels will perform best for it, your spot may never run and you may not know it until it has jeopardized your entire selling program.

Bonus-to-pay-out involves a special arrangement with the station to deliver a certain number of responses. A schedule is negotiated with the station to guarantee a certain minimum schedule. If, at the end of the schedule, the response goal has not been reached, the station must continue to run the commercial until it is reached. This method provides a better planning base for the direct marketer.

With television time in high demand, such opportunities are not as available as they once were. But, if they can be located, they can be a superb vehicle for direct marketers.

TV Schedules

What kind of broadcast television schedule is most productive and/or efficient for the direct marketer? It depends on the objective. For direct sale or lead generation commercials, which require the viewer to get up and take some action within minutes, certain criteria apply. For example, the television viewing day is divided into various *day-parts*. There is weekday daytime, early evening or fringe, prime time, late night or fringe, and weekend. Each day-part tends to reach one group or combination of viewers better than the others.

It is important to know your primary target group so you can select the most appropriate day-part. Prime time is so called because it reaches the largest audience with the most exciting shows. It is also the most expensive. The more attentive viewers are to the show, the less likely they are to respond immediately. Therefore, times of lower viewer involvement and attentiveness are better and less expensive for the advertiser who expects a direct response. Reruns, talk shows, old movies, and the like often are the best vehicles for direct response advertising. These tend to run predominantly in daytime, fringe, and late night time slots. (See Table 11-1.)

Similarly, because independent stations tend to run a higher percentage of syndicated reruns and movies, their viewers tend to have a lower level of attentiveness to the programming. But even on independent stations, avoid news shows and other high-interest programming. Check the ratings. They are a good guide.

Seasonality is another factor in direct response TV. The first quarter and third quarter respectively are the best seasons for television response, just as they are for print and mail. Moreover, television time pricing is related to viewing levels, which are seasonal and vary month to month as well as by day-part. (See Table 11-2.)

Market Performance

Some geographic locations are good for certain products or offers. Others are simply not receptive. It pays to know ahead of time what a market's propensity is. Previous experience with mail or print can be a reasonably reliable guide.

In any event, it is not necessary to jump in up to your neck. Start with a handful of markets, two to five, say, and test the waters. Try a one- or two-week schedule. As few as 10 commercials per week can give you a reading. Monitor your telephone response daily. You'll know within two or three days if it's bust or boom. After a week or so you'll have an even more precise fix on how well your commercial is doing. If it holds up, stay with it— until it starts to taper off. Then stop. Don't try to milk a stone.

Meanwhile, move on to other markets in the same methodical and measured way. You always can return to your most successful markets later in the marketing year after your commercial has had a rest. Or come back with a new offer.

Table 11-1. Viewer Attention Levels by Program Type
Percent at Full Attention

	Total Audience		
	Adults	Men	Women
Weekday Daytime			
"Today Show"	43	50	38
Serials	64	61	64
Quiz/Game shows	66	76	61
Situation comedies	57	60	56
Early Evening			
Situation comedies	64	64	63
Action/adventure	69	69	69
Talk shows	68	76	67
News	68	77	65
Prime Time			
Movies	77	76	77
Variety	70	74	68
Drama	72	74	70
Situation comedies	66	67	64
Sports	62	65	52
Late Night			
News	70	71	67
Talk shows	66	66	67
Movies	76	75	77

Source: Simmons 1981.

Direct Response Radio

Radio, too, is a mass medium. But it is possible to buy radio on a more selective basis than broadcast television. There are many more radio stations than television stations, and each has its own personality, which is reflected in its programming. Some stations feature rock and roll music, some classical music, some are "talk" or "all news" stations. Each selects its audience (or vice versa) by its programming format. And, of course, radio costs less to use—both in media charges and production.

With radio as a direct response or support medium, audience selection is important. Radio measurement, unlike television, is not based on households, but on individual listeners. This is a testimony to the individual way that radio is listened to and to the fact that the average home has 5.5 radios in it, often one or more per person or room.

While radio ratings can tell you the demographics of a station's audience, station formats give you some idea of the psychographics of that audience. So if you know who your target customers are, you can determine what station or stations to use to reach them. (See Table 11-3.)

Day-parts are as important in radio as they are in television. Certain times of day have larger audiences. And listenership varies by age throughout the day. With most radio formats, the audience peaks at "drive times." These are in the morning (6 to 10 A.M.) and evening (3 to 7 P.M.). These are

Table 11-2. Index of Seasonality of Viewing, by Day-Part (Annual Average = 100)

	Day	Early Evening	Prime	Late Evening	Sat. & Sun. Morning
Households					
January-March	108	**112***	113	105	**111**
April-June	92	91	98	99	93
July-September	98	82	83	98	81
October-December	102	**115**	107	97	**115**
Men					
January-March	**113**	**115**	113	109	104
April-June	89	87	96	101	85
July-September	90	77	80	91	74
October-December	107	**120**	**111**	98	**132**
Women					
January-March	106	107	113	105	103
April-June	96	93	96	99	86
July-September	91	82	80	98	86
October-December	105	**118**	**111**	98	**122**

Source: A. C. Nielsen Audience Demographic Report, 1974.
*Levels in bold-face type are 10 percent or more above the average viewing index.

the most expensive times to buy on radio, but they usually are not the best times for direct response advertisers. The person behind a wheel cannot run to the phone, or even get a pencil to write a number down.

Radio is inherently a low-reach, high-frequency medium. People tend to listen regularly to the same station, with little switching, and many different stations divide up the total radio audience. Maximum reach potential is about 60 percent and only when several stations are bought. Reach builds slowly while frequency increases quickly: 50 GRPs in one week of daytime television will achieve 30 percent reach at a frequency of 1.7. Those same 50 GRPs in radio will take four weeks to reach 31 percent, but the frequency level will be 6.5.

When buying radio for direct marketing purposes, be sure to consider your communications objective and the reach and frequency of various stations ratings and formats by day-part. If radio is being used for direct response, its frequency and targetability provide plenty of opportunity to achieve good response rates at low cost. If it is being used for support, several stations will have to be purchased across all day-parts to obtain the desired reach. Radio also can be used to support TV, adding frequency to television's reach.

Time lengths for messages on radio are fairly standardized at sixty seconds. This is the most economical unit. Thirty-second spots cost proportionately more (75 percent of the sixty-second rate).

One advantage of radio for the direct marketer is its combination of low cost and quick turnaround time, making it easy and economical to experiment. You can be extremely topical or exploit fast-breaking events. A thoroughly respectable radio commercial can be on the air within twenty-four hours of a decision to use it.

Table 11-3. Radio Listening by Station Format

Total Audience	Age Groups					
	18-24	*25-34*	*35-44*	*45-54*	*55-64*	*65+*
Men						
Adult Contemporary	225	128	53	36	82	26
All News	32	76	111	166	119	123
Beautiful Music	44	39	165	123	175	100
Black	207	141	120	51	2	9
Classical/Semi-Classical	40	53	105	256	133	40
Country	65	102	174	93	116	47
Golden Oldies	327	73	87	12	17	29
Middle of the Road	63	121	142	124	66	70
Progressive	190	227	26	11	47	8
Soft Contemporary	235	157	50	43	68	11
Standard	69	57	145	141	105	109
Talk	41	51	83	172	178	124
Top 40	205	149	69	44	33	40
Women						
Adult Contemporary	199	151	82	65	22	42
All News	41	52	48	136	167	184
Beautiful Music	18	100	130	169	126	76
Black	199	139	118	85	19	7
Classical/Semi-Classical	60	61	262	171	36	34
Country	63	90	181	111	107	63
Golden Oldies	195	221	61	30	25	2
Middle of the Road	97	137	95	126	87	46
Progressive	260	134	109	19	41	—
Soft Contemporary	235	157	50	43	68	11
Standard	30	68	126	157	139	106
Talk	15	24	96	170	137	198
Top 40	223	126	127	64	24	5

Source: RAB, Research Dept., 1980.

Creating for Direct Response TV and Radio

Creating for TV

In wrestling with concepts for television, remember it is a visual medium and an action medium. And you are using it in a time of great video literacy. Your concept must be sharp, crisp. It must be designed to jar a lethargic and jaded audience to rapt attention. So your concepts require the best and most knowledgeable of talent.

When you have arrived at your concept, it's time to write a script and do a storyboard. The script format is two adjacent columns, one for video descriptions and one for copy and audio directions. The two columns track together so that the appropriate words and sounds are shown opposite the pictures they will accompany. Video descriptions should make it possible to understand the general action in any given scene. It is not necessary at this point to spell out every detail.

The storyboard follows from and accompanies the script. It is a series of artist's drawings of the action and location of each scene. There should be enough individual pictures (called frames) to show the flow of the action and important visual information. Most concept storyboards run eight to sixteen frames, depending on the length of the commercial, the complexity of the action, and the need to show specific detail.

Novices make two important errors when doing television storyboards. One is a failure to synchronize the words and the pictures. At no point should the copy be talking about something different than what the picture is showing, nor should the picture be something that is unrelated to the words.

The second mistake is a failure to realize most people who evaluate a storyboard equate frames with the passage of time. Each frame in an eight-frame storyboard will often be interpreted as 1/8th of commercial time. If some intricate action takes place over five seconds, it could take four or five frames to illustrate. Meanwhile, a simple scene that may run ten seconds can often be illustrated with one or two frames. Imagine the confusion the reviewer of the storyboard faces. Make sure your storyboards show elapsed time. Often an elapsed time indicator next to the picture will do the trick.

Once you have developed a television storyboard you feel is a good representation of what you want to accomplish, it is possible to evaluate it in the following fashion.

The first thing to look for is AQRI (Acquire Quick Related Interest). You have five seconds or less to capture and hold your target prospect's attention. Have you used those five seconds well? The attention must be related to the subject of the commercial. An irrelevant attention-getting device will only lose the viewer after the proposition begins to develop. And you may miss the very people you want to interest. Get the viewer's attention. Do it quickly. But do it relevantly.

Next you can score your commercial from 1-5 (1 being poor, 5 being excellent) against these criteria.

- Is it simple, clear, easy to understand?
- Is it credible, believable?
- Is it original in its approach, commanding interest with its freshness?
- Is it relevant to the benefit of the product or service?
- Is it empathetic, giving your audience a good feeling about the product, the company, and the advertising as being appropriate to the way they live their lives?

If it can pass this quiz with a score of twenty-five, you should have a winner. A score of twenty would pass, too. But can't you do better?

Of course, these are only guidelines. They are not rules. Even if they were, the essence of all great advertising, including direct response, is to break the rules to reach people in a way they haven't been reached before. But it is something quite different to violate *principles* that have been developed over years of observation. Do so only at your own peril.

There is a set of rules that relates to the law. Various industry self-regulatory bodies and instruments of the government watch over the airwaves. They require that advertising be truthful and not misleading. Don't say (or picture) anything in your commercial that you can't substantiate or replicate in person. And don't make promises your product or service can't deliver on.

As you design your direct response commercial, there are some important techniques to keep in mind. If at all possible, integrate your offer with the remainder of your commercial. It will make it easier for the viewer to comprehend and respond. And it will give your offer, and your product or service, the opportunity to reinforce each other in value and impression.

Also, if possible, integrate the 800 toll-free number into the commercial. You should plan to have the telephone number on the screen for at least twenty-five seconds, and more, depending on the length of the commercial. Try to find ways to make it "dance" on the screen. Bring it on visually as it is announced on the sound track. Highlight it will flairs or color or find some other way to make it an integral but highly visible part of the commercial and the offer. The following is a good example of a commercial designed to generate an immediate response.

A support television commercial differs from a straight response commercial in ways worthy of note. Since it seeks to reach the largest number of people, it usually runs in time periods when thirty seconds is the prevalent availability. It must have a greatly condensed message, placing a premium on simplicity. It almost must pay a larger than usual tribute to the image considerations of the client. As it seeks no immediate response, but directs the viewer elsewhere, memorability and a positive attitude about the advertiser become extremely important.

Video	*Audio*
1. *Open on MCU of professional demonstrator in kitchen, hacking at wooden block.*	**Demonstrator**: I'm purposely chopping this hardwood block to smithereens to demonstrate an amazing new product: Miracle Mac Knives!
2. *Zoom to ECU of demonstrator still hacking at block. Super card 1 (flashing: warning).*	**Dem (VO)**: Ladies and gentlemen, please don't try this on the knives in your kitchen drawer. Miracle Mac Knives are the *only* knives in the world that can take this kind of punishment . . .
3. *Cut to demonstrator cutting paper into strips.*	and keep coming back for more!!
4. *Cut to ECU of demonstrator: gestures to blade.*	The secret is space-age, chrome molybdenum steel—the hardest steel ever made—that stays sharp, for *life*, without any grinding or sharpening tools!
5. *Hands demonstrate sharpening.*	Imagine! Just a simple pass over the back of china plate restores the original cutting edge.
6. *Pull back for MCU of demonstrator.*	**Demonstrator**: Grab a pencil and paper folks because I want to send you a set of these amazing Mac Knives for 30 days *free!* But first, watch.
7. *Demonstrate tomato.*	**(VO)**: You can cut a tomato paper-thin slice after slice, and never lose a drop of juice;
8. *Demonstrate roast.*	carve meat from the bone as clean as a whistle;
9. *Demonstrate radishes.*	decorate radishes like an expert;
10. *Demonstrate bread in mid-air.*	cut bread a sixteenth of an inch thin;
11. *Demonstrate turkey.*	carve a turkey clear down to the bone in seconds;
12. *Demonstrate potato.*	even take an eye out of a potato so easy you won't believe it!
13. *Cut to ECU of hands demonstrating blade.*	And just look at this: Each knife is scientifically designed to keep your fingers away from the cutting board,

Video	Audio
14. *Hands demonstrate tips.*	with safe rounded tips,
15. *Hands demonstrate hole.*	and handy hanging hole,
16. *Hands demonstrate handles.*	plus teak handles that are permanently bonded to the steel for super strength.
17. *Pull back to demonstrator who displays knives one at a time.*	**Demonstrator:** And now, during this special TV offer, you can own one, two, three, four Miracle Mac Knives for just $19.95.
18. *Dissolve to knives and box. Super card 2: 30-day free trial.*	**Dem (VO):** But first, try them at home for 30 days free! No need to send any money!
19. *Cut to knife rack demonstration. Super card 3: Free! When you send $19.95 plus one dollar shipping and handling.*	However, if you use your credit card or include payment with your order, we'll include this handsome hardwood knife rack at no extra cost! If not fully satisfied, return the knife set, keep the knife rack, and we'll refund your purchase price of $19.95.
20. *Demonstrator assembles sandwich and cuts it.*	Try the knives that are so hard, so sharp, they slice through a Dagwood sandwich in one stroke!
21. *Cut to slide of phone number and address. Super card 4: offer for cable TV viewers only.*	**Demonstrator:** Order your set today. Give the knives a real workout for 30 days. Here's how: Call 000-0000 right now or write Mac Knives, care of Station OOO, Charleston, West Virginia. Send only $19.95 plus one dollar shipping and handling. That's Mac Knives, care of Station OOO, Charleston, West Virginia, or call 000-0000 now.

Contrast this thirty-second support TV commercial with the preceding direct sale commercial (audio portion only):

Look for this brochure in Sunday's paper; because 9 out of 10 of these homes have no guarantee they'll be rebuilt if destroyed by fire. But with Allstate's new home replacement guarantee, your home will be rebuilt completely even if rebuilding costs more than you're covered for. Take the first important step to get Allstate's Home Replacement Guarantee. Look for this brochure in Sunday's paper because you never know when fire will strike.

Creating for Radio

In its early days, television was perceived by many copywriters as nothing more than illustrated radio. With the evolution of the medium we learned how limited that vision was. Now, in this age of video, there is a tendency to think of radio as television without the pictures. That perception is equally wrong.

Radio is the "writer's medium" in its purest sense. Words, sounds, music, even silence are woven together by the writer to produce a moving tapestry of thought, image, and persuasion. Connection with the listener is direct, personal, emotional, primal. In fact, research by educational groups has found that information taken in through the ear is often remembered more readily and more vividly than that received visually.

In writing for radio, it is important to consider a station's format. The "country and western" station has a different listening audience from the "all-news" station. Different people listen to classical music versus talkback or rock programming. Tailor your message and its style to the format of the station it is running on. That doesn't necessarily mean make it sound exactly like the station's programming. Sometimes it makes sense to break the flow of programming to stand out as a special message, but only within the framework of the format that has attracted the station's listeners.

Remember also that radio is more personal than TV. Radios are carried with the listener, in a car, at the beach, at the office, in the bathroom, even joggers with their earphones are tuned into the radio cosmos. Moreover, because the radio listener can supply important elements in the message mosaic, the conclusion drawn from it is likely to be more firmly held than that which the individual has not participated in. Do not fill in all the blanks for your listeners. Let them provide some of the pieces. At the same time, be sure the words you use are clear in their meaning and emotional content. Be sure the sounds are clearly understandable and recognizable. If not, find some way to augment them with narrative or conversation that establishes a setting that is easy to visualize.

Use music whenever you can justify its cost and consumption of commercial time. Music is the emotional common denominator. Its expression of joy, sorrow, excitement, romance, action, and so forth, is as universally understood as any device available to you. When it comes time to consider music, contact a music production house. There usually are several in every major city. Los Angeles, New York, and Chicago have scores of them. They usually will consult at no charge. Or consider library music that can be purchased outright at low cost. If you can live with its often undistinguished quality, it can be an excellent value.

Another aspect of radio is its casualness. Whereas television tends to command all of our attention and concentration, radio usually gets only a portion of it. It is important to keep radio commercials simple and stopping. Devices such as special sounds (or silence) can arrest your listener's attention. To hold it, the idea content must be cohesive and uncomplicated. Better to drive one point home than to flail away at many. If many points must be covered, they all should feed to a strong central premise. This advice is appropriate for all advertising. But for radio it is critical.

The length a radio commercial runs is usually sixty seconds. This not only should be adequate for most commercial messages but also is the time length listeners have become accustomed to. Thirty-second commercials are available but are not a good buy for direct response purposes.

One other thing that everyone who listens to radio will appreciate is that radio lends itself to humor. For some reason we have become used to hearing humor on radio, and we respond positively to it. The following radio commercial employs humor effectively to address small business owners, while talking to the public at large.

Husband:	How did we get into this anyway?
Wife:	Who knows, we tried to make it work.
Husband:	Well, I guess it's over.
Wife:	We better get on with it.
Husband:	Okay, you get the car.
Wife:	Right.
Husband:	I get the sofa bed. You get the fridge.
Wife:	Right.
Husband:	I get the Bell System Yellow Pages Directory. You get the . . .
Wife:	Hold on—that doesn't mean the Gold Pages Coupon Section does it?
Husband:	Why sure it does.
Wife:	I get the Gold Pages Coupons.
Husband:	Well come on—you're getting the bedroom set too.
Wife:	You can have the bedroom set. I want the Gold Pages Coupons good for discounts at local merchants.
Husband:	I'll tell you what.
Wife:	What?
Husband:	I'll throw in the oil painting and the end tables.
Wife:	I want the Gold Pages.
Husband:	Look you can have everything else. Just let me keep the Gold Pages Coupons.
Wife:	Get off your knees. You really want them that bad?
Husband:	I do absolutely.
Wife:	We could split them.
Husband:	You mean . . . tear them apart?
Wife:	You're right—it won't work.

Husband:	No. Neither will this.
Wife:	It won't work.
Husband:	You mean . . .
Wife:	We'll just have to stay together.
Husband:	Dolores—what a mistake we almost made.
Wife:	Lorraine!
Husband:	Lorraine—what a mistake we almost made.
Wife:	Who's Dolores?

Self-Quiz

1. Which of these two TV audiences is *highly defined?*

   ☐ Broadcast TV   ☐ Cable TV

2. HBO is a premium subscription TV channel. They offer subscribers:

   a. Movies

   b. _____

   c. _____

3. HSN is a leading home shopping show offering, for the most part, liquidated merchandise. QVC, another home shopping show, features _____ merchandise.

4. Radio has two things going for it over broadcast TV:

   a. Program _____.

   b. Lower _____ for like time periods.

5. How might direct response advertisers benefit from video cassettes and video discs?

   _____

   _____

   _____

   _____

6. Define gross rating points (GRPs).

   _____

   _____

7. Define *reach* and *frequency*.

   Reach: _____

   _____

   Frequency: _____

   _____

8. Within what time frame can a direct response advertiser learn how well a commercial is doing?

   ☐ Within a week

   ☐ Two to three weeks

   ☐ A month

9. The day parts of radio are:

   a. Day

   b. Early evening

   c. Prime

   d. _____

   e. _____

10. If you use a toll-free number as part of your TV commercial you should plan to have the telephone number on the screen at least:

    ☐ 10 seconds   ☐ 25 seconds   ☐ 60 seconds

11. Name three types of radio program formats:

    a. Country and Western

    b. _____

    c. _____

Pilot Project

Your assignment is to sell an album of rock music by a "hot" group for $19.95. The medium you are to use is radio. Prepare a sixty-second commercial for a rock station.

CHAPTER TWELVE

Co-ops

Package goods firms, for the most part, disavow direct marketing as a part of their marketing mix. And yet, a direct marketing vehicle—the cents-off coupon—is integral to most of their marketing programs.

Cents-off coupons qualify as direct marketing, in my opinion, because they meet the three requirements of a direct response proposition: (1) a definite offer (a discount on a specified product), (2) all the information necessary to make a decision (all cents-off coupons contain complete information), (3) a response device (the coupon, when presented at the checkout counter, becomes the transaction device).

Promotions come and go. But cents-off coupons continue to grow. (See Table 12-1.)

When consumers are asked why they continue to redeem coupons, they give three major reasons:

1. Coupons save money.

2. Coupons inform consumers about old-line products and give encouragement to try new products.

3. Coupons reduce the cost of the products consumers buy.

Table 12-1. Growth of Coupon Distribution (Excludes In-Ad Coupons)

Year	Number (Billions)
1981	102.4
1982	119.5
1983	142.9
1984	163.2
1985	179.8

Marketers use coupons:

- To improve competitive penetration in a market
- To move out-of-balance inventories
- To stimulate product demand at the retail level as a means of obtaining retailer agreements to stock a product
- To accelerate the introduction and widespread use of a new product
- To get new users for an old product

Mass Market Penetration

The dominant force in cents-off coupon distribution is Donnelley Marketing, publisher of the Carol Wright mail co-op, distributed to more than 35 million selected households nine times a year.

Although Carol Wright distribution is indeed huge, it is a carefully segmented distribution carved from Donnelley's 78 million household residential data base. Carol Wright gives the following demographics for the typical homemaker who receives their co-op:

> A married woman (81%) between 25 and 49 years old (65%) whose household income exceeds $25,000 (66%) and whose family size is three or more persons (68%). She is at least a high school graduate (86%, with 53% having attended college). Her children are under 18 years old (58%), she lives near one or more high-volume supermarkets (91%) and collects and uses cents-off coupons on a regular basis (92%).

Donnelley has identified the households they select as "heavy users." These "heavy users," surprisingly, skew to families with annual incomes over $25,000 rather than those of poverty income under $10,000. And, quoting from readership studies they have conducted, nearly all (95 percent) open and look through the Carol Wright ensemble. Each coupon is seen, on average, by more than two-thirds (71 percent) of the recipients. Better than a third (40 percent) indicate a positive brand message response. And of those who redeem the coupons, more than three quarters (78 percent) buy new brands or brands they do not regularly use, depending on product category.

Media and Redemption Rates

Mail distribution of cents-off coupons, while highly effective, is dwarfed by distribution in other media. Table 12-2 shows the latest distribution figures available in the DMA "Fact Book."

While direct mail coupon distribution is, by far, the most expensive distribution channel on a cost-per-thousand basis, this is compensated for by a much higher average redemption rate. (See latest DMA figures in Table 12-3.)

Table 12-2. Distribution of Coupons by Media

Media	Percentage
Daily Newspapers/ROP Solo	12.2
Magazines	8.6
Direct Mail	4.4
In/On Packs	4.8
Sunday Supplements	2.1
Sunday Free-standing Inserts	50.4
Daily Free-standing Inserts	9.5
Daily Co-op/All	8.0

Table 12-3. Average Coupon Redemption Rates

Media	Percentage Average Redemption
Direct Mail	7.0
Magazines (on-page)	2.0
Newspapers ROP/Solo	2.3
Sunday Supplements/Solo	2.0
Daily Newspaper Free-standing Inserts	4.0
Sunday Newspaper Free-standing Inserts	4.2
Newspaper Comic Section	1.8
Magazines (Pop-Ups)	4.3
Co-op (All)	2.4

Traditional Co-ops

While the vast majority of participants in Carol Wright co-ops are package goods firms, some direct marketers include mail order offers in their co-ops. However, most direct marketers who use co-ops tend to use those that have a greater number of direct response offers. Types of direct response co-ops available break into the following categories.

1. *Mail order co-ops.* These are arranged by direct marketers who put their own co-ops together. They induce other direct marketers to join forces with them and make combined mailings to their buyer list. The income from other marketers naturally reduces mail circulation cost for the sponsor.

2. *In-house co-ops.* A variation of the commercial co-op is the in-house co-op. In this case the sponsor (marketer) co-ops only products or services that he or she sells. The advantage is that selling costs are spread over several offers, rather than one.

3. *Vertical co-ops.* Here we are talking about specific groups, such as business people, college students, new mothers, school teachers, accountants, lawyers, engineers, and so forth.

4. *Magazine co-ops.* Many magazines sponsor a co-op of their own, their circulation list serving as the channel of distribution. This service offers two major advantages to the sponsoring magazine: (1) a chance for additional revenue from regular magazine advertisers, and (2) an inducement to prospective advertisers to test the responsiveness of the magazine's market. (See Exhibit 12-1.)

Standard Rate & Data Service (SRDS) has an entire section devoted to co-op mailings in its periodic directory called *Direct Mail List Rates and Data.* The listings contain much valuable information.

Sales/Costs Ratios

Quoting averages is always dangerous, but as a rule-of-thumb response for individual pieces in a co-op is about one-fourth the response of a solo mailing. The cost, however, is likewise about one-fourth. Response rates do vary, of course. A 50 percent discount offer from *Time*—so well known that little explanation is necessary—is likely to pull much better than that for an unknown publication. Also a new product offer, because of restricted space in a co-op, is likely to pull far less than one-fourth of a solo mail effort.

Co-op Formats

Direct marketers have two basic formats available to them: postcard and "loose" inserts. (See Exhibit 12-2.) Most postcard publications carry three postcards to the page, the reply card unit size measuring approximately 6″ × 3⅝″. An advertiser can purchase a single card or two or three adjacent cards (Exhibit 12-3).

Sponsors determine the size and weight limitations for loose inserts. Typically the weight limitation is one-quarter ounce, and the size limitation is 5″ × 8″. If the advertiser exceeds the weight limitation, he or she is usually subject to a surcharge.

Exhibit 12-1. A Co-op Mailing

A Store Redemption Coupon and a direct response offer among forty-three inserts in a typical Carol Wright co-op.

Getting Co-ops Read

Participants in co-ops face fierce readership competition. You can greatly improve your chances for getting your piece read and acted on by knowing the behavior patterns of people who receive co-ops. Phil Dresden, an expert on co-ops, provides a valuable insight:

> I have witnessed a number of focus group research interview sessions through a one-way mirror. Different groups of housewives were brought in and handed co-op envelopes filled with coupons and offers. There was an amazingly consistent behavior pattern. The participants, without exception, sorted each envelope's contents into two piles. Later when they were asked what was the basis for the two piles, they answered: "Interesting-not interesting; like-dislike; value-no value." Your offer must find its way to the right pile during that initial sorting.
>
> The way to get into the first pile is to have a simple message clearly stated with effective graphics. The more alternatives you offer, the

less your response will be. In a phrase, don't get sorted out; keep it simple. You only have a few seconds to make an impact. Inserts in direct mail co-ops are more like ads in a magazine than like regular direct mail. If the offer appears to be too much trouble, if it appears that the message is going to take some time and effort to get at, the housewife goes to the next offer.

Before you release your final mechanical to the printer, write two questions down on a piece of paper and see if you can answer them honestly: (1) Have you given the potential respondent an opportunity for dialog with you? (2) What precisely are you asking the potential respondent to believe and to do?

Generally, in co-op direct response advertising the recipient sees little and remembers less. Any purchase is basically made on impulse, and response levels can be seriously impacted if the potential respondent does not act within a short time span. The products and services should fall into the pattern of something wanted or needed now.

Testing a Co-op

As Phil Dresden points out, testing co-ops is a tricky business. When you test an insert in a co-op, you are doing so with one group of partners; when you "roll out," you are likely to be participating with a different group of partners. So you must live with this variable. Here are a few simple rules for testing co-ops based on the Dresden experience:

1. Because testing is a trial for a subsequent major promotion, it is important to ensure conditions such that the major promotion will be as close to the original as possible.

2. Know what your break-even point is and test a sample large enough so your result can be acted upon.

3. Test the co-op first and leave the segments for later unless your product clearly suggests a particular segment. For example, if your product is aimed entirely at a female market, test only the female portion of a co-op mailing.

4. Test a cross section of the complete co-op list. If no "nth" sample is available, request distribution in several different markets—all widely dispersed.

5. Don't let too much time elapse between your test and your continuation, especially if the item you are testing is of a seasonal nature.

Exhibit 12-2. Three Examples of Participants in *Advertising Age*'s Loose Pack Postcard Deck

SUPER SALESMAN

Need a sales rep who's hard working, loyal, who never gets tired and always delivers your sales message just the way you intended it?

Panasonic's new CT-130V Monitor/VCR is all of these and more. It combines a compact VHS video recorder and big 13" color monitor for **foolproof** delivery of your important sales presentations.

For details, send in this card or call Midwest Visual, Chicago's largest and most respected audio-visual dealer, at (312) 478-1250.

Authorized Dealer
Panasonic

Name _____ Title _____

Company _____ Phone _____

Address _____ City _____ State _____ Zip _____

WIN A VACATION FOR TWO IN SUNNY SOUTHERN CALIFORNIA!

Yes, I would like the opportunity to win a vacation for two, courtesy of Western Airlines and Disneyland Hotel. Please include my name in the June 14 drawing.

Name _____

Title _____

Company _____

Address _____

City _____ State _____ Zip _____

Daytime Telephone (_____) _____

Disneyland Hotel
OFFICIAL HOTEL OF THE MAGIC KINGDOM
A MOBIL ★★★★ AND AAA ★★★★ RESORT
ANAHEIM, CALIFORNIA 92802 • A WRATHER HOTEL

Western Airlines
Count on us

All entry forms must be received by June 10, 1985. Drawing will be held on June 14, 1985. Reservations for travel and lodging must be completed by December 31, 1985 and are subject to availability. Crain Communications employees, suppliers and their families ineligible to participate.

Steal this color copier.

Not a sale. Not a bargain. At 29% savings, it's a steal. For only $995 a brand new Savin 7010 gives you:

- One of the smallest personal copiers made.
- Two-sided copying.
- Book copying.
- Letter and legal size copies.
- Faithfully reproduces solids and halftones.
- Copies on label stock and transparencies.

- Fastest 1st copy speed in its class 10 seconds.
- 10 crisp copies per minute.
- Microprocessor controls.
- Fiber optics.
- 100 sheet paper tray.
- Short jamproof paper path.
- Reliability.
- Color copies.

Only $995*
Was $1395 — you save $400.

FOR MORE INFORMATION CALL:
Jim Cook, Sales Manager (312) 640-9595
Or return this card filled out.

savin
The Dependable Decision

NAME _____ TITLE _____
COMPANY _____
ADDRESS _____
CITY _____ STATE _____
ZIP _____ PHONE _____

*Price valid if purchased by phone or demonstrated at Savin sales offices.
*Savin and Savin logotype are registered trademarks of Savin Corporation.
© Copyright 1983 Savin Corporation. Stamford, CT 06904

Exhibit 12-3. Three Examples of Postcard Advertisers in *Physicians Market Place*

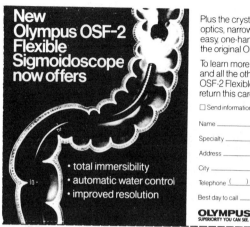

Package Inserts

The never-ending quest for reducing selling costs has led many major direct marketers to offer package insert programs to noncompeting advertisers. A sample array of package insert programs is shown in Exhibit 12-4.

Jack Oldstein, president of Dependable Lists, Inc., states, "Package inserts offer immediacy, guaranteed mail order buyers, with no waste circulation, the understood endorsement by the mailer of your product to his loyal customers, and the names used are fresher than the next update."

The late Virgil D. Angerman, formerly sales promotion manager of Boise Cascade Envelope Division, gave this sage advice about package insert programs. "The planning of a package insert program is much like planning a direct mail campaign. The advertiser should evaluate the type of person who will receive the package insert. The advertiser should ask if he or she is the logical prospect for a particular merchandise or service. The questions should be raised, will the insert do a thorough selling job? Is the offer attractive? Have you made it easy to send an inquiry or order?"

Just as with mailing lists, best results are realized when you match your offer to the market. If you are selling insurance to older people, using package inserts with vitamin shipments makes sense. If you are selling sports apparel, using package inserts with shipments going to fishermen and hunters makes sense, and so forth.

Professional mailing list brokers will provide list cards of firms who accept package inserts just as they supply list cards of direct marketers who make their mailing list available for rental.

Other Co-ops

While special interest, package insert, and newspaper co-ops offer mass distribution opportunities to direct marketers at low cost, there are also several off-beat co-ops available.

Many paperback book publishers make card inserts available to direct response advertisers. Circulation can run into the millions. Direct response advertisers can select distribution by title. Thus, the advertiser can fairly well estimate the demographic profile of readers by the type of book they are buying. *Gone with the Wind* would probably be a good distribution channel for an offer to women, *The Parsifal Mosaic* for an offer to men, and so forth.

One of the more recent developments is co-op distribution via grocery stores. Producers of grocery bags have devised manufacturing facilities whereby inserts can be pre-inserted in grocery bags. Thus, when shoppers empty their grocery bags, they find the direct response offers inside. Another medium available through retail grocery stores is what is commonly called the "supermarket rack." Shoppers are exposed to a variety of literature in racks adjacent to check-out counters.

Exhibit 12-4. Co-ops and "Piggybacks"

LIST TYPE, SOURCE, DESCRIPTION & SIZE	COST & MINIMUM	CONTACT YOUR BROKER OR	ENTER NUMBER ON INFO CARD
StarCrest Package Insert Program. Direct-response customers receptive to home-centered offers. Average unit of sale: $20. Sex: 93% female. Source: 100% direct mail. Four SMPs required. Total: **150,000-200,000 monthly.**	$40/M No Test	Woodruff-Stevens 40 East 34th Street New York, NY 10016 (213) 725-1555	177
Mail-Order Buyers Package Insert Program. Individuals have responded to package inserts, direct mail, and inserts in newspaper supplements. Items are moderately priced and cover a variety of interests. Sex: 70% female. Average unit of sale: $10. SMP required. Total: **65,000 per month**	$35/M Test 10,000	Nora Nelson Inc. 621 Avenue of the Americas New York, NY 10011 (212) 924-7551	178
Bank Systems & Equipment Action Reply Card Mailing. Fall mailing to top-qualified bank/thrift purchasing decision makers. October 1 deadline for Fall program. Mailing frequency: 2/year. Total: **35,025**	$33/M No Test	Gralla Publications 1515 Broadway New York, NY 10036 (212) 869-1300	179
Frederick's of Hollywood Package Insert Program. August mailing to women who are buyers of high style apparel, beauty and health aids, shoes, and jewelry. SMP required. Mailing frequency: 6/year. Total: **41,000 in August.**	$35/M Test 10,000	List Services Corp. P.O. Box 2014 Ridgefield, CN 06877 (203) 438-0327	180
Xerox Education Publications Package Insert Program. Inserts placed into the introductory packages of weekly reader books, including children's clubs and continuity buyers. Source: 100% direct response. SMP required. Total: **3,500,000**	$45/M Test 25,000	Qualified List Corp. 135 Bedford Road Armonk, NY 10504 (212) 324-8900	181
Alves Photo Service Package Inserts. Nationwide audience of mail-order buyers of film processing. Unit of sale: $5-$15. Source: 50% direct mail, 50% space ads. SMP required. Total: **10,000 weekly.**	$20/M Test 25,000	Leon Henry Inc. 455 Central Avenue Scarsdale, NY 10583 (914) 723-3176	205
Popular Club Package Insert Program. Credit-oriented homemakers buying a broad spectrum of products from a merchandise catalog. Unit of sale: $70. Sex: 98% female. Median age: 35. Average income: $15,000. Mailing frequency: 1/year. Total: **810,000**	$30/M Test 10,000	E.J. Krane Inc. P.O. Box 663 Princeton Junction, NJ 08550 (609) 452-2885	183
Sunset House Insert Program. Buyers of beauty products, jewelry, health aids, horticulture items, housewares and novelty items. Source: 90% direct mail. Average unit of order: $10-$13. Sex: 78% female. Total: **100,000**	$40/M Test 10,000	Woodruff-Stevens & Associates 40 East 34th Street New York, NY 10016 (212) 725-1555	217

Co-ops are a major tool for direct response advertisers when used correctly. They are not suitable for selling a $400 calculator, but are excellent for getting inquiries about a $400 calculator. Co-ops are highly preferred for in-store coupon redemptions and for scores of direct response offers requiring a minimum of information for a targeted audience.

Self-Quiz

1. Why do cents-off coupons qualify as direct marketing?

2. Heavy users of cents-off coupons skew toward families with:

   ☐ Annual income under $10,000

   ☐ Annual income over $25,000

3. Which is the largest distribution channel for cents-off coupons?

   ☐ Newspapers   ☐ Magazines   ☐ Direct mail

4. Which medium shows the highest average redemption rate:

   ☐ Newspapers   ☐ Magazines   ☐ Direct mail

5. Name four types of traditional co-ops.

   a. _____

   b. _____

   c. _____

   d. _____

6. A co-op is likely to pull about one-fourth that of a solo mailing at about

   _____ the cost.

7. What is the difference between "loose" insert co-ops and postcard co-ops?

   _____

   _____

   _____

8. Describe how homemakers tend to sort out the contents of co-op envelopes.

   _____

   _____

   _____

   _____

9. What is the one variable you must live with in scheduling the continuation of a co-op you tested previously?

   _____

   _____

_____

_____

10. Name five advantages of package inserts.

a. _____

b. _____

c. _____

d. _____

e. _____

Pilot Project

You have become promotion director of the *Advertising Age* postcard program, which is distributed several times a year to its 70,000 plus subscribers.

As a prelude to developing your promotion program, it is your assignment to develop a list of prospects whose propositions you feel will appeal to advertising agency personnel, marketing executives, advertising managers, advertising research executives, and graphic arts personnel.

Please break your prospect categories into two segments: primary and secondary. Expand the list for each to twelve, using the first three as starting points.

Primary

1. Advertising and marketing books
2. Premiums
3. TV production
4. _____
5. _____
6. _____
7. _____
8. _____
9. _____
10. _____
11. _____
12. _____

Secondary

1. Investment opportunities
2. Office forms
3. Office equipment
4. _____
5. _____
6. _____
7. _____
8. _____
9. _____
10. _____
11. _____
12. _____

CHAPTER THIRTEEN

Telemarketing

Telemarketing is an advertising medium for direct response advertisers just as is print, broadcast, and direct mail. Telemarketing is particularly powerful when it is integral to other mediums. The 800 toll-free number in a direct response commercial, a direct response ad, or a direct mail package becomes a major force in overcoming human inertia.

The power of telemarketing begets a responsibility to use the medium with discretion. Intrusive, high-pressure calls at inconvenient times are most often counterproductive. Telemarketing is most effective when helpful dialogues are maintained with existing customers and qualified prospects.

The Spectrum of Telemarketing Applications

One way to explore telemarketing opportunities is to look at a tele-marketing sales continuum as a means to identifying applications.

Order taking usually begins with a catalog or other promotion mailed

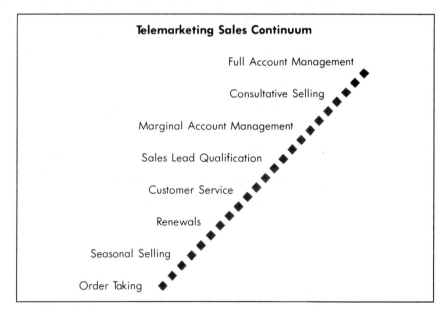

Telemarketing Sales Continuum

Full Account Management
Consultative Selling
Marginal Account Management
Sales Lead Qualification
Customer Service
Renewals
Seasonal Selling
Order Taking

Material for this chapter has been extracted from Successful Telemarketing *by Bob Stone and John Wyman, published by NTC Business Books, Lincolnwood, Illinois, 1986.*

to potential customers. The prospect is encouraged to use the convenience of calling an 800 number to place an order.

For example, when Fotomat introduced a new product—videotape sales and rentals—it publicized an 800 number for customers to place orders and to get directions to the nearest local Fotomat Hut.

Additionally, an order-taking operation offers the possibility of upgrading by including limited cross-selling, new product couponing, and even simple marketing research.

Seasonal selling is another telemarketing application. The Swim Shop—a company in Nashville, Tennessee, that supplies gear to summer swim teams—offers an example of how to extend a limited sales season. Since the peak swimming season lasts about twelve weeks—too short a period for the shop to rely on traditional methods to fill orders—it made available an 800 number so orders could be received and filled promptly late in the season. Avoiding the mail stretched out the firm's sales season.

Renewals are another widely used aspect of telemarketing. These applications are now an integral part of a magazine's circulation subscription program. One phone call can produce what it might take several subscription renewal letters to accomplish. The technique has been used successfully also for selling other products—fruit, cheese, even plants.

As a major user of telemarketing for policy renewals, one insurance company's "conservation program" saves about $20,000 per month by using telemarketing to conserve policies about to lapse.

Customer service, another area for improved effectiveness and cost control, is the next step up the telemarketing continuum. Using a unique system, the 3M Company offers an 800 number to assist their telecommunication equipment customers. The 3M National Service Center, located in St. Paul, Minnesota, is manned 365 days a year, twenty-four hours a day, with skilled technicians and coordinators. Through systematic questioning and a variety of facsimile, ASCII communication terminals, store and forward electronic message distribution terminals, the latest electronic monitoring and testing equipment, and a sophisticated on-line computer system, the staff can isolate the failure to an equipment problem or operator error. The 3M center has found that on more than 30% of the calls, the equipment failure can be solved in minutes, without dispatching a service technician.

Sales lead qualification is designed to reduce the number of wasted in-person sales visits. With an estimated $205 average for each industrial sales call, companies cannot afford to send salespeople to unqualified prospects. The better qualified a prospect is, the greater the sales call's potential for success. When a prospect is prequalified by telephone, telemarketing helps to direct outside salespeople to where the highest sales potential exists.

Reliance Electric, a Cleveland-based manufacturer of electric and mechanical power distribution equipment and weighing scales and systems, uses telemarketing to qualify half of the 125,000 sales leads received annually. Because almost all sales require customized products, Reliance's field sales force of 700 are all highly trained engineers; Reliance utilizes telemarketing to focus their sales team on new business potential.

By incorporating an 800 number into all of its advertising, Reliance generates lead responses into its telemarketing center—called the Marketing Information Center. Telemarketing specialists qualify these prospects—notifying field sales of the "hot" prospects for follow-up within twenty-four hours. Reliance also utilizes outbound WATS follow-up to qualify nontelephone generated leads (i.e., letters, reply cards, trade show contacts, and so on). The M.I.C. system, in its first year of operation, increased quotation activity of field sales by one million dollars. In its second year, Reliance is expecting that figure to further increase by 50 percent.

Marginal account management allows a marketer to capitalize on the revenue potential of smaller accounts without the high cost burden of face-to-face sales visits. Banding together marginal accounts spread over a wide geographic area permits profitable coverage at low cost.

To handle such targeted accounts profitably, Hallmark Cards, Inc., the social expression company, uses telemarketing. Hallmark uses a combination of direct mail and telemarketing to give its remote outlets the same highly personal, current card selection as any urban, large card shop or department store.

Consultative selling is a highly personal involved sales technique. With telemarketing, a customer's needs are probed by a specially trained sales representative. Personalized solutions are designed during the phone contact, when possible.

Full account management is at the very zenith of the marketing spectrum. It involves order taking, answering questions about order status, inventory availability, shipment scheduling and billing, credit checking and product consultation. This full-service operation includes both selling and customer service.

Telemarketing in the Advertising Mix

We mentioned at the outset that telemarketing is unique in that it hypes response when integrated with other advertising mediums. Let us now explore some of the applications.

Direct Mail

Telemarketers learned early on that if you give direct mail recipients the choice of either making a toll-free call or returning a reply card total response is usually increased. And AT&T has found, as have many others, that those who inquire by phone are more likely to order. Exhibit 13-1 is a good example of how long-distance services emphasize their toll-free number in both their letter and reply card. The bottom line is that those who respond by phone prequalify themselves as better prospects. Closure rates are often four-to-six times greater than mail response.

Of all the advertising applications of the 800 number none have proved more successful than toll-free phone order privileges for catalog buyers. Catalog director after catalog director reports the average phone order to be 20 percent greater than the average mail order. Thus, if a catalog firm gets an average order of $70 by mail, they can expect an average phone order of $84.

The reason for the larger order is easy to explain. A woman ordering a dress by phone, for example, puts the telephone communicator into a natural consultative selling situation. Consider this dialogue:

> Fine, Mrs. Smith. You want size 18 in the royal blue. Have you considered the scarf on page 32, item number 1628? This would really look beautiful with the royal blue. . . . Good. I'll include it with your order. Shipment will go out via UPS tonight. Thank you.

Consultative selling increases the average catalog order. No doubt about it. But here is another unique way to increase the average phone order: Jack Schmid, a catalog consultant in Kansas City, Missouri, came up with this idea when he was catalog manager of Halls, a division of Hallmark.

Jack printed the following legend in his catalog—"When you place your order by phone, ask our telephone communicator for the special of the week." Dialogue between the customer and the telephone communicator went along these lines.

Customer:	I'd like to order items number 1202 and number 1842. Also I'd like to know what your special of the week is.
Communicator:	Our special of the week is the set of six tumblers on page 21. If you will turn to that page you will note that the catalog price is $24. Our special price this week is $18.
Customer:	Okay. Add the tumblers to my order.

This program was a great success. Depending upon the special of the week, up to 29 percent of those who placed phone orders added the special of the week to their orders.

Print Advertising

It is so common today to see in newspapers and magazines ads that feature either a local number or 800 number to get information or to place an order. As a matter of fact the 800 number has changed the way many marketers do business. All to the good.

Exhibit 13-1. Illustration of a Letter from AT&T with a Reply Card

AT&T

2301 Main Street • P.O. Box 549 • Kansas City, Missouri 64141 • 1 800 821-2121, ext. 626

Dear Executive,

We are pleased to be able to present our special AT&T long distance services in one comprehensive "Business Services Guide."

This gives you the opportunity to review just what the new AT&T is offering. From AT&T Long Distance Service to AT&T Data Services, we bring you the best telecommunications network anywhere.

Our services are designed to help your business grow, and grow with your business, no matter how small or large your company is.

And along with the thorough outline of our services in your enclosed Business Services Guide, we're also offering a free consultation with a professional Consultant, to help you choose the AT&T long distance services that are right for you.

Simply call us toll-free at 1 800 821-2121, ext. 626 to speak to an AT&T Network Consultant.

Our Consultants have worked with businesses of all sizes across the country, so we can help you decide which services make sense for your company. And your Consultant will offer personalized service and advice to help your business use them to cut costs, increase your sales, and help your business grow faster. He or she can even coordinate implementation of the services for you.

So take some time to read through your Business Services Guide. And be sure to contact your Network Consultant at our toll-free number, or mail the enclosed postpaid card, to put these services to work for your business.

Sincerely,

Judy DeVooght

Judy DeVooght
Manager, Network Consultants

FIND OUT HOW YOUR BUSINESS CAN CUT COSTS AND IMPROVE PROFITABILITY WITH AT&T LONG DISTANCE SERVICES

CALL TOLL-FREE

1 800 821-2121, ext. 626
OR MAIL THIS POSTPAID CARD

YES! Please tell me more about AT&T long distance services.

Please fill in Phone Number _____
(Area Code)

If address is incorrect, fill out information below

Name/Title _____

Company _____

Address _____

City _____ State _____ Zip _____

33U-073

Exhibit 13-2. Monex International Advertisement

To illustrate the power of integrating the 800 number into print advertising let us look at two unique examples:

It's not unusual for consumers to order merchandise by phone in the $10 to $100 range. But it is most unusual for consumers to order gold or silver by phone in units of $1,500, $2,500, $5,000, $10,000, and more. And yet they do in the aggregate of millions of dollars. By phone!

Exhibit 13-2 is typical of the sort of advertisement that Monex International runs consistently in the *Wall Street Journal* and other publications appealing to the serious investor.

What is so unique about Monex's use of print and phone is that major purchases of precious metals are consumated entirely by phone.

The second example of a unique application of print and phone involves what is commonly referred to as "dealer-locater advertising."

Consider the problem a major marketer with hundreds or thousands of dealers faces when a very special service is offered only through a select number of their dealers. Telemarketing turns out to be the ideal solution.

The Chevron ad in Exhibit 13-3 is a classic example of the solution. Note how Chevron makes it easy for the consumer to learn the name and address of the nearest dealer offering "6-Point Car Service Warranty Protection."

More and more national advertisers are offering a dealer locater service by providing a toll-free number in their print advertising. It's faster, more economical, and more cost efficient.

TV Advertising

There are few direct response TV commercials these days that do not include an 800 number. The 800 number makes instant response a reality. In the very first chapter of this book due reference was made to the impact of telephone upon TV's home shopping shows. Millions and millions in merchandise is being sold via TV with the phone as the catalyst.

But direct response TV, with the toll-free number as an adjunct, goes well beyond the sale of merchandise. Consider this example.

New York Telephone Company is a major TV advertiser. Among the many services they have offered their customers are information and entertainment services, such as Sports Phone, Dial-A-Joke, and Weather.

Exhibit 13-4 shows a thirty-second commercial promoting Sports Phone. In the short span of thirty seconds, the viewer sees fifteen frames with accompanying audio. It is significant to note that the phone number is superimposed over four of the frames with the area codes for a ten-cent call superimposed over two of the frames.

Were these direct-response TV commercials successful? And how! In a twelve-month period New York Telephone Company received millions of incremental phone calls.

The Mathematics of Telemarketing

The power of telemarketing is beyond question. It's place in the totality of direct marketing is firmly established. But the mathematics of telemarketing is not clearly understood by many. For starters we face up to the fact that the telephone is *the most expensive* advertising medium on a per thousand basis outside of face-to-face selling. So telemarketing has to be very cost effective to be successful. And for thousands of marketers it is.

To get to the numbers we went to Rudy Oetting, President of R. H. Oetting & Associates, Inc., a leading telemarketing operation in New York City.

Exhibit 13-3. Chevron "Dealer-Locater" Ad

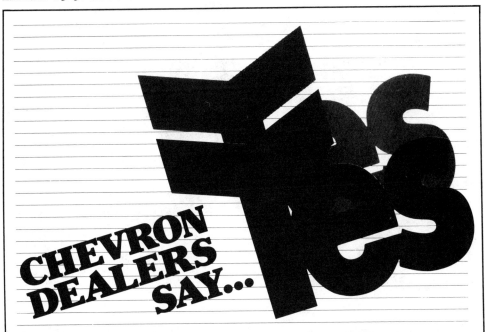

6-Point Car Service
Warranty Protection

While many gas stations are saying no to choices
and services, Chevron Dealers say Yes. Yes to a *6-point
warranty protection plan* on many car care services at
Chevron Hallmark Award Stations.

1. **90 DAYS or 4,000 MILES GUARANTEED**
Whichever comes first. Warranty covers all
parts and labor.

2. **PROBLEM SOLVED OR MONEY
REFUNDED**
If a problem occurs, either the work will be
done over at no cost to you, or the entire cost will be
refunded, at the dealer's option.

3. **ADVANCE WRITTEN ESTIMATES**
You'll know the cost before work begins. If
additional repairs are needed, your approval
will be obtained first.

4. **RETURN OF REPLACED PARTS**
At your request, all replaced parts will be
returned for your inspection.

5. **HONORED AT HALLMARK AWARD
STATIONS WITH REPAIR FACILITIES**
If a problem occurs, take your car back to the
station where the service was performed. If you're
more than 50 miles from that station, your warranty
will be honored by any Hallmark Award Dealer who
performs that type of service.

6. **ON-THE-ROAD HOTLINE**
There are over 1000 Hallmark Award Dealers
with service facilities in the U.S. You can call
toll-free **(800) 227-1677** for the nearest station which
will honor your warranty.
You'll find that all Chevron Hallmark Award Dealers—
including those who do not offer car care service—
maintain the highest standards of customer service.
For the nearest Chevron Hallmark Award Station
call:

(800) 227-1677

Complete Details of Warranty available at your Chevron Hallmark Award Station.

Exhibit 13-4. New York Telephone TV Spot

WRK

CLIENT: NEW YORK TELEPHONE CO.   TITLE: "FIELD TALK"   DATE: 4/8/81
PRODUCT: SPORTS PHONE   LENGTH: 30 SECONDS   CODE NUMBER: AXSP 0333

1. COACH: (OC) Rocky,
   (SFX: SNAP)

2. go back out there and run the trap reverse.

3. Green T45R

4. wide out set.

5. Got it?

6. ROCKY: Got it.

7. COACH: Now let's call Sports Phone and find out how the competition's doing.

8. It's 976-1313.

9. ROCKY: Got it!

10. COACH: Now run that play boy.

11. ROCKY: (VO FROM FIELD) 976-1313 Hut!

12. COACH: (SFX: GRUNT) ....that's wrong.... ...that's wrong...

13. ANNCR: (VO) It's no more than a dime in these area codes

14. for all the major scores.

15. On Sports Phone.

Inbound/Outbound Costs

There are two sets of numbers that are key to estimating telemarketing costs: (1) cost per call for handling *inbound* calls from business firms and consumers, and (2) cost per call per decision-maker contact in making *outbound* calls to business firms and consumers. Mr. Oetting provided the following range of costs for each.

Approximate Inbound Cost per Call

Category	Range of Cost
Business	$2.50 to $5.00
Consumer	$1.50 to $3.00

Approximate Outbound Costs per Decision-Maker Contact

Category	Range of Cost
Business	$7.00 to $14.00
Consumer	$2.50 to $4.00

The difference in cost range between inbound and outbound calls should be explained. In the case of inbound calls, the initiator is always a prospect or customer: The caller phones at a time of his/her convenience with a view to getting further information or negotiating an order: In the case of outbound calls, the initiator is always the marketer: The call may be made at an inconvenient time for the prospect and the caller may have to generate awareness about a new product or service. Consequently, outbound calls are usually of longer duration and often require more experienced, higher paid personnel.

The range of costs, whether for inbound or outbound, depends a great deal upon the telemarketing application and the complexity involved for each application.

The following indicates where ranges of costs are most likely to fall, on average, by application.

Application	Low Range	High Range
Order processing	X	
Customer service	X	
Sales support		X
Account management		X
Sales promotion	X	

Developing Worksheets

Knowing the average range of costs for inbound and outbound calls is key, but it is just the start. The operation of an in-house telemarketing center requires a full range of personnel. And it is subject to taxes, fringe benefit costs, incentive costs, equipment costs and collateral material costs as well. To get a true picture of all monthly costs, worksheets are advised.

Rudy Oetting has provided us with two representative worksheets (Exhibits 13-5, 13-6): one for inbound and one for outbound.

Exhibit 13-5. Monthly Expense Statement—Inbound: 9:00 A.M. to 5:00 P.M.

Representative Phone Hours (1235) Direct Expenses	Cost	Cost/Phone Hour
Labor		
Manager (⅓ time)	$ 1,250	$ 1.01
Supervisor (full time)	2,750	2.23
Representatives (10 full time)	16,000	12.95
Administration (2 full time)	2,426	1.96
Tax and fringe (⅓ of wages)	8,134	6.59
Incentives	2,000	1.62
Subtotal	$32,560	$26.36
Phone		
Equipment and service	1,489	1.21
Lines:		
• WATS	12,819	10.38
• *MTS (Message Toll Service)*	—	—
Subtotal	$14,308	$11.59
Other		
Lists	—	—
Mail/Catalogs	2,470	1.00
Postage	1,235	.50
Miscellaneous	1,000	.81
Subtotal	$ 4,705	$ 2.31
Total Direct	51,573	41.76
G&A (15%)	7,736	6.26
Totals	$59,309	$48.02

Basis for Expense Statement

Labor

Manager	Annual − $45,000 × 1/3 allocation − $1,250/month
Supervisor	Annual − $33,000 at full allocation − $2,750/month
Representatives	$9.23/hour × 40 hours/week × 52 weeks full allocation = $1,600/month 6.5 phone hours/day × 19 days/month − 123.5 phone hours/month
Administration	$7.00/hour × 40 hours/week × 52 weeks full allocation = $1,213/month
Tax and fringe	33.3% of wages (including contest incentives)
Incentives	Reps only = $2,000/month
Phone *ACD + Sets*	$65,000 depreciated over 5 years plus $4,875 annual maintenance
WATS (800) =	Step Rate 18 plus Band 5* 42 minutes (70%) per labor hour *WATS* Connect Time: 1235 hours × 0.70% = 865 billable *WATS* hours plus 10 lines @ $36.80/line access

Note: The average number of calls handled per rep phone hour is 12 @ 2.3 minutes each. As high as 15 per phone hour during peaks.

Computations
1. @ 12 calls/hour = $3.93/call
2. @ 15 calls/hour = $3.14/call
3. @ 1 Order/rep phone hour = $47.00 per order
4. @ 6 Orders/rep phone hour = $7.85 per order

*Step Rate 18 (Local State) plus Band 5 (all other continental states plus Puerto Rico and Virgin Islands).

It is easy to see how worksheets lead to capturing all the numbers. The key numbers to explore are (1) cost per phone hour, (2) cost per call, and (3) cost per order (or response). A review of the computations for Exhibit 13-5 (inbound) shows a significant difference in cost, for example, when phone representatives are able to handle fifteen incoming calls per hour as contrasted to twelve calls per phone hour. And the cost per order drops dramatically if the representative is able to close six orders per phone hour, for example, as contrasted to one per phone hour.

Likewise for Exhibit 13-6 (outbound) significant differences are to be noted in costs at differing levels relating to total dialings per phone hour, total decision-maker contacts per phone hour and total orders per phone hour. Such computations provide a realistic approach to determining breakeven point.

Exhibit 13-6. Monthly Expense Statement—Outbound: 9:00 A.M. to 5:00 P.M.

Representatives Phone Hours (1235) Direct Expense	Cost	Cost/Phone Hour
Labor		
Manager (1/3 time)	$ 1,500	$ 1.21
Supervisor (full time)	3,000	2.43
Representatives (10 full time)	18,000	14.58
Administration (2 full time)	2,426	1.96
Tax and fringe (1/3 of wages)	12,296	9.96
Incentive	12,000	9.72
Subtotal	$49,222	$39.86
Phone		
Equipment and service	350	.28
Lines:		
•WATS	9,228	7.47
•MTS (Message Toll Service)	3,075	2.50
Subtotal	$12,653	$10.25
Automation		
Depreciation	4,950	1.58
Maintenance	731	.59
Subtotal	2,681	2.17
Other		
Lists	3,088	2.50
Mail/Catalogs	617	.50
Postage	309	.25
Miscellaneous	1,235	1.00
Subtotal	$ 5,249	$ 4.25
Total Direct	$69,805	$56.53
G&A (15%)	10,471	8.48
Totals	$80,276	$65.01

Basis for Expense Statement

Labor

Manager   Annual = $54,000 × 1/3 allocation = $1,500/month

Supervisor   Annual = $36,000 at full allocation = $3,000/month

Representatives $8.65/hour × 40 hours/week × 52 weeks full allocation = $1,800/month
6.5 phone hours/day × 19 days/month = 123.5 phone hours/month

Administration $7.00/hour × 40 hours/week × 52 weeks at full allocation = $1,213/month

Tax and fringe 33.3% of wages (including contest incentives)

Incentives Reps only—40% of Total Renumeration

Phone

WATS = Step Rate 18 plus Band 5*
35 minutes (50%) per labor hour WATS connect time:
1235 × 50% = 617 billable WATS hours
plus 10 lines @ $31.65/line access

MTS
(Message Toll
Services) = 5 minutes per labor hours connect time:
1235 × 8.3% = 102.5 Message Toll @
0.50 Min. = $3,075

Computations
1. @ 12 TDs (total dialings) per rep phone hours cost per dial = $5.42
2. @ 15 TDs (total dialings) per rep phone hour cost per dial = $4.33
3. @ 5 DMCs (decision-maker contacts) per phone hour cost per DMC = $13.00
4. @ 6 DMCs (decision-maker contacts) per phone hour cost per DMC = $10.83
5. @ 1 Order per rep phone hour cost per order = $65.00
6. @ 3 Orders per rep phone hour cost per order = $21.67

*Step Rate 18 (Local State) plus Band 5 (all other continental states plus Puerto Rico and Virgin Islands).

While these two worksheets relate to the sale of products or services, the same type of arithmetic can be structured to determine likely costs for literature requests, product information, customer service calls, sales support, full account management, or sales promotion. The calls handled or made per hour might vary by application, but the principles are the same.

Call Ratios Favor Telemarketing

When comparing outbound sales calls to field sales calls the pure ratios favor telemarketing. On the average, a field salesperson can make five to six calls a day—twenty-five to thirty a week; on the average, a telemarketing salesperson can make twenty-five to thirty decision-maker contacts (DMCs) a day—125 to 150 week.

Put another way, to achieve the same contact level, on average five field salespeople would have to be added for every telemarketing salesperson.

Making the In-House/Service Organization Decision

Understanding the mathematics of telemarketing is a key to success, but the numbers that evolve are affected dramatically, pro or con, by the caliber of personnel involved. The telephone communicator becomes the "voice" of the company and the way he or she handles the phone conversation has both immediate and long-term impact.

The major question marketers face when contemplating a telemarketing operation is: "Should I develop my own in-house operation, or should I use an experienced service organization?" To put this important question into focus we went to Jim McAllister, president of Telephone Marketing Services of Cincinnati, Ohio. His organization performs full account management services for a wide variety of prestigious clients.

When an In-House Telemarketing Operation Is Indicated

The first question put to McAllister was a *zinger:* Under what conditions is it more appropriate for an organization to test and/or maintain a telemarketing center in-house? His answer was candid and precise:

1. Situations which involve a great deal of technical knowledge.

2. Programs which require a high degree of integration with other internal support departments; close coordination of shipping schedules, inventories, credit, and so forth.

When a Service Organization Is Indicated

Jim McAllister then turned to situations in which, in his opinion, an outside service organization is indicated.

1. Situations in which flexibility is required, such as several concurrent campaigns with varying objectives; seasonal selling programs or promotional campaigns.

2. Situations in which a full-time staff is either inadequate or cannot be justified, such as contacting a large universe over a short period of time; new product introductions; periods of exceptionally high incoming 800 number response; any short-term program.

3. Most sales support systems such as prospect qualification, lead generation, and new business or account campaigns.

4. Situations in which there is a lack of, or an unwillingness to commit, internal resources such as quality management and personnel, administrative cost control, equipment, and so forth.

Speaking further on the inside versus outside issue McAllister observed, "When first considering telemarketing, most companies initially turn to some form of outside assistance. This can range from various publications and seminars to training manuals and consultants. Many times this fact-finding process leads to the misconception that telemarketing can provide spectacular results with very little effort and that it's relatively simple."

This perception not only creates unrealistic expectations, but often biases or prevents a thorough evaluation process that should include all the elements necessary for a successful program as well as all the factors which will create pitfalls and obstacles.

"The decision to do telemarketing internally or through an outside supplier is often made prematurely," he said. "It should be determined *after* the evaluation process has led to the decision to test a specific program. The test phase definitely favors a good outside supplier. They have the organization in place, whereas the internal expertise, resources available and commitment at this stage are not normally sufficient to provide a valid test of potential.

"The decision to do telemarketing inside or outside need not be a permanent 'either-or' decision," McAllister concluded, "since the variety and timing of telemarketing applications can require outside support of in-house programs."

Telemarketing in the Training Process

For those who opt for an in-house telemarketing operation it must be emphasized that there is far more involved than putting a successful sales person on the phone. As a matter of fact, more often than not, the worst thing one can do is put a successful staff salesperson into a telemarketing center. A field salesperson thrives on face-to-face interaction, resists being desk bound.

To establish the traits of a successful telemarketing person and to learn what is involved in the on-going training process we went to the AT&T training center in Cincinnati, Ohio. We are indebted to Nancy Lamberton, staff manager, for sharing her experience with us.

Traits of a Telemarketing Person

Our first question to Nancy Lamberton was "When recruiting, what traits do you look for?" She listed five traits.

1. Good communication skills—voice quality is clear and pleasant; articulate.

2. Persistent and able to bounce back from rejection.

3. Good organization skills.

4. Ability to project telephone personality—enthusiasm, friendliness.

5. Flexibility. Can adapt to different types of clients and new situations.

"We have potential applicants for telemarketing sales positions go through a 1½-hour telephone assessment process," Nancy continued. "Applicants are put in several sales situations to determine if they have the dimensions we are looking for."

Training for New Hires

"Nancy, once a person is hired, what type of training program is that person put through?" She then proceeded to outline their training program covering a period of 18½ days.

1. Orientation (4 days)—Salesperson learns overall structure and goals of AT&T Communications as well as general business functions.

2. Network Services (2½ days)—Salesperson receives basic knowledge of AT&T Communications products and services. This is what the salesperson will be selling. This course is delivered via computer-based education.

3. Selling Skills (3½ days)—Salesperson learns sales skills through the interactive video disc, then goes through four hours of role playing with an instructor.

4. Telemarketing (2 days)—Salesperson learns how to identify client's needs and telemarketing applications. Through casework, the salesperson practices implementing an application for a client.

5. Account Management (3 days)—Each salesperson has 400 accounts, which means that priortizing accounts by revenue potential, cycling accounts, and time management are critical.

6. Advanced Account management (3½ days)—After three to eight months of experience, the salesperson gets advanced training on how to manage the highest potential accounts.

The Seven-Step Selling Process

Students are schooled thoroughly in a seven-step selling process, a process developed over time, which leads the salesperson in logical steps from precall planning to the close and wrap-up. The outline that follows details these steps.

1. Precall Planning
   a. Reviewing client information.
   b. Planning objective for the call.
   c. Psyching—getting mentally ready for the call!

2. Approach/Positioning
   a. Identify who you are and where you're from.
   b. Purpose of the call.
   c. Interest-creating statement.
   d. Build rapport.
   e. Getting the decision maker.
   f. Getting through the receptionist/screener.

3. Data Gathering
   a. Gain general understanding of the client's business.
   b. Move from general to specific types of questions.
   c. Questioning techniques.
   d. Identifying a client business need.

4. Solution Generation
   a. Tailor communication solution to specific client need.
   b. As in-depth questions to test the feasibility of the solution.
   c. Gather data for cost/benefit analysis.
   d. Prepare client for the recommendation.

5. Solution Presentation
   a. Get client agreement to area of need.
   b. Present recommendation in a clear and concise manner.
   c. Use benefits.

6. Close
   a. Timing—when to close.
   b. Buying signals.
   c. Handling objections.
   d. Closing techniques.

7. Wrap-up
   a. Implementation issues.
   b. Thank client for the business.
   c. Confirm client commitment.
   d. Leave name and number.
   e. Position next call.

Applying the Seven-Step Selling Process

Now let us see how this selling process might be applied outside of the field of communications. For our example, we'll create a wholesaler who specializes in veterinary drugs. The call is to introduce a new drug to a regular customer.

1. Precall Planning

    The telemarketer reviews the account file of the Whiteside Veterinary Clinic. He notes that Dr. Sargent ordered her usual order of drug supplies last month, but that she hasn't tried a new drug that L.L.M. Pharmaceutical has recently introduced via direct mail.

    The telemarketer reviews his introduction briefly, takes a deep breath, and says "Smile!"

2. Approach/Positioning

    "Hello. This is Mark Wiley with L.L.M. Pharmaceutical. Dr. Sargent is usually available about this time. May I speak with her?"

    "Good morning, Dr. Sargent. This is Mark Wiley with L.L.M. How have things been going at your clinic since I last talked to you? (Pause) I'm certainly glad to hear that! Dr. Sargent, as a buyer of many of our quality products, I knew you'd be interested in hearing about one of our innovative new drugs. If you have a minute, I'd like to ask you a couple of questions. . . ."

3. Data Gathering

    "Doctor, your practice pretty much covers a suburban area, doesn't it?"

    "Right now when a dog is suffering from hookworm, what drug are you prescribing?"

4. Solution Generation

    "Many vets also used to prescribe that particular drug. Have you had many dogs suffering from various side effects from that drug?"

    "Would you be interested in prescribing a new drug that has few, if any, side effects?"

5. Solution Presentation

    "L.L.M. has introduced Formula XYZ that not only has fewer side effects, but extensive laboratory tests have shown that the medicine takes effect twenty-four hours more quickly than similar drugs."

6. Close

    "I'm sure that your customers would appreciate faster relief for their pets. Can I add a case of Formula XYZ to your regular order?"

7. Wrap-up

    "I'm sure that you will be pleased with the results, Dr. Sargent. We've gotten excellent comments back from many vets around the country. I'll get that shipment to you by early next week. Thank you for your business. I'll be calling you again the first of next month. Have a good day!"

Role Playing: A Key Teaching Device

"One of the most effective ways to teach proper telemarketing procedures is to get students involved in role playing," Nancy Lamberton pointed out.

"Role playing is an excellent way to acclimate the student to the job," she said. "By putting students in different selling situations, we accelerate the learning curve. Students make their first mistakes with the instructor rather than the prospect."

Role-playing Examples

"Our instructors put students through role playing situations and then evaluate their performance," Nancy continued. We asked her to give us a poor example and a good example of a telephone dialogue with an evaluation for each. (These are abbreviated versions for demonstration purposes.) First we will give you the poor example.

Heritage Village Furniture
Poor Example

Sue: Hello. May I speak to Steve Rooney?

Steve: This is he.

Sue: Oh, this is Steve? Well, Steve, this is Sue Jones, your new account executive. I'd like to talk to you about your phone services. Do you have a minute?

Steve: I didn't catch the company you're with. . . .

Sue: Oh, gosh, I'm sorry . . . I'm with AT&T.

Steve: Well, I'm pretty busy today. . . .

Sue: That's okay, I won't take much of your time. Can I just ask you a few questions about your business?

Steve: If it only takes a minute. . . .

Sue: So, are you a furniture retail store?

Steve: No, actually we manufacture furniture.

Sue: Do you then sell it to retail furniture stores?

Steve: Yes, we do.

Sue: What is your sales volume a year?

Steve: I don't see what business that is of yours. Anyhow, why are you asking me all these questions? What has it got to do with my phone service?

Sue: Well, it helps me better understand your company so I can show you how to use telemarketing.

Steve: I'm not interested in telemarketing. The way our business works, you can't sell furniture over the phone.

Sue: A lot of companies are doing it.

Steve: Well, not my company! Maybe you should call me back when you can tell me how to save on my phone bill. I'm really quite busy. . . .

Sue: Can I call you tomorrow, Mr. Rooney?

Steve: Why don't you just send something in the mail? That would be quicker.

Sue: Oh, okay. I'll do that today. Thanks for your time, Mr. Rooney.

Now for the evaluation. (See Exhibit 13-7.)

Let's deal with the same selling opportunity, but with a good example of how it might be handled.

Heritage Village Furniture
Good Example

Sue: Hello. This is Sue Jones with AT&T Communications. May I speak to Steve Rooney?

Steve: This is he.

Sue: Oh, good. How are you doing today, Mr. Rooney?

Steve: Well, actually I'm pretty busy today. . . .

Sue: I understand that you're a busy person, Mr. Rooney, but if I can show you how to get the most out of your communication dollars would you have a few minutes to discuss some ideas?

Steve: Well, I guess I do have a couple of minutes, but what can AT&T do for me?

Sue: As your account executive, I will be working with you to show you how AT&T long-distance services can be a valuable part of Heritage's profit picture. To see exactly how I can be of service to you, it would be helpful if I understood your business better. Tell me a little about Heritage Village Furniture, if you would. . . .

Exhibit 13-7. Role-playing Evaluation (Poor Example)

ACCOUNT EXECUTIVE
TELEMARKETING SELLING SKILLS
Evaluation Sheets

ROLE PLAY/SKILL PRACTICE

Trainee: Sue Jones   Date: 6/16/84

Which call (1st, 2nd, etc.) 2nd

Instructor/Evaluator: M. Dambraton   Case-Company name: Heritage Village

Skill	ST	SAT	NI	NO	COMMENTS
Performance rating					
APPROACH POSITIONING					
Managed screener: polite, persistent, used as a resource				✓	Sue obviously didn't have a plan going into this call. She confused the client by not explaining who she represented and the purpose of the call. She also didn't get the client's attention.
Completed positioning statement: who, where from, why calling			✓		
Made interest-creating opening statement			✓		
Asked for appropriate contact (if no name given prior to call)		✓			The poor introduction set the tone of the entire call — Sue never recovered.
Explained consultative role			✓		
Used listening skills		✓			
DATA GATHERING					
Made appropriate transition from AP		✓			Sue assumed Heritage was a retail store, which brought a negative response from the client. A series of close-ended questions then followed. Sue needs to ask more open-ended questions to get the client involved in the conversation.
Verified existing LD services				✓	
Asked about immediate concerns			✓		
Learned about business operations			✓		
Structured questioning strategy			✓		

Performance rating: ST - Strong; SAT - Satisfactory; NI - Needs Improvement; NO - Not observed.

(continued)

Exhibit 13-7. Role-playing Evaluation (Poor Example)

Skill / Performance rating	ST	SAT	NI	NO	COMMENTS
Used open/closed questions appropriately			✓		The strategy was poor. Before she got the client comfortable, Sue asked about sales volume.
Questions appeared directed toward objective(s)			✓		At this point, the client's frustration with the call came out.
Attempted to build credibility				✓	
Maintained conversational tone		✓			
Maintained control of dialogue			✓		
Demonstrated listening skills:					
-Probed and clarified					
-Paid attention to client					
-Followed client leads					
-Used silence			✓		
-Demonstrated empathy					
-Tied together ideas					
SOLUTION GENERATION/DEVELOPMENT					
Identified relevant/appropriate applications					
Collected appropriate specific data					
Dropped interest-creating hints					
Tailored application(s) to business operations & expressed needs					
SOLUTION PRESENTATION					
Reviewed & got agreement on client's objectives & concerns					
Tailored solution to client					
Focused on relevant benefits					
Demonstrated cost-effectiveness					
Anticipated impact of solution on client's business					

Exhibit 13-7. Role-playing Evaluation (Poor Example)

Skill	ST	SAT	NI	NO	COMMENTS
Made an organized presentation				✓	Sue tried to overcome the objection by talking about telemarketing. Many clients have preconceived notions about telemarketing. Don't throw the term around — show the client how it can benefit him!
Created interest and continuity in pres'n				✓	
Handled resistance & objections			✓		
Responded to buying signals				✓	
THE CLOSE					
Timed the close right				✓	Sue let the client off the hook, which was probably a good choice considering how the call was going.
Used appropriate technique(s)				✓	
Handled objections successfully				✓	
Gave client time to respond to close				✓	
Got clear commitment/Got an order				✓	
Wrapped up call:					
-Summarized call					
-Reinforced close					
-Arranged for next call		✓			
-Clarified what client would do					
-Clarified what AE would do					
FOLLOW-UP (if appropriate)					
Inquired about progress of implementation				✓	
Responded to client concerns				✓	

Steve: We're a manufacturer of traditional home furnishings.

Sue: Who do you sell to, Mr. Rooney?

Steve: Various retail outlets such as local furniture stores. A lot of it is custom work, special orders.

Sue: Where are these outlets located?

Steve: Mostly in the eastern part of the country.

Sue: That's a large area. How do you reach all of your customers?

Steve: We have a sales force that visits the stores to keep our name in front of them. The salespeople show new samples of fabrics and promote sales we have going. The most important thing is that the furniture retailer remembers our name when his customer walks in the door.

Sue: Is that because you have a lot of competition?

Steve: You bet. I mean there are all sorts of furniture manufacturers. A lot of them with their own stores. We have to rely on the independent furniture store to sell our line.

Sue: Let's go back to your sales process. How do you get your orders?

Steve: Well, since most of the work is custom and we can never predict when an order will come in, most of the orders are mailed to us by the retailer. We have a form in the back of our sample book.

Sue: How long does it take to get that order in from the time it's mailed?

Steve: Oh, probably four days.

Sue: And how long does it take you to get the piece of furniture delivered to the customer once you've gotten the order?

Steve: Anywhere from six to eight weeks . . . depends if we have all the materials in stock.

Sue: I remember when I ordered a chair recently, that sure seemed like a long time. Would you be interested in cutting down that delivery time?

Steve: Well, sure, but it takes that long to make the furniture—that can't be cut down.

Sue: Oh, I understand, Mr. Rooney. But perhaps we could cut down the time it takes you to get the order from the retailer. Would you be interested if I could show you a way to shorten those four days to just a few minutes to get that valuable order?

Steve: What do you have in mind?

Sue: Instead of using the mail for your orders, you could use a toll-free number for your retailers to call in their orders. Not only would you receive the order immediately, but you could also check on inventory while the retailer was on the line. If you were out of a fabric, say, the retailer could consult his customer to see what they wanted to do. This would save additional time and perhaps even the sale. Don't you think a toll-free number would give you a competitive edge?

Steve: Well, I don't know of anyone else doing that. But what kind of costs are we talking about?

Sue: I think you'll be surprised to see how inexpensive it is to provide this service to your customers. Our 800 toll-free number actually costs less than a regular long-distance phone call. So for a couple of dollars for the phone call, you'll be making a sale worth hundreds of dollars, plus improving your long-term relationship with the retailers. Can I place that order for you today?

Steve: How can I say no? Let's give it a try.

Sue: I'm sure you'll see immediate results. I'll give you a call in a few days to set the installation date. I really appreciate your business, Mr. Rooney. I look forward to working with you on this and perhaps other ideas.

Steve: Sounds good. Be talking to you soon.

Sue: Thanks again, Mr. Rooney. Goodbye.

Exhibit 13-8 reflects a much better evaluation than Exhibit 13-7.

Telemarketing is a dynamic medium, without a doubt. When integrated into the total marketing process, it will increase sales efficiency and profits by qualifying leads, increasing response from catalogs, direct mail, print and broadcast advertising and maintaining contact with the direct marketer's most priceless asset—his or her customer base!

Exhibit 13-8. Role-playing Evaluation (Good Example)

ACCOUNT EXECUTIVE
TELEMARKETING SELLING SKILLS
Evaluation Sheets

ROLE PLAY/SKILL PRACTICE

Trainee: _Sue Jones_

Which call (1st, 2nd, etc.) _2nd_   Case—Company name: _Heritage Village_

Instructor/Evaluator: _D. Pemberton_   Date: _6/16/84_

Skill	ST	SAT	NI	NO	COMMENTS
APPROACH POSITIONING					
Managed screener: polite, persistent, used as a resource				✓	Sue got the decision-maker to talk to her by showing some empathy and creating some interest. This was very effective without being too pushy.
Completed positioning statement: who, where from, why calling		✓			
Made interest-creating opening statement	✓				
Asked for appropriate contact (if no name given prior to call)		✓			
Explained consultative role	✓				
Used listening skills	✓				
DATA GATHERING					Sue twist her questions off the client's remarks, although she still kept the focus on her objectives. Some more incisive questions may have been helpful, but Sue identified a business need.
Made appropriate transition from AP		✓			
Verified existing LD services				✓	
Asked about immediate concerns		✓			
Learned about business operations	✓				
Structured questioning strategy	✓				

Performance rating ST – Strong; SAT – Satisfactory; NI – Needs improvement; NO – Not observed.

Exhibit 13-8. Role-playing Evaluation (Good Example)

Skill	ST	SAT	NI	NO	COMMENTS
Made an organized presentation	✓				Good timing and aggressiveness. Client's tone indicated that he was interested, but he was worried about cost. Sue overcame the cost issue, and went for the close. Very effective!
Created interest and continuity in pres'n	✓				
Handled resistance & objections		✓			
Responded to buying signals		✓			
THE CLOSE					
Timed the close right	✓				
Used appropriate technique(s)	✓				
Handled objections successfully		✓			
Gave client time to respond to close		✓			
Got clear commitment/Got an order	✓				
Wrapped up call:					
-Summarized call					
-Reinforced close					
-Arranged for next call		✓			
-Clarified what client would do					
-Clarified what AE would do					
FOLLOW-UP (if appropriate)					
Inquired about progress of implementation				✓	
Responded to client concerns				✓	

Performance rating

(continued)

Exhibit 13-8. Role-playing Evaluation (Good Example)

Skill / Performance rating	ST	SAT	NI	NO	COMMENTS
Used open/closed questions appropriately		✓			
Questions appeared directed toward objective(s)	✓				
Attempted to build credibility		✓			
Maintained conversational tone	✓				
Maintained control of dialogue		✓			
Demonstrated listening skills: -Probed and clarified -Paid attention to client -Followed client leads -Used silence -Demonstrated empathy -Tied together ideas	✓				
SOLUTION GENERATION/DEVELOPMENT					Overall, Sue did a good job. A few specific facts I like the value of a sale — would have helped build even a stronger case.
Identified relevant/appropriate applications	✓				
Collected appropriate specific data		✓			
Dropped interest-creating hints		✓			
Tailored application(s) to business operations & expressed needs		✓			
SOLUTION PRESENTATION					Sue used specific benefits to sell the client on the solution. Although she didn't use specific cost figures, her point was well made to the client.
Reviewed & got agreement on client's objectives & concerns	✓				
Tailored solution to client		✓			
Focused on relevant benefits	✓				
Demonstrated cost-effectiveness		✓			
Anticipated impact of solution on client's business				✓	

Self-Quiz

1. There are eight major applications of telemarketing. Complete this list.

   a. Order taking
   b. Seasonal selling
   c. Renewals
   d. Customer service

   e. _____
   f. _____
   g. _____
   h. _____

2. People who inquire by phone are ☐ more likely to order ☐ less likely to order.

3. What is the function of "dealer-locater" advertising?

   _____

   _____

   _____

4. Why are outbound calls more expensive than inbound calls?

   _____

   _____

   _____

5. On the average, a field salesperson can make ___ to ___ sales calls a day; a telemarketing salesperson can make ___ to ___ calls a day.

6. Under what conditions is it more appropriate for an organization to test or maintain a telemarketing center in house?

   _____

   _____

   _____

7. Name two situations where it makes more sense to use an outside telemarketing organization.

   a. _____

   _____

   _____

   b. _____

   _____

   _____

8. Field salespeople are most likely to succeed at telemarketing.
   ☐ True   ☐ False

9. Name two desirable skills of a successful telephone communicator.

   a. _____

   _____

   b. _____

   _____

10. Complete this list of seven steps involved in the telemarketing selling process.

   a. Precall planning   e. _____
   b. Approach/Positioning   f. _____
   c. Data gathering   g. _____
   d. Solution generation

Pilot Project

You are the marketing director of an envelope company. You have a customer base of 100,000 small business firms, all secured by direct mail. You have decided to test the efficiency of telemarketing.

Your assignment is to develop a telemarketing test plan. In developing this plan, please answer the following questions.

1. Will you use a commercial organization to structure your test, or will you structure the test in house? And why?

2. What data, or measures, will you use to estimate when inventories might be depleted for each customer?

3. What information might you request from each customer in the process of your calls?

4. What special offers might you make in an effort to get repeat business by telephone?

Creating and Producing Direct Marketing

CHAPTER FOURTEEN

Techniques of Creating Direct Mail Packages

Direct mail is an expensive advertising medium. It costs you fifteen to twenty times as much to reach a person with a direct mail package as it does to reach him with a thirty-second TV commercial or a full-page ad in a newspaper. But direct mail has certain unique advantages that more than compensate for its higher cost. If you understand what these advantages are and use them properly, you will be able to bring in orders or responses at a cost equal to or below that of space or broadcast. And, as a general rule, customers acquired by direct mail are usually better customers in terms of repeat business than those acquired by space or broadcast advertising.

Selectivity

Through careful list selections and segmentation, direct mail can give you pinpoint selectivity unmatched by any other advertising medium (with the exception of the telephone). You can literally pick out households one by one, mailing only to those that are the best prospects for your offer. The fundamentals of list selection and segmentation are discussed in Chapter 5. Review these carefully.

Virtually Unlimited Choice of Formats

In direct mail, you are not restricted to thirty seconds of time or a 7″ × 10″ page. You can use large, lavishly illustrated brochures. You can have any number of inserts. You can use pop-ups, fold-outs, swatches—even enclose a phonograph record. What you can do is limited only by your imagination and budget constraints. For example, one enterprising mailer used a unique response device: he mailed a carrier pigeon to each prospect. The respondent taped his reply to the pigeon's leg and released the pigeon. The mailer didn't even have to pay a return postage charge!

Personal Character

Even though you mail in the millions, you are still mailing individual pieces to individually addressed human beings. Every recipient knows that an ad or TV commercial was not created specifically for him, but for a mass audience. Direct mail approaches the prospect on a personal level that, with personalized letters, even extends to a greeting by name. As any salesperson will agree, you can sell much better when you are talking to an individual rather than to people en masse.

No Competition

In most advertising media, the advertising is an adjunct, not the main reason the person is watching the TV channel or reading the magazine. In direct mail, advertising arrives all by itself to be opened and read at the recipient's leisure. When it is read, there is nothing to compete with it for your prospect's attention.

Most Testable Medium

With direct mail you can virtually simulate laboratory conditions for testing. You control exactly when the mail is dropped; you control exactly who gets which test package. Many magazines and newspapers can give you an A/B split, but direct mail will give you as many "splits" as you care to have.

Unique Capability to Involve the Recipient

Direct mail offers a wide choice of devices that involve the recipient, such as tokens, stamps, questionnaires, and quizzes. And with direct mail, you can literally get the recipient to "talk back" to you—to open a dialogue—by asking him questions and giving him space to respond on the reply device.

Selecting the Format

Because direct mail offers an unlimited choice of format, a good place to start is deciding which basic format you wish to use. There are three basic formats to choose from:

The *classic format* utilizes a separate outer or mailing envelope. The size of that envelope, the material from which it is made (paper, plastic, foil), and the number of colors in which it is printed can vary widely. And what goes inside that envelope can vary even more widely. Classic formats range from simple, dignified, businesslike letters (Exhibit 14-1) to lavish packages stuffed with brochures, inserts, gift circulars—even pop-ups and phonograph records (Exhibit 14-2). The classic format is the most personal of the direct mail formats. For this reason, it almost always includes a separate letter, either preprinted or personalized.

The *self-mailer* does not have an outer envelope. These mailers vary from a single sheet of paper folded once for mailing to wonderfully complex pieces with multiple sheets and preformed reply envelopes (Exhibit 14-3). Generally, a self-mailer comes off the press complete, ready to address and mail. As a rule, self-mailers are less expensive than classic mailing packages. There is only one component to produce and no inserting is needed since the piece is completed on press.

Exhibit 14-1. A Classic Direct Mail Format

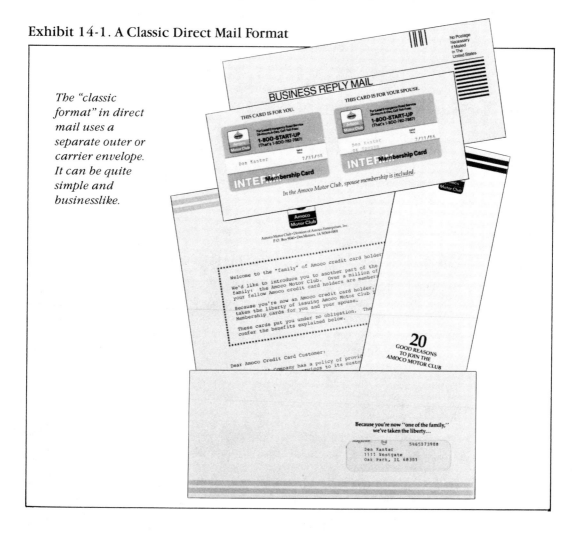

The "classic format" in direct mail uses a separate outer or carrier envelope. It can be quite simple and businesslike.

The "classic format" can also be lavish, exciting, and packed with different pieces, as illustrated by this mailing by American Family Publishers.

Exhibit 14-2. Expanded Classic Direct Mail Format

The "publisher's letter" or "second letter" has become a proven results booster in direct mail today.

Exhibit 14-3. Self-Mailer

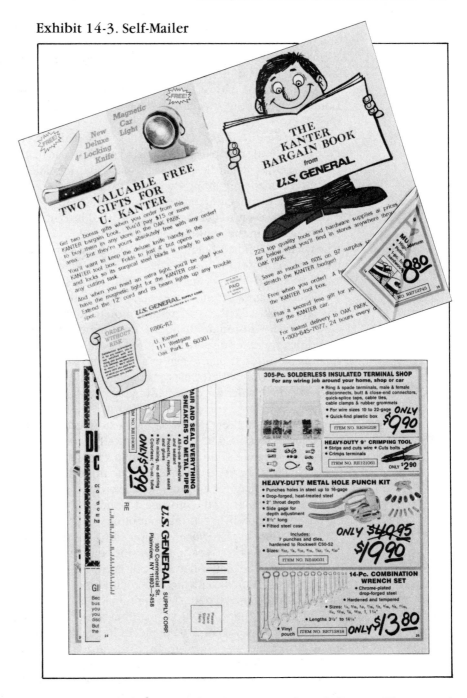

Shown here, a self-mailer, produced on one pass through the press. When opened it contains individual, personalized premium (gift) slips, order form, and bound-in forty-four-page catalog. Even a preformed order envelope is included!

The *catalog* is literally a magazine, with up to many hundreds of pages, stitched, glued, or perfect-bound. Catalogs require a highly specialized format, and their use is subject to many important guidelines. Catalogs are discussed in detail in Chapter 15.

No discussion of direct mail formats would be complete without mentioning some of the specialized devices that are used regularly in direct mail.

Involvement devices include stamps, tokens, rub-offs, sealed envelopes—one company even used a jigsaw puzzle that the recipient had to put together. Regardless of the format you use, reader involvement can make it dramatically more effective. If you get the reader involved with your offer and message, you're well on your way to a sale (Exhibit 14-4). A most effective way to get the reader involved is to include a product sample or swatch in the mailing. Obviously this device is not suitable for all types of merchandise, but nothing beats letting somebody touch, feel, and try what you're selling.

Specialized devices include die-cut shapes, tip-ons, and pop-ups. These can be great attention-getters. But be careful: you don't want to let the "gimmick" take the reader's attention from your basic sales message. One company tested an elaborate (and expensive) pop-up device and found that the mailing actually pulled better without it! The pop-up was stealing attention from the mailer's message.

In connection with formats, there are several tried-and-true variations you should consider for your mailing package.

The *second letter,* or "publisher's letter" (Exhibit 14-5), has become almost a "must" in direct mail today. Repeated testing indicates that such a letter boosts response 10 percent or more. This is either a folded letter or a letter in a separate sealed envelope that warns sternly: "Open this letter *only* if you have decided not to respond to this offer." Of course everybody opens it immediately. This gives you the chance to do a little extra selling, primarily in reassuring the prospect that he really has nothing to lose and everything to gain in accepting your offer.

The *closed-face envelope* (Exhibit 14-6) has the name and address of the recipient "typed" right on the envelope; there is no window or "slot" through which the name shows. Inside there are two or three other pieces (letters, applications) on which the recipient's name, address, and other information are also "typed." The mailing looks like it was typed individually, but not so: these ingenious mailings are run on computer, then the outer envelope is matched to the pieces inside. Because they look so personal, closed-face packages are rarely discarded without opening.

Invitation formats have been around for a long time (see Exhibit 14-7). But they are very effective, especially for publishers, club memberships, and credit card solicitations. The format simulates a formal invitation ("You are invited to accept. . . ."). The outside of the invitation usually carries a letter explaining the offer. Naturally, an RSVP—a call to action—is included in the mailing.

The *simulated telegram* is less formal but carries a lot of urgency (see Exhibit 14-8). It's been popular as a follow-up mailing or part of a renewal series and has worked well for credit card solicitation, insurance, and loans-by-mail offers. However, with the decline in the use of real telegrams, the simulated telegram is being used less and less. The simulated telegram is usually printed on yellow stock and, more often than not, is computer-filled. (Caution: the basic telegram format is copyrighted by Western Union. You are not allowed to "lift" it.)

Exhibit 14-4. Involvement Device

A typical involvement device: the reader is asked to lift the peel-off stickers from the outer envelope and affix them to the order form, thereby "validating" the free gift and free trial membership.

Exhibit 14-5. The Publisher's Letter

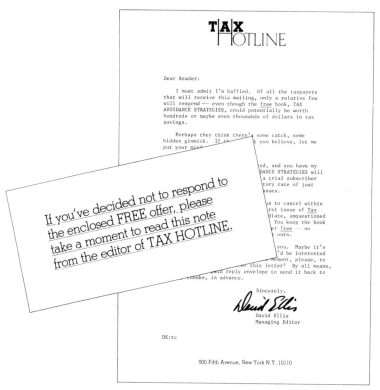

The "publisher's letter" or "second letter" has become a proven results booster in direct mail today.

Exhibit 14-6. Closed-Face Envelopes

The "closed-face" envelope has no slot or window through which the recipient's name shows. It looks like it was personally typed, but it's actually a computer-generated envelope that is matched to the pieces inside.

Exhibit 14-7. The Invitation Format

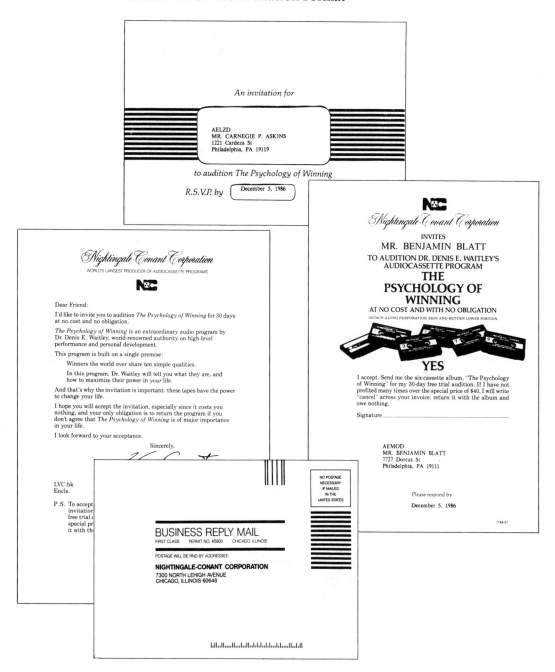

Invitation formats remain an effective technique. After all, who can turn down an invitation?

Exhibit 14-8. The Simulated Telegram

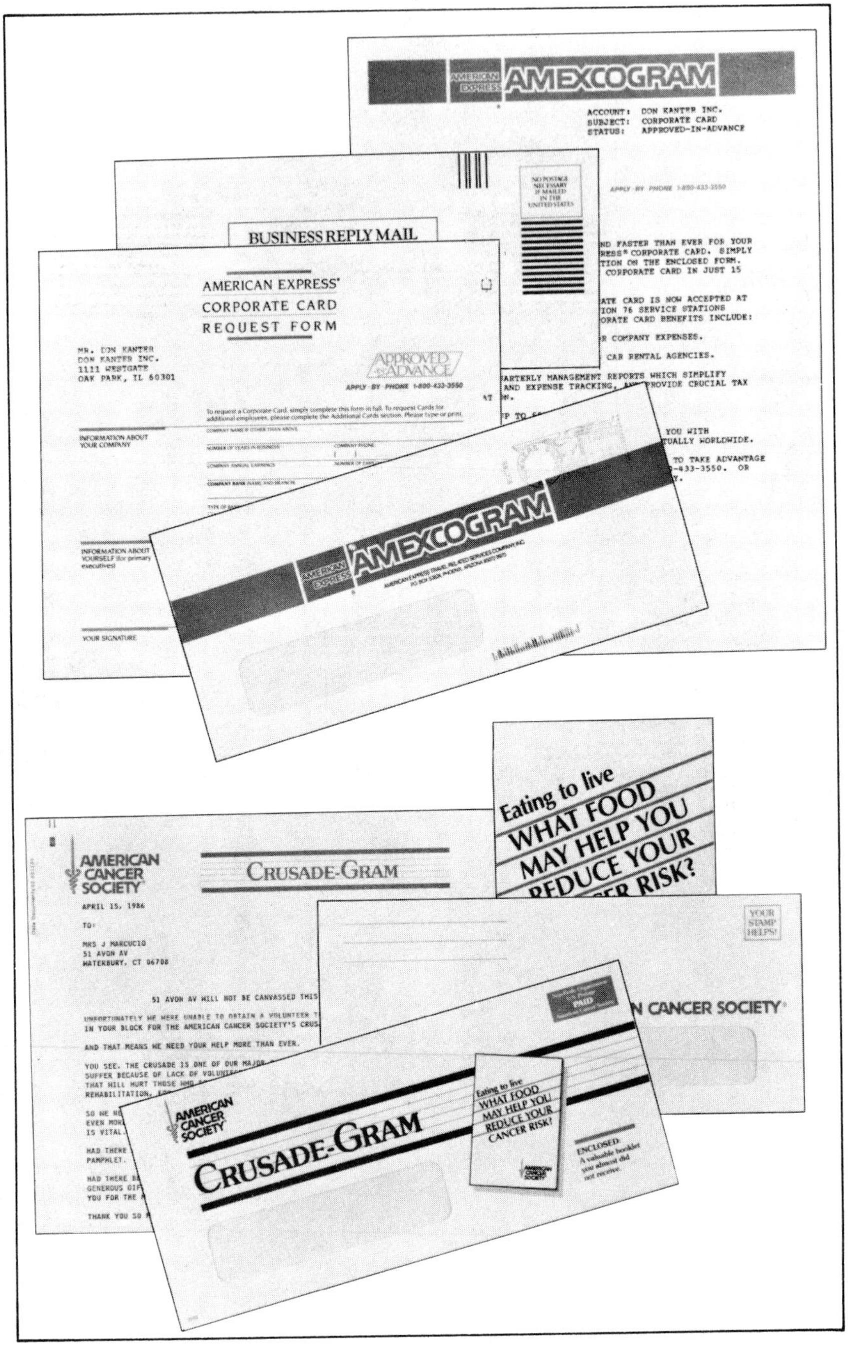

Although not as popular as it was a few years ago, the simulated telegram retains the look—and the urgency—of the real thing.

Exhibit 14-9. Personalized Letters

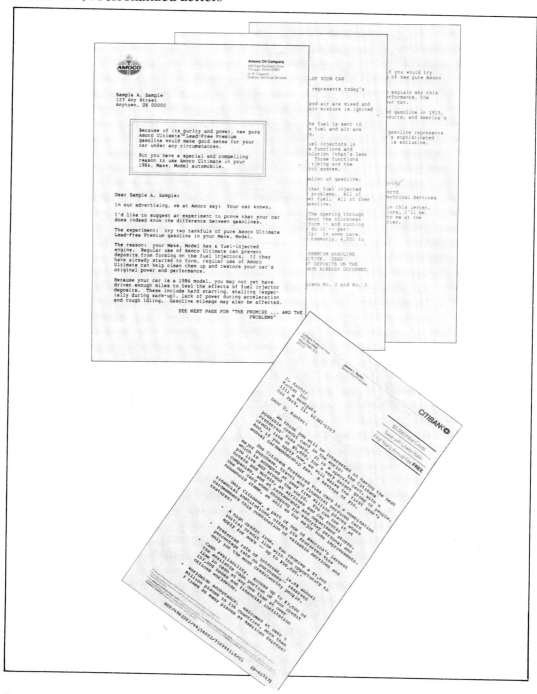

Personalized letters appear to be individually typed. New personalization techniques can vary the size and face of the type, and "laser" personalization permits economical small-run personalization.

Personalization is common today regardless of what format you use. Personalization is done by computer, by ink-jet imaging or by laser printing (Exhibit 14-9). Each method has its advantages and its particular requirements. Each method requires specific preparation of materials, so you would be well advised to seek professional production help if you are planning a personalized mailing.

When you run into somebody who tells you that personalized letters "always" outpull nonpersonalized ones, be skeptical. In my experience, personalized letters *usually* outpull nonpersonalized ones, but not always. Also, they have to outpull by enough to pay for the extra cost of personalization. When you use personalization, use all the information you can. But don't scatter the person's name indiscriminately throughout the letter. A good rule to follow is to write a personalized letter as you would write a letter to any person you know fairly well.

Which format for your mailing piece? That depends. It depends on your budget. It depends on whom you're trying to reach. Do you want a package that will stand out on the businessman's desk? Or is it something designed for leisurely reading by the consumer at home? If you're not sure, you should use the classic format with a separate outer envelope and a separate letter. The great preponderance of direct mail today uses this format, and while it is more expensive than a self-mailer, it will usually pull better.

One further caution on formats: postal regulations, which govern the mailability of any given piece, change regularly. You are well advised to check the layout of your mailing piece with your local post office before you produce it. There are few things in life more disheartening than a phone call that begins: "This is the post office, and we're holding your mailing because . . . ."

Creative Strategy

Now that we have the product or service, our offer (proposition) and our format, we're ready to create the mailing piece. Right? Wrong. And therein lies a basic failing in a lot of direct mail produced today. The writer is too anxious to dash to his typewriter, and the artist is too anxious to get to his drawing board. Why does this occur? Marketing is "work," but creative effort is *fun*, and we all tend to do what we like to do. But unless the creative work is strategically grounded, it is not going to work—or at least, not as well as it should.

As one sage observed: "If you don't know where you're going, any road will take you there." Advertising, general or direct response, has to know exactly where it is going, and the "road map" that points the way is called *creative strategy*.

Every large advertising agency and virtually every large company has its own creative strategy, under one name or another. They all share a common objective: they focus the efforts of the creative persons. It is the discipline of creative strategy that prevents advertising from trying to be all things to all people—and, in reality, being nothing to any of them.

Following is an outline for a typical creative strategy, which organizes the information about the product or service into a disciplined format. Remember: to be useful, this outline must be *written*.

- *The product.* What it is, what it does, how it works, what it costs, what its features are, what its *benefits* are, what makes it different, what makes it better—even what its weaknesses are.
- *Competitive products.* How they compare with ours in terms of features, benefits, and price.
- *The market.* How big is it and what share of it do we have? Who buys the product today and why? Who else *should* buy it and why? Who are our present customers and future prospects in terms of demographic characteristics, such as age, sex, marital status, income, and education. Who are they in psychographic terms? Are they liberal or conservative, avante garde, or traditional?
- *The media.* What's going to carry our message? If space or broadcast media are to be used, which ones, how often, and in what space or time units? If direct mail is the only medium, what lists will we be using— specifically or in general? What do we know or assume about quantities, formats, colors?
- *The budget.* What limitations should govern our creative thinking in terms of creative staff time, layout costs, photography, illustrations, production costs?
- *Objectives.* As specifically as possible, what are we trying to *do*, in terms of overall goals and specific goals, in accordance with the total program, and in line with specific components within the program? Among all possible goals, what are our priorities? Which ones are primary and vital; which are secondary and merely desirable; which are nice but expendable?
- *Creative implementation.* How do we propose to organize what we know or assume about the product, the competition, and the market to achieve our stated objectives? How will we position the product? What relative emphasis will we give to product features and product benefits? What do we anticipate as our central copy theme? How will it be executed visually? And how will it be orchestrated among various elements of the program? Most important of all from a response standpoint, what will our offer be and how will it be dramatized?

How your creative strategy document addresses these questions, the order in which you address them, and the format in which you cast them are all minor matters. They can be varied according to circumstances. When the creative strategy is thoroughly digested by both the writer and the artist, they both have a good idea of what the mailing package should accomplish, how, and why.

Precreative Work

With a creative strategy in place, we're ready to start creative work. Well . . . almost ready.

First, there are some important "precreative" matters to be taken care of before one word of copy is written or one piece of the mailing is designed. Listen to Gene Schwartz, a professional direct response writer, as he describes how he listens first with his ears, and then with his eyes:

1. Sit down with the owner of the product or service—the man who's hiring you—and pump hell out of him. Put it on a tape recorder and have him talk for three or four hours.

Ask him where the product comes from, what it does, what are its problems and how he's tried to cure them, why it's better than its competitors, who likes it, who doesn't like it, what proof he's got that it works, what strange uses people have got out of it, what funny stories he has accumulated in regard to its manufacture or use, what problems he was trying to solve when he created it, how he would improve it if he had unlimited money, what causes most of his refunds, who works for him to help him make it, how it is made, how he keeps up the quality, who writes him what about it, etc.

2. Talk to his customers. Do it in person, or on paper. See if they agree with him. If they don't, find out why.

3. Listen to his competitors. They often tell you more about the opportunities they're missing in their ads than the opportunities they're seeing and therefore seizing. Let them write a possible head or two for you—out of the body copy of their ads.

4. Then put all the material down, in one big pile, and underline it. Start blending it together, like you'd make a cake. Give first priority to your head and subheads, then the body claims. And then type it up, preferably adding little of yourself except as selector and condenser.

Direct response creative pros use a variety of techniques for approaching the moment of truth. But they all have one thing in common: They dig, dig, dig. The hack, on the other hand, just sits down to write. Miracle performances don't happen by accident—they're created.

The Copywriter as Salesperson

Listen to Don Kanter, long-time vice president of Stone & Adler, who now owns his own direct response creative service. He has a unique way of describing some copywriters. "The trouble with many copywriters," he says, "is that they think their job is to write copy." Kanter quickly explains this by adding, "That is equivalent to a salesperson saying, 'My job is to talk.' The job is not to 'talk.' For a writer, the job is not to 'write.' For both, the job is to *sell*. Selling is the end result; writing is merely the means a copywriter uses to reach that end. This is true of all advertising copywriting; it is especially true of direct response copywriting because the writer is usually the only salesperson with whom the prospect will ever come in contact. If he or she doesn't make the sale, there is nobody else to do it."

The Benefit/Price/Value Equation

To sell effectively, the direct response writer must know why people buy. They buy, essentially, when they consider something to have value. This is often expressed in a simple equation: benefit divided by price equals value. In other words, every time a person is confronted with a buying decision, he subconsciously assigns a worth to the benefits he perceives. At the same time, he assigns a worth to the price he must pay. And subjectively, very subconsciously, he divides one into the other to reach his buying decision. If, in his mind, the benefits outweigh the price, he will buy. If the price outweighs the benefits, he will not buy.

What Is Price?

To most people, *price* is the monetary amount asked for the goods or services being sold: the $29.95, or $39.95, or $5.00 per month, or whatever. But there is more to price than that. There's time. We are asking the customer to wait before he or she can enjoy the benefits of what he or she buys. There's the factor of buying the product sight unseen (unlike retail purchasing, where you can see, touch, and often try what you are buying). There's a factor of buying from a company the customer may not know. There's the risk that the product or service may not deliver the benefits that have been promised. In direct marketing, all of these are part of the price that must be paid. While we may not be able to do much about the actual price (the $29.95, or $39.95, or $5.00 a month), we can (and we must) do everything possible to reduce the other factors of price to the minimum.

How? By using the proven techniques that direct marketing has pioneered:

- Testimonials
- Guarantees
- Free trial offers or cancellation privileges
- Reassurance about the stature and reliability of the selling company

What Is a Benefit?

Let's assume we are selling a stereo system. This system has two three-way speakers, each with a big "woofer" and "tweeter" and a midrange. That's a benefit. Right? Wrong. That's a selling point or product feature. It's a distinction that every writer must recognize and keep in mind. A benefit is something that affects the customer personally. It exists apart from the merchandise or service itself. A selling point or product feature is something in the product or service that makes possible and supports the benefit. Our stereo system with two three-way speaker systems is a selling point. It is a quality in the product itself. That I can enjoy lifelike, three-dimensional sound is the benefit. It is this benefit that affects me personally. This benefit is made possible by the fact that this stereo system has two three-way speakers. Remember, it is the benefit that the customer really wants to have. It is the selling point that proves to him that he can really have it.

Translate Selling Points into Benefits

Before you write any copy, therefore, it is very important to dig out every selling point you can and translate each selling point into a customer benefit. The more benefits the customer perceives (i.e., the more benefits you can point out to him), the more likely he will buy. Here's an example: Suppose you're writing copy to sell a portable counter-top dishwasher. These are some of the selling points in this merchandise. And alongside each is the benefit which that selling point makes possible:

Selling Point	*Benefit*
1. Has a 10-minute operating cycle.	1. Does a load of dishes in 10 minutes; gets you out of the kitchen faster.
2. Measures 18 inches in diameter.	2. Small enough to fit on a counter-top; doesn't take up valuable floor space.
3. Transparent plastic top.	3. Lets you watch the washing cycle; you know when the dishes are done.
4. Has universal hose coupling.	4. Fits any standard kitchen faucet; attaches and detaches in seconds.

Copy Appeals and Basic Human Wants

With your benefits down on paper, you now have to decide on the appeals that will do the best selling job. Creative people refer to this in different ways. Some talk about how you "position" the product in the prospect's mind. Others refer to "coming up with the big idea" behind the copy. What is it about your offer and benefit story that is most appealing? When you stop to think about it, people respond to any given proposition for one of two reasons: to gain something they do not have or to avoid losing something they now possess. As you can see from the accompanying chart, basic human wants can be divided into these two categories. The professional copywriter carefully sifts and weighs the list of basic human wants to determine the main appeal of his proposition. (In Chapter 16 you'll see how the same product can be slanted to employ many different appeals just by changing your headline.)

The desire to gain:	The desire to avoid loss:
To make money	To avoid criticism
To save time	To keep possessions
To avoid effort	To avoid physical pain
To achieve comfort	To avoid loss of reputation
To have health	To avoid loss of money
To be popular	To avoid trouble
To enjoy pleasure	
To be clean	
To be praised	
To be in style	
To gratify curiosity	
To satisfy an appetite	
To have beautiful possessions	
To attract the opposite sex	
To be an individual	
To emulate others	
To take advantage of opportunities	

Eleven Guidelines to Good Copy

Does your proposition offer the promise of saving time and avoiding hard or disagreeable work? Most people like to avoid work. Saving time is almost a fetish of the American people. Appeal to this basic want, if you can.

Does your proposition help people feel important? People like to keep up with the Joneses. People like to be made to feel that they are part of a select group. A tremendous number of people are susceptible to snob appeal. Perhaps you can offer a terrific bargain by mail and capitalize on the appeal of saving money. The desire to "get it wholesale" is very strong.

Don Kanter uses these guidelines as checkpoints for good, professional copy:

1. Does the writer know his product? Has he or she dug out every selling point and benefit?

2. Does the writer know his market? Is he or she aiming the copy at the most likely prospects rather than at the world in general?

3. Is the writer talking to the prospect in language that the prospect will understand?

4. Does the writer make a promise to the prospect, then prove that he or she can deliver what was promised?

5. Does the writer get to the point at once? Does he or she make that all-important promise right away?

6. Is the copy, especially the headlines and lead paragraphs, germane and specific to the selling proposition?

7. Is the copy concise? There is a great temptation to overwrite, especially in direct mail.

8. Is the copy logical and clear? Does it "flow" from point to point?

9. Is the copy enthusiastic? Does the writer obviously believe in what he or she is selling?

10. Is the copy complete? Are all the questions answered, especially obvious ones like size and color?

11. Is the copy designed to sell? Or is it designed to impress the reader with the writer's ability? If somebody says "that's a great mailing," you've got the wrong reaction. What you want to hear is, "That's a great product (or service). I'd love to have it."

The Changes in Direct Mail

Only a few years ago, direct mail was a "set" medium, with its own rules that you broke at your peril. A direct mail package had an outer envelope, a reply envelope, a letter (at least two pages and probably more), a brochure, an order form—at the minimum.

But change is coming. In fact, it's here, according to Don Kanter, who has been doing direct response creative work for twenty years. The changes, he says, are focused on one objective: faster, stronger, more telegrahic communication with the prospect.

Why? Two reasons, Kanter says. First, "Mailbox Clutter" is becoming real, just as "TV Clutter" did some years ago. Only a direct mailing that grabs and holds the prospect's attention—from the envelope through every component—has a chance of working. Second, we are now talking to the TV generation, which grew up with visual symbols. Unlike us older folks who grew up reading books, the TV generation is less inclined to stay with you if you don't get your message across very quickly.

Basically, the specific changes are in two areas:

1. *Shorter copy and better copy.* Kanter believes that direct mail historically has been overwritten, because direct mail does not impose the discipline for tight, concise writing that space or broadcast does. Now that discipline is being imposed by outside factors, it means that the direct mail writer must edit and polish copy, making every word justify its existence. A four-page letter (or longer) may still be the best way to go, but it must be a beautifully written, meticulously polished, and lovingly edited four-page letter.

2. *Quicker communication through graphics.* At long last, the designer is becoming an equal partner in the direct mail creative process, as we learn what our brethren in general advertising have always known: graphics communicate more quickly and more forcefully than words.

   An added benefit of the designer's involvement is that we are improving the appearance of direct mail, as well as the level of taste. The old "direct mail look" which was distinguished by type piled up on virtually every component, is slowly disappearing.

Creating the Classic Mailing Package

Now that we've looked at formats and discussed copy, let's turn to the individual pieces in a so-called classic mailing package.

The Outer Envelope

The outer envelope, or carrier envelope (Exhibit 14-10), has one job: to get itself opened. To accomplish this, the envelope can use many techniques.

- It can dazzle the reader with color, with graphics—and with promises of important benefits (including wealth, in the case of sweepstakes offers) if the reader will only open it.
- It can impress the reader with its simplicity and lead him to believe that the contents must be very important.
- It can tease the reader and so excite his curiosity that he simply must open it.

To help accomplish its purpose, the envelope can be the traditional paper envelope (perhaps with extra cut-outs or "windows"), or it can be made of transparent polyethylene or foil. Whatever it's made of, and whatever it says, the outer envelope sets the tone of your mailing. It must harmonize with the materials inside.

The Brochure

As noted, most mailing packages require a good brochure or circular in addition to a letter. It can be a small, two-color affair or a beautiful, giant circular that's almost as big as a tablecloth. But the job it has to do is the same, and it deserves your best creative effort.

   One way or another your circular has to do a complete selling job. To give yourself every chance for success, review the appearance, content, and preparation of your circular. The following is a handy checklist for this purpose.

Appearance

1. Is the circular designed for the market you are trying to reach?

2. Is the presentation suited to the product or service you are offering?

3. Is the circular consistent with the rest of the mailing package?

Content

4. Is there a big idea behind your circular?

5. Do your headlines stick to the key offer?

6. Is your product or service dramatized to its best advantage by format and/or presentation?

7. Do you show broadly adaptable examples of your product or service in use?

8. Does your entire presentation follow a logical sequence and tell a complete story—including price, offer, and guarantee?

Preparation

9. Can the circular be cut out of regular size paper stock?

10. Is the quality of paper stock in keeping with the presentation?

11. Is color employed judiciously to show the product or service in its best light?

The Order Form

If Ernest Hemingway had been a direct response writer, he probably would have dubbed the order form "the moment of truth." Many prospects make a final decision on whether to respond after reading it. Some even read the order form before anything else in the envelope because they know it's the easiest way to find out what's being offered at what price. The best advice I can offer on order forms comes from Henry Cowen, a direct marketing specialist. He says, "There are direct mail manuals around that recommend simple, easy-to-read order forms, but my experience indicates the mailer is far better off with a busy, rather jumbled appearance and plenty of copy. Formal and legal-looking forms that appear valuable, too valuable to throw away, are good." The key words in Cowen's statement are "too valuable to throw away." The order form or reply form that appears valuable induces readership. It impels the reader to do something with it, to take advantage of the offer. High on the list of devices and techniques that make order forms look valuable are certificate borders, safety paper backgrounds, simulated rubber stamps, eagles, blue handwriting, seals, serial

Exhibit 14-10. Various Envelope Formats

The outer
envelope can be
vibrant and
exciting . . .

dignified and
businesslike . . .

TRUE OR FALSE?

1. It's OK to use an asterisk next to "FREE" to explain the strings attached.

2. Two lift letters outpull one.

3. The best way to find out a customer's age on the order form is to ask for the birth date.

Inside:
11 more challenges
to your Direct Marketing IQ

Plus, **get the answers FREE**

or it can tease
the reader.

numbers, receipt stubs, and so on. And sheet size alone can greatly add to the valuable appearance of a response form (Exhibit 14-11). (You've seen examples of many of these techniques on the order forms shown in Chapter 4.)

By all means, don't call your reply device an order form. Call it a Reservation Certificate, Free Gift Check, Trial Membership Application, or some other benefit heading. It automatically seems more valuable to the reader.

Getting back more inquiry and order forms starts with making them appear too valuable to throw away. But to put frosting on the cake, add the dimension of personal involvement. Give the reader something to do with the order form. Ask him to put a token in a "yes" or "no" slot. Get him to affix a gummed stamp. Have him tear off a stub that has your guarantee on it. Once you have prodded the prospect into action, there is a good chance you will receive an order.

Finally, the order form should restate your offer and benefits. If a prospect loses the letter or circular, a good order form should be able to stand alone and do a complete selling job. And if it's designed to be mailed back on its own (without an envelope), it's usually worthwhile to prepay the postage.

Gift Slips and Other Enclosures

In addition to the letter, brochure, and order form, one of the most common enclosures is a free gift slip. If you have a free gift offer, you'll normally get much better results by putting that offer on a separate slip rather than building it into your circular (Exhibit 14-12).

If you insert an extra enclosure, make sure it stands out from the rest of the mailing and gets attention. You can often accomplish this by printing the enclosure on a colored stock and making it a different size from the other mailing components. Most free gifts, for example, can be adequately played up on a small slip that's 3½″ × 8½″ or 5½″ × 8½″.

Another enclosure that's often used is a business reply envelope. This isn't essential if the order form can be designed as a self-mailer. But, if you have an offer that the reader might consider to be of a private nature, an envelope is usually better. Buying a self-improvement book, for example. Or applying for an insurance policy, where the application asks some personal questions. Also, the extra expense of a reply envelope is often justified if you want to encourage more cash-with-order replies.

The Letter—The "Key Ingredient" of Direct Mail

If any one piece in a direct mail package is key, that piece is the letter. One of the prime advantages of direct mail is its capacity for personal, one-on-one communication, and the letter provides that personal communica-

Exhibit 14-11. Order Form

The order form (which should never be called an order form) is the moment of truth in a direct mail package. It must look too valuable to throw away.

tion. It's no wonder, then, that more has been written about how to create a good direct mail letter than any other part of the direct mail package.

Exhibit 14-12. Free Gift Offers

If you have a free gift with you offer, you'll get better results by highlighting it with a separate slip.

Seven-Step Formula

Here's a letter-writing formula that has served me well. I believe it follows a more detailed route than most formulas. And, used wisely, it should not stifle your creativity.

1. *Promise a benefit in your headline or first paragraph—your most important benefit.* You simply can't go wrong by leading off with the most important benefit to the reader. Some writers believe in the slow buildup. But most experienced writers I know favor making the important point first. Many writers use the "Johnson Box": short, terse copy that summarizes the main benefits, in a box above the salutation.

2. *Immediately enlarge on your most important benefit.* This step is crucial. Many writers come up with a great lead, then fail to follow through. Or they catch attention with their heading, but then take two or three paragraphs to warm up to their subject. The reader's attention is gone! Try hard to elaborate on your most important benefit right away, and you'll build up interest fast.

3. *Tell the reader specifically what he or she is going to get.* It's amazing how many letters lack details on such basic product features as size, color, weight, and sales terms. Perhaps the writer is so close to his proposition he assumes the reader knows all about it. A dangerous assumption! And when you tell the reader what he or she's going to get, don't overlook the intangibles that go along with your product or service. For example, he's getting smart appearance in addition to a pair of slacks, knowledge in addition to a 340-page book.

4. *Back up your statements with proof and endorsements.* Most prospects are somewhat skeptical about advertising. They know it sometimes gets a little overenthusiastic about a product. So they accept it only with a grain of salt. If you can back up your own statements with third-party testimonials or a list of satisfied users, everything you say becomes more believable.

5. *Tell the reader what he or she might lose if he or she doesn't act.* As noted, people respond affirmatively either to gain something they do not possess or to avoid losing something they already have. Here's a good spot in your letter to overcome human inertia—imply what may be lost if action is postponed. People don't like to be left out. A skillful writer can use this human trait as a powerful influence in his or her message.

6. *Rephrase your prominent benefits in your closing offer.* As a good salesperson does, sum up the benefits to the prospect in your closing offer. This is the proper prelude to asking for action. This is where you can intensify the prospect's desire to have the product. The stronger the benefits you can persuade the reader to recall, the easier it will be for him or her to justify an affirmative decision.

7. *Incite action. Now.* This is the spot where you win or lose the battle with inertia. Experienced advertisers know once a letter is put aside or tossed into that file, you're out of luck. So wind up with a call for action and a logical reason for acting now. Too many letters close with a statement like "supplies are limited." That argument lacks credibility. Today's consumer knows you probably have a warehouse full of merchandise. So make your reason a believable one. For example, "It may be many months before we go back to press on this book." Or "Orders are shipped on a first-come basis. The sooner yours is received, the sooner you can be enjoying your new widget." (See Exhibit 14-13 for a famous direct mail letter that follows this seven-step formula.)

Writing a Winning Letter
Choosing the Lead

Whatever formula or philosophy you adopt, the first task is to decide on the lead for the letter. Nothing is more important. Numerous tests have shown that one lead in a letter can pull substantially better than another. Let's look at six of the most common types of leads used in sales letters. To help you compare them, let's take a sample product and write six different leads for that product. The product we'll use is a businessman's self-improvement book, which includes biographical sketches of a dozen prominent business leaders.

1. *News.* If you have a product that is really news, you have the makings of an effective lead. There is nothing more effective than news. If you have a product or service that's been around a while, perhaps you can zero in on one aspect of it that's timely or newsworthy.

   Example: Now you can discover the same success secrets that helped a dozen famous business leaders reach the top!

2. *How/what/why.* Any beginning newspaper reporter is taught that a good story should start out by answering the main questions that go through a reader's mind—who, what, when, where, why, and how. You can build an effective lead by promising to answer one of these questions and then immediately enlarging on it in your opening paragraphs.

   Examples: How successful people really get ahead; what it takes to survive in the executive jungle; or why some people always get singled out for promotions and salary increases.

3. *Numbered ways.* This is often an effective lead because it sets the stage for an organized selling story. If you use a specific number, it will attract curiosity and usually make the reader want to find out what they are.

   Example: Seventeen little-known ways to improve your on-the-job performance—and one big way to make it pay off!

4. *Command.* If you can use a lead which will command with authority and without offense, you have taken a big step toward getting the reader to do what you want.

   Example: Don't let the lack of education hold you back any longer!

5. *Narrative.* This is one of the most difficult types of leads to write, but it can prove to be one of the most effective. It capitalizes on people's interest in stories. To be effective, a narrative lead must lead into the sales story in a natural way and still hold the reader's interest. Ideally, the lead should also give the reader some clue to where the story is going or why he or she should be interested.

   Example: When he started in the stock room at IBM, nobody ever thought Tom Watson would some day be president of this multibillion dollar corporation.

6. *Question.* If you start with the right type of question, you can immediately put your reader in the proper frame of mind for your message. But be sure the question is provocative. Make it a specific question, promising benefits—one that's sure to be answered in the affirmative.

Example: If I can show you a proven way to get a better job, without any obligation on your part—will you give me a few minutes of your time?

It is impossible to put too much emphasis on the importance of working on your leads. The lead is the first thing your reader sees. Usually he or she makes a decision to read or not read at this point. I always write out at least three or four different leads, then choose the one I think will do the best job of appealing to the reader's basic wants.

Make a Letter Look Inviting

Here's a final, very important tip from top professional writers. They try to make their letters look attractive, inviting, and easy to read. (See Exhibit 14-14.) The pros keep paragraphs down to six or seven lines. They use subheads and indented paragraphs to break up long copy. They emphasize pertinent thoughts, knowing that many readers will scan indented paragraphs before they decide whether to read a letter clear through. They use underscoring, CAPITAL LETTERS, and a second ink color to make key words and sentences stand out. And they skillfully use leader dots and dashes to break up long sentences.

Scan the two versions of the AMA letter in Exhibit 14-14. Notice how much more inviting the letter on the left is compared to the original typewritten version. Same copy, but one letter encourages reading and the other doesn't.

Finally, I recommend that you type your letter, or, if you insist on having it typeset, have it set in typewriter type. To me, a letter should *look* like a letter, and "real" letters are done on typewriters.

Letter Length and the Postscript

"Do people read long copy?" The answer is Yes! People will read something for as long as it interests them. An uninteresting one-page letter can be too long. A skillfully woven four-pager can hold the reader until the end. Thus, a letter should be long enough to cover the subject adequately and short enough to retain interest. Don't be afraid of long copy. If you have something to say and can say it well, it will probably do better than short copy. After all, the longer you hold a prospect's interest, the more sales points you can get across and the more likely you are to win an order.

Regardless of letter length, however, it usually pays to tack on a postscript. The P.S. is one of the most effective parts of any letter. Many prospects will glance through a letter. The eye will pick up an indented paragraph here, stop on an underlined statement there, and finally come to rest on the P.S. If you can express an important idea in the P.S., the reader may go back and read the whole letter. This makes the P.S. worthy of your best efforts. Use it to restate a key benefit. Or to offer an added inducement, like a free gift. Even when somebody has read the rest of the letter, the P.S. can make the difference between whether the prospect places an order. Use the P.S. to close on a strong note, to sign off with the strongest appeal you have.

The Value of Versioned Copy

Suppose, just suppose, that instead of sending exactly the same letter to all your prospects, you could create a number of versions for each major segment of your market. And rather than talking about all the advantages and benefits of the product, you could simply zero in on those that fit each market segment. Sounds like a logical idea that should increase response, doesn't it?

Yet my own experience with versioned or segmented copy has been mixed. Sometimes I've seen this technique work very effectively; other times it's a bomb. So I suggest that you test it for yourself. If your product story should be substantially different for certain audience segments— and you can identify and select them on the lists you're using—develop special versions of your regular copy and give the technique a try.

One type of versioned copy that generally does pay off is special copy slanted to your *previous* buyers. Customers like to think a firm remembers them and will give them special treatment. In going back to your satisfied buyers, there's less need to resell your company. You can concentrate on the product or the service being offered.

How to Improve a Good Mailing Package

So far we've been talking about how to create a new mailing package. Let's suppose you've done that, and you want to make it better. Or you've got a successful mailing package you've been using for a couple of years (your control) and you want to beat it. How do you go about it? One of the best ways I know is to come up with an entirely different appeal for your letter. For instance, suppose you're selling an income tax guide and your present letter is built around saving money. That's probably a tough appeal to beat. But to develop a new approach you might write a letter around a negative appeal, something people want to avoid. Experience with many propositions has proved that a negative appeal is often stronger than a positive one. Yet it's frequently overlooked by copywriters. An appropriate negative copy appeal for our example might be something like, "How to avoid costly mistakes that can get you in trouble with the Internal Revenue Serv-

Exhibit 14-13. The Kiplinger Letter

STANLEY R. MAYES *ASSISTANT TO THE PRESIDENT*

THE KIPLINGER WASHINGTON EDITORS, INC.

1729 H STREET, NORTHWEST, WASHINGTON, D. C. 20006   TELEPHONE: 887-6400

THE KIPLINGER WASHINGTON LETTER   THE KIPLINGER TAX LETTER
THE KIPLINGER AGRICULTURAL LETTER   THE KIPLINGER FLORIDA LETTER
THE KIPLINGER CALIFORNIA LETTER   THE KIPLINGER TEXAS LETTER
CHANGING TIMES MAGAZINE

More Growth and Inflation Ahead...
and what YOU can do about it.

     The next few years will see business climb to the highest
level this country has ever known. And with it...inflation.

     This combination may be hard for you to accept under today's
conditions. But the fact remains that those who do prepare for both
inflation AND growth ahead will reap big dividends for their foresight,
and avoid the blunders others will make.

     You'll get the information you need for this type
of planning in the Kiplinger Washington Letter...
and the enclosed form will bring you the next 26
issues of this helpful service on a "Try-out" basis.
The fee: Less than 81¢ per week...only $21 for the
6 months just ahead...and tax deductible for business
or investment purposes.

     During the depression, in 1935, the Kiplinger Letter warned
of inflation and told what to do about it. Those who heeded its advice
were ready when prices began to rise.

     Again, in January of 1946, the Letter renounced the widely-
held view that a severe post-war depression was inevitable. Instead
it predicted shortages, rising wages and prices, a high level of
business. And again, those who heeded its advice were able to avoid
losses, to cash in on the surging economy of the late '40s, early '50s
and mid '60s. It then kept its clients prepared for the swings of the
'70s, keeping them a step ahead each time.

     Now Kiplinger not only foresees expansion ahead, but also
continuing inflation, and in his weekly Letter to clients he points
out profit opportunities in the future...and also dangers.

     The Kiplinger Letter not only keeps you informed of present
trends and developments, but also gives you advance notice on the
short & long-range business outlook...inflation forecasts...energy
predictions...housing...federal legislative prospects...politics...
investment trends & pointers...tax outlook & advice...labor, wage
settlement prospects...upcoming gov't rules & regulations...ANYTHING
that will have an effect on you, your business, your personal finances,
your family.

     To take advantage of this opportunity to try the Letter and
benefit from its keen judgments and helpful advice during the fast-

                             (Over, please)

(continued)

One of the most famous letters in direct mail, the Kiplinger letter. With minor changes it has been running (and working) for almost forty years! Notice how it follows the "seven-step formula" for writing sales letters.

Exhibit 14-13. The Kiplinger Letter

changing months ahead...fill in and return the enclosed form along
with your $21 payment. And do it with this guarantee: That you may
cancel the service and get a prompt refund of the unused part of
your payment any time you feel it is not worth far more to you than
it costs.

I'll start your service as soon as I hear from you, and
you'll have each weekly issue on your desk every Monday morning
thereafter.

Sincerely,

Stanley Mayes
Assistant to the President

SAM:kga

P. S.   More than half of all new subscribers sign up for a full year
at $42. In appreciation, we'll send you FREE five special Kiplinger
Reports on receipt of your payment when you take a full year's service,
too. Details are spelled out on the enclosed slip. Same money-back
guarantee and tax deductibility apply.

Exhibit 14-14. Effective Letter Design

This November, you're invited to take an exciting look at what computers can do for you...

...at the landmark course that will give you--as it's given thousands of executives--the confidence and know-how you need to:

* Clear up the mystery and confusion of data processing!
* Make your computer work harder for you!
* Tell your systems people what <u>you</u> want--instead of the other way around!
* Make computers your partner in management

Dear Executive:

If you're baffled by computers...baffaloed when systems people use words like "byte" and "nanosecond"...if you're tired of the data processing department telling <u>you</u> what can be done, because you don't know enough to give the orders...

...it's time you took the American Management Associations' course that's cured thousands of "computer phobia"...

FUNDAMENTALS OF DATA PROCESSING FOR THE NON-DATA PROCESSING EXECUTIVE

Not for programmers or DP professionals...this 3-day course is one of the few computer seminars just for you, the data processing <u>user</u>! One at which you'll take a fascinating look at what computers can do for you...and learn how to utilize them to become a more effective manager...

...And this November, you can attend any of 12 sessions in 10 major cities across the country--<u>including a city near you!</u>

Thousands of managers and executives have attended this landmark course and, without hesitation, many have called it "the best course they've ever taken." <u>Here's what just a few of the recent attendees had to say:</u>

"I got terrific ideas and concepts that I can implement and

(inside...)

American Management Associations · 135 West 50th Street · New York, N.Y. 10020 · (212)586-8100

(continued)

Notice how much more inviting the letter on page 342 is, even though the letters have identical copy.

Exhibit 14-14. Effective Letter Design

```
* * * * * * * * * * * * * * * * * * * * * * * * * * * * * * *
*                                                           *
*     This November, you're invited to take an exciting look *
*             at what computers can do for you...            *
*                                                           *
*  ...at the landmark course that will give you--as it's given *
*  thousands of executives--the confidence and know-how you need to: *
*                                                           *
*   * Clear up the mystery and confusion of data processing! *
*   * Make your computer work harder for you!                *
*   * Tell your systems people what you want--instead of the *
*     other way around!                                      *
*   * Make computers your partner in management              *
*                                                           *
* * * * * * * * * * * * * * * * * * * * * * * * * * * * * * *
```

Dear Executive:

      If you're baffled by computers...buffaloed when systems people
use words like "byte" and "nanosecond"...if you're tired of the data
processing department telling you what can be done, because you
don't know enough to give the orders...

...it's time you took the American Management Associations' course
that's cured thousands of "computer phobia"...

                 FUNDAMENTALS OF DATA PROCESSING
               FOR THE NON-DATA PROCESSING EXECUTIVE

            Not for programmers or DP professionals...
            this 3-day course is one of the few computer
            seminars just for you, the data processing
            user! One at which you'll take a fascinating
            look at what computers can do for you...and
            learn how to utilize them to become a more
            effective manager...

            ...And this November, you can attend any of
            12 sessions in 10 major cities across the
            country--including a city near you!

      Thousands of managers and executives have attended this landmark
course and, without hesitation, many have called it "the best course
they've ever taken." Here's what just a few of the recent attendees
had to say:

      "I got terrific ideas and concepts that I can implement and

                                              (inside...)

American Management Associations · 135 West 50th Street · New York, N.Y. 10020 · (212)586-8100

ice." Or, "Are you taking advantage of these six commonly overlooked tax deductions?"

Another good technique is to change the type of lead on your letter. Review the examples of six common types of leads given earlier. If you're using a news lead, try one built around the narrative approach. Or develop a provocative question as the lead. Usually a new lead will require you to rewrite the first few paragraphs of copy to fit the lead, but then you can often pick up the balance of the letter from your control copy. A top creative man who has a well-organized approach for coming up with new ideas is Sol Blumenfeld, a veteran direct mail professional. Here are some of the approaches Blumenfeld uses:

The Additive Approach

This means adding something to a control package that can increase its efficiency in such a way as to justify the extra cost involved. Usually, this entails using inserts. Inserts that can be used to heighten response include testimonial slips, extra discounts, a free gift for cash with order, and a news flash or bulletin. Other additive ideas include building stamps or tokens into the response device. And, if you have a logical reason to justify it, add an expiration date to your offer.

The Extractive Approach

This copy exercise requires a careful review of your existing mailing package copy. You often can find a potential winning lead buried somewhere in the body copy.

The Innovative Approach

Unlike the extractive approach, this is designed to produce completely new ideas. If you are testing three or four new copy approaches, at least one of them should represent a potential breakthrough, something that's highly original, perhaps even a little wild. I encourage writers to let themselves go, because we've seen them produce real breakthroughs this way—dramatic new formats, exciting copy approaches, and offers that have really shellacked the old control!

Some Final Tips

When you create your own direct mail, you might check it against the following list of pointers. Remember that these are *guidelines*, not rigid rules, and that when I say "X will usually outpull Y," that means every so often X will not outpull Y.

With that caution in mind, here are the guidelines:

Mailing Format

- The letter ranks first in importance.
- The most effective mailing package consists of outside envelope, letter, circular, response form, and business reply envelope.

Letters

- Form letters using indented paragraphs will usually outpull those in which paragraphs are not indented.
- Underlining important phrases and sentences usually increases results slightly.
- A separate letter with a separate circular will generally do better than a combination letter and circular.
- A form letter with an effective running headline will ordinarily do as well as a filled-in letter.
- Authentic testimonials in a sales letter ordinarily increase the pull.
- A two-page letter ordinarily outpulls a one-page letter.

Circulars

- A circular that deals specifically with the proposition presented in the letter will be more effective than a circular of an institutional character.
- A combination of art and photography will usually produce a better circular than one employing either art or photography alone.
- A circular usually proves to be ineffective in selling news magazines and news services.
- In selling big-ticket products, deluxe large-size, color circulars virtually always warrant the extra cost over circulars $11'' \times 17''$ or smaller.

Outside Envelopes

- Illustrated envelopes increase response if their message is tied into the offer.
- Variety in types and sizes of envelopes pays, especially in a series of mailings.

Reply Forms

- Reply cards with receipt stubs will usually increase response over cards with no stub.
- "Busy" order or request forms that look important will usually produce a larger response than neat, clean-looking forms.
- Postage-free business reply cards will generally bring more responses than those to which the respondent must affix postage.

Reply Envelopes

- A reply envelope increases cash-with-order response.
- A reply envelope increases responses to collection letters.

Color

- Two-color letters usually outpull one-color letters.
- An order or reply form printed in colored ink or on colored stock usually outpulls one printed in black ink on white stock.
- A two-color circular generally proves to be more effective than a one-color circular.
- Full color is warranted in the promotion of such items as food items, apparel, furniture, and other merchandise if the fidelity of color reproduction is good.

Postage

- Third-class mail ordinarily pulls as well as first-class mail.
- Postage-metered envelopes usually pull better than affixing postage stamps (and you can meter third-class postage).
- A "designed" printed permit on the envelope usually does as well as postage metered mail.

Self-Quiz

1. What unique advantages permit direct mail to do a better selling job than any other advertising medium?

   a _____

   b. _____

   c. _____

   d. _____

   e. _____

2. What are the three basic formats of direct mail?

   a. _____

   b. _____

   c. _____

3. Complete the following true-false quiz:

   a. Personalized letters will always outpull nonpersonalized ones. _____

   b. A "publisher's letter" will usually boost response 10 percent or more. _____

   c. A pop-up device is a sure-fire way to increase response. _____

   d. Invitation formats are "passé." _____

4. Complete this equation for making a sale:

   Benefit *divided by* _____ *equals* _____.

5. What is the difference between a benefit and a selling point?

   _____

   _____

   _____

   _____

6. What are some of the basic wants inherent in most people?

   a. _____   f. _____

   b. _____   g. _____

   c. _____   h. _____

   d. _____   i. _____

   e. _____   j. _____

7. What do most people desire to avoid?

   a. _____   d. _____

   b. _____   e. _____

   c. _____   f. _____

8. Name eleven guidelines to good direct mail copy.

   a. _____   g. _____

   b. _____   h. _____

   c. _____   i. _____

   d. _____   j. _____

   e. _____   k. _____

   f. _____

9. What is the key objective in preparing an order form? Make order forms look _____

   _____

10. Name four typical involvement devices.

   a. _____

   b. _____

c. _____

d. _____

11. Name the six most common types of leads used in sales letters.

a. _____   d. _____

b. _____   e. _____

c. _____   f. _____

12. List the points in the seven-step letter writing formula in sequence:

a. _____   e. _____

b. _____   f. _____

c. _____   g. _____

d. _____

13. What are the two best applications of a P.S.?

a. To restate _____

b. To offer an added _____

14. Define each of these approaches for improving a good mailing package:

a. The additive approach _____

_____

_____

b. The extractive approach _____

_____

_____

c. The innovative approach _____

_____

_____

Pilot Project   You are the advertising manager of a major national chain store group (e.g., Sears, Wards, J.C. Penney, etc.) Your company wants to get more of its credit cards in the hands of qualified persons. Your assignment: prepare a direct mail package to "sell" your store's credit card.

Assumptions:

- The credit card is free; there is no yearly charge or fee to have one.
- It is honored in your company's stores from coast to coast for anything sold in those stores.
- In addition to your company's own credit card, your company's stores also accept the two bank credit cards (VISA and MasterCard).

The objective of your direct mail package is to get creditworthy persons to fill out an application for the card. They will be credit-checked, and a certain number of persons will be turned down. Another obvious objective is that, when a person has applied and been approved for the card, you want him or her to *use* it.

There are some steps to guide you through the decisions you will have to make:

1. Write a creative strategy. Pay particular attention to *competitive products, market,* and *creative implementation.*

2. Which format would you select: classic or self-mailer. Why?

3. Here are some selling points (or product features) of the card. Below each one, list the *customer benefit* made possible by that selling point. (To get you started, the first one is filled in.) Note: more than one benefit can usually be derived from a single selling point.

   a. Lets you charge purchases.
      You don't need to carry cash.

   b. Card is good nationwide.

      _____

   c. Card is good for anything sold at our stores.

      _____

4. What is the "big idea" behind your mailing package? How will you implement this theme in the letter? Circular? Outer envelope? Order form (application)?

5. Are you going to use any additional pieces, such as gift slips or a publisher's letter?

6. Write your sales letter. Pay particular attention to the "seven-step formula."

7. How could you use versioned copy in your letter?

CHAPTER FIFTEEN

Techniques of Creating and Marketing Catalogs

America's long-standing love affair with the catalog has intensified over the past decade. The consumer—the employed female in particular—has turned to the catalog as a way to save shopping time. Business firms, engaged in the sale of equipment and supplies to other businesses, have turned to the catalog as a means of reducing the high cost of person-to-person selling.

With the expansion of catalog marketing, more sophisticated marketing methods are being applied. Mailings to direct response lists—primarily buyers from other catalogs—have long been the major mode of circulation for consumer catalog marketers. Catalog marketers in the business-to-business field have used a mix of direct response lists and compiled lists. But some of the major consumer catalog marketers have also established their own retail and catalog stores in high density shopping areas.

How Consumers Perceive Successful Catalogs

Catalog circulation is, of course, the final act in the catalog process. There's got to be a reason for being for every catalog, a niche to fill. And merchandise selection and position, creative concepts, copy and graphics are all critical to the total catalog process. In the final analysis your catalog must be *perceived* as worthy to browse and act upon.

Dick Hodgson, a noted direct marketing consultant and catalog specialist, points out that there are four key perceptions that must be held by the consumer in order for the catalog operation to be successful.

Perceived Availability

Mr. Hodgson points out that while the product or service being sold may be available from a neighborhood merchant, this becomes a major competitive issue only if the potential buyer is aware of this fact and thus determines it would be easier to purchase from a nearby source.

The Brookstone Company offers a catalog that carries the slogan: "Hard To Find Tools." Actually, many of the tools Brookstone sells—or similar tools that will do the same jobs—are available through local hardware merchants. But they're the type of articles merchants keep in those bins under their counters or in the stockroom, "just in case somebody asks for them." Thus, the reader of a Brookstone catalog perceives such tools to be truly "hard to find." Brookstone has had steady and profitable growth serving buyers who have come to depend on its catalog rather than the local merchants as a source for tools and, as Brookstone puts it, "Other Fine Things."

Direct marketers have developed many special techniques to encourage their customers to perceive their products or services as being unique and thus not easily available elsewhere. Marketers emphasize their exclusive colors, designs, and packaging; special combination of products; attractive and easily understood credit plans; early introductions of new or improved products; and a variety of other effective techniques that traditional retailers have been reluctant to adopt.

Perceived Authority

The second of Dick Hodgson's benchmarks for a successful catalog is *perceived authority.* Successful catalog operations, Dick points out, either trade on an area of established authority or go to great lengths to build a base of authority from which to sell. Take, for example, those successful airline seatback catalogs. Note how much space they devote to luggage and other travel-related items. With their years of experience in handling luggage, airlines are perceived by the consumer as having clearly established themselves as authorities on the durability of luggage. And when the airline says a bag is durable, the consumer has got to believe it knows what it is talking about.

One sometimes wonders why so many catalogs seem to waste so much space on seemingly ego-centered editorial material about the facilities and the people of the companies behind them. It's not just an ego trip in most cases, but rather it's a carefully calculated effort to build authority in the minds of customers and prospects to encourage buying with confidence. And such space is far from wasted when it eliminates the need for a lot of back-up copy for each item in the book.

Perceived Value

The third of Dick Hodgson's points is perceived value. Suppose that you are a consumer interested in a jade necklace. You go to the leading department store in your city and look at a small assortment of jade necklaces. Then you "shop" the Gump's catalog which is produced twice a year by the famous Gump's store in San Francisco. You know the reputation of Gump's for its precious items from the Far East, including jade. If you are typical, your perception of value would be heavily swayed toward Gump's because of its "authority" with respect to jade.

Perceived Satisfaction

As previously mentioned, a guarantee of satisfaction is a key in mail order. The American consumer has been trained in the perception that if he is unhappy with his purchase he can return it for replacement, full credit, or full refund.

The customer's perceived satisfaction doesn't start and end with the guarantee. Smart direct marketers are very selective in the merchandise they offer to forestall potential fears customers might have about dissatisfaction. In fashions, for example, direct marketers often purposely select styles that don't involve critical fits. They select colors that reproduce well and are easily visualized from printed illustrations. And they prepare copy which not only romances the product, but carefully spells out details which, if misunderstood, could result in dissatisfaction.

Four Types of Catalogs

The function of catalogs can be better understood by categorizing the types of catalogs and examining the characteristics of each. There are four general types of catalogs: retail catalogs, full-line catalogs, business-to-business catalogs, and consumer specialty catalogs. Each type bears special considerations.

Retail Catalogs

A recent phenomenon on the marketing scene has been the interest in catalogs by retailers. Some stores, most notably Neiman-Marcus, have been famous for their catalogs for decades. For most stores, the principal objective has been to build in-store traffic. Now, however, emphasis is shifting to other objectives. A major new goal is generation of mail and phone orders from customers outside the retailers' trading area.

So the objectives of the retailer are not necessarily similar to those of the mail order catalog entrepreneur who does not have a retail store. The retailer usually wants store traffic inside his trading area and mail order sales outside it. Also, the retailer can opt for a catalog largely underwritten by vendor money, vendors considering such funds to be "advertising allowances." But the store pays a price when the vendor pays to "advertise" an item in the store's catalog.

The vendor catalog. Some time ago, someone got the idea that the "smart" way for a retail catalog operation to go was to sell "advertising" in the catalog to vendors, with vendors underwriting all, or most, of the cost. You can't argue with the arithmetic. But with each "ad" a retailer accepts, he compromises mail order principles. Vendors dictate the catalog makeup. Retailers don't.

A giant step closer to a true mail order catalog is the well-executed "store traffic" catalog. Many stores produce such catalogs and mail them to charge customers in their trading areas. The prime objective is to produce mail order sales.

This creates a dilemma. For example, a store might be a leader in the sale of sterling silver in its trading area so it features sterling silver in its catalog. The result might be big in-store sales, but zero mail order sales. For another example, a department store that is a leader in "high fashion" apparel finds that only staple apparel sells in its catalog. Dilemma: Should it leave "high fashion" out of its catalog and risk losing some of its big in-store sales?

The problem isn't severe if the retailer restricts distribution to his trading area with building store traffic being the prime objective. But suppose the retailer decides to mail the catalog outside his trading area, soliciting "pure" mail orders? His mail order sales are certain to be diluted to the extent he has violated sound mail order principles.

The extent to which retailers build healthy mail order operations in the future will be dependent upon two basics: the application of sound mail order principles and long-term commitment.

Full-Line Merchandise Catalogs

In the purest sense there are only a handful of full-line merchandise catalogs in this country, catalogs that, in effect, are complete department stores. Among these are Sears, Spiegel, and J. C. Penney. Among the subcategories of full-line merchandise catalogs is the "wholesale" catalog, which features selections of merchandise such as appliances, electronics, and jewelry. Most such catalogs are backed by vendor money, the vendors paying all or a portion of the cost for running catalog pages featuring their merchandise.

Business-to-Business Catalogs

A real phenomenon of the past decade has been the growth of business catalogs through which business sells to business. But in spite of phenomenal growth during the past decade, the potential in this area has hardly been scratched. (See Chapter 6, "Business-to-Business Direct Marketing.")

Consumer Specialty Catalogs

The most dramatic growth over the past decade has occurred in the area of consumer specialty catalogs—catalogs that fill special needs or cater to identifiable lifestyles. The great Sears, Roebuck and Company, for example, in addition to its basic full-line merchandise catalog now publishes some twenty special-interest catalogs offering auto parts, western apparel, tall men's clothing, winter sporting goods, convalescent products, and similar groups of products for market segments.

Catalog Creativity

The tremendous growth in catalog sales, both in the business market and the consumer market, has brought unprecedented competition. This has created a paradox: unprecedented growth accompanied by unprecedented failure.

Reasons for failure are many, with shortage of capital being high on the list. But even an abundance of capital does not assure success. The X factor, the one distinguishing mark that makes one catalog stand out from all others in its class, is *creative execution*, without doubt.

And if I were asked to identify the one person who has done the most to raise the level of catalog creativity, I would say without a moment's hesitation, "She is Ms. Jo-Von Tucker, president of Jo-Von Tucker & Associates of New York City." Jo-Von has created more upscale catalogs than anyone. The pages that follow capture her incisive thinking about catalog creativity.

Before a graphic marketing solution can be found for a catalog, a certain amount of "homework" should be done. A thorough understanding of the specific market is as important as knowing the product or service line well. Any available research regarding the lifestyle of the prospective customer should be considered as valuable marketing input. By learning upfront about habits and leisure activities we simultaneously gain access to needs and requirements of the consumer.

Vignette of the Upscale Market

Market research data gives us a profile of an affluent mail order customer. As high as 85 percent of upscale catalog buyers are female. The national work force in America currently reflects that in excess of 55 percent are women.

In order to define "upscale," one must look beyond Webster's contribution and resort to demographic monetary measures of income. By today's inflationary standards, a single income of $35,000 annually qualifies, as does a two-income annual total of $50,000. The key to consider (and the most difficult to track) is discretionary income. A family that earns $50,000 annually but has living commitments of $45,000 does not necessarily reflect a $5,000 discretionary income, because of unscheduled commitments or other unplanned living expenses.

Discretionary income can be tracked by numbers of mail order purchases and projected by average dollar order of each purchase. A mail order company can program its computers to track buying behavior of its own customers, but must rely on conjecture or sharing of information to expand the portrait beyond their area of control.

Assuming from industry statistics that 50 percent of mail order customers are married and that they have an average of 1.5 children per household, we know that the prospects have *needs* for their children as well as for themselves. During the course of a year they will purchase clothing, sports equipment, toys, learning supplies and gifts—some via the mail. Time is a priority to this customer because with today's active lifestyle there exists less leisure time than in our recent history. People choose to do other things with available leisure time than traditional retail shopping. Many opt for the convenience of mail order as an alternate shopping style.

The Quality-Style-Conscious Upscale Buyer.

Photo: Courtesy of The Photographers, Inc.

An ideal prequalification consideration for customer acquisition is one of having bought through the mail previously, either from competition or from a similar offering. An established inclination to purchase quality products from catalogs gives us insight into how this customer responds, both to merchandise categories and to graphic selling techniques.

A complete study of an upscale mail order customer should be used to fill in a canvas for a portrait, each bit of data completing another segment of the sketch. The types of stores at which consumers hold charge cards will help identify "quality of lifestyle"; active sports participation, home entertaining. Knowledge about civic and/or political activities, charity involvement, travel frequency and many other factors can be used to fill in the blanks—to educate direct marketers to their customers' needs.

The Competitive Mailbox

With the recent deluge of mail order catalogs comes a challenge to the producers of such marketing tools: to be better, more unique, slicker, and more credible than the catalog that arrives in the prospect's hands at the same time as yours. Catalogs have evolved to a high level of sophistication during the past ten years, and the customer has been educated through multiple exposures to expect this kind of presentation. Clean, contemporary graphics combined with dramatic photography and understated copy, all wrapped up in shiny high-gloss printing on quality paper. The look of today's catalogs—a creatively produced marketing vehicle designed to present, excite, motivate and, ultimately, to sell.

The importance of establishing both an image and credibility for a catalog cannot be emphasized too strongly. On any given day, three or more catalogs may arrive simultaneously. There's no likelihood a prospect will order from all catalogs received on a given day: more likely a single catalog will capture attention and interest. In order for the chosen catalog to be yours, the most creative marketing decisions must have been made at each step of production, culminating in an outstanding catalog presentation.

To put your catalog to the supreme test, conduct your own private survey. Select three or four competitive catalogs and lay them out next to your most recent issue. Try to be objective, and put yourself in the customer's frame of mind as you glance at each catalog. Which one do you reach for first, and why? Does your catalog make a definitive statement about your company and about what's inside the pages? Does it entice you to open it and to scan through? When you pick it up, does it give you a tangible impression of quality?

Now here is the crucial test: open your catalog and that of a competitor to any spread. Compare the two presentations. Do they look alike? Could your two-page spread be pulled from your catalog and dropped into the competitive book and still blend in? If so, you've got a problem! You have produced a "me too" book, and the customer will know it.

Filling a Niche

"Me too" books are all too common in the industry. And what a waste, considering the cost of catalog production today!

To establish a niche in an overcrowded marketplace, you must have a "raison d'être," a reason for being. It should begin with the selection and editing of merchandise, and conclude with the physical presentation. Additionally, a niche is enhanced by special techniques in fulfillment and customer service. Set yourself apart from your competition by continually seeking new items (even more reason for merchandise exclusivity and product development) and by refinement of your catalog creative efforts.

Think of the mailbox as a crowded marketplace where many vendors are milling around, setting up displays of their wares. To simply spread a blanket on the ground and dump your products in a heap is not enough. Instead, use each spread within your catalog as a window display. It is, of course, your decision whether to opt for a Neiman-Marcus-type presentation or that of a variety store. I firmly believe (based on twenty years' experience in cataloging) that quality sells better! It does not matter whether you are selling caviar or pots and pans, *tasteful graphics are more successful* because the prospective customer is receptive to them.

The Bon Appétit *appeal to the good life.*

Photo: Courtesy of Bon Appétit *and Knapp Communications.*

The Bon Appétit *appeal to the good life. Photo: Courtesy of* Bon Appétit *and* Knapp Communications.

The Paper Store

Catalogs are effective for a variety of reasons. First, they provide a convenient way of shopping. Second, they are capable of provoking an emotional response. Third, due to around-the-clock, toll-free telephone numbers and available order forms, there is no time limit for the customer. Fourth, an edited selection can be presented. And, fifth, a catalog can be ultimately considerate.

In relation to the fifth point, the catalog medium has an inherent advantage. It will never be rude, and it is always accessible when the customer is ready to buy. As a sales force it can be totally controlled to reflect company policy and image, as opposed to the retail store personnel situation. Mail order has an opportunity to be a thoughtful selling process because of editing. The customer is not asked to go through racks and racks of clothing items or to peruse hundreds of shelves of decorator items. Instead, an experienced, knowing merchant has done the editing for her or him, eliminating duplicates and offering a narrow array of products that are tastefully designed and quality produced.

In fact, we have learned a valuable lesson about the importance of editing mail order merchandise; customers have shown us that too many

The Paper Store: Convenience and Multiple Appeals.

Photos: Courtesy Creme de la Creme (top), Gucci (middle), American Express (bottom).

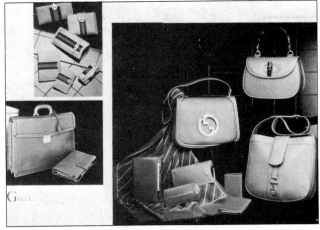

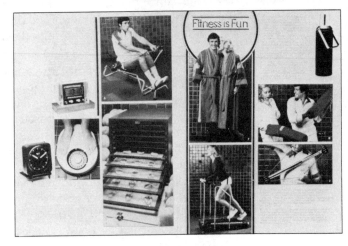

choices of a product category tend to confuse a prospective buyer. Many times a prospect will decide not to buy at all, rather than make a choice from too many similar items.

Catalog Psychology

The application of psychology to catalog marketing is an important element in being considerate of the customer and in motivating a decision to buy. It is understood by very few cataloguers and actually applied by even fewer.

Consideration involves showing the merchandise most effectively—scaling it with a simple prop or accessory so that the customer immediately understands the size of the item; showing it in use, so its benefits are readily grasped; answering any possible questions about the product in the copy, succinctly, so as not to take advantage of the prospect's time; controlling the reproductions in separations and printing, so that the item is shown in the actual color that the customer will receive. The design and graphics of the catalog are clean, with ample white space for framing the photography and providing relief for the prospect's eyes. The type is also clean, with limited reverse copy used, and no reverses out of busy photographic backgrounds.

The use of color is another application of catalog psychology. Research tests have proved that people respond predictably and emotionally to colors. Certain colors, such as warm earth tones, are comfortably perceived and provide pleasurable backgrounds for merchandise. And there are some colors that work negatively, provoking an unpleasant reaction from a viewer. Bright pinks and orchids are such colors and should be avoided for photographic backdrops.

Nature's colors and tints seem to be the most acceptable to the eye. The human eye functions much like a camera lens, seeing all colors made up of a combination of red, yellow, blue, and black. A mechanical tint is less believable to the eye than a photographic one, which has shades from light to dark, and all four colors from the spectrum as opposed to a screen combination of one or two colors. Using mechanical tints cheapens a catalog and costs credibility.

Conceptualizing a Catalog

If a catalog is to qualify as being convenient, unique, and considerate, it must be well thought out. An effective catalog does not begin at the drawing board with pen on layout paper, but much in advance of that. It begins with conceptualizing.

Each of the key people involved in the production of a catalog must allocate adequate thinking time. The merchant must think about the products; the art director must plan the creative approach; print production must think about the preparation of specifications and the desired end result of reproduction. But the head of direct marketing is usually the one responsible for the up-front conceptualizing called "direction" or "point of view."

Point-of-view conceptualizing involves finite review of the target audience, the kind of merchandise to be offered, the image desired, the concept of graphics and format, the degree of credibility and quality reproduction, and many other determining factors. Communication of these weighed decisions is imperative to each of the members of the production team, so that directions can be followed and conceptualizing achieved.

I find it most helpful to make notes as I begin to seek a concept for a catalog. The notes help to move thoughts to paper and to hold them as they are refined and polished. From the notes I begin to make thumbnail sketches, again to help crystallize thoughts into a less fleeting form. The sketches needn't be works of art; they are there to help communicate thoughts. Neither should they be inflexible. Improvement will naturally come in the progression of the development and as other people are brought into the thinking process.

As conceptual thinking brings direction, it should be equally applied to merchandising, format, and reproduction. A catalog can present a schizophrenic image if one area is well thought out and others are simply thrown together without the proper conceptual foundation. Conceptualizing is a technique of *theorizing* a catalog. From theory you must move to reality, or the *realization* of the book.

To Theme or Not to Theme

Part of the conceptualizing process is deciding whether or not your catalog will be presented in a theme mode. There are endless subjects for theming, from seasons to lifestyle, from needs to special interests. Themes provide you with a logical format for presentation. (Some catalog marketers opt for no-theme presentation, a potpourri mixing of merchandise lending interest to the book.)

A catalog does not have to be strictly themed. A combination presentation can be equally effective, using themes for special sections or spreads. Or, in reverse, a themed catalog can present one spread of merchandise in potpourri fashion, breaking the pacing of the book and making it more interesting for the customer.

If a theme is used, it should be carried out subtly as a cohesive element. Using a seasonal theme, like springtime, fresh spring flowers can be used as props (never to detract from the merchandise) and pastel spring colors can be selected as backgrounds for shots. Birds, bird nests, robins' eggs, green leaves, raindrops, clouds: nature's props are infinite in variety, but don't cheat! Fake flowers will look exactly like what they are. Use the real thing, or forget it. Otherwise, you will destroy the credibility that you are working so hard to achieve.

The Cover Story

A catalog cover must work harder than any other ingredient in the medium. It must instantaneously make a statement of believability and credibility for the company, as well as entice the prospective customer to open the pages of the catalog.

Approximately 3 seconds is the amount of time each catalog cover is given by the recipient. That translates to an equivalent of 1½ seconds to establish credibility and 1½ seconds to intrigue the customer with a promise of what is inside the catalog. An incredible selling job must be accomplished in a short span of time.

Because the allotted interest time is small, it generally pays off for a catalog company to establish a recognizable format for their covers. If your catalog is instantly recognizable by its cover, more of the customer's attention can be called to the promise of exciting merchandise offerings inside the book. Formats can be developed that say, at a glance, this is the new American Express Catalog or the Holiday Issue of Bachrachs.

A cover format need not be inflexible; it is entirely possible to design a cover concept that will allow variations within a general framework. Subject matter may vary, while type style and placement of the logo remain the same with each issue.

Covers may be editorial or merchandised, depending on your point of view. Most cataloguers currently produce merchandised covers because of the value of the front cover selling space potential. It is difficult to give up what usually proves to be the number one selling space in the catalog just to make an editorial statement.

A combination cover can also be used. An item of merchandise can be selected for the cover and shown somewhat esoterically, which results in an editorial look. American Express samples shown here demonstrate a continuity of look or image, with merchandise shown editorially. In addition, the American Express card (even more recognizable than the logo) is worked into the cover each time.

Bachrachs covers are merchandised, with the selling copy shown on the back cover and referenced again on the inside front cover. Since Bachrachs is a man's specialty clothing catalog, men's wear is shown on the front cover, usually treated seasonally in background and atmosphere.

It is a good idea to date your covers for identification purposes. Holiday 1988 or Summer 1988 will do for the wording, or you can be very specific if you produce seven or eight books a year, and label each issue with date of publication.

Very little space is devoted here to editorial covers because I would rather promote the sale of merchandise for any catalog. Additionally, I feel that it is more considerate of the customer to give an indication of what kind of items are inside the book. Editorial treatment of merchandise accomplishes both goals; that is, to make a statement for the company image-

Successful Covers

*Combination
Look.*

*Photos: Courtesy
of American
Express.*

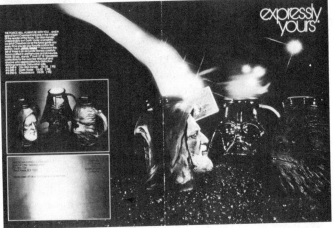

wise and to let the customer know what to expect. And, it sells merchandise.

Selection of an item for the cover should be done carefully. Some generic guidelines are:

1. The item under consideration should be unusual, not generally found in other catalogs or stores. (Exclusive is even better.)

2. It should be deemed photographable by the creative staff.

3. It should be representative of the line of products offered inside the book.

4. It should be understandable, requiring only one depiction to show its features.

Creative Cover Techniques

The main ingredient that should be sought for a cover depiction is that of *drama.* A dramatic portrayal of a product lends impact to your cover efforts and will work harder for you than a pedestrian version. Williams-Sonoma chooses items that are representative, yet newsworthy, and features them dramatically with a Chuck Williams-prepared dish.

Drama can be obtained through lighting and composition of photography. Communicate to your creative director and photographer precisely what you are trying to achieve with your cover portrayal. And then allow them some creative license to bring back an outstanding cover shot. When composing the photograph they might discover a better angle that will enhance and further dramatize the product.

Good photography is your key to the finest reproduction. Be sure that you capture in photography the essence and quality of your point-of-view statement. Don't expect the separator, regardless of how accomplished he may be, to build something into the shot that is missing.

The Japanese have a phrase that relates to image and perception; they put great value in "presenting face." A catalog cover does exactly that to your customers. Although it requires weeks to create and is only recognized for a few brief seconds, the fact that is presented has a lasting impression. It is important to present face by producing a unique, dramatic, quality-oriented cover. It is your official invitation to the customer to browse the pages of your paper store.

Graphic design is another important element. It can make the difference between a tasteful cover and a distasteful one. No matter how effective your cover photograph is, without good graphic treatment it will be wasted. Graphic format can vary from bold to subtle and understated and can change your statement from a shout to a whisper. Both kinds of statements can be successful, but rarely should you bounce from one to the other. Select your statement by knowing your customer, and sticking with the appropriate one. Refine it as you go along; each cover that you do should be better than the one preceding.

Dramatic Covers: A Key Ingredient

Photos:
Courtesy of
American
Express.

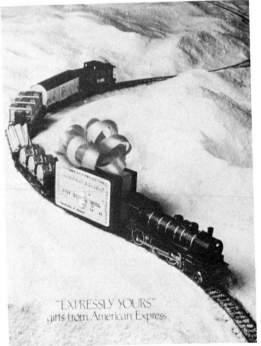

Catalog Design Techniques

A catalog is perceived by spreads, two facing pages. Customers do not see single pages one at a time, but rather the two facing pages as a visual element. Layout of pages should always be done bearing this in mind. The two-page spread should be worked as a unit, not individual pages as stand-alones.

If you imagine the spread as a black canvas, then your mind (not your pencil) automatically begins to compose the white space as a physical frame for the items to be shown. Treatment of products does not have to be democratic. Drama in page layout is best achieved by varying the sizes of the depictions, so that at least one item on the spread is shown quite large and treated as important. Varying the size of the photographs also provides relief for the prospect's eyes, eliminating the monotony of a "comic book format" where all the photographic boxes are the same size.

A layout format should blend from spread to spread, although it is not wise to repeat the exact same layout all the way through the book. Grid system layout is an easy way out—too easy! In fact, it reflects laziness or lack of creativity on the part of the designer. If you opt for grid system layout, you needn't pay the price of an accomplished catalog designer; a draftsman can do a grid system well.

The placement and arrangement of the elements should be done pleasingly and should help direct the eye to encompass the entire spread. This technique is called eye movement direction. The shape of the articles within the photographic boxes may have direction itself and should be used to subtly direct the eye at all times around or back into the spread. Even the gaze direction of the models can help to lead the prospect to the next depiction, which will lead to the next, and so forth, until every item on the spread has been perceived. A designer should not be a slave to eye movement direction, but should maintain an awareness of the power of being able to gently direct a prospect's attention.

Use of White Space

Unused white space can be the cleanest, most effective frame to set off the photography in a catalog. Type reads best when printed in black on white paper, and four-color photography stands out most dramatically when framed with white space. Use it effectively, and do not feel that because the white paper is there, it must be filled with another product. The proper allotment of space is just as important to the visual impact of a spread as the use of typography and photography.

Pacing and Pagination

The speed at which a prospect thumbs through a catalog is called pacing. Designers and planners of catalogs can, to a degree, control that page-turning speed. By placing some full-page impact shots spaced throughout the book you can gain the reader's attention for long spans of time. Addi-

Effective Catalog Layout and Design

Photos: Courtesy of Artisans of China/Fingerhut Corporation (top), Nieman-Marcus (middle), and C & P Telephone (bottom).

tionally, the use of color can achieve the same thing; that is, a reverse black spread sandwiched between several light, white spreads. A book that is all white tends to be perceived much like a long piece of staccato music. Varying the presentation gets better receptivity from the customer.

Pagination, or the assignment of items to a spread, helps to pace the catalog. An intriguing special interest spread, or grouping of items by theme, will capture attention and make the book more interesting. Sometimes the color of merchandise itself will suggest a theme, like primary colors, or natural earth tones. An entire spread of items can be put together for a patio party, including buffet servers, patio or garden candles, informal napkins, invitations, and patio dresses. Or how about a spread of products to make communicating easier? You could offer personalized stationery (formal and informal), electronic items like a telephone answering machine, a personal desk journal with appointment calendar, etc. And then accessory items for your at-home desk, like picture frames, small calculators, covered coffee mug, letter opener, and so on. Prospects accept pagination when it is done logically.

Copy as a Supportive Element

Without denigrating the role of copy, I must state for the record that catalogs are primarily a photographic medium. The pictures must first capture the prospect's attention. The copy should never detract from the graphic presentation but should be used subliminally to inform and enhance. Columnar copy, if keyed properly to the photography, is accepted as easily understandable and less distracting than cut copy, or copy that appears in individual blocks directly under the item. Cut copy tends to give a catalog a "chopped up" look.

Typography should be clean and well planned and used supportively as a graphic element. Type size should be readable, preferably nine point with pleasing leading. Limit the number of type faces used to a bare minimum. If headlines are used, they should either explain or entertain. Usually a themed spread should be identified as such by a headline. Don't ask the prospect to guess why you grouped certain items together.

The content of catalog copy should be succinct, informative, descriptive, and, above all, accurate. In directing the writing of copy for catalogs, one usually must remind the copywriter of the need for discipline. It is more difficult to use fewer words to describe an item than it is to use more words. It is also important to develop an acceptable format for the listing and sequence of the item name, s.k.u. (stock keeping unit) number, price, and postage and handling charge.

Design Innovation

The preceding observations on catalog design are not to be considered ironclad or self-sustaining. They are intended as guidelines and generic

Dramatic Product Shots through Lighting and Props

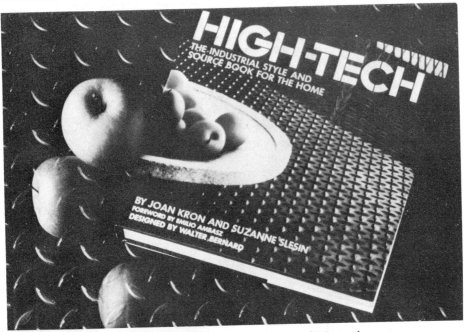

Photos: Courtesy of Edmund Scientific.

Photo: Courtesy Gucci.

Dramatic Product Shots through Lighting and Props

directions, possibly even as a foundation for your own individual style. There are endless ways to design a catalog, and each catalog deserves its own graphic identity. Don't be a look-alike, and don't rely on someone else's creative thinking for your catalog image. Formulate your own success story with innovation and refinement. Let others copy you, and feel good about it.

But if you are already an established leader in the field, do not be complacent about your standing. Continue to seek new solutions. Don't be afraid to experiment. Polish your presentation so that each catalog is better. And concentrate on customer consideration—not for the sake of graphic awards, but to help the merchandise sell better!

Keep your knowledge up to date on state-of-the-art technology. Advancements in reproduction are being made daily and are opening new doors to design techniques.

Photography Techniques for Catalog Marketing

Photography for catalogs should be used as a sculptor uses clay—a vital ingredient in the make-up of a marketing tool. It can be expressive and is definitely motivational. Densities and composition may be molded and formed to give lifelike quality to inanimate objects, while shots involving models may be softly persuasive, yet show stunning clarity of detail.

Dramatization

As in cover photography, all of the product shots inside a catalog must sell one-to-one, and drama can be your best ally in accomplishing this. Emphasis on an item can be gained by lighting—special lighting that can spotlight, halo, or sculpt with dimension. Flat, overall lighting is not as effective for catalog work. Instead, get the maximum dramatic impact for each item by lighting to pick up details and shadows. Aim for crisp, clean highlights, but be careful not to drop the important middle tones!

The product should determine the lighting technique to be used. Different approaches are required to light a piece of crystal and a leather book. Keep your backgrounds as consistent across a spread as possible, and adjust the lights to best enhance the item being shot. Whether it is a table top shot on a small sweep or a location shot involving models, think the entire spread through before photography begins. That way you can communicate with the photographer to make your wishes known. Guesswork is costly and frustrating to everyone involved.

The Subtle Use of Props

Props should be used in photography to scale an item for size or to help explain its use. In a major setup shot that has plenty of room it's all right to use props in the background or foreground just to make the shot more interesting, as long as the props don't overpower the merchandise. When selecting a prop for scale, choose something that is easily understood at a glance. Commonly used props for scaling are flowers, fruit, and hands. You can also select stamps, coins, jelly beans, paper clips, or popcorn. Avoid using something that could be a variety of sizes, like books, candles, leaves, handbags, and ashtrays.

There is danger of overpropping at all times, and it is advisable to use props only when necessary and then prudently and tastefully. If the props overpower, the product gets lost. The example of the glass bowl (p. 369) demonstrates overpropping. We had lots of requests for the recipe, but we sold very few glass bowls!

Maximizing Location Shootings

Location shootings for showing fashion items are effective in catalogs because (a) they allow us to utilize nature's perfect lighting (which we cannot totally simulate in a studio); and (b) their background subject matter adds the element of entertainment for our prospects.

Whether you are shooting at the local park or halfway around the world, the rules should be the same. Don't crop out all of the background! If you have that in mind to start with (and most merchants do) save wear and tear on the shooting crew and stay in the studio. Location shots are difficult to plan and execute because of logistics, obtaining shooting permission, and moving merchandise, crew, equipment, and models around. Remember that the model needn't be centered in every shot. Allow some room for interesting composition, and don't tight-crop out all of the atmosphere. I once had a client who dragged me, merchandise, crew, models, and photographic equipment all over the world to shoot. And then insisted on cropping out all backgrounds. The books easily could have been shot in my backyard instead of in a foreign country!

Basics for Success

Catalog creativity has been emphasized in this section of the chapter. But this should not diminish in any way the vital ingredients of marketing, research, merchandising, list selection, print production, mailing, order forms, computers, toll-free numbers, customer service, and fulfillment. Each has a priority role in the production and distribution of a successful catalog.

But catalog creativity seems to be the most misused and the most misunderstood of the necessary elements. By dissecting some of the major areas of creativity, perhaps we can eliminate some of the mystique and replace it with a more professional application of common sense rules. Although there is nothing common about creativity, neither is there anything sacred about it. It requires intense effort to crystallize an idea into a sound marketing piece. And not only is the marketplace ever changing, but so are the opportunities for presentation.

Photo: Courtesy of Neiman-Marcus.

Creativity, as Jo-Von Tucker has so capably expressed, is the X factor necessary for leadership in a catalog category. Creative execution transcends the basics of a successful catalog operation. There are ten basics important to success.

1. *Right market positioning.* Every catalog must have a reason for being, must fill an identifiable, a reachable niche in the marketplace.

2. *Right merchandise selection.* Merchandise selection must fit the profile of the identified market. (Exclusive products, in particular, build customer loyalty.)

3. *Right positioning and grouping of merchandise.* Most professionals have found the best way to position merchandise is by popularity of categories, the most popular categories appearing up front in the book. Merchandise grouping should be arranged to achieve related buying opportunities and to maintain reader interest throughout the book.

4. *Right graphics.* To quote Jo-Von Tucker, "Catalogs are primarily a photographic medium." The graphics you use express the degree of authority you bring to the specific market you choose to serve.

5. *Right use of color.* Colors should provide pleasurable backgrounds for merchandise. Nature's colors and tints are considered to be the most acceptable to the eye.

6. *Right size.* Business-to-business catalogs should most always be 8½″ × 11″ in size for convenience in placing in industrial catalog reference files. The most popular consumer catalog size is 8½″ × 11″ — thirty-two pages. However, a smaller page size, such as 5½″ × 8½″, should be considered if an 8½″ × 11″ page size would come in at less than twenty-four pages. ("Heft"—thickness—denotes authority and encourages browsing.)

7. *Right copy.* Copy is subordinate to photography in catalog marketing, but it is vital. Copy must be disciplined, but it must include the basics: sizes, colors, materials, weight—if a factor, price. And, in a minimum of words, copy must appeal to the emotions for consumer catalogs and to rationalization for business catalogs.

8. *Right sales stimulators.* It can't be said too often: A catalog must sell on its own. Many catalogs just arrive and lie there. Other catalogs are live, vibrant, exciting—truly creative. Adroit sales stimulation, appropriate to the targeted market is often the ingredient that pushes response beyond the norm. Sales stimulators warrant special attention.

9. *Right order forms.* Experience has proved that a bound-in order form with return envelope stimulates more orders than an on-page order form.

10. *Right sales analysis.* It's sad but true—the most beautiful, most imaginative catalog ever conceived turns downright "ugly" if sales don't meet projections. Every catalog should and must be analyzed page by page to avoid future failures, to build upon success.

Building a Customer Relationship

The six sales stimulators in wide use by catalog marketers are

1. The Overwrap—a sheet wrapped around the front and back cover, allowing extra space to encourage browsing and to stimulate ordering by offering incentives

2. Early order stimulators—free gifts for ordering by a specific date, or an extra sweepstakes incentive for ordering by a specific date

3. Toll-free phone orders—a convenience and cost-free incentive to order

4. Charge privileges—an encouragement to buy without cash through use of bank cards and travel-and-entertainment cards

5. Free trial periods—an incentive to examine and try merchandise with privilege to return

6. Free gifts, or discounts tied to size of order—a stimulant to larger average orders

Where most catalog marketers fail, however, is in establishing a *customer relationship* that, when done right, hypes sales over time. Dick Hodgson, the catalog marketing expert, points out some of the subtle ways astute catalog marketers build customer relations.

Order acknowledgments: Very few catalog marketers acknowledge orders. Yet, an acknowledgment of a mail order answers a nagging question. "Did they get my order?" Publishers Clearing House is an exception: they acknowledge all magazine orders with a "thank you" letter. Then, when payment is received they send a receipt with another letter and another chance to make a sale.

Better packaging: When a shipment arrives from a mail order house your first impression—good or bad—comes from the packaging. Kraft bags may offer economies, but do they give the impression "your order was packed with loving care"?

Brownstone Studio does package with loving care. A blouse ordered from them, for example, arrived in a corrugated box with their logo printed on the tape. And when the box was opened the purchaser was greeted by imprinted tissue. (No plastic peanuts!) But it was how the merchandise was packed inside the tissue that really made a favorable impression: the blouse was on a hanger inside a transparent bag. Conclusion: Brownstone cares.

Ship letters: Another unique way to establish a customer relationship is to use what are referred to as "ship letters"—a letter enclosed with the shipment showing interest in the customer. Few catalog marketers grasp this opportunity.

Ann Taylor, a consumer catalog marketer, is an exception. Upon opening the package the purchaser will find a brief letter along these lines.

> The Ann Taylor philosophy is based on quality, taste, and service. If, for any reason, you wish to contact us regarding your purchase, please write to us. We always appreciate hearing from our customers. Your comments will help to make Ann Taylor an even better place to shop. Address your remarks to Mark Shulman, President.

Customer service enclosures: Understandably, the last thing a catalog marketer wants is *returned merchandise.* That may explain why most don't even hint at the possibility of returned merchandise. Nor do they provide any instructions for returns. That is shortsighted: it is no way to build a customer relationship.

Spiegel, a giant mail order house, understands the importance of building customer relations: they have no hesitancy in providing precise instructions for returns. Enclosed with their shipments is a slip that reads:

> This sheet provides step-by-step instructions for merchandise returns ... gives you a "hot line" number to call ... and offers to arrange a UPS or freight pick-up for you. And if you don't think that's a valuable service, you haven't talked with many of Spiegel's growing list of customers.

Little extras: One of the strongest techniques for building a relationship with a customer is to surprise the customer with little, unexpected extras in the shipment.

Quill Corporation, the office supply and equipment catalog firm, for example, included a set of colorful pens in their package along with a special offer for additional sets.

Lillian Vernon, the specialty catalog people, offer a unique premium for each $10 or $15 of merchandise ordered.

Austad's, another specialty catalog firm, regularly enclose free gifts with their shipments—a five-function LCD watch designed to snap onto your golf glove, for example.

Joan Cook, also a specialty catalog firm, hypes future business by enclosing an envelope with shipments labeled "money inside." The "money" is a $5 discount certificate which can be used on a future order.

William-Sonoma, the cooking equipment and supplies people take advantage of package enclosures to liquidate remainders. Not only do they include bargain-loaded sale flyers in many of their packages, but they also enclose an added sheet offering further reductions.

Personal touch: Mail order customers appreciate the personal touch. The ultimate is a phone call, particularly after a first order.

There is the example of a friend who placed an order with a computer supply firm. A few days after receiving shipment he received a phone call from the president of the company asking his reaction to his recently developed product. He showed genuine interest in my friend's reactions. And the president was enough of a salesman to ask if he could use more of the product. He got the order right then and there.

Building a customer relationship: there is nothing more important.

How to Analyze Results

The catalog sales manager looks at item exposure in a catalog the same way an advertising manager looks at space advertising in print media. Every inch of space you use in a catalog costs a certain amount of money. The cost of space is charged to the item being advertised.

Table 15-1 illustrates the importance of analyzing by item and by page. Let's examine these pages, starting with page 23. Note that three items are offered, one getting a space allocation of a half page and the other two each getting one-fourth page. Note the half-page allocation has an advertising cost of $968 as compared to an advertising cost of $484 for the quarter-page units.

It is significant that item 1618, with a space allocation of one-half page, did $6,699 in sales, over 80 percent of the total sales for the page. Item 1619 lost a small amount of money. Item 1620 made a minimum profit. If profits were calculated for the total page, ignoring the contribution of each item, then item 1619 would not show up as a loser and item 1620 would not show up as a minimum profit item.

Page 47 is also a profit maker. But note that only item 2612 shows a profit, whereas the other two items are losers.

Page 67 is a bad page. Two of the items lost money and the other just broke even. Total loss for the page was $1,040.

Finally let's look at page 69. Both items were profitable. But take careful note that the item allocated three-fourths of a page produced $290 in profit, whereas item 4622, which was allocated only one-fourth of a page, produced $428 in profit.

Let's take a closer look at these figures through the eyes of the catalog sales manager. The first thing he will do is to look at his big winners. From the four pages he has two big winners: items 1618 and 2612. He allocated one-half page to item 1618. For the next edition of his catalog, he well may consider increasing the space to three-fourths of a page or even a full page. He allocated two-thirds of a page to item 2612. For the next edition, he may consider going to one full page.

Now let's look at the losers. Item 1619 was a small loser. He may consider dropping this to one-sixth of a page or eliminating it entirely. On page 47 he had two losers: items 2613 and 2614. Since he allocated only the minimum one-sixth of a page, he can go one of two ways: either eliminate the items entirely or give them more space with the hope that additional space will put them in the profit column.

On page 67 he also had two losers: items 3499 and 3501. He gave one-half page to item 3499. Now he must decide whether it should be eliminated entirely. Since he gave only one-fourth page to item 3501, it is a moot question whether he can put it in the profit column by reducing the space further. These are difficult decisions to make.

One factor that will influence a catalog sales manager's decision is whether the catalog features full-line selection or not. The general merchandise house with full-line selections often must live with losers, whereas the specialty merchandise house (like Miles Kimball, Foster & Gallagher, and Hanover House) is rarely confronted with the problem.

The sophisticated catalog sales manager sees things in numerical results that the neophyte rarely sees. For the sake of illustration, let's assume

Table 15-1. Analysis of Sales Results for Selected Pages from a Typical Catalog

Page Number	Item Number	Space Allocation	Dollar Volume	Advert. Cost	Product Cost	Total of Costs	Item Profit	Item Loss	Page Profit (Loss)
23	1618	1/2 page	$6,699	$ 968	$1,608	$2,576	$4,123		
	1619	1/4 page	556	484	133	617		$ 61	
	1620	1/4 page	1,004	484	241	725	279		
Totals for page			$8,259	$1,936	$1,982	$3,918	$4,402	$ 61	$4,341
47	2612	2/3 page	$8,592	$1,291	$3,007	$4,298	$4,294		
	2613	1/6 page	386	323	135	458		72	
	2614	1/6 page	193	323	68	391		198	
Totals for page			$9,171	$1,937	$3,210	$5,147	$4,294	$ 270	$4,024
67	3499	1/2 page	$ 817	$ 968	$ 531	$1,499		$ 682	
	3500	1/4 page	925	484	426	910	$ 15		
	3501	1/4 page	316	484	205	689		373	
Totals for page			$2,058	$1,936	$1,162	$3,098	$ 15	$1,055	($1,040)
69	4621	3/4 page	$3,226	$1,452	$1,484	$2,936	$ 290		
	4622	1/4 page	1,689	484	777	1,261	428		
Totals for page			$4,915	$1,936	$2,261	$4,197	$ 718		$ 718

Source: Stone & Adler.

item 1618, a big winner, was a sport sweater. The catalog sales manager asks himself, "If sport sweaters sell so well, why shouldn't we test sport jackets, sweatshirts, and jacket emblems?" Thus he builds on a winner.

The State of Catalog Marketing

The state of catalog marketing overall is rosy: catalogs fit today's lifestyle. But there are clouds on the horizon.

Catalog glut. Slow delivery. Back orders. Shoddy packaging. Wrong merchandise. Failure to establish favorable customer relationships. Poor catalog execution. Lack of catalog marketing know-how. These are the major problems that turn consumers away and have an adverse effect on catalog marketing in its totality.

Sobering evidence of the fact that expertise in catalog marketing has a long way to go is provided by a catalog buying study conducted by Dick Hodgson with his daughter Lisa and the Catalog Retail Corporation's Jay Walker.

Hodgson placed 101 orders (mostly by phone). Ten percent of his orders arrived in four days, 20 percent within the first week. As a matter of fact, 70 percent of total orders placed arrived in two weeks. That's the good news.

The bad news is that after four weeks a heavy percentage of the remaining orders still hadn't arrived. Among the guilty marketers were some of the better known names in the catalog field. Many first-time mail order buyers who ordered from any of these firms likely concluded, "I'll never order from a catalog again." So everybody suffers.

A really surprising outcome of the study was that only seven of ninety-two companies with whom phone orders were placed tried to upsell other merchandise during the phone conversation. Golden opportunities lost!

Jay Walker placed 320 orders, mostly by mail. Fourteen companies cancelled the orders; twelve companies were guilty of total back orders.

Walker's delivery patterns were somewhat similar to those experienced by Dick Hodgson. Seven orders arrived within four days; 35 within the first week. Fifty percent of the orders placed arrived within two weeks. Forty-six companies took more than four weeks for delivery.

Hodgson and Walker both experienced service problems, particularly on the phone. Examples: Callers, put on hold; a recorded message every 30 seconds, repeated seven times before operator answered; an unfriendly voice answered the phone. Ordered two shirts, only one arrived. Called again and was told it was shipped the same day. Shirt arrived five days later . . . the wrong color! Sent back for exchange. They called to say they can't exchange items when paid for by cash. Place another order!

One of the significant findings in the study was that delivery time for phone orders averaged eleven days versus nineteen days for merchandise ordered by mail. This gives credence to promoting, "For quicker delivery, order by phone."

But when one hears the horror stories about slow delivery, merchandise snafus, inept phone operations, and back orders, it's amazing that catalog marketing is as successful as it is. Perhaps the positive way to look at it is to say, "Just think how successful I can be if I do it right!"

Self-Quiz

1. What are the four key perceptions that must be held by the consumer in order for a catalog operation to be successful?

   a. Perceived_____   c. Perceived_____

   b. Perceived_____   d. Perceived_____

2. What are the four general types of catalogs?

   a. _____   c. _____

   b. _____   d. _____

3. What is the X factor—the one distinguishing mark—that makes one catalog stand out from all others in its class?

   _____

4. As high as _____ percent upscale catalog buyers are female.

5. To establish a niche in an overcrowded marketplace, you must have

   _____.

6. Bright pinks and orchids work ☐ positively ☐ negatively for photographic backdrops.

7. What is meant by conceptualizing?

   _____

   _____

   _____

8. A catalog cover must instantaneously make a statement of

   _____ and _____ for the company.

9. The main ingredient that should be sought for a cover depiction

   is _____.

10. Catalogs are primarily a (n) _____ medium.

11. Catalog results should be analyzed ☐ by items ☐ by pages.

12. Name three ways you can improve *customer relationships* in a catalog operation.

    a. Order acknowledgments

    b. _____

    c. _____

13. Name four factors effecting catalog growth:

    a. Slow delivery   c. _____

    b. _____   d. _____

Pilot Project

You have a favorable connection with a leisure apparel manufacturer who has agreed to make available his line of leisure apparel and to also develop some exclusive fashions for you, if you can find a niche for a catalog operation.

You have done some basic research and believe that there is a niche for you among people who jog, particularly singles in the $35,000 and above income bracket, and marrieds in the $50,000 and above income bracket.

Realizing there are just so many jogging outfits you can offer for various ages, and both sexes, you determine that you should also offer other leisure apparel that might appeal to those whose lifestyle includes jogging.

With this as a background develop a marketing plan that will include the following:

1. An appropriate name for the catalog.

2. A list of twenty leisure apparel items, other than jogging outfits, that might appeal to joggers.

3. What publications you might use to get catalog requests.

4. What mailing lists you might test.

5. Whether you would opt for location photography and, if so, where?

CHAPTER SIXTEEN

Techniques of Creating Print Advertising

Many of the creative techniques needed for creating a successful direct mail package (Chapter 14) are also necessary in creating productive direct response ads in magazines and newspapers. But the space available for words and pictures is much more severely limited, and most of the gimmicks, gadgets, showmanship, and personal tone of direct mail do not apply here. This throws a heavy load of responsibility for the success of the ad on a carefully worded headline, a compelling opening, tightly structured copy, and appropriate visual emphasis.

Before the actual work of creating an ad begins, two important questions should be answered: Who is the prospect? What are the outstanding product advantages or customer benefits?

Often there is no single clear answer but, rather, several distinct possibilities. Then the profitable course of action is to prepare ads embodying all your most promising hypotheses and split-test as many of them as your budget permits.

Visualizing the Prospect

Every good mail order or direct mail piece should attract the most attention from the likeliest prospects, and every good creator of direct response advertising visualizes his or her prospects with varying degrees of precision when he or she sits down at his typewriter or drawing board.

Good direct response advertising makes its strongest appeal to its best prospects and then gathers in as many additional prospects as possible.

And who are the prospects? They are the ones with the strongest desire for what you're selling. You must look for the common denominators.

For instance, let's say you are selling a book on the American Revolution. Here are some of the relevant common denominators that would be shared by many people in your total audience.

1. An interest in the American Revolution in particular

2. An interest in American history in general

3. A patriotic interest in America

4. An interest in history

5. An interest in big, beautiful coffee table books

6. An interest in impressing friends with historical lore

7. A love of bargains

8. An interest in seeing children in the family become adults with high achievement

Now, out of the total audience of 1,000 some readers would possess all eight denominators, some would possess some combination of six, some a different combination of six, some just one of the eight, and so on.

If you could know the secret hearts of all 1,000 people and rank them on a scale of relative desire to buy, you would place at the very top of the list those who possessed all eight denominators, then just below them those who possessed just seven, and so on down to the bottom of the scale, where you would place people who possessed none.

Obviously, you should make as many sales as possible among your hottest prospects first, for that is where your sales will be easiest. Then you want to reach down the scale to sell as many of the others as you can. By the time you get down to the people possessing only one of the denominators, you will probably find interest so faint that it would almost be impossible to make your sales effort pay unless it were fantastically appealing.

Obvious? Yes, to mail order professionals who learned the hard way. But to the tenderfoot, it is not so obvious. In his eagerness to sell everybody, he may muff his easiest sales by using a curiosity-only appeal that conceals what is really being offered.

On the other hand, the veteran but uninspired pro may gather up all the easy sales lying on the surface but, through lack of creative imagination, fail to reach deeper into the market. For instance, let's say that of 1,000 readers, 50 possess all eight denominators. A crude omnibus appeal that could scoop up many of them would be something like, "At last—for every liberty-loving American family, especially those with children, whose friends are amazed by their understanding of American history, here is a big, beautiful book about the American Revolution you will display with pride—yours for only one-fifth of what you'd expect to pay!" A terrible headline, but at least one that those possessing the eight denominators of interest would stop to look at and consider. You may get only 5 percent readership, but it will be the right 5 percent.

Now, on the other hand, suppose you want to do something terribly creative to reach a wider market. So you do a beautiful advertising message headed "The Impossible Dream," in which you somehow work your way from that starting point to what it is you're selling. Again, you may get only 5 percent readership, but these readers will be scattered along the entire length of your scale of interest. Of the fifty people who stopped to read your message, only two or three may be prime prospects possessing all eight denominators. Many people really interested in books on the American Revolution, in inspiring their children with patriotic sentiments, and in acquiring big impressive books at big savings will have hurried past unaware.

The point: don't let prime prospects get away. In mail order you can't afford to. Some people out there don't have to be sold; they already want what you have, and if you tell them that you have it, they will buy it. Alone they may not constitute enough of a market to make your selling effort pay, but without them you haven't got a chance. So, through your clarity and directness, you gather in these prime prospects; then through your creative imagination you reach beyond them to awaken and excite mild prospects as well.

Once the prospect is clearly visualized, a good headline almost writes itself. For example, here is an effective and successful headline from an ad by Quadrangle/New York Times Book Company. It simply defines the prospect so clearly and accurately that the interested reader feels an instant tug:

> For people who are almost (but not quite) satisfied with their house plants . . . and can't figure out what they're doing wrong

A very successful ad for Washington School of Art, offering a correspondence course, resulted from our bringing the psychographic profile of our prime prospect into sharp focus. We began to confront the fact that the prospect was someone who had been drawing pictures better than the rest of us since the first grade. Such people are filled with a rare combination of pride in their talent and shame at their lack of perfection. And their goal is not necessarily fame or fortune, but simply to become a "real artist," a phrase that has different meanings to different people. So the winning headline simply reached out to the right people and offered them the right benefit:

> If you can draw fairly well (but still not good enough) we'll turn you into a real artist

Of course, a good headline does not necessarily present an explicit definition of the prospect, but it is always implied. Here are some classic headlines and the prospects whom the writer undoubtedly visualized:

> Can a man or woman my age become a hotel executive?

The prospect is—probably—a middle-aged man or woman who needs, for whatever reason, an interesting, pleasant, not too technically demanding occupational skill such as hotel management, and is eager for reassurance that you *can* teach an old dog new tricks. Note, however, how wide the net is cast. No one is excluded. Even a person fearing he may be too young to be a hotel executive can theoretically read himself into this headline:

Don't envy the plumber—be one

The prospect is a poorly paid worker, probably blue collar, who is looking for a way to improve his lot and who has looked with both indignation and envy at the plumber, who appears not much more skilled but earns several times as much per hour.

How to stumble upon a fortune in gems

The prospect is everybody, all of us, who all our lives have daydreamed of gaining sudden wealth without extreme sacrifice.

Is your home picture-poor?

The prospect is someone, probably a woman, with a home, who has a number of bare or inadequately decorated walls, and who feels not only a personal lack but also, perhaps more important, a vague underlying sense of social shame at this conspicuous cultural "poverty." Whether she appreciates it or not, she recognizes that art, books, and music are regarded as part of the "good life" and are supposed to add a certain richness to life.

Be a "nondegree" engineer

This is really a modern version of "don't envy the plumber." The prospect is an unskilled or semiskilled factory worker who looks with a mixture of resentment and grudging envy on the aristocracy in his midst, the fair-haired boys who earn much more, dress better, and enjoy special privileges because they are graduate engineers. The prospect would like to enjoy at least some of their job status but is unwilling or unable to go to college and get an engineering degree.

Are you tired of cooking with odds and ends?

The prospect is that Everywoman, or Everyman, who has accumulated over the years an enameled pan here, an aluminum pot there, an iron skillet elsewhere, and to whom a matched set of anything represents neatness, order, and elegance.

Can you call a man a failure at 30?

The prospect is a young white-collar worker between twenty-five and thirty-two years old who is deeply concerned that life isn't turning out the way he dreamed and that he is on the verge of failing to "make it"—permanently.

Selecting Advantages and Benefits

Advantages belong to the product. Benefits belong to the consumer. If the product or service is unique or unfamiliar to the prospect, stressing benefits is important. But if it is simply a new, improved model in a highly competitive field where there already exists an established demand, the product advantage or advantages become important.

Thus, when pocket electronic calculators were first introduced, such benefits as *pride, power,* and *profit* were important attributes. But, as the market became flooded with competing types and brands, product advantages such as the floating decimal became more important.

There are two kinds of benefits, the immediate or obvious benefit and the not-so-obvious ultimate benefit—the real potential meaning for the customer's life of the product or service being sold. (See Exhibit 16-1.) The ultimate benefit often proves to have a greater effect, for it reaches deeper into the prospect's feelings.

Victor Schwab, one of the great mail order pioneers, was fond of quoting Dr. Samuel Johnson's approach to auctioning off the contents of a brewery: "We are not here to sell boilers and vats, but the potentiality of growing rich beyond the dreams of avarice."

It pays to ask yourself over and over again, "What am I selling? Yes, I know it's a book or a steak knife, or a home study course in upholstering—but what am I *really* selling? What human values are at stake?"

For example, suppose you have the job of selling a correspondence course in advertising. Here is a list of ultimate benefits and the way they may be expressed in headlines for the course. Some of the headlines are patently absurd, but they illustrate the mind-stretching process involved in looking for the ultimate benefit in your product or service.

- *Health:* "Successful ad people are healthier and happier than you think—and now you can be one of them."
- *Money:* "What's your best chance of earning $50,000 a year by the time you are 30?"
- *Security:* "You are always in demand when you can write advertising that sells."
- *Pride:* "Imagine your pride when you can coin a slogan repeated by 50 million people."

Exhibit 16-1. Classic Direct Response Ad

"Can he really play?" a girl whispered. "Heavens no!" Arthur exclaimed. "He never played a note in his life."

They Laughed When I Sat Down At the Piano But When I Started to Play!—

ARTHUR had just played "The Rosary." The room rang with applause. I decided that this would be a dramatic moment for me to make my debut. To the amazement of all my friends, I strode confidently over to the piano and sat down.

"Jack is up to his old tricks," somebody chuckled. The crowd laughed. They were all certain that I couldn't play a single note.

"Can he really play?" I heard a girl whisper to Arthur.

"Heavens, no!" Arthur exclaimed. "He never played a note in all his life. . . But just you watch him. This is going to be good."

I decided to make the most of the situation. With mock dignity I drew out a silk handkerchief and lightly dusted off the piano keys. Then I rose and gave the revolving piano stool a quarter of a turn, just as I had seen an imitator of Paderewski do in a vaudeville sketch.

"What do you think of his execution?" called a voice from the rear.

"We're in favor of it!" came back the answer, and the crowd rocked with laughter.

Then I Started to Play

Instantly a tense silence fell on the guests. The laughter died on their lips as if by magic. I played through the first few bars of Beethoven's immortal Moonlight Sonata. I heard gasps of amazement. My friends sat breathless—spellbound!

I played on and as I played I forgot the people around me. I forgot the hour, the place, the breathless listeners. The little world I lived in seemed to fade—seemed to grow dim—unreal. Only the music was real. Only the music and visions it brought me. Visions as beautiful and as changing as the wind blown clouds and drifting moonlight that long ago inspired the master composer. It seemed as if the master musician himself were speaking to me—speaking through the medium of music—not in words but in chords. Not in sentences but in exquisite melodies!

A Complete Triumph!

As the last notes of the Moonlight Sonata died away, the room resounded with a sudden roar of applause. I found myself surrounded by excited faces. How my friends carried on! Men shook my hand—wildly congratulated me—pounded me on the back in their enthusiasm! Everybody was exclaiming with delight—plying me with rapid questions. . . . "Jack! Why didn't you tell us you could play like that?". . . "Where did you learn?"—"How long have you studied?"—"Who was your teacher?"

"I have never even seen my teacher," I replied. "And just a short while ago I couldn't play a note.'.

"Quit your kidding," laughed Arthur, himself an accomplished pianist. "You've been studying for years. I can tell."

"I have been studying only a short while," I insisted. "I decided to keep it a secret so that I could surprise all you folks."

Then I told them the whole story.

"Have you ever heard of the U. S. School of Music?" I asked.

A few of my friends nodded. "That's a correspondence school, isn't it?" they exclaimed.

"Exactly," I replied. "They have a new simplified method that can teach you to play any instrument by mail in just a few months."

How I Learned to Play Without a Teacher

And then I explained how for years I had longed to play the piano.

"A few months ago," I continued, "I saw an interesting ad for the U. S. School of Music—a new method of learning to play which only cost a few cents a day." The ad told how a woman had mastered the piano in her spare time at home—and without a teacher! Best of all, the wonderful new method she used, required no laborious scales—no heartless exercises—no tiresome practising. It sounded so convincing that I filled out the coupon requesting the Free Demonstration Lesson.

"The free book arrived promptly and I started in that very night to study the Demonstration Lesson. I was amazed to see how easy it was to play this new way. Then I sent for the course.

"When the course arrived I found it was just as the ad said — as easy as A.B.C! And, as the lessons continued they got easier and easier. Before I knew it I was playing all the pieces I liked best. Nothing stopped me. I could play ballads or classical numbers or jazz, all with equal ease! And I never did have any special talent for music!"

Play Any Instrument

You too, can now teach yourself to be an accomplished musician—right at home—in half the usual time. You can't go wrong with this simple new method which has already shown 350,000 people how to play their favorite instruments. Forget that old-fashioned idea that you need special "talent." Just read the list of instruments in the panel, decide which one you want to play and the U. S. School will do the rest. And bear in mind no matter which instrument you choose, the cost in each case will be the same—just a few cents a day. No matter whether you are a mere beginner or already a good performer, you will be interested in learning about this new and wonderful method.

Send for Our Free Booklet and Demonstration Lesson

Thousands of successful students never dreamed they possessed musical ability until it was revealed to them by a remarkable "Musical Ability Test" which we send entirely without cost with our interesting free booklet.

If you are in earnest about wanting to play your favorite instrument—if you really want to gain happiness and increase your popularity—send at once for the free booklet and Demonstration Lesson. No cost — no obligation. Right now we are making a Special offer for a limited number of new students. Sign and send the convenient coupon now — before it's too late to gain the benefits of this offer. Instruments supplied when needed, cash or credit. U. S. School of Music, 1031 Brunswick Bldg., New York City.

U. S. School of Music,
1031 Brunswick Bldg., New York City.

Please send me your free book, "Music Lessons in Your Own Home", with introduction by Dr. Frank Crane, Demonstration Lesson and particulars of your Special Offer. I am interested in the following course:

....

Have you above instrument? ....

Name ....
        (Please write plainly)

Address ....

City .... State ....

Pick Your Instrument

Piano
Organ
Violin
Drums and Traps
Banjo
Tenor Banjo
Mandolin
Clarinet
Flute
Saxophone
Voice and Speech Culture
Automatic Finger Control
Piano Accordion
'Cello
Harmony and Composition
Sight Singing
Ukulele
Guitar
Hawaiian Steel Guitar
Harp
Cornet
Piccolo
Trombone

This ad, written by John Caples, a member of the Direct Marketing Hall of Fame, is considered one of the classics of direct response writing.

- *Approval:* "Did you write that ad? Why I've seen it everywhere."
- *Enjoyment:* "Get more fun out of your daily job. Become a successful ad writer!"
- *Excitement:* "Imagine working until 4:00 A.M.—and loving every minute of it!"
- *Power:* "The heads of giant corporations will listen to your advice—when you've mastered the secrets of advertising that works." (Just a wee bit of exaggeration there, perhaps.)
- *Fulfillment:* "Are you wasting a natural talent for advertising?"
- *Freedom:* "People who can get million dollar advertising ideas don't have to worry about punching a time clock."
- *Identity:* "Join the top advertising professionals who keep the wheels of our economy turning."
- *Relaxation:* "How some people succeed in advertising without getting ulcers."
- *Escape:* "Hate going to work in the morning? Get a job you'll love—in advertising!"
- *Curiosity:* "Now go behind the scenes of America's top advertising agencies—and find out how multimillion dollar campaigns are born!"
- *Possessions:* "I took your course five years ago—today I own two homes, two cars, and a Chris-Craft."
- *Sex:* "Join the people who've made good in the swinging advertising scene."
- *Hunger:* "A really good ad person always knows where his next meal is coming from."

Harnessing the Powers of Semantics

A single word is a whole bundle—a nucleus, you might say—of thoughts and feelings. And when different nuclei are jointed together, the result is nuclear fusion, generating enough power to move the earth.

A whole new semiscience, semantics, has been founded on this unique property of words. The late newspaper columnist, Sydney Harris, popularized it with his occasional feature, "Antics with Semantics." A typical antic goes something like this: "I am sensible in the face of danger. You are a bit overcautious. He is a coward." The factual content may be the same, but the semantic implications vary widely.

Semantics is the hydrogen bomb of persuasion. In politics, for example, entire election campaigns sometimes hinge on the single word "boss." If one side manages to convince the public that the other side is controlled by a boss or bosses, but that the first side has only "party leaders," it will probably win the election.

In direct marketing, clear understanding and skillful use of semantics can make a powerful contribution to ad headlines (Exhibit 16-2). Here are a few examples.

What do you think when you read the word "Europe"? Perhaps there are certain negative connotations—constant military squabbles, lack of Yankee know-how, and so on. But far more important in the psyche of most Americans are the romantic implications—castles, colorful peasants, awesome relics of the past, charming sidewalk cafes, all merging into the life-long dream of making the Grand Tour of Europe.

Another semantically rich word is "shoestring." A man is a fool to start a business of his own with inadequate capital. But if he succeeds, he is a "wizard," and his inadequate capital is seen in retrospect as a "shoestring." Harian Publications got the idea of linking these two words with a couple of modest connectives and achieved verbal nuclear fusion that sold thousands of books on low-cost travel: *Europe on a Shoestring.*

Because there is no copyright on semantic discoveries, Simon and Schuster could capitalize on Harian's discovery and publish their *$1 Complete Guide to Florida.* In fact, they were so successful they broke the mail order "rule" that a product selling for only $1.00 cannot be profitably sold in print ads.

For the word "Europe" they simply substituted another semantically rich word, "Florida," and came up with another powerful winner. A one-inch advertisement using this headline drew thousands of responses at a profitable cost per order, even when this tiny ad appeared to be completely lost on a 2,400-line page filled with larger ads screaming for attention.

The fascinating thing about this kind of verbal nuclear fusion is that once it has been achieved it can be repeated almost endlessly—not only in the same form but in other forms as well.

For example, a real breakthrough in selling *Motor's Auto Repair Manual* was achieved many years ago with the headline, "Now You Can Lick Any Auto Repair Job." Every single word made a contribution to the power of the headline, as indeed each word always does in an effective headline. "Now" made the ad a news event, even after it had been running for years. "You," perhaps the sweetest word ever sounded to the ears, made it clear that the benefit included the reader and not just professional auto mechanics. "Can," another great word, promises power, achievement. "Lick" promises not only sure mastery but sweet triumph. Notice how much richer it is than "do." "Any" increases the breadth of the promise to the outermost limit. "Auto" selects the prospect and defines the field of interest. "Repair" defines the proposition, and "Job" emphasizes the completeness of its scope.

Once this breakthrough had been achieved, it was possible to make the same statement in many different ways with equal success. "Now Any Auto Repair Job Can Be 'Duck Soup' for You," "Now Any Auto Repair Job Can Be Your 'Meat,'" and so on.

"Engineer" is a rich, many-faceted word. To an artist or a writer, the word may connote a literal-minded square. To an engineer's prospective

Exhibit 16-2. The Power of a Strong Headline

This classic ad, appearing in scores of publications over a period of years, consistently outpulled all ads tested against it. Its success may well be attributed to the major headline's strong appeal to parental pride.

mother-in-law, it may connote a good provider. To an engineer, it means a degree in engineering and professional standing earned by hard study at college.

But to the manual and semiskilled workers in an electronics plant, our agency reasoned, in developing appeals for the Cleveland Institute of Electronics, the word "engineer" suggests the college-educated wise guy who is the fair-haired boy in the plant—an object both of envy on the part of the worker and of secret derision born of envy. We couldn't promise "You too can be an engineer," because "engineer" by itself is taken to mean a graduate engineer, and completion of CIE courses doesn't provide college credits or a college degree. However, many of the job titles in our promotion, such as "broadcast engineer," "field engineer," or "sales engineer," have the word "engineer" in them without requiring a college degree. So we were legitimately able to promise prospective enrollees the prestige and other rewards of being an engineer in an ad headed, "Be a Non-Degree Engineer." (See Exhibit 16-3.)

Semantic considerations like these cause mail order people to spend hours discussing and tinkering with a single headline or even a single word in the headline. It will pay you to study the mail order headlines you see used over and over again and try to analyze and apply the semantic secret of their success.

Building in the "Hook"

A successful direct marketing ad must compete fiercely for the reader's time and attention. No matter how great the copy is, it will be wasted if the headline does not compel reading. So most successful headlines have a "hook" to catch the reader and pull him in. The most common hooks are such words as *why, how, new, now, this, what.* They make the reader want to know the answer. *Why* it is? *How* does it? *What* is it?

Consider the flat statement:

Increasing your vocabulary can help you get ahead in life

This is merely an argumentative, pontifical claim. It doesn't lead anywhere. But notice how the addition of just one word changes the whole meaning and the mood:

How increasing your vocabulary can help you get ahead in life.

This unstylish, uncreative headline, and the copy that followed sold hundreds of thousands of copies of a vocabulary book. It selected the prospect (people who were interested in larger vocabularies), it promised an ultimate benefit (*success*), and it built in a hook (*how*).

Exhibit 16-3. The Power of Semantics

How to Become a "Non-Degree" Engineer in the Booming World of Electronics

Thousands of real engineering jobs are being filled by men without engineering degrees. The pay is good, the future bright. Here's how to qualify...

By G. O. ALLEN

President, Cleveland Institute of Electronics

THE BIG BOOM IN ELECTRONICS—and the resulting shortage of graduate engineers—has created a new breed of professional man: the "non-degree" engineer. He has an income and prestige few men achieve without going to college. Depending on the branch of electronics he's in, he may "ride herd" over a flock of computers, run a powerful TV transmitter, supervise a service department, or work side by side with distinguished scientists designing and testing new electronic miracles.

According to one recent survey, in military-connected work alone 80% of the civilian field engineers are not college graduates. Yet they enjoy officer status and get generous *per diem* allowances in addition to their excellent salaries.

In TV and radio, you qualify for the key job of Broadcast Engineer if you have an FCC License, whether you've gone to college or not.

Now You Can Learn at Home

To qualify, however, you do need to know more than soldering, testing circuits, and replacing components. You need to really know your electronics theory—and to prove it by getting an FCC Commercial License.

Now you can master electronics theory at home, in your spare time. Over the last 30 years, here at Cleveland Institute of Electronics, we've perfected AUTO-PROGRAMMED™ lessons that make learning at home easy, even if you once had trouble studying. To help you even more, your instructor gives the homework you send in his undivided personal attention—it's like being the only student in his "class." He even mails back his corrections and comments the same day he gets your work, so you hear from him while everything is still fresh in your mind.

Does it work? I'll say! Better than 9 out of 10 CIE men who take the U.S. Government's tough FCC licensing exam *pass it on their very first try.* (Among non-CIE men, 2 out of 3 who take the exam *fail.*) That's why we can promise in writing to refund your tuition in full if you complete one of our FCC courses and fail to pass the licensing exam.

Students who have taken other courses often comment on how much more they learn from us. Says Mark E. Newland of Santa Maria, Calif.:

"Of 11 different correspondence courses I've taken, CIE's was the best prepared, most interesting, and easiest to understand. I passed my 1st Class FCC exam after completing my course, and have increased my earnings by $120 a month."

Mail Coupon for 2 Free Books

Thousands of today's "non-degree" engineers started by reading our 2 free books: (1) Our school catalog "How to Succeed in Electronics," describing opportunities in electronics, our teaching methods, and our courses, and (2) our special booklet, "How to Get a Commercial FCC License." To receive both without cost or obligation, mail coupon below.

CIE Cleveland Institute of Electronics
1776 E. 17th St. Dept. PS-6, Cleveland, Ohio 44114

Cleveland Institute of Electronics
1776 East 17th Street, Dept. PS-6, Cleveland, Ohio 44114

Please send me without cost or obligation:

1. Your 40-page booklet describing the job opportunities in Electronics today, how your courses can prepare me for them, your methods of instruction, and your special student services.
2. Your booklet on "How to Get a Commercial FCC License."

I am especially interested in:

☐ Electronics Technology   ☐ Electronic Communications
☐ First Class FCC License   ☐ Industrial Electronics
☐ Broadcast Engineering   ☐ Advanced Engineering

Name .... Age ......
(Please print)

Address...

City .... State .... Zip.......

Present Job Title ....

Accredited Member National Home Study Council
A Leader in Electronics Training...Since 1934

The power of semantics is shown in this strong headline. It incorporates many favorable connotations in the promise to become a "Non-Degree Engineer."

Of course, the hook can be merely implied. There is no hook word in the headline, "Be a Non-Degree Engineer." But there is a clear implication that the copy is going to tell you how to achieve this.

Writing the Lead

Perhaps the most troublesome and important part of any piece of mail order copy is the lead, or opening. A lead that "grabs" the reader doesn't guarantee that he will read the rest of the copy. But one that fails to grab him does practically guarantee that he *won't* read the rest.

Always remember in writing or judging a lead that your reader has better things to do than sit around and read your advertising. He doesn't really want to read your copy—until you make him want to. And your lead has got to make him want to.

A common error in writing leads is failure to get to the point immediately—or at least to *point* to the point. Haven't you had the experience of listening to a friend or associate or public speaker who is trying to tell you something but not able to get to the point? Remember how impatient you felt as you fumed inwardly, "Get to the point!" Your readers feel that same way about copy—and can very easily yawn and turn away. A good roundabout lead is not impossible, but it takes a brilliant writer.

A good principle to follow is that the copy should proceed from the headline. That is, if your headline announces what you are there to talk about, then you should get down to business and talk about it. Although it is true that some successful advertising merely *continues* the message started by the headline or display copy, there is far less danger of confusion if the copy *repeats* and *expands* the headline message, exactly the way a good news item does.

Notice how marvelously these leads from the *Wall Street Journal* news columns form a bridge between the headlines and the rest of the stories:

New Postage-Stamp Ink to Speed Mail Processing

NEW YORK—U.S. postage stamps will soon be tagged with a special luminescent ink that will permit automatic locating and cancelling of the stamps to speed processing of the mail.

Affluent Americans Awash in Documents Snap Up Home Safes

NEW YORK—There's a popular new home appliance that won't wash a dish, dry a diaper, or keep a steak on ice. It's a safe. And it's being propelled into prominence by a paperwork explosion.

Notice, too, that although the lead restates the thought of the headline, it does it in a different way, recapping the thought but also advancing the story.

Classic Copy Structure

In a classic mail order copy argument, a good lead should be visualized as the first step in a straight path of feeling and logic from the headline or display theme to the concluding call for action. In that all-important first step, the reader should be able to see clearly where the path is taking him or her. Otherwise he or she may not want to go. (This is the huge error of ads that seek to pique your curiosity with something irrelevant and then make a tie-in to the real point. Who's got time for satisfying that much curiosity these days?)

The sections of a classic copy argument may be labeled *problem, promise of solution, explanation of promise, proof, call to action.* However, if you're going to start with the problem, it seems like a good idea at least to hint right away at the forthcoming solution. Then the reader won't mind your not getting to the point right away, as long as he or she knows where you're going. A generation ago, when the pace of life was slower, a brilliant copywriter could get away with spending the first third of his copy leisurely outlining the problem before finally getting around to the solution. But in today's more hectic times, it's riskier.

Here is an ad seeking Duraclean dealers in which the problem lead contains the promise of solution.

I found the easy way to escape from being a "wage slave"

I kept my job while my customer list grew . . . then found myself in a high-profit business. Five years ago, I wouldn't have believed that I could be where I am today.

I was deeply in debt. My self-confidence had been shaken by a disastrous business setback. Having nobody behind me, I had floundered and failed for lack of experience, help, and guidance.

Now the copy could have simply started out, "Five years ago, I was deeply in debt," and so on. But the promise of happier days to come provides a carrot on a stick, drawing us down the garden path. You could argue that the headline had already announced the promise. But in most cases, good copy should be able to stand alone and make a complete argument even if all the display type were removed.

Here, from an ad for isometric exercises, is an example of the flashback technique referred to earlier:

[Starts with the promise]

Imagine a 6-second exercise that helps you keep fit better than 24 push-ups. Or another that's capable of doubling muscular strength in 3 weeks!

Both of these "quickie" exercises are part of a fantastically simple body-building method developed by Donald J. Salls, Alabama Doctor of Education, fitness expert and coach. His own trim physique, his family's vigorous health and the nail-hard brawn of his teams are dramatic proof of the results he gets—not to mention the steady stream of reports from housewives, athletes, even school children who have discovered Dr. Salls' remarkable exercises.

[Flashback to problem]

Most Americans find exercise a tedious chore. Yet we all recognize the urgent personal and social needs for keeping our bodies strong, shapely, and healthy. What man wouldn't take secret pride in displaying a more muscular figure?

What woman doesn't long for a slimmer, more attractive figure? The endless time and trouble required to get such results has been a major, if not impossible hurdle for so many of us. But now [return to the promise] doctors, trainers, and physical educators are beginning to recommend the easy new approach to body fitness and contour control that Dr. Salls has distilled down to his wonderfully simple set of 10 exercises.

Of course a really strong, exciting promise doesn't necessarily need a statement of the problem at all. If you're selling a "New Tree That Grows a Foot a Month," it could be argued that you don't actually have to spell out how frustrating it is to spend years waiting for ordinary trees to grow; this is well known and implied.

Other Ways to Structure Copy

There are as many different ways to structure a piece of advertising copy as there are to build a house.

But response advertising, whether in publication or direct mail, has special requirements. The general advertiser is satisfied with making an impression, but the response advertiser must stimulate immediate action. Your copy must pile up in your reader's mind argument after argument, sales point after sales point, until his resistance collapses under the sheer weight of your persuasiveness, and he does what you ask.

One of the greatest faults in the copy of writers who are not wise in the ways of response is failure to apply this steadily increasing pressure. This may sound like old-fashioned "hard sell," but, ideally, the impression your copy makes should be just the opposite. The best copy, like the best salesperson, does not appear to be selling at all, but simply to be sharing information or proposals of mutual benefit to the buyer and seller.

Of course, in selling certain kinds of staple merchandise, copy structuring may not be important. There the advertising may be compared to a painting in that the aim is to convey as much as possible at first glance and then convey more and more with each repeated look. You wouldn't sell a thirty-five-piece electric drill set with a 1,000-word essay but, rather, by spreading out the set in glowing full-color illustrations richly studded with "feature call-outs."

But where you are engaged in selling intangibles, an idea or ideas instead of familiar merchandise, the way you structure your copy can be vitally important.

In addition to the classic form mentioned above, here are some other ways to structure copy.

With the "cluster-of-diamonds" technique, you assemble a great many precious details of what you are selling and present them to the reader in an appropriate setting. A good example is the "67 Reasons Why" subscription advertising of *U.S. News & World Report,* listing sixty-seven capsule descriptions of typical recent news articles in the magazine. The "setting"—the surrounding copy containing general information and argumentation—is as important as the specific jewels in the cluster. Neither would be sufficiently attractive without the other technique.

The "string-of-pearls" technique is similar but not quite the same. Each "pearl" is a complete little gem of selling, and a number of them are simply strung together in almost any sequence to make a chain. David Ogilvy's "Surprising Amsterdam" series of ads is like this. Each surprising fact about Amsterdam is like a small-space ad for the city, but only when all these little ads are strung together do you feel compelled to get up from your easy chair and send for those KLM brochures. This technique is especially useful, by the way, when you have a vast subject like an encyclopedia to discuss. You have not one but many stories to tell. And, if you simply ramble on and on, most readers won't stay with you. So make a little list of stories you want to tell, write a tight little one-paragraph essay on each point, announce the subject of each essay in a boldface subhead, and then string them all together like pearls, with an appropriate beginning and ending.

The "fan dancers" technique is like a line of chorus girls equipped with Sally Rand fans. The dancers are always about to reveal their secret charms, but they never quite do. You've seen this kind of copy many times. One of the best examples is the circular received in answer to an irresistible classified ad in *Popular Mechanics.* The ad simply said "505 odd, successful enterprises. Expect something odd." The circular described the entire contents of a book of money-making ideas in maddening fashion. Something like: "No. 24. Here's an idea that requires nothing but old coat hangers. A retired couple on a Kansas farm nets $240 weekly with this one." "No. 25. All you need is a telephone—and you don't call them, they call you to give their orders. A bedridden woman in Montpelier nets $70.00 a week this way." And so on.

With the "machine gun" technique, you simply spray facts and arguments in the general direction of the reader, in the hope that at least some of them will hit. This may be called the no-structure structure, and it is the first refuge of the amateur. If you have a great product and manage to convey your enthusiasm for it through the sheer exuberance of your copy, you will succeed, not because of your technique, but despite it. And the higher the levels of taste and education of your readers, the less chance you will have.

Establishing the Uniqueness of Your Product or Service

What is the unique claim to fame of the product or service you are selling? This could be one of your strongest selling points. The word "only" is one of the greatest advertising words. If what you offer is "better" or "best," this is merely a claim in support of your argument that the reader *should* come to you for the product or services offered. But, if what you are offering is the "only" one of its kind, then the reader *must* come to you if he or she wants the benefits that only you can offer.

Here are some ways in which you may be able to stake out a unique position in the marketplace for the product or service you are selling: "We're the largest." People respect bigness in a company or a sales total—they reason that, if a product leads the others in its field, it must be good. Thus "No. 1 Best-Seller" is always a potent phrase, for it is not just an airy claim but a hard fact that proves some kind of merit.

But what if you're *not* the largest? Perhaps you can still establish a unique position.... "We're the largest of our kind." By simply defining your identity more sharply, you may still be able to claim some kind of size superiority. For example, there was the Trenton merchant who used to boast that he had "the largest clothing store in the world in a garage!"

A mail order photo finisher decided that one benefit it had to sell was the sheer bigness of its operation. It wasn't the biggest—that distinction belonged, of course, to Eastman Kodak. But it was second. And Eastman Kodak was involved in selling a lot of other things, too, such as film and cameras and chemicals. Their photo finishing service was only one of many divisions. So the advertiser was able to fashion a unique claim: "America's Largest *Independent* Photo Finisher."

"We're the fastest-growing." If you're on the way to *becoming* the largest, that's about as impressive a proof of merit as being the largest—in fact, it may be even *more* impressive, because it adds the excitement of the underdog coming up fast. *U.S. News & World Report* used this to good effect during the 1950s while its circulation was growing from approximately 400,000 to about three times that figure: "America's Fastest-Growing News-magazine." Later, the same claim was used effectively for Capitol Record Club, "America's Fastest-Growing Record Club."

"We offer a unique combination of advantages." It may be that no one claim you can make is unique, but that none of your competitors is able to equal your claim that you have *all* of a certain number of advantages.

In the early 1960s, the Literary Guild began to compete in earnest with the Book-of-the-Month Club. They started offering books that compared very favorably with those offered by BOMC. But the latter had a couple of unique claims that the Guild couldn't match—BOMC's distinguished board of judges and its book-dividend system, with a history of having distributed $375 million worth of books to members.

How to compete? The Guild couldn't claim the greatest savings; one of Doubleday's other clubs actually saved the subscriber more off the publisher's price. It couldn't claim that it had books offered by no other club; some of Doubleday's other clubs were offering some of the same books, and even BOMC would sometimes make special arrangements to offer a book being featured by the Guild.

But the Guild was able to feature a unique *set* of advantages that undoubtedly played a part in the success it has enjoyed: "Only the Literary Guild saves you 40 percent to 60 percent on books like these as soon as they are published." Other clubs could make either of these two claims, but only the Guild could claim both.

"We have a uniquely advantageous location." A classic of this was James Webb Young's great ad for "Old Jim Young's Mountain Grown Apples— Every Bite Crackles, and the Juice Runs Down Your Lips." In it Jim Young, trader, tells how the natives snickered when his pappy bought himself an abandoned homestead in a little valley high up in the Jemes Mountains. But "Pappy" Young, one of the slickest farmers ever to come out of Madison Avenue, knew that "this little mountain valley is just a natural apple spot—as they say some hillsides are in France for certain wine grapes. The summer sun beats down into this valley all day, to color and ripen apples perfectly; but the cold mountain air drains down through it at night to make them crisp and firm. Then it turns out that the soil there is full of volcanic ash, and for some reason that seems to produce apples with a flavor that is really something."

Haband Ties used to make a big thing out of being located in Paterson, New Jersey, the silk center of the nation. Even though most of the company's ties and other apparel were made of synthetic fibers, somehow the idea of buying ties from the silk center made the reader feel he was buying ties at the very source. In the same way, maple syrup from Vermont should be a lot easier to sell than maple syrup from Arizona.

Finally, suppose you believe that you have something unique to sell, but you hesitate to start an argument with your competitors by making a flat claim that they may challenge. In that case you can *imply your uniqueness* by the way in which you word the claim. "Here's one mouthwash that keeps your mouth sweet and fresh all day long" doesn't flatly claim that it's the only one. It simply says, "at least *we've* got this desirable quality, whether any other product does or not." *Newsweek* identified itself as "the news magazine that separates fact from opinion"—a powerful use of that innocent word "the" which devastates the competition.

Exhibit 16-4. A/B Copy Test

The makers of Wynn's Friction Proofing Oil wanted to test two different sales appeals: (1) Get more power with less gas; (2) save one gallon of gas in every ten. These two "reader ads" were written to test the appeals. The second appeal brought twice as many sample requests as the first one.

ADD THIS PRODUCT TO ANY MOTOR OIL FOR MORE POWER WITH LESS GAS

Sluggish motors get a new lease on life with Wynn's Friction Proofing Oil. This new chemical compound added to your present brand of motor oil every 1000 miles, bonds a super-slick surface to engine parts. This virtually eliminates the friction drag that wastes up to half your car's power, and gives you so much extra mileage from gasoline that it's like getting one gallon free with every ten you buy. Besides paying for itself in gasoline savings, Wynn's cuts carbon and sludge, frees sticky valves, reduces wear and repairs. Try Wynn's for new pep, power, economy from your car. We're so sure you'll continue to use it that we make this special introductory offer of a regular 1000-mile size 95¢ can of Wynn's for only 10¢. Just send your name and address, enclosing 10¢ in coin or stamps. By return mail you'll get a certificate entitling you to a 95¢ can of Wynn's without additional charge at any Wynn dealer. Limit one. Offer expires April 30. Write today—Wynn Oil Company, Dept. A-4, Azusa California.

AT SERVICE STATIONS, GARAGES, NEW CAR DEALERS

CAR OWNERS! SAVE ONE GALLON OF GAS IN EVERY TEN

Sluggish motors get a new lease on life with Wynn's Friction Proofing Oil. This new chemical compound added to your present brand of motor oil every 1000 miles, bonds a super-slick surface to engine parts. This virtually eliminates the friction drag that wastes up to half your car's power, and gives you so much extra mileage from gasoline that it's like getting one gallon free with every ten you buy. Besides paying for itself in gasoline savings, Wynn's cuts carbon and sludge, frees sticky valves, reduces wear and repairs. Try Wynn's for new pep, power, economy from your car. We're so sure you'll continue to use it that we make this special introductory offer of a regular 1000-mile size 95¢ can of Wynn's for only 10¢. Just send your name and address, enclosing 10¢ in coin or stamps. By return mail you'll get a certificate entitling you to a 95¢ can of Wynn's without additional charge at any Wynn dealer. Limit one. Offer expires April 30. Write today—Wynn Oil Company, Dept. C-12, Azusa, California.

AT SERVICE STATIONS, GARAGES, NEW CAR DEALERS

Effective Use of Testimonials

If you have a great product or service, you have an almost inexhaustible source of great copy practically free—written by your own customers. They will come up with selling phrases straight from the heart that no copywriter, no matter how brilliant, would ever think of. They will write with a depth of conviction that the best copywriters will find hard to equal.

The value of testimonials in mail order advertising has been recognized for nearly 100 years, is generally taken for granted, and nonetheless is frequently overlooked. If a survey were conducted of companies dependent on responses by mail the survey would undoubtedly reveal that a shockingly high percentage of those companies have no regular, methodical system of soliciting, filing, and using good testimonials. Yet a direct marketing enterprise may often stand or fall on whether it makes a good use of testimonials.

Many years ago the Merlite Company was founded to sell the Presto midget fire extinguisher, entirely through agents. The advertising job was to pull inquiries from prospective agents, who were then converted to active salespeople by the followup direct mail package. One of the first efforts for Merlite was the creation of a testimonial-soliciting letter. From this letter, which was mailed to a fair number of their best agents, came the story which formed the basis for a successful small space ad which ran for years and resulted in the sale of thousands of units. The headline: "I'm Making $1,000 a Month—and Haven't Touched Bottom Yet!" In those days, $1,000 a month was big money—it represented just about the top limit of the wildest dreams of people of modest means. If the ad had claimed, "Make $1,000 a month selling this amazing little device," it would have sounded like a hard-to-believe get-rich-quick scheme. But the fact that an actual agent said it (his name and picture appeared in every ad) made the possibility a fact, not a claim. And the "haven't touched bottom yet" was a homey additional promise that probably no city slicker copywriter would have thought of if he were creating a fictional testimonial.

Many U.S. School of Music ads in the past were built around testimonials. Being able to play a musical instrument has a deep meaning for people that could best be expressed by the students themselves. One ad bore a headline extracted from an ecstatic student's comments: "I Can't Believe My Ears—I'm Playing Music! My friends all think it's me, but I keep telling them it's your wonderful course."

One of the most appealing and effective stories used in art school advertising was that of a Florida mother who enrolled in the course and became one of the state's best-known painters. Her story was filled with more joy of fulfillment, credible praise for the course, and identification for other women than could be used in the ad. For instance, the day her textbooks arrived, she felt like a "child with a new toy." Her instructors were "just wonderful. I actually came to feel they were my friends." But what if you're a homemaker tied down with housework and babies? Isn't it hard to find time to paint? "It's not as hard as it sounds. When you have something exciting to look forward to, the housework flies. It's like when you're expecting a guest. You seem to get through the chores easily because you're looking forward to the visit." But won't hubby and kids be resentful if Mom spends a lot of time painting? Not her family. "They're so enthusiastic. Everytime I complete a painting, it's like a wonderful family party at our home." Isn't this reassuring? Isn't this what every creative woman would enjoy? And doesn't she make it all sound wonderfully possible and attainable?

You may have received some unsolicited testimonials that you have gotten permission to use and are already using. But, if you expand this by setting up a methodical testimonial-soliciting program, you can increase tenfold your effective use of testimonials. Because the quality and usefulness of testimonials vary widely, the more testimonials you pull in, the more pure gold you should be able to pan from the ore. Of course, it's important to get the testimonial donor's signature on some kind of release giving you permission to use his comments, name, and photo, if any. The wording of the releases varies. Some companies are content with a very simple "You have my permission" sentence; others use a more elaborately foolproof legal form. You should consult your attorney about the kind you choose to use.

Your testimonial-soliciting letter should drop a few gentle hints about your interest in hearing of actual benefits and improvements from your product. Otherwise you'll get too many customers writing similar lines of empty praise such as "it's the greatest" and "it's the finest."

Justify the Price

"Why Such a Bargain? The Answer Is Simple." These eight magic words constitute one of the most important building blocks in the mail order sale. They have been expressed hundreds of different ways in the past, and will appear in hundreds of new forms in the future. But whether in the mail order ads of magazines and direct mail yesterday and today, or the televised home-printed facsimile transmission of tomorrow, the *price justification argument* will always be with us. It does an important job of making the low price seem believable and the high price not really so high.

Here are a number of examples of price justification from the past. As you read through them, ask yourself if it isn't likely that similar arguments will still be used in the year 2000.

Doubleday Subscription Service: "How can the Doubleday Subscription Service offer these extremely low prices? The answer is really quite simple. Not everyone wants the same magazines. By getting all the publishers to allow us to make their offers in one mailing, each subscriber has a chance to pick and choose; each magazine gets its most interested readers at the lowest possible cost. The savings are passed on to you in the lowest possible prices for new, introductory subscriptions."

Reader's Digest (Music of the World's Great Composers): "How is this low price possible? Without the great resources of RCA and the large 'audience' of *Reader's Digest,* such a collection would have to cost about $60.00. This sum would be needed to cover royalties to musicians, the cost of recording, transferring sound from tape to records, manufacturing and packaging. But because a single large pressing of records brings down the cost of manufacturing, and because the entire edition is reserved in advance for *Digest* subscribers, you can have these luxury-class records now at a fraction of the usual price for records of such outstanding quality!"

Singer (socket wrench and tool set): "This set is not available in stores—but sets like these sell regularly in stores at a much higher price. You save the difference because—unlike the usual store which sells just a few sets at a time, we sell many hundreds, thus enabling us to purchase large quantities at big savings which we pass on to you."

American Heritage (History of the Civil War): "The post-publication price of the standard edition will be $19.95; it can be kept down to this level because of the exceptionally large first printing. But if you reserve a copy before publication (a great help with shipping, storage, inventory, etc.) we shall be glad to reduce the $19.95 price by 25 percent." (Notice the double whammy here. First, the value of the post-publication edition is justified, and then the even greater value of the pre-publication edition is justified.)

Book-of-the-Month Club (Pre-Publication Society): "Like the 'limited edition'—a very old custom in publishing—'pre-publication' offerings are designed to help *underwrite* the costs of any publishing project where there is an exceptionally high risk and heavy investment. Under modern printing conditions, if a publisher can be assured of a relatively large edition, the per-copy cost is reduced with almost every extra thousand copies printed. In recent years the usual procedure has been for the publisher, himself, to print an elaborate circular announcing the 'pre-publication offer' (similar to the one enclosed) and to permit booksellers, at a slight cost, to mail these announcements to select good customers. Rarely, however, do more than a few hundred booksellers over the country participate in this kind of promotion, with the result that comparatively few book lovers ever learn of it, and usually only in large cities. The efforts of the Pre-Publication Society will be far more thorough and widespread."

Visual Reinforcement of Words and Ideas

All our powers of comprehension are built on our earliest sensations and associations. First comes touch, but that won't be much help to advertising until Aldous Huxley's "Feelvision" is invented. Next, when we are several months old, comes image, as we learn to associate Mama's smiling face with getting fed, burped, and changed. Then comes the spoken word, when we learn to call Mama by name. This early experience with the image and the spoken word is what makes television such a potent advertising force.

Our earliest experience with the printed word is usually in our heavily illustrated first reader (or preschool picture book). It is printed in large clear serif type, in lowercase—which is why serif body types seem more readable than sans serif, and lowercase more comfortable than upper. And when the book says, "oh! see the boy!" sure enough, there is usually a picture of a boy. This makes it less likely that we would stand up in class and read aloud, "oh! see the doy!"

Advertising has seized on this fact of human development and developed it into an astonishingly effective tool of communication. It has learned, probably far more than ever before in human history, to team words and pictures for greater impact than either alone can achieve. Sometimes it's a *rebus,* in which a picture is substituted for some of the words. For instance, instead of saying *"(a summons, a will, a deed, a mortgage, a lease) are a few of the reasons why every family should have a lawyer,"* an ad for New York Life Insurance Company substituted a picture of such documents as a will and a mortgage, for the words in parentheses.

Sometimes, it's a *pantomime,* with the words providing only the necessary minimum of explanation. An Itkin Brothers office furniture ad showed in four pictures what the subhead promised: "In less than 45 minutes you can have four new offices without changing your address, increasing rent, or interrupting work." The pictures were the headline, and the four captions under the photos of the partitions being installed simply read: "8:45 . . . 8:50 . . . 9:15 . . . and 9:25."

Sometimes it's a *visual literalism.* For instance, our small-space ad for U.S. School of Music, headed "Are You Missing Half the Fun of Playing the Guitar?" showed only half a guitar. The instrument was literally sawed in half.

Sometimes it's an *abstract picture.* How the devil can you picture the abstract concept "two," for instance? Avis made it literal with a photo of two fingers.

Also, the overall appearance of the ad provides visual reinforcement. Even if there are no illustrations, which is often true, the typography and design can convey a great deal about what kind of company is behind the advertising. For decades most mail order advertising was notorious for being less attractive than general advertising; much of it still is. Whether this helps or hurts results is hotly debated. It may be that a certain homey or buckeye look adds an air of unsophisticated honesty and sincerity. But for any company involved in starting an *ongoing relationship with a customer,* the appearance of its direct marketing advertising should convey that it is a responsible, tasteful, and orderly company with which to do business.

The Response Device

Most direct response ads carry a reply coupon or card for ease of responding. The significant exception is small-space ads. A two-inch ad would have to be about twice as big to accommodate a coupon. Many advertisers find that it does not produce twice as many results.

A black-and-white page with an insert card (a postpaid reply post card inserted next to the ad) costs about two and a half times more than a black-and-white page alone but usually pulls at least four times as much as a page with coupon. (Advantages of insert cards were explored in Chapter 9.)

There are many variations of the postpaid reply envelope, depending on cost and publication policy: oversize card insert, full-page insert with detachable card, four-page card stock insert with detachable card, eight-page newspaper advertising supplement with bound-in or stuck-on card or envelope, loose envelope (such as for film processing) inserted in Sunday newspapers, and so on.

The creative problem in preparing coupon or card copy is to summarize the message from the advertiser to the prospect as clearly, succinctly, and attractively as possible. Many readers tear out a card or coupon and leave it in a pocket or drawer for days or even weeks before deciding to send it in. At that point, the reader wants to know what this minicontract entails. It is important to provide as much resell and reassurance as possible.

If the advertiser is a club, the coupon copy should clearly spell out terms of membership.

Check boxes, numbers to be circled, and other aids to make completing the form easy should be provided wherever possible.

Any money-back guarantee, whether already mentioned in the adjoining copy or not, should be clearly stated.

"Telescopic" Testing

Standard practice in direct mail for many years is to test simultaneously as many as five or six or even ten or twelve different copy appeals, formats, or offers. Giving each package equal exposure over a representative variety of lists is probably the most scientifically precise research method in advertising. But this practice has *not* been so common in publication advertising. There, for a long time, advertisers were limited to the simple *A/B split-run* test, in which every other copy of a given issue of a publication would contain Ad A and every other copy Ad B (separately keyed, of course). (See Exhibit 16-4.) This, too, is very precise. The main thing is to make sure that the circulation purchased is large enough to provide a statistically significant variation in results between the two ads. But for testing your way to a breakthrough, it can be *slow.*

If you test two ads, wait for the results; then test two more, and so on. A year or so may pass before you discover the "hot button." On the other hand, if you test the control against one ad in publication A and another in publication B (we often do), it is useful, but it does introduce *another variable,* the difference in the two publications. And a truly scientific test has only one variable.

All our experience and common sense tell us that six or eight tests are far more likely to product a hit than only two. To solve this problem, direct marketing advertisers are turning increasingly to multiple ad testing. We call it "telescopic" testing, because it permits the advertiser to telescope a year's testing experience into a single insertion. Telescopic testing simply applies the direct mail principle of multiple testing to publication advertising. But it requires publications or formats with the *mechanical capability* of running such tests. Perhaps the first magazine to offer this capability was *TV Guide.* Because television programs are different in each region, *TV Guide* publishes over eighty different regional editions. Theoretically, you could do *over eighty different split-runs,* one in each regional edition, in a single week. (But you wouldn't, because the circulation for each test would be too small.) By testing Ad A vs. Ad B in the first region, Ad A vs. Ad C in the next region, and so on, it is possible to test as many as ten or fifteen different ads or ad variations simultaneously. By assigning to Ad A results the numerical value of 100, we can give the other ad results proportionate numerical values and rank them accordingly.

An easier way to do multiple testing is by intermixed card stock inserts bound into a magazine so that Ad A appears in copy No. 1, Ad B in copy No. 2, Ad C in copy No. 3, and so on.

Advertisers began testing new appeals and offers by doing A/B regional splits of *black-and-white pages* and even *half-pages* in the local program section of *TV Guide.* The following examples illustrate what can be done:

- A book series achieved a 252 percent improvement.
- A correspondence course inquiry ad was improved 209 percent.
- A name-getting giveaway program brought its advertising cost per coupon down to nineteen cents!

The technique of applying telescopic testing is discussed in Chapter 19. Today there are three basic methods of running multiple tests:

1. *Simultaneous split-runs in regional editions* of a magazine that offers such a service, with one ad used as a control in all the splits.

2. *Free-standing stuffers* or loose newspaper preprints, intermixed at the printing plant before being supplied to the publication.

3. *Full-page card inserts in magazines,* intermixed at the printing plant.

Exhibit 16-5. Control Ad A in Insert Test

Exhibit 16-6. Ad B in Insert Test

Exhibit 16-7. Ad C in Insert Test

Exhibit 16-8. Ad D in Insert Test

Exhibit 16-9. Ad E in Insert Test

Exhibit 16-10. Ad F in Insert Test

Exhibit 16-11. Ad G in Insert Test

It's a rather expensive game to play, but major direct marketers today are playing for multimillion dollar stakes. And all it takes is one breakthrough to pay for all the necessary research in a very short time.

A dramatic example of the application of telescopic testing is provided by a series of six ads created for *Consumer Reports* and tested simultaneously against the control ad via intermixed bound-in inserts in *TV Guide*. Shown in Exhibits 16-5 through 16-11 is the first page of each of the seven insert tests. Study each carefully and see if you can give ratings for Ads A through G.

Have your rated the ads? Okay, let's review the actual results by coupon count. Ranking Ad A—the control ad—as 100, here is the relative pull of each ad, courtesy of Joel Feldman, who was director of Marketing/ Circulation for the magazine at the time.

Ad A—100 (control)
Ad B—107
Ad C—101
Ad D—82
Ad E— 65
Ad F— 61
Ad G—33

While the 7 percent gain scored by the winner, Ad B, may not seem like a startling improvement, it is important to keep in mind that this 7 percent was on top of the impressive gains scored by Ad A, the winner in previous tests. And the circulation of 500,000 given to each ad resulted in a sufficiently large number of responses to make the results highly significant statistically. So thanks to this test, the client could be confident that future publication advertising would be 7 percent more efficient—a substantial gain when applied to millions of dollars worth of advertising.

Self-Quiz

1. Good direct response advertising should make its strongest appeal to

_____

_____

2. Who are the best prospects?

_____

_____

_____

3. Advantages belong to the _____

_____.

Benefits belong to the _____

_____.

4. When are benefits more important?

_____

_____

5. When are advantages more important?

_____

_____

6. Fill in this list of ultimate benefits.

a. _____   j. _____

b. _____   k. _____

c. _____   l. _____

d. _____   m._____

e. _____   n. _____

f. _____   o. _____

g. _____   p. _____

h. _____   q. _____

i. _____

7. Semantics is the hydrogen bomb of _____.

8. Most successful headlines have a "hook" to catch the reader and pull him or her in. The most common hooks are such words as:

a. _____   d. _____

b. _____   e. _____

c. _____   f. _____

9. A common error in writing leads is that the writer _____

_____.

10. A good writing principle is that body copy should _____

_____.

11. What labels may be applied to the section of a classic copy argument?

   a. _____

   b. _____

   c. _____

   d. _____

   e. _____

12. Name four other ways to structure copy.

   a. _____

   b. _____

   c. _____

   d. _____

13. What four-letter word is one of the greatest advertising words?

   _____

14. Name five unique claims to fame that may prove to be the strongest selling points for a product or service.

   a. _____

   b. _____

   c. _____

   d. _____

   e. _____

15. What is the major advantage of using testimonials in direct response advertising?

   _____

   _____

   _____

   _____

16. Name one of the most important building blocks in the mail order sale.

   _____

   _____

   _____

   _____

17. Name four ways you can give visual reinforcement to words and ideas.

 a. _____

 b. _____

 c. _____

 d. _____

18. When is a coupon not indicated for a direct response ad?

 _____

 _____

 _____

 _____

19. What is the definition of "telescopic" testing?

 _____

 _____

 _____

 _____

20. What are the three basic methods of running multiple tests?

 a. _____

 b. _____

 c. _____

Pilot Project

You are a copywriter by profession. You have just been employed by a direct response advertising agency. The agency has been appointed by a home study school offering a course in *accounting*. Your copy supervisor has asked you to come up with headlines designed to get inquiries. Develop one headline for each of these ultimate benefits:

Health: _____

_____

Money: _____

_____

Security: _____

_____

Pride: _____

_____

Approval: _____

_____

Enjoyment: _____

_____

Excitement: _____

_____

Power: _____

_____

Fulfillment: _____

_____

Freedom: _____

_____

Identity: _____

_____

Relaxation: _____

_____

Escape: _____

_____

Curiosity: _____

_____

Possessions: _____

_____

Sex: _____

_____

Hunger: _____

_____

Managing Your Direct Marketing Operation

Managing a Lead Generation Program

Many products and services cannot be sold cost effectively through a one-step sales effort. A two-step, or multistep, program is usually necessary when a significant customer investment is required, or when personal interaction is necessary to complete a transaction. The two major uses of a lead generation program are:

1. Identifying prospect/customer interest or potential prior to committing to the cost of a face-to-face sales visit

2. Generating interest and stimulating traffic into a local retail outlet

The first instance is *lead qualification* and the second is *lead* (or traffic) *generation.* If your needs can be met by either of these activities, you need a lead generation program.

Types of Lead Generation Programs

There are three overall types of lead generation programs. Although the principles that govern are the same, the needs that dictate the programs differ.

Business-to-Business

The primary objective in business-to-business lead generation is to get qualified leads from prospects who, in effect, raise their hands and say, "I'd like more information about your proposition." The thrust of the promotion can be as simple as encouraging prospects to request literature with an inducement to order by mail. Telephone follow-ups of those who request literature is often an integral part of the lead generation program.

For more complex propositions, requiring interaction with a live salesperson, the objective is to get a request for a salesperson to call. However, the cost of an industrial sales call being what it is today—McGraw-Hill estimates in excess of $200—mail and phone follow-up is more and more becoming the norm, rather than the exception.

A recent development, in the office equipment field in particular, is the establishment of office equipment stores. In this case manufacturers like IBM and Xerox use direct marketing methods to induce qualified prospects to visit their stores to discuss their needs and to see live demonstrations.

Business-to-Consumer

The feasibility of lead generation programs for consumer products is most always dictated by price point and available channels of distribution. The unit of sale inherent in package goods, for example, obviates the practicality of a lead generation program except in the case of a cents-off coupon co-op. (See Chapter 12, "Co-ops.")

However, lead generation programs do make eminent sense for the likes of a lawn care service where the annual expenditure is in the area of $100. Or for electronic equipment like VHS. Or for refrigerators, or air conditioning, or freezers, or insulation—each a considered purchase of magnitude for the consumer.

Some manufacturers sell major equipment directly to the consumer. Most sell through traditional retail channels. In the former, the objective is to get qualified leads and to complete the transaction by mail and/or telephone follow-up. In the latter, the objective is to drive a qualified prospect into a retail outlet.

Public Relations

A third type of lead generation program uses public relations as the medium for getting leads. Done right, PR is an extremely effective method of producing leads in both the consumer and business field.

As a matter of fact, more often than not, editorial mention of a free booklet offer or a new product is likely to produce more leads than a space ad. The theory is that the reader puts more stock in editorial mentions than in ads. The other side of the coin is that conversions to orders are more likely from space ads than from editorial mentions.

The policies of publishers vary when it comes to giving free editorial mention. Some publishers give editorial mention only if an ad is placed; others give editorial mention irrespective of space advertising. Many firms prepare and distribute their own news releases to likely publications. However, there is no substitute for a good public relations agency in getting news releases placed.

Adjusting Quality and Quantity of Leads

No matter what the type of lead generation program, all marketers have an option to produce what are commonly referred to as "loose" or "tight" leads. Loose lead offers can be expected to produce a higher "front-end" response; tight lead offers can be expected to produce a lower front-end response, but a higher closure percentage. Listed below are ten lead "looseners" and ten lead "tighteners."

Looseners:

1. Tell less about the product
2. Add convenience for replies
3. Give away something
4. Ask for less information
5. Highlight the offer
6. Make the ad "scream"
7. Don't ask for a phone number
8. Increase the offer's value
9. Offer a contest or sweeps
10. Run in more general media

Tighteners:

1. Mention a price
2. Mention a phone or sales call
3. Tell a lot about the product
4. Ask for a lot of information
5. Specify rules for the offer
6. Ask for postage on the reply
7. Bury the offer in the copy
8. Tie the offer to a sales call
9. Change the offer's value
10. Ask for money

The decision as to whether you want loose leads or tight leads must be dictated by experience. If salespeople close only one out of ten loose leads, for example, they may become discouraged and abandon the program. On the other hand if salespeople close three out of ten loose leads versus five out of ten tight leads with twice as many leads to draw from, they and management too might opt for the loose lead program.

Gathering Input from the Sales Force

When planning a promotion, marketers often overlook the most valuable tie to their customer base—the sales force. No source will be able to relate to the specific needs and product application for a market as well as the sales force. They are on the "firing line." They know what is going on out in the territory, who their competition is, the spheres of influence among their prospects. Even the message in your communications can be influenced in both tone and content by the sales force.

Setting the Objectives of the Program

The special need for objectives in a lead generation program relates to the quality of leads. An abundance of leads can be meaningless if an insufficient number convert to sales. The key question is, What ratio of sales to inquiries do we need to make this program profitable? This must be spelled out when setting objectives.

Determining the Promotion Strategy

Strategies should identify the steps required for accomplishing the program's objectives. They are the road map for getting from where you are to where you want to be. In addition, they should mesh with the strategies being applied by the sales force and other distribution channels. For example, if the sales force's strategy is soliciting the legal profession to sell word processors, then the promotion's strategy may be to develop a direct mail/lead generation campaign directed at the legal profession. This, in turn, would provide qualified leads from the legal profession for the sales force to convert into sales.

Planning the Implementation Stage of the Lead Generation Program

Once objectives and strategies are established, the time to implement the program—make it come alive—arrives. Implementation involves consideration of the following areas:

- *Sales Force Involvement.* Any sales force can make or break a lead generation program. Front-end involvement, as stated, is essential. So is foreknowledge of the full promotional effort, including media selection, samples of ads and/or mailing packages, and detailed explanations of any offers or incentives. Finally, a feedback loop should be established for a qualitative assessment of positive and negative results of the promotion.

- *Capacity and Lead Flow Planning.* Lead flow is not a faucet that can be turned on or off at will. Lead flow must be planned so that leads come in at a rate equal to the sales force's capacity to handle. Although there will be more on this subject later in this chapter, the key point to remember is that either too few leads or too many leads will work to the detriment of the program.
- *Creative Strategy.* Creative strategy for a lead generation program should reflect the creative strategies applied for other advertising efforts, including general advertising, but the look and feel of the communication should be consistent with the overall image of the company to get the full benefits of an integrated campaign.
- *Media Strategy.* The key question is, given the target market and the product offering, what media will most effectively accomplish the task? Whether it be mail, print, broadcast, cable—whatever the medium— key considerations such as penetration, key prospects reached, number of contacts, and so forth, must be considered.
- *Fulfillment Strategy.* As simple as it sounds, one must know exactly what will happen to a lead, once it's received. If there is to be a brochure, for example, ample quantities must be in stock before the initial communication occurs. Measurement systems must be in place (covered later in this chapter). Systems must be in place for scheduling sales calls, referring leads to the field, call-back programs, and so forth. Failure to be ready to fulfill promptly can kill the best of promotions.

You've informed your sales force, planned capacity, made your offer, and the leads start coming in. How do you manage this process to ensure the maximum effectiveness and efficiency for the entire program?

Capacity Planning

Let's begin by taking a closer look at capacity planning. We said that it was a critical component of the up-front planning process, but it is also key to managing on an ongoing basis. No matter how carefully planned, a program can change because of internal and external variables.

For instance, postal deliveries might be slower or faster than anticipated, a computerized customer file might malfunction, a new product could take twice as much time to sell to a lead than anticipated. The possibilities are endless, but the point is simple: Plan your capacity to be flexible to change.

Let's look at a typical capacity planning chart that indicates an optimum lead flow. (See Table 17-1.) Assuming a salesperson can average one cold prospect call a day, Table 17-1 shows how many calls each office can make in a working month of twenty days (twenty calls per person). This information determines what quantity of mail is required at a 5 percent return to furnish leads for these calls, given that probably 20 percent of them will be qualified calls and the rest will be screened out prior to a sales call.

Thus, control can be exercised over mailings so that the two salespersons in Denver, for example, will not be suddenly swamped by scores of sales leads. In their district, 4,000 mailing pieces would be needed to furnish them with forty qualified leads, as many as the two salespersons can follow up in one month. ZIP code selectivity helps to target mailings within a district.

To keep a constant flow of leads moving to the field at an average of 3,500 a month would require 70,000 mailing pieces per month. A year's campaign (twelve months multiplied by 70,000) requires 840,000 mailing pieces.

Of course, all of this up-front planning and development is directed towards providing the sales center with an even flow of qualified leads. In simple terms, the sales center is a centralized location that houses your telemarketing sales force. This subject will be covered in detail throughout the telemarketing section of this book.

Table 17-2 illustrates a sales center with a need for about 450 leads per week. Direct mail, television, radio, and print are all being utilized.

Table 17-1. Capacity Planning Chart

District Offices	Number of Salespeople in Each	Total Qualified Calls Needed Each Month	Total Leads Required (at 20% Qualified)	Mailings Required (at 5% Return)
Indiana	10	200	1,000	20,000
Tennessee	14	280	1,400	28,000
Virginia	10	200	1,000	20,000
Michigan	10	200	1,000	20,000
Illinois	16	320	1,600	32,000
West Virginia	13	260	1,300	26,000
New Jersey	5	100	500	10,000
San Francisco	8	160	800	16,000
Maine	9	180	900	18,000
Seattle	9	180	900	18,000
New York City	10	200	1,000	20,000
Ohio	10	200	1,000	20,000
Texas	7	140	700	14,000
Utah	3	60	300	6,000
Connecticut	6	120	600	12,000
Pittsburgh	9	180	900	18,000
Philadelphia	11	220	1,100	22,000
Miami	3	60	300	6,000
Des Moines	7	140	700	14,000
Los Angeles	2	40	200	4,000
Denver	2	40	200	4,000
Atlanta	3	60	300	6,000
Totals	175	3,540	17,700	354,000

Table 17-2. Lead Flow Report

Program Code	Map	Class	Post Drop Date	Resp. %	Drop Quant.	Resp. Quant.	1/02	1/09	1/16	1/23	1/30	2/06	2/13	2/20	2/27	3/06	3/13	3/20	3/27
Payroll-Control Pkg.																			
CB-85555-001	1	1	1/02	3.00	35000	1050		74	179	273	263	53	53	53	53	32	21		
Payroll-Test Pkg.																			
CB-85556-T01	1	1	1/02	2.00	10000	200		14	34	52	50	10	10	10	10	6	4		
CB-85556-T02	1	1	1/02	2.00	10000	200		14	34	52	50	10	10	10	10	6	4		
Accounting-Control																			
CB-86666-002	2	1	2/06	1.50	50000	750							53	128	195	188	38	38	38
Accounting-Test																			
CB-86667-T03	2	1	2/06	1.00	10000	100							7	17	26	25	5	5	5
CB-86667-T04	2	1	2/06	1.00	10000	100							7	17	26	25	5	5	5
CB-86667-T05	2	1	2/06	1.00	10000	100							7	17	26	25	5	5	5
CB-86667-T06	2	1	2/06	1.00	10000	100							7	17	26	25	5	5	5
Direct Resp. T.V.							275	200	125			225	225	100			190	225	225
Direct Resp. Radio							100	75				75				50	100	100	100
Direct Resp. Print							75	75	75	75	75	75	75	75	75	75	75	75	75
Lead Flow Totals							450	452	447	452	438	448	453	443	447	456	452	458	458

Note: This is a hypothetical case.

Lead Qualification

It is no secret that in any lead generation program lead quality varies a great deal. In fact, generally speaking, about 20 percent of total leads will result in about 80 percent of total sales revenue. Given this, it makes sense to optimize time and effort with a good lead qualification system. There are two good reasons for optimizing time and effort.

1. Time is money: Given the cost of an industrial sales call (over $200 by a McGraw-Hill estimate) it costs too much to have a salesperson call on unqualified prospects.

2. Good leads get "cold": While salespeople are pursuing low-quality leads, high-quality leads get "cold." Each day a lead is not acted upon makes the likelihood of sales conversion less likely.

How can leads be qualified? The best way is to build screening devices into the upfront media selection.

Lists in the business field, for example, can be selected by sales volume, number of employees, or net worth. It must be recognized, however, that while such selectivity can produce a better qualified lead, it can also reduce the number of leads, sometimes significantly. If a product or service tends to have more of a mass application, this may not be desirable.

There are a number of ways to handle lead qualification after leads are received. The following is a prototype of a telephone script for lead qualification. A well-structured telephone script can help a telemarketing specialist to immediately "weed out" low-potential prospects prior to initiating a sales call.

Sales Representative:	Thank you for calling us, Mr. Johnson. My name is Valerie Gelb. How can I help you?
Prospect:	Well, I saw your advertisement and I'm interested in your (product).
Sales Representative:	I'm pleased to hear that, Mr. Johnson. You know we have several models. It would help me to recommend the most efficient one for your needs, if I knew a little more about your company. *Just what product or service do you offer?*
Customer Response:	
Sales Representative:	That's interesting. You know we have quite a few customers in the same business in (City) who find our (product) does an unusually good job for them. *Where are you located?*
Customer Response:	
Sales Representative:	Well, in a business like yours, with so many locations, you must have used products similar to ours before. *Just how did they work out for you?*

Customer Response:

Sales Representative: Did they do what you expected of them or did you have any particular problems?

Customer Response:

Sales Representative: Well, I can assure you you won't have those kinds of problems with our product. Especially since we can offer you a model more suited for the way your company uses it.
By the way, is there more than one division in your company that might be using (product)?

Customer Response:

Sales Representative: That means you will need a considerable quantity to begin with—and a continuing supply.
Just how many (products) do you regularly use each month?

With this series of six simple questions, a sales representative can qualify a prospect's sales potential in three important categories: the appropriateness of the product for the prospect's needs, the potential sales volume the prospect represents, and the ability of the company to fulfill the sale and service the account.

This questionnaire approach can also be an excellent means of capturing marketing information about prospects and customers. Demographic and psychographic information can be part of the feedback loop to the media selection and targeting of the initial "up-front" communication.

Table 17-3. Lead-Sorting Form

Code	Lead Disposition	Analysis	Follow-up Action	Result
A	High Potential	Refer to outside sales force		
B	Medium Potential	Sell by telephone		
C	Low Potential	Resurface at later date		
D	No Potential	No potential-information seekers		

The most efficient way to sort leads is by degrees of potential. Table 17-3 shows how one very successful advertiser sorts leads.

Lead Flow Monitoring

As mentioned earlier in this chapter, the more quickly a lead is acted upon, the higher the likelihood of conversion. The theory behind this is that the interest is highest when a prospect has first responded to an offer. The longer that lead sits, the "colder" the prospect becomes. (While it differs by offer, a rule of thumb is that a lead should be acted upon within ten days *maximum.* Sooner, if possible.)

But, as anyone who has worked with a lead generation program will tell you, sometimes leads come in at a greater rate than anticipated, no matter how carefully planned. Or, sometimes less than anticipated. The latter will not cause "cold" leads, but they could have impact on sales personnel morale, overhead costs, and so on. Whether too high or too low, it pays to have contingency systems in place.

Contingency Planning

Let's look at a typical lead flow planning model to see the normal distribution of leads into a sales center.

In the case of this illustration, we have learned over time that the response to mailings will almost always follow this response curve with 50 percent of total response in the first four weeks, the balance over the next six weeks.

 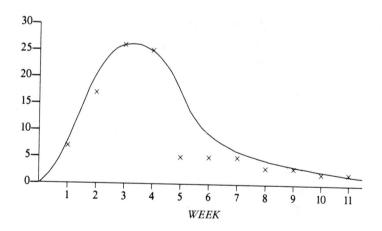

The next illustration is simply a series of these response "waves," each representing mailings. If print or broadcast were being used, a different formula for each would have to be developed.

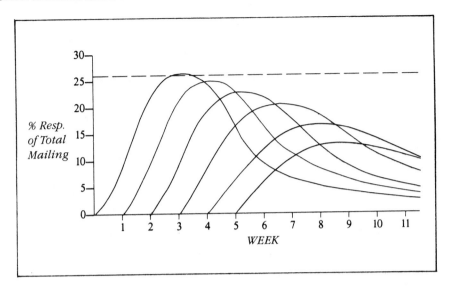

At best, our planning will keep us within 90 to 110 percent of the dotted line, our stated capacity. But what if some of the internal or external events mentioned earlier should change our response curve and create a shortfall? There are two basic systems that can be employed to effectively manage around this.

"In Queue" or "Lead Bank" System

Many companies create a "lead bank" system, which is a purposeful manner of always being above capacity. When a lead enters the sales center, it first enters the lead bank before being dispatched for follow-up. If there is always an extra week's worth of leads, and they are handled first in, first out, no leads are penalized or allowed to get "cold." Naturally, the "lead bank" would be stocked with mail responses. You must handle telephone responses immediately.

If and when there is an underdelivery of leads, the lead bank is drawn down until additional leads can be driven into the center. Or, the bank can be increased temporarily, when an overdelivery occurs until the up-front solicitation can be decreased.

Shelf Contingency

It is always wise to have additional up-front communications "on the shelf"—that is, produced and ready to go—in the event of an underdelivery. If the lead generation program is direct mail, for example, two weeks of additional mail packages in reserve will assure a timely response to an underdelivery problem. And, after normal capacity resumes, the lead bank can be replenished.

Tracking and Results Reporting

Tracking and results reporting are as important as management of leads in the sales center. These activities will result in quantification of the actual effort, relating the success of the program to its objectives, and making management aware of the degree of efficiency, market penetration, and revenue streams.

Tracking

Which information an advertiser decides to track is largely a function of individual needs. However, the following information data may be considered essential.

1. *Number of leads by effort.* Whether for a mailing, print ad, or broadcast spot, the number of leads responding to each effort should be captured. This is usually handled by a specific code of each.

    For instance, a mailing with a split copy test is actually two mailings. Therefore, each response device should have a specific code, so when it's received at the sales center, the proper mailing can be credited. If telephone response is encouraged, as it should be, a specific phone extension code should be given for each mailing, thus making it possible to credit the proper promotion effort.

    By capturing information by code, the winning test promotions will emerge.

2. *Quality of lead/conversion information.* The best pulling mailing or ad isn't always the most successful, for it is conversion to sales that is the true measure of success. The following comparison of two mailing packages illustrates the point.

	Number Mailed	Percent Response	Number Responses	Percent Conversion	Number Sales
Package A	20,000	2.0	400	6	24
Package B	20,000	1.0	200	15	30

As you can see, package A would seemingly be the more successful package. But when conversion is factored in, the greatest number of sales actually came from package B. Other data captured might include: list utilization, demographic information, sales volume, and number of employees.

Once this data is captured, it is critical that it be maintained on a system. The critical element of this system is the customer file. This file should include all information captured from various offers, as well as follow-up information such as calls made, time between providing leads and sales calls, and cost per sale. The ideal is to be able to determine sales efficiency through cost per sale by office, individual salesperson, and by source of lead.

Results Reporting

There's little question that an efficient lead generation program will increase sales and cut sales costs. But it is essential that results be measured and reported. Documentation of results is essential for three basic reasons: (1) to measure against original objectives of the lead generation program, (2) to prove value to the sales force, and (3) to prove value to management.

Anatomy of a Business-to-Business Lead Generation Program

To this point we have distilled the factors involved in building a lead generation program. But knowing the factors is one thing: making the factors work is often quite another thing.

We must start with the realization that sales representatives in general loath and avoid paperwork. They often resent any intrusion in their territory and scorn measurement and control. So the question is, knowing the inherent resistance, is it possible to develop a model program that will really work?

For the answer to the question we go to Bob Hutchings, advertising advisor, IBM Corporate Advertising, White Plains, New York. In a career with IBM spanning almost four decades, Bob has held many positions. He is renowned for the expertise he brought to IBM Instruments, Inc., in the development of a computerized inquiry and sales lead qualifying system. His system faces and solves the problems of lead generation. What follows is an explanation of the Hutchings system and, equally important, what is behind it.

Business-to-business buying in general, is an evolutionary decision-making process and not an impulse process, as evidenced by consumer marketing. Many salespeople use the traditional AIDA formula in the persuasion process: they (1) create **A**ttention, (2) generate **I**nterest, (3) develop **D**esire, and (4) initiate **A**ction.

Advertising has accepted a similar model developed by researchers Lavidge and Steiner to explain how advertising works. Their model, like the AIDA formula, is based on a hierarchy of effects in the communication process. It is possible to borrow from this model and establish a hierarchy of effects for the selling process (Exhibit 17-1). The model assumes that before purchasing action occurs, an evolution takes place: mentally, the prospect moves through a series of steps starting with awareness and ending in the purchase action.

There are a number of discreet steps in-between. It is here that the opportunities to increase the efficiency of personal selling efforts exist. It is here that advertising plays a more important role in the selling process.

Salespeople and advertising efforts both start at the information level. However, advertising can do a more cost-efficient job of creating awareness, developing knowledge, and generating interest. These are the areas of opportunity for advertising in the hierarchy of effects.

The attitude and behavioral levels of evaluation, conviction, and purchase are more appropriately handled by salespeople. These steps often require a face-to-face dialogue or a product demonstration to facilitate the decision-making process.

To increase efficiency and cut costs, salespeople should do what they do best, and advertising should do what it does best. An effective inquiry system assigns specific roles to both.

Exhibit 17-1. Purchasing-Decision Process Hierarchy of Effects

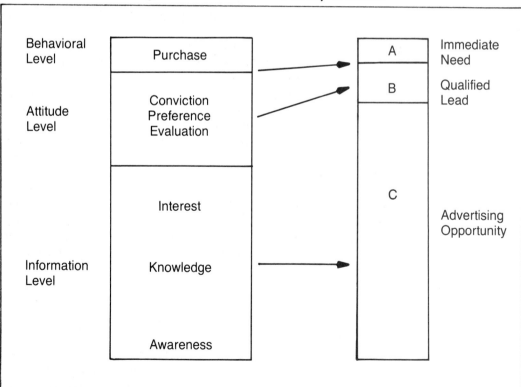

Requirements for Success

It is advisable to locate the computer for the inquiry system in the advertising department. Advertising people are good caretakers for the system; they have a natural interest in justifying advertising programs. The personal computer, with its easy to use inquiry-handling software makes the decision to install it in the advertising department a relatively easy one.

When the system resides in the advertising department, controls can be structured to eliminate delays in responding to inquiries. When inquiries are handled by other departments, delays are often experienced because of other priorities. Other departments often do not associate sales value with the inquiry handling, not understanding that with time the inquiries "cool." Thus, sales opportunities are lost.

Sales representatives frequently believe that leads generated by headquarters are questionable. Cold inquiries sent for a follow-up contribute to that belief. An unfortunate reality is that salespeople often discard the entire bundle of sales leads when the first few are unproductive.

The inquiry system will survive if emphasis is placed on the ability of the system to measure the promotion and identify its contribution to sales.

Advertising objectives should be inquiry-oriented. Advertising objectives must be clearly defined as inquiry-driven advertising. The creation of advertising that employs known response techniques should be the mission of agency and/or staff copywriters and art directors. Their advertising should be measured against response-oriented goals. The inquiry system starts with the offer.

A response-oriented advertisement should employ alternative offers. Responses to hard offers, such as "Send a Salesperson," and soft offers, such as "Send Information," position the inquirer's interest in an obvious way. Requests to send a salesperson indicate an immediate need. Requests for information indicate a lower interest level. Frequently overlooked are additional offers that can position the inquirer within other steps of the buying-decision hierarchy. One such offer is "Put me on your mailing list." This type of offer identifies continuing interest in the product or subject presented in the advertising.

Responses to hard offers are associated with an immediate need and require no further qualification before they are sent as sales leads. Most inquiries, however, are responses to soft offers. Unfortunately, about 77 percent of such responses are not yet qualified for a personal follow-up. Respondents to soft offers must be investigated and qualified before the leads are released to the salespeople.

Qualifying Soft Offers

The mailing package that is used to fulfill an inquiry has more value than just supplying product information. It is a vehicle that can be used to gather information about the inquirer's level of interest in buying. The fulfillment package is often misused. It is frequently a haphazard collection of material assembled as an afterthought. Too often a response card with an offer similar to the original is used. It is unlikely that the same person will respond to the same offer twice. The fulfillment package must be an integral part of the initial creative planning process for the direct response advertising program.

A bounce-back card should be inserted with the mailing package. This card is the key to qualifying inquiries (Exhibit 17-2). This reply card differs from an inquiry business reply card. Its purpose is to get information about inquirers, their ability to buy, and their potential as prospects. The bounce-back card is not offer-oriented and therefore a reason must be given as to why it should be returned. Here is one way to position it:

> We hope your inquiry has been answered to your complete satisfaction. If it hasn't we'd like to know about it. We would appreciate you taking a minute to respond to these few questions. This will help us to provide you with the thorough service we want you to have.

The bounce-back card questions are easily answered. A simple check mark does most of the job with room for comments.

From these questions a profile can be drawn which places the respondent in one of a series of follow-up categories (Exhibit 17-3).

Monitoring the Fulfillment Follow-up

The computer monitors the time from the shipment date of the fulfillment package. If the bounce-back card is not returned within a specified time, a follow-up letter and another bounce-back card are sent. The letter appeals for response by asking, "Has your recent inquiry been answered properly?" If there is still no response, a second follow-up is sent within thirty days. This letter is more direct: "We're back again because we haven't heard from you." The envelope includes another bounce-back card.

The bounce-back card has now been exposed three times to the inquirer. Additional follow-up is usually nonproductive.

Data from the bounce-back cards are analyzed; it is the compilation of information drawn from the original inquiry card and the bounce-back card that identifies an inquirer as a qualified sales lead.

Some inquiry management systems use the telephone to qualify all inquiries. However, the telephone can prove costly when the volume of inquiries is extensive. These systems managers who use the telephone to upgrade and further qualify promising bounce-back respondents, consider this method to be more cost efficient.

Classifying Responses

When a sales representative is requested on either the inquiry card or the bounce-back card, the card is classified as "A" in the computer and sent for follow-up as "immediate need." The "A" will be used for forecasting sales potential and generating management reports.

Exhibit 17-2. Lead Qualifier

BOUNCE BACK BRC

We hope your inquiry has been answered to your complete satisfaction. If it hasn't, we'd like to know about it and would appreciate your taking a minute to respond to these few questions. This will help us to provide you with the thorough service we want you to have.

1. Was the information you received adequate?
   ☐ Yes   ☐ No

2. If you need additional information, please specify.
   _____

3. Are you contemplating purchasing analytical instruments?   ☐ Yes   ☐ No   If yes, are your requirements   ☐ immediate   ☐ 3-6 months   ☐ 6-12 months   ☐ over 12 months

4. What is your application?   _____

5. Would you like an IBM Technical Marketing Representative to call?   ☐ Yes

   Phone No. _____

6. Do you wish to remain on our mailing list?
   ☐ Yes   ☐ No

7. Comments _____

   _____

If your address is incorrect,
please make corrections.

Baker80208B NMR2
B Baker
Sr Research Physicist
Denver University
University Park
Denver CO 80208

Please help us by completing this postage free card and returning it to us.

Bounce-back cards that are analyzed as "continuing interest" are classified as "B." They are sent to the sales representative as qualified sales leads that need development through personal contact.

All other inquiries reside in the computer and are classified as "C." They are the emerging market, and a very responsive mailing list.

It is the "C" group that represents the advertising opportunity. Advertising follow-up with direct mail programs drive the group up the purchasing-decision hierarchy at less cost than personal selling. When they arrive at the qualification level, the sales representative takes over.

Too often companies discard inquiry names if they are not immediately productive. This is a major error and a waste of excellent business potential.

Sales Representative Follow-up

When unqualified inquiries are sent to salespeople, they are, for the most part, unproductive and tend to lower sales morale. With a qualification system a dramatic change in attitude can take place. Better sales leads stimulate a cooperative spirit and make the follow-up reports easier to obtain.

Advertising management and marketing management need to know the potential of sales leads to future business. In most companies, it is unlikely that an order is closed on the first call. The follow-up report is critical to the evaluation of the various advertising programs. Many inquiry systems have failed because accurate information was not supplied about the follow-up process.

Exhibit 17-3. Inquiry Classification

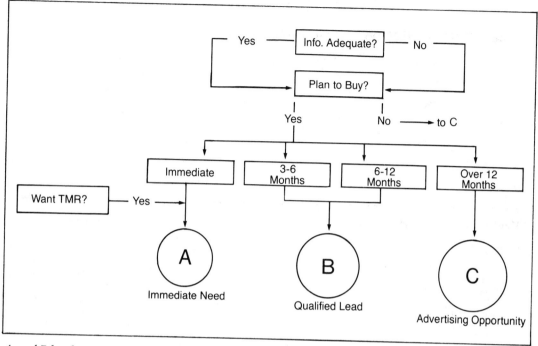

A and B leads sent to TMR; C lead in data base for advance follow-up.

Getting salespeople to report on the follow-up call is a problem. One way to overcome it is to design a simple, easy to use report form. The follow-up report form illustrated in Exhibit 17-4 is a self-mailer which requires only a check mark in a box in the "Excellent" or "Good" columns within the four categories. The four categories represent the segments for forecasting the closing of the order. Each box is assigned a number. These numbers become the basis for advertising evaluations and other management reports.

Inquiry systems seldom have all follow-up reports returned for evaluation; a return of 75 percent is good. However, harassing salespeople for delinquent reports can do more damage to sales department support of the inquiry system than the missing data can.

Inquiry System Reports

The information collected provides a data base from which a wealth of useful information is available. The computer summarizes the results of the advertising and sales effort. It can sort in countless ways and will produce printed reports or graphs.

This information can be put to work in many ways and can help provide advertising accountability. Reports prove useful in researching and evaluating new markets. They can evaluate publication effectiveness and pro-

Exhibit 17-4. Inquiry/Follow-up Report Form

Sales Inquiry Information Record

Today's Date:	04/6/84	Product Interest:	CS
Territory	DANIEL SPARKS	Fulfillment Sent:	03/15/84

INQUIRY
FROM: H. BARGER

Inquiry Classification: B

GENERAL ELECTRIC COMPANY
175 Curtner Ave.
San Jose, CA 95125

Special Requests:

SOURCE: CHEM & ENG NEWS

Follow Up Report: BARGER95125H

Product Interest: CS

Contact Date:

Responded By: ☐ Phone ☐ On Site ☐ Other
Next Step Planned:
☐ Demonstration
☐ CSC Visit
☐ Sample Evaluation
☐ Price Quote
☐ Proposal

COMMENTS: _____

_____

_____

_____

Return Follow Up Report

Closing Potential
(check one box)

1-3 Months*	① Excellent	② Good
3-6 Months	③ Excellent	④ Good
6-12 Months	⑤ Excellent	⑥ Good
Over 12 Months	⑦ Excellent	⑧ Good
No Potential	☐ Excellent	

*Forecast? ☐ Yes ☐ No If Yes, $ _____ Revenue

Type of Funding
☐ Internal   ☐ Grant   Seeking funds
☐ No Funding   ☐ Don't Know

What competition if any? _____

_____

Marketing Rep. Sig. _____

---

vide insight into the value of various creative appeals. Some reports can be used to evaluate the effectiveness of sales follow-up activity, and even the equity of sales territory assignments. Reports can be generated as needed, but they should be prepared and circulated on a monthly basis.

Here are reports that are especially helpful to sales representatives:

1. *The Company Profile Report* (Exhibit 17-5). This report documents a historical record of inquiries received from a single company. People who respond to the advertising are listed with their qualification rating, date of inquiry, and product interest. This report also has value in maintaining sales territory coverage when representatives change.

2. *The Trip Planning Guide.* The inquiry data can be sorted in Zip code sequence and supply a reference to the sales representative planning

a more orderly coverage of territory. When appointments are scheduled in one Zip code location another nearby company can be called upon.

3. *Quarterly Inquiry Listing.* An inquiry report can be prepared that lists the total respondents by territory. Labels can be made and used for local mailing programs.

Exhibit 17-5. Company Profile Report

```
REPORT UXM010                          ***COMPANY PROFILE***                           PAGE: 1
SPEC ID: 1047                                                                          DATE:
-------------------------------------------------------------------------------------------------
WILLIAM H RORER INC                                                           SIC: 283-DRUGS
500 VIRGINIA DRIVE                                                            REGION: NORTHEAST
PORT WASHINGTON PA 19034                                                      TERRITORY JIM CIOBAN


---------------------------------------INQUIRIES RECEIVED FROM: -----------------------------------

                                                     PROD     PROM/       DATE/        INQRY
NAME              PHONE             TITLE            INT      MEDIA       SOURCE*       CLASS
L  M SATTLER      215/628-6388                        LO       12 PF     03/11/82 TS      B

E KELLY           215/628-6621                        LO       12 PF     03/15/82 TS      B

L  M SATTLER      215/628-6388     CHEMIST            LO       17 VG     09/22/82 S       A


------------------------------ LAST INQUIRY FOLLOW UP RECORD ------------------------------------

              NAME:  L  M SATTLER

     CONTACT DATE:   9/28/82
 PRODUCT INTEREST:   LO
           ACTION:   PROP PLANNED
      COMPETITION:
        POTENTIAL:   1
  TYPE OF FUNDING:   INTERNAL
     RESPONDED BY:   ON SITE

         COMMENTS:

*CODES:
(TS) TRADE SHOW — (S) SPACE — (L) LIT — (DM) DIR MAIL — (BB) BOUNCE BACK
```

These reports are useful to sales management:

1. *The Purchase Potential Report* (Exhibit 17-6). The source of information for the purchase potential report is the sales lead follow-up card. The closing potential numbers assigned by the sales people establish a ratio norm against which other programs are evaluated. This norm becomes a stronger management tool as the inquiry system data base grows.

   Norms are useful in comparing current month activity against previous month activity and comparing achievements against year-to-date objectives. They are also useful in comparing sales region and sales representative effectiveness.

Exhibit 17-6. Purchase Potential Report

NAME	COMPANY	CITY	ST	POT	PROD	TER	REG
R P SLOANE	HONEYWELL	PHOENIX	AZ	1	E2	RK	DW
A P MASINO	HANSENS LAB INC.	ROCHESTER	NY	1	VO	CD	PC
D HALPERN	EATON CORP	MURRAY HILL	NJ	1	U1	JK	PC
C A CHANG	WYETH LABS	TOLEDO	OH	1	I3	LL	HD
G LARSON	A W LYONS	RARITAN	NJ	1	LO	LC	PC
C K KIM	ORTHO PHARM CORP	SPRING HOUSE	PA	1	I9	JC	TM
J R BRECO	SHERWIN WILLIAMS	PHILADELPHIA	PA	2	NB	JC	TM
C T KITCHEN	KITCHEN MICROTECH	MORGAN TOWN	WV	2	L9	GC	HD
F RANDA	PARKER CORP	DES PLAINES	IL	2	G1	GO	HD
S G WEBER	PENNWALT CORP	AURORA	IL	2	VO	DC	TM
D JUNG	GENERAL GRAIN	CRANBURY	NJ	2	VO	JK	PC
R LA CORTE	SMITH KLINE & FRENCH	PITTSBURGH	PA	2	VO	DC	TM
B PEPPE	UNIV. PITTSBURG	PITTSBURGH	PA	2	VO	DC	TM
E N PLOSED	S C JOHNSON CO	RACINE	WI	2	13	GO	HD
B SWARIN	CITY OF BARTLESVILLE	BARTLESVILLE	OK	3	E2	JB	JM
K P KOSITIO	GLYCO CHEMICALS	PASADENA	CA	3	I3	SB	DW
P LENAHAN	ELECTRONIC PROP. CO	ALBUQUERQUE	NM	3	RO	FH	JM
A C SHAIKI	AVACARE	PLANO	TX	3	VO	JB	JM
K NOMURA	UNIV. CALIFORNIA	PACIFIC PAL	CA	3	I3	JB	JM
H L WALDRAM	PROPELLANT LAB	WARREN	PA	3	N8	MF	HD
R E LIVINGS	GENERAL MOTORS	WILLIAMSPORT	PA	3	U9	DC	JM
M T LITTLE	NORTHROP CORP	IRVINE	CA	3	E2	FS	DW
C M OAKLEY	PARKER CHEMICAL CORP	LANCASTER	PA	3	VO	DC	TM
J F SHALLA	CARTER WALLACE CORP	GLENVILLE	IL	3	VO	GO	HD
R W CASE	RIVERFRONT MERTS	COVINGTON	KY	4	P2	GC	HD
M W KIRBY	FOOD MATERIALS	HAWTHORNE	CA	4	I3	FS	DW
F N FRY	ALLIED CHEMICAL	MIDLAND	MI	4	U9	LL	HD
G J BEYER	UPJOHN COMPANY	CRANBURY	NJ	4	VO	JK	PC
T C ALLEN	SQUARE DEAL CO	NEWARK	DE	4	U9	JC	TM
W E BRAKES	COOK COUNTY HOSPITAL	CHICAGO	IL	4	I3	GO	HD
R C BUTTERHOP	DUPONG CORP	NEWARK	NJ	4	VO	JK	PC
J R BOLANDS	ECHO SOUND CORP	CHICAGO	IL	4	VO	GO	HD
B N AMAND	US FDA	WASHINGTON	DC	4	U1	BG	TM
I SIEGE	ARMSTRONG WORK CORP	LEWISTOWN	PA	4	VO	DC	TM
J ROP	CARTER WALLACE	SANTA CLARA	CA	4	VO	DD	DW
T W ALLEN	DRAFT INC	NORWOOD	PA	4	I3	DC	TM
L GOLHY	ALLERGAN PHARM	INDIANAPOLIS	IN	4	VO	JV	HD
M JUHA	BTI CORPORATION	DUARTE	CA	4	VO	FS	DW
F LIPARI	GENERAL STORE COMPANY	PEORIA	IL	4	VO	GO	HD
W E BAKER	UNIV. CINCINNATI	CINCINNATI	OH	4	VO	GC	HD
J PARHUA	KEYSTONE CARBON CO	READING	PA	4	VI	DC	TM

NATIONAL POTENTIAL FOR LEAD CLOSING — DATE: JUNE PAGE: 1

The purchase potential identifies the volume of potential sales. This report is useful for manufacturing planning. The same report also helps sales managers plan for appropriate sales closing action. For instance, a potential rating of "1" may require only a special incentive to get the order, while a "3" may need more sales contact including a product demonstration.

2. *The Product Inquiry Report* (Exhibit 17-7). The product inquiry report maintains a running record of the numbers of inquiries for each

product in the line. Quite often, there is a correlation between product inquiries and product sales volume. This report can highlight those areas where more advertising is needed to increase the number of inquiries.

3. *The Regional Inquiry Report* (Exhibit 17-8). This report compares the effectiveness of one region with another in scoring inquiry potentials. A similar report compares sales representatives within a region on their record.

Exhibit 17-7. Product Inquiry Report

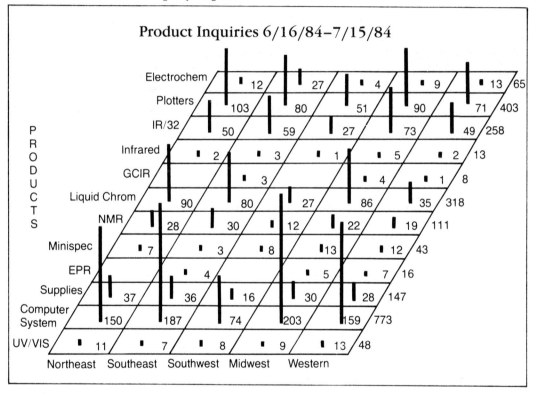

These reports are useful to advertising management:

1. *The Daily Flash Report* (Exhibit 17-9). This report identifies the daily status of each promotion. The daily mail count is recorded by a bar chart. A trend line that records the total inquiries for the campaign is overlayed. As time progresses, the bar chart forms a bell-shaped curve that can be used to identify the halfway point of the inquiry returns. Identifying this point is useful in projecting the life of the promotion.

2. *The Publication Effectiveness Report.* This report lists the various publications used and identifies the total exposure of a promotion. This is done by multiplying the circulation of the publication by the number of insertions. The report determines the comparative pulling power of each publication, while at the same time comparing the cost effectiveness of them all. Thus the groundwork is established for determining future use of each publication.

3. *The Cost-to-Potential-Revenue Report.* This report identifies the cost per thousand to reach the market with a promotion, the cost per inquiry, the percent of qualified inquiries, the cost per qualified inquiry, the sales potential resulting from the inquiries, and the forecast revenue-to-advertising cost ratio.

Reporting with Graphic Charts Has Many Advantages

Charts add a dimension to the meaning of a report. Responsible managers who need to know the progress of inquiry promotion programs, and those responsible for support of the inquiry system, generally have limited time to review results. Submitting hard copy reports loaded with columns of figures is a mistake.

Most managers manage by comparison. Graphic charts present easy-to-see relationships and encourage deeper involvement in the report. It is easier to compare a present position against a past position and the intended objective with a chart than it is with a printout of hundreds of numbers.

Exhibit 17-8. Regional Inquiry Report

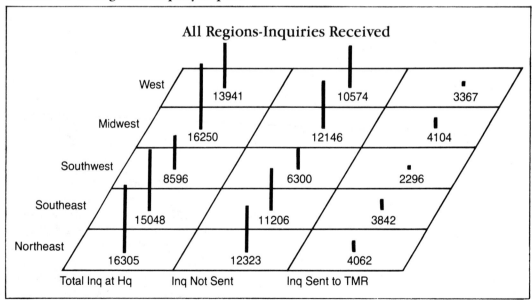

Summary

The efficient handling and managing of inquiries in business-to-business marketing is a major problem for many companies. An inquiry management system can be a solution and also become a valuable company asset.

- An inquiry system helps advertising to become more accountable for its expenditures; it integrates the advertising and selling functions into a unified whole.
- The system can increase sales productivity by the elimination of unproductive follow-up calls; it is a position aid in finding prospects ready to buy.
- The application of an inquiry system to the advertising and marketing functions can become a valuable management tool, one that is useful in assessing progress toward objectives.

In summary, an inquiry management system works because it measures results—the ingredient most wanted in advertising and marketing activity today.

Exhibit 17-9. Daily Flash Report

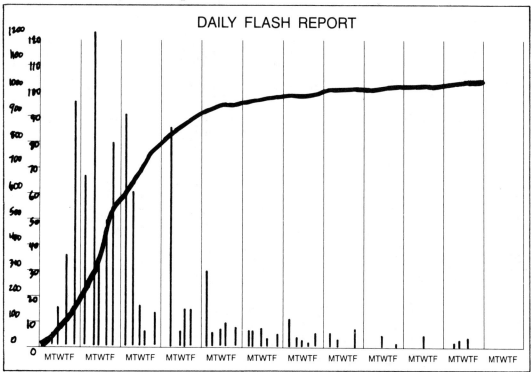

Self-Quiz

1. What are the three overall types of lead generation programs?

   a. _____

   b. _____

   c. _____

2. Name three ways to "loosen" a lead.

   a. _____

   b. _____

   c. _____

3. Name three ways to "tighten" a lead.

   a. _____

   b. _____

   c. _____

4. There are four basic tasks that must be managed up front before any lead generation program is introduced. What are the four tasks?

   a. _____

   b. _____

   c. _____

   d. _____

5. What is the best way to make certain that the sales force isn't over-supplied or undersupplied with leads?

   _____

   _____

   _____

   _____

6. Usually about 20 percent of total leads will result in about _____percent of total sales revenue.

7. McGraw-Hill estimates the cost of an industrial sales call to be over $_____.

8. The most efficient way to sort leads is by degrees of potential. With

high potential as the very best, name the three remaining degrees of potential.

a. high potential

b. _____

c. _____

d. _____

9. Most lead generation programs will produce _____percent of total response over the first four weeks.

10. What are the two best systems that can be used to manage around a shortfall in lead generation?

a. _____

b. _____

11. There are two ways that leads should be tracked. What are they?

a. _____

b. _____

12. Sales people seldom return all follow-up reports to headquarters. What is considered to be a *good* percentage?
☐ 25%   ☐ 50%   ☐ 75%

13. What is the value of a Purchase Potential Report?

_____

_____

_____

_____

Pilot Project

You work for a firm that manufactures central air conditioning systems for the home. A minimum sale comes to $5,000. All sales are handled through a sales force. The target market is home owners with a median income of $50,000.

Your firm has decided to test the viability of a lead generation program and has selected Milwaukee, Wisconsin, as a test market. Your assignment is to develop a marketing plan for management review.

In preparation for actually writing the marketing plan, please answer the following questions:

1. What information will you need from the sales force?
   Examples might be: (a) Who is their major competitor? (b) Who is the

decision maker in the home? (c) What are the major objections the sales force has to overcome? What additional information will you need from the sales force?

2. What objectives will you set for the program?
For example, how many leads per day would you propose to furnish each salesperson? How would you propose to screen leads so you could classify between high potential and low potential? What other objectives would you set?

3. What would your strategies be for obtaining highly qualified leads?
One strategy, for example, might be an offer to conduct a free survey to determine the cost of central air conditioning in a home. Another strategy might be a special promotion aimed at customers in Milwaukee, asking them to provide names of friends whom they consider most likely to have an interest in central air conditioning. What other strategies might you employ?

4. How will you implement your lead generation program? Here are some key questions you should answer in your marketing plan:

   a. Will you ask your sales force to provide names of key prospects? How else will you involve the sales force?
   b. What media strategies will you employ?
      • Will you use compiled lists of home owners? At what median income level?
      • Will you use direct response lists? If you will—what kinds of direct response lists? (Lawn care subscribers, for example?)
      • Will you use newspapers? Which ones?
      • Will you use magazines? Which ones?
      • Will you use radio? Which stations?
      • Will you use TV? Which stations?
      • Will you use cable TV? Which stations?

CHAPTER EIGHTEEN

Mathematics of Direct Marketing

Until 1967 there weren't many places to turn to for the development and application of advanced mathematical formulas to measure the many facets of direct marketing that go to make up its accountability and profitability. Indeed many of the most successful practitioners of the period, in spite of their seemingly satisfactory profitability, were using only the most rudimentary of mathematical principles.

It was typical to be able to state that promotion of a *total* customer file was profitable but to be unable to identify profitability by segments based upon various criteria, including frequency of purchase, recency of purchase, amount of purchase, and type of merchandise purchased.

Seeing this void in the direct marketing field, Robert Kestnbaum launched a unique management consulting firm not only to serve existing direct marketing operations but to provide feasibility studies for major corporations who wished to explore direct marketing. Since 1967, Bob Kestnbaum and his organization, Kestnbaum & Company, have served such distinguished firms as L. L. Bean, Sears Roebuck, American Express, IBM, Hewlett-Packard, Johnson & Johnson, Moore Business Forms, and AT&T. This chapter, a key chapter I might add, distills the mathematical formulas and principles developed by this unique management consulting firm.

Creativity in direct marketing brings recognition, awards, and applause. Unfortunately, profitability and success do not always accompany the recognition and the awards. Some of the attributes of direct marketing that appeal most to those who engage in it are the accuracy with which profitability can be evaluated and the careful way that a program can be expanded with predetermined financial risk. Accountability and analysis lie at the heart of successful direct marketing.

Profitability and Break Even
Establishing Unit Profitability

The most convenient starting point for establishing the profitability of an activity is to determine the contribution associated with each unit sold or with the average order handled. This process begins with separation of costs into variable and fixed.

For this purpose, variable costs are those which relate primarily to each order processed or each unit sold. They may be classified into merchandise costs which include everything related to making, delivering, and packaging the product and operating costs which include order processing, warehousing, shipping, and the cost of computer processing.

It is a good idea to use a worksheet to help identify all revenue and the variable and fixed cost items that come into play. Try to think of every possible cost that could be incurred and document the sources or components of each for future reference. Exhibit 18-1 illustrates a simple worksheet that can be prepared easily. Exhibit 18-2 illustrates a more detailed analysis that can be programmed on any size computer. It has the advantage of forcing attention on smaller units of activity and the frequency with which each kind of activity occurs.

Regardless of the form used, the output of the first part of the analysis (Exhibit 18-1 or 18-2) is the amount of money associated with each unit or each order that is available to pay for selling costs and other fixed costs. After the latter are recovered, the same amount of money becomes profit. This amount is labeled *order margin* by some people or *contribution* to selling cost, overhead, and profit by others. Regardless of the name used, note two things about its composition:

1. Some companies may include an allocation to cover overhead, thus making it a contribution to selling cost and profit only. This is the way the figures are treated in these exhibits.

2. No advertising or selling costs are included. The reasons are dealt with in the next section.

Selling Costs

In direct marketing the costs of placing advertisements, making mailings, or using the telephone should be considered as selling expense rather than advertising. The messages delivered by whatever media are chosen are the salespeople of direct marketing. As we will see in a minute, it is convenient to consider these selling costs as a special kind of semifixed expense in that a commitment is made to a given program before any sales are obtained.

When catalogs or other mailed materials are being used, it is customary to express selling costs on the basis of each thousand pieces mailed or otherwise distributed. When an advertisement is placed in a magazine or a broadcast medium, the cost of each advertising appearance or group of appearances is used.

Often it is advisable to test variations in advertisements and/or mailing packages. Because variations are tested in small quantities, inordinate costs occur for printing and extra creative efforts. It would be misleading to include these one-time costs as part of the regular profitability calculation. (An exception would be the development expense of a catalog to be used only during a single selling season.) It is generally preferable to consider the added costs of creative and small printing quantities as part of overhead expense. Evaluation of potential profitability of a total direct marketing effort should be computed on the basis of selling costs one expects to encounter in an on-going program of the size normally conducted for a roll-out.

Relationship between Contribution per Order, Selling Cost, and Response Rate

Break even and profitability are determined by the interrelationship between contribution to selling cost, overhead, and profit associated with an average order, the selling cost per thousand or per advertisement, and the response rate.

The total available contribution to selling cost, overhead, and profit may be viewed as a pie. Whatever portion of the pie is used to recover selling cost and overhead leaves the remainder for pretax profit. In the examples shown in Exhibits 18-1 and 18-2, an allocation to cover overhead has been included in the applicable costs. The contribution shown in lines 16 and 240, respectively, need to be applied only to selling cost and profit. If the available contribution equals 35 percent of net sales, as in this case, then that 35 percent must be divided between selling cost and profit. Thus a selling cost of 20 percent, or $8 per order, leaves 15 percent, or $6 per order, for profit. Conversely, a selling cost of 25 percent, or $10 per order, leaves a 10 percent pretax profit equal to $4 per order.

The relationship between selling cost and required response rate can be seen quickly. Assuming that we are satisfied with a 25 percent selling cost and 10 percent pretax profit, we have $10 per order to pay for whatever advertising medium is used. As is shown in the bottom portion of Exhibit 18-3, a statement insert costing $60 per thousand to print and place would produce the targeted profit if net sales equal six orders per thousand or 0.6 percent, while a catalog or brochure costing $400 per thousand in the mail would require net sales of forty orders per thousand or 4 percent.

Note that these calculations are based on *net sales*. If returns are 2.1 percent, then six net orders per thousand will require 6.1 gross orders or 0.61 percent response and 40 net orders per thousand will require 49.9 gross orders or 4.09 percent.

Exhibit 18-1. Direct Mail Profitability Work Sheet

Promotion *Sample Catalog Test Mailing*

Line

1	Selling Price	$ 35.40	
2	Plus Service Charge	$ 4.60	
3	Total Selling Price		$ 40.00
4		$ 40.00	
5			
6	Merchandise Cost	13.05	
7	Drop Shipping & Delivery	2.30	
8	*Goods Lost in Shipment*	.13	
9	*Processing, Credit Check, & Collection Cost	2.68	
10	*Cost of Returns	.06	
11	*Bad Debt	.31	
12	*Money Cost (Installment Receivable)	—	
13	*Exchange Handling*	.21	
14	*Overhead & Inventory Carrying Cost*	7.26	
15	*Total Cost*		26.00
16	*Net Order Contribution*		$ $14.00 (P)

Exhibit 18-1 is a simple work sheet that can be used to calculate the profitability of a direct mail promotion. There are four primary calculations involved:
1. *Contribution per net order to selling cost, overhead and profit* (line 16). *Total selling price including shipping and handling or service charge revenue is shown in line 3.*

All order-related variable costs are itemized in lines 6 through 14 and summed in line 15. These costs are calculated on a net order *basis. If certain overhead/fixed costs are estimated as a percent of sales, they can also be included as has been done here in line 14.*

The second part of Exhibit 18-1 provides the detail calculations of those items marked with an asterisk. It appears on pages 446-447.

Order processing and collection costs are derived by multiplying the unit costs by the appropriate base assuming 100 gross orders. Order processing unit costs are multiplied by gross orders. Credit card discount costs are applied to net orders. The total is then divided by net orders to obtain the cost per net order.

Cost of returns are calculated in a similar fashion. Unit costs are summed and multiplied by the return percentage. The result is then divided by the net orders expressed as a percentage of gross orders.

Bad debt is calculated by multiplying the estimated bad debt percent of sales by the total selling price.

Contribution per net order (line 16) *is derived by subtracting total variable cost* (line 15) *from the total selling price* (line 3).

Exhibit 18-1. Direct Mail Profitability Work Sheet

Circularization Costs per M

#		
17	Circular	$ _____
18	Inserts	_____
19	_____	_____
20	_____	_____
21	Letters	_____
22	Order Forms	_____
23	Envelopes	_____
24	_____	_____
25	_____	_____
26	List Rental	_____
27	Inserting, Addressing, Mailing	_____
28	_____	
29	*Catalog Printing & Mailing*	291
30	Postage	109
31	_____	_____
32	Total Circularization Cost	$ 400.00
33	Fixed Overhead per M	allocation incl. above
34	Total Circ. & Overhead	$400.00 (C)
35	Break-even Net Sales per M (C) ÷ (P)	2.86% 28.57 orders

(continued)

2. Promotion and fixed overhead cost per thousand (line 34). *This involves a summing of the costs of all relevant promotional components and an estimate of the fixed overhead per thousand pieces mailed* (lines 17 through 33). *Total cost per thousand is summed in line 34.*

3. Net orders per thousand required to break even (line 35). *This is calculated by dividing the promotion and overhead cost per thousand* (line 34) *by the net order contribution to selling cost, overhead, and profit* (line 16).

4. Total profit at various levels of response (top of page 446). *Total profit at given response levels is calculated as follows:*

Convert the response level to a projected net orders per thousand (line 37).

Subtract the orders required to break even (line 35) *to obtain the unit sales per thousand earning full profit* (line 39).

Multiply by net order contribution (line 16) *to obtain net profit per thousand* (line 41).

Multiply this figure by the total circulation quantity in thousands (line 42) *to obtain total net profit* (line 43).

Divide net pretax profit per M (line 41) *by net sales per M* (line 37) *and multiply the quotient by 100 to obtain net pretax profit as a percent of sales* (line 44).

Exhibit 18-1. Direct Mail Profitability Work Sheet

Total Profit at Various Levels of Net Pull

		1,200.00	1,600.00	1,800.00
36	Projected Net Sales per M (dollars)	1,200.00	1,600.00	1,800.00
37	Projected Net Sales per M (units)	30.00	40.00	45.00
38	Less: Break-even Net Sales (units)	28.57	28.57	28.57
	(Line 35)			
39	Unit Sales per M Earning Full Profit	1.43	11.43	16.43
40	Net Order Contribution (Line 16)	× 14.00	14.00	14.00
41	Net Pretax Profit per M	$ 20.02	160.02	230.02
42	M Circulars Mailed	× 200.00	200.00	200.00
43	Total Net Profit	$ 4,004.00	32,004.00	46,004.00
44	Net Pretax Profit % to Sales	1.7%	10.0%	12.8%

Supporting Calculations and Assumptions

PROMOTION TERMS ASSUMPTIONS

Sample Catalog Test Mailing

1. No. Pieces Mailed   200 M
2. Credit Check   _____Yes   X No
3. Gross Orders Rejected   0 %
4. Gross Shipments Returned   2.1 %
5. Net Sales Uncollectable   .78 %

Order Processing and Collection Costs (Line 9)

a. Gross Orders   100 × $ 2.54 = $ 254[a]

   Less: Credit Rejects   ___ × _____ = _____

b. Gross Sales   ___ × $_____ = $_____

   Less: Returns   ___ × _____ = _____

c. Net Sales   (A)97.9 × $ .08 = $ 8[b]

   Total $ 262 (B)

   Cost Per Net Sale (B ÷ A) $ 2.68

[a] Includes mail order processing, phone order processing, and order picking/packing.
[b] Credit card discount of 2 percent applied to.

Exhibit 18-1. Direct Mail Profitability Work Sheet

*Cost of Returns (Line 10)

Return Service Charge $_____.68_____

_____

Drop Shipment Charge   _____

Shipping Out   _____

Shipping Back   _____2.25_____

Missing Items   _____

Total $____2.93____(A)

% Returns Projected   _____2.1___%(B)

Return Cost per Net Sale (A × B) ÷ (100 − B) $_____.06_____

*Bad Debts (Line 11)

Total Selling Price $____40.00____(A)

% Reserve for Bad Debts   _____.78___%(B)

Bad Debt Cost per Net Sale (A × B) $_____.31_____

*Money Cost (Line 12)

Contract term plus _____ months   _____(A)

Times Sales Decimal (if A is 12 or under divide by 12;
   if 13 to 24 dived by 24; etc.)   (A) ÷_____ = _____(B)

Total Sales Price (Line 3) $_____(C)

Money Employed (B × C) $_____(D)

Effective Interest Rate   _____%(E)

Money Cost (D × E)   _____

Exhibit 18-2. Direct Marketing Profitability Analysis Average Contribution per Order

Line No.		Base Cost 1	Factor % 2	Weighted Cost/Unit 3[a]	Net Cost per Unit 4[b]
201.0	Selling Price	35.40	100.00	35.40	35.40
202.0	Installment Price	—	—	—	—
203.0	Shipping & Handling Revenue	4.60	100.00	4.60	4.60
204.0	Additional Options & Accessories	—	—	—	—
205.0	Total Average Sale	—	—	40.00	40.00
206.0					
207.0	Merchandise Cost	13.05	100.00	13.05	13.05
208.0	Premium for Purchase	—	—	—	—
209.0	Options or Accessories	—	—	—	—
210.0	Credit Card Discount	0.80	10.00	0.08	0.08
212.0	Sales Tax Not Collected	—	—	—	—
213.0	Bad Debt	40.00	0.78	0.31	0.31
214.0	Subtotal	—	—	13.44	13.44
215.0					
216.0	Order Card Postage	—	—	—	—
217.0	Order Processing	0.68	95.00	0.65	0.66
218.0	Order Picking/Packing	1.80	100.00	1.80	1.84
219.0	Shipping Cost	2.25	100.00	2.25	2.30
220.0	Premium for Examination	—	—	—	—
221.0	Credit Check	—	—	—	—
222.0	Return Handling	0.68	2.10	0.01	0.01
223.0	Return Refurbishing	—	2.10	—	—
224.0	Shipping Exchanges	4.73	3.00	0.14	0.14
225.0	Postage Refund, Return, & Exchange	2.25	5.10	0.11	0.12
226.0	Goods Lost in Shipment	13.05	1.00	0.13	0.13
227.0	Telephone Order Processing	1.75	5.00	0.09	0.09
228.0	Subtotal	—	—	5.18	5.30
229.0					
230.0	Total Direct Costs	—	—	18.63	18.74
231.0					

Exhibit 18-2 is part of the output of a computer-programmed profitability analysis which is a more sophisticated counterpart to the work sheet in Exhibit 18-1. It involves much greater detail on the individual cost components and the frequency with which they occur.

Revenue components are itemized in lines 201 through 205, while direct costs are itemized in lines 207 through 230.

Lines 232 through 238 detail the overhead and indirect costs. Contribution per order is derived in lines 240 and 242, while lines 243 and 244 calculate different combinations of selling cost and pretax profit which correspond to the 35% contribution to selling cost and profit (line 240).

Column 1 lists the base cost for each component.

Column 2 displays the weighting factor which is applied to the base cost. This factor is expressed either in terms of:

Exhibit 18-2. Direct Marketing Profitability Analysis Average Contribution per Order

Line No.		Base Cost 1	Rate % 2	Weighted Cost/Unit 3[a]	Net Cost per Unit 4[b]
232.0	Cost of Money—Installment Receivables	—	12.00	—	—
233.0	Cost of Money—Receivables	—	12.00	—	—
234.0	Product Inventory	2.17	12.00	0.26	0.26
235.0	Overhead—Departmental	40.00	—	—	—
236.0	Overhead—Corporate	40.00	17.50	7.00	7.00
237.0	Subtotal	—	—	7.26	7.26
237.5					
238.0	Total Cost	—	—	25.89	26.00
239.0					
240.0	Contribution to Selling Cost & Profit	—	35.00	14.11	14.00
241.0					
242.0	Contrib. to Selling Cost, OH & Profit	—	53.15	21.37	21.26
243.0	Selling Cost if Pretax Profit Target Is	10.00	25.00	—	10.00
244.0	Pretax Profit if Selling Target Is	20.00	15.00	—	6.00

Line No.	Supporting Calculations and Assumptions	Constant Assumptions
11.0	Selling Price	$35.40
13.0	Installment Terms: No. of Payments	—
14.0	Installment Terms: Amount of Payment	—
15.0	Total Installment Price	—
15.1	Implied Interest Charges	—
15.2	Simple Interest Rate "Reg Z"	—
16.0	Shipping & Handling Charge	$ 4.60
17.0	Additional Price of Option of Accessory	—
21.0	Merchandise Cost	$13.05
22.0	Cost of Premium, Free with Purchase	—
23.0	Cost of Option or Accessory	—
24.0	Cost of Premium, Free for Examination	—
25.0	Average Inventory Value	$ 2.17
31.0	Order Card Postage	—
32.0	Order Processing	$ 0.68
33.0	Order Picking/Packing	$ 1.80
34.0	Shipping Cost	$ 2.25
36.0	Telephone Order Processing	$ 1.75
41.0	Return Handling	$ 0.68
42.0	Return Refurbishing	—
43.0	Postage Refund on Returns & Exchanges	$ 2.25

(continued)

Frequency of occurrence expressed as a percentage as in lines 201 through 230, or
An interest rate as in lines 232 through 234, or a percentage of sales, as in lines 235 through 244.
Column 3 contains the weighted cost per gross unit obtained by multiplying column 1 by column 2.
Column 4 derives the cost per net unit by adjusting the values in column 3 by the return rate factor.
[a] *Column 1 × Column 2.*
[b] *Based on returns of 2.1%.*

Exhibit 18-2. Direct Marketing Profitability Analysis Average Contribution per Order

Line No.		% Freq/% Rate **1**	Discount /Uncollect **2**
51.0	Cash with Order	90.00	0.87
52.0	Net 30 Days	—	—
61.0	Charge to American Express	—	4.10
62.0	Charge to Diners Club	—	—
63.0	Charge to MasterCard	5.00	2.00
64.0	Charge to Visa	5.00	2.00
65.0	Charge to Other Cards	—	—
67.0	Total Charge Cards	10.00	2.00
71.0	Installment Receivables	—	—
73.0	Sales Tax—Not Collected	—	—
81.0	Percent Purchased w/Option or Accessory	—	—
82.0	Percent Lost in Shipment	1.00	
83.0	Percent Returned Goods	2.10	—
84.0	Percent Exchanges	3.00	
85.0	Percent Paying Shipping & Handling	100.00	—
86.0	Percent Order Card Postage	—	
87.0	Percent Postage Refunds	100.00	
88.0	Percent Telephone Orders	5.00	
89.0	Percent Interest Paid	12.00	
91.0	Percent Corporate Overhead	17.50	
92.0	Percent Departmental Overhead	—	
92.5	OVHD=(0)%(Avg. Price+S&H) or (1)%Price	—	
93.0	Percent Selling Cost Target	20.00	
94.0	Percent Pretax Profit Target	10.00	

The second part of Exhibit 18-2 lists the input assumptions used to derive the profitability analysis report.

Lines 11 through 43 list the unit costs associated with each order, return, and exchange.

The first column of lines 51 through 94 contains the weighting factors used in the profitability calculations:

Frequency of occurrence, in lines 51 through 88.

Interest rate, in line 89.

Percent of sales, in lines 91 through 94.

The second column contains the bad debt rate and credit card discount rates that are applied to each applicable transaction (lines 51 to 73).

Exhibit 18-3. Break-even and Profitability Analysis

Average Order		$ 40.00	
Contribution	35%	$ 14.00	

	Statement Insert	Catalog
Promotion Cost Per 1000	$ 60.00	$ 400.00
Net Orders per 1000 Required to Break Even	4.30	28.60
Net Response %	.43%	2.86%
Net Sales Per 1000	172.00	$1,144.00

	Case A		Case B	
Target Profit	15%	$ 6.00	10%	$ 4.00
Promotion Cost Target	20%	$ 8.00	25%	$10.00

	Statement Insert	Catalog	Statement Insert	Catalog
Net Orders per 1000 Required to Make Target Profit	7.50	50.0	6.0	40.0
	.75%	5.0%	.6%	4.0%
Net Sales Per 1000	$ 300	$2,000	$ 240	$1,600

Break-even orders = Promotion cost per thousand ÷ contribution order.
Net orders per 1000 required to reach selling cost target = promotion cost per 1000 ÷ promotion cost target per order.
Net sales per 1000 = orders × $40.

Exhibit 18-3 displays the calculation of the response required either to break even or to meet certain profitability targets.

The first part of the exhibit displays the contribution per net order, both as a percent of sales and as a dollar figure. This figure was calculated in line 16 of Exhibit 18-1 and in line 240, column 4 of Exhibit 18-2.

The second part of the exhibit shows break-even calculations for two media: a statement insert and a catalog. For each medium:

The promotion cost per thousand is divided by the dollar contribution per order to obtain the net orders per thousand required to break even.

Response percent is simply orders per thousand divided by 10.

Net sales per thousand are calculated by multiplying net orders per thousand by the average order size, which in this case is $40.

The third part of the exhibit presents similar calculations for response required to meet different profitability targets.

Targeted profit per order is first established. For example, when the average order is $40 and targeted pretax profit is 15%, then $6 per order must be set aside as profit.

Allowable promotion cost equals total contribution per order less the targeted profit per order.

The promotion cost per thousand is divided by this new allowable promotion cost per order to obtain net orders per thousand required, to achieve the targeted profit.

Net sales per thousand are obtained by multiplying the required net orders by the $40 average order size.

Profitability of a Continuity Program

The same calculation can be applied to determine the profitability of a continuity program. Suppose, for example, that a set of five $40 items is being sold, each successive item being shipped only when the preceding one is paid for. Exhibit 18-4 summarizes the figures for each shipment in the program individually as well as for the total program. Revenue and expenses are calculated for each shipment in exactly the same way as was illustrated in Exhibits 18-1 and 18-2, except that return and bad debt rates are much higher for the continuity.

Results for the total program are the sum of transactions made to the average customer starting in the program. Total net sales per starter are $124.74 and, after applicable expenses, contribution to selling cost and profit per starter is $29.51. Again, the marketer in this example can target how much of this contribution he wants to devote to acquiring a starter and how much he wants to leave as pretax profit. Since the total value of the sale is higher, the *absolute* amount that can be spent to acquire a starter and the *absolute dollar profit* per starter are greater.

Arithmetic of Two-Step or Inquiry-Conversion Promotions

Up to this point, we have assumed that the seller uses an individual mailing or ad to produce sales. Very often it is more profitable to generate inquiries with various low-cost methods and then convert those inquiries into sales by using special mailings, by telemarketing (Chapter 13), or by a combination of these methods. In the example of the continuity offer, an average sale of $124.74 opens the possibility of using an inquiry-conversion approach.

Inquiries can be generated through any of the media available to the direct marketer. For example, if an advertisement costing $2,000 placed in a magazine produces 1,000 inquiries, the cost per inquiry would be $2. In addition, there will be a cost of perhaps $30 or $40 per thousand to process inquiries into a usable mailing list. As shown in the top portion of Exhibit 18-5 the seller must convert 14.4 percent of inquiries costing $2 each in order to generate a 10 percent pretax profit on sales.

Varying the media, kinds of advertisements, appeals, and offers will affect the cost of generating inquiries. Typically, the more highly qualified an inquiry, the more costly it will be to generate, but the higher the conversion rate will be. The thoughtful direct marketer will experiment continuously with various ways of producing inquiries and various means of converting them in order to fine-tune a program and to maximize profits.

Most companies find that an inquiry list will support repeated conversion mailings. There is likely to be a fall-off in response to each successive effort, but it is profitable to continue making conversion mailings until the incremental cost of the last mailing is greater than the contribution it generates.

The bottom portion of Exhibit 18-5 illustrates the results of a series of conversion mailings costing $225 per thousand to execute. Given the 10 percent objective for pretax profit, $17.04 is available from each order to pay for the order acquisition cost. This means in order to maximize short-term profit, a conversion series can be continued until the last mailing pulls 13.2 net orders or 14.3 gross orders per thousand or 1.4 percent, assuming returns of 7.4 percent. Short-term profit is maximized after the third conversion mailing since the actual selling cost for the fourth mailing exceeds the allowable cost. However, the total program would exceed the profit target until a fifth conversion mailing.

Improving the Figures

To improve the bottom line, the direct marketer must focus on at least one and preferably on all of the three factors affecting profitability: unit contribution, selling cost, and response rate. Unit contribution can be improved by raising the gross margin, perhaps by upgrading the product or offering sets or combinations of items. Opportunities for cost reduction in every aspect of the business should be explored continuously. Chapter 4 deals with the importance of testing alternative advertisements, packages, appeals, and offers in order to improve response and performance.

A special kind of analysis can be applied by catalog marketers. Not only can overall results be analyzed, but each item or category of products can be subjected to the same type of profitability analysis as well. When sales and profitability of items in a category or in a price range are aggregated, the performance of that group of items can be determined. Unprofitable individual items or categories of items can be eliminated, remerchandised, or given different amounts of space in order to improve their performance.

Return on Investment

So far, we have looked at direct marketing programs as though they occur at one point in time. Actually, of course, the events associated with the program take place over a period of several months or even years. When we consider the timing of revenues and costs, we can begin to obtain a picture of cash flows that are vital to the health of any business, as well as of return on investment, which may well be the best indicator of long-term business success.

Compared to other businesses, direct marketers do not have large investments in buildings and equipment. Often the most important considerations for direct marketers are the expenditure for inventory and the commitment that must be made to advertisements, catalogs, or other selling materials before any sales are received. For these reasons, several different ways of thinking about return on investment have been advanced. The more important ones will be reviewed here.

Return on Selling and Inventory Investment

For a company that is already in business, the major decisions that must be made in advance of each season or selling period are the size of the selling campaign to be undertaken and the amount of inventory to be purchased. Consider the case of a catalog marketer whose average order value is $40 including shipping and handling revenue and whose profitability is identical to that shown in Exhibits 18-1 and 18-2. Assume this company has two selling seasons a year and that it turns its inventory six times each year or three times each season. Its catalogs cost $400 per thousand, for which the bills are paid thirty days after mailing and from which most orders are received within ninety days of mailing.

Exhibit 18-6 shows a simplified profit and loss statement for 1,000 catalogs. The company is investing $400 for its catalogs, plus one-third of the $510 cost of goods, or a total of $570. Within a ninety-day period it receives back this entire amount plus $148 in pretax profit. Some people calculate the return on the investment in inventory and selling cost as $148 ÷ $570 or 26 percent. However, this return is actually received within ninety days, and theoretically the investment could be rolled over four times each year. The actual return is closer to four times 26 percent, or 104 percent. While this calculation has the advantage of being quick and easy to make, it is not only imprecise, but erroneous.

A better way to consider the mathematics of direct marketing and return on investment is to try to simulate revenues and expenses month-by-month as they are expected to occur. Exhibit 18-7 presents a simple financial model for the same catalog effort. Revenues flow in according to the historic response pattern that this cataloger has experienced. One-third of the needed inventory is purchased each month beginning one month in advance of mail date and catalogs are paid for thirty days after mail date. The total sales, costs, and pretax profit for the nine months involved are the same as in Exhibit 18-6. This analysis identifies a maximum monthly cash drain of $221 per thousand catalogs in month three and a cumulative cash drain that peaks in the first and again in the third months. Cash flow will be an important consideration to the management of this company. The internal rate of return* on these cash flows is 303.6 percent, which is a much more accurate way of stating return on this company's investment and is very different from the 104 percent calculated by the simple method in the preceding paragraph.

---

* Internal rate of return is the single rate at which the discounted value of all cash flows is zero. It is a good measure of the true rate of return on cash flows.

Exhibit 18-4. Direct Marketing Continuity Program Profitability Work Sheet Average Contribution to Selling Cost and Profit per 100 Starters[a]

Line No.	1	2	3	4	5	Total
			Shipment Number			
1 Starters/Gross Shipments	100.00	76.50	61.93	52.39	45.79	336.61
2 Returns %	10%	8%	6%	5%	5%	7.40%
3 Net Shipments	90.00	70.38	58.21	49.77	43.50	311.86
4 Bad Debt %	15%	12%	10%	8%	8%	11.30%
5 Units Bad Debt	13.50	8.45	5.82	3.98	3.48	35.23
6 Net Sales	$3,600	$2,815	$2,328	$1,991	$1,740	$12,474
7 Merch. Cost	1,175	918	760	650	568	4,070
8 Operating Costs	1,052	738	564	442	387	3,183
9 Fixed Costs	655	512	424	362	317	2,270
10 Contrib. to Selling Cost & Profit	$ 718	$ 646	$ 581	$ 537	$ 469	$2,951
11 Cum. Net Sales per Starter	36.00	64.15	87.43	107.34	124.74	
12 Cum. Contrib. per Starter	$ 7.18	$13.63	$19.44	$24.81	$29.51	

Exhibit 18-4 calculates the cumulative profit per starter for a five-ship continuity program by tracing all activity associated with 100 starters and calculations a mini P&L for each shipment.

Line 1 contains the gross shipments for each item in the series. For each shipment after the first, the gross shipments equal the gross shipments for the previous item less returns and bad debt (lines 2 through 5). In a typical continuity program there would also be voluntary cancellations which would reduce subsequent shipments. These have been ignored here to simplify the example.

Line 6 contains net sales which are calculated by multiplying the net shipment by the $40 average order size.

Costs for each shipment are summarized in lines 7 through 9. Operating costs include bad debt. These costs are developed using the same cost factors illustrated in Exhibits 18-1 and 18-2. For example, fixed costs are calculated as 18.2 percent of net sales.

Contribution to selling cost and profit (line 10) is obtained by subtracting operating and fixed costs from net sales.

Cumulative net sales and profit are calculated in lines 11 and 12, respectively.

When the figures, other than percentages, in the total column are divided by 100, the value per starter is obtained. Thus there are 3.37 gross shipments per starter, $124.74 net sales per starter, and $29.51 contribution per starter.

[a] *Columns and rows may not foot exactly due to rounding.*

Exhibit 18-5. Inquiry-Conversion Profitability

A. REQUIRED RESPONSE RATE FOR ONE FOLLOW-UP MAILING

	$/Order	%
Net Sales	$ 124.74	100.0%
Contribution to Selling Cost and Profit	29.51	23.7
Pretax Profit at 10%	12.47	10.0
Allowable Selling Cost at 10% Profit	$ 17.04	13.7%

	Cost per 1,000 Inquires
Advertising Cost at $2.00 per Inquiry	$2,000
Processing Cost	40
Total Acquisition Cost	2,040
First Follow-up Mailing	225
Total Initial Investment	$2,265

Net orders required to generate 10% Profit = $2,265 ÷ $17.04 = 132.9 or 13.3%

Gross orders required assuming 7.4% returns = 132.9 ÷ 92.6% = 143.5 or 14.4%

Exhibit 18-5 highlights the profitability calculations for inquiry-conversion programs. It uses the net sales per starter and contribution per starter derived in Exhibit 18-4.

Part A displays the calculation of the required response rate for a single follow-up mailing to an inquiry generation effort. The allowable selling cost at a 10% profit is calculated by subtracting the allocation for profit from the contribution to selling cost and profit per order. The initial investment per thousand inquiries is calculated by summing the

Advertising cost

Inquiry processing cost

Cost of the first follow-up mailing

Net orders required to generate the targeted profit are calculated by dividing the initial investment per thousand by the allowable selling cost per order

Gross orders required per thousand are calculated by factoring up the net orders by a return rate assumption

Exhibit 18-5. Inquiry-Conversion Profitability

B. CONVERSION SERIES PROFITABILITY FOR 1,000 INQUIRIES

	Acquisition	Conversion Mailings				
		#1	#2	#3	#4	#5
Quantity Mailed		1,000	880	838	822	815
Response Percent		12.0%	4.8%	1.9%	.8%	.3%
Orders		120	42	16	7	2
Less Returns		9	3	1	0	0
Net Orders		111	39	15	7	2
Cumulative Net Orders		111	150	165	172	174
Allowable Selling Cost at $17.04		$1,891	665	256	119	34
Cumulative Allowable Selling Cost		$1,891	2,556	2,812	2,931	2,965
Actual Selling Cost	$2,040	225	198	189	185	183
Cumulative Actual Selling Cost	2,040	2,265	2,463	2,652	2,837	3,020
Cum. Balance Available for Selling Cost	($2,040)	($ 374)	$ 93	$ 160	$ 94	($ 55)

Part B outlines the profitability calculation for a series of five conversion mailings subsequent to the inquiry generation effort.

The quantity mailed on each subsequent mailing is equivalent to the previous quantity mailed less orders produced from the previous mailing. Often it is not practical to extract buyers and most of the conversion series is mailed to all inquirers.

Net orders are derived by subtracting returns. The 7.4% return rate was calculated in line 2 of Exhibit 18-4.

Allowable selling cost is calculated by multiplying the net orders by the allowable selling cost per order at a 10% profit, i.e., $17.04.

Actual selling cost includes the acquisition cost and the cost of each conversion mailing.

The cumulative balance available to spend on conversion mailings, taking into account the 10% profit target, is shown in the last row. A negative balance after the fifth conversion effort indicates that selling cost exceeds the allowable 13.7% by $55. Since total selling costs will equal $3,019.88 (total acquisition cost plus $225/M for conversion mailings), and total net sales are $21,704.76 (174 net orders × $124.74), the overall selling cost would be 13.9% if the last conversion effort were retained. Those last two orders, however, would cost $91.50 each to obtain ($183÷2) and would be very unprofitable.

Long-Term or Lifetime Value of a Customer

Most direct marketing businesses are based on the proposition that it may be worthwhile to spend money to acquire a new customer because that customer will buy again from the company at which time a profit will be generated. Since different customers will make repeat purchases at different times and different rates, how can we determine the long-term value of a customer or a group of buyers?

One could approach this problem historically. Supposing that a catalog marketer were able to track all activity from 1,000 customers who were acquired at the same time in January, five years ago. During the five-year period examined, the company did not change its distribution policy. Catalogs were sent to all customers who had purchased within three years. While this simple catalog circulation policy has been used by many direct marketers, it is by no means recommended as the best or even as a desirable approach. (See Chapter 2 for a discussion of direct marketing data bases and segmentation.)

The same technique illustrated in Exhibit 18-7 is applied to each individual catalog mailing. All the revenues, costs, and cash flows associated with this group of 1,000 customers are analyzed month-by-month for 120 months until there are so few active customers left from the original 1,000 that their additional purchases would have negligible impact.

While this model is created on a monthly basis using a computer, Exhibit 18-8 summarizes the results for each year. Let us say that the owners of this company have targeted a long-term return on their investment of at least 25 percent per year. If we discount the annual pretax profit shown in this schedule at a 25 percent rate, then the value in that first January of all future profits in excess of a 25-percent per year return is $2,848 per thousand customers or $2.85 per customer. This means that, given the company's historic catalog circulation policy and actual sales results, the company could afford to have spent $2.85 in that first January to acquire each customer with the expectation of earning a 25-percent per year return on all such customers acquired.

Most companies are not in a position to track all of the sales and costs associated with each customer over an extended period of time. Moreover, companies change their policies with respect to the number and content of mailings sent and the rules used to determine who will receive each mailing. The sophisticated direct marketer today can build computer models that calculate the statistical probability of purchases in each season by customers having different profiles, can estimate the results of changing the nature, number, and effectiveness of mailings or other contacts, and can incorporate assumptions as to changes in order size, margins, and costs.

Such computer models can then be used to simulate the consequences of changes in strategy or policy. Exhibit 18-9 illustrates the impact on return on investment of the pursuit of three different strategies to build a catalog mail order business. The model assumes that the same amount of money is invested in each strategy. The strategies are to:

1. Mail more catalogs to rented lists to acquire more customers.

2. Expand the catalog by adding more products and increasing the number of pages.

3. Create an extra catalog to be mailed to better customers during the fall season.

The chart in Exhibit 18-9 illustrates that over the five-year horizon for which results are simulated, the company in question would invest most advantageously in expanding its product line. You will notice, however, that the customer acquisition strategy appears to be closing the gap quickly at the end of the period and might be expected to outperform the product line expansion strategy in the sixth or seventh year. Further study might indicate that this particular company could blend the two approaches by expanding the size of some of its catalogs and also enlarging its customer acquisition activities.

Exhibit 18-6. Income and Expense Statement for 1,000 Catalogs

40 Orders at $40 per Order *(including shipping and handling revenue)*		*Percent*
Gross Sales	$1,600	
Returns	34	
Net Sales	1,566	100.0%
Merchandise Cost	510	32.6
Operating Cost	223	14.2
Fixed Cost	285	18.2
Contribution to Selling Cost & Profit	548	35.0
Selling Cost	400	25.5
Pretax Profit	$ 148	9.5%

Exhibit 18-6 illustrates a mini P&L for 1,000 catalogs mailed, assuming: 40 gross orders at $40 per order, returns at 2.1% of gross, and cost factors identical to those shown in Exhibits 18-1 or 18-2.

Measurements and Analysis

Calculating profitability. Determining lifetime value of customers. Developing long-range strategies for building businesses. Building models. These are the instruments sophisticated direct marketers use. But only well-planned and -executed campaigns produce the desired results.

The direct marketer builds on the strongest foundation if he plans each campaign around efforts that have been tested previously. (See Chapter 19 for more discussion of the statistics and strategy of testing.) Of course, a company launching a new business has no prior testing experience to use as the basis for its planning. Such a company must proceed cautiously, placing relatively few ads or mailing only the number of pieces required to determine whether a package, or an offer, or a list is successful.

Established direct marketers, however, plan their campaigns to achieve a predetermined balance between contacting former customers who would be expected to purchase at a high rate and seeking to acquire new customers. The balance that each company strikes is dependent on the relative profitability of each type of effort and its long-range growth strategy.

Exhibit 18-10 illustrates a mail plan for the same catalog marketer we have used as an example throughout this chapter. The total mail plan calls for sending one million catalogs which produce a 4.63 percent gross response overall and an average order of $41. Prior experience with the company's own list of customers and rented lists range widely, as shown. Several new lists are included as tests. In order to keep expanding the business, it is wise for most direct marketers to utilize 10 percent to 15 percent of each campaign to test new lists, or packages, or offers.

Some aspects of this mail plan are worth pointing out. House lists totaling 200,000 former buyers are expected to produce approximately $3,200 sales per thousand. With an average order of $45, they are expected to produce a 7.25 percent gross response and 24.5 percent pretax profit. In contrast, mailings to proven rented lists are expected to show an average order size of $38 to $42 and response rates of 3.73 percent to 4.45 percent and 10 percent pretax profit. Test mailings of 5,000 to each of 20 new lists are expected to break even.

Using the same profitability calculation as is shown in Exhibits 18-1 and 18-2, the individual profitability of the mailing to each list is estimated. This is easy to do, since we know the selling cost associated with each list, namely catalog, postage, and mailing expense plus list rental where applicable. And we are estimating the response rate and average order size based on experience.

What is the actual profitability of this mailing? Exhibit 18-11 shows the actual results as of the report date and projected results at the end of the season. The company has been very careful to code its order forms to indicate the list to which each catalog was sent and has asked those customers placing their order by phone to look at the mailing label on the catalog and provide the list code shown thereon. By dint of these efforts, 80 percent of the orders received can be attributed to a specific list. The remaining 20 percent of orders that could not be coded by list must be allocated in the same proportion as attributed orders. This step is extremely important since one would otherwise underestimate the response from each list mailed and might be tempted to stop mailing lists that would then appear marginal.

Since this analysis is being prepared at a time when historic order response patterns indicate that the catalog is 80 percent done or that orders received to date represent 80 percent of all orders that will be received, the actual results for each list after allocation of uncoded orders are divided by 0.8 to produce projected results at the end of the order cycle. Resulting profitability is based on projected results, not on orders received to date.

Exhibit 18-7. Financial Model for 1000 Catalogs

	Month									
	1	**2**	**3**	**4**	**5**	**6**	**7**	**8**	**9**	**Total[a]**
Gross Sales	—	$608	$528	$208	$ 96	$ 80	$ 48	$ 16	$ 16	$1,600
Returns	—	13	11	4	2	2	1	0	0	34
Net Sales	—	595	517	204	94	78	47	16	16	1,566
Merchandise Cost	170	170	170	—	—	—	—	—	—	510
Operating Cost	—	85	74	29	13	11	7	2	2	223
Fixed Cost	—	108	94	37	17	14	9	3	3	285
Contribution to Selling Cost & Profit	(170)	232	179	138	64	53	32	11	11	548
Selling Cost	—	—	400	—	—	—	—	—	—	400
Cash Flow	($170)	$232	($221)	$138	$ 64	$ 53	$ 32	$ 11	$ 11	$ 148

Monthly internal rate of return (IRR) = 25.3%; Annualized IRR = 303.7%

Exhibit 18-7 displays a simplified financial model corresponding to the situation shown in Exhibit 18-6. The difference is that this model displays the timing of the revenues, costs, and cash flows as they occur over nine months.

The monthly internal rate of return is the monthly rate at which the present value of the cash flows equates to zero.

The annualized internal rate of return is the monthly rate multiplied by 12.

[a] *Columns may not total exactly due to rounding.*

Exhibit 18-8. Lifetime Value of 1000 New Buyers

	Yr 1	Yr 2	Yr 3	Yr 4	Yr 5
Gross Sales	$11,086	$7,505	$6,173	$2,830	$1,739
Returns	233	158	130	59	37
Net Sales	10,854	7,348	6,044	2,770	1,703
Merchandise Cost	3,538	2,395	1,970	903	555
Operating Costs	1,541	1,043	858	393	242
Fixed Costs	1,975	1,337	1,100	504	310
Contribution to Selling Cost & Profit	3,799	2,572	2,115	970	596
Selling Cost	1,600	1,600	1,600	625	408
Cash Flow	2,199	972	515	345	188
Discounted at 25%	1,759	622	264	141	62
Present Value	2,848	—	—	—	—
Lifetime Value per Customer	2.85	—	—	—	—

Exhibit 18-8 summarizes the long-term revenues, costs, and cash flows associated with a group of 1,000 new buyers to a catalog operation similar to that displayed in Exhibit 18-7. These values were derived using a financial model like that shown in Exhibit 18-9 with the following significant differences:

It is assumed that there are four catalog mailings each year to this group of 1,000 customers.

Response rates to the catalog mailings vary by the recency of purchase starting with 9% for customers who purchased in the most current six-month season down to 3% for customers who have not purchased for 3 years.

The exhibit displays the annual totals resulting from the financial modeling technique applied to each catalog mailing.

The allowable investment to acquire a customer is derived by:

Discounting each year's cash flow at 25% to obtain a present value for the 5-year stream of cash flows.

Dividing the present value by 1,000 to obtain a lifetime value customer.

The average order and cost structure of the catalog mailings is identical to that displayed in Exhibit 18-7.

Basing the analysis simply on orders to date again would understate final sales and profitability very significantly. Finally, this analysis calculates the statistical probability of exceeding the minimum 10 percent target for pretax profit. What a handy tool this final column provides. It synthesizes into a single number the likelihood of achieving the desired profit by mailing to that list again assuming, of course, that all other conditions remain the same.

That last assumption should not be skipped over quickly. Conditions in the economy shift. Some companies make radical changes in the composition of their product line. Some companies whose lists you rent may have made important changes resulting in customers who behave differently. A direct marketer can make better use of statistics and arithmetic than can a person engaged in any other form of marketing. But it is not all science. The tools discussed in this chapter will help you, but they will not substitute for careful decision making based on good business judgment. Learn the tools well—and then apply your own good sense.

Exhibit 18-9. Return on Investment

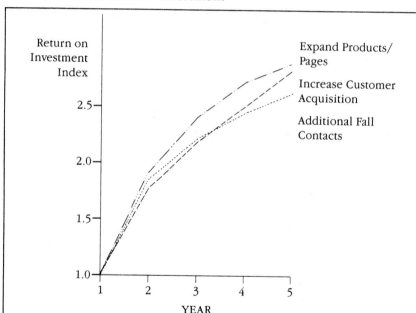

Exhibit 18-9 displays the performance of three alternative growth strategies, as measured by return on investment.
The three strategies are:
Expand products or pages for each catalog
Increase customer acquisition efforts by mailing to more rented lists and expanding the space advertising budget
Introduce an additional fall catalog each year
The actual return on investment has been indexed to the return in the first year to disguise the actual figures.

Exhibit 18-10. Catalog Mail Plan

1 Code	2 List Description	3 Mail Qty	4 Avg Order	5 Resp %	6 Gross Sales/M	7 Gross Sales	8 Net Sales/M	9 Selling Cost[a]	10 Sell Cost%[b]	11 Pretax Profit	12 Profit per M	13 Profit %[b]
1000	House List	200000	$45.00	7.25	$3262	$652400	$3193	$67000	10.49	$156544	$782	24.51
2010	Rollout List 1	70000	40.00	4.36	1744	122080	1707	28000	23.43	13830	197	11.57
2020	Rollout List 2	70000	40.00	4.27	1708	119560	1672	28000	23.92	12967	185	11.08
2030	Rollout List 3	70000	40.00	3.73	1492	104440	1460	28000	27.38	7786	111	7.61
2040	Rollout List 4	70000	42.00	4.09	1717	120190	1680	28000	23.80	13183	188	11.20
2050	Rollout List 5	70000	40.00	4.18	1672	117040	1636	28000	24.44	12103	172	10.56
2060	Rollout List 6	70000	38.00	4.09	1554	108780	1521	28000	26.29	9273	132	8.71
2070	Rollout List 7	70000	40.00	4.45	1780	124600	1742	28000	22.95	14694	209	12.05
2080	Rollout List 8	70000	40.00	3.82	1528	106960	1495	28000	26.74	8649	123	8.26
2090	Rollout List 9	70000	40.00	4.00	1600	112000	1566	28000	25.54	10376	148	9.46
2100	Rollout List 10	70000	40.00	3.91	1564	109480	1531	28000	26.12	9513	135	8.88
20	Subtotal	700,000	$40.00	4.09	1636	1,145,130	1602	280,000	25.00	112,374	161	10.02
3001	Test List 1	5000	37.00	3.25	1202	6010	1176	2000	34.00	59	11	1.00
3002	Test List 2	5000	37.00	3.07	1135	5675	1111	2000	36.00	−55	−11	−0.99
3003	Test List 3	5000	40.00	3.16	1264	6320	1237	2000	32.33	165	33	2.67
3004	Test List 4	5000	34.00	3.16	1074	5370	1051	2000	38.04	−160	−32	−3.04
3005	Test List 5	5000	37.00	3.16	1169	5845	1144	2000	34.95	2	0	0.03
3006	Test List 6	5000	37.00	3.16	1169	5845	1144	2000	34.95	2	0	0.03
3007	Test List 7	5000	37.00	3.21	1187	5935	1162	2000	34.42	33	6	0.57
3008	Test List 8	5000	37.00	3.11	1150	5750	1125	2000	35.53	−29	−5	−0.52
3009	Test List 9	5000	37.00	3.16	1169	5845	1144	2000	34.95	2	0	0.03
3010	Test List 10	5000	37.00	3.16	1169	5845	1144	2000	34.95	2	0	0.03
3011	Test List 11	5000	38.00	3.16	1200	6000	1174	2000	34.05	55	11	0.94
3012	Test List 12	5000	37.00	3.16	1169	5845	1144	2000	34.95	2	0	0.03
3013	Test List 13	5000	36.00	3.16	1137	5685	1113	2000	35.94	−52	−10	−0.93
3014	Test List 14	5000	37.00	3.16	1169	5845	1144	2000	34.95	2	0	0.03
3015	Test List 15	5000	37.00	3.26	1206	6030	1180	2000	33.88	66	13	1.12
3016	Test List 16	5000	37.00	3.06	1132	5660	1108	2000	36.09	−60	−12	−1.08
3017	Test List 17	5000	42.00	3.16	1327	6635	1299	2000	30.79	273	54	4.20
3018	Test List 18	5000	32.00	3.16	1011	5055	989	2000	40.42	−268	−53	−5.42
3019	Test List 19	5000	37.00	3.16	1169	5845	1144	2000	34.95	2	0	0.03
3020	Test List 20	5000	37.00	3.16	1169	5845	1144	2000	34.95	2	0	0.03
30	Subtotal	100,000	37.00	3.16	1169	116,885	1144	40,000	34.96	43	0	0.04
	Total/Average	1,000,000	$41.36	4.63	$1915	$1,914,415	$1874	$387,000	20.65	$268,961	$269	14.35%

[a] Assumes rollout catalog cost of $335/M and list rental cost of $65/M.
[b] Percent of net sales assuming 2.1% returns.

Exhibit 18-11. Catalog Mail Report

Mail Date:
Percent Done: 80%

Catalog No:
Week Ending:

Code	List Description	Mail Qty	Cum Orders	Cum Sales	Avg Order	Adj Sales	Adj Sales/M	Sales	Sales/M	Projected Resp%	Projected Sell Cost%	Projected Profit	Proj Prof/M	Prob of 10% Profit[a]
1000	House List	200000	8500	$385000	$45.29	$481249	$2406	$601561	$3007	6.64	11.38	$139124	695	100.00%
2010	Rollout List 1	70000	1899	74665	39.32	93331	1333	116663	1666	4.24	24.52	11974	171	83.12
2020	Rollout List 2	70000	2272	80000	35.21	100000	1428	125000	1785	5.07	22.89	14831	211	99.99
2030	Rollout List 3	70000	1735	73632	42.44	92040	1314	115050	1643	3.87	24.87	11421	163	57.69
2040	Rollout List 4	70000	2048	99225	48.45	124031	1771	155038	2214	4.57	18.45	25123	358	100.00
2050	Rollout List 5	70000	2028	70400	34.71	88000	1257	110000	1571	4.53	26.01	9691	138	5.27
2060	Rollout List 6	70000	2240	90880	40.57	113600	1622	142000	2028	5.00	20.15	20656	295	100.00
2070	Rollout List 7	70000	1822	85360	46.85	106700	1524	133375	1905	4.07	21.45	17700	252	100.00
2080	Rollout List 8	70000	1830	84825	46.35	106031	1514	132538	1893	4.08	21.58	17414	248	100.00
2090	Rollout List 9	70000	2311	87440	37.84	109300	1561	136625	1951	5.16	20.94	18814	268	100.00
2100	Rollout List 10	70000	2112	84748	40.13	105935	1513	132418	1891	4.71	21.61	17373	248	100.00
3001	Test List 1	5000	120	5500	45.83	6875	1375	8593	1718	3.75	23.78	944	188	74.13
3002	Test List 2	5000	80	3175	39.69	3968	793	4960	992	2.50	41.19	-300	-60	0.00
3003	Test List 3	5000	125	5550	44.40	6937	1387	8671	1734	3.90	23.56	971	194	78.12
3004	Test List 4	5000	96	3596	37.46	4495	899	5618	1123	3.00	36.38	-74	-14	0.00
3005	Test List 5	5010	140	4925	35.18	6156	1228	7695	1535	4.37	26.62	632	126	25.07
3006	Test List 6	5000	98	3877	39.56	4846	969	6057	1211	3.05	33.74	75	15	0.00
3007	Test List 7	5000	90	5575	61.94	6968	1393	8710	1742	2.80	23.45	984	196	74.62
3008	Test List 8	5000	79	3549	44.92	4436	887	5545	1109	2.45	36.84	-100	-20	0.00
3009	Test List 9	5015	130	4890	37.62	6112	1218	7640	1523	4.04	26.83	611	121	14.90
3010	Test List 10	5000	88	3765	42.78	4706	941	5882	1176	2.75	34.74	15	3	0.00
3011	Test List 11	5000	100	5590	55.90	6987	1397	8733	1746	3.13	23.40	992	198	79.50
3012	Test List 12	5000	89	3699	41.56	4623	924	5778	1155	2.77	35.37	-20	-4	0.00
3013	Test List 13	5000	150	6200	41.33	7750	1550	9687	1937	4.67	21.09	1319	263	99.01
3014	Test List 14	5000	134	5235	39.07	6543	1308	8178	1635	4.17	24.99	802	160	48.64
3015	Test List 15	5002	130	4325	33.27	5406	1080	6757	1350	4.05	30.27	314	62	0.15
3016	Test List 16	5000	135	4375	32.41	5468	1093	6835	1367	4.20	29.98	342	68	0.21
3017	Test List 17	5008	135	5440	40.30	6800	1357	8500	1697	4.19	24.08	909	181	67.12
3018	Test List 18	5000	98	3997	40.79	4996	999	6245	1249	3.05	32.71	139	27	0.01
3019	Test List 19	5000	155	6015	38.81	7518	1503	9397	1879	4.82	21.74	1219	243	97.41
3020	Test List 20	5000	85	5255	61.82	6568	1313	8210	1642	2.65	24.88	813	162	51.70
	Total/Average	1,000,035	31,054	$1,310,708	$42.20	$1,638,375	$1638	$2,047,959	2048	4.85	19.30	$314,708	$315	100.00%

[a] Based on net sales assuming a 2.1% return rate.

Exhibit 18-10 Mail Plan—Notes *Exhibit 18-10 shows a sample mail plan which would be put together before a mailing. The primary purpose of putting together such a plan is to build the sales and profits projection for the total mailing by estimating the performance of each list separately.*

Column 1 contains the key code used on the response device to indicate the list from which each order is obtained.

Column 2 contains a written description of the list.

Column 3 shows the mail quantity of each list.

Columns 4 through 6 detail the expected average order size, response rate, and resulting gross sales per thousand for each list. These results applied to the mail quantity provide the expected total gross sales for each list, which are displayed in column 7.

Column 8 contains the expected net sales per thousand which is estimated from the gross sales by applying a return factor.

Column 9 indicates the total catalog mailing cost, while column 10 expresses that selling cost as a percentage of net sales.

Column 11 displays the expected pretax profit which is derived by subtracting the merchandise cost, operating cost, fixed cost allocation and selling cost from the expected net sales. All of these calculations can be approximated readily using the procedure shown in Exhibits 18-1 and 18-2.

Column 12 gives the resulting profit per thousand and the final column shows profit as a percent of net sales.

Exhibit 18-11 Mail Report—Notes *Exhibit 18-11 shows a sample mail report which would be generated during the course of a mailing.*

Columns 1 through 3 include the source code, list description, and actual mail quantity, respectively.

Columns 4 and 5 display the actual cumulative orders and sales as of the date of the report.

Column 6 contains the average order size derived by dividing the cumulative sales by the cumulative orders.

Column 7 displays the adjusted sales, which are obtained by adding a prorata allocation of the uncoded sales to each list. The adjusted sales per thousand in column 8 are derived by dividing the adjusted sales by the mail quantity.

Column 9 shows projected sales which are derived by dividing the adjusted sales by the estimated percentage done for the catalog at the time of the report. Historic order response patterns are applied to the mail dates for each list to determine the percent done. Column 10 divides column 9 by the mail quantity in thousands.

Column 11 contains the projected response rate which is obtained by projecting cumulative orders to completion in the same way that sales were projected, and dividing the projected orders by the mail quantity.

Column 12 contains the estimated selling cost percent of net sales obtained by dividing the promotional cost by the projected net sales for each list.

The projected profit and profit per thousand in columns 13 and 14 are derived by applying the relevant costs to the projected sales.

The last column contains the probability of meeting the 10% profit target. This figure is derived by comparing the projected response rate with the response rate required to produce a 10% profit given the average order size for each list. Taking the actual mail quantity into consideration, this figure represents the statistical probability that each list would achieve or exceed the target response rate when mailed again under similar conditions.

Self-Quiz

1. Contribution per unit or per average order is calculated by subtracting _____ from average unit selling price or from average order value.

2. Selling cost in direct marketing is the expense of _____ _____

3. It is helpful to treat creative expense and the extra cost of _____ _____ by budgeting them as part of _____ expense.

4. Typically, the more highly qualified an inquiry is the
   ☐ more costly it will be to generate.
   ☐ less costly it will be to generate.

5. In the short run, it is profitable to continue making conversion mailings to an inquiry list until the _____ of the last mailing is _____ the contribution it generates.

6. What are the three factors that determine profitability?
   a. _____
   b. _____
   c. _____

7. Catalog marketers should not only analyze overall results, but they should analyze results for each _____ and _____ of items as well.

8. A practical way to compute return on investment is to try to simulate _____ and expenses _____ as they are expected to occur.

9. Name three strategies that might be applied to improving return on investment for a catalog operation.

   a. _____

   b. _____

   c. _____

10. In order to expand an ongoing direct marketing program, it is wise to devote a portion of each campaign to _____.

11. When analyzing results of a campaign, uncoded response should be _____ to _____ in the same proportion as _____.

12. Making rollout promotion decisions is greatly aided by calculating the statistical probability of that each test will exceed _____.

Pilot Project

You have a mail order item that sells for $45. Your total cost, including product cost, shipping and handling costs, estimated returned goods, and overhead is $29. Your mailing cost is $350 per thousand.

Considering your unit profit per sale and your cost per thousand mailed, perform the following calculations.

1. Number of orders required per thousand to break even.

2. Number of orders required per thousand to make a 10 percent profit.

CHAPTER NINETEEN

Idea Development and Testing

"We've got to develop ideas with breakthrough potential and test their validity" is an oft-repeated statement in direct marketing circles. The never-ending thirst for the breakthrough is motivated by fantastic pay-off potentials. "Book-of-the-Month Club" was a breakthrough concept. It led to billions of dollars of book sales. Newspaper and magazine inserts. The "Gold Box" concept. TV support for other media. Ink-jet imaging. Each a gigantic breakthrough.

But how does one develop breakthrough ideas? Are there techniques to be applied? Yes.

Brainstorming

Brainstorming, first popularized in the 1950s by Alex Osborne of BBD&O, continues to be one of the most effective methods of finding new creative solutions to difficult problems. Scores of examples could be cited of breakthroughs that have resulted from brainstorming, but a few will suffice. First, some house rules for brainstorming.

House Rules for Brainstorming

Select a leader. Let the leader take all responsibility for contact with reality; everyone else in the brainstorming meeting is to "think wild." In the brainstorming meeting, the leader plays a low-key role. It's important to avoid an influence on the participants. The duties of the leader are:

- To see that detailed notes are taken on all ideas expressed
- To see that the agenda and time schedule are adhered to
- To admonish any critical thinkers in the group—no negative thinking is allowed during the brainstorming session
- To see that the group takes time to "build up" each idea
- To keep all participants involved and contributing

Rules during Brainstorming

1. Suspend all critical judgment of your own—or other people's—ideas. Don't ask yourself if this is a *good idea* or a *bad idea*. Accept it and rack your brain for ways to improve the concept.

2. Welcome "freewheeling," off-the-wall thinking. Wild, crazy, funny, far-out ideas are important. Why? Because they frequently shock us into a totally new viewpoint of the problem.

3. Quantity, not quality, is the objective during the brainstorm session. This may sound contradictory. It's not. Remember, every member of the group has been briefed on the problem in advance. You have a carefully planned agenda of material to cover. Consequently, your group is well directed toward the right problem. Therefore we can say, "Go for quantity in the idea session."

4. Build up each idea. Here's where most so-called brainstorm sessions fail. They just collect ideas as fast as they come and let it go at that. The leaders should carefully slow the group down so they stop with each idea and help build it up. Enhance each idea, no matter how crazy or off-beat it may seem.

It's the leader's responsibility to see that these four guidelines are adhered to in every meeting, but he or she should do this in a very low-key, informal manner. It is important that the leader does not become a dominant, authority figure in meetings.

Brainstorming is part of a three-phase process.

1. Before you start, create an agenda and carefully define problem(s) in writing.

2. Set quotas for ideas and a time limit for each section of the agenda.

3. Review the house rules with participants before each brainstorming session.

After the session is over, then—and only then—use your normal everyday judgment to logically select ideas with the most potential from all available alternatives.

Brainstorming: Example 1

The problem: Insurance companies are not allowed to give free gifts as an incentive for applying for an insurance policy. How can we offer a free gift and stay within the law? That was the brainstorming problem. Sounds like an impossible problem. Right? Wrong. Brainstorming participants broke through with a positive solution, a blockbuster.

The breakthrough: The brainstorming idea that hit pay dirt was to offer the free gift to everyone, whether they apply for the policy or not.

Result: A 38 percent increase in applications.

Brainstorming: Example 2

The problem: How can we avoid paying postage for sending prizes to "no" entrants in an "everybody wins" sweepstakes? (Possible savings in postage to the marketer—if the problem could be solved—was about $250,000.)

The breakthrough: We asked "no" entrants to provide a stamped, self-addressed envelope. We included a prize in the shipping carton for those who said "yes." (The Post Office Department approved the requirement at the time.)

Result: This was the most successful sweepstakes contest the sponsor ever conducted. The sponsor also enjoyed savings of $250,000 in postage.

Brainstorming: Example 3

The problem: We have thirty-six competitors selling to schools. They all promise "prompt shipment" of their pompons. How can we dramatize the fact that we ship our pompons in twenty-four hours and thus capture the bulk of the market?

The breakthrough: We inserted a Jiffy Order Card in the catalog, in addition to the regular order form, featuring Guaranteed Shipment Within 24 Hours.

Result: Pompon sales increased a dramatic 40 percent!

Brainstorming: Example 4

The problem: A leading agricultural chemical company manufactures both a corn herbicide and corn insecticide. Each product has its own positioning in the farm market, and each product has a different share of market in various geographic areas across the nation. How can new users for each product be won over from competition?

The breakthrough: Create a combination rebate program. Because the ratio of herbicide to insecticide remains relatively constant regardless of farm size, offer a rebate on *both* products when purchased at the same time.

Result: A significant number of farmers who had planned to purchase the two products from different manufacturers took advantage of the rebate offer and purchased both products from one manufacturer, with an average order of $25,000.

Fantasy Games

Of all the games creative people play, my favorites are fantasy games. These can be defined as games that enable one to reach out for satisfaction of his or her most fervent wishes. Here's a fantasy game anyone can play in a group or alone. The rules are simple: before you charge into the solution to a direct marketing problem, write three words on the top of a piece of paper—"I wish that. . . ." Then complete the sentence with your most fervent wish. Let's take some examples:

Fantasy 1. Some time ago, someone probably said, "I wish I could find a way to spread my advertising sales cost over several books rather then one." Out of it came the negative option and the Book-of-the-Month Club. A marketing triumph.

Fantasy 2. A client recently expressed this wish: "I wish we could cut our bad debts in half." A fantasy? Not at all. Brainstorming provided a way to cut the client's bad debts by 80 percent!

Fantasy 3. "I wish that we could find a way to contact customers just one week before their supplies are depleted." A unique computer system to accomplish exactly that came out of this wish.

Lateral Thinking

Recently I sent a memo to all of our writers, asking the question, "What do you do when your creative process turns blah?" Here is the reply of one of our senior writers: "I use the principles of random word technique and lateral thinking. I also like to use the Think Tank, a piece of gadgetry, designed by Savo Bojicic of University of Ontario. It forces the user to break the habit of logical, vertical thinking and opens the mind to creative, uninhibited lateral thought. Here's how I use the Think Tank:

First, I twist the dials on the sides of the Think Tank to jumble up the words inside. Second, I copy down six random words that appear in the window of the Think Tank. Third, I spend at least five minutes with each word, using word associations and so forth, that relate to the problem I'm trying to solve. Usually one or more of the words will "trigger" an idea. Here's an example:

My problem was to come up with some new ideas on how to get more credit card holders for Amoco. I twirled the dial on the Think Tank and the word "water" popped into the window. In a matter of milliseconds my free, stream-of-consciousness thinking was set in motion and led to a unique idea. Water made me think of boats. Boats need gasoline, just as cars do (a good-size cruiser may spend $75 to $100 or more for a fill-up). There are Amoco gas pumps at marinas on the water. Why not send our regular credit card solicitation package with a special letter and special appeal to a list of boat owners? (Credit the lateral thinking process with this breakthrough idea.)

Creative Stimulators

The degree of truly creative output is directly related to two factors: clear and specific definitions of problems to be solved and the right "atmosphere" for developing creative solutions.

Frank Daniels, a former creative director with Stone & Adler, has a system for stimulating creative people. Using a long-established technique for idea stimulation, he provides creative people with eight "stimulators" designed to expand their thinking. The examples that follow were applied to the Lanier Company, manufacturers of dictating equipment. Creativity was being stimulated for promoting a minirecorder, Lanier's Pocket Secretary. Each of the eight stimulators is accompanied by a key thought and a series of questions designed to promote creative solutions.

Can We Combine?

Combining two or more elements often results in new thought processes. These questions are designed to encourage brainstorming participants to think in terms of combinations.

Key thought: Combine appropriate parts of well-known things to emphasize the benefits of our product. "Think of owning a Rolls-Royce the size of a Volkswagen" (Lanier Pocket Secretary).

- What can be combined physically or conceptually to emphasize product benefits?
- Can the product be combined with another so that both benefit?
- Where in the product offer would a combination of thoughts be of most help?
- What opposites can be combined to show a difference from competitive products?
- What can we combine with our product to make it more fun to own, use, look at?
- Can part of one of our benefits be combined with part of another to enhance both?
- Can newness be combined with tradition?
- Can a product benefit be combined with a specific audience need through visual devices? Copy devices?
- What can we combine from the advertising and sales program to the benefit of both? Can salespersons' efforts be combined into advertising?
- Can we demonstrate product advantages by using "misfit" combination demonstration?
- Can we combine manufacturing information performance tests with advertising to demonstrate advantages?

Time Elements

Saving time and having extra time are conventional human wants. This series of questions is designed to expand one's thinking toward making time a plus factor in the product offer.

Key thought: Alter time factor(s) in present offer, present schedules, and present product positioning to motivate action.

- Does seasonal timing have an effect on individual benefits?
- Can present seasonal timing be reversed for special effect?
- Can limited offers be effective?
- Can early buyers be given special consideration?
- Can off-season offers be made?
- Are there better days, weeks, or months for our offers?
- Can we compress or extend present promotional sequencing?
- Can our price be keyed to selected times of the week, month, year?
- Can we feature no-time-limit offers?
- Can we feature limited time offers?
- Can we feature fast delivery or follow-up?

Can We Add?

An axiom of selling is that the customer often unconsciously compares the added benefits of a competitor's product with those of your product. The products with the most added benefits traditionally sell better. These questions are designed to ferret out added benefits for a particular product.

Key thought: Look for ways to express benefits by relating functional advantages of unrelated products or things. "We've taken all the best cassette recorder features and added one from the toaster" (pop-out delivery).

- What has been added to our product that's missing from others?
- Do we have a deficiency due to excess that can be turned into advantage?
- Is our product usable in many different ways aside from the intended use?
- Is our product instantly noticeable? Is it unusual in terms of size, shape, color? What unrelated symbols can we use to emphasize this unique characteristic?
- Does our product make something easier? What have we added by taking this something away?
- Does our product make order out of chaos or meaningful chaos out of total chaos? What have we added by taking this something away?
- What does the purchase of our product add to the buyer's physical situation, mental condition, subconscious condition, present condition, future condition?
- Where would the buyer be if he or she does not purchase? What would be missing from the buyer's life?
- Does our product give its full benefit to the buyer immediately or does he or she build up (add to) his well-being through continued possession?

Can We Subtract?

Taking away can often be as appealing as adding to. Less weight, less complexity, less fuss, less bother are fundamental appeals. These questions steer brainstorming participants in that direction.

Key thought: Subtract from the obvious to focus attention on benefits of our product/service. "We've weighed all the minirecorders and made ours lighter."

- What deficiencies does our product have competitively?
- What advantage do we have?
- What features are the newest? The most unusual?
- How can our product use/cost be "minimized" over time?
- Can a buyer use less of another product if he or she buys ours?
- Can the evidence of total lack of desire for our product be used to illustrate benefits?
- Can the limitations of our benefits be used as an appeal?
- What does lack of our product in the buyer's living habits do to her or him?
- Does our product offer a chance to eliminate any common element in all competitive products?
- Does our product reduce or eliminate (subtract) anything in the process of performing its work?
- Will our product deflate (subtract from) a problem for the buyer?

Can We Make Associations?

Favorable associations are often the most effective way to emphasize product benefits. "Like Sterling on silver," a classic example of a favorable association, is an [observation] [saying] [remark] [comment] that accrues to the benefit of the product being compared with other products.

Key thought: Form a link with unrelated things or situations to emphasize benefits.

- Can we link our product to another already successful product to emphasize benefits?
- Can we appeal to popular history, literature, poetry, art to emphasize benefits?
- What does the potential buyer associate with our product? How can we use this association to advantage?
- When does the potential buyer associate our product with potential use?
- Can associations be drawn with present or future events?
- Can associations be made with abstractions that can be expressed visually, musically, with words and so forth?
- Can funny, corny, challenging associations be made?

- Can associations be made with suppliers of component parts?
- Is our product so unique it needs no associations?
- Can our product be associated with many different situations?

Can We Simplify?

What is the simple way to describe and illustrate our major product bene-fit? As sophisticated as our world is today, the truism persists that people relate best to simple things. These questions urge participants to state benefits with dramatic simplicity.

Key thought: Dramatize benefits individually or collectively with childishly simple examples, symbols, images.

- Which of our appeals is strongest over our competition? How can we simplify to illustrate?
- Is there a way to simplify *all* our benefits for emphasis?
- Where is most of the confusion about our product in the buyer's mind?
- Can we illustrate by simplification?
- Is our appeal abstract? Can we substitute simple, real visualizations to emphasize?
- Could a familiar quotation, picture, be used to make our appeal more understandable?
- Is our product complex? Can we break it up (literally) into more under-standable pieces to emphasize benefits?
- Can I overlap one benefit with another to make product utility more un-derstandable?
- Can I contrast an old way of doing something with the confusing part of our product to create understanding?
- Is product appeal rigidly directed at too small a segment of the market? Too broad a segment?
- Can we emphasize benefits by having an unskilled person or child make good use of the product in a completely out-of-context situa-tion?

Can We Substitute?

The major product benefit for our product is often so similar to major product benefits of competitive products that it is difficult for the con-sumer to perceive the difference. Substituting another theme, such as Avis did when the company changed its theme to "We Try Harder," can often es-tablish a point of difference. These questions inspire participants to think in terms of substitution.

Key thought: Substitute the familiar for another familiar theme for em-phasis; substitute the unfamiliar for the familiar for emphasis.

- Can a well-known theme for another product be substituted for our theme, or can a well-known benefit for another product be substituted for our benefit?

- Can an incongruous situation be used to focus emphasis on our theme or benefits?
- Can a series of incongruous situations be found for every benefit we have? Can they be used in one ad? Can they form a continuity series of ads?
- What can be substituted for our product appeal that will emphasize the difference between us and our competitors?
- Can an obviously dissimilar object be substituted for the image of our product?
- Can a physical object be used to give more concrete representation of a product intangible?
- Is our product replacing a process rapidly becoming dated? Can we substitute the past for the present, the future for the past or the present?
- Can we visualize our product where the competitor's product is normally expected to be?
- Can we visualize our product as the only one of its kind in the world, as if there were no other substitutes for our product?

Can We Make a Reversal?

The ordinary can become extraordinary as usual situations are reversed. A man doing the wash. A woman pumping gas. A trained bear pushing a power mower. These questions are designed to motivate participants to think in terms of reversing usual situations.

Key thought: Emphasize a benefit by completely reversing the usual situation.

- What are the diametrically opposed situations for each of our product benefits?
- For each copy point already established, make a complete reverse statement.
- How would a totally uninformed person describe our product?
- Can male- and female-oriented roles be reversed?
- Can art and copy be totally reversed to emphasize a point?
- How many incongruous product situations can be shown graphically? Verbally?
- Can we find humor in the complete reversal of anticipated product uses or benefits?

Test the Big Things

Whether testable ideas come out of pure research, brainstorming, or self-developed creativity, the same picture applies: *test the big things.* Trivia testing, for example, testing the tilt of a postage stamp or testing the effect of various colors of paper stock, are passé. Breakthroughs are possible only when you test the big things. Six big areas from which breakthroughs emerge are:

1. The products or services you offer

2. The media you use (lists, print, and broadcast)

3. The propositions you make

4. The copy platforms you use

5. The formats you use

6. The timing you choose

Five of the areas for testing appear on most published lists these days. But testing new products and new product features is rarely recommended. Yet everything starts with the product or service you offer.

Many direct marketers religiously test new ads, new mailing packages, new media, new copy approaches, new formats, and new timing schedules season after season with never a thought to testing new product features. Finally, the most imaginative of creative approaches fails to overcome the waning appeal of the same old product. And still another product bites the dust.

This need not happen. For example, consider the most commonplace of mail order items, the address label. Scores of firms offer them in black ink on standard white stock. Competition is keen: prices all run about the same. From this variety of competitive styles, however, a few emerge with the new product features: gold stock, colored ink, seasonal borders, and so forth. Tests are made to determine appeal. The new product features appeal to a bigger audience.

Projectable Mailing Sample Sizes

Determining mail sample sizes for testing purposes was covered thoroughly in Chapter 8, "Mailing Lists." As we pointed out, a 5,000 test of a given list is usually adequate to get a "feel" of responsiveness but continuations are almost certain to vary because of time lapse, seasonality, change in list sources, economics, weather conditions, consumer behavior, and a host of other factors.

Some direct marketers live by probability tables that tell the mailer what the sample size must be at various response levels within a specified error limit, such as 5 or 10 percent. No one argues the statistical validity of probability tables. Probability tables can't be relied on too heavily because it is impossible to construct a truly scientific sample. However, such tables, within limits, can be helpful. Table 19-1 is based on a 95 percent confidence level at various limits of error.

Testing Components versus Testing Mailing Packages

In the endless search for breakthroughs, the question continually arises: In direct mail, should we test components or mailing packages? There are two schools of thought on this. The prevailing one is that the big breakthroughs come about through the testing of completely different mailing packages as opposed to testing individual components within a mailing package. Something can be learned from each procedure, of course. In my opinion, however, the more logical procedure is to first find the big difference in mailing packages and then follow with tests of individual components in the losing packages, which can often make the winning packages even better.

In package testing, one starts with a complete concept and builds all the components to fit the image of the concept. Consider the differences between these two package concepts:

	Package 1	*Package 2*
Envelope	9″ × 12″	No. 10
Letter	Eight-page, stapled	Four-sheet (two sides) computer written
Circular	None	Four-page, illustrated
Order form	8½″ × 11″, perforated stub	8½″ × 3⅔″

The differences between these two packages concepts are considerable. Chances are great that there will be a substantial difference in response. Once the winning package evolves, component tests make excellent sense. Let us say the 9″ × 12″ package is the winner. A logical subsequent test would be to fold the same inserts into a 6″ × 9″ envelope. A reply envelope may be considered as an additional test. Computerizing the first page of the eight-page letter could be still another test.

How to Test Print Advertising

For direct marketing practitioners who are multimedia users, testing print advertising is just as important as testing direct mail. And, as with direct mail, it is important that the tests be constructed in such a way as to produce valid results.

Gerald Schreck, media director of Doubleday Advertising Company, New York, gave the following pointers on A/B split tests in an *Advertising Age* feature article.

The split helps you determine the relative strengths of different ads. For example, you can run two ads, A and B, in a specific issue or edition of a publication so that two portions of the total run are equally divided and identical in circulation. The only difference is that ad A will run in half of the issue and ad B will run in the other half. For measuring the strength of the ads, a split includes an offer requiring your reader to act by writing or sending in a coupon. Then all you need do is compare the responses with the individual ads. If done properly this method can be accurate to two decimal points. You also have the advantage of real-world testing to find out what people actually do, not just what they say they'll do. And, because all factors are held equal, the difference in results can be attributed directly to your advertising. (See Exhibit 19-1.)

Exhibit 19-1. Variations in the Uses of Splits

A/B Split	Clump Split	Flip-Flop Split
A	A	A
B	A	B
A	A	B
B	B	A
	B	
	B	

A/B splits. In an ideal situation, an issue of a split-run publication will carry ad A in every other copy with ad B in the alternate copies.

Clump splits. Most often, however, publications cannot produce an exact A/B split. They will promise a clump. That is, every lift of fifty copies, for instance, will be evenly split or even every lift of twenty-five or ten. The clump can be very accurate when the test is done in large circulations.

Flip-flops. For publications that offer no split at all, you can create your own. Take two comparable publications, X and Y. Run ad A in X and ad B in Y for the first phase. Then for the second phase, reverse the insertions: Ad B in X and ad A in Y. Total the respective results for A and B and compare.

The split that isn't. We recently asked one magazine publisher if he ran splits. The production manager told us, "Oh, yes, we run a perfect split. Our circulation divides exactly—one-half east of the Mississippi and one-half west." Look out. That is not a valid split.

Although the A/B split can't tell you why individuals respond to your ad, the technique can tell you what they responded to. And a real bonus is that when you have completed your tests, you'll have a list of solid prospects.

In the A/B split, how can you compare one run against another run of the same ad? You can "key" coupons or response copy by:

1. *Dating.* On your coupons, try JA388NA for January 3, 1988 in *Newsweek* for ad A and JA388NB for the same insertion of ad B.

2. *Department numbers.* Use Dept. A for ad A and Dept. B for B in your company's address.

3. *Color of coupon.* One color for A, another for B.

4. *Color of ink.*

5. *Names.* In ad A, ask readers to send correspondence to Mr. Anderson, for B, have them write to Mr. Brown.

6. *Telephone numbers.*

7. *Shape of coupon.*

8. *IBM punches.* You don't even need a computer. Just select a pattern you can read.

9. *The obvious.* Right on the coupon, use "For Readers of *Glamour*" in A and "For *Glamour* Readers" in B.

10. *Address information.* Mr., Mrs., Miss in A; Mr., Ms., for B.

11. *Abbreviations.* In your address, New York for A, N.Y. for B.

12. *Typeface.* In coupon A, all caps for NAME, and so forth, and in Coupon B, upper-and lower-case for Name, and so forth.

The possibilities are virtually unlimited. All you need is a code that's in keeping with your ad and the publication, one you find is easy to understand and use.

Telescopic Testing

While it is certainly necessary to construct meaningful A/B split tests, they do have limitations. When the advertiser runs an A/B split test he or she doesn't know what would have happened if she or he had been able to run ad C against ads A and B and, additionally, ads D, E, F, and G—all simultaneously, all in the same edition, all under measurable conditions.

Today, testing to find the best ad among a multiplicity of ads all tested under the same conditions is quite feasible. The method is widely known as *telescopic testing*. Telescopic testing is simply the process of telescoping an entire season of test ads into one master test program. (Examples of telescopic testing were given in Chapter 16.) Regional editions of publications and other developments make telescopic testing possible. Indeed,

Table 19-1. Test Sample Sizes Required for 95 Percent Confidence Level for Mailing Response Levels from 0.1 to 4.0 Percent

R (Response)	.02	.04	.06	.08	.10	.12	.14	.16	.18	.20	.30	.40	.50	.60	.70
							Limits of Error (expressed as percentage points)								
.1	95,929	23,982	10,659	5,995	3,837	2,665	1,957	1,499	1,184	959	426	240	153	106	78
.2	191,666	47,916	21,296	11,979	7,667	5,324	3,911	2,994	2,366	1,917	852	479	307	213	156
.3	287,211	71,803	31,912	17,951	11,488	7,978	5,861	4,487	3,546	2,872	1,276	718	459	319	234
.4	382,564	95,641	42,507	23,910	15,303	10,627	7,807	5,977	4,723	3,826	1,700	956	612	425	312
.5	477,724	119,431	53,080	29,858	19,109	13,270	9,749	7,464	5,987	4,777	2,123	1,194	764	530	390
.6	572,693	143,173	63,632	35,793	22,908	15,908	11,687	8,948	7,070	5,727	2,545	1,432	916	636	467
.7	667,470	166,867	74,163	41,717	26,699	18,541	13,622	10,429	8,240	6,675	2,966	1,669	1,068	741	545
.8	762,054	190,514	84,673	47,628	30,482	21,168	15,552	11,907	9,408	7,621	3,387	1,905	1,219	847	622
.9	856,447	214,112	95,160	53,528	34,258	23,790	17,478	13,382	10,573	8,564	3,806	2,141	1,370	951	699
1.0	950,648	237,662	105,628	59,415	38,026	26,407	19,401	14,854	11,736	9,506	4,225	2,376	1,521	1,056	776
1.1	1,044,656	261,164	116,072	65,291	41,786	29,018	21,319	16,322	12,897	10,446	4,643	2,611	1,671	1,160	853
1.2	1,138,472	284,618	126,496	71,155	45,539	31,624	23,234	17,788	14,055	11,385	5,060	2,846	1,821	1,265	929
1.3	1,232,097	308,024	136,899	77,006	49,284	34,225	25,145	19,251	15,211	12,321	5,476	3,080	1,971	1,369	1,006
1.4	1,325,529	331,382	147,280	82,845	53,021	36,820	27,051	20,711	16,364	13,255	5,891	3,314	2,121	1,473	1,082
1.5	1,418,769	354,692	157,640	88,673	56,751	39,410	28,954	22,168	17,515	14,188	6,305	3,547	2,270	1,576	1,158
1.6	1,511,818	377,954	167,980	94,489	60,473	41,995	30,853	23,622	18,664	15,118	6,719	3,780	2,419	1,680	1,234
1.7	1,604,674	401,168	178,297	100,292	64,187	44,574	32,748	25,073	19,811	16,047	7,132	4,012	2,567	1,783	1,310
1.8	1,697,338	424,334	188,592	106,083	67,894	47,148	34,639	26,521	20,955	16,973	7,543	4,243	2,716	1,886	1,385
1.9	1,789,810	447,452	198,868	111,863	71,592	49,717	36,526	27,966	22,096	17,898	7,955	4,474	2,863	1,988	1,461
2.0	1,882,090	470,523	209,121	117,631	75,284	52,280	38,410	29,407	23,235	18,821	8,365	4,705	3,011	2,091	1,536

Table 19-1. Test Sample Sizes Required for 95 Percent Confidence Level for Mailing Response Levels from 0.1 to 4.0 Percent

R (Response)	Limits of Error (expressed as percentage points)														
	.02	.04	.06	.08	.10	.12	.14	.16	.18	.20	.30	.40	.50	.60	.70
2.1	1,974,178	493,544	219,352	123,386	78,967	54,838	40,289	30,846	24,372	19,742	8,774	4,935	3,158	2,193	1,611
2.2	2,066,074	516,518	229,564	129,129	82,643	57,391	42,165	32,282	25,507	20,661	9,182	5,165	3,306	2,295	1,686
2.3	2,157,778	539,444	239,753	134,861	86,311	59,938	44,036	33,715	26,638	21,578	9,590	5,394	3,452	2,397	1,761
2.4	2,249,290	562,322	249,920	140,581	89,972	62,480	45,903	35,145	27,769	22,493	9,997	5,623	3,599	2,499	1,836
2.5	2,340,609	585,152	260,068	146,288	93,624	65,017	47,767	36,572	28,896	23,406	10,403	5,851	3,745	2,600	1,911
2.6	2,431,737	607,934	270,192	151,983	97,269	67,547	49,627	37,996	30,021	24,317	10,807	6,079	3,891	2,702	1,985
2.7	2,522,673	630,668	280,296	157,667	100,907	70,074	51,483	39,416	31,144	25,227	11,211	6,307	4,036	2,803	2,059
2.8	2,613,416	653,354	290,380	163,339	104,537	72,595	53,335	40,834	32,264	26,134	11,615	6,534	4,181	2,904	2,133
2.9	2,703,968	675,992	300,440	168,998	108,159	75,110	55,183	42,249	33,382	27,039	12,017	6,760	4,326	3,004	2,207
3.0	2,794,328	698,582	310,480	174,645	111,773	77,620	57,026	43,661	34,497	27,943	12,419	6,986	4,471	3,105	2,281
3.1	2,884,495	721,124	320,499	180,281	115,380	80,125	58,867	45,070	35,611	28,845	12,820	7,211	4,615	3,205	2,355
3.2	2,974,470	743,618	330,496	185,904	118,979	82,623	60,702	46,476	36,721	29,745	13,220	7,436	4,759	3,305	2,428
3.3	3,064,254	766,063	340,471	191,516	122,570	85,118	62,535	47,878	37,830	30,642	13,619	7,660	4,903	3,404	2,501
3.4	3,153,845	788,461	350,427	197,115	126,154	87,607	64,364	49,278	38,936	31,538	14,017	7,884	5,046	3,504	2,574
3.5	3,243,244	810,811	360,360	202,703	129,730	90,089	66,188	50,675	40,040	32,432	14,414	8,108	5,189	3,603	2,647
3.6	3,332,452	833,113	370,271	208,278	133,298	92,568	68,009	52,069	41,141	33,325	14,811	8,331	5,332	3,702	2,720
3.7	3,421,467	855,367	380,163	213,842	136,859	95,041	69,825	53,460	42,240	34,214	15,207	8,554	5,474	3,801	2,793
3.8	3,510,290	877,572	390,031	219,393	140,412	97,507	71,638	54,848	43,336	35,103	15,601	8,776	5,616	3,900	2,865
3.9	3,598,921	899,730	399,878	224,932	143,957	99,969	73,446	56,233	44,430	35,989	15,995	8,997	5,758	3,998	2,938
4.0	3,687,360	921,840	409,706	230,460	147,494	102,426	75,252	57,615	45,522	36,874	16,388	9,218	5,900	4,097	3,010

with regional editions you can telescope a year's testing sequences into a single insertion, testing many ads simultaneously. *TV Guide* offers the best opportunity for telescopic testing. *TV Guide* publishes over 100 different editions. *Woman's Day* offers twenty-six regional editions. *Time,* with eight regional editions, makes it possible to test nine different ads or ad variations simultaneously.

Tom Collins, a pioneer in telescopic testing, has established a rule of thumb for estimating the minimum circulation you should buy for your ad tests to make results meaningful. First, start by assuming you need an average of 200 responses per appeal to be statistically valid. Then, multiply your allowable advertising cost per response by 200. Finally, multiply that figure by the number of key numbers in the test. This will give you the total minimum expenditure required to get meaningful results.

To clarify the technique further, let's say you want to test four new ads against a control ad, which we will call ad A. Your tests for the four new ads against the control ad will be structured as follows: A vs. B; A vs. C; A vs. D; A vs. E. Thus we have a total of five ads requiring eight different keys. (Ad A, the control ad, is being tested against a different ad in four separate instances and therefore requires four different keys.)

To read the results in this kind of test, we simply convert ad A to 100 percent, depending on the results achieved. In this way, ad C can be compared with ad E, for instance, even though they are not directly tested against one another. Now, let's say we want to test the four new ads in *TV Guide* against the control ad. Further, using the Collins formula, let's assume we need a circulation of two million to get 200 or more replies for each side of each two-way split. The type of schedule that would be placed in *TV Guide* to accomplish this objective appears on the previous page. Note that a careful review of the markets selected for each split (region) shows that all markets are balanced geographically.

Telescopic testing is not limited to regional editions of publications. Newspaper inserts serve as an ideal vehicle for such testing. The test pieces are intermixed at the printing plant before being shipped to the newspaper. All test pieces, however, must be exactly the same size. Otherwise, newspapers cannot handle them on their automatic inserting equipment.

Using full-page card inserts in magazines is still another way to test simultaneously a multiplicity of ads. Scores of magazines now accept such inserts. It is important to remember that in telescopic testing we are looking for breakthroughs, not small differences. As Collins puts it, "We are not merely testing ads, we are testing hypotheses. Then when a hypothesis appears to have been proved by the results, it is often possible to construct other, even more successful ads, on the same hypothesis."

Test hypotheses tend to fall into four main categories:

1. What is the best price and offer?

2. Who is the best prospect?

3. What is the most appealing product advantage?

4. What is the most important ultimate benefit? (By "ultimate benefit" we mean the satisfaction of such basic human needs as pride, admiration, safety, wealth, peace of mind, and so on.)

Idea development and testing are soul mates. The two things to keep uppermost in mind are: (1) strive for breakthrough ideas and (2) test the big things.

Split 1—Ad A vs. Ad B		*Split 2—Ad A vs. Ad C*	
Edition	Circulation	Edition	Circulation
San Francisco-Metro	750,000	Northern Wisconsin	170,000
Pittsburgh	225,000	Philadelphia	230,000
Detroit	225,000	Cleveland	55,000
South Georgia	67,000	Kansas City	230,000
Iowa	210,000	Western New England	175,000
Phoenix	275,000	North Carolina	272,000
Western Illinois	87,000	Colorado	139,000
Northern Illinois	186,000	Illinois/Wisconsin	225,000
	2,025,000	Gulf Coast	125,000
		Minneapolis/St. Paul	126,000
		Central California	115,000
		Southeast Texas	64,000
		West Virginia	165,000
			2,091,000

Split 3—Ad A vs. Ad D		*Split 4—Ad A vs. Ad E*	
Edition	Circulation	Edition	Circulation
Central Ohio	210,000	Eastern New England	665,000
Michigan State	309,000	Chicago Metro	475,000
Western New York State	65,000	Orlando	140,000
Central Indiana	230,000	Oklahoma State	184,000
San Diego	255,000	St. Louis	235,000
New Hampshire	141,000	Eastern Illinois	100,000
Portland	195,000	Missouri	141,000
Eastern Virginia	160,000	Eugene	45,000
Kansas State	92,000	Idaho	57,000
Tucson	70,000		2,042,000
North Dakota	65,000		
Eastern Washington St.	145,000		
Evansville-Paducah	104,000		
	2,041,000		

Self-Quiz

1. What are the duties of the leader in brainstorming?

   a. _____

   b. _____

   c. _____

   d. _____

   e. _____

2. What are the three phases of the brainstorming process?

   a. _____

   b. _____

   c. _____

3. One way to solve a difficult problem is to fantasize. The first three words of your expressed desire should be: _____

   _____.

4. What is lateral thinking?

   _____

   _____

   _____

5. What are the six big things to test?

   a. _____

   b. _____

   c. _____

   d. _____

   e. _____

   f. _____

6. What is the safest rule to follow in testing mailing lists?

   _____

   _____

   _____

7. In direct mail testing, which is preferable?

   ☐ Testing components   ☐ Testing complete mailing packages

8. Name six ways to key a print ad.

   a. _____

   b. _____

   c. _____

   d. _____

   e. _____

   f. _____

9. Define telescopic testing.

   _____

   _____

   _____

10. Name the four categories into which hypotheses seem to fall.

   a. _____

   b. _____

   c. _____

   d. _____

Pilot Project

You are engaged in a fantasy game. Three wishes follow. Come up with at least three solutions for each of the wishes.

1. *I wish that* I could get all my customers to suggest friends who would likewise become customers.

2. *I wish that* I could get all my customers to pay their bills within forty-five days.

3. *I wish that* I could reach all the people in this country who are over six-feet tall.

CHAPTER TWENTY

Research for Direct Marketers

Overview

Since the inception of direct marketing, the primary method for assessing direct marketing programs has been the "in market" or "in-mail" test.

What has made the direct marketing process particularly appealing to marketers is that the results produced by these tests have been *measurable, quantifiable,* and *predictable.* In other words, these results have provided a quantified measurement of *overt* response in terms of "making the sale," "producing a qualified sales lead," or "stimulating someone to request further information."

By overlaying this overt behavior with geodemographic data, it has been possible to build statistical models that can define high-propensity-response groups, providing far more precise methods for marketing and prospecting.

Testing and the Total Marketing Research Process

The first and most important point to understand in marketing research for direct marketing, however, is that testing is an integral part of the total marketing research process. Testing is not an isolated marketing research activity and should not be treated as such.

The testing process consists of four phases:

1. Exploratory research

2. Pretest research

3. Tests

4. Posttests

(See Exhibit 20-1.)

Phase I: Exploratory Research

The *exploratory phase* deals with defining and understanding your target audience as well as the marketplace in which you compete. The focal point of the exploratory phase is *situation analysis* which deals with understanding the geodemographic characteristics of your target audience as well as the attitudes, habits, and needs—particularly those characteristics that are most influential on heavy, regular usage of your product or service. The situation analysis should also cover an understanding of the competition and market dynamics in terms of what attributes and benefits each competitive product or service brings to market, and why consumers are attracted to them. The end result of this situation analysis should be points of maximum leverage on which a direct marketing program can be developed. Such leverage points usually center on special ways of segmenting a target audience, ways or methods for reaching each specified target audience segment, and special ways of segmenting products or services.

Exhibit 20-1. The Total Marketing and Research Process

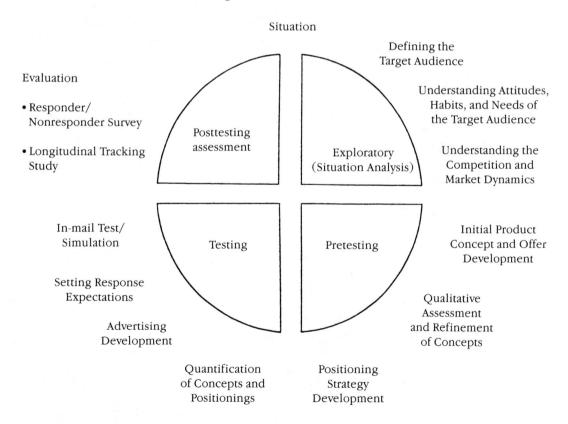

Phase II: Pretesting

The *pretesting phase* consists of developing, assessing, and refining the marketing and creative products before in-market testing. There are several issues which should be addressed in this phase:

- Determine that your product or service is offering an attribute or benefit that the consumer really wants—that is, something that is preemptive, setting it apart from the competition.
- Develop and refine the creative and the offer. In this area, qualitative research such as focus groups or in-depth individual interviews can help determine whether the creative approach is communicating information about the product or service and the offer in a manner that is clear, believable, and relevant to consumers in the target audience.
- Research usually referred to as copy testing can be used to assess alternative creative executions and offers. This research is usually quantitative, that is, a survey, in nature and is used to develop comparative profiles of the creative and the offer. Such research is useful in two ways. It helps to provide objective criteria for improving the creative or the offer, rather than giving them some subjective grade. Of even greater importance, however, is that this research can reduce the number of alternatives to be tested, thus greatly reducing test costs and increasing the accuracy of reading back-end results. Research done in the pretest phase can often help to uncover variables or clarify issues which should be addressed in the *testing phase.*

Phase III: Testing

One of the first questions asked by those businesses new to direct marketing is, "When can we stop testing?" And the answer of course is, "Never!" The testing process is dynamic and continuous (which is why the diagram on page 489 is a circle). The main objective in all testing is to learn, modify, and improve.

The *testing phase* brings together five key variables for assessment in the market:

- The product or service
- The media or method of accessing the defined target audience
- The time or season
- The advertising/communication
- The offer or promotion

The test plan consists of the combinations in which these variables will be tested as well as the determining of response expectations and financial objectives.

Although all of the elements of the test plan are crucial, the most important single variable in direct marketing is the media, or the access to the consumer, since this access provides the strongest point of leverage for all other test variables. In fact, if the media cannot provide access to qualified consumers in sufficient quantities, the remainder of the elements in the direct marketing mix become almost irrelevant by comparison. That is why testing is so critical to finding the lists that will access high-propensity prospects in sufficient quantities.

An alternative method of testing is simulation, which can be used in conjunction with live testing. Simulation systems such as STAR (Simulator Testing Advertising Response—a system developed by Direct Marketing Research Associates and Erard Moore Associates) predict response without running actual space advertising, package/statement inserts, or direct mail packages. Simulation can save time and costs by reducing the number of variables to be tested in market and often by eliminating the need to address variables or issues that are of little importance to the direct marketing mix.

Simulation uses a close facsimile of an actual ad or direct mail package mailed to a sample of consumers with a questionnaire and letter. Separate packages are mailed to test and control cells. Data from the questionnaires are combined with actual responses to the simulated mailing to develop a prediction of relative response performance.

Phase IV: Posttesting Assessment

Posttesting assessment is potentially the area of greatest strength for direct marketing research. Assessment attempts both the analysis of test response and the development of diagnostic information in order to determine *why* the response rate was achieved and *what* can be done to achieve higher response rates.

The analysis of response rates is a measurement of overt behavior in terms of making a sale, a request for more information, or qualifying a sales lead. Marketing research can also provide diagnostic insights which can help to measure the quality of the response For example, Responder/ Nonresponder surveys can help pinpoint issues:

- *Incremental sales:* The degree to which new consumers were attracted to the offer versus the sales' merely subsidizing current customers, particularly heavy or frequent buyers
- *Competitive conquest:* the degree to which competitive customers tried your product or service and were converted to regular customers
- *Attitudinal shifts:* the degree to which the brand image of your product or service was enhanced by direct advertising

In addition, questionnaires, which can help provide much added value to both the consumer and the marketer, can be included as an integral part of the mailing package.

- The response to relevant questions about the product or service helps to establish a vital two-way communication or dialogue between the marketer and the consumer.
- This dialogue can help establish a relationship with the consumer which can give the product or service a preemptive position in the mind of the consumer.
- The information provided by the consumer can be used to qualify or segment them, giving the marketer valuable insights into subsequent positioning of products or services and more precisely targeting the appropriate message to the appropriate segment.

Marketing Research for Traditional and Nontraditional Direct Marketers

Let's begin by comparing the key direct marketing problems faced by traditional direct marketers versus those confronting nontraditional direct marketers. Once these issues are appreciated, it will be easier to understand the role that marketing research needs to play in each of the two areas.

It has been said that in the land of the blind, the one-eyed man is king. Traditional direct marketing today finds itself in exactly the opposite environment: how to compete when everyone has the eyesight of an eagle. Thus traditional direct marketers today find themselves in a maturing industry in which the major competitors are experienced and sophisticated, many of the market segments are glutted with similar products and services, and everyone's mailbox is cluttered with very similar looking pieces.

Within such an environment, marketing research should address such issues as:

- Developing mailing pieces that cut through the mailbox clutter by more discretely and relevantly being targeted to specific consumer segments in terms of the offer and the visual and message elements. This could certainly help to dramatically increase response rates and help enhance the marketer's image while making the sale.
- More effectively prospecting for new customers by developing an in-depth understanding of the types and numbers of "high-propensity prospects" available, and translating these consumer segments into targetable groups which can be directly accessed. This could help reduce quantities mailed as well as mailing costs.
- Providing strategic direction for growing traditional direct marketing businesses in terms of identifying new product and service categories with high growth potential; assessing the most dynamic segments within each category; screening for the most viable products and services within each segment.

Nontraditional direct marketers such as consumer goods manufacturers and retailers are just beginning to explore the many possible applications which direct marketers can offer their businesses. These applications include:

- Institutional direct marketing programs in which the use of major consumer brands can be extended from home consumption to include institutional consumption.
- The use of direct marketing for a direct distribution system as an alternative or supplement to retail distribution. A direct marketing distribution system can be quite effective for name brands of clothing and gourmet food items that may require an inordinate number of stock keeping units (SKUs) and a great deal of copy and illustration in order to sell successfully.
- The use of direct marketing as a vehicle for testing new positionings for a brand economically and discretely, without telling the media or competitors and without disturbing your current franchise.
- Targeted promotions that can be used by retailers and manufacturers to provide specific measurable, projectable promotional programs to selected prospects and customers.
- Customized communications that can be used by retailers and manufacturers to deliver discrete, measurable messages targeted to specific customer or prospect profiles.
- The use of direct marketing as a media vehicle to provide direct access to selected customers and prospects for retailers and manufacturers.

The role of marketing research, as it relates to a number of nontraditional direct marketing approaches (see a description of the research process on page 488), can include two broad areas: the front-end, or development of programs; and the back-end, dealing with the measurement and assessment of these programs.

Direct Marketing Research for Consumer Products
Front-End Research

Let us now examine some specific examples in which marketing research can support direct marketing efforts for consumer products and services.

The first example will demonstrate the use of research in the initial phases, the *exploratory* and *pretest* phases, by defining target audience segments; and providing an understanding of these segments; translating this understanding into product/service positionings, an offer, and a relevant, believable, understandable message.

In the past, direct marketers have centered their research activities on analyzing consumers' geodemographic characteristics and purchase behaviors. Direct marketers used these approaches, because these two variables are most readily linked with list and prospect selection. Attitudinal, psychographic, and lifestyle data have been much underutilized by direct marketers because these factors are not readily translated to list or prospect selection.

To realistically define, understand, reach, and communicate with target audiences, however, it is imperative that research deal with consumers on all four relevant levels:

- Geodemographics
- Psychographics and lifestyles
- Attitudes
- Purchase behavior

All four factors must be dealt with. They must all be integrated to form pictures of "real" consumers, who they are and where they live (geodemographics); what their basic attitudes and values toward life are and how these attitudes are translated into the way these persons live (psychographics and lifestyles); their perceptions, attitudes, and values with respect to various product and service categories (attitudes); and how these perceptions, attitudes, and values translate into selection making in the marketplace (purchase behavior).

The *Stone & Adler Study of Consumer Behavior and Attitudes toward Direct Marketing* was the first attempt to perform such an interdisciplinary synthesis. The study was designed, fielded, and analyzed with the help of Goldring & Company, Inc., and the Home Testing Institute. Once the data was collected within each of the four levels, it was integrated through a software program called PAG (Positive Attribute Group); copyrighted by Goldring & Company, Inc., 1986.

PAG is a comprehensive analytical technique for determining the *combination* of purchase activities, demographics, psychographics and lifestyles, and attitudes toward direct marketing at work in the direct marketing environment. PAG enabled us to segment the direct marketing environment and identify the four variables and their combinations active in each segment.

The PAG program subsequently produced six consumer clusters arrayed in an order (of importance) which breathed life into each of the clusters.

Cluster 1: Mailbox Gourmets

Let us begin with the most important cluster for direct marketers: "Mailbox Gourmets." If anyone wonders who the magical 20–30 percent that almost all direct marketers target are, the answer is the Mailbox Gourmets (26 percent of the population).

In terms of psychographics and lifestyles, Mailbox Gourmets perceive themselves to be sophisticated. They want more of everything—especially travel. They are extremely active and involved and perceive themselves as not having enough leisure time.

Mailbox Gourmets are affluent. Their demographics show them to be above average in education, income, and engaged in white-collar occupations. This cluster is also female-intensive. Although three-fourths are married, this percentage is slightly below marriage averages. The family structure is less traditional with more two-paycheck families or single professionals, particularly women.

It is not surprising that their attitudes toward direct marketing are extremely positive. They enjoy it, are comfortable with it, and although most people perceive themselves to be novices when transacting by mail or phone, these people perceive themselves to be experts.

All of this information translates into direct marketing purchasing behavior that earns this cluster its name: they spend a lot (significantly more than any other cluster) and they buy often.

Cluster 2: Young Turks
In terms of psychographics and lifestyles, the "Young Turks" are very trendy, as one would expect. They also consider themselves to be—whether they are, in fact, or not—sophisticated and worldly.

Demographically, this group accounts for 10 percent of the households and form a perfect yuppie profile: they are single and male-intensive, well educated, and economically aspiring.

Although Young Turks are also very positive toward direct marketing, they tend to be cautious because they are emerging consumers. This makes them very "presentation sensitive." Because they are so active, they are more likely to order via 800 number than any other cluster group. The Young Turks are the second highest group in terms of dollars spent and purchase frequency, but their expenditures are significantly less than those of the Mailbox Gourmets.

Cluster 3: Life Begins at 50
The "Life-Begins-at-50" cluster comprised 7 percent of households and was completely middle-of-the-road in terms of psychographics and lifestyle.

Demographics indicate that these older consumers are "empty nesters": their children are grown and away at college or married. As a group they are engaged in a mixture of blue and white collar occupations.

Like the Young Turk, the Life-Begins-at-50 cluster is also quite positive but cautious toward direct marketing. The cautiousness, in this case, is due to the fact that these people are the experienced "old pros" who have been shopping direct for twenty to thirty years. This experience is, therefore, transformed into a demanding attitude. They know what they want and the marketer had better give it to them.

These data translate into direct marketing dollar expenditures and purchase frequencies just below those of the Young Turks; but the products this cluster is likely to buy are vastly different. The Life-Begins-at-50 cluster is more likely to buy higher ticket items such as home furnishings or housewares. They are also more likely to buy vitamins and minerals, and to belong to a book club. Young Turks, on the other hand, are more likely to purchase products related to self-indulgence such as electronic "toys" and sports equipment.

Cluster 4: Dear Occupant Now we come to the great faceless, nameless masses that account for 14 percent of households—"Dear Occupant." Actually, they are the leftovers in the clustering process and, therefore, represent those who were:

- Neither too positive nor negative in their attitudes
- Neither affluent nor destitute
- Neither the lightest nor heaviest buyers

As such they are truly the mundane, moderate, middle.

Cluster 5: Kitchen Patriots When members of these households (23% of total) are not out shopping at their favorite shopping mall or mass merchandiser, they are likely to be home reading the daily newspaper, a magazine, or their mail at the kitchen table à la Archie and Edith Bunker.

In terms of lifestyles and psychographics, this cluster is the backbone of traditional American morality and values:

- They are extremely patriotic.
- Home, family, and community are extremely important to them.
- They have sufficient leisure time, which is one reason they shop so much. In fact, many of them have more time than money.

Demographically, this group is blue-collar intensive, middle in income and education, and indexes highest among those fifty-five years old and older.

Although the Kitchen Patriots' attitudes toward direct marketing are basically negative, they like to browse through their mail, including direct mail pieces and catalogs. But because of these negative attitudes toward direct marketing, coupled with their propensity toward retail shopping, Kitchen Patriots tend to be non-direct-marketing buyers or light selective buyers at best.

Cluster 6: Above-It-Alls Finally, we have the most negative, the proretail cluster, the "Above-It-Alls." They are nearly a carbon copy of the Mailbox Gourmets with a major difference: while they are gourmets, they are antimailbox.

In terms of lifestyles and psychographics, this cluster is career-oriented, active and involved in fads and causes, perceives itself as taking a leadership position, and is athletic.

Demographically, they are somewhat more affluent than Mailbox Gourmets. They tend to be more traditional in household composition, wives are more often than not, full-time homemakers—which, of course, gives them more time for retail shopping. This cluster also tends to be more strictly suburban than the Mailbox Gourmets who are more split between suburbs and cities. The Above-It-Alls' attitude toward direct marketing is basically negative. In fact, not only do Above-It-Alls like mail, in general, much less than any other group, they don't like to browse, and, in particular, they don't see direct marketing as a convenience. Not surprisingly, this cluster rates as non-direct-marketing buyers or light, selective buyers, at best. They want to *see* and *touch* the merchandise first, try it on, and obtain instant gratification both in purchasing and returning merchandise.

Putting Attitudinal Research to Work for Your Business

If information is to be useful to a business, it must be analyzed and interpreted for strategic implications which lead to specific actions. Let us now take a look at how attitudinal data can be directly applied to business in terms of:

1. Profiling target audiences and product categories

2. Segmenting customers for precise file selection, and developing highly targeted products, services, and creative appeals

Profiling Target Audiences and Categories

There are two major reasons why a business may want to use target audience and category profiling:

1. For new business development

2. For expanding an established business

For new business development, it is important to know *who* are the users within a category. Not only is it important to know who they are geo-demographically for the purpose of list selection, but it is also important to know who they are attitudinally. Attitudinal understanding leads to meaningful positioning to the target audience. Thus the target audience can be communicated with in the most relevant, believable, and understandable manner.

For expanding an established business, profiling can provide an important perspective to the direct marketer by showing how high is up. Unfortunately, too many direct marketers are trapped by their house files;

they don't have the necessary information to make the best strategic use of media when prospecting.

Profiling can provide these insights by allowing direct marketers to compare customers on their files against category users on a national basis. Thus direct marketers can then judge whether they are obtaining their fair share of the "target audience pie." If they are not, they can then fine-tune their demographics for media selection. Even more importantly, they can fine-tune their creative approach and offer so that they have a better chance of being seen and read by their target audience prospect.

Let us briefly examine how such profiling and segmentation can be done. The first step is for the marketer to perform a buyer concentration analysis from her or his customer file as shown in Exhibit 20-2. Such a buyer concentration study will segment the file into groups of Heavy or Frequent Buyers, Medium Buyers, and Light or Infrequent Buyers.

Exhibit 20-2. Buyer Concentration Analysis

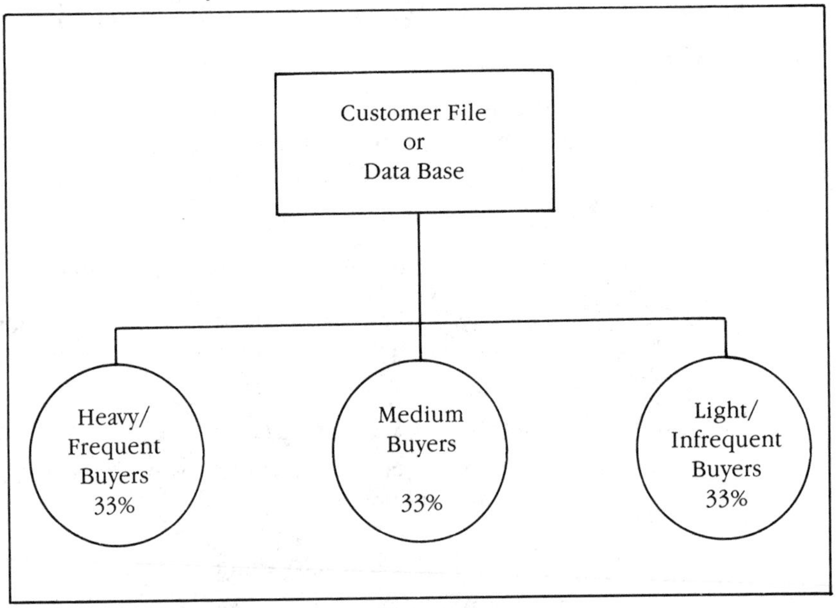

The second step consists of overlaying the buyer segments with attitudinal and lifestyle data, and developing a second level of segmentation as shown in Exhibit 20-3. This segmentation is accomplished by selecting a sample of names from the house file and administering a survey questionnaire containing attitudinal and lifestyle questions. By combining the answers to these questions with the geodemographic and purchase behavior data already on the file, PAG clusters can then be developed. At this stage, two analyses are critical: (1) the percentage of the customer file that comprises each of the six clusters; (2) the percentage of Light, Medium, and Heavy Buyers that comprised each of the six clusters.

Exhibit 20-3. Attitudinal and Lifestyle Overlay

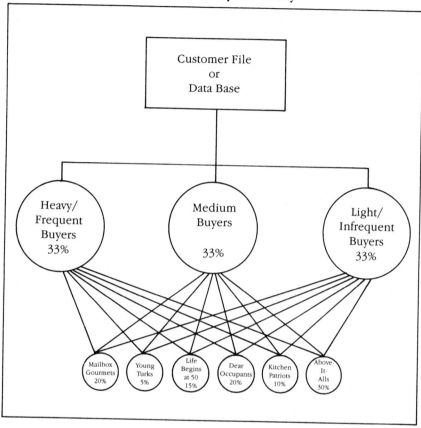

The third step consists of developing a profile comparing your customer file and a nationally representative sample of consumers (i.e., a consumer data base). This comparison allows you to determine whether or not you are getting your fair share of such groups as:

- Affluent/upscale consumers
- Younger or emerging consumers entering the marketplace
- Transitional consumers who are changing their lifestyles and their purchasing habits

For example, the comparative profile shown in Exhibit 20-4 points to a possible problem with the highest propensity direct marketing consumers who are significantly under-represented on the customer file. There could be similar problems if the buyer concentration analysis shows that a disproportionate number of Mailbox Gourmets, Young Turks, and Life-Begins-at-50 consumers are merely medium and light buyers.

The use of national consumer data bases can bring additional strategic marketing insights to your business when applied across a variety of product and service categories as well as segments within these categories.

Exhibit 20-4. Comparative Consumer Profile

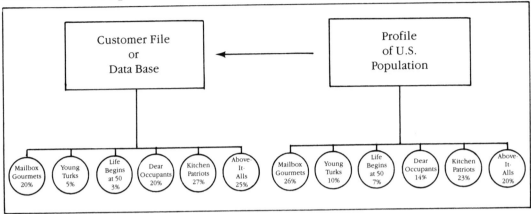

(See Chapter 2, "Data Base Marketing.") Let us review some examples of such applications in three diverse categories: Insurance, Credit Cards, and Clothing Catalogs.

Insurance Profiles   The *Stone & Adler Study of Behavior and Attitudes Toward Direct Marketing* examined both the incidence of insurance inquiries and insurance purchases (by mail or phone) during the preceding twelve-month period. The total incidence of inquiries was higher than expected at 25.9 percent. When the incidence of inquiries was analyzed by individual consumer clusters, it was observed that inquiries were relatively flat across all six clusters. (Exhibit 20-5; information for Exhibit 20-5 to 20-13 drawn from the Stone & Adler National Profile.)

Exhibit 20-5. Insurance Inquiries by Consumer Cluster

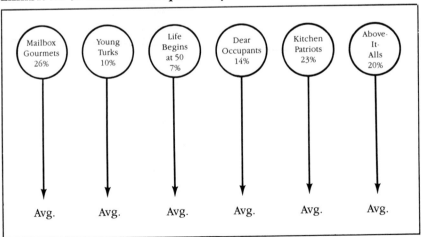

Thus, inquiries were not skewed toward those clusters that were direct mail responsive. In other words, of the total inquiries, the extremely direct marketing-positive Mailbox Gourmets accounted for 26 percent of the inquiries, while the extremely direct marketing-negative Above-It-Alls accounted for 20 percent of the inquiries, which is directly proportional to their representation in the general population. If the inquiries were indexed by cluster, therefore, each cluster would index at 100.

The incidence of insurance conversions by mail or phone totaled approximately 44 percent of the conversions, or 11 percent of the total sample (Exhibit 20-6). When the incidence of conversions was analyzed by individual consumer clusters, the same pattern emerged for conversions as for inquiries.

Exhibit 20-6. Insurance Conversions by Consumer Cluster

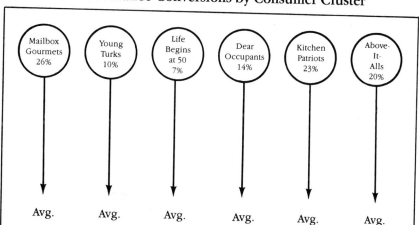

Conversions were also relatively flat across all six clusters. That is, conversions were not skewed toward those clusters that were the most direct mail responsive in other categories. Again, conversions were proportionate to each cluster's representation in the total U.S. population. All six clusters would, therefore, index at or near 100.

The conclusion drawn was that insurance was one of the *least* direct marketing responsive of all the twenty-six product and service categories surveyed in the *Stone & Adler Study*. However, the potential direct marketing audience for insurance is much larger than many other categories because it has a less negative bias toward direct marketing.

But to take advantage of such an opportunity, direct marketers must strategically use research data of the type shown above to:

- Define the highest propensity consumer segments for each type of insurance product
- Understand the needs for each type of insurance product from the perspective of each consumer segment

- Communicate the positioning, offer, and benefits of each insurance product in a manner that is understandable, relevant, and believable to the targeted consumer segments

Credit Card Acquisition Profiles   Credit card acquisition in the *Stone & Adler Study* included only new credit cards from new credit card sources that were obtained within the past twelve months. Acquisition did not include any credit cards that had expired and for which the company sent a new one. Acquisitions were based upon either a solicitation received in the mail or a coupon sent in from a newspaper or magazine ad.

Acquisition profiles were developed for the four major categories of cards:

- Bank cards such as Visa and MasterCard
- Travel and entertainment cards such as American Express, Carte Blanche, and Diners Club
- Department store cards such as those from Sears, J.C. Penney, Wards, Nieman Marcus, Saks Fifth Avenue, Bonwit Teller, and local department stores
- Gasoline cards such as Amoco, Shell, and Texaco

The total incidence of bank card acquisition was 20 percent. As you can see (Exhibit 20-7), the incidence by cluster was heavily skewed toward the clusters that are the most positive toward dirct marketing (Exhibit 20-7).

Exhibit 20-7. Bank Card Acquisition Patterns

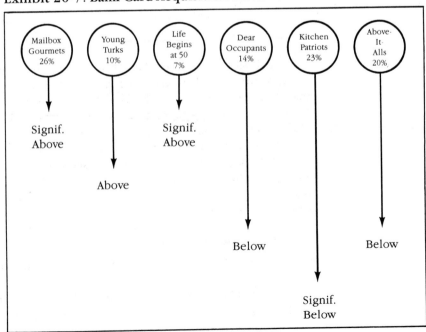

The total incidence of travel and entertainment card acquisition was 5 percent, which was the lowest of all four credit card market segments, and a good indication of the maturity that this segment is displaying. Again, acquisition of travel and entertainment cards, for the most part, is skewed toward the most direct marketing positive clusters. (See Exhibit 20-8.)

Exhibit 20-8. Travel and Entertainment Card Acquisition Patterns

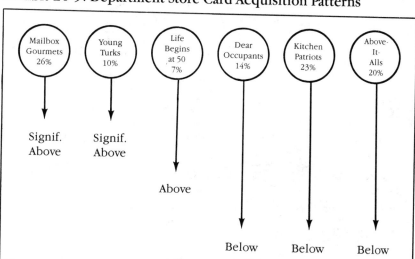

The total incidence of department store card acquisition was 23 percent. This percentage was the highest of all four credit card segments. The same skewed pattern that we observed in bank and travel and entertainment cards persists, except that it is even more accentuated. (See Exhibit 20-9.)

Exhibit 20-9. Department Store Card Acquisition Patterns

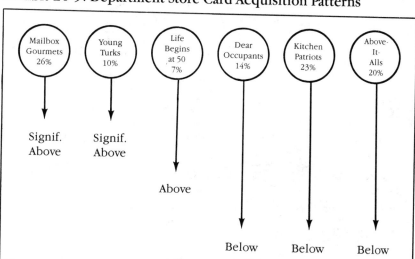

The gasoline credit card segment also showed a degree of maturity similar to that of travel and entertainment cards, with an incidence of acquisition at 12 percent. The skewing of acquisition toward positive direct marketing clusters is the least pronounced in this market segment. (See Exhibit 20-10.)

Exhibit 20-10. Gasoline Card Acquisition

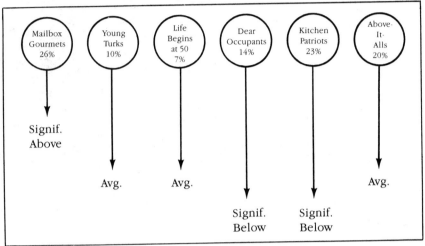

In summary, when above-average acquisition patterns are observed across all four credit card segments, clearly the most positive direct marketing clusters demonstrate the highest propensity to obtain credit cards. (See Exhibit 20-11.)

Exhibit 20-11. Above Average Acquisition Patterns

	Mailbox Gourmets 26%	Young Turks 10%	Life Begins at 50 7%	Dear Occupants 14%	Kitchen Patriots 23%	Above-It-Alls 20%
Bank cards	X	X	X			
T and E cards	X	X	X			
Department store cards	X	X	X			
Gasoline cards	X					

What are the implications of credit card acquisition being so heavily skewed toward positive direct marketing consumers? First, there is an "overall" need for credit. Clearly there is a new need for total credit in the form of multiple cards, not merely one card. But who are these high-propensity credit card acquirers? Supplementary work in this area shows that there are identifiable, targetable groups such as emerging and transitional consumers.

Emerging consumers can be found in the Young Turk cluster and among the younger Mailbox Gourmets. Demographically, these are recent college or technical school graduates, young aspiring professionals, newlyweds, and new parents (Full Nest I).

Transitional consumers can be most readily found in the Life-Begins-at-50 cluster and among the older Mailbox Gourmets. These people are undergoing major lifestyle changes such as divorce, remarriage, or a midlife career change, which affect their credit needs.

Catalog Clothing Buyer Profiles

Respondents to the *Stone & Adler Study* were asked whether they had purchased any clothing within the past *three* months either at retail outlets or through mail order (where "you sent in a mail order form or phoned in your order, and the item was delivered to your home, office, or elsewhere"). The total incidence of purchasing clothing from all sources, both retail and direct, was the highest of all 26 categories measured in the *Stone & Adler Study* at 74 percent.

As can be seen in Exhibit 20-12, the Mailbox Gourmets and Young Turks, the two most positive direct marketing clusters, demonstrated the highest incidence; the Kitchen Patriots and Above-It-Alls, the most negative direct marketing groups, showed the lowest incidence.

Exhibit 20-12. Clothing Buyer Profiles—Retail and Direct

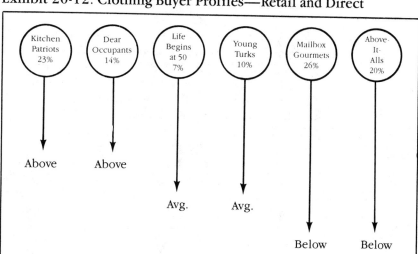

When you isolate catalog clothing purchases, a somewhat different pattern emerges (Exhibit 20-13). The incidence of purchase among Mailbox Gourmets registers significantly above average at 52 percent or an index of 200. Conversely, the incidence among Young Turks slips below average at 8 percent. And the incidence among Kitchen Patriots slips to under one half of their representation in the sample of 11 percent, while purchase incidence of Above-It-Alls registers a mere 5 percent or one quarter of their representation in the sample.

Exhibit 20-13. Catalog Clothing Buyer Profiles

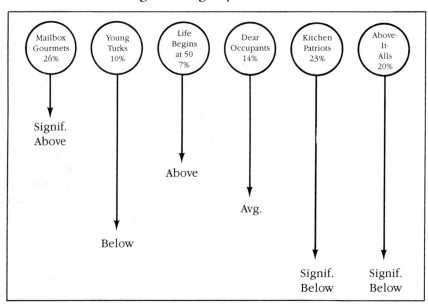

Several strategic implications can be drawn from this data:

- Mailbox Gourmets are conspicuous consumers in the clothing category. They buy more at both retail and catalog. Unfortunately, the growing mailbox clutter is also centering on this group because Mailbox Gourmets are on "everyone's" mailing list. Research should be used, therefore, to develop intrusive catalogs and mass media advertising to break through the clutter; and to develop unique types or lines of merchandise that continues to attract the loyalty of Mailbox Gourmets.

- Although the Life-Begins-at-50 cluster exhibited the second highest propensity to buy clothing from catalogs, their purchases tend to be concentrated on a much narrower range of merchandise than the Mailbox Gourmets. Research should be used, therefore, to develop creative messages that motivate this cluster to try products they have not purchased by mail before; and select the merchandise with the highest propensity to generate trial.

- The underperformance by the Young Turks represents a major lost opportunity to clothing catalog marketers, particularly in terms of an extremely high net present value. Research could help by directing catalog marketers on the best ways of communicating with and reassuring them about the key issues of styling and fit.
- Although the Kitchen Patriots and Above-It-Alls do not represent a major opportunity for direct mail clothing sales, they should not be summarily dismissed by direct marketers. Since direct mail, particularly catalogs, are used by both of these groups as reference materials for retail shopping, direct marketing can be used effectively among both groups as a targeted advertising vehicle to increase retail traffic.

Direct Marketing Research for Business-to-Business Applications

Many people ask whether the principles of marketing and research are the same for business-to-business products and services as they are for consumer products and services. After all, this line of reasoning goes, the people making purchases for businesses are the same consumers who buy television sets, automobiles, and toothpaste, aren't they? The answer is, "Not exactly."

When John Q. Consumer begins buying products for a business, the situation becomes much more complicated than it is for consumer products. In a business environment, he is part of a much larger, more complex institutional hierarchy. Thus, responsibility for the purchase decision, as well as the ultimate consumption of the products or services, is a much more involved process.

For example, regardless of the organization of the business, the target audience within a business will normally have at least three hierarchical levels. (See Exhibit 20-14.) The purchaser is the person responsible for recommending and making the purchase whether he or she is the purchasing agent, office manager, or director of human resources. The gate keeper is a CEO or chief financial officer from whom the purchaser must often obtain approval. The end user is often a department manager in the production, accounting, or marketing department whose department will actually be using the products or services purchased. In fact, either the gate keeper or end user may originate the purchasing process as well as influencing it.

To make matters even more difficult, there are problems with finding qualified prospects on each of these three levels. First, we must understand that not everyone we contact is in the market for our products or services. At one extreme are those prospects who are simply not interested, either in our product or service category, or in the particular brand we are selling.

Exhibit 20-14. Business-to-Business Purchasing Process

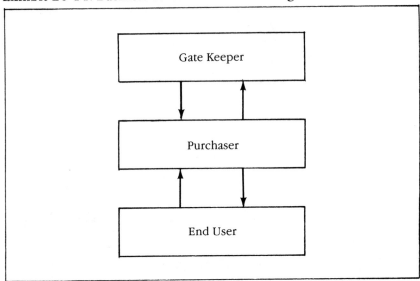

Others may have recently purchased and made long-term commitments. Thus, while these prospects are in our category, they are not available to us for an extended period of time.

At the other extreme are those who are left, a group of prospects we call active considerers. And not even all of these prospects are available to us because they must first be converted from prospects to serious shoppers.

Thus, when direct marketers approach business-to-business marketing problems by merely testing and retesting rather than carefully defining and thoroughly understanding each level of prospect audience being targeted, you can readily see why the odds of success are so often slight.

How can marketing research raise the odds of obtaining the highest propensity prospects? Let's review a couple of examples.

Profiling

Business-to-business house files can be matched against a national data base of businesses such as Dun & Bradstreet. This process will result in a more thorough knowledge of the current client base—a well-defined target market for future prospecting. With this knowledge comes a better understanding of the marketing and communications programs necessary to more effectively penetrate the desired segments.

The information and insights obtained through profiling can help the business-to-business marketer accomplish a number of objectives:

- Marketing and Creative Objectives—to define and target business segments of the highest propensity; to provide creative and marketing guidance in communicating with high propensity target audience segments on a clearer, more relevant, and believable basis

- Promotional—to provide creative and marketing guidance in developing specific reactivation and increased activity programs to the current customer file
- Sales—to help increase the efficiency of the sales force, by directing them to concentrate their efforts on the highest propensity segments of the prospect universe
- Media—to attain greater efficiency in direct mail and other media

Business-to-business profiling is usually developed on a three-phased basis:

- Phase I—Account identification and matching. This phase consists of linking the national data base operations files to the business-to-business house file.
- Phase II—Appending data from the national data base to the business-to-business house file. This phase utilizes the existing compiled business establishment data (e.g., geographic, type of business, size of business, and type of location) from the national database.
- Phase III—Development of market segmentation profiles. This phase consists of analyzing the business-to-business customer file on the basis of the distribution and concentration of customers within specific market segments (e.g., to what extent are your current best customers concentrated within certain areas such as SIC codes, geographic areas, company size, and revenue contribution groups).

Another way of analyzing the activities of current customers and assessing their potential is through drawing maps or creating matrixes of current purchasing activities as shown in Exhibit 20-15.

Based upon the purchase activity quadrant in which the customer falls, we are then in a position to segment our customer file and target specific messages and offers to best leverage the different opportunities:

- Quadrant 1—represents our best customers who spend the most dollars and purchase the most frequently. Clearly the emphasis in this segment is to maintain loyalty and provide rewards for continuity.
- Quadrant 2—represents customers who spend a lot of dollars, but infrequently. Large average order sizes combined with low levels of purchase frequency indicate that they may be using us for a few specialized purchases. Supplementary research, such as in-depth personal interviews among a sample of customers in this quadrant, can help uncover the reasons we are being used on an infrequent, specialized basis. These issues can then be addressed in both the creative and offer to move them into Quadrant 1.
- Quadrant 3—represents customers who spend just a few dollars, but make purchases relatively frequently. Small average order sizes combined with high levels of purchase frequency indicate that these customers are "cherry picking" our inventory, concentrating on the lowest

Exhibit 20-15. Purchase Activity Matrix

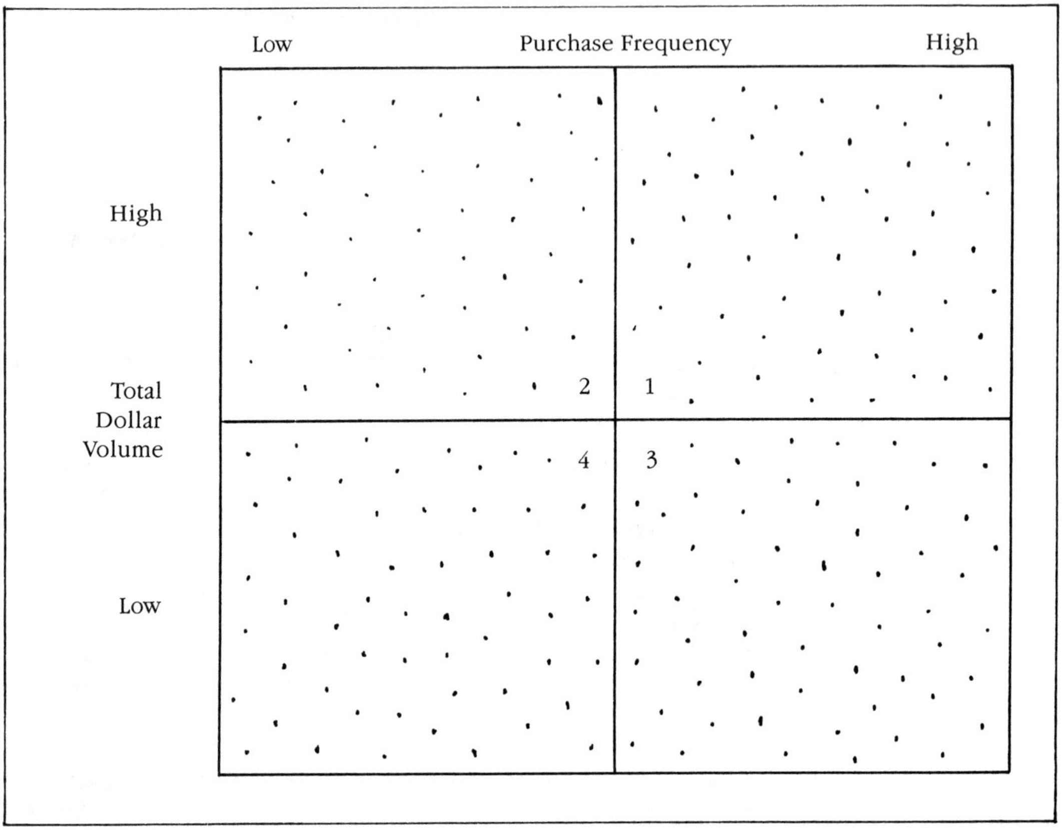

cost sales items. Again supplementary research, such as in-depth personal interviews among a sample of customers in this quadrant, can help us uncover problems that can be addressed with both creative and offers to stimulate purchases of a wider range of merchandise, particularly higher-ticket items.

- Quadrant 4—represents the worst of all possible worlds, the customer who doesn't spend very much or very often. The potential payoff in identifying such customers is in saving money by targeting a higher proportion of your spending toward those customers in the first three quadrants.

We can further assess the potential of these customers by observing the degree to which companies with certain characteristics such as SIC code, size, and geographic location, tend to be concentrated in certain quadrants. For example, if customers from four SIC codes are predominant within Quadrant 1 (highest sales volume, greatest purchase frequency), we should then analyze what our share of market or degree of penetration is in each of the four SIC codes. When this is done by comparing the customers in our house file against the total number of businesses within each SIC code on the national data base, a profile of our market penetration can be drawn as in Exhibit 20-16.

Exhibit 20-16. Company Penetration in Selected Market Segments

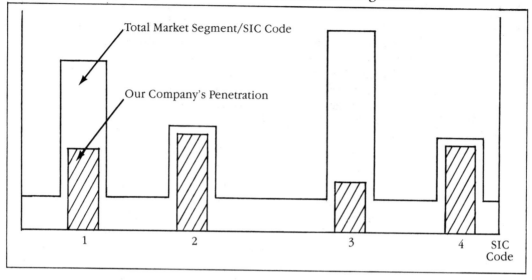

Primary Research for Marketing and Creative Development

Sometimes there is insufficient information available for profiling, particularly when a new market or segment is being entered. Such situations call for the marketer to obtain primary information directly from prospects in the form of qualitative information (focus groups or in-depth personal interviews) and/or quantitative data (surveys).

Research for a New Marketing Venture

This situation occurred when the Harris Corporation called on Stone & Adler to develop qualified leads for marketing a state-of-the-art office automation system. This unique system performed both word processing and data processing functions from a single work station and could function as a compatible component of the current user's data processing network.

Since this represented a new marketing venture for Harris, research was needed to provide a basic understanding of the attitudes toward, and the decision-making process involved in, selecting office automation systems, such as:

- How the need for office automation systems is arrived at (i.e., how the purchase process is initiated)
- Who is involved in the decision-making process
- Criteria used in the decision-making process
- Informational sources used in the decision-making process

Research was also needed to understand what the affect of the low recognition level of Harris Corporation as an entrant in this market would have upon key prospects.

Since the proposed target audience for this system was the "*Fortune 1,000*" companies, the research process began with focus groups consisting of "key decision makers" of office automation systems selected from a sample of these companies. A wide variety of industry groups was included.

To begin with, the exercise of finding the real "key decision maker" in the sample corporations became a survey unto itself. Often, three to five contacts had to be made before the actual decision maker was reached. This knowledge had major implications for our ultimate targeting because the actual titles of the decision makers varied widely. Some had traditional titles such as manager/director of Management Information Systems, manager/director of Office Automation Systems, or manager/director of Information Services. But the majority of decision makers had titles which appeared to be unique to each sample company and contained several functions under one hat such as: manager of Office Information Systems and Corporate Planning and Administration, manager of Office Automation Systems and Information Center, director of Office Automation Systems and Information Technology.

Decision-Making Process   Regardless of the decision maker's title, however, he or she (approximately 20 percent of the persons in our sample were female) formed one level within a three-level purchase process hierarchy (Exhibit 20-17).

The purchase process centered around the manager/director of Management Information Systems or Office Automation Systems as the functional leader, the technical expert. The CEO or president's involvement in the decision-making process tended to revolve around the issue of financial considerations and the effect of the computer systems on the operating efficiencies of the departments obtaining the equipment. In some instances, however, the CEO or president was the originator of the purchasing process.

The perspective of the staff managers was specifically applications oriented in terms of "What functions will the machine perform for my department?" "How easy is the equipment for my people to learn—since they aren't EDP experts?" "How compatible is the software with our current software?" "What happens if something breaks?" The purchase process frequently began from this perspective. Usually one of three scenarios occurs:

1. The department manager wishes to have an additional piece of equipment that is already in another department of the company.

2. The department manager wishes to have an additional piece of equipment from a "nonapproved" vendor.

3. The department manager requests a major new system which requires a system study to be conducted.

Exhibit 20-17. Purchase Process Hierarchy

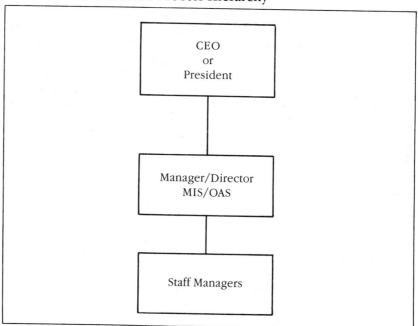

Scenarios two and three will require major involvement on the part of the MIS (Management Information Systems)/OAS (Office Automation Systems) director.

Current Marketing Environment The Harris Corporation was facing a marketing environment in which much of the investment in major office automation equipment had already been made. Hence, for the majority of target prospects, the emphasis was on updating and refining the systems already in place. (Current systems were generally decentralized. Each division operated its own mainframe; a few were without mainframes.)

The procedures for purchasing this type of equipment appear to be ritualized and formal. Many corporations have ongoing equipment investigation committees. Purchases are often made based on an "approved vendor list" consisting of large well-known companies such as IBM, WANG, and DEC (Harris was not on approved vendor lists). Since these decisions are of such high visibility, most MIS and OAS key decision makers tend to be relatively conservative in terms of not looking to be "the first" to try a product or system. In the eloquent words of one battle-scarred OAS director, "I have no desire to be on the bleeding edge."

Major Criteria for Office Automation System Selection

A major requirement when purchasing new equipment appears to be system compatibility, for two basic reasons. First, a significant amount of money has been spent on the current equipment, and additions must, therefore, be able to interface with it. Second, most systems purchases involve software rather than hardware, and are being purchased for ordinary managers and clerical workers rather than data processing people. Therefore, new equipment must require minimum training and run current software programs. The second major requirement is for equipment and systems that satisfy basic functional needs of the department.

Other key requirements of office automation equipment that decision makers looked for during their last purchase of equipment included:

- Ease of use
- Ability to share system among other operators
- Support with installation, software, and maintenance
- Communication with other equipment
- Staying power of the vendor company

Sources of Information in Decision Making

When looking for information on new products, key decision makers tended to rely on:

- Word of mouth from peers in the field and other technical people at work, which was viewed as the most important source of information
- Marketing representatives and their companies' literature
- Seminars
- Trade publications

Other Information Developed

A variety of other information was developed from the study. Included were reactions to concept statements describing the proposed office automation system on a blind (nonbrand) basis, research to determine which current competitors would most likely market such a system, and reactions to the Harris Corporation's marketing such a system.

Conclusions and Implications   The conclusions and implications upon which the subsequent advertising strategy was developed revolved around four issues:

- Credibility, or the ability to convince prospects that the Harris Corporation's high level of experience and technical expertise in other markets was being transferred to the office automation equipment market
- Complexity of the decision-making process with multiple levels of target audiences, each having its own needs and points-of-view
- Conservatism on the part of key decision-makers because of the high visibility of the decision with the concomitant need for risk reduction through vendor approval lists
- Compatibility with current systems in terms of both hardware and software

In Chapter 6, "Business-to-Business Direct Marketing," you saw the lead-generation program that evolved from the research conducted for the Harris Corporation. Without this research the agency and the client would have simply guessed their way through.

The Future of Research in Direct Marketing

The future of research will be dictated by the problems that it is asked to address. For example, as traditional marketing categories continue to mature and competitors face increasing clutter in the mailbox, print, and TV, the problem of identifying, understanding, and reaching the highest propensity prospects looms larger and larger.

Hence, the major problem common to both traditional and nontraditional direct marketers, given the current environment, is *identifying* and *understanding* key target audience *segments*. This is particularly true in terms of focusing on points of greatest strategic leverage, and developing techniques to gain *direct access* to these segments. The problem is shared and must be jointly solved by research and media working in tandem. While this may, at first glance, seem to be a relatively simple, straightforward problem to solve, it isn't.

Consumer Insights and Delivery Process

As long as the disciplines of research and media are treated as separate functions, they will not be able to perform the integrated process of "Consumer Insights and Delivery" which is needed to address the problems of both traditional and nontraditional direct marketers.

As you can see by the integrated process shown in Exhibit 20-18, the process begins with research defining *who* the target audience is, and *why* they behave the way they do.

Exhibit 20-18. Consumer Insights and Delivery Process

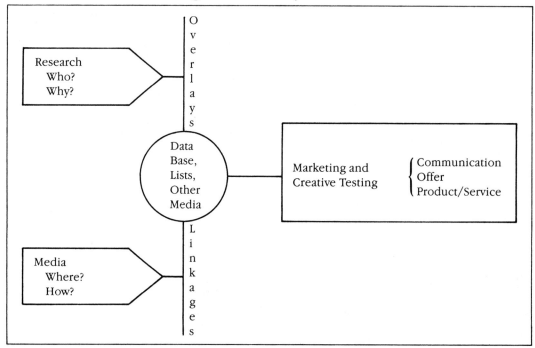

The primary purpose of this chapter has been to show direct marketers and would-be direct marketers the true value of research and the types of research that can identify target markets and lead to well-executed direct response advertising. Conducting the actual research is best left to professional researchers. For the direct marketer, knowing what should be researched is the imperative.

Self-Quiz

1. Name the four phases in the marketing research process.

   a. Exploratory research   c. _____

   b. Pretest   d. _____

2. The exploratory phase deals with defining and understanding your _____ audience.

3. The pretesting phase consists of developing, assessing, and refining the _____ and _____ products before in-market testing.

4. The testing phase consists of bringing together five key variables for assessment in the market.

    a. The product or service

    b. The media or method of assessing the defined target audience

    c. The time or season

    d. _____

    e. _____

5. Posttesting assesses reactions of both responders and nonresponders. Responder/nonresponder surveys can help pinpoint such issues as:

    a. Incremental sales

    b. Competitive conquest

    c. _____   _____

6. Define "high-propensity prospects":

    _____

    _____

    _____

7. Define these terms:

    Geodemographics:_____

    _____

    Psychographics and lifestyles:_____

    _____

8. PAG identifies six consumer clusters. Name them.

    a. Mailbox Gourmets   d. _____

    b. Young Turks   e. _____

    c. Life Begins at 50   f. _____

9. Why is it important to "profile" a target audience?

_____

_____

_____

10. Research principles ☐ are the same ☐ are not the same for business-to-business products and services as they are for consumer products and services.

Pilot Project

Suppose that your company acquired a product line in a category with which you were totally unfamiliar. No information exists as to who used such products or why. Consumer attitudes toward the line and competitive products are unknown. Prepare a research plan that will provide the basic information necessary to market the line. This plan should include a statement of research objectives for each project item and the specific type of technique best suited to meet the objectives.

CHAPTER TWENTY-ONE

Direct Marketing in the Total Marketing Mix

Pete Hoke, publisher of *Direct Marketing* magazine, often refers to direct marketing as "a subset of marketing," which is to say it is integral to the total marketing mix. There is a tendency by many to regard direct marketing as an isolated method of selling—mail order—but what remains to be understood and applied is the melding of direct marketing with other marketing methods.

Exhibit 21-1 graphically shows the elements involved in a total marketing situation. Company objectives relate directly to marketing objectives. Marketing objectives relate directly to market definition and marketing mix definition. And these definitions have a direct bearing on the four Ps: product, price, place, promotion.

The famous Professor Theodore Levitt, of the Graduate School of Business Administration, Harvard University, is of the school who puts businesses into one of two classes: those who are marketing driven, favoring the consumer, and those who are production driven, favoring the manufacturer. The professor and his legion of followers clearly favor businesses who are marketing driven. And they are right.

Exhibit 21-2 neatly delineates the attitudes of the two camps: marketing and production. As one can see the two camps can be poles apart. That's why marketing must have top management status in the company structure to achieve maximum success. (Exhibit 21-3.)

And, finally, marketing must have a strong hand in company procedures (Exhibit 21-4). I can say, without fear of contradiction, that a major deterrent to direct marketing success where other marketing disciplines are primary is the failure to give direct marketing proper status in the marketing mix.

Perhaps the best way to dramatize opportunities for melding direct marketing with other marketing methods is to give live examples of applications.

Airlines

The primary marketing channel for the sale of airline tickets is through travel agencies, accounting for about 65 percent of total airline revenue. Secondary channels are airline ticket offices and airport ticket counters. Prime advertising mediums for driving consumers and business people to these outlets are television, newspapers, and radio, with magazines as a secondary medium.

Exhibit 21-1. The Elements of a Total Marketing Situation

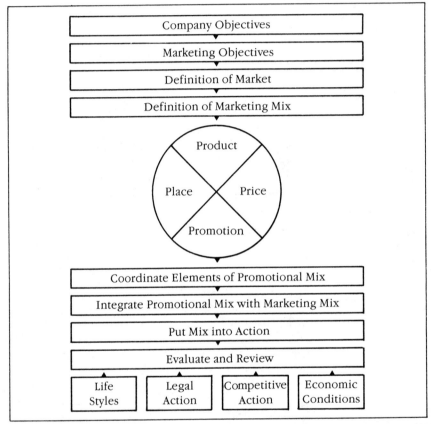

Source: Readings in Promotion Management, *James U. McNeal, editor (New York, Appleton-Century-Crofts, 1966).*

Newspaper advertising, in particular, is used to promote specific destinations such as ski areas, summer vacation areas, and exotic places like Hawaii. Thousands of inquiries are received annually, requesting information about specific trips. When these names are captured the airline can build a data base by specific interests: skiing, Hawaii, European destinations, and so forth. Data about advertising source, date of inquiry, can and should be included in the data base.

Exhibit 21-2. Marketing and Production Orientations

Marketing Orientation	Attitudes	Production Orientation
[C O N S U M E R]		[M A N U F A C T U R I N G]
Consumer forces dominate; emphasis on long-range planning.	Objectives	Internal forces dominate; emphasis on efficiency and technology in the short run.
Decision-making starts with the consideration of the consumer.	Place of the consumer	Decisions are imposed on the consumer.
Company makes what it can sell.	Product mix	Company sells what it can make.
Used to determine customer needs and test how product satisfies these needs.	Role of marketing research	Used to determine consumer reaction, if used at all.
Create new markets as well as serve present markets.	Marketing strategy	Satisfy existing markets.
Focus on market opportunities.	Innovation	Focus on technology.
Sometimes lead, sometimes follow; offensive posture.	Competition	Always follow, react; defensive posture.
An objective.	Profit	A residual, what's left over after all costs are paid.
Focus on marketing problems.	Other corporate functions	Focus on manufacturing and finance problems.

Source: Robert F. Vizera, Thomas F. Chambers and Edward J. Cook, Adoption of the Marketing Concept—Fact or Fiction, *Sales Executive Club of New York, 1967.*

It is the use of the data base that brings direct marketing into play. For now there can be an annual target mailing to all who raised their hands and said in effect, "We have a special interest in ski vacations." Prime prospects, to be sure. The same may be said of those who have inquired about Hawaii, or European destinations, or other special destinations.

Unique to the airline industry is the marketing fact that about 80 percent of their revenue comes from about 20 percent of their customers commonly known as "frequent flyers." It is to this choice market—frequent flyers—that the airlines give special recognition. And they employ direct marketing methods to single them out.

Direct marketing methods have been used, very successfully, to gain memberships for airline key clubs: United Airlines Red Carpet Club, American Airlines Admirals Club, and TWA Ambassador Club, for example. Club members receive trip news and special offers at frequent inter-

Exhibit 21-3. Marketing and Production Orientations

Marketing Orientation	Structure	Production Orientation
[C O N S U M E R]		[M A N U F A C T U R I N G]
Marketing personnel.	**Top management**	Production or finance personnel in top job.
On same level as heads of production, finance and personnel.	**Place of Marketing Executive**	On lower level.
Reports to top Marketing Executive.	**Sales Executive, Advertising Department, Marketing Research**	On same level, or higher, than the top Marketing Executive; sometimes not a separate department.
Reports to top Marketing Executive.	**Product planning**	Reports to engineering, production, top executive; sometimes not a separate function.
In the marketing group; seen as customer service.	**Customer credit**	In the controller's department; seen as necessary evil.
Reports to marketing department.	**Inventory function, transportation**	Reports to production department.

Source: Martin Baier, Adjunct Professor, University of Missouri, Kansas City.

vals. Other direct marketing applications by airlines include mailings to travel agencies—their number one sales outlet—encouraging them to recommend their airlines over competition and mailings to their data bases encouraging consumers to go to travel agencies to inquire about passage on their airlines over competition.

But perhaps the best illustration of melding direct marketing with other marketing methods in the airline industry was exemplified in Chapter 1, "The Scope of Direct Marketing." Here you learned the direct marketing approach United Airlines and other major airlines are using to maintain customer loyalty.

Automobile Manufacturers

Automobiles have been marketed to the consumer in the same way for decades: from manufacturer to the dealer to the consumer. Manufacturer advertising budgets are huge. The Lincoln Mercury division of Ford Motor Company, for example, had a 1987 advertising budget in the neighborhood of $100 million. The huge manufacturer budget does not include dealer association budgets or individual dealer budgets. More millions.

Manufacturer budgets are heavy in television, radio, magazines, and newspapers. Local dealer associations go heavy in TV with some newspaper and radio. Leading local dealers tend to go heavy in local TV and newspapers, while lesser dealers tend to put most of their advertising dollars into newspapers.

It is at the manufacturer and dealer association levels that direct marketing applications are most likely to be initiated. The manufacturer has

Exhibit 21-4. Marketing and Production Orientations

Marketing Orientation	*Procedures*	*Production Orientation*
[C O N S U M E R]		[M A N U F A C T U R I N G]
Begins with determination of customer needs; seeks to identify a market opportunity.	*Product planning*	Begins with consideration of production and technological capacities; looks to utilize excess capacity and waste material.
Customer determines prices; price determines costs.	*Price*	Costs determine price.
A co-ordinated approach including all aspects of the Marketing Mix. Marketing integrated into all functions of the business.	*Marketing campaign*	Individual efforts by each department, often resulting in conflict and wasted effort. No integration of marketing and other functions.
Designed for customer convenience; seen as sales tool.	*Packaging*	Seen as protection and a container for the product.
Communicates need-satisfying benefits of the product; consumer motivations paramount.	*Advertising*	Emphasizes product features, quality and ego of the producer. Producer motives paramount.
Level set with customer requirements in mind.	*Inventory*	Levels set with production requirements in mind.
Seen as customer service.	*Transportation*	Seen as extension of production and storage functions.
Helps the buyer to buy; seeks to match product to customer needs; co-ordinates with advertising, promotion, distribution; determines unfilled customer needs.	*Sales*	Seeks to "sell" to the buyer; often unaware of advertising, promotion research and distribution activities.

the most targeted mailing list of all: he or she has an exact list of all owners of the cars by year, by model. And because present owners are the best prospects for future sales automobile manufacturers make it a practice to invite present owners to see the new models as introduced at their dealers each year.

Second to efforts to maintain customer loyalty are efforts to encourage car owners to switch. Direct marketing efforts in this regard are quite sophisticated.

All automobile manufacturers have available to them lists of owners of competitive makes of cars by model, by year. Applying marketing logic, manufacturers deduce that an owner of a Toyota is not likely to be a prime prospect for a Lincoln or a Cadillac. But a Toyota owner could be a good prospect for a Honda. A Lincoln owner could be a good prospect for a Cadillac. An Oldsmobile Cutlass owner could be a good prospect for a Mercury Cougar. These matchups offer the best opportunities for encouraging switching.

Thus mailing efforts through dealer associations—names of neighborhood dealers are often featured—targeted to best prospects for switching can produce dealer traffic. Rebate certificates and free gifts for test drives are often key factors in inducing car owners to switch.

The dealer's best defense against losing customers to competition is to keep his present customers coming back to his dealership for maintenance services. And, here again, direct marketing methods are best suited to achieving the objective. Many dealers use a planned program to remind owners of various checkup periods in relation to the age of their cars. And they offer incentives to have the checkups and maintenance services done at their dealership.

Insurance Companies

Not counting merchandise sales of huge mail order companies such as Sears, J.C. Penney, and Spiegels, insurance companies lead the pack in sales via direct marketing methods. Annual sales of insurance via direct marketing methods are estimated to be in excess of four billion dollars. Leading "mail order" insurance companies include Colonial Penn, National Liberty, Physicians Mutual, and Old American Insurance Company. For these firms direct marketing is their prime marketing method. But most of them have a secondary marketing channel—an agent organization who engages in person-to-person selling.

There is a natural synergism between direct marketing and agent marketing. The millions of dollars spent by mail order insurance companies on TV, on radio, in newspapers and magazines, and in direct mail serve as "advertising" for the agent organization, thus building an "image" for agent prospects.

But astute insurance direct marketers carry the synergism a lot further than the impact of advertising. Some use their mail order policyholder list as a "prospect list" for their agent organization. For example, an agent who has a policyholder card, indicating the policyholder now has an A&H (accident and health) policy with the company, might attempt to sell a life insurance policy or an add-on to the existing A&H policy. Experience shows that the agent's closure rate is far greater when she or he works existing policyholders as contrasted to "cold" prospects.

Another important application of direct marketing in the insurance field is "cross-selling"—selling other policies to existing policyholders direct by mail. Some insurance companies pay a commission to agents even though they're not involved in such sales; others don't.

Most insurance companies today, whether they sell insurance direct to the consumer, or not, use direct marketing methods for "upgrading" or "downgrading" existing policyholders. Allstate Insurance Company, for example, uses direct mail to upgrade bodily injury coverage for automobile policyholders. And I have seen mailings where they use direct mail suggesting downgrading of deductibles.

But of all the applications of direct marketing methods as part of the total marketing mix of insurance companies, none is more dramatic than "third-party selling." The success of third-party selling is dependent upon the recommendation of an affinity group, such as a union, a fraternal organization, an oil company credit card group, an alumni association, or a senior citizen organization. Allegiance to the organization, and therefore respect for their recommendation, plus common interests, account for the better-than-average response to third-party selling efforts (Exhibits 21-5 and 21-6).

The most dramatic application of third-party selling has been done against the AARP (American Association of Retired People) membership list. The insurance needs of older people are unique and common to the membership list. Thus third-party insurance offers, catering to the needs of AARP's millions of members, are highly productive.

Oil Companies

Oil companies saw the advantages of adding direct marketing to their marketing mix early on—the catalyst for profiting from direct marketing methods has been, and continues to be, the oil company credit card.

The credit card grew out of a desire to have a device that would build gasoline station loyalty for a particular brand of gasoline. The credit card filled that need. So most of the oil companies—Shell, Exxon, Texaco, Amoco, Gulf and many of the smaller ones—issued their own gasoline credit cards—free. This spur to gas station marketing had its rewards, but cementing customer loyalty became muted, to a major degree, by the fact that any credit-worthy person could hold cards from all the major oil companies. Maintenance of the credit program became a financial burden for many of the oil companies.

Then in the late 1950s, direct marketing provided a way to bring added income to oil company credit card operations, thus absorbing major portions of credit file costs. Someone correctly deduced that oil company credit card holders would be ideal prospects for selected merchandise offers, particularly if payment could be made on the installment plan through the oil company credit card.

The chief exponents of this revolutionary marketing method were syndicators, many of whom underwrote test mailing costs for the oil companies. One of the pioneers in syndication was Al Sloan of Chicago, who underwrote the first syndicated mailing package test program for the $149.95 Bell & Howell movie camera outfit. Thousands and thousands of movie outfits were sold to oil company credit card holders.

But this was just the beginning of merchandise offers to oil company credit card holders. There were scores of successful offers. Wrist watches—for men and women. Flatware. China. Cameras—Polaroid and others. Lounge chairs. Lawn mowers. You name it. Oil companies collected a handsome profit on each sale, plus interest on installment sales.

Syndication isn't the force today it once was because as selling costs have increased over the years there has been a profit squeeze, rarely leaving enough room for two profits: the syndicator and the oil company. However, oil companies have not gone out of the merchandise business. Their major channel for merchandise sales today is the remittance envelope enclosed with monthly statements (Exhibit 21-7). The selling cost is so nominal that when a "hot" item is offered profits are almost certain.

Inflation and the high cost of money added to the cost burden of maintaining oil company credit card operations. As a matter of fact one of the majors—Atlantic Richfield (Arco)—dropped its credit card operation entirely, offering a cash discount in lieu of charge privileges. But most other oil companies decided not to give up their credit card franchises, although many aped Arco's offer of a discount for cash purchases. One alternative to be considered was converting the free oil company credit card to a fee card. The only problem there was that, at best, oil companies would probably end up with no more than half of the credit card file they had had. Another alternative would be to drop the free cards in lieu of bank card privileges: VISA or MasterCard, or both. The negative to this move was loss of identity of the oil company as against competing oil companies.

Faced with these dilemmas American Oil Company (Amoco) came up with a brilliant marketing alternative: a new fee card, called "Multicard," with advantages over their regular free oil company card. Thus, using direct marketing methods, they were able to move hundreds of thousands of free card holders to the status of fee card holders.

Retailers

While most retailers have been slow to make direct marketing a part of their marketing mix, others have achieved remarkable success. The opportunity for department stores to increase store traffic and expand markets

Exhibit 21-5. Third-Party Letter

"Third-party" letter from Shell Oil Company, recommending hospital income plan underwritten by National Home Life Assurance Company.

SHELL OIL COMPANY
SHELL CREDIT CARD CENTER
TULSA, OKLAHOMA 74102

Dear Customer:

Have you ever wondered, "Could I ever cover medical bills and day-to-day expenses for my family if I was hospitalized for any length of time?"

Now there's a Plan available for Shell Credit Card Customers that pays you regardless of what you collect from Medicare, Workers' Compensation or any other company's plans. This Group Hospital Income Plan was designed to help you pay your hospital and medical bills when you're hospitalized.

These benefits may help you to budget your other income for those every day living expenses that don't stop just because you're in the hospital.

In inflationary times like these, many good plans don't pay all the medical bills. That's why it's particularly important to consider a Group Hospital Income Plan like this.

We selected one of the leaders in the direct-to-consumer health and hospital insurance products, National Home Life Assurance Company, to underwrite and offer this Plan especially for our Credit Card Customers.

I urge you to read the enclosed letter for all the details on the many benefits of this low group rate Plan. You will then see why I recommend you consider this valuable opportunity to help protect yourself and your loved ones.

Sincerely,

E.E. Cassady
Manager, Customer Services
Shell Credit Card Center

EEC:il
LY4521R

P.S. Good News--As a Shell Credit Card Customer--you are automatically eligible for low group rates. And, you can charge it to your Shell Credit Card Account.

Exhibit 21-6. Application Form Included in Third-Party Mailing

GUARANTEED ACCEPTANCE FORM FOR THE

Group Hospital Income Plan

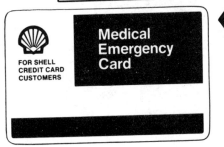

◀ **Your Medical Emergency Card**

Medical Emergency Card

FOR SHELL CREDIT CARD CUSTOMERS

LARRY STONE
605 LAUREL
WILMETTE, IL 60091

is eligible to enroll in this low-cost Group Hospital Income Insurance Plan for only $1 for your first month—and then continue for as little as $3.92 a month depending on the plan you choose.

PLEASE REPLY BY AUG 13, 1982

It's So Easy To Enroll!

1. Check the Hospital Income Plan that is best for you. Then...

2. Complete and sign the form below.

3. Send no money. Mail your completed form in the postage paid envelope.

☐₀₀ Plan A

$**60.00** a day

☐₀₁ Plan B

$**30.00** a day

Plans A and B pay from the very first day for covered accident and illness.

If you would prefer to have coverage from the very first day for covered accidents and after the fifth day for illnesses, please check one of the plans at right. Please see brochure for benefits, rates, limitations and renewability for all plans.

☐₀₂ **Plan C, $60.00 a day** ☐₀₃ **Plan D, $30.00 a day**

GROUP ENROLLMENT APPLICATION TO
NATIONAL HOME LIFE ASSURANCE COMPANY

RXRBNXRMD

34304139

(Please Print)

Name ___ LARRY STONE

Address ___ 606 LAUREL

City ___ WILMETTE

Your Date of Birth ___ Month ___ Day ___ Year

Telephone ( )

State ___ IL ___ Zip ___ 60091

Age ___ Male ☐ Female ☐

☐ I want coverage for children ☐ I want coverage for maternity benefits ☐ I want coverage for children and maternity benefits

List all dependents to be covered under this Plan: (DO NOT include name that appears above.)

Name Please print name and indicate relationship (for example husband, wife, son etc.)	Relationship	Sex M/F	Date of Birth			Age
			Month	Day	Year	
1.						
2.						
3.						

FOR ADDITIONAL DEPENDENTS: Please use separate sheet if necessary.

Please enroll me in the Group Hospital Plan for Shell Credit Card Customers and charge my Shell account. I understand that the initial billing will be for the first two (2) months coverage.

I understand that no insurance will be in effect until I am issued my certificate by the underwriter (National Home Life Assurance Company. Administrative Offices Valley Forge, Pa 19493). I also understand that injury or sickness for which I or any person listed have been medically advised or treated or where distinct symptoms were evident during the 12 month period immediately prior to the effective Date of my coverage will not be covered during the first year. Any such pre-existing conditions will, however, be covered for daily hospitalization benefits after the first year, provided that hospitalization begins more than one year from the Effective Date of coverage.

Date ___

Signature X ___

NHGA-780

GROUP ENROLLMENT FORM

NHGC-780-1080 60/30 EP0/5

Underwritten by National Home Life Assurance Company

SIGN & MAIL THIS FORM TODAY. SEND NO MONEY. CHARGE IT!

Exhibit 21-7. Merchandising through Credit Card Billings

*This offer was
included with
monthly
remittance
statements to
Amoco credit
card holders.*

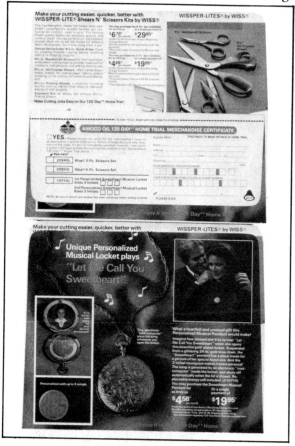

via the catalog medium was covered thoroughly in Chapter 15. But there are other opportunities. Many, in fact.

Surprisingly, many retailers who say they don't use direct marketing methods are doing so without realizing it. For example, every time a local department store runs a newspaper ad stating, "Telephone Orders Accepted," a direct marketing technique is being applied. Traditionally retailers "talk" to their publics—prospects and customers—through newspaper advertising. Retailers, as a category, do not talk to their identifiable customers—the backbone of their businesses—as effectively as they might.

The smallest of retail businesses—a neighborhood apparel store, for example—can profit by applying direct marketing methods. Direct mail and telephone are the two ideal mediums for giving special recognition to customers.

It's hard to beat the appeal of an advance announcement of a forthcoming sale, as an example. Many merchants run sales for customers only, closing the store for a given period to all who do not have a customer admittance card. This technique can be dynamite. And the telephone is a natural for personal contact with regular customers. There's the story of the leading salesman of an upscale clothing store in Kansas City, Missouri. He maintains a card file of all his customers. Knows their size, color preferences, whether they prefer vests or not, whether they prefer cuffs or not. Everything. So when the new spring line, or summer, or winter line comes in, this salesman goes through the stock and picks out suits for his customers. Then he gets on the phone. This marketing concept is easily expandable to chains like Brooks Brothers and Capper & Capper.

Retailers have three big advantages that cannot be matched by those who do not have retail stores.

1. *The advantage of local identity.* This is a big plus in the local trading area. The reluctance to order by mail from an unknown firm in a distant city is overcome when a mailing comes from a local retailer.

2. *The advantage of additional traffic.* A firm that sells solely through mail order either gets an order direct by mail or phone, or it's dead. Retailers, on the other hand, can have their cake and eat it too. Orders are generated direct by mail or by phone. And they can expect additional store traffic as well.

3. *Buying power.* Giant retailers and buying groups have buying power going for them. They have the sources of supply and the possibility of volume discounts.

There are three disadvantages which retailers must overcome.

1. *Lists.* Most retail customer lists consist of charge customers, those who have charged purchases at the retail store. They are *not,* for the most part, mail order buyers. Few retail charge lists are arranged by recency, frequency, or amount of purchase. Most retail direct mail promotions are across-the-board: metro and suburban areas alike. And you just don't sell many power mowers to apartment dwellers! The merchandise retailers stock in suburban stores is different from that in downtown stores to cater to different preferences. But retailers seem to ignore this necessity when it comes to direct mail.

2. *Installment credit.* Without installment credit, the sale of big ticket merchandise by mail is a virtual impossibility. There is a real hang-up for retailers who want to retain their identity with their own charge card—offering thirty-day terms—to the exclusion of other charge cards which allow for installment payments. The answer lies in choosing one of two alternatives: instituting a revolving credit plan for the existing store credit card, or working through one of the bank credit card systems.

3. *Merchandise selection.* Selecting merchandise for mail order sales and selecting merchandise for sale over the counter can be as different as day and night. Few mail order practitioners could sit in the chair of the retail store buyer and vice versa! The types of merchandise to be selected, the manner of promotion, the economics involved, differ greatly.

Since the retailer enjoys the great advantages of store traffic resulting from his direct marketing effort, there are many objectives that can be explored.

1. *Activating existing charge customers.* The area with the most sales potential in any business is existing customers. And the charge card list is the prime list. There's no more effective way to activate a charge list than to give special recognition to charge customers and to show this recognition with special offers.

2. *Getting new customers.* Close behind the objective of activating existing customers is the goal of getting new customers. And here's where direct marketing methods can prove a bonanza. Pinpoint marketing makes it possible to seek new customers in most trading areas with the most potential around existing stores. Merchandise offers can be tied to efforts to acquire new customers, with the objective of making such efforts break even or do better.

3. *Increasing store traffic.* Store traffic is still the name of the game. Direct marketing efforts will automatically create store traffic spillover. But beyond this, the retailer can direct mail a special offer not generally advertised, designed to increase store traffic. A well-organized store traffic program can pay off big.

4. *Leveling out sales volume.* The retail sales cycle has been a fact of life ever since the early days of Wanamaker, the Penneys, and the Fields. It still is today. Direct marketing efforts can be a big factor in filling in the valleys of the cycle.

5. *Pretesting merchandise and price.* Direct marketing methods offer perhaps the most accurate means of pretesting the appeal of merchandise and the most appealing price level. I have yet to see retailers use direct marketing for this purpose, but it could prove to be imaginative and profitable.

6. *Selling a wider range of merchandise.* This can be the most desirable and most profitable objective of all. Mail order thrives on the sale of merchandise and merchandise combinations not generally available in the retail store. But who is to say that retailers should not sell merchandise *not generally available in their retail store?* It's being done right now—successfully. Cameras, radios, dinnerware, tool sets, delicacies, paint guns, magazine subscriptions, insurance—an endless variety of merchandise and services, and all extra business.

So the time is ripe for retailers to get on the direct marketing bandwagon. The elements are all here for those who will grasp the opportunities and run with them.

The applications of direct marketing methods by airlines, automobile manufacturers, insurance companies, oil companies, and retailers are widely adaptable to other industries as part of their marketing mix. Here are additional direct marketing applications that can be melded into the marketing mix.

Introducing New Products

It is a fact of marketing that most manufacturers limit new product development to the restraints of their present channels of distribution. A manufacturer who markets major equipment through a small sales force does not attempt to develop low cost equipment that appeals to thousands of prospects. Nor rarely does a package goods manufacturer, whose major channel of distribution is the grocery trade, show interest in developing new products for another channel of distribution, such as department stores.

And yet the same research department that has the ability to develop a major breakthrough for a new computer might well have the ability to develop a new pocket calculator that would appeal to the masses. If the manufacturer decides against such development because the product doesn't fit his or her present distribution channel—a small sales force dedicated to the sale of major equipment—a big profit opportunity may be passed by.

Following is a classic case history where direct marketing made it possible for a major equipment manufacturer—Hewlett-Packard—to introduce an exciting new product that did not fit their selling mode. The year was 1970. Hewlett-Packard had just invented the first scientific pocket calculator. The basic markets were determined to be scientists and engineers. And an appropriate selling price was determined to be $395. There was no way that the small sales force of H-P, accustomed to making sales in the thousands of dollars, could cover a market of thousands of scientists and engineers. What to do?

Direct marketing proved to be the answer to the problem. The target market was scientists and engineers. There was a wide array of publications and mailing lists available to reach these target markets. So a space and direct mail campaign was developed. (See Exhibits 21-8 and 21-9). The results were sensational. About 10 percent of inquiries were converted to sales: the direct mail package pulled an incredible $40,000 in sales for every 1,000 inquiries.

Hewlett-Packard soon found other markets. And they rapidly developed other specialized pocket calculators. Direct marketing was a major factor in opening the college book store market, for example, and it proved highly successful.

Exhibit 21-8. Space Ad Designed to Get Inquiries for the HP-35 Pocket Calculator

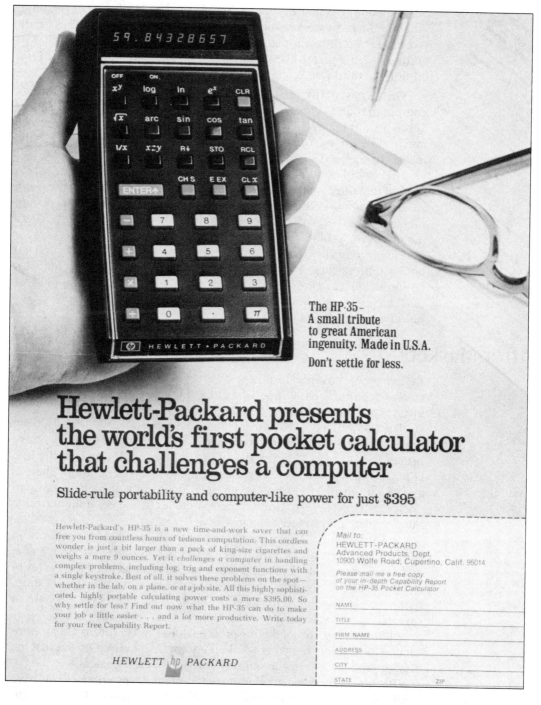

The HP-35—
A small tribute
to great American
ingenuity. Made in U.S.A.

Don't settle for less.

Hewlett-Packard presents the world's first pocket calculator that challenges a computer

Slide-rule portability and computer-like power for just $395

Hewlett-Packard's HP-35 is a new time-and-work saver that can free you from countless hours of tedious computation. This cordless wonder is just a bit larger than a pack of king-size cigarettes and weighs a mere 9 ounces. Yet it *challenges a computer* in handling complex problems, including log, trig and exponent functions with a single keystroke. Best of all, it solves these problems on the spot— whether in the lab, on a plane, or at a job site. All this highly sophisticated, highly portable calculating power costs a mere $395.00. So why settle for less? Find out now what the HP-35 can do to make your job a little easier . . . and a lot more productive. Write today for your free Capability Report.

Mail to:
HEWLETT-PACKARD
Advanced Products, Dept.
10900 Wolfe Road, Cupertino, Calif. 95014

*Please mail me a free copy
of your in-depth Capability Report
on the HP-35 Pocket Calculator*

NAME

TITLE

FIRM NAME

ADDRESS

CITY

STATE   ZIP

HEWLETT hp PACKARD

But the marketing story doesn't end there. As H-P developed a complete line of specialized calculators, the development of a catalog covering the complete line became a logical extension of the solo mailing program. And this worked too. So successful was the Hewlett-Packard direct marketing program that they went from sales of approximately $20 million the first year to about $60 million the second year to almost $100 million the third year. A true success story.

The success of H-P, however, brought on serious competition—foreign competition and domestic competition from such prestigious firms as Texas Instruments. And with competition, lower prices. Much lower. The much lower prices greatly reduced the viability of direct marketing as the major channel of distribution.

This would be a sad ending to a great marketing story if it weren't for the fact that direct marketing popularized pocket calculators to the point where distribution through retail stores—electronic stores and department stores, in particular—became viable and successful. So H-P followed the marketing evolution.

This case history dramatizes three important points. (1) A firm need not limit product development to products which fit their present distribution mode. (2) Direct marketing can be the most effective method for introducing a new product. (3) Direct marketing can popularize a new product and lead to other channels of distribution.

After-Markets

In Chapter 6, "Business-to-Business Direct Marketing," we explored after-market opportunities. A firm in the office duplicating equipment field was given as an example. Here are others.

The 3M Company is a major manufacturer and seller of overhead equipment for showing transparencies. Their prime markets are businesses and schools. Their modes of distribution are through dealer and company salespeople. Selling the equipment is just the first step. There is a great after-market for supplies. Supplies include not only blank transparencies for conversion to printed transparencies by the equipment owner, but complete preprinted programs as well.

As an example, 3M has complete packaged programs for schools on subjects such as math for various grade levels, languages, safety, hygiene, and scores more. Sales in the aggregate are substantial, but there is a problem: dollar sales are small compared to dollar sales for original equipment. So salespeople tend to concentrate their efforts on the sale of original equipment.

A big answer to the marketing problem for 3M was to prepare a supplies catalog to go direct to owners of their equipment. And a plus was that the catalog produced "over-the-transom" orders for their dealers.

IBM, the huge manufacturer of computers and typewriters, today has a companywide commitment to direct marketing as a part of their total mar-

Exhibit 21-9. H-P Mailing to Engineers

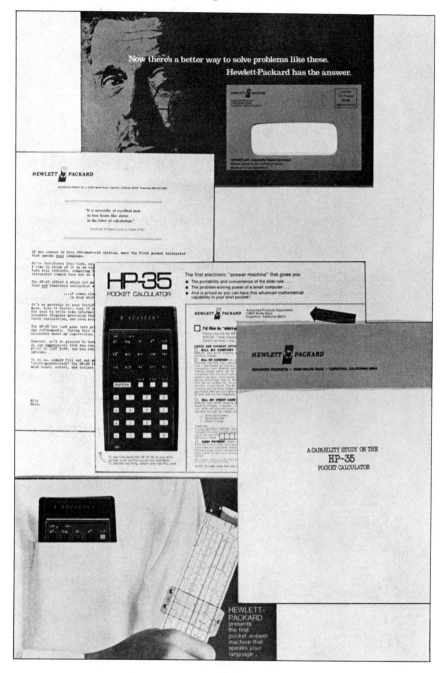

Hewlett-Packard's mailing for its pocket calculator was carefully designed to appeal to engineers. Package pulled an incredible $40,000 in sales for every 1,000 inquiries.

keting mix. Getting qualified leads for salespeople is just one of several direct marketing applications. The cost of person-to-person selling being what it is, IBM too has found they can no longer afford to have their salespeople sell after-market supplies except to the largest of customers. So today IBM has their own office and computer supply catalog. And they even sell typewriters direct to small businesses. What's more, IBM uses direct marketing methods to drive prospects into computer shows that they conduct in the U.S. and Canada.

Direct Marketing in the Advertising Mix

So, as we have seen, there are scores of ways to meld direct marketing with other marketing methods. But what about melding direct marketing advertising with general advertising? Here the opportunities for improvement are considerable.

More often than not, I've seen direct response advertising for given firms that has little resemblance to their general advertising. Different typography. Different look. Inappropriate handling of logos. No tie-in with central campaign themes. Lost opportunities, for sure.

Major general advertisers spend millions of dollars establishing their franchises, building their images. To pass up the opportunity to ride established images is to dilute the effectiveness of direct response advertising. To fail to tie in to campaign themes—"The Friendly Skies of United"—"You're in Good Hands with Allstate"—"The Knowledge Business"—is to lose identity.

The applications of direct marketing as a single marketing method or as a part of the total marketing mix are almost endless. With strategic planning and professional execution, the opportunities are almost endless. Best of success to you in all your direct marketing efforts!

Self-Quiz

1. What are the four Ps of marketing?

a. _____

b. _____

c. _____

d. _____

2. Basically, managements dictate that their companies be:

   a. _____ driven, or

   b. _____ driven.

   c. _____ driven is preferable.

3. Name a prime source for building a data base for airlines.

   _____

4. What is an automobile dealer's best defense against losing customers to competition?

   _____

   _____

   _____

5. Define "third-party selling" in the insurance field.

   _____

   _____

   _____

6. What is the major advantage of an oil company credit card from the standpoint of the oil company?

   _____

   _____

   _____

7. Using direct marketing as a part of the total marketing mix offers three big advantages to retailers over nonstore marketers. Name them.

   a. _____

   b. _____

   c. _____

8. Why is direct marketing a logical marketing method for capturing major equipment after-markets?

   _____

   _____

   _____

9. Why should direct response advertising ride on the coattails of general advertising used by traditional marketers?

_____

_____

_____

Pilot Project

Assume you are the assistant marketing director of the Lincoln-Mercury Division of Ford Motor Company. You have been given a key task that lends itself to direct marketing applications: to switch owners of competitive cars to the Mercury Cougar.

Prepare a marketing plan that will identify:

1. Owners you consider to be your best prospects to switch, by competitive make of car.

2. Your marketing strategy for getting these prospects into Mercury dealer showrooms (incentives, offers, etc.).

3. Prepare a sales letter to accomplish your objective.

Careers in Direct Marketing

Laurie Spar
Vice President
Direct Marketing Educational Foundation

Individuals who have read Bob Stone's book, but who previously were unfamiliar with direct marketing, will probably be very enthusiastic about the potential of the field and may be thinking about career possibilities.

Indications are that direct marketing will continue to increase in scope, expenditures, and technology. This will require a steady stream of fresh, new, trained talent not only to fill positions in companies which are expanding their direct marketing efforts, but in companies entering the direct marketing stream for the first time.

Those who have read this book, who have taken a course in direct marketing, or who have a basic understanding of the principles and practices of direct marketing, will have a chance to start a very exciting career. Those who are aware of specific position categories, where they are, and how to find them will have an edge over competition for jobs. Discussed in this appendix are some of the many career opportunities, why a career in marketing is a good choice, how to get experience, where the jobs are and how to find them, and some basic tips on the marketing of the most important product—YOU!

Advantages of a Direct Marketing Career

As recently as a few years ago, most people entered direct marketing not by choice, but by chance. Once they got involved in direct marketing, they were here to stay. Direct marketing is growing daily, changing constantly. It offers challenges that are testable, measurable, and accountable. The constant emphasis on testing offers a chance to try new offers, new premiums, new lists, and so on along with a constant opportunity to learn. It's fun, can be financially rewarding, and is never dull.

Although almost every first job is difficult to get because of a lack of experience, direct marketing has an advantage that most other industries do not: it is testable, measurable, and accountable. Accountability is what makes for rapid advancement—much more so than in other fields. Direct marketers know almost immediately what's working. They can compute the return on their investment (ROI). Those who consistently add to the ROI (return on investment) are promoted quickly.

Direct marketing offers you the opportunity to test new ideas quickly—and relatively inexpensively. It's a chance for you to broaden your advertising and marketing experience. When you realize who's using direct marketing, you'll realize why a background in its techniques is advantageous and why it's a sound career choice.

Who's Using Direct Marketing?

Virtually any kind of organization can use direct marketing to sell its products and services, to raise funds, to generate inquiries, to call attention to issues, to elect candidates, to build store traffic, to generate leads for salespeople. These organizations include consumer product manufacturers; financial service organizations (banks, savings & loan companies, personal credit and insurance companies); consumer mail order marketers; business and industrial mail order marketers; publishers (newspapers, magazines, books); book-and-tape clubs; industrial manufacturers; business equipment manufacturers; retailers; public utilities; travel and transportation companies; package goods manufacturers and distributors; fund raisers, service organizations (public relations, trade associations, management consultants, etc.). Many of these include *Fortune* 500 and 1000 companies.

Even companies that have traditionally used image-building general advertising are now integrating direct marketing into their marketing and advertising mix. The entry-level person who has a background in direct marketing will be an asset to companies that need to make sound business decisions as to their choice of advertising methods.

Direct marketing is not only being used more and more extensively within the United States, but throughout the world as well. Global opportunities—companies using direct marketing within other countries, as well as U.S. firms doing business direct in foreign countries—represent yet another example of the growth of the field, and a good reason for you to be in it.

Direct Marketing Careers

Because job functions often vary from company to company, standard job titles and descriptions are difficult to define. New techniques, new segmentation methods, and technology may result in new job titles. Some of the general direct response career areas that offer great opportunities are described as follows:

Careers in Direct Response Advertising Agencies

In a speech at a major industry conference, David Ogilvy advised agency leaders not to hire anyone unless they had direct response experience. "Direct marketers know what works!" When he made this comment in the 1970s, there were only a handful of direct response agencies. Indicative of the growth of direct marketing is the fact that every major advertising agency has formed or acquired a direct response division. In addition, there are many "independent" agencies that specialize in direct response.

Job titles and departments in direct response advertising agencies are similar to those in general advertising agencies, but the opportunity for advancement is more rapid in direct.

Depending on background, interests, and career goals, an individual can choose a direct response agency career in traffic, account management/client services, media, creative, or production. With increased sophistication in the profession, many agencies now have a research department, or will probably form one shortly. The new emphasis on more narrowly defined target audiences means new emphasis on data base marketing; several agencies are developing data base services for their clients. Many agencies have become what is called "full-service" agencies, with additional departments to service client needs in telephone marketing, list consulting, and lettershop services.

There are direct response agencies that deal solely with the consumer market or business-to-business market or fundraising, as well as agencies that deal solely with catalog marketing. Obviously, an understanding of these markets and of direct marketing techniques is critical to success in an agency career.

As an entry-level applicant, you should decide whether to begin on the agency side or the client side and/or whether to work for a large agency or a small agency. Obviously, there are pluses and minuses on both sides, but the applicant will have to compare her or his goals, aspirations, and personality with information gleaned from research about individual companies.

Traffic   Traffic is an excellent entry-level opportunity—a chance for an aspiring account executive or creative person to get a foot in the door and learn the agency business. The traffic coordinator is responsible for coordinating the component parts of a total advertising project with each of the agency's departments.

Account Executives   Account executives are responsible for liaison with the client, involvement in marketing strategy, and coordinating with various other departments involved in the creation of the advertising and its implementation. In general, account executives must have a marketing, business, advertising, or communications background. These backgrounds are not necessarily prerequisites, but they are extremely helpful.

Creative   The creative department of a direct response agency involves copywriters and graphic arts people. A course in copywriting is not a prerequisite for copywriters, but the individual must have a love of words and possess the proven ability to communicate them clearly and concisely. The more you have written, the better.

Unlike general advertising which seeks to create awareness, often through clever, creative ads, direct response advertising must sell. The copywriter must have a thorough knowledge of the target audience—what it wants, why it buys, and how it reacts—and must work closely with all departments of the agency. Direct response copywriters must always remember that they are first, last, and always . . . salespeople. Their copy, along with the proper offer and media, is what does the selling. In order to gain experience, newcomers should write, write, and continue to write! Collecting samples of direct mail and direct response print advertising is good training. And, of course, a portfolio is a must.

A career as a copywriter can begin as an assistant or junior, then advance to copywriter, senior copywriter, copy supervisor/director. Often, copywriters become vice presidents/creative directors, supervising both copywriters and graphic arts people.

Art and Layout   Those with artistic talents can find jobs as artists, layout artists, or product photographers, working closely with the copywriters in developing the creative concept and "marrying" the copy to the graphics. Obviously, talent demonstrated by a portfolio and then through experience is positively required for this department.

Media Buying and Production   There are many opportunities for entry-level positions in media buying. Media include mail, print, broadcast, and the new electronic media, and telephone.

There are several agencies that handle direct response broadcast production. When hiring, these departments generally look for people who have a background in direct response, broadcast, communications, and sometimes, liberal arts. Knowledge of direct response broadcast techniques is helpful (there are books which deal solely with this topic). Students who have worked in production or management of campus radio or TV stations will have had some valuable applicable experience. On-the-job-training will familiarize them with the direct response details.

The advent of all the new electronic media, such as cable TV, shopping on home computers, videotex, and home shopping channels means that the individual interested in the future technology will have to keep up with the constantly changing times by reading trade press such as *Broadcasting, Cablevision, Channels, Electronic Media, Millimeter, Multichannel News, Television and Radio Age*, the *Media Industry Newsletter*, and the *Home Video Publisher*. Many such new electronic media are in the experimental stage: there is a constant flux of corporate newcomers and much room for success or failure.

The media people must coordinate with all departments. They are responsible for the selection and the purchase of lists, space, or time, and analysis of the results. Media orders must be coordinated with brokers and publications and placed on a timely basis. Media people must be good negotiators when bargaining for print space or broadcast time, getting not only the lowest rates, but also the best positions or times. An analytical mind is critical, along with the ability to effectively communicate recommendations based on the results.

Production   Production people in direct response agencies are integral to meeting deadlines. They must be detail oriented and able to work under the pressure of deadlines. They are responsible for working with the various suppliers such as printers and lettershops. They must see to it that the advertising message's component parts are complete, that the colors are correct, that there are no typographical errors (imagine what a misplaced decimal point could do to the client's bottom line!), and that postal regulations and size standards are adhered to.

Research   Careers in research departments begin at the assistant level and can work up to senior management. Because of the statistical nature of research, courses in research methodology, quantitative and behavioral statistics, psychology, sociology, and the like are obligatory. Unlike some other areas of direct response marketing, an MBA may be required for success in the research department.

A Final Word   A career at a direct response agency is exciting and very challenging. The constant emphasis on testing means that there is always an opportunity to try new ways of getting that immediate response. A change in a word in the offer, a different premium or list, a change in the advertising medium, or any one of many other variables can mean significant increases (or decreases!) in response rates. Those responsible know immediately what worked and what did not.

Yes, an agency career can be exciting, but extremely demanding. Only you can decide if this is the career for you. If you're a "nine-to-fiver," if you cannot work under the pressure of client demands and deadlines, if you are not a risk-taker and open to criticism, then an agency career is not for you.

Career Opportunities in Mailing Lists

Once the direct mail package or catalog has been completed in-house or by an outside agency, it must reach the right prospects. The most creative mailing will be a failure if it is not sent to the right target audience. That's where mailing lists come into the picture. Depending on an individual's qualifications, goals, and credentials, there are three (or possibly four) areas involved in the list business. An individual with a bent for numbers, for research, computers, analysis, or sales will find challenging and lucrative careers as a broker, manager, or compiler, as well as with computer service bureaus and data base companies.

List Brokers   Like brokers in other industries, the list broker serves both the list owner and the mailer (user). The list broker helps the marketer select the lists that will work best for the particular product/offer. The broker helps in the planning of the mailings, the analysis of the response, the forecasting for future mailings, and is often involved in the clients' marketing strategy. Brokers are accountable, too, measured by their clients on the success of their recommendations.

List brokers must also be familiar with data bases. They must know where they can be obtained and what they can do. They may make recommendations on when to overlay demographic and lifestyle data on "house" (the mailer's own) or rented lists.

Entry-level jobs in list brokerage often begin either at the administrative assistant level or assistant account manager (or executive) on up to senior account manager and vice president/account supervisor. The successful account executive has a great deal of client contact and must be ambitious and eager to learn about new lists, pay attention to detail, and have good oral and written communications skills.

Lists are rented to the broker or directly to the mailer by an internal or external manager. The broker performs a sales function for the list owner, and is also concerned with clerical and detail work and follow-up with the list owner (in the case of external list managers) and with the mailer. The manager must explain why the list should be tested/used, which companies have used it successfully in the past, and what the indications are for other clients.

For both manager and broker careers, a marketing background is helpful; strong communications skills are essential even for those with marketing backgrounds.

List Compilers   List compilers can specialize in business and professional markets or consumer markets. Compilers "capture" data from a variety of commercial and public sources such as directories, and voter and automobile registration lists. They must have experience in developing sources for names and a methodology for producing lists with a high degree of accuracy. This end of the business tends to be more technical in nature, requiring the services of data processors, computer programmers, program analysts, software engineers, and the like. The very large compilers have data bases with marketing-oriented information on millions of individuals and households.

Service Bureaus Service bureaus are connected with all these list areas. The advent of ZIP codes and customer information files has brought the list maintenance service bureau to prominence. Service bureaus perform sophisticated data processing and data conversion tasks such as merge/purge, personalized computer letters, postal presorting, model development and analysis, and list rental fulfillment, requiring the services of individuals with a computer and technical background. In addition, they require salespeople to sell their services to brokers, managers, and mailers.

Lettershops

With the billions and billions of pieces of direct response advertising that go into the mail, lettershops perform an absolutely necessary function for the direct mail field. They represent a sales area that is often ignored by job applicants. Lettershops, which can be independently owned and operated, or part of full-service, direct response agencies, represent the last link in the direct mail process.

Although many of the jobs are mechanical or clerical in nature, lettershops require salespeople to sell the services of the company. The sales personnel give advice on exactly how names and addresses should be delivered to the lettershop. They specify the requirements for insertion and labeling and furnish mailers with written reports indicating receipt of materials and mailing costs. Because many salespeople work on a commission or salary plus commission basis, the more cost efficient they are to their client, the more the client will use their services and recommend them to others.

Catalogs

Catalogs are probably the most visible medium of direct response advertising. You have only to open your own mailbox to realize the number of catalogs—and the number of job opportunities. Those interested in the catalog field may think first of consumer mail order catalogs, but should also consider business-to-business catalogs and those used by retailers.

Some mail order companies produce their catalog(s) "in-house," at agencies that specialize in catalog production, or at direct response agencies that create catalogs for some of their clients. Corporate research will tell the job seeker which catalogs are produced in-house and which ones utilize the services of outside agencies.

If you've studied retailing, a career with a retail catalog organization offers some exciting possibilities. In addition to merchandising, there's marketing and creative, production, testing, list maintenance and management, data base operations—all on the "front end" of this business.

There is also the "back-end" or "fulfillment" function of the business. The most beautiful catalog in the world will be a dismal failure if the inventory, delivery, and customer service departments are inadequate. These present some excellent entry-level training opportunities for newcomers who want to learn the catalog business and see what's working and what isn't. (Customer service reps and inventory people are often in a position to make recommendations for improvement, thereby getting their names known to the management personnel who make promotion and hiring decisions.)

Jobs in catalog agencies are similar to those in direct response agencies. Some mail order companies create their own marketing strategies, develop and rent their own lists, do their own testing, and so forth. If they have only some of the agency capabilities, they then utilize the services of agencies that specialize in design and production for the rest.

Telemarketing

Telemarketing agencies are structured like advertising agencies, but their medium is the telephone. A client will hire a telemarketing agency to make or receive calls. A marketing representative or the executive responsible for new business development will develop leads, make the "sales" presentation to the client, and formalize the "pitch" with a written marketing plan or proposal. The marketing rep is then responsible for client communications. Previous experience in telemarketing is helpful, but sales experience is certainly required.

A telemarketing account executive organizes and manages the client's program within the agency. Good written and oral communication, organizational, and analytical skills are required. The account executive coordinates scriptwriting, testing, list preparation, and client reports.

Scriptwriters are the creative people of the telemarketing agency. Different copy skills are required in telemarketing because the script must be written to be heard, anticipating questions and preparing responses to prospects' questions in advance. Journalism and creative writing are helpful backgrounds for this line of work.

Some direct marketing companies do their own telemarketing in-house; others utilize telemarketing agencies which have "centers." It is the telemarketing center manager's responsibility to supervise the making or receiving of calls based on the client's marketing strategy, lists, and script requirements. The center manager must recruit, train, schedule, and motivate the center's "communicators."

A center manager should have a background in business administration and human resources. Telemarketing operations experience is essential, along with people management skills, logistics, and scheduling. Due to the increased automation technology in telemarketing, a background in computer science is advantageous.

Telemarketing trainers instruct the communicators about the client's products or services. In addition, they teach listening skills and sales techniques. They often monitor the communicators during the sales call to make sure all goes according to the script and marketing plan; they make adjustments in the script if necessary.

An individual interested in sales will therefore get terrific training as a telephone communicator. Very often communicators work part time and come from all walks of life—students, homemakers, actors. Good communications skills are essential, but a business or marketing background is not required. For this reason, telemarketing is a good entry-level job for those who wish to advance.

Where Do I Go from Here?

Now that you've read this book and are familiar with some of the many career choices in direct marketing, where do you go from here? How do you find out about the different companies? How can you gain the experience that every employer looks for?

First, anyone interested in this field should read specialty books on the various aspects of direct response. Be familiar with the "lingo" of direct marketing. Be acquainted with its techniques. Read the trade press, keep up with who's doing what, with mergers and acquisitions, with promotions and career changes. Make lists of people and companies. Do research on individual companies by contacting them for copies of their promotion pieces and annual reports.

To build your résumé or contact mailing list, refer to the *Direct Marketing Market Place* (published by Hilary House). This directory lists hundreds of companies in the direct marketing field by business category. It lists key contacts, addresses, and phone numbers, and gives a brief description of what the company does. The Direct Marketing Association also publishes service directories (which list direct response agencies, list brokers, compilers, managers, research firms, and international organizations). These directories are available for sale or they can be consulted in the DMA library.

The DMA's very extensive library is available by appointment to DMA members (free of charge), to full-time students with ID (free of charge), and to individuals (charge for one-time use). The person interested in learning about direct marketing will find a wealth of information, including all the books dealing with the subject, trade press, business category files containing reprints of articles, company files, portfolios of DMA's award winning ECHO campaigns, and much, more more.

Next, join local direct marketing organizations. There are over forty of these scattered throughout the country and the world. Most of these groups have local Direct Marketing "Days" which often include trade shows. These events offer wonderful opportunities for you to expand your education and make contacts.

Internships help you gain actual work experience in direct marketing—a chance to turn theory into practice. The Direct Marketing Educational Foundation and some of the local clubs sponsor internship programs with local members, and some positions can be obtained by writing individually to local companies.

Full-time students interested in gaining hands-on experience might want to enter the Leonard J. Raymond Collegiate ECHO Awards Competition. This is a direct response advertising competition in which student teams act as a direct response agency, plan the marketing and creative strategies, plan the campaign, construct the budget, and project the results for a corporate sponsor. Valuable prizes aimed at furthering direct response education (including attendance at a DMA Annual Conference or a local Direct Marketing "Day" or reference books) are available for the winning teams and their faculty advisors.

Full-time seniors or graduate students can apply for the Foundation's Collegiate Institute. This is a week-long seminar on all aspects of direct response. Included as part of the program is a session on resume writing and interviewing, as well as an "Interview Afternoon" at which time direct marketing companies are encouraged to interview scholarship recipients for entry-level jobs.

Individuals interested in this field should collect various forms of direct response ads. Pay attention to format, copy, order forms, positioning, and so forth. These "real-world" examples are excellent educational tools. Of course, your own portfolio should be maintained in a highly professional manner.

In addition, the Direct Marketing Educational Foundation conducts programs for students and professors geared at expanding the scope of direct marketing education. It also has additional career information, course listings, sample course outlines, a bibliography of direct marketing texts and career resources, a listing of local direct marketing clubs, and an informal resume referral service (Direct Marketing Educational Foundation, 6 East 43rd Street, New York, NY 10017, 212/689-4977).

Where Are the Jobs?

Although the majority of direct marketing companies are located in New York, Chicago, and Los Angeles, others can be found throughout the U.S. and abroad, and in increasing numbers. Local direct marketing clubs often list position openings; many will print your "Positions Wanted" ad free of charge in the classified section of their newsletter. Otherwise, consult the *Direct Marketing Market Place*, local classifieds, and/or trade press. There are several executive recruiters that deal with direct response positions, but they rarely deal with entry-level openings.

A Word about Salaries

This appendix has deliberately eliminated salary information. There are so many variables for each job function that it would be practically impossible even to give accurate ranges. Salaries depend upon the location of the company, its size, the responsibilities, benefits, and so forth. Probably the best thing for a job seeker to do to determine a reasonable range would be to consult local classifieds to determine the "going rate."

Remember that entry-level salaries in direct marketing are competitive with salaries in other areas of marketing and advertising, but due to direct marketing's testability, measurability, and accountability, the opportunities for advancement are much greater.

Marketing Yourself

The most important thing to remember about your résumé is that understanding of direct response techniques will help you market yourself.

Just as you would do research before marketing a product, you must do research about your own likes and dislikes, strengths and weaknesses. You must also do research about prospective employers. The information you glean from directories, annual reports, through personal contacts, will serve to make up your own personal "data base" of prospects. The research will help you target your efforts to the best prospects rather than blanketing the universe with résumés!

Just as you would want your prospect to act immediately and buy your product or service, you want that employer to act—by calling you for an interview and then by hiring you.

Remember that your résumé is your ad; your cover letter is your sales pitch; your interview is your sales call; and your thank-you letter is your follow-up. Don't do anything in marketing yourself to a prospective employer that you wouldn't do in marketing a product or service. Remember to keep your résumé benefit oriented, stressing accomplishments rather than responsibilities. List only relevant information, information that will help you get the job you are seeking.

Glossary*

Access Time: The time it takes a computer to locate a piece of information in memory or storage and to take action, that is, the "read" time. Also, the time it takes a computer to store a piece of information and to complete action, that is, the "write" time.

Action Devices: Items and techniques used in a mailing to initiate the response desired.

Active Buyer: A buyer whose latest purchase was made within the last twelve months. (*See* **Buyer**.)

Active Customer: A term used interchangeably with "active buyer."

Active Member: Any member who is fulfilling the original commitment or who has fulfilled that commitment and has made one or more purchases in the last twelve months.

Active Subscriber: One who has committed for regular delivery of magazines, books, or other goods or services for a period of time still in effect.

Actives: Customers on a list who have made purchases within a prescribed time period, usually not more than one year; subscribers whose subscriptions have not expired.

Additions: New names, either of individuals or companies, added to a mailing list.

Address Coding Guide (CG): Contains the actual or potential beginning and ending house numbers, block group and/or enumeration district numbers, ZIP codes, and other geographic codes for all city delivery service streets served by 3,154 post offices located within 6,601 ZIP codes.

Address Correction Requested: An endorsement which, when printed in the upper left-hand corner of the address portion of the mailing piece (below the return address), authorizes the U.S. Postal Service, for a fee, to provide the known new address of a person no longer at the address on the mailing piece.

A.I.D.A.: The most popular formula for the preparation of direct mail copy. The letters stand for Get Attention, Arouse Interest, Stimulate Desire, Ask for Action.

Alphanumeric: A contraction of "alphabetic" and "numeric." Applies to any coding system that provides for letters, numbers (digits), and special symbols such as punctuation marks. Synonymous with Alphameric.

Assigned Mailing Dates: The dates on which the list user has the obligation to mail a specific list. No other date is acceptable without specific approval of the list owner.

Audience: The total number of individuals reached by a promotion or advertisement.

Audit: Printed report of the counts involved in a particular list or file.

Back End: The activities necessary to complete a mail order transaction once an order has been received and/or the measurement of a buyer's performance after he has ordered the first item in a series offering.

Bangtail: Promotional envelope with a second flap which is perforated and designed for use as an order blank.

---

* Source: Direct Marketing Association.

Batch Processing: Technique of executing a set of computer programs/selections in batches as opposed to executing each order/selection as it is received. Batches can be created by computer programming or a manual collection of data into groups.

Batched Job: A job that is grouped with other jobs as input to a computing system, as opposed to a transaction job entry where the job is done singly to completion.

Bill Enclosure: Any promotional piece or notice enclosed with a bill, an invoice, or a statement not directed toward the collection of all or part of the bill, invoice, or statement.

Binary: Involves a selection, choice, or condition in which there are two possibilities such as the use of the symbols "0" and "1" in a numbering system.

Bingo Card: A reply card inserted in a publication and used by readers to request literature and samples from companies whose products and services are either advertised or mentioned in editorial columns.

Bit: A single character or elements in a binary number (digit). The smallest element of binary machine language represented by a magnetized spot on a recording surface or a magnetized element of a storage device.

Bounce Back: An offer enclosed with mailings sent to a customer in fulfillment of an order.

BPI (Bytes Per Inch)**:** Characters, represented in bytes, per inch.

Broadcast Media: A direct response source that includes radio, television, and cable TV.

Broadside: A single sheet of paper, printed on one side or two, folded for mailing or direct distribution, and opening into a single, large advertisement.

Brochure: Strictly, a high-quality pamphlet, with especially planned layout, typography, and illustrations. Term is also used loosely for any promotional pamphlet or booklet.

Bucktag: A separate slip attached to a printed piece containing instructions to route the material to specific individuals.

Bulk Mail: A category of third-class mail involving a large quantity of identical pieces but addressed to different names which are specially processed for mailing before delivery to the post office.

Business List: Any compilation or list of individuals or companies based upon a business-associated interest, inquiry, membership, subscription, or purchase.

Buyer: One who orders merchandise, books, records, information, or services. Unless another modifying word or two is used, it is assumed that a buyer has paid for all merchandise to date.

Burst: To separate continuous form paper into discrete sheets.

Byte: Sequence of adjacent binary digits operated upon as a unit and usually shorter than a computer word. A character is usually considered a byte. (A single byte can contain either two numeric characters or one alphabetic or special character.)

Cash Buyer: A buyer who encloses payment with order.

Cash Rider: Also called "cash up" or "cash option" wherein an order form offers installment terms, but a postscript offers the option of sending full cash payment with order, usually at some saving over the credit price as an incentive.

C/A: Change of address.

Catalog: A book or booklet showing merchandise, with descriptive details and prices.

Catalog Buyer: A person who has bought products or services from a catalog.

Catalog Request (Paid or Unpaid): One who sends for a catalog (prospective buyer). The catalog may be free; there may be a nominal charge for postage and handling, or there may be a more substantial charge that is often refunded or credited on the first order.

Census Tract: Small geographical area established by local committees, and approved by the Census Bureau, which contains a population segment with relatively uniform economic and social characteristics with clearly identifiable boundaries averaging approximately 1,200 households.

Cheshire Label: Specially prepared paper (rolls, fanfold, or accordion fold) used to reproduce names and addresses to be mechanically affixed, one at a time, to a mailing piece.

Circulars: General term for printed advertising in any form, including printed matter sent out by direct mail.

Cleaning: The process of correcting and/or removing a name and address from a mailing list because it is no longer correct or because the listing is to be shifted from one category to another.

Cluster Selection: A selection routine based upon taking a group of names in series, skipping a group, taking another group, etc. For example—a cluster selection on an nth name basis might be the first 10 out of every 100 or the first 125 out of 175, etc.; a cluster selection using limited ZIP codes might be the first 200 names in each of the specified ZIP codes, and so forth.

Coding: (1) Identifying devices used on reply devices to identify the mailing list or other source from which the address was obtained. (2) A structure of letters and numbers used to classify characteristics of an address on a list.

Collate: (1) To assemble individual elements of a mailing in sequence for inserting into a mailing envelope. (2) A program which combines two or more ordered files to produce a single ordered file. Also the act of combining such files. Synonymous with merge as in merge/purge.

Commission: A percentage of sale, by prior agreement, paid to the list broker, list manager, or other service arm for their part in the list usage.

Compile: The process by which a computer translates a series of instructions written in a programming language into actual machine language.

Compiled List: Names and addresses derived from directories, newspapers, public records, retail sales slips, trade show registrations, etc., to identify groups of people with something in common.

Compiler: Organization which develops lists of names and addresses from directories, newspapers, public records, registrations, and other sources, identifying groups of people, companies, or institutions with something in common.

Completed Cancel: One who has completed a specific commitment to buy products or services before cancelling.

Comprehensive: Complete and detailed layout for a printed piece. Also: "Comp," "Compre."

Computer: Data processor that can perform substantial computation, without intervention by a human.

Computer Compatibility: Ability to interchange the data or programs of one computer system with one or more other computers.

Computer Letter: Computer-printed message providing personalized, fill-in information from a source file in predesignated positions. May also be full-printed letter with personalized insertions.

Computer Personalization: Printing of letters or other promotional pieces by a computer using names, addresses, special phrases, or other information based on data appearing in one or more computer records. The objective is to use the information in the computer record to tailor the promotional message to a specific individual.

Computer Program: Series of instructions or statements prepared to achieve a certain result.

Computer Record: All of the information about an individual, company, or transaction stored on a specific magnetic tape or disc.

Computer Service Bureau: An internal or external facility providing general or specific data processing services.

Consumer List: A list of names (usually at home address) compiled, or resulting, from a common inquiry or buying activity indicating a general or specific buying interest.

Continuity Program: Products or services bought as a series of small purchases, rather than all at one time. Generally based on a common theme and shipped at regular or specific time intervals.

C.T.O.: Contribution to overhead (profit).

Contributor List: Names and addresses of persons who have given to a specific fund raising effort. (*See* **Donor List**.)

Controlled Circulation: Distribution at no charge of a publication to individuals or companies on the basis of their titles or occupations. Typically, recipients are asked from time to time to verify the information that qualifies them to receive the publication.

Controlled Duplication: A method by which names and addresses from two or more lists are matched (usually by computer) in order to eliminate or limit extra mailings to the same name and address.

Continuous Form: Paper forms designed for computer printing that are folded, and sometimes perforated, at predetermined vertical measurements. These may be letters, vouchers, invoices, cards, etc.

Conversion: (1) Process of changing from one method of data processing to another, or from one data processing system to another. Synonymous with Reformatting. (2) To secure specific action such as a purchase or contribution from a name on a mailing list or as a result of an inquiry.

Co-op Mailing: A mailing of two or more offers included in the same envelope or other carrier, with each participating mailer sharing mailing costs according to some predetermined formula.

C.P.I. (Cost Per Inquiry): A simple arithmetical formula derived by dividing the total cost of a mailing or an advertisement by the number of inquiries received.

C.P.O. (Cost Per Order): Similar to Cost Per Inquiry except based on actual orders rather than inquiries.

C.P.M. (Cost Per Thousand): Refers to total cost-per-thousand pieces of direct mail "in the mail."

Coupon: Part of an advertising promotion piece intended to be filled in by the inquirer or customer and returned to the advertiser.

Coupon Clipper: One who has given evidence of responding to free or nominal-cost offers out of curiosity, with little or no serious interest or buying intent.

Deadbeat: One who has ordered a product or service and, without just cause, hasn't paid for it.

Decoy: A unique name especially inserted in a mailing list for verifying list usage.

Delinquent: One who has fallen behind or has stopped scheduled payment for a product or service.

Delivery Date: The date a list user or a designated representative of the list user receives a specific list order from the list owner.

Demographics: Socioeconomic characteristics pertaining to a geographic unit (county, city, sectional center, ZIP code, group of households, education, ethnicity, income level, etc.).

Direct Mail Advertising: Any promotional effort using the Postal Service, or other direct delivery service, for distribution of the advertising message.

Direct Response Advertising: Advertising, through any medium, designed to generate a response by any means (such as mail, telephone, or telegraph) that is measurable.

Donor List: A list of persons who have given money to one or more charitable organizations. (*See* **Contributor List**.)

Doubling Day: A point in time established by previous experience when 50% of all returns to a mailing will normally be received.

Dummy: (1) A mock-up giving a preview of a printed piece, showing placement and nature of the material to be printed. (2) A fictitious name with a mailable address inserted into a mailing list to check on usage of that list.

Dupe (Duplication): Appearance of identical or nearly identical entities more than once.

Duplication Elimination: A specific kind of controlled duplication which provides that: no matter how many times a name and address is on a list, and how many lists contain that name and address, it will be accepted for mailing only once by that mailer. Also referred to as "dupe elimination."

Editing Rules: Specific rules used in preparing name and address records that treat all elements the same way at all times. Also, the rules for rearranging, deleting, selecting, or inserting any needed data, symbols, and/or characters.

Envelope Stuffer: Any advertising or promotional material enclosed in an envelope with business letters, statements, or invoices.

Exchange: An arrangement whereby two mailers exchange equal quantities of mailing list names.

Expire: A former customer who is no longer an active buyer.

Expiration: A subscription that is not renewed.

Expiration Date: Date a subscription expires.

Field: Reserved area in a computer which services a similar function in all records of the file. Also, location on magnetic tape or disc drive which has definable limitations and meaning: e.g., Position 1-30 is the Name Field.

File Maintenance: The activity of keeping a file up-to-date by adding, changing, or deleting data (all or part). Synonymous with List Maintenance. (*See* **Update**.)

Fill-In: A name, address, or other words added to a preprinted letter.

First-Time Buyer: One who buys a product or service from a specific company for the first time.

Fixed Field: A way of laying out, or formatting, list information in a computer file that puts every piece of data in a specific position relative to every other piece of data, and limits the amount of space assigned to that data. If a piece of data is missing from an individual record, or if its assigned space is not completely used, that space is not filled (every record has the same space and the same length). Any data exceeding its assigned space limitation must be abbreviated or contracted.

Former Buyer: One who has bought one or more times from a company with no purchase in the last twelve months.

Free-Standing Insert: A promotional piece loosely inserted or nested in a newspaper or magazine.

Frequency: The number of times an individual has ordered within a specific period of time. (*See* **Monetary Value and Recency**.)

Friend-Of-A-Friend (Friend Recommendation)**:** The result of one party sending in the name of someone considered to be interested in a specific advertiser's product or service; a third-party inquiry.

Front End: Activities necessary, or the measurement of direct marketing activities, leading to an order or a contribution.

Fund Raising List: Any compilation or list of individuals or companies based on a known contribution to one or more fund raising appeals.

Geographics: Any method of subdividing a list, based on geographic or political subdivisions (ZIP codes, sectional centers, cities, counties, states, regions).

Gift Buyer: One who buys a product or service for another.

Gimmick: Attention-getting device, usually dimensional, attached to a direct mail printed piece.

Guarantee: A pledge of satisfaction made by the seller to the buyer and specifying the terms by which the seller will make good his pledge.

Hot-Line List: The most recent names available on a specific list, but no older than three months. In any event, use of the term "hot-line" should be further modified by "weekly," "monthly," etc.

House List: Any list of names owned by a company as a result of compilation, inquiry or buyer action, or acquisition, that is used to promote that company's products or services.

House-List Duplicate: Duplication of name-and-address records between the list user's own lists and any list being mailed by him on a one-time use arrangement.

Inquiry: One who has asked for literature or other information about a product or service. Unless otherwise stated, it is assumed no payment has been made for the literature or other information. (*Note: A* **Catalog Request** *is generally considered a specific type of inquiry.*)

Installment Buyer: One who orders goods or services and pays for them in two or more periodic payments after their delivery.

Interlist Duplicate: Duplication of names and address records *between* two or more lists, other than house lists, being mailed by a list user.

Intralist Duplication: Duplication of name and address records *within* a given list.

K: Used in reference to computer storage capacity, generally accepted as 1,000. Analogous to M in the direct marketing industry.

Key: One or more characters within a data group that can be used to identify it or control its use. Synonymous with Key Code in mailing business.

Key Code (Key)**:** A group of letters and/or numbers, colors, or other markings, used to measure specific effectiveness of media, lists, advertisements, offers, etc., or any parts thereof.

Keyline: Can be any one of many partial or complete descriptions of past buying history codes to include name-and-address information and current status.

KBN (Kill Bad Name): Action taken with undeliverable addresses; i.e., nixies. You KBN a nixie.

Label: Piece of paper containing the name and address of the recipient which is applied to a mailing for address purposes.

Layout: (1) Artist's sketch showing relative positioning of illustrations, headlines, and copy. (2) Positioning subject matter on a press sheet for most efficient production.

Letterhead: The printing on a letter that identifies the sender.

Lettershop: A business organization that handles the mechanical details of mailings such as addressing, imprinting, collating, etc. Most lettershops offer some printing facilities and many offer some degree of creative direct mail services.

List (Mailing List): Names and addresses of individuals and/or companies having in common a specific interest, characteristic, or activity.

List Broker: A specialist who makes all necessary arrangements for one company to use the list(s) of another company. A broker's services may include most, or all, of the following: research, selection, recommendation, and subsequent evaluation.

List Buyer: Technically, this term should apply only to one who actually buys mailing lists. In practice, however, it is usually used to identify one who orders mailing lists for one-time use; a List User or Mailer.

List Cleaning: The process of correcting and/or removing a name and/or address from a mailing list because it is no longer correct. Term is also used in the identification and elimination of house list duplication.

List Compiler: One who develops lists of names and addresses from directories, newspapers, public records, sales slips, trade show registrations, and other sources for identifying groups of people or companies with something in common.

List Exchange: A barter arrangement between two companies for the use of a mailing list(s). May be: list for list, list for space, or list for comparable value—other than money.

List Maintenance: Any manual, mechanical, or electronic system for keeping name-and-address records (with or without other data) up-to-date at any specific point(s) in time.

List Manager: One who, as an employee of a list owner or as an outside agent, is responsible for the use, by others, of a specific mailing list(s). The list manager generally serves the list owner in several or all of the following capacities: list maintenance (or advice thereon), list promotion and marketing, list clearance and record keeping, collecting for use of the list by others.

List Owner: One who, by promotional activity or compilation, has developed a list of names having something in common; or one who has *purchased* (as opposed to rented, reproduced, or used on a one-time basis) such a list from the developer.

List Rental: An arrangement whereby a list owner furnishes names to a mailer, together with the privilege of using the list on a one-time basis only (unless otherwise specified in advance). For this privilege, the list owner is paid a royalty by the mailer. ("List Rental" is the term most often used although "List Reproduction" and "List Usage" more accurately describe the transaction, since "Rental" is not used in the sense of its ordinary meaning of leasing property.)

List Royalty: Payment to list owners for the privilege of using their names on a one-time basis.

List Sample: A group of names selected from a list in order to evaluate the responsiveness of that list.

List Segmentation: (*See* **List Selection**.)

List Selection: Characteristics used to define smaller groups within a list (essentially, lists within a list). Although very small, select groups may be very desirable and may substantially improve response; increased costs, however, often render them impractical.

List Sequence: The order in which names and addresses appear in a list. While most lists today are in ZIP code sequence, some are alphabetical by name within the ZIP code; others are in carrier sequence (postal delivery); and still others may (or may not) use some other order within the ZIP code. Some lists are still arranged alphabetically by name or chronologically, and in many other variations or combinations.

List Sort: Process of putting a list in a specific sequence or from another sequence or no sequence.

List Test: Part of a list selected to try to determine the effectiveness of the entire list. (*See* **List Sample**.)

List User: One who uses names and addresses on someone else's list as prospects for the user's product or service; similar to Mailer.

Load Up: Process of offering a buyer the opportunity of buying an entire series at one time after the customer has purchased the first item in that series.

Magnetic Tape: A storage device for electronically recording and reproducing, by use of a computer, defined bits of data.

Mail Date: Date a list user, by prior agreement with the list owner, is obligated to mail a specific list. No other date is ac-ceptable without specific approval of the list owner.

Mailer: (1) A direct mail advertiser who promotes a product or service using lists of others or house lists or both. (2) A printed direct mail advertising piece. (3) A folding carton, wrapper, or tube used to protect materials in the mails.

Mailgram: A combination telegram-letter, with the telegram transmitted to a postal facility close to the addressee and then delivered as first class mail.

Mailing Machine: A machine that attaches labels to mailing pieces and otherwise prepares such pieces for deposit in the postal system.

Mail Order Action Line (MOAL): A service of Direct Marketing Association which assists consumers in resolving problems with mail order purchases.

Mail Order Buyer: One who offers, and pays for, a product or service through the mail. (Generally, an order telephoned in response to a direct response advertisement is considered a direct substitute for an order sent through postal channels.)

Mail Preference Service (MPS): A service of the Direct Marketing Association for consumers who wish to have their names removed from national commercial mailing lists. The name-removal file is made available to subscribers on a quarterly basis.

Master File: File that is of a permanent nature or regarded in a particular job as authoritative, or one that contains all sub files.

Match: A direct mail term used to refer to the typing of addresses, salutations, or inserts onto letters with other copy imprinted by a printing process.

Match Code: A code determined either by the creator or the user of a file for matching records contained in another file.

MOAL: Acronym for Mail Order Action Line.

Monetary Value: Total expenditures by a customer during a specific period of time, generally twelve months.

"More Mail": Portion of the Direct Marketing Association's Mail Preference Service for consumers requesting information on how to receive more advertising mail.

MPS: Acronym for Mail Preference Service.

Multiple Buyer: One who has bought two or more times (not one who has bought two or more items, one time only); also a Multibuyer or Repeat Buyer.

Multiple Regression: Statistical technique used to measure the relationship between responses to a mailing with census demographics and list characteristics of one or more selected mailing lists. Used to determine the best types of people/areas to mail. This technique can also be used to analyze customers, subscribers, and so forth.

Name: Single entry on a mailing list.

Name Acquisition: Technique of soliciting a response to obtain names and addresses for a mailing list.

Name-Removal Service: Portion of DMA's Mail Preference Service for consumers who wish to have their names removed from mailing lists used by MPS subscribers.

Negative Option: A buying plan in which a customer or club member agrees to accept and pay for products or services announced in advance at regular intervals *unless* the individual notifies the company, within a reasonable time after announcement, not to ship the merchandise.

Nesting: Placing one enclosure within another before inserting into a mailing envelope.

Net Name Arrangement: An agreement, at the time of ordering or before, whereby the list owner agrees to accept adjusted payment for less than the total names shipped to the list user. Such arrangements can be for a percentage of names shipped or names actually mailed (whichever is greater) or for only those names actually mailed (without a percentage limitation). They can provide for a running charge or not.

Nixie: A mailing piece returned to a mailer (under proper authorization) by the Postal Service because of an incorrect, or undeliverable, name and address.

No-Pay: One who has not paid (wholly or in part) for goods or services ordered. "Uncollectable," "Deadbeat," and "Delinquent" are often used to describe the same person.

North/South Labels: Mailing labels that read from top to bottom and can be affixed with Cheshire equipment.

Novelty Format: An attention-getting direct mail format.

Nth Name Selection: A fractional unit that is repeated in sampling a mailing list. For example, in an "every tenth" sample, you would select the 1st, 11th, 21st, 31st, etc., records—or the 2nd, 12th, 22nd, 32nd, etc., records, and so forth.

OCR (Optical Character Recognition): Machine identification of printed characters through use of light-sensitive devices.

Offer: The terms promoting a specific product or service.

One-Time Buyer: A buyer who has not ordered a second time from a given company.

One-Time Use of a List: An intrinsic part of the normal list usage, list reproduction, or list exchange agreement in which it is understood that the mailer will not use the names on the list more than one time without specific prior approval of the list owner.

Open Account: A customer record that, at a specific time, reflects an unpaid balance for goods and services ordered, without delinquency.

Optical Scanner: An input device that optically reads a line of printed characters and converts each character into its electronic equivalent for processing.

Order Blank Envelopes: An order form printed on one side of a sheet, with a mailing address on the reverse. The recipient simply fills in the order, folds, and seals like an envelope.

Order Card: A reply card used to initiate an order by mail.

Order Form: A printed form on which a customer can provide information to initiate an order by mail. Designed to be mailed in an envelope.

Package: A term used to describe all of the assembled enclosures (parts or elements) of a mailing effort.

Package Insert: Any promotional piece included in a product shipment. It may be for different products (or refills and replacements) from the same company or for products and services of other companies.

Package Test: A test of part or all of the elements of one mailing piece against another.

Paid Cancel: One who completes a basic buying commitment, or more, before cancelling the commitment. (*See* **Completed Cancel**.)

Paid Circulation: Distribution of a publication to individuals or organizations which have paid for a subscription.

Paid During Service: Term used to describe a method of paying for magazine subscriptions in installments, usually weekly or monthly, and, usually, collected in person by the original sales person or a representative of that company.

Peel-Off Label: A self-adhesive label attached to a backing sheet which is attached to a mailing piece. The label is intended to be removed from the mailing piece and attached to an order blank or card.

Penetration: Relationship of the number of individuals or families on a particular list (by state, ZIP code, SIC, etc.) compared to the total number possible.

Personalizing: Individualizing of direct mail pieces by adding the name or other personal information about the recipient.

Phone List: Mailing list compiled from names listed in telephone directories.

Piggy-Back: An offer that hitches a free ride with another offer.

Poly Bag: Transparent polyethylene bag used in place of envelopes for mailing.

Pop-Up: A printed piece containing a paper construction pasted inside a fold and which, when the fold is opened, "pops up" to form a three-dimensional illustration.

Positive Option: A method of distributing products and services incorporating the same advance notice technique as Negative Option but requiring a specific order each time from the member or subscriber. Generally, it is more costly and less predictable than Negative Option.

Postal Service Prohibitory Order: A communication from the Postal Service to a company indicating that a specific person and/or family considers the company's advertising mail to be pandering. The order requires the company to remove from its own mailing list and from any other lists used to promote that company's products or services all names listed on the order. Violation of the order is subject to fine and imprisonment. Names listed on the order are to be distinguished from those names removed voluntarily by the list owner at an individual's request.

Post Card: Single sheet self-matters on card stock.

Post Card Mailers: Booklet containing business reply cards which are individually perforated for selective return, to order products or obtain information.

Premium: An item offered to a buyer, usually free or at a nominal price, as an inducement to purchase or obtain for trial a product or service offered via mail order.

Premium Buyer: One who buys a product or service to get another product or service (usually free or at a special price), or who responds to an offer of a special product (premium) on the package or label (or sometimes in the advertising) of another product.

Preprint: An advertising insert printed in advance and supplied to a newspaper or magazine for insertion.

Private Mail: Mail handled by special arrangement outside the Postal Service.

Program: A sequence of steps to be executed by the computer to solve a given problem or achieve a certain result.

Programming: Design, writing, and testing of a program.

Prospect: A name on a mailing list considered to be a potential buyer for a given product or service but who has not previously made such a purchase.

Prospecting: Mailing to get leads for further sales contact rather than to make direct sales.

Protection: The amount of time, before and after the assigned mailing date, a list owner will not allow the same names to be mailed by anyone other than the mailer cleared for that specific date.

Psychographics: Any characteristics or qualities used to denote the lifestyle(s) or attitude(s) of customers and prospective customers.

Publisher's Letter: A second letter enclosed in a mailing package to stress a specific selling point.

Purge: The process of eliminating duplicates and/or unwanted names and addresses from one or more lists.

Pyramiding: A method of testing mailing lists, in which one starts with a small quantity and, based on positive indications, follows with increasingly larger quantities of the list balance until the entire list is mailed.

Questionnaire: A printed form to a specified audience to solicit answers to specific questions.

Random Access: An access mode in which records are obtained from, or placed into, a mass storage file in a non-sequential manner so that any record can be rapidly accessed. Synonymous with Direct Access.

Recency: The latest purchase or other activity recorded for an individual or company on a specific customer list. (*See* **Frequency** and **Monetary Value**.)

Reformatting: Changing a magnetic tape format from one arrangement to another, more usable format. Synonymous with Conversion (list or tape).

Renewal: A subscription that has been renewed prior to, or at, expiration time or within six months thereafter.

Repeat Buyer: (*See* **Multiple Buyer**.)

Rental: (*See* **List Rental**.)

Reply Card: A sender-addressed card included in a mailing on which the recipient may indicate his response to the offer.

Reply-O-Letter: One of a number of patented direct mail formats for facilitating replies from prospects. It features a die-cut opening on the face of the letter and a pocket on the reverse. An addressed reply card is inserted in the pocket and the name and address thereon shows through the die-cut opening.

Reproduction Right: Authorization by a list owner for a specific mailer to use that list on a one-time basis.

Response Rate: Percent of returns from a mailing.

Return Envelopes: Addressed reply envelopes, either stamped or unstamped —as distinguished from business reply envelopes which carry a postage payment guarantee—included with a mailing.

Return Postage Guaranteed: A legend imprinted on the address face of envelopes or other mailing pieces when the mailer wishes the Postal Service to return undeliverable third class bulk mail. A charge equivalent to the single piece, third class rate will be made for each piece returned. (*See* **List Cleaning**.)

Return Requested: An indication that a mailer will compensate the Postal Service for return of an undeliverable mailing piece.

Returns: Responses to a direct mail program.

RFMR: Acronym for Recency-Frequency-Monetary Value Ratio, a formula used to evaluate the sales potential of names on a mailing list.

Rollout: To mail the remaining portion of a mailing list after successfully testing a portion of that list.

R.O.P. (Run of Paper or Run of Press): Usually refers to color printing which can be placed on any page of a newspaper or magazine.

Rough: Dummy or layout in sketchy form with a minimum of detail.

Royalties: Sum paid per unit mailed or sold for the use of a list, imprimatur, patent, etc.

Running Charge: The price a list owner charges for names run or passed, but not used by a specific mailer. When such a charge is made, it is usually to cover extra processing costs. However, some list owners set the price without regard to actual cost.

Run of Paper: (1) A term applied to color printing on regular paper and presses, as distinct from separately printed sections made on special color presses. (2) Sometimes used to describe an advertisement positioned by publisher's choice—in other than a preferred position—for which a special charge is made.

Salting: Deliberate placing of decoy or dummy names in a list to trace list usage and delivery. (*See* **Decoy** and **Dummy**.)

Sample Buyer: One who sends for a sample product, usually at a special price or for a small handling charge, but sometimes free.

Sample Package (Mailing Piece): An example of the package to be mailed by the list user to a particular list. Such a mailing piece is submitted to the list owner for approval prior to commitment for one-time use of that list. Although a sample package may, due to time pressure, differ slightly from the actual package used, the list user agreement usually requires the user to reveal any material differences when submitting the sample package.

Scented Inks: Printing inks to which a fragrance has been added.

Sectional Center (SCF or SCF Center): A Postal Service distribution unit comprising different post offices whose ZIP codes start with the same first three digits.

Selection Criteria: Definition of characteristics that identify segments or subgroups within a list.

Self-Cover: A cover of the same paper as the inside text pages.

Self-Mailer: A direct mail piece mailed without an envelope.

Sequence: An arrangement of items according to a specified set of rules or instructions. Refers generally to ZIP codes or customer number sequence.

SIC (Standard Industrial Classification): Classification of businesses, as defined by the U.S. Department of Commerce.

Software: A set of programs, procedures, and associated documentation concerned with operation of a data processing system.

Solo Mailing: A mailing promoting a single product or a limited group of related products. Usually it consists of a letter, brochure, and reply device enclosed in an envelope.

Source Code: Unique alphabetical and/or numeric identification for distinguishing one list or media source from another. (*See* **Key Code**.)

Source Count: The number of names and addresses, in any given list, for the media (or list sources) from which the names and addresses were derived.

Split Test: Two or more samples from the same list—each considered to be representative of the entire list—used for package tests or to test the homogeneity of the list.

State Count: The number of names and addresses, in a given list, for each state.

Statement Stuffer: A small, printed piece designed to be inserted in an envelope carrying a customer's statement of account.

Step Up: The use of special premiums to get a mail order buyer to increase his unit of purchase.

Stock Art: Art sold for use by a number of advertisers.

Stock Cut: Printing engravings kept in stock by the printer or publisher for occasional use.

Stock Formats: Direct mail formats with preprinted illustrations and/or headings to which an advertiser adds his own copy.

Stopper: Advertising slang for a striking headline or illustration intended to attract immediate attention.

Stuffer: Advertising enclosures placed in other media—that is, newspapers, merchandise packages, mailings for other products, etc.

Subscriber: Individual who has paid to receive a periodical.

Swatching: Attaching samples of material to a printed piece.

Syndicated Mailing: Mailing prepared for distribution by firms other than the manufacturer or syndicator.

Syndicator: One who makes available prepared direct mail promotions for specific products or services to a list owner for mailing to his own list. Most syndicators also offer product fulfillment services.

Tabloid: A preprinted advertising insert of four or more pages, usually about half the size of a regular newspaper page, designed for inserting into a newspaper.

Tape Density: The number of bits of information (bytes) that can be included in each of a specific magnetic tape—for example, 556 BPI, 800 BPI, 1600 BPI, etc.

Tape Dump: A printout of data on a magnetic tape to be edited and checked for correctness, readability, consistency, etc.

Tape Layout: A simple "map" of the data included in each record and its relative, or specific, location.

Tape Record: All the information about an individual or company contained on a specific magnetic tape.

Teaser: An advertisement or promotion planned to excite curiosity about a later advertisement or promotion.

Telecommunications: Data transmission between a computer system and remotely located devices via a unit that performs the necessary format conversion and controls the rate of transmission over telephone lines, microwaves, etc. Synonymous with Transceive.

Telephone Preference Service (TPS): A service of the Direct Marketing Association for consumers who wish to have their names removed from national telemarketing lists. The name-removal file is made available to subscribers on a quarterly basis.

Terminal: Any mechanism which can transmit and/or receive data through a system or communications network.

Test Panel: A term used to identify each of the parts or samples in a split test.

Test Tape: A selection of representative records within a mailing list that enables a list user or service bureau to prepare for reformatting or converting the list to a form more efficient for the user.

Throwaway: An advertisement or promotional piece intended for widespread free distribution. Generally printed on inexpensive paper stock, it is most often distributed by hand to passersby or from house-to-house.

Tie-In: Cooperative mailing effort involving two or more advertisers.

Til Forbid: An order for continuing service which is to continue until specifically cancelled by the buyer. Also "TF."

Title: A designation before (prefix) or after (suffix) a name to more accurately identify an individual. (Prefixes—Mr., Mrs., Dr., Sister, etc.,: Suffixes—M.D., Jr., president, sales manager, etc.)

Time Sharing: Multiple utilization of available computer time, often via terminals, usually shared by different organizations.

Tip-On: An item glued to a printed piece.

Token: An involvement device, often consisting of a perforated portion of an order card designed to be removed from its original position and placed in another designated area on the order card, to signify a desire to purchase the product or service offered.

Town Marker: A symbol used to identify the end of a mailing list's geographical unit. (Originated for "towns" but now used for ZIP codes, sectional centers, etc.)

TPS: Acronym for "Telephone Preference Service."

Traffic Builder: A direct mail piece intended primarily to attract recipients to the mailer's place of business.

Trial Buyer: One who buys a short-term supply of a product, or buys the product with the understanding that it may be examined, used, or tested for a specific time before deciding whether to pay for it or to return it.

Trial Subscriber: A person ordering a publication or service on a conditional basis. The condition may relate to: delaying payment, the right to cancel, a shorter than normal term and/or a special introductory price.

Uncollectable: One who hasn't paid for goods and services at the end of a normal series of collection efforts.

Unit of Sale: Description of the average dollar amount spent by customers on a mailing list.

Universe: Total number of individuals that might be included on a mailing list; all of those fitting a single set of specifications.

Update: Recent transactions and current information added to the Master (main) list to reflect the current status of each record on the list.

Up Front: Securing payment for a product offered by mail order before the product is sent.

UPS: Acronym for United Parcel Service.

Variable Field: A way of laying out for formatting list information that assigns a specific sequence to the data, but doesn't assign it specific positions. While this method conserves space on magnetic tape, it is generally more difficult to work with.

Verification: The process of determining the validity of an order by sending a questionnaire to the customer.

WATS: Acronym for Wide Area Telephone Service. A service providing a special line allowing calls within a certain zone, on a direct dialing basis, for a flat monthly charge.

White Mail: Incoming mail that is not on a form sent out by the advertiser. All mail other than orders and payments.

White Envelope: Envelope with a die-cut portion on the front that permits viewing the address printed on an enclosure. The "die cut window" may or may not be covered with a transparent material.

Wing Mailer: Label-affixing device that uses strips of paper on which addresses have been printed.

ZIP Code: A group of five digits used by the U.S. Postal Service to designate specific post offices, stations, branches, buildings, or large companies.

ZIP Code Count: The number of names and addresses in a list, within each ZIP code.

ZIP Code Sequence: Arranging names and addresses in a list according to the numeric progression of the ZIP code in each record. This form of list formatting is mandatory for mailing at bulk third class mail rates, based on the sorting requirements of Postal Service regulations.

Index

Inquiry system reports, 431–36
Insert cards
    bind-in, 207–8
    co-ops, 274
    and position factor, 217–18
Institutional advertising, 133
Insurance companies, use of direct mail by, 279, 524–25
Internal lists, 164
Internships, 547–48
Investment method of fund-raising, 142–43
Invitation format, 316, 319
Involvement devices, 316, 317

J
JFY, 38
Joan Cook catalog, 375
Johnson & Johnson, 441

K
Kestnbaum & Company, 441
Kiosks, as direct marketing tool, 5, 7, 72
Kiplinger letter, 339
Kobs & Brady Advertising, 243, 244
Krupp/Taylor USA, 130–31

L
Lateral thinking, 472
Lead
    in direct mail letters, 336–37, 343
    in print advertising, 392
Lead bank system, 424
Lead flow monitoring, 423
Lead flow planning, 418
Lead generation, 11, 16–18, 414
    in business-to-business program, 124–25, 414–15, 426–36
    in business-to-consumer program
    capacity planning, 418–20
    contingency planning, 423–24
    lead flow monitoring, 423
    and public relations, 415
    qualification, 421–22
    tracking and results reporting, 425–26
    tracking sources for, 27–28
    types of programs for, 414–15
Lead qualification, 124–25, 279–80, 414, 416–18, 421–22
Letters. *See also* Direct mail letters

form, 344
    personalized, 321, 322
    second, 316, 318
    ship, 374
Lettershops, careers in, 545
Lifestyle analysis, 494
    and data base marketing, 33, 35–39
    in selecting merchandise for offer, 113–14
Lifestyle Selector®, 36, 180
Lifetime cumulative gifts, 143–44
Lifetime membership offer, 68
Lillian Vernon, 375
List. *See* Mailing lists
List brokers
    career as, 544
    role of, 170–71
List compilers, career as, 544
List managers, role of, 171–72
Literary Guild, 67, 397
Load-ups, 68, 70
Location shootings, 371

M
Machine gun technique, 395–96
Madison House, 88
Magazine(s)
    listing of consumer with mail order and or shopping advertising pages, 196–205
    renewal campaigns, 279
Magazine advertising, 192
    advertising response pattern, 210–12
    bind-in cards in, 207–8
    bingo cards in, 208–10
    buying space, 218–19
    categories in, 206
    color advertising in, 215–16
    determining proper ad size in, 213–15
    mathematical modeling in, 188
    pilot publications of, 195, 206–7
    position factor in advertising, 216–18
    regional editions of, 193–95
    testing response to, 193–94
    timing and frequency analysis for advertising in, 212–13
Magazine co-ops, 269
Mailing lists. *See also* Lead generation
    careers in, 543–45
    and choice of merchandise, 111, 113–14
    definition of, 164
    and demographics, 169–70